INSIDE
AUTOCAD® 14

MICHAEL E. BEALL
BILL BURCHARD
JOJO GUINGAO
MICHAEL TODD PETERSON
DAVID M. PITZER
MARK SAGE
SURYA SARDA
CRAIG W. SHARP
FRANCIS SOEN
DON SPENCER

New Riders Publishing, Indianapolis, Indiana

Inside AutoCAD® 14

By Michael E. Beall, Bill Burchard, Jojo Guingao, Michael Todd Peterson, David M. Pitzer, Mark Sage, Surya Sarda, Craig W. Sharp, Francis Soen, Don Spencer

Published by:
New Riders Publishing
201 West 103rd Street
Indianapolis, IN 46290 USA

Library of Congress Cataloging-in-Publication Data

```
Inside AutoCAD release 14 / Michael E. Beall ... [et al.].
      p.   cm.
    Includes index.
    ISBN 1-56205-755-3
    1. Computer graphics. 2. AutoCAD (Computer file)  I. Beall,
  Michael E.,  1953-   .
  T385.I47655   1997
  620'.0042'02855369—dc21                              97-11550
                                                          CIP
```

Warning and Disclaimer

Publisher	Don Fowley
Associate Publisher	David Dwyer
Marketing Manager	Mary Foote
Managing Editor	Carla Hall
Director of Development	Kezia Endsley

Product Director
Alicia Buckley

Senior Editors
Sarah Kearns, Suzanne Snyder

Development Editors
Laura Frey, Naomi Goldman

Editors
Gail Burlakoff, Sandy Doell, Mitzi Foster, Wendy Garrison, Noelle Gasco, Krista Hansing, Cricket Harrison, Brad Herriman, Dayna Isley, Matt Litten, Karen Walsh, Michelle Warren, Phil Worthington

Technical Editors
John Crawford, Jim Fisher, David Harrington

Software Specialist
Steve Flatt

Assistant Marketing Manager
Gretchen Schlesinger

Acquisitions Coordinator
Stacey Beheler

Administrative Coordinator
Karen Opal

Manufacturing Coordinator
Brook Farling

Cover Designer
Karen Ruggles

Cover Production
Aren Howell

Book Designer
Anne Jones

Director of Production
Larry Klein

Production Team Supervisors
Laurie Casey, Joe Millay

Graphics Image Specialists
Todd Wente, Clint Lahnen

Production Analysts
Dan Harris, Erich J. Richter

Production Team
Lori Cliburn, Laure Robinson, Susan Van Ness, Christy Wagner

Indexer
Nick Schroeder

About the Authors

Michael E. Beall is the owner of Computer Aided Management and Planning in Shelbyville, KY, near Louisville. Mr. Beall offers contract services and professional training on AutoCAD as well as CAP and CAP.Spex from Sweets Group, a division of McGraw-Hill. He is the co-author of *AutoCAD Release 13 for Beginners* and *Inside AutoCAD LT for Windows 95* from New Riders Publishing and author of *AutoCAD Release 13 for Professional: Level I* courseware for New Riders, certified for use at Autodesk Authorized Training Centers. Mr. Beall has been presenting CAD training seminars to architects and engineers since 1982 and is currently an instructor at the University of Louisville ATC. As owner of the former Computer Training Services in San Jose, CA, Mr. Beall developed a highly successful six-month Architecture and Facility Planning program for re-entry adults at The Copper Connection, an ATC in Santa Clara, CA. He now offers contract services and training exclusively on AutoCAD and products from Sweet's Group, the leading furniture specification software for use with AutoCAD. He received a Bachelor of Architecture degree from the University of Cincinnati and is an Affiliate member of the International Facility Manager's Association.

Bill Burchard is a CAD systems specialist with David Evans & Associates. He has been in the civil engineering business for 20 years. He has extensive experience in computer modeling and applications for civil engineering projects, including plan preparation, technical publications, engineering design, FMS/GIS systems, 3D modeling, 3D photorealistic renderings, and 3D animations. Additionally, Mr. Burchard is a registered Autodesk author/publisher, and is a consulting author and technical editor with New Riders Publishing. In these capacities, he has worked on several book projects regarding the use of AutoCAD, including *Inside AutoCAD Release 13c4* and *AutoCAD Performance Tuning Toolkit*. Mr. Burchard is also a contributor to *Inside AutoCAD*, a monthly newsletter published by the COBB Group.

Jojo Guingao has over 10 years of consulting, application development, training, and support experience in the CAD industry. He is the Technical Account Manager for the Product Support and Services Group at Autodesk and is considered an in-house expert on Autodesk Data management applications such as AutoCAD Data Extension (ADE), AutoCAD SQL Environments (ASE), and Autodesk WorkCenter.

As a Technical Account Manager, Jojo is responsible for managing Autodesk strategic accounts such as Ford, Southwestern Bell, U.S. Fish and Wildlife, and U.S. Navy Facilities Projects. Before coming to Autodesk, Jojo was an Application

Programmer with Softdesk, Inc., where he worked on a project for Pella Designer, Silver Catalog, and Fleetwood Project. His experience also includes working as a CAD consultant for several Autodesk Resellers in Silicon Valley and Saudi Arabia.

Jojo hold a B.S. in electronics and Communications Engineering from Mapua Institute of Technology in Manila, Philippines.

Michael Todd Peterson is currently an instructor at Pellissippi State Community College, an ATC. He previously taught at the University of Tennessee College of Architecture. Todd also owns MTP graphics, a rendering and animation firm that specializes in architectural visualization and mulitmedia. In addition to this book, Mr. Peterson has authored or co-authored *Inside AutoCAD for DOS*, *3D Studio for Beginners*, *3D Studio Max Fundamentals*, *Inside AutoCAD Release 13c4*, *Windows NT for Graphics Pro*, and *AutoCAD in 3D*.

David M. Pitzer is an AutoCAD instructor and consultant. He currently serves as an Adjunct Professor at Santa Rosa Junior College in Santa Rosa, CA, where he teaches AutoCAD Customization, AutoLISP, and 3D Modeling and Rendering. Mr. Pitzer is a Contributing Editor of CADalyst Magazine where his articles frequently appear. His articles have also appeared in CADENCE magazine and the AutoCAD Tech Journal. He has been a lecturer at Autodesk University on two occasions. He was a co-author of Inside

AutoCAD Release 13 for Windows and Inside AutoCAD Release 13c4, served as technical editor for AutoCAD Performance Tuning Toolkit and as development editor for Inside AutoCAD LT for Windows 95, all published by New Riders Publishing, and is currently serving as technical editor for two other AutoCAD books. He currently serves as an officer with the Sonoma County AutoCAD Users' Group. He has been writing about and using AutoCAD since 1987. Mr. Pitzer received a Bachelor of Science degree from The Citadel in Charleston, S.C., and makes his home in the wine country north of San Francisco, CA.

Mark Sage has been an employee with Autodesk for over eight years. Mr. Sage currently serves as a Product Manager for AutoCAD. At Autodesk, Mark has managed various aspects of AutoCAD components through five product development cycles beginning with Release 10. Along with his AutoCAD responsibilities, Mark is the Product Manager for the AutoCAD Release 13 Internet Publishing kit, WHIP! and the AutoCAD Internet Utilities. Mr. Sage's involvement with AutoCAD is extensive, dating back to 1983. Mark recalls selling one of the earliest releases of the product—AutoCAD version 1.02—for a Victor 9000 running CPM/86!

Surya Sarda is the Program Manager for ActiveX Automation and VBA at Autodesk, Inc. He is a veteran of nine years at Autodesk, Inc. Before working on ActiveX Automation, he was involved with the MCAD division and worked on AME, AutoSurf, and Designer products. He holds bachelor's and master's degrees in Mechanical Engineering. You can reach him at surya@autodesk.com.

Craig W. Sharp, AIA, is an architect with over 24 years of international experience. He is an author and lecturer on the use of computers in architecture and daily faces the challenge of producing projects on a computer. He is prin-cipal with Motley + Associates in Roan-oke, VA, an architectural, interior design, and planning firm that specializes in educational facility design. He has been using AutoCAD since version 2.1.

Francis Soen is an independent AutoCAD Consultant serving Pittsburgh and the surrounding tri-state area. With more than 14 years of experience working with AutoCAD, Francis provides customized training, LISP and menu customization services, network and drawing management services, and database programming expertise. Mr. Soen has been a co-author on several AutoCAD books. As an instructor at the Authorized AutoCAD Training Center at the Community College of Allegheny County, he has provided training to many members of the Pittsburgh CAD community. With degrees in Civil Engineering from Lehigh University and UC Berkeley, Mr. Soen has developed an expertise in using AutoCAD for civil engineering, AEC applications, and Digital Terrain Modeling. Francis can be contacted through CompuServe at

73232,760 or by phone at 412-922-0412, and is always happy to hear from other local users.

Don Spencer is the Senior Partner for the VisualiZation Group, a consulting partnership specializing in design, visualization, and training with Autodesk products. He is also Director of Technical Development for Digitoe, Inc., computerized Footwear Systems, and Autodesk Registered Application Developer for the footwear industry. He is currently serving as Education & Training Industry Chair on the Autodesk User Group International Board of Directors. He is an Autodesk Training Center Manager and has been teaching AutoCAD, AutoCAD Designer, AutoSurf, and related AutoCAD, rendering, and animation courses for ATCs, colleges, and industry for seven years. He has 18 years of manufacturing, drafting, 3D design, and consulting experience, the last nine years using Autodesk products.

Trademark Acknowledgments

All terms mentioned in this book that are known to be trademarks or service marks have been appropriately capitalized. New Riders Publishing cannot attest to the accuracy of this information. Use of a term in this book should not be regarded as affecting the validity of any trademark or service mark. AutoCAD is a registered trademark of Autodesk, Inc.

Contents at a Glance

Table of Contents

Part IV: Annotating, Dimensioning, and Plotting with R14

Part VII: Reference Materials

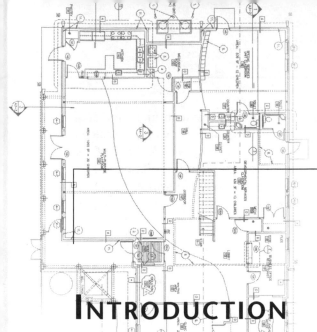

INTRODUCTION

AutoCAD is a software phenomenon; its users far outnumber those of any other CAD system. Since its introduction, AutoCAD has grown from a micro-curiosity to a full-fledged CAD system by any set of standards. AutoCAD also has grown from a relatively simple program to a large and complex one, but do not be intimidated by its size and complexity. More than one million designers and drafters have learned to use AutoCAD with the help of Inside AutoCAD, *the best-selling AutoCAD book for more than 10 years.*

Inside AutoCAD 14 *is your guide to a significant step in the evolution of AutoCAD: AutoCAD Release 14. Because AutoCAD Release 14 utilizes the flexibility of Windows, it offers you a far more productive design environment and interface than AutoCAD under DOS, and includes several advanced features not available in the DOS version.*

Inside AutoCAD 14 *is organized to be of primary benefit to professional AutoCAD users—those who use AutoCAD on a regular basis in the course of their work. It assumes some understanding of the AutoCAD and Windows user interfaces, and aims at sharpening the skills you need to grow as a professional AutoCAD user.*

AutoCAD Release 14 has over 100 new features and improvements in it, including raw performance, drawing productivity, presentation-quality drawings, enhanced data sharing, improved customization, and management tools. *Inside AutoCAD 14* provides extensive coverage of these new features and includes information on integrating the new features with the old. This book provides real-world examples, tips, and tricks to help you be more productive and more competitive in your job.

How This Book Is Organized

Inside AutoCAD 14 is designed to help you master AutoCAD and sharpen the professional skills you need to use AutoCAD effectively and efficiently, beyond simply understanding the basics of the program. To accomplish this goal, the book is organized into parts, each of which covers a specific group of concepts and operations. Each part is a collection of related chapters, presented more or less in order of increasing complexity.

Part I: Introducing AutoCAD Release 14

Part I brings you up-to-speed on the new interface changes and tools introduced in Release 14. It is a quick introduction to the newest AutoCAD release.

Part II: Starting New Projects with R14

To gain the competitive edge over other drafters and designers, you must have an organized working environment. Part II lays the groundwork for planning and organizing projects, setting up the drawing environment, and using layers and linetypes to manage your drawings. When you complete Part II, you will have your AutoCAD system tuned to your design and drafting needs so you can begin drawing more productively.

Part III: Creating and Editing Drawings

Part III covers the creation and editing of your drawings—the core of AutoCAD. Each chapter builds upon the previous one to help you build and reinforce your skill set. Learn how to create and edit blocks, complex objects, polylines, splines, and more. This section not only provides the techniques but also includes tips and tricks from AutoCAD experts on how to use these techniques more effectively, giving you the competitive advantage.

Part IV: Annotating, Dimensioning, and Plotting with R14

The details make the drawing. Part IV discusses the details of text annotation, dimensioning, hatch patterns, and plotting. Learn techniques that save time and effort, and give high-quality, professional results.

Part V: Customization and Advanced Concepts

Part V takes you to the next level with AutoCAD 14 by presenting customization techniques for your workstation and drawings. Part V also presents the powerful, advanced features of AutoCAD, including 3D, AutoLISP, ActiveX, AutoCAD SQL Environment (ASE), scripts, and slide libraries.

Part VI: CAD on the Internet

The latest vehicle of collaborative drafting is the Internet. Part VI investigates the newest features of AutoCAD that enable you to work with colleagues over the web and on the Internet. Instead of being frustrated with the web, use it to your advantage with tools and techniques presented in Part VI.

Part VII: Reference Materials

Inside AutoCAD 14 is equipped with three appendices and two reference indices. Appendix A covers the AutoCAD 14 Bonus Pack. It includes detailed information on the Bonus Pack as well as tutorials that will help you master the Bonus Pack. Appendix B is the System Variables reference and Appendix C is the Dimensioning Variables reference. Use these handy references to save time and effort. Appendix D, the exercise index, lists the title and page number of every exercise in the book.

Chapter Exercises

Each part of *Inside AutoCAD 14* contains hands-on, real-world exercises that demonstrate each technique or command being discussed. These exercises not only enable you to gain familiarity with the Release 14 interface and commands, but they serve to reinforce the discussion in the text. Each exercise strives to bring you one more step ahead of your competition by including tips and tricks from industry leaders and experienced CAD professionals.

The exercises are set up as numbered steps. By following along through the steps and using the explanatory text and figures for support, you will increase your efficiency and effectiveness with AutoCAD.

You should save your drawings when instructed to help you build a habit of saving drawings at regular intervals. If you want to proceed at a leisurely pace, you can save and close your drawing whenever you see the save instruction and reload your drawing later.

If you just read the text and exercises and look at the illustrations, you will learn a great deal about the program. But if you want to gain a greater mastery of AutoCAD, you need to sit down at your computer and work through the exercises.

Special Sidebars

Inside AutoCAD 14 features special sidebars that are set apart from the normal text as follows. This book includes four distinctive types of sidebars: Notes, Insider Tips, Warnings, and New for R14. These passages have been given special treatment so that you can instantly recognize their significance and easily find them for future reference.

NOTE

A Note includes extra information you should find useful. A Note might describe special situations that can arise when you use AutoCAD under certain circumstances, and might tell you what steps to take when such situations arise.

INSIDER TIP

An Insider Tip provides quick instructions for getting the most from your AutoCAD system. Often these tips will be written in first person because the author is imparting special information that he has gained after many years of experience of AutoCAD use. An Insider Tip might show you how to speed up a procedure, or how to perform one of many time-saving and system-enhancing techniques.

WARNING

A Warning tells you when a procedure can be dangerous—that is, when you run the risk of a serious problem or error, even losing data or crashing your system. Warnings generally tell you how to avoid such problems or describe the steps you can take to remedy them.

The New for R14 icon appears whenever the text describes a feature that is new to AutoCAD Release 14. This icon is present to help upgraders master the new features quickly, and to point out to users the increased benefits of the latest release of AutoCAD.

New Riders Publishing

The staff of New Riders Publishing is committed to bringing you the very best in computer reference material. Each New Riders book is the result of months of work by authors and staff who research and refine the information contained within its covers.

As part of this commitment to you, New Riders invites your input. Please let us know if you enjoy this book, if you have trouble with the information and examples presented, or if you have a suggestion for the next edition.

Please note, however: New Riders staff cannot serve as a technical resource for AutoCAD or for questions about software- or hardware-related problems. Please refer to the documentation that accompanies your software or to the application's Help systems.

If you have a question or comment about any New Riders book, there are several ways to contact New Riders Publishing. We will respond to as many readers as we can. Your name, address, or phone number will never become part of a mailing list or be used for any purpose other than to help us continue to bring you the best books possible.

You can write us at the following address:

New Riders Publishing
Attn: Publisher
201 W. 103rd Street
Indianapolis, IN 46290

If you prefer, you can fax New Riders Publishing at 317-817-7448.

You can also send electronic mail to New Riders at the following Internet address:

abuckley@newriders.mcp.com

New Riders Publishing is an imprint of Macmillan Computer Publishing. To obtain a catalog or information, or to purchase any Macmillan Computer Publishing book, call 800-428-5331 or visit our web site at http://www.mcp.com.

Thank you for selecting *Inside AutoCAD 14*!

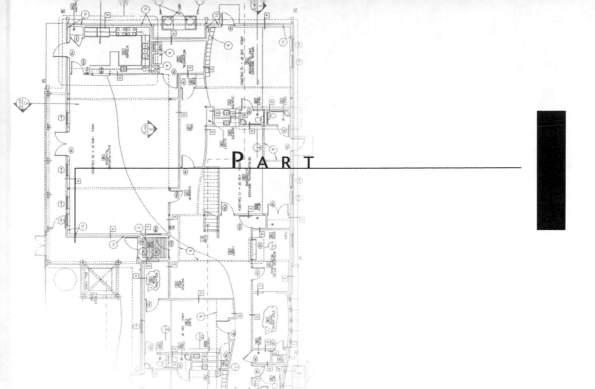

PART

INTRODUCING AUTOCAD RELEASE 14

Chapter 1: Exploring the New R14 Interface

EXPLORING THE NEW R14 INTERFACE

by David M. Pitzer

With the introduction of AutoCAD Release 14, Autodesk has made a significant move toward bringing AutoCAD's Graphical User Interface (GUI) even further in line with the standards found in Windows 95/NT 4.0 applications. Although AutoCAD Release 13 adopted some of the standards established by Microsoft Corporation, Release 13's early development took place simultaneously with the introduction of the Windows 95 operating system, so R13 was unable to adopt many of the new Windows 95 GUI innovations. Not so with Release 14; with both Windows 95 and Windows NT 4.0 as well-established operating systems, AutoCAD Release 14 is able to take full advantage of the now-familiar GUI features.

In adopting these standards and conventions, Release 14 not only has a new look to most of its dialog boxes and many of its toolbars, but it also has a more efficient "feel." Most of the efficiency increase can be objectively measured. It is largely the result of architectural changes to AutoCAD's core program, significant changes in the graphics system, and the more efficient use of memory. This chapter discusses many of the new elements and features and a few of the new Release 14 commands, particularly as they relate to the user interface. This chapter covers the following topics:

- Standard toolbar and menus

- New Explorer-style dialog boxes

- Object Properties toolbar

- Toolbar editing

- Some of Release 14's new commands

Standard Toolbar and Menus

Release 14's Standard toolbar and pull-down menus conform closely with those of other modern Windows applications, especially those in the Microsoft Office Suite. Figure 1.1 shows Release 14's Standard toolbar and menus juxtaposed with those for Microsoft Word 7.0. The first six pull-down menu titles and the first 11 icons in the Standard toolbars are identical.

Figure 1.1

Comparison of Release 14 and MS Word menus and Standard toolbars.

Having this degree of standardization among applications has an obvious advantage of making new applications much easier to learn; the skills gained in one application can be easily transferred to another. In addition, "usability" is enhanced because many of the basic functions common to both applications are found in the same familiar locations or are identified with standard icons.

Pull-Down Menus

Some of the labels of the Release 14 pull-down menus have been changed from previous releases, and the placement of unchanged labels has been modified. In Release 14, however, these changes point to an overall scheme intended to provide better functionality and easier to use pull-downs. Changes within the menus exist as well. For example, although the number of three-level cascades has increased, two-level cascades with repeating terms or words have been eliminated. In figure 1.2, for example, compare the difference between the cascading menu structure for controlling the UCS icon in Release 13 and 14.

Figure 1.2

 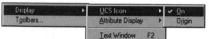

Comparison of Release 13 (left) and Release 14 cascade menus.

In addition, some pull-down menu consolidation can be seen in Release 14. Items found in the Construct pull-down of Release 13's Acadfull menu, for example, have been integrated into Release 14's Modify pull-down menu and rearranged so that often-used commands appear toward the top of the menu. At first, these pull-down menu modifications may seem awkward for both Release 13 and Release 12 users. With continued usage, however, most users will find them to represent an overall better arrangement.

NOTE

Resist the temptation to use menus from previous releases in Release 14 because new commands have been added and some old commands have been deleted. Although you may feel more comfortable with older, more familiar menus, the Release 14 pull-down menu structure is well thought-out. After a short acclimation period, you will find it easier to work with.

Screen Menu

AutoCAD's Release 14 Screen menu remains essentially unchanged, except for the order of command appearance on individual pages, which closely tracks the order found on the Standard toolbar. Some further minor modifications have been incorporated, but those who use the Screen menu will notice little significant change in this menu's layout and functionality.

INSIDER TIP

The close correlation between Release 14's pull-down menus and the Screen menu enables those who want to make the transition away from the use of a Screen menu to do so in an efficient, fairly "painless" manner. Although I was a staunch advocate of the Screen menu over many releases, I now find it cumbersome and distracting and I dislike the amount of screen "real estate" it consumes.

Tablet Menu

For users of tablets and Tablet menus, Release 14 offers good and bad news. The bad news is that layout of the Release 14 Tablet menu has been extensively modified, especially in Tablet menu areas 2 and 4. The good news is that the Release 13 menu design has been included as an alternate Tablet drawing in the shipping Release 14 files. To take advantage of the many new Release 14 commands and options, however, the newest arrangement should be used. The large Tablet area 1 is retained for those who want to use this area for menu customization. The modified tablet overlay presents the new Release 14 commands and functions in a manner more consistent with the pull-down menus.

INSIDER TIP

Tablet menu overlay users should seriously consider switching from this method of command entry to Release 14's extensive toolbar to avoid unnecessary, repetitive eye, arm, and shoulder movements you encounter when using the tablet menu overlay method. The toolbars customization capabilities provide an excellent means of retaining or incorporating customization into a far more ergonomically efficient presentation. For those who prefer the absolute mode of screen cursor movement, Release 14 supports standard WinTab drivers that allow a tablet puck to be used as a mouse but in an absolute movement mode.

Toolbars

The toolbars in Release 14 have been extensively re-designed and reduced in number from 50 in Release 13 to 16 in Release 14. The number of flyout tools has also been drastically reduced. Flyouts have been retained on such command groups as the ZOOM command options and the Inquiry tools group (DISTANCE, AREA, LIST, ID, and Mass Properties) found on the Standard toolbar, but they appear nowhere else. This reduction in the number of flyouts, as well as the consolidation of other toolbars, greatly reduces the complexity of the overall toolbar layout and organization scheme.

NOTE

If you are a fan of flyout tools, don't despair; you can still add flyouts to any of the out-of-the-box toolbars or construct your own toolbars with flyouts using the toolbar customization facility in R14. See Chapter 22, "Customizing without Programming," for more information on customizing toolbars.

To facilitate the handling of toolbars, Release 14 introduces a new command, TOOLBAR. This command displays a dialog box that makes it much easier to display and hide toolbars. This new command is demonstrated in the following exercise.

DISPLAYING AND HIDING TOOLBARS WITH THE TOOLBAR COMMAND

1. Start AutoCAD. Double-click on the Release 14 AutoCAD icon to display the Start Up dialog box (the multiple start-up methods, including wizards, will be discussed in a later chapter). For now, simply click on the Cancel button located on the right-hand side of the dialog box. This starts a blank session of AutoCAD.

2. To activate the TOOLBAR command in any active drawing, choose View, Toolbars.

3. The Toolbars dialog box lists all the toolbars available in any menu group (see fig. 1.3). Placing or removing an X in the check box associated with any toolbar causes that toolbar to be displayed or hidden.

4. Scroll down the list and place an X in the Inquiry Toolbar check box. The Inquiry toolbar appears.

5. Now remove the X from the Inquiry Toolbar check box and notice that the Inquiry toolbar disappears or is "hidden."

Figure 1.3

*Release 14's new Toolbars
dialog box.*

From the Toolbars dialog box, you can click on the Customize button to activate
additional dialog boxes that enable you to customize toolbars. Additional buttons
enable you to control the size of tool icons and display or hide tooltips. See Chapter
22, "Customizing without Programming," for more information on customizing
toolbars.

NOTE

The TOOLBAR command is new in Release 14, replacing the TBCONFIG command in
Release 13. The overall functionality of the Toolbars dialog box, however, remains
unchanged.

A New Style of Dialog Box

Release 14's close adherence to Windows GUI standards is obviously apparent in the
many new Windows "Explorer-type" dialog boxes that appear throughout Release
14. These dialog boxes closely follow the appearance and functionality of the
Explorer applet in Windows 95 and NT 4.0, and they impart much of the same
functionality to many essential AutoCAD operations. Beyond increased functionality, however, these new dialog boxes have the advantage of being familiar to veteran
Windows 95/NT users and are easy to learn for those who are new to Windows.

This chapter introduces you to the Layer & Linetype Properties dialog box. After you
learn the new functionality and features of this dialog box, many of the other new
Release 14 dialog boxes will be easy to learn and use. These other dialog boxes and
their operation within AutoCAD Release 14 are examined in the remainder of this
book.

Layer and Linetype Management

Perhaps the most significant example of Release 14's new dialog boxes is the Layer & Linetype Properties dialog box shown in figure 1.4. This dialog box's resemblance to the Windows Explorer dialog box is immediately apparent. With this redesigned dialog box, all the attributes of layers and linetypes are displayed in a logical, accessible, and usable manner.

Figure 1.4

Release 14's new Layer & Linetype Properties dialog box with the Layer tab selected.

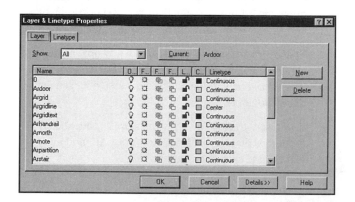

The dialog box consists of two tabs, one for Layer properties and one for Linetype properties. The Layer tab, which is examined in this chapter, presents all the functions needed to create, rename, delete, and assign properties to your drawing's layers. You can carry out the majority of these functions from the central "window" listing the drawing's layers as shown in the following exercise.

CONTROLLING LAYER PROPERTIES FROM THE LAYER & LINETYPE PROPERTIES DIALOG BOX

1. Open the drawing file Chap01.dwg from the accompanying CD-ROM.

2. Click on the Layers tool of the Object Properties toolbar to display the Layer & Linetype Properties dialog box. (It's the second tool from the left.)

3. Notice that the current layer, Ardoor, is identified next to the Current button located above the layer list.

   Highlight the Argrid layer, and click on the Current button to make it current. Notice that the Argrid layer name remains highlighted.

4. Under the C column of the layer list, select the color box associated with the Argrid layer. The Select Color dialog box appears.

5. Select a new color from the Select Color dialog box, and click on OK. Notice that the color box for the Argrid layer changes to the new color.

6. Next, highlight the name of the linetype associated with the Argrid layer. The Select Linetype dialog box appears.

7. Click on the Load button. The Load or Reload Linetypes dialog box appears. Scroll down the list box and highlight the Dashdotx2 linetype. Notice that both a Linetype and a Description column are visible. Click on OK to close the dialog box.

8. You return to the Select Linetype dialog box. Notice Dashdotx2 is now available for assignment. Highlight the Dashdotx2 linetype and click on OK. Notice that layer Argrid has linetype Dashdotx2 now assigned. Leave the Layer & Linetype Properties dialog box open.

9. If you want to close the drawing at this point, click on Cancel in the Layer & Linetype Properties dialog box. Now, exit AutoCAD, and click on the No button when asked if you want to save changes.

In this exercise you should have noticed several new features, such as the method of setting the current layer, the presence of layer state icons, and the redesigned Select Linetype dialog box. Release 14 has many other features that are not as immediately apparent—some of which fall within the functionality of Windows 95/ NT Explorer dialog boxes in general—and are not necessarily documented in Release 14's online help. Some of these features are demonstrated in the following exercises.

CREATING, DELETING, AND RENAMING LAYERS

1. Return to the Layer & Linetype Properties dialog box from the previous exercise, or open it by typing **Layer** at the command prompt.

2. Click on the New button. Notice that a new layer named Layer1 is added to the bottom of the list of layers and that the name is highlighted and boxed, indicating that the name can be changed from the keyboard.

3. Type the name **previous-non–compliant-heating-ducts** and press Enter. An error message stating that the maximum layer name length has been exceeded appears. Close the error message by clicking on its OK button.

4. Notice that the new layer name is still highlighted. Position your cursor at the end of the highlighted name and click the left mouse button to unhighlight the name. Now backspace until heating-ducts is removed. Add **heatduct** to the remaining name and press Enter. The new layer is added.

    Notice that the new layer has the default settings of color White, linetype Continuous, and Thawed, Unlocked, and On states.

5. Select the layer named Stmetal by clicking on the name. Notice that the Stmetal layer is highlighted.

6. Now click on the New button again. Notice that a new Layer1 appears directly beneath the previously highlighted layer. Also note that the default settings of the new Layer1 are the same as the previously highlighted layer.

7. Type the name **bmetal** for the new layer name and press Enter. A new layer, Bmetal, is created with the same settings as the Stmetal layer.

8. Notice that the layer Bmetal is hightlighed. Now click again to the right of the layer name. Notice that the layer name is boxed and highlighted.

9. Type a new layer name of **cmetal** and notice that the layer is renamed to Cmetal.

10. With the layer Cmetal still highlighted, click on the Delete button. Notice that the layer is deleted.

11. Click on the New button. Type **hv-aux1,hv-aux2,hv-aux3** and press Enter. Notice that as you type the comma, AutoCAD adds the previous layer name and creates a new layer named Layer1, which you immediately begin renaming as you continue typing the next layer's name. Three new layers have now been created.

12. Click on the layer Text to highlight it. Click on the Delete button. A message box appears informing you `You cannot delete this layer because it contains objects`. Close the message dialog box by clicking on OK.

As you can see, the methods of creating, renaming, and deleting layers are fast, simple, and straightforward. For users already familiar with Windows 95/NT, this dialog box has most of the familiar Explorer-type functionality. For Release 14 users who are new to Windows 95/NT, it is easy to learn and use.

NOTE

Notice that in this dialog box when a layer name is both highlighted and boxed, you can edit the highlighted text by typing. Standard Windows keyboard functionality—such as the ability to use the arrow, Home, and End keys, deleting, backspacing, and retyping—is available. To terminate your editing, press the Enter key.

Performing operations on a group of layers is also easy in this new dialog box. You can easily select a group of layers that shares an attribute and then operate on this group globally. In addition, an easy means of ordering or filtering the display of layers based on layer names or other attributes exists. These are demonstrated in the following exercises.

PERFORMING OPERATIONS ON GROUPS OF LAYERS

1. Continue from the previous exercise. In the Layer & Linetype Properties dialog box, scroll to the top of the layer list.

2. Now single-click the Name column heading (see fig. 1.5). Notice that the list of layers is displayed in a reverse alphabetical order.

Figure 1.5

Changing the display order in the layer list.

3. Move the screen pointer to the C column heading and single-click. Notice that the layer list is now ordered by layer color.

4. Scroll to the bottom of the list. Now place the screen pointer on the line separating the C and Linetype column divisions as shown in figure 1.6. Notice that the pointer changes to a "resize" format.

Figure 1.6

Expanding and contracting layer display columns.

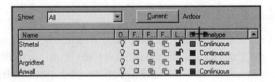

5. Now expand the width of the C column by clicking and dragging the pointer to the right. Notice that the C column expands to show the color name or number. Notice that layer Arhandrail is assigned a color of yellow. Drag the column back to its original, minimized width.

6. Click on the down arrow to display the Show drop-down list. From the displayed list, select All unused. Notice than only the new, unused layers containing no objects are displayed.

7. With only All unused layers still displayed, right-click anywhere in the layer list area. A Select All/Clear All pop-up menu appears. Choose Select All and notice that all displayed layers become highlighted.

8. Now rest the screen pointer over any of the "light bulb" icons in the O column. After a moment, notice the tooltip indicating that these icons control the On/Off state of a layer.

9. Click on any On/Off icon and notice that all highlighted layers change to an Off state (the icons change color). Right-click again and choose Clear All. Previously selected layers become unhighlighted.

INSIDER TIP

As an alternative to the Select All/Clear All pop-up menu demonstrated in the previous exercise, I often find the keyboard short-cut equivalents to be more handy; while the screen pointer is inside the layer list, press Ctrl+A to select all displayed layers and F2 to clear all but the last layer picked, which remains highlighted and boxed.

You can also use the standard Windows Explorer dialog box selection aids of Shift+click and Ctrl+click to select two or more layers. Shift+click will select layers in a noninterrupted series while Ctrl+click enables you to select a series of layers at random.

The preceding exercise showed you several ways to filter and display only certain layers based on standard predefined layer characteristics—such as alphabetically by the first character in the name, color, or On/Off state, and so on. You can work with yet another powerful means of filtering the layers. Using the Set Layer Filters dialog box, you can use the preceding criteria in combination with the wild-card character (*) to build very specific filters based on layer name prefix or suffix characteristics. This is shown in the following exercise.

BUILDING MORE SOPHISTICATED LAYER FILTERS

1. Continue from the preceding exercise. From the Show drop-down list, select All. Note that all layers are displayed.

2. Again in the Show drop-down list, select Set Filter Dialog. The Set Layer Filters dialog box is displayed as shown in figure 1.7.

Figure 1.7

The Set Layer Filters dialog box.

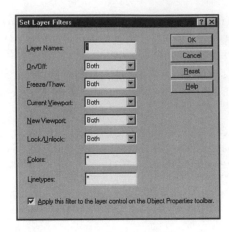

3. In the Layer Names edit box, type **ar*** and then click on OK. The Set Layer Filters dialog box closes, and only layers matching the filter are displayed. Note that both layers Arnorth and Arnote are currently locked.

4. Return to the Set Layer Filters dialog box and display the choices in the Lock/Unlock drop-down list by clicking on the arrow. Click on Locked, and then click on OK. Note that only locked layers beginning with the characters ar are now displayed.

5. Display all layers by selecting All in the Show drop-down list. All layers are displayed.

Using the Set Filter dialog box enables you to build very specific layer filters and can speed up your work with layers significantly. This filtering capability also emphasizes the importance of developing or adopting an intelligent layer naming scheme. With the proper, consistent application of meaningful layer name prefixes, for example, it is easy to display only the layers meeting a set of criteria that you define.

Referring to figure 1.4, the Details button at the bottom of the dialog box is a toggle that causes the dialog box to "unfold" and show an additional dialog section, as shown in figure 1.8. The expanded dialog box provides a more apparent or entry-level method of changing layer settings intended primarily for the new or casual user. Experienced users will more likely use the direct toggling of layer properties and the "in-place" editing offered in the layer list. The expanded dialog box also provides a means to have any changes to Xref-dependent layers retained in the referenced drawing by selecting a check box.

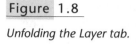

Figure 1.8

Unfolding the Layer tab.

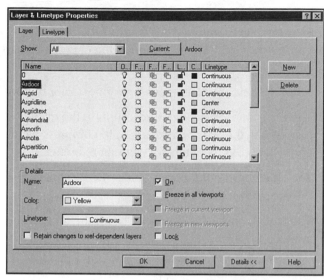

You have closely examined the Layer tab of the Layer & Linetype Properties dialog box early on in the book for two reasons. First of all, it is representative of all the new Explorer-type dialog boxes found throughout Release 14. Understanding the features of this dialog box will enable you to approach other important dialog boxes with a knowledge of their basic functionality. After all, one of the major advantages of these new dialog boxes is that in knowing the features and operation of one, you can transfer this knowledge to others. Secondly, this particular dialog box deals with one of the most important elements in any AutoCAD drawing: handling layers. Knowing how to easily and efficiently work with layers—even a large number of layers—should increase the productivity of anyone working in AutoCAD.

You will encounter the Layer & Linetype Properties dialog box again when you learn more about using layers in Chapter 4, "Organizing Drawings with Layers," and linetypes will be covered in Chapter 5, "Using Linetypes Effectively." The next section looks at some of the other new features found in Release 14.

Object Properties Toolbar

Although at first glance the Object Properties toolbar in Release 14 may look very much like that in Release 13, a closer examination shows several significant changes. Three command icons have either been removed or relocated, one icon representing a new command has been added, and another icon has been changed into a drop-down list. Release 14's new Object Properties toolbar is shown in figure 1.9. Enhancements include the following:

- A new Color control replaces the former Color button.

- The Layer and Linetype controls support the display of layer and linetype names with the use of ellipses (…) to compress names longer than 32 characters (31 characters for external references).

- The Linetype control always places the By Layer and By Block at the top of the drop-down list.

- The Layer control displays Tooltips for the four layer state icon and the color swatch.

Figure 1.9

Release 14's new Object Properties toolbar.

Make Object's Layer Current Command

 The new icon at the far left of the Object Property toolbar calls a new command. This new command is actually an AutoLISP function—(ai_molc)—defined in Release 14's menu Lisp file. (Ai_molc) makes the layer of a selected object current. This rather straightforward function has long been on many AutoCAD users' "wish lists," and it is frequently one of the first AutoLISP functions added by those customizing their AutoCAD installation. It is demonstrated in the following exercise.

USING THE MAKE OBJECT'S LAYER CURRENT COMMAND

1. Continue in or open this chapter's Chap01.dwg file found on the accompanying CD-ROM. Perform a Zoom, Extents by typing **Zoom** and pressing Enter, then **E** and Enter. Referring to figure 1.9, notice at ① that the current layer is Ardoor.

2. Rest the screen pointer on top of the first icon of the Object Properties toolbar ②. Notice that the tooltip reads `Make Object's Layer Current`.

3. Click on the Make Object's Layer Current icon ②. You see the following prompt:

    `Select object whose layer will become current:`

4. Select anywhere on the text "HVAC PLAN" at the bottom of the drawing.

5. Notice at ① that the current layer has changed to the Text layer.

6. Undo the layer change by typing **U** at the Command: prompt and then press Enter. Notice that the current layer reverts back to Ardoor.

7. If you want to close this drawing at this point, click on the No button when asked if you want to save changes.

Object Properties Toolbar Editing

In AutoCAD Release 13, the Object Properties toolbar contained three custom controls to set the layer, color, and linetype defaults for newly created objects. In Release 14, these controls add the capability to list and edit Layer, Color, and Linetype properties for objects selected while AutoCAD is at the Command: prompt. This significant change enables the toolbar controls in Release 14 to behave in a manner similar to the equivalent property toolbars in such Windows 95/NT applications as Word, Excel, and other Microsoft Office applications. AutoCAD's Object Properties toolbar can now provide immediate feedback of such vital information as the layer, color, and linetype of selected objects. This immediate, visual feedback is faster and more direct than that provided by the LIST and DDMODIFY commands available in previous editions of AutoCAD, and represents a major Release 14 enhancement. This more efficient method of editing objects could be termed "toolbar editing." Toolbar editing is much more efficient because you are not required to access a dialog box that obscures the drawing window in order to edit common object properties. The speed and efficiency of toolbar editing is shown in the following exercise.

NOTE

As efficient as toolbar editing is, it has one potential drawback: an object, or objects, must first be selected, and there must be no command in progress for this method to work. This means that the AutoCAD system variable PICKFIRST must be enabled, or set to a value of 1. This setting yields the so-called noun/verb mode of editing and is not the traditional method employed by most AutoCAD users. Keep in mind that having AutoCAD's Grips feature enabled is *not* the same as having noun/verb selection mode enabled, although they are often both enabled by those who use Grips editing. Because having noun/verb editing enabled does not preclude using the more traditional verb/noun methodology (the two are not mutually exclusive), however, many Release 14 users will, no doubt, find themselves wanting to now enable the PICKFIRST feature by default in order to take advantage of the efficiency of toolbar editing. The speed and efficiency of this form of object property editing is shown in the following exercise.

THE ADVANTAGES OF "TOOLBAR EDITING"

1. Continue in or open this chapter's Chap01.dwg file on the accompanying CD-ROM. Perform a Zoom, Extents by typing **Zoom** and pressing Enter, then **E** and pressing Enter.

2. Ensure that the noun/verb edit mode is active by opening the Tools menu and choosing Selection. In the Object Selection Settings dialog box, ensure that a check mark appears in the Noun/Verb Selection check box. Click on the box if necessary to place a check mark in the check box. Click on OK to close the dialog box.

3. Referring again to ① in figure 1.9, check that the current layer is Ardoor.

4. Now perform a Zoom, Center by typing **Z** and pressing Enter and then **C** and pressing Enter. At the prompt for Center point, type **40,45** and then press Enter. At the Magnification or Height prompt, type **3x** and press Enter. Your view should resemble that shown in figure 1.10.

5. Pick the grid centerline shown at ① of figure 1.10. Note that the line is highlighted, showing that it has been picked. Notice that the line's layer, Argridline, appears in the layer list box at ② of figure 1.10. Also notice at ③ that the state of the layer, On, Thawed, Unlocked, cyan color, is displayed in the list box. The list boxes at ④ and ⑤ show that, for the selected object, color (cyan) assignment is ByLayer and linetype (center) is also ByLayer.

Figure 1.10

Using the Object Properties toolbar for "toolbar editing."

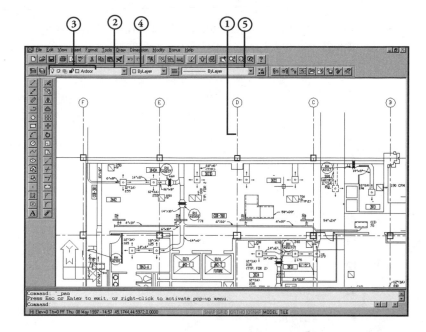

6. To change the line's layer assignment, click on the down arrow in the layer drop-down list ② and select layer Argridtext. Notice that the layer assignment of the selected line changes to Argridtext and that the line remains highlighted.

7. Next, click on the down arrow for the color assignment drop-down list ④. Select the color Red. Notice that the line is now explicitly assigned a color of red. The line remains highlighted.

8. Now click on the down arrow in the linetype assignment drop-down list ⑤. Select linetype Dashdot2. Notice that the line is now explicitly assigned a linetype of Dashdot2. The line remains highlighted.

9. End toolbar editing by pressing Esc. This unhighlights the line showing it is no longer selected. Notice that the Object Properties toolbar now reverts to a display of the current layer, color, and linetype, the default settings for any newly created objects.

10. Now select the same line again. Notice that the layer, layer states, color, and linetype of the line are displayed. Repeat steps 6 through 9 and return the line to layer Argridline, color ByLayer, and linetype ByLayer.

11. If you want to close the drawing at this point, click on the No button when asked if you want to save changes.

The preceding exercise shows the speed, power, and utility of toolbar editing. As you can see, AutoCAD's Grips feature need not be enabled to allow this more efficient way of editing. Using the Object Property toolbar enables you to perform real-time object editing that in previous releases could have required the following commands:

- CHANGE
- CHPROP
- COLOR
- DDCHPROP
- DDCOLOR
- DDEMODES
- DDLMODES
- DDLTYPE
- DDMODIFY
- LINETYPE
- LIST
- VPLAYER

In fact, the DDEMODES command in the preceding list has been discontinued because its functionality is now largely supplanted and is more easily accomplished by toolbar editing.

NOTE

You can "toolbar edit" two or more objects at a time. If the selected objects do not share all properties in common, the appropriate Object Properties toolbar display appears to be blank. But you can still use the drop-down lists to select color, layer, and linetype attributes. All the selected objects will, of course, end up with the same attributes.

INSIDER TIP

Many AutoCAD users, including myself, have not used the Noun/Verb selection method previously, mainly because of the way we learned AutoCAD. With the power of toolbar editing in Release 14, however, having Noun/Verb as your default selection method has a definite advantage. Even if you prefer to use Verb/Noun for editing operations such as Move, Copy, and so on, set or leave the Noun/Verb selection enabled from now on.

Release 14's New Tools

 Other than the usability of the Explorer-type dialog boxes and the efficiency of toolbar editing, Release 14 contains a number of new tools to speed your work. Some of these, such as the Make Object's Layer Current (ai_molc) command discussed previously, are actual commands that can be used at the Command: prompt. Others fall into the category of new features or enhancements to commands found in previous AutoCAD releases. Used together, these tools increase the efficiency of working in Release 14. Many of these new commands and tools appear on the Standard Toolbar as new icons. Figure 1.11 shows the Release 14 Standard Toolbar with these new tools identified.

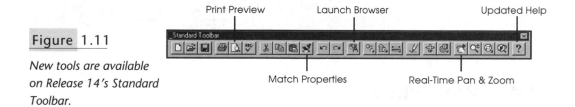

Figure 1.11

New tools are available on Release 14's Standard Toolbar.

Print Preview

Release 14 adds an updated plot (or print) preview facility (see fig. 1.12). It is directly accessible from an icon on the Standard Toolbar without going through the Print dialog box. You can also access it from the Command: prompt with Release 14's new PREVIEW command. The Preview option of the Print/Plot Configuration dialog box also uses this new preview mode. The previewed output is displayed as a white sheet on a gray background, which is a similar layout to preview features in applications such as Microsoft Word. The ability to see the overall presentation aids in visualizing the finished plot or print and represents a further step toward attaining a true What-You-See-Is-What-You-Get (WYSIWYG) on-screen preview.

The new preview facility supports dynamic, Real-Time Pan & Zoom with both Zoom Window and Zoom Previous options that enable you to quickly check layout and output accuracy. Overall, this preview feature is not only faster than its counterpart in AutoCAD 13, but more representative of the finished print. Its features are also more standard and therefore easier to use.

Figure 1.12

*Release 14 has an
enhanced plot/print
preview.*

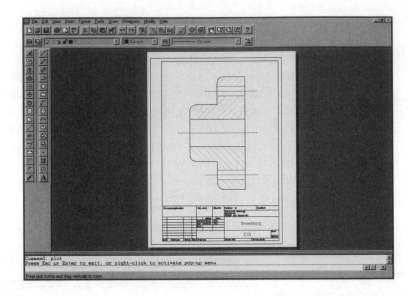

Match Properties

Release 14's Match Properties command is a new AutoCAD Runtime Extension (ARX) command (match.arx) that provides a one-step, easy-to-use command and dialog box interface for copying properties, such as color and linetype, from one AutoCAD object to another. It emulates the "Format Painter" feature found in most Microsoft Office applications. Match Properties (the actual command name is MATCHPROP) performs the equivalent function in a CAD context. Unlike most format painter features, however, Release 14's Match Properties has the additional functionality of enabling the user to specify which properties to copy. The Match Properties feature is demonstrated in the following exercise.

CHANGING PROPERTIES WITH MATCH PROPERTIES COMMAND

1. Continue in or open Chap01.dwg found on the accompanying CD-ROM. Perform a ZOOM, Extents by typing **Z** and pressing Enter, and then **E** and pressing Enter at the Command: prompt. Check that the noun/verb selection mode is enabled by choosing Tools, Selection from the pull-down menu and ensuring that a check mark appears in the Noun/Verb check box; then close the Object Selection Settings dialog box by clicking on OK.

2. Next perform a ZOOM, Center by typing **Z** and pressing Enter, followed by **C** and pressing Enter. At the Center prompt, type **61,45** and press Enter. At the Magnification or height prompt, type **6x** and press Enter. Your screen should resemble figure 1.13.

Figure 1.13

Matching Properties with the MATCHPROP command.

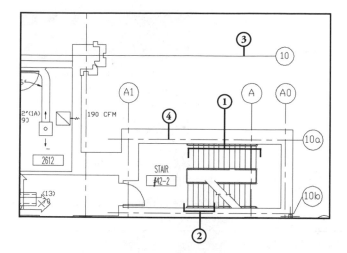

3. Several objects in this portion of the drawing have properties improperly assigned. Select one of the lines at ① and notice in the Object Properties toolbar that these lines are incorrectly assigned to the Arwall layer with color and linetype ByLayer. They need to match the properties of the other stair lines ②. Press ESC key to cancel the selection.

    Referring to figure 1.11, click on the Match Properties icon. The following prompt appears:

    ```
    Select Source Object:
    ```

4. Select one of the lines at ② in figure 1.13. These are the lines whose properties you want to match. The following prompt appears:

    ```
    Settings/<Select Destination Object(s)>:
    ```

5. Select all the lines at ① and press Enter. The destination objects change appearance. Verify the new properties by selecting one of the lines at ①. Notice in the Object Properties toolbar that the layer is now Arstair.

6. Next notice that the line at ③ needs to match the line at ④. Select the line at ③. Notice that its layer assignment is correct (Argridline, ByLayer) but that its linetype is Continuous. Press ESC key to cancel the selection.

7. Click on the Match Properties icon again and select the line at ④ as the source object. The following prompt appears:

    ```
    Settings/<Select Destination Object(s)>:
    ```

8. Type **S** and press Enter to display the Property Settings dialog box shown in figure 1.14. Remove the check marks from all the check boxes except Linetype, which is the property you want to match, and close the dialog box by clicking on OK.

Figure 1.14

Selecting the properties to match.

9. Now select the line at ③ and press Enter. Verify the property change by selecting the line. Notice in the Object Property toolbar that the linetype is now ByLayer.

10. If you want to close the drawing at this point, click on the No button when asked if you want to save changes.

INSIDER TIP

Although the Settings option of the MATCHPROP command offers a great deal of flexibility in filtering exactly which properties you want to transfer to the target objects, it is often more efficient to transfer *all* properties of the source object, even though most of the target object properties may already match.

As you can see from the preceding exercise, the Match Properties feature is very flexible. In combination with the new "listing" ability of the Object Properties toolbar, Match Properties is frequently more convenient and efficient than using several other commands such as CHANGE, CHPROP, DDCHPROP, LIST, and DDMODIFY.

Shortcut Menus

In Release 14, right-clicking grip-selected objects displays a standard Windows-type shortcut menu that enables you to directly edit and modify the selected objects and their properties. This feature is demonstrated in the following exercise.

EDITING GRIP-SELECTED OBJECTS WITH A SHORTCUT MENU

1. Continue in or open this chapter's Chap01.dwg available on the accompanying CD-ROM. Restore the "shortcut" view by selecting View, Named Views. In the View Control dialog box, select SHORTCUT, click on Restore, and then click on OK. Your screen should resemble figure 1.15.

Figure 1.15

Using the shortcut menu on grip-selected objects.

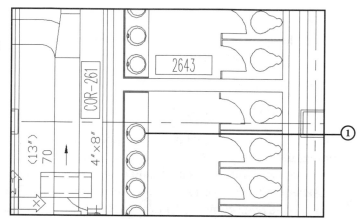

2. Turn on Ortho mode by pressing F8. Next check that the Grips feature is enabled by choosing Grips from the Tools pull-down menu and ensuring that a check mark appears in the Enable Grips check box; then click on OK.

3. Now select the lavatory block at ①, and click on the grip to turn it solid. The lavatory block is now "grip-selected."

4. Right-click to display the shortcut menu shown in figure 1.16 and choose Copy. Drag the highlighted copy of the lavatory block anywhere directly above the grip-selected block.

Figure 1.16

The grip-selected object shortcut menu.

5. Using direct distance entry, type **.68** and press Enter twice. Notice that the block is copied .68 units at 90 degrees to the original. Press Esc twice to exit the grip-selected mode.

6. If you want to close the drawing at this point, click on the No button when asked if you want to save changes.

Using the shortcut menu on grip-selected objects increases productivity by offering a standard Windows method of direct object manipulation without the intervention of additional dialog boxes or the need to choose options via keyboard entry. Figure 1.16 shows several editing choices available on the shortcut menu. The Properties option offers additional modification possibilities by displaying the Modify Properties dialog box appropriate for the selected object.

Real-Time Pan & Zoom

Real-time pan & zoom features were quietly introduced into AutoCAD mid-way through the Release 13 cycle as separate commands. Their implementation was somewhat awkward and their existence was never well-documented. Many Release 13 users didn't know of their existence. In Release 14, real-time pan and zoom features have been combined into a single command and tightly integrated into the overriding ZOOM command structure. Real-time pan & zoom is demonstrated in the following exercise.

USING REAL-TIME PAN & ZOOM

1. Open or continue in this chapter's Chap01.dwg. Perform a ZOOM, Extents by typing **Z** and pressing Enter followed by **E** and Enter.

2. Re-enter the ZOOM command by pressing Enter. The following prompt appears:

```
All/Center/Dynamic/Extents/Previous/Scale(X/XP)/
Window/<Realtime>:
```

3. Notice that the default option in R14 is Realtime, not Scale, as it was in previous releases.

   Accept the default by pressing Enter. Note that the screen cursor changes to the real-time zoom symbol shown in figure 1.17.

Figure 1.17

The real-time pan & zoom symbol.

4. Position the symbol at the top of the screen, and then click and drag the symbol toward the bottom of the screen. Notice the zoom magnification decreases. Repeat the click and drag, moving the symbol toward the top of the screen. Notice that the magnification increases.

5. Perform a series of bottom-to-top click and drag zoom-in motions until your screen resembles figure 1.18. This represents an approximate 400× zoom factor above the Zoom Extents level.

Figure 1.18

Zooming to a 400× zoom factor.

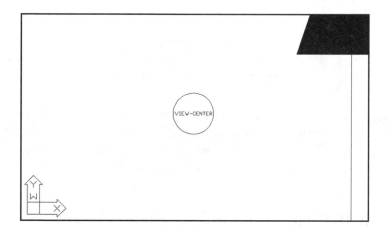

6. Now right-click. The real-time pan & zoom pop-up menu appears as shown in figure 1.19. From this menu, choose Zoom Previous. Notice that the display reverts to the Zoom Extents view.

Figure 1.19

The real-time pan & zoom pop-up menu.

7. Right-click again and choose Pan from the pop-up menu. The real-time pan symbol appears. Use a click-and-drag motion to pan around the drawing.

8. Display the pop-up menu with a right-click, and choose Zoom Extents.

9. Display the pop-up menu and choose Exit. Real-time pan & zoom ends.

10. If you want to close the drawing at this point, click on the No button when asked if you want to save changes.

Notice that the Zoom, Extents in these exercises did not trigger a regen and that the image was centered after the Zoom, Extents operation. In Release 14, zooming to the extents of a drawing no longer causes a regen in most cases, and the resulting image is centered instead of being shifted to the lower-left corner of the display. These changes eliminated the two major complaints against this otherwise useful ZOOM option.

NOTE

Although not shown in the previous exercise, real-time pan & zoom can be accessed from the Standard Toolbar as shown in figure 1.11. If another command is in progress, real-time pan & zoom will automatically be entered transparently.

In Release 14, real-time panning and zooming operations are quick, smooth, and easy to carry out. The real-time mode is now the default mode for both the PAN and ZOOM commands, which makes viewing and navigating around even large drawings much more intuitive and faster.

Running Osnap Toggle and Snap Override

Release 14 introduces several enhancements to the operation of object snaps. The running object snap toggle, for example, is an enhancement that enables you to toggle off any running object snaps prior to selecting a point without losing the running osnap settings. Although running osnaps are a powerful and useful drawing aid, their use in previous releases has been hampered by the inability to quickly disable them on a temporary basis. Release 14 corrects this limitation.

To access the running osnap toggle feature, double-click the OSNAP tile on the Release 14 status bar (see fig. 1.20). To provide additional functionality, if no running osnaps are set, double-clicking the OSNAP tile will display the Osnap Settings dialog box in which you can specify running osnaps.

Figure 1.20

The OSNAP tile used to access, specify, and override OSNAP.

OSNAP MODEL TILE

Insider Tip

When either setting or disabling running osnaps, it is frequently more desirable to use keyboard entry instead of double-clicking a tile outside the drawing area. In Release 14, the F3 key or Ctrl+F enables you to do this.

Prior to Release 14, it was often difficult to explicitly enter coordinate data while a running osnap was set; the osnap took precedence. In Release 14, an option is provided to enable explicit coordinate entry to take precedence over any running osnap. With this option (enabled by default), direct coordinate entry is enhanced, and you can be confident that such entries are given priority over any running osnap in effect. This option is controlled by the new system variable OSNAPCOORD.

AutoSnap

The use of object snaps is one of the most common operations in AutoCAD; without the capability to snap to specific points on drawing object geometry, it would be virtually impossible to make precise drawings. The basic operation of AutoCAD's osnap feature has not essentially changed since the feature was first introduced in Release 2. Release 14, however, supports a new enhancement to the basic osnap feature. AutoSnap enables you to preview and confirm snap point candidates before picking a point during drawing and editing operations. Even though it is a powerful tool, Osnap selection is often pick-intensive, time-consuming, and occasionally ambiguous. AutoSnap rectifies these drawbacks by providing visual and tactual confirmation of snap points, which enables you to know beforehand if you have locked onto the desired point, even when multiple snap modes are set or when the underlying drawing geometry is visually dense. The AutoSnap feature is demonstrated in the following exercise.

AN INTRODUCTION TO THE AUTOSNAP FEATURE

1. Continue in or open this chapter's Chap01.dwg, which can be found on the accompanying CD-ROM. Restore the "autosnap" view by choosing View, Named Views from the pull-down menu. In the View Control dialog box, choose AUTOSNAP, click on Restore, and then click on OK. Your screen should resemble figure 1.21.

Figure 1.21

A demonstration of the AutoSnap feature.

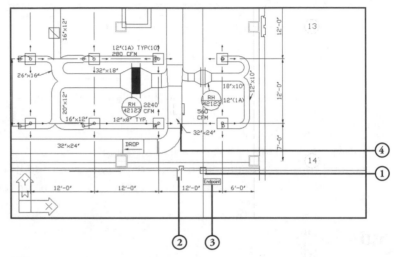

2. Next, ensure that the AutoSnap feature is turned on. Choose Tools, Object Snap Settings. Select the AutoSnap(TM) tab of the Object Settings dialog box. Ensure that a check mark appears in all the AutoSnap feature check boxes as shown in figure 1.22.

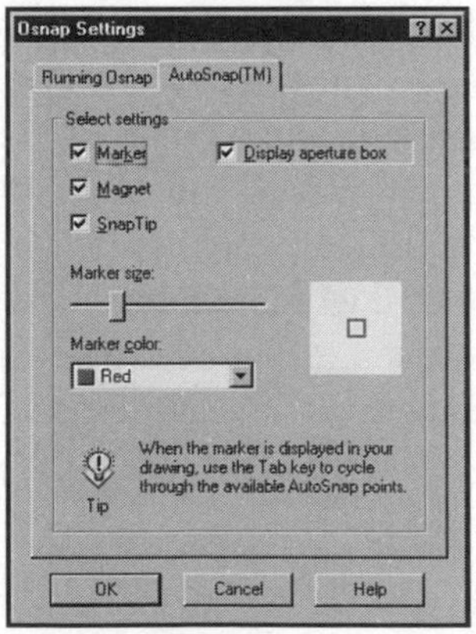

Figure 1.22

Setting the features of AutoSnap.

3. While still in the Object Settings dialog box, select the Running Osnap tab and place a check mark in the check box next to the Endpoint setting. Close the dialog box by clicking on OK.

4. Begin the LINE command by typing **L** and pressing Enter. Now move and rest the aperture located at the center of the screen cursor over the line shown at ① in figure 1.21. Notice the distinctive Marker that appears at ② and the Snap Tip at ③.

5. Move the aperture to the Marker at ②. Notice that the aperture "snaps" into place when in close proximity to the marker.

6. With the LINE command still in progress, continue to move the aperture around the drawing. Notice the behavior of the Marker as the aperture contacts a line object.

7. Now set a MIDpoint snap in effect by either typing **mid** and pressing Enter or using Shift+right-click and selecting Midpoint from the cursor pop-up menu.

8. Move the aperture across several line objects and note the position of the Midpoint AutoSnap Marker and the Snap Tip.

9. End the LINE command by pressing the Esc key. Then restart the LINE command by pressing the spacebar.

10. Move the aperture to the position shown at ④. Depending on the size and exact position of your aperture box, as many as six line endpoints fall within the aperture. The Endpoint Marker will snap to one of these endpoints.

11. With the aperture still at ④, repeatedly press the keyboard's Tab key and notice how the Endpoint Marker switches among the possible endpoint choices. Also note that the line to whose endpoint the marker snaps becomes highlighted, giving an unambiguous means of identification.

12. With any one of the line objects highlighted, press the Pick button and move the cursor toward the lower-left corner of your display. Note the endpoint to which you snapped. Cancel the LINE command by pressing Esc.

13. If you want to close the drawing at this point, click on the No button when asked if you want to save changes.

Object snapping is an important capability. The AutoSnap feature provides the first significant enhancement to this frequently used drawing aid. It removes much of the guesswork from entering object snaps. For veteran AutoCAD users, it makes object snapping that much more efficient. For new users, the basic concept of object snapping is easier to comprehend and learn. You will use AutoSnap in several exercises in this book.

Launch Browser

A new BROWSER command in Release 14 enables you to easily launch your Internet web browser from within AutoCAD. The BROWSER command launches whatever browser application is associated with .HTM in your system registry. This command is available from the Standard Toolbar (see fig. 1.23) as well as from the Command: line. The following exercise shows how easy this command is to use.

NOTE

If you do not have a connection to the Internet configured, you can skip this exercise.

USING THE BROWSER COMMAND

1. Open any drawing.

2. From the Standard Toolbar, click on the Launch Browser icon shown in figure 1.23. The following prompt appears:

   `Location   <www.autodesk.com>:`

3. Press Enter. Note that your configured Internet browser starts and goes to the default location (URL).

4. You also can type another address at the prompt shown in step 2.

Launch Browser

Figure 1.23

Release 14's new Launch Browser icon.

INSIDER TIP

The default location for the BROWSER command is determined by the system variable INETLOCATION. It is useful to set this to your Internet Service Provider's home page. This enables you to access any of a number of your favorite CAD web sites quickly without first going to the Autodesk home page. If you want to go directly to Autodesk's home page, choose Connect with Autodesk from the Help pull-down menu.

INSIDER TIP

When typing an address at the command line for the BROWSER command, it is permissible, but unnecessary, to type the *http://* prefix. This shortcut is useful when pasting an abbreviated URL address for this command to the command line. If the prefix is absent, it is automatically added before being sent to your browser application.

Being able to quickly access the Internet from within AutoCAD is a great time-saver. Its importance will become more and more apparent as the capability to share drawing file information on the Internet develops. The importance of the link between AutoCAD and the Internet is the subject of Part VI, "CAD on the Internet."

Updated Help

The entire Help facility in Release 14 is updated to conform more closely to Windows standards and conventions. The Help Topics: AutoCAD Help dialog box shown in figure 1.24 contains a Contents tab in addition to the Index and Find tabs introduced in Release 13. The topics, or books, listed on the Contents tab are intended primarily to offer help with more general topics, such as a listing of all Release 14 command and system variables along with definitions and usage information. Other general topics include subjects such as an Installation Guide and a Customization Guide.

Figure 1.24

Release 14's Help topics can be found on the Contents tab.

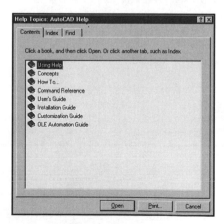

The Find and Index tabs enable you to search for or go directly to a large number of topics. They operate much like a search of a book's index pages. As you type in a subject, the number of topics is automatically limited and narrowed down. Clicking on the Display button displays the expanded help topic page or pages.

INSIDER TIP

In both the Index and Find tabs, typing the name of an AutoCAD command in UPPERCASE letters narrows your search to the topic page covering the basic command. Topics relating to that command's usage under specific circumstances are listed under or near the basic command topic. This is helpful when you are uncertain of the sub-topics any given command may offer.

Figure 1.25 shows a typical help topic page, the sub-page from the ALIGN command topic. Any given topic page may be copied to the Windows Clipboard or printed. In addition, you can add your own annotations to a topic and place bookmarks on pages you want to be able to return to quickly.

Figure 1.25

A typical page from the enhanced Help facility.

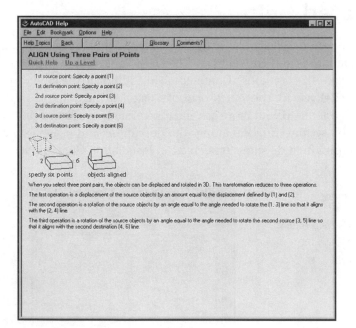

INSIDER TIP

If you've never or rarely used AutoCAD's Help, I urge you to start taking advantage of this vastly improved facility. Release 14's Help is both extensive and easy to use.

Release 14's Learning Assistance

Within the overall Help facility, but new to Release 14, is AutoCAD Learning Assistance. You can access this facility by choosing Learning Assistance from the Help pull-down menu. This new addition to Help is actually a stand-alone application that ships with Release 14 as a separate CD. It represents a very sophisticated use of multimedia learning/teaching technology. It is, in effect, an extensive online multimedia tutorial. With the aid of both animation and voice tracks, basic and advanced AutoCAD topics are fully explained and demonstrated. Users can interrupt and replay an animation and even exit Learning Assistance to practice or apply a concept in an actual AutoCAD session using the lesson's drawing from the tutorial's CD. Figure 1.26 shows a page from a typical Learning Assistance tutorial. To utilize Learning Assistance, you must have a compatible sound card and a configured animation application.

Figure 1.26

A page from Release 14's Learning Assistance CD.

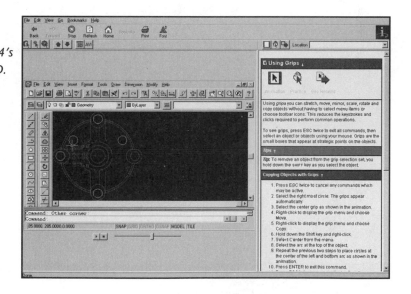

Learning Assistance is intended for use by both veteran and new AutoCAD users as well as for those moving to a Windows environment. It is an effective learning tool that enables you to set your own pace and concentrate on topics or concepts that are of interest to you.

Summary

Many of the new features in AutoCAD Release 14 are visual in nature and are related directly or indirectly to the user interface. Because AutoCAD is, primarily, a visual design application heavily dependent on a useful interface, these new features serve to increase your efficiency while using AutoCAD. Several of Release 14's enhancements are not mentioned in this chapter but are covered in later chapters. Other features, such as the new Layer & Linetype Properties dialog box discussed in this chapter, represent improvements in usability and functionality that are seen in many other dialog boxes within Release 14. The move toward full Windows integration that started in Release 13 is completed in Release 14. This more efficient "look" helps bring about more efficient operation.

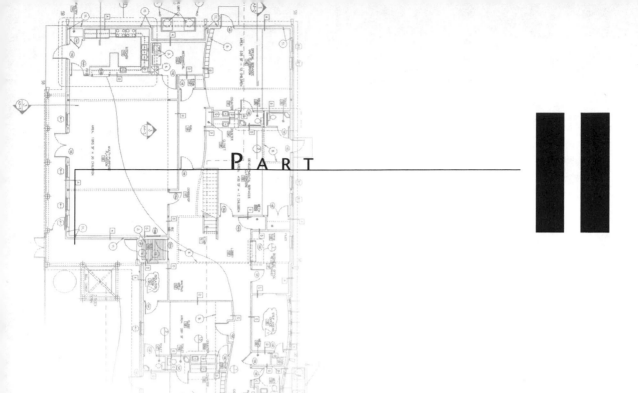

P A R T

II

STARTING NEW PROJECTS WITH R14

Chapter 2: Before the Drawing Begins: Planning and Organizing Projects

Chapter 3: Setting Up the AutoCAD 14 Drawing Environment

Chapter 4: Organizing Drawings with Layers

Chapter 5: Using Linetypes Effectively

BEFORE THE DRAWING BEGINS: PLANNING AND ORGANIZING PROJECTS

by Craig W. Sharp

You might have been attracted to AutoCAD because this program can save you time in creating the drawings and images associated with your work. In this chapter, you will learn techniques that are not necessarily drawing-based, but that have a lot to do with saving time. This chapter is about the process of organizing your thoughts and your work to save time, both on your current project(s) and on your future projects. Whether your work is organized into work orders, purchase orders, shop drawings, tool and die, CNC, or the AEC industry, it generally is organized around "project delivery" efforts. In this chapter, you will learn to use AutoCAD and Windows 95/Windows NT to help you deliver your projects more effectively and more predictably. Among the topics discussed are:

- Key organization factors

- Initial drawing setup

- AutoCAD project organization features

- Creating title blocks and template files

If you're like most of us, you probably swear each New Year's Eve that you will get organized. You probably swear that you will do some filing, back up old files, save some special drawings for reuse, or learn how to better manage your software and files. This chapter will give you the tools that should become part of your daily work habits and that will automate many of your New Year's resolutions...at least where project and file organization is concerned. By the way, spring cleaning, weight loss, and developing new social skills are beyond the scope of this book.

Getting Started: Key Factors to Organize First

The ultimate goal of project organization is to save time. In general, you can save time in three ways:

- Don't repeat what you have already done.

- Locate what you have already done faster than you can re-create it.

- Don't make mistakes.

These foundations of time saving are part of a larger picture called Total Quality Management. The next sections discuss factors that you can organize to start saving time and help achieve the goals in the preceding bullets. These preliminary organization factors include determining the following: how many drawings are needed, how much detail is required, or what is an efficient method of workflow management, how many different ways the drawing will be displayed, and what elements you can use more than once.

Determining How Many Drawings Are Necessary

When you sit down to start drawing a project, one of your earliest tasks is to determine just how many and what type of drawings you will need. Two important issues should be considered when establishing the number of drawings to create.

First and foremost, you should address the computing power versus drawing size factor. Computing power consists of storage space, both long-term (such as with hard disk, tape, and network server) and short-term (such as how much RAM you have), coupled with the speed of your graphics card and CPU. Autodesk and other experts toss about many factors relating to how much memory and hard disk you need to handle each megabyte of drawing. Unfortunately, no hard-and-fast rule exists. If you use xrefs, extended entity data, attributes, and 3D solids, and if you like to open multiple copies of AutoCAD at once, then your needs vary substantially from someone who stores 2D vector information in a drawing without any bells and whistles. Therefore, you must ascertain your ideal drawing size through experience and simple trial and error. A good set of guidelines, for example, would be to use 32 times your drawing size in memory and 64 times your drawing size in free disk space. When you have a good feel for how large your drawings can be before the performance of your system hinders your work, you can determine how you want to organize your drawing data into drawings. The following examples discuss various options for organizing a project into drawings with AutoCAD:

■ Your drawing is contained in one model, and you can view the model through various paper space viewports. (Keep in mind that a model can be 3D or 2D.) In this case, your entire project might be in one drawing, or in a series of drawings that attaches the model to each drawing via AutoCAD's xref capability. The model can then be viewed and annotated differently in each viewport or drawing.

■ Each of your drawings comprises a very detailed portion of a much larger product. You can use an xref that is a component grid for your product. This xref organizes the location of and junction between each drawing.

■ Each of your drawings can be developed by viewing one or two other drawings. You can use multiple copies of AutoCAD and keep multiple drawings open at one time.

■ Your drawings are only a small portion of your project documentation, and the drawings are linked to text documents, images, and other multimedia-media products using Object Linking and Embedding (OLE).

You will learn more about the use of xrefs in Chapter 13, "External References," and the use of paper space in Chapter 15, "Paper Space." It is important that you consider a variety of approaches when creating your drawings and that you develop a tried-and-true method that delivers exactly what you need a majority of the time. After you develop your approach to building your drawings, you can begin to predict how many drawings you will need and what their contents will be.

Developing Drawing and Task Lists

Using this approach, you should develop a list of drawings and a task list that goes with each drawing. This list of drawings and the associated tasks should be flexible and expandable. One of the best ways to accomplish this feat is to link a spreadsheet into the paper space of each of your drawings. In this way, you can have a central storehouse for your task list that is visible in each of your drawings. You also can plot this task list with your drawing so that you can easily measure your progress when you create progress prints of your project. Finally, you can update this task list as you work in each drawing. Your to-do list probably expands as you work in your drawings and as tasks come to mind. Using a linked spreadsheet enables you to add to your list for any drawings while remaining in the current drawing. You will learn some simple steps for creating a linked spreadsheet task list in an exercise later in this chapter. Figure 2.1 shows a sample task list, and figure 2.2 shows the placement of the spreadsheet task list within a drawing.

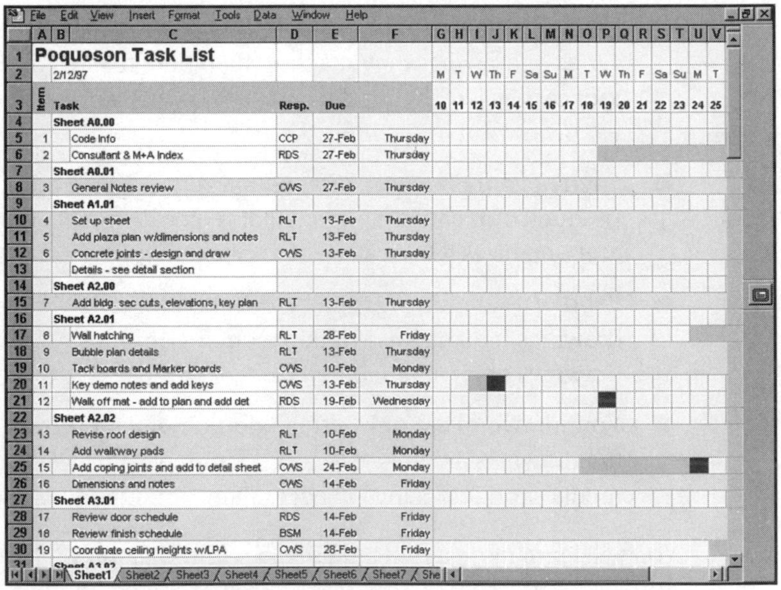

File Edit View Insert Format Tools Data Window Help

	A	B	C	D	E	F	G	H	I	J	K	L	M	N	O	P	Q	R	S	T	U	V
1	Poquoson Task List																					
2		2/12/97					M	T	W	Th	F	Sa	Su	M	T	W	Th	F	Sa	Su	M	T
3	Item	Task		Resp.	Due		10	11	12	13	14	15	16	17	18	19	20	21	22	23	24	25
4		Sheet A0.00																				
5	1		Code Info	CCP	27-Feb	Thursday																
6	2		Consultant & M+A Index	RDS	27-Feb	Thursday																
7		Sheet A0.01																				
8	3		General Notes review	CWS	27-Feb	Thursday																
9		Sheet A1.01																				
10	4		Set up sheet	RLT	13-Feb	Thursday																
11	5		Add plaza plan w/dimensions and notes	RLT	13-Feb	Thursday																
12	6		Concrete joints - design and draw	CWS	13-Feb	Thursday																
13			Details - see detail section																			
14		Sheet A2.00																				
15	7		Add bldg. sec cuts, elevations, key plan	RLT	13-Feb	Thursday																
16		Sheet A2.01																				
17	8		Wall hatching	RLT	28-Feb	Friday																
18	9		Bubble plan details	RLT	13-Feb	Thursday																
19	10		Tack boards and Marker boards	CWS	10-Feb	Monday																
20	11		Key demo notes and add keys	CWS	13-Feb	Thursday																
21	12		Walk off mat - add to plan and add det	RDS	19-Feb	Wednesday																
22		Sheet A2.02																				
23	13		Revise roof design	RLT	10-Feb	Monday																
24	14		Add walkway pads	RLT	10-Feb	Monday																
25	15		Add coping joints and add to detail sheet	CWS	24-Feb	Monday																
26	16		Dimensions and notes	CWS	14-Feb	Friday																
27		Sheet A3.01																				
28	17		Review door schedule	RDS	14-Feb	Friday																
29	18		Review finish schedule	BSM	14-Feb	Friday																
30	19		Coordinate ceiling heights w/LPA	CWS	28-Feb	Friday																

Sheet1 Sheet2 Sheet3 Sheet4 Sheet5 Sheet6 Sheet7 She

Figure 2.1

A sample task list for a series of drawings.

Figure 2.2

You can use the task list in a non-plotting area of the drawing. If you want the task list to appear in your plots, simply pick it up and move it into the plot area of your drawing.

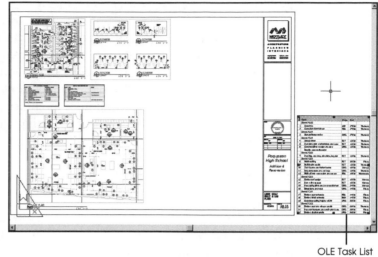

OLE Task List

Determining How Much Detail Is Required

Another important factor in the organization of your project is determining how much detail is required for the drawing. Because AutoCAD is so accurate, you can easily fall into the trap of creating minuscule details that might not have anything to do with the actual production of your project from your drawings. It is important that you describe only what the ultimate user of your drawing(s) will need in order to accomplish the specific job. In addition, you should keep in mind that the person actually creating your project might have better, more effective methods of building the product in the field than you do on the drawing. The following list of questions will be discussed in the following section to help you determine the extent of the detail in each drawing and in your project as a whole:

- What should be explained?
- When should it be explained?
- How should it be explained?
- Who should explain it?
- Where should it be explained?

The answers to each of these might seem obvious to you at first glance, but after you take a look at how they affect your project organization, you will realize how many factors are involved in answering each question.

Answering the Questions

In answering the first question, you should not be concerned with only the parts of your project that you will draw. You also should consider how to organize your drawings in a way that describes your project in the most efficient and effective manner. For example, you might need to define a continuous chamfer that surrounds a face plate, as well as the location of the holes in the face plate and the specific location of tooling on the face plate. To adequately describe these conditions, you would need two sections—one horizontal and one vertical through the face plate—as well as a front view of the face plate. Two isometric views can accomplish the same thing with one less drawing required.

The second question might mean that you won't need to draw some details of your project at all because you will get back a set of shop drawings from a vendor who determines how the detailing will be done. Answering this second question also might determine the order of the drawings within a set of project drawings.

It might be obvious to you that the third question concerns the type of drawing (such as isometric and plan and section drawings) that you need. However, you also should think about using photographs, notation, and shaded 3D models as part of the explanation.

This fourth question might mean that you can have a vendor finish your work for you in the form of shop drawings, but it also involves finding a person within the project team to work on a design or a drawing. A conceptual designer, for example, might not have the CAD skills that are ultimately needed to complete a detailed 3D model. Therefore, you might have to alter your preferred choice of drawing technique based upon who is doing the design and drawing.

After you have completed the first four questions, you are prepared to ask the final question, which is the ultimate determination of the organization of your drawings. For example, you must determine whether you have so many details that they must be on their own sheets or whether these details should be included as blow-ups on the same sheet as the larger scale drawing. You also must establish a systematized approach to the order of your drawings that works every time. Furthermore, you should address whether you can readily insert drawings into the drawing sequence if you discover that one is needed well into your project. Two key concepts can help you manage this portion of your effort:

■ Developing an efficient numbering system used within the drawings

■ Developing a file naming/folder naming system that corresponds with the drawing numbering system

Developing an Efficient Numbering System

You need a way to name or number your drawings that works the same way every time and allows flexibility in the order of your drawings and the number of each type of drawing. A perfect example of a system that works in this way is a library catalogue, better known as the Dewey Decimal System. If you can organize your drawings into categories and sequence the drawings within a category, then this type of system might work for you. For example, in the AEC industry, drawings have categories, such as Cover Sheet and General Information Sheets, Floor Plans, Elevations, and Sections. Each category might contain a sequence of drawings, such as the First Floor Plan and the Second Floor Plan. Following this format, you could define a drawing numbering system that meets the goals of predictability, flexibility, and expandability. The following list details a numbering system you could implement:

0.00, 0.01, 0.02, and so on—Cover Sheets and General Information

1.00, 1.01, 1.02, and so on—Floor Plans

2.00, 2.01, 2.02, and so on—Elevations

3.00, 3.01, 3.02, and so on—Sections

...and so forth.

NOTE

Note that a floor plan can be added into the middle of the set at any time—the limitation here is that only 9 drawing categories and 99 drawings can exist within each category. If you want more, simply add more numbers to your file names, as in 01.000.

Developing a File and Folder Naming System

You can carry this system a bit further and use it to name the drawing files while also adding project numbers and a drawing description. If you design your drawing-numbering and file-naming conventions with some forethought, the file names will sort themselves in the Open or Save File dialog boxes in order, so you will know what a drawing contains without opening the drawing. The only limitation in Windows 95/Windows NT is that the file name can't contain more than 255 characters, and it can't contain any of the following characters: \ / : * ? " < > |. Of course, if you make your file names 255 characters long, you can't have the files in a folder, you will spend a lot of time typing the file names, and many file dialog boxes won't display the entire name within them. Therefore, a responsible file-naming system might include a project or work-order number, a drawing number, and a predictable maximum number of characters for a description. The example illustrates the format of the filename following this system:

<project number><drawing number><revision number><drawing owner><sheet title>.dwg

9701-1.00-01cws-OVERALL BUILDING PLAN.dwg

Note that Windows 95 also remembers the upper-case letters separately from lower-case letters. Using upper- and lower-case letters can help with the legibility of the drawing file name. Also note that the final extension for the file name is always .dwg, because AutoCAD must see the .dwg file extension to load the file. Even if you can see only the first 15 characters of this file name, you would know that the file belongs to project number 9701, that it's a plan of some type, that it's revision number 1, and that someone with the initials "cws" originated the drawing. This file naming convention also first sorts the drawing files by project number, then by drawing number, then by revision, and then by author. Figure 2.3 shows an example of what the results might be.

Figure 2.3

Using file names with built-in intelligence will save you time and help organize your project.

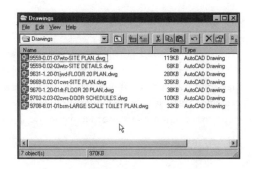

INSIDER TIP

If you create new drawings on a regular basis, an involved file name might become counter-productive. In other words, the amount of information that you include in your file name is partly based upon the shelf life of your drawings.

If you organize your drawings into folders that have some logical hierarchy to them, the file names also can become simpler. For instance, the previous example could have a folder structure similar to the one shown in figure 2.4.

Figure 2.4

The judicious use of folders can simplify file-naming needs.

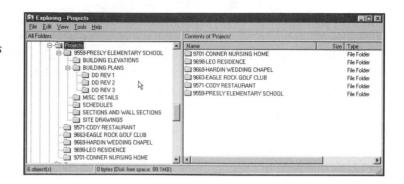

Using the folders in figure 2.4, the file name used previously could become 9701-1.00cws-OVERALL.dwg.

It's always a good idea to keep the project number or work order number as part of the drawing file name so that drawings that might be accidentally stranded can be tied to their project with relative ease. You also must consider how many versions of any one portion of the file name you might have. For example, the project number 9701 enables you to have 99 projects in the year 1997. If you think you will have more than 99 projects, you would have to number the projects with 5 digits, as in 97001. Likewise, 1.00 means that only 99 floors can exist in the building (1.01 through 1.99), and using 01 for a revision marker means that up to 99 revisions can exist. Make sure that you don't limit yourself and have to change your file-naming scheme in a year or two. Take the time to study the types and number of events that you need to record in your file name by looking over past projects that you or other members of your company have completed. Don't hesitate to run your ideas by others to see if they can spot any shortcomings.

Determining How Your Drawings Relate

This topic can become very complex, because AutoCAD can be linked to other documents—in addition, complex relationships can exist within your project between drawings. You can organize your thoughts about the interrelationships between your drawings and other drawings or documents by asking a few simple questions:

- What information must be shared between drawings?

- What other documents will be included in the drawings?

- What other documents will the drawings be included within?

At this point, it might be a good idea to create a mock-up set of drawings using a standard form. If you have a number of drawings and documents that make up your project and your sheets are standard and uniformly sized, then a mock-up is easy to do and beneficial. If your projects are small in terms of document count or widely varied in document format and size, you may not find a mock-up on a form to be that helpful.

You can create this mock-up as a basis for your drawing set in AutoCAD, or you can free-hand the mock-up using preprinted sheets and a pencil. Creating electronic mock-ups of your project will be helpful in the long run because the effort will contribute to the creation of the final documents.

However you choose to create a mock-up, it should organize key information. In the section, "Determining Which Elements Can Be Used More Than Once," figure 2.8 shows an example of a mock-up form that contains places that provide the information to answer the three questions just reviewed. This shared information is placed in the drawing window on the form by using callouts—or bubbles—that reference another drawing. Lists that describe what documents also will be included from outside the drawing, as will documents that contain the drawing represented by this mock-up page. Additionally, such useful information as drawing number, drawing name, date, project name, and author is included on the form.

If you want to create your mock-ups electronically, you can place the mock-up right on the drawing to aid in its creation. This can be set up ahead of time by using a form in place of a title block in a template drawing. (This process will be discussed a bit later in this chapter.) After the mock-up has served its purpose, you can substitute a real title block for the mock-up form. If you keep your mock-ups separate from your drawings, then it's a good idea to create your mock up as an $8\frac{1}{2} \times 11$ sheet so that you can plot "mini" sets of your entire project until you complete the mock-up.

Using Object Linking and Embedding (OLE)

When you include your drawing in another document or include a document within your AutoCAD drawing, you use Object Linking and Embedding (OLE). When you link a file within another file, you can stipulate whether you want to update the object each time you open the file that contains the embedded object. In this way, the object is always current, which offers a powerful benefit to you if multiple people are working on a project. When someone makes a change to the embedded object, all the documents containing the embedded object are updated. If you want to freeze the embedded object in time so that it doesn't change within the drawing, you can change the link between the object and the document to a manual link so that you can control the updates. This is done with the OLE Links command found on the Edit pull-down menu. Figure 2.5 shows an example of using OLE in an AutoCAD drawing.

Figure 2.5

OLE either updates or freezes objects in an AutoCAD drawing.

Bitmap images are easy to include in your drawings

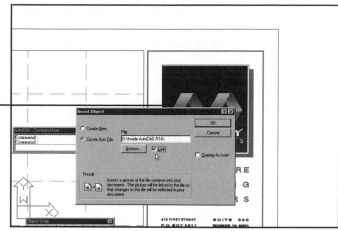

The method shown in figure 2.5 uses Insert OLE Object from the Insert menu in AutoCAD, which is fine as long as you want to place all the objects from a file into your drawing. You also can use the Windows clipboard to insert objects. The following example illustrates how to create a task list and insert it into a drawing.

NOTE

This exercise uses a spreadsheet to create a task list because a spreadsheet makes insertion and numbering of tasks relatively simple. If you don't have a spreadsheet product, you can use WordPad (which comes with Windows 95 and Windows NT 4.0) to accomplish the same feat.

USING OLE TO EMBED TASK LISTS IN YOUR DRAWINGS

1. First, create a task list with a few drawings listed. If you have a current project for which you need a task list, that would be a good place to start—otherwise, just make one up. The task list can be any width and length, but Windows products limit the size of the embedded object to approximate a printed $8\frac{1}{2} \times 11$-inch page size. If you create a large spreadsheet, you must piece it together using more than one object in order to see the entire list in your drawing. For ease, model your task list on the sample shown in figure 2.1, which appears earlier in this chapter.

2. After you have highlighted the tasks, open the Edit pull-down menu and choose Copy to copy the spreadsheet contents to the clipboard.

3. Minimize the spreadsheet and start AutoCAD. The Start-Up dialog box should appear (unless you have disabled this). Click on the Use a Template button. From the Select a Template List, choose Ansi_d.dwt. Then click on OK. For this exercise, you may choose another template if desired.

4. From the Edit pull-down menu, choose Paste Special. Select Paste Link, and you should see only your spreadsheet listed in the dialog box. Click on OK in the Paste Special dialog box and your task list should be inserted into the AutoCAD drawing.

5. Type **ZOOM A** at the Command: prompt, and press Enter.

6. Move the cursor into the center of the OLE object, and select the object. The object's grips are enabled and the cursor becomes a four-headed arrow. Press and hold down the left mouse button while you move the object to the right of the drawing area.

7. With the object still selected, move the cursor over one of the corners. The cursor will turn into a diagonal two-headed arrow.

8. Hold the Shift key down and grab one of the corners of the object. You can resize the object and maintain the correct aspect ratio of the object by holding down the Shift key.

The result should appear similar to figure 2.2, shown earlier in this chapter. Now you can add any variety of objects to your drawings from the Windows clipboard.

Developing Efficient Workflow Management

If more than one person will work on a drawing, you must determine how each person will know which drawing is the current drawing. This aspect of project delivery is known as *workflow management*. Consider, for example, the scenario if outside consultants or contractors work on the drawings and you want to make changes to them. How will you know which drawing contains the most recent information? If you do not address this concern, you might have two drawings that each contain some of the information that you need to create the correct drawing. As an even more complicated scenario, two people might need to work on the drawing at the same time.

Proper Network File Control

Your organization of the project and its documents and your management of file access are key to avoiding disaster with multiple document users or authors. If you work on a network that provides multiple access to a drawing, then your network software must support file locking. Most contemporary network products enable you to open files in Read Only mode and won't let you overwrite the file on which someone else is working. Proper network file control means that the first person to open a drawing is the only editor that can actually save changes to the drawing. All subsequent users can open the drawing only in Read Only mode. If someone absolutely must record changes to a drawing that is currently open by someone else, they must save their changes as a new drawing. Recording these changes on a unique layer name and saving the changes as a new drawing enables the changes to be merged with the original drawing later.

Using Redlines

Users also can record redlines on a unique layer that can be merged with a drawing. Redlines record comments, questions, and instructions over a drawing that are acted upon by someone else later. Figure 2.6 shows an example of redlines.

Figure 2.6

Creating redlines as instructions for revision to a drawing does not require the use of sophisticated AutoCAD commands.

Create redline layers

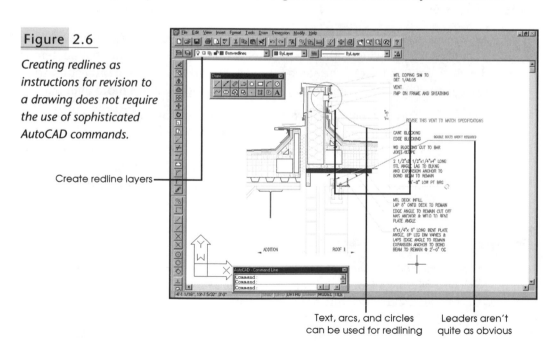

Text, arcs, and circles can be used for redlining

Leaders aren't quite as obvious

INSIDER TIP

Because redlines can be created using basic AutoCAD commands, you could create your own toolbar that contains basic redlining commands such as text, lines, arcs, circles, and leaders. In this way, individuals who are not sophisticated AutoCAD users still can contribute to your drawings electronically, saving time and paper.

Another way to avoid multiple file-use problems is to xref the drawing into a new drawing and create the redlines in the new drawing. In either event, you should name the drawing file and the layers used for redlines based upon a standard. For example, the file name could include the redliner's initials, a date, and the term *redlines* in the file name. The layer also could include the redliner's initials and redlines in the layer name.

Determining Which Elements Can Be Used More Than Once

As you saw earlier in this chapter, you can use xrefs to create more than one drawing from the same drawing. Although the use of xrefs can help ensure that numerous drawings contain exactly the same information and reduce total project drawing storage needs, xrefs also can help you avoid drawing elements more than once.

If you use a drawing template, as discussed earlier, you might not want to include a drawing border in the template drawing. Instead, you could devise a project border sheet that contains the project name, issue date, project number, project address, your firm's logo, address, and other information as an xref. Each new project drawing then would include the border as an xref so that changes need to be made only once.

NOTE

Using this method, you should create the xref so that it contains only the information common to all project drawings. You can also use AutoCAD Blocks for the same purpose. The question is, do you expect to make project-wide changes in the repetitive objects in your project. If the answer is yes, then you need to use xrefs.

Using an element more than once can mean more than creating an exact duplicate of objects. You might want to use guides in all your project drawings, such as the format of text, a key plan with different portions hatched in each drawing, or a sheet grid that doesn't plot. For example, you can create a block that contains only attributes that fill in your title block. The drawing author, checker, sheet number, sheet name, and date can be filled in for each drawing, but such elements as the text style, height, and layer will always be the same. (You will learn more about blocks in Chapter 12, "Creating and Using Blocks.") In fact, if your projects usually involve a large number of drawings, you can help the entire project team by creating a template drawing that contains the border and project as an xref, the sheet specific text as attributes, and a grid on layer DEFPOINTS (a default AutoCAD layer that never plots). Figure 2.7 shows an example of a template drawing that incorporates a number of unifying features.

Figure 2.7

A template drawing can contain project-specific information if you create a new template for each of your projects.

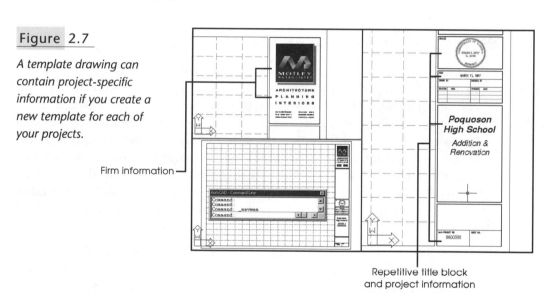

An important factor to consider is that, at the start of a project, you must map out as many multiple-use opportunities as you can, including organizing portions from drawings that you can reuse from earlier projects or from standard drawings that you have developed over numerous projects. Using the mock-up set discussed earlier, you also should map out the use of viewports to create numerous views of your model. Figure 2.8 shows an example of a mock-up of a portion of an architectural project.

Figure 2.8

A mock-up of a project.

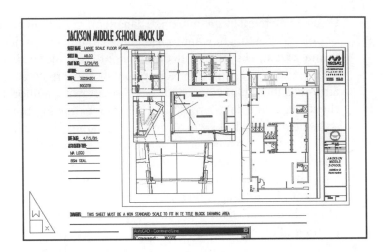

Determining How a Drawing Will Be Displayed

The final, and possibly most complex, issue to consider when laying out a project is the number of ways that a drawing will be displayed. As discussed in Chapter 27, "Publishing on the Web," Release 14 enables you to publish your drawings on the Internet. In addition, you might need to plot the drawing on a number of different sheet sizes, or you might need to create both drawings and renderings of the drawings for the project. Finally, as is the case for many drawings in this book, you might need to publish your drawings in a shop manual or a technical publication. As you can imagine, large drawings with a significant amount of detail don't publish very well on computer screens (if they did, the AutoCAD Zoom command wouldn't exist).

If you will create documents that will be displayed on the Internet, published in a technical publication, and plotted on a sheet of paper, something will have to give. You might need to create completely different drawings for each type of media due to one single factor: your text and symbols won't work for each and every possible publishing method. Although a perfect solution doesn't exist for these broad publishing requirements, planning for the project's needs from the start can save a lot of time and headaches. If your publication needs vary from project to project, it might be a good idea to obtain a drawing from a previous project that is similar to the one you will use for the current project. Using this drawing, you could try to publish it under all the conditions that you must meet. This process will help you uncover any problems that you might encounter.

Setting Up Your Drawing

After you have pondered each of the issues discussed so far, it is time to set up your drawings. You must follow a sequential set of steps to determine how you can accomplish this task. If you follow these steps, you will avoid revisiting text sizes, drawing configurations, and a number of other complications later in a project:

- Determining paper size
- Determining drawing scale
- Developing title blocks
- Determining units and angles

Determining Paper Size

The first and foremost determination you must make is what size the ultimate product will be. If you will plot your drawings to paper, the paper sizes that your plotter handles define your options for the drawing. Using a mock-up process—whether a formal one, such as the process discussed earlier, or simply figuring out how much paper area is required for an appropriate scale of your drawings—is the first step. Paper comes in an extensive set of sizes, and each industry generally settles upon a set of standard sizes. One important factor to consider about paper is whether you can create a modular approach to your paper sizes. Figure 2.9 shows a progression of paper sizes that will expand or contract between sheet sizes while maintaining the same aspect ratio between sheets. Maintaining the same aspect ratio means that you can blow up or minimize your drawings without concern for whether the drawing will fit the same way on the larger or smaller sheet.

Figure 2.9

Using paper sizes that are modular is an important consideration.

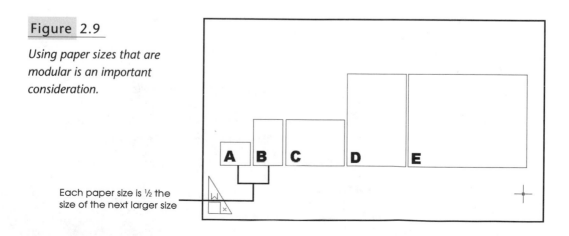

Each paper size is ½ the size of the next larger size

Obtaining modular sheet sizes might not be an easy task. If you are in the AEC industry, for example, nothing about standard AEC sheet sizes is modular. The AEC industry is hopelessly antiquated in this area and is making no rapid movement toward changing the system. While they have a modular set, no copier or standard envelope will use a 9×12-inch paper size. Table 2.1 lists standard paper sizes that are available.

Table 2.1

Standard Paper Sizes

Paper Size	Standard	MM	In
Eight Crown	IMP	1461×1060	57½×41¾
Antiquarian	IMP	1346×533	53×21
Quad Demy	IMP	1118×826	44×32½
Double Princess	IMP	1118×711	44×28
Quad Crown	IMP	1016×762	40×30
Double Elephant	IMP	1016×686	40×27
B0	ISO	1000×1414	39.37×55.67
Arch-E	USA	914×1,219	36×48
Double Demy	IMP	889×572	35×22½
E	ANSI	864×1118	34×44
A0	ISO	841×1189	33.11×46.81
Imperial	IMP	762×559	30×22
Princess	IMP	711×546	28×21½
B1	ISO	707×1000	27.83×39.37
Arch-D	USA	610×914	24×36
A1	ISO	594×841	23.39×33.11
Demy	IMP	584×470	23×18½
D	ANSI	559×864	22×34
B2	ISO	500×707	19.68×27.83
Arch-C	USA	457×610	18×24
C	ANSI	432×559	17×22
A2	ISO	420×594	16.54×23.39

Paper Size	Standard	MM	In
B3	ISO	353×500	13.90×19.68
Brief	IMP	333×470	13⅛×18½
Foolscap Folio	IMP	333×210	13⅛×8¼
Arch-B	USA	305×457	12×18
A3	ISO	297×420	11.69×16.54
B	ANSI	279×432	11×17
Demy quarto	IMP	273×216	10¾×8½
B4	ISO	250×353	9.84×13.90
Crown quarto	IMP	241×184	9½×7¼
Royal octavo	IMP	241×152	9½×6
Arch-A	USA	229×305	9×12
Demy octavo	IMP	222×137	8¾×5⅜
A	ANSI	216×279	8.5×11
Legal	USA	216×356	8.5×14
A4	ISO	210×297	8.27×11.69
Foolscap quarto	IMP	206×165	8⅛×6½
Crown Octavo	IMP	181×121	7⅛×4¼
B5	ISO	176×250	6.93×9.84
A5	ISO	148×210	5.83×8.27
	USA	140×216	5.5×8.5
	USA	127×178	5×7
A6	ISO	105×148	4.13×5.83
	USA	102×127	4×5
	USA	76×102	3×5
A7	ISO	74×105	2.91×4.13
A8	ISO	52×74	2.05×2.91
A9	ISO	37×52	1.46×2.05
A10	ISO	26×37	1.02×1.46

Determining Drawing Scale

After the paper sizes have been established, the next step is to determine the appropriate scale for your drawings. The scale of a drawing is a deceptively simple concept, and it involves more than simply figuring out what size your drawing must be to fit on the paper. The real issue about drawing scale is that the information contained on the drawing must be legible, yet the drawing scale must be standard in your industry and the sheet size must be as convenient to handle as possible. Your drawing must place the model, notes, dimensions, hatching, and symbols in their most favorable and legible light. If you have to cram a drawing full of symbols and text, you could lose the linework that represents the object of your drawing. Creating the drawing at the appropriate scale allows for space between text, dimensions, and symbols both within and around your drawing.

Of course, if you always create drawings at full-scale, then the only option is in the selection of sheet size for your paper. Using the appropriate scale might require you to cut your drawing up into sections rather than display the entire model on one sheet of paper. You might think that a drawing spanning more than one sheet seems inconvenient, but legibility is more important in this case.

Using Paper Space Viewports to Scale a Model

You can scale your model in two ways. You can either provide a scale factor at plot time or you can view your model through paper space viewports. Release 14 has eliminated regens when panning and zooming in paper space, so the only intelligent choice is to use paper space. You will learn to set up a paper space viewport later in the exercises for this chapter. The best part about paper space viewports is that you get instant feedback from your drawing as to what drawing scale fits on your sheet. To use a paper space viewport for plotting to scale, you must zoom in on your model at a predetermined scale factor. The following steps summarize the entire process:

1. First, you must calculate the required scale factor. If your drawings use a decimal scale, this is a relatively simple feat. For example, a drawing created at 1:10 uses a scale factor of .10. The AEC industry uses nondecimal scale factors, however, and the calculation requires a few more steps. A $1/8$-inch =1 foot scale drawing requires a scale factor of $1/96$. To convert AEC scales, simply multiply your drawing scale (in this case, $1/8$) by $1/12$. Therefore, the scale factor for a $1/4$-inch = 1 foot drawing is $1/48$, and a 3-inch = 1 foot drawing is $1/4$.

2. Next, from a paper space view (Tilemode=0), make sure that you are in model space by clicking on the Status Bar to display Model, as shown in figure 2.10.

Figure 2.10

Use the Status Bar to access model space through a paper space viewport.

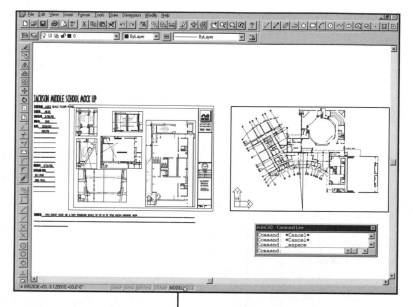

Double-click here to switch between model and paper space

3. You should see the crosshairs in the desired viewport. If you don't, click within the boundaries of the desired viewport to make this the current viewport.

4. Use Zoom Extents so that you can see all your model. Then use Zoom Center and select a point in the approximate graphic center of your model (the center of a rectangle that contains your entire model)(see fig. 2.11).

5. When you are prompted for magnification or height, enter your scale factor, followed by **XP** (see fig. 2.12).

Figure 2.11

Select the center of the drawing portion you want to view.

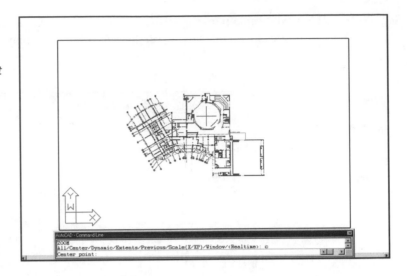

Figure 2.12

Enter the scale factor when prompted.

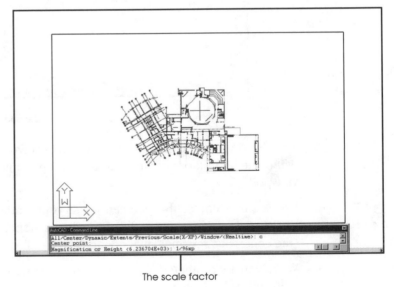

The scale factor

The area of the drawing you selected is centered in the viewport at the desired scale, as seen in figure 2.13.

Using this technique, you can set up numerous plot scales of your drawing for any specific needs that you might have. Note also that any text, symbols, or other elements placed in model space will be scaled as well. If you want to display the same model at different scales, you must create symbols, dimensions, and text on different layers or draw them all in paper space. The great thing about drawing symbols, text, or other elements in paper space is that you can create them at their actual size without having to convert for scale. This means, for example, that text that is ⅛ inch is ⅛ inch high in all drawings, no matter what scale is used to plot the model. Keep in mind, though, that when you put text and symbols in paper space, no permanent lock exists between the model space view and the paper space contents. In this way, the view of your model might somehow shift within the viewport, which will ruin the alignment of the dimensions, text, or other elements in paper space with that of the model.

Figure 2.13

The selection is centered with the correct scale.

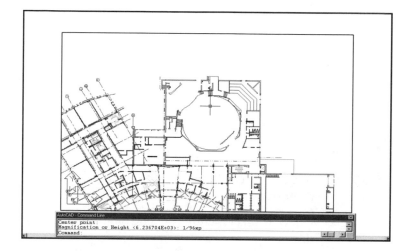

Developing Title Blocks

Almost any drawing, whether a work order, a maintenance drawing, or a sophisticated manufacturing document, should have a title block. A title block provides informational—and often legally required—verification of what the drawing represents in terms of the object of the drawing, the time of day the drawing was created, and the origin of the drawing. If you only publish your drawings electronically, then the title block might differ considerably from one that eventually will be used for plotting or printing. For now, it will be assumed that a paper output is the ultimate goal of an AutoCAD drawing. The following list serves as a guide for the elements your title block should include:

- The name, address, and phone numbers of the firm originating the drawing

- The name, address, and phone numbers of any consultants working on the drawing

- The date that the drawing was originally created and approved for use

- A revision history, including who performed the revision, what the revision was, and when the revision occurred

- A drawing title

- A project name or work order title

- A location for seals, stamps, and/or approval signatures

- A drawing number

- A project or work order number

- The author of the drawing and the name of individual(s) who checked the drawing, if required

- The name of the AutoCAD drawing file

- The date that the drawing was printed or plotted

- A copyright notice, if required

- Additional general information, such as a project address, plant name, and owner's name

- Linework that organizes the title block information and its relationship to the drawing

The design of title blocks is often the source of great debate within a company. No perfect title block design exists, and your needs might include items not listed in the above guide. Generally, the more information (either critical or organizational in nature) that you can place in the lower-right corner of the sheet, the easier it will be for others to quickly find the desired drawing. The title block should provide the information legibly for all size plots, but not dominate the sheet. You also might need to develop a title block for multiple sheet sizes. Most likely, you will not be able to use the same title block for an $8\frac{1}{2}\times11$-inch sheet as you can for a 34×44-inch sheet. You will need to experiment with different designs until you have a set of title blocks that works for all possibilities.

Additionally, the title block can contain a grid design that promotes the modular development of your drawings. For example, if you typically develop details that can be printed on $8\frac{1}{2}\times11$-inch paper, then you could develop a drawing module that enables you to piece together a number of small modular drawings into a larger drawing. In this case, you should be concerned with the drawing area within the title block for the module size, not the sheet of paper size. This is because you will transfer the drawing area from one sheet to the next. Figure 2.14 shows one example of a modular approach to the drawing area.

Figure 2.14

Using a modular grid for drawing development enables you to use modular drawings more effectively.

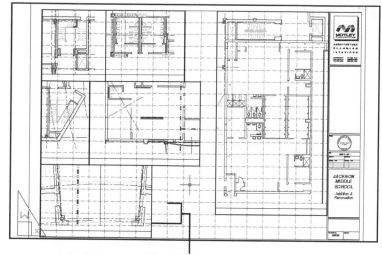

Align viewports with modular divisions of the drawing area to save time

As this chapter has discussed, you probably will want to create template drawings for each of your title blocks. The use of template drawings will be discussed later, and you will have the chance to create a template drawing in upcoming chapter exercises.

Determining Units and Angles

The discipline and country in which you work determines whether you'll use fractional inches, feet and fractional inches, decimal feet, decimal inches, meters, or centimeters in the creation of drawings. Additionally, you must determine how accurately to display the dimensions. AutoCAD does not understand any specific system of the division of distance—the program simply draws using units. As a result, you must tell AutoCAD how you want those units displayed. To change the display of units and angles in AutoCAD, you can open the Format pull-down menu and choose Units. The Units Control dialog box will be displayed, as shown in figure 2.15.

You should set up the default units that you will use in your template drawings so that when you save the template drawings, all your new drawings will use the default units and angles settings that you have selected in the Units Control dialog box. You also should note that you can select the precision of the display of your units and angles.

INSIDER **T**IP

Don't confuse this setting with the precision of dimensions, because you will set the dimension precision when you create dimensioning defaults. Chapter 18, "Productive Dimensioning," discusses dimensioning in greater detail.

Figure 2.15

The Units Control dialog box is used to set AutoCAD units and angles.

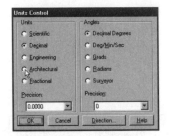

Your primary concern should be how much precision you need to see when you create your AutoCAD drawings. High-precision settings often cause AutoCAD to display the drawing coordinates using scientific notation, such as 1.07E+10, which usually isn't much help. On the other hand, if you're trying to track down a drafting error, high-precision settings can tell you that a line has been drawn at an angle of 179.91846 degrees instead of 180 degrees. The simple process of trial and error can help you determine the best settings for your needs. You also might have noticed that you can set the direction for angles in the Units Control dialog box. The Direction option sets the origin of 0 degrees in your drawing, as well as the direction, Counter-Clockwise or Clockwise, that angles will be positive. When you select the Direction option, the Direction Control dialog box appears, as shown in figure 2.16.

Figure 2.16

The Direction Control dialog box is used to set the origin of 0 degrees, as well as the direction of positive angles.

Converting Between Units

You also should set up the default origin and direction for your angles in template drawings. You will be asked to set up your Units, Angles, and Precision in the exercise that sets up a template drawing later in this chapter.

You should note that if you will need to convert your drawings from feet and inches to metric units, the units in which you create your drawing will not automatically convert. This is because you are drawing in units, not in real-world sizes. For example, when you create a drawing in feet and inches, one unit is an inch. When you convert to a metric drawing, you must change units to decimal units and convert the drawing to a metric drawing by scaling the drawing by the proper conversion factor (2.54 to convert inches to centimeters or 25.4 to convert inches to millimeters). As a result of this component of AutoCAD's design, you must determine what the drawing should represent before you start creating lines, circles, and arcs. You can instruct AutoCAD to dimension objects by scaling them between different units of measure (accomplished by setting a linear scale factor for dimensioning), but the model will not be drawn true to size in the converted units.

Using AutoCAD Features That Help in Project Delivery

In this book, you will learn how to use many AutoCAD features that will help you deliver a project more effectively. When you set up your projects, you must keep the capability of certain AutoCAD features or commands in mind as you develop your approach to a project or to project standards. This chapter also discusses the use of these commands as they relate to project setup, but later on, you should develop your skills for using these commands in later chapters. For now, concentrate on the concepts that are being presented instead of concerning yourself with the detailed use of a command or concept. When you learn how to use these commands later in the book, think about how they relate to project delivery. After you have learned to use these commands, you can return to this chapter to review their use in terms of project delivery.

Drawing Layers

One of the most powerful features offered by AutoCAD—and a feature that can make project delivery more efficient—is the use of drawing layers. Drawing layers are created using AutoCAD's LAYER command and are used to set up drawing data in hierarchical groups that can be turned on or off or locked from editing. In this way, you can, for example, create text that controls how the shop manufactures a part on one layer and text that helps a salesman explain the product on a different layer. By turning one layer or the other off, you can plot two drawings that serve different purposes from the same drawing. You also can use AutoCAD's capability to freeze layers (a condition in which the layer information isn't displayed or loaded into memory) to save drawing load-time, as well as display various portions of the same model. You can freeze layers of drawings that are xref'd into the current drawing, or you can freeze layers within individual paper space viewports. This means that one AEC drawing or viewport could contain a floor plan, while another drawing or viewport could contain a reflected ceiling plan—yet you could use the same model for both drawings. In addition, you can develop nonprinting layers for information that you don't want plotted, but will use with the drawing.

Using the DEFPOINTS Layer

AutoCAD has a default layer called DEFPOINTS that will never plot. The DEFPOINTS layer automatically is added to your drawing when you create an associative dimension. You can draw information for reference purposes, such as floor plan areas, thread counts, or volumes and weights that you won't plot on a drawing. You also can create nonplotting layers. To do so, simply assign a color to the layer on which your plotter won't plot. During the process, use a pen width of 0 or a pen that doesn't have a tip installed, but that is placed in the carousel. Nonplotting areas help you avoid replotting drawings because you won't have to remember to freeze or turn off layers that you don't want to plot.

NOTE

The configuration setup is in the plotter menu. The colors of the drawing are coordinated with the plotter. Not all ink jet and electrostatic plotters have the capability to set a 0 line width, but many do. A very fine line will usually work, too.

Other Uses for Layers

As discussed earlier in this chapter, you also can use layers for redlining purposes. Additionally, you can store information to be used for project data or design on informational layers that can be read by other software. For example, point data from a site survey must be on a specific layer so that the site contours can be generated by a third-party software product. You must take these types of informational layers into account if you use third-party products when you develop your prototype drawings.

Furthermore, you can separate different portions of your model and allocate them to different layers. Using different layers helps you to quickly set a color (as well as plotting pen size) and linetype for all objects placed on any one layer. You also should consider different layers for actual model components versus model linework. For example, hidden lines show something beyond or above the model and are not actually part of the model linework. Thus, you could separate the hidden lines from the actual model lines by putting them on different layers. If you want to create a template to be used for cutting out a plate of a portion of a machine, the hidden lines could easily be ignored yet displayed in a plot of the entire piece of equipment.

Meeting Industry Standards

Finally, your industry might have organizations that have developed layering standards for use in electronic drawings. If your drawings are required to meet certain industry standards, you must set up your layers accordingly. Other industries, such as the AEC industry, might have guidelines only for layer names and use, but these guidelines will help you in developing your own layering standards. The point is that some research is required before you develop your use of layers in your projects. After you have developed layering standards, you can easily store them in your template drawing. Layers in AutoCAD are developed and managed by accessing the Layer tab of the Layer & Linetype Properties dialog box shown in figure 2.17. You will learn more about layer creation and management in Chapter 4, "Organizing Drawings with Layers."

Figure 2.17

The AutoCAD Layer & Linetype Properties dialog box manages layers in AutoCAD.

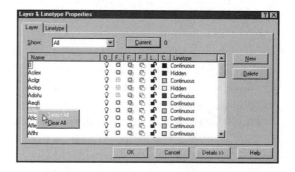

Defining Linetypes

Linetypes represent different things for different industries. AutoCAD comes with a variety of linetypes, and AutoCAD also enables you to define a wide variety of linetypes that can contain symbols within the linetype or that have varying spacing between line components. Linetypes can be part of an industry drafting standard, so you should create a set of linetypes that meet your industry's requirements and include them in the linetype file. If you don't have a wide variety of rarely used linetypes, you can load them into your template drawing so that they are readily available. It is not absolutely necessary to preload linetypes, however, because they are relatively easy to retrieve from the AutoCAD linetype file. You will learn more about creating and loading linetypes in Chapter 5, "Using Linetypes Effectively." Figure 2.18 shows some examples of the types of lines that you can create and use in AutoCAD.

Figure 2.18

A variety of linetypes can be created within AutoCAD.

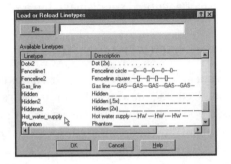

Selecting Text Styles

AutoCAD enables you to use any font that comes with Windows, as well as text fonts that are supplied with AutoCAD. You must select the font or fonts that best work with your drawing size and plotter or printer. It is equally important that the fonts that you use are legible for a wide variety of reproduction sizes. For example, many drawings are placed on microfilm as a matter of storage. To ensure that the lettering is visible on the microfilm, you should use text styles that are a minimum of ⅛ inch in plotted height. Establishing text style standards also will make your project delivery more predictable. After you have experimented with a variety of plotted output and text styles, you will want to select a few styles to serve for general text, sheet title block information, drawing titles, and emphasized text. Everyone has distinct taste in text appearance, so AutoCAD supports a host of variations in the appearance of text. Therefore, it might be best for you to find examples of text that you and your firm find acceptable and then find text settings and fonts in AutoCAD that best approximate your desired results. Text can have different angles, line spacing, heights, weights, effects (upside down, backwards, and/or vertical), and width factors. Figure 2.19 shows examples of what can be accomplished with a single text font in AutoCAD. You will learn more about the use of text in Chapter 16, "Text Annotation."

Figure 2.19

The variety of text effects in AutoCAD creates many opportunities for expression.

Saving Views

AutoCAD enables you to save views of your drawings to which you can return time and time again. The reuse of views can result in considerable time savings if you have a predictable set of views upon which all drawing users can rely. For example, everyone will need a view of the entire drawing, including its title block. You could save this view as a view named Overall by using the AutoCAD VIEW command. Views can be saved in either paper space or model space. You might want to save standard views that are ¼ portions of the drawing and call them UL, UR, LL, and LR for upper-left, upper-right, lower-left, and lower-right. Saving these views in a template drawing ensures that they are available in all your drawings.

Paper Space versus Model Space Viewports

AutoCAD uses paper space for real-world paper sizes and model space for real-world model sizes. The proper use of these two spaces means that you never need to be concerned about scaling a drawing up or down for a plot. In pre-paper space days, users had to remember the scale of each drawing so that when the drawings were plotted, the users could enter the correct scale factor in response to plot setup questions presented by AutoCAD.

Proper use of paper space takes some getting used to because you view your model through ports from paper space to model space. You create your model and work on the model in model space, so you must be able to view the model as close to full-screen as possible. Figure 2.20 shows how a model appears within a paper space viewport that does not fill the screen.

Figure 2.20

A paper space viewport does not always provide a full-screen view of your model.

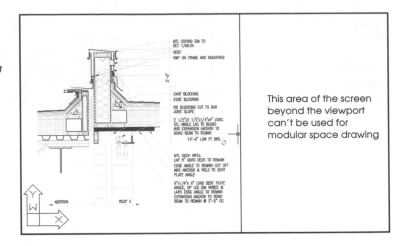

If you have more than one viewport set up to create a number of drawings on a sheet, then, of course, you must zoom in on each viewport to show the model as full-screen as possible.

INSIDER TIP

You might want to consider creating a viewport that is as big as the drawing area within your title block to store with your template drawing. This viewport can provide a good starting place for any drawing and can be resized, copied, or turned off as the drawing develops.

Unless your drawings are very predictable, you won't be able to create multiple viewports that will work every time. Using the overall viewport saves some time when you create a drawing, however. You will learn more about the use of paper space in Chapter 15. In addition, you will add a paper space viewport in the next drawing exercise.

AUTOMATING PAPER SPACE VIEWPORTS

Certainly, it would be nice if you didn't have to do all that math in your head to figure out what viewports you can use at what scale. Included on the CD accompanying this book are VPMAKR.LSP and VPMAKR.DCL, both of which automate the process for you. Copy these files to a location on the AutoCAD path.

1. Start a new drawing by choosing File, New. Use the Ansi_d.dwt template drawing that accompanies AutoCAD. Double-click on the Model button on the status line to switch to paper space. Use the ERASE command and select the inside line on the border to

erase the existing paper space viewport. To verify that all viewports have been erased, try to double-click the Paper button on the status line—AutoCAD should say: `There are no active Model Space Viewports`.

2. Zoom .5X and then use the PAN command until your title block rests off to the left-hand side of the screen. Right-click the mouse and select Exit from the pop-up menu to exit the real-time PAN command.

3. Make sure you're in paper space, and use the MVIEW command to create a large viewport, as shown in figure 2.21.

Figure 2.21

Set up a large viewport that shows a model in model space to the side of the title block.

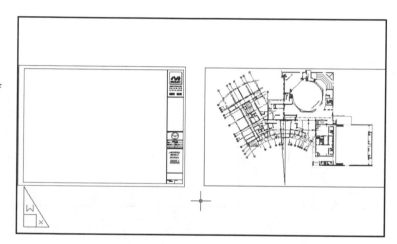

4. Switch to model space by double-clicking on the Paper button on the status bar. Now draw some quick rectangles and circles that are approximately as large as your normal drawings. (For example, if you design buildings, create some that are 200 feet long.) If you have an existing model that you can insert into the new drawing, you can use that, too.

5. Perform a Zoom Extents on the drawing.

6. Choose Load Application from the Tools pull-down menu. Select File from the Load AutoLISP, ADS, and ARX Files dialog box. Locate and select the VPMAKR.LSP file from the accompanying CD. Click on OK to return to the Load AutoLISP, ADS, and ARX Files dialog box. With the VPMAKR.LSP file highlighted in the Files to Load list, click on the Load button and load VPMAKR.LSP, as shown in figure 2.22.

7. Make sure you are still in model space, and type **VPMAKR** at the Command: prompt.

8. Select a window around the portion of the drawing that you want to display to scale in a viewport, as shown in figure 2.23.

Figure 2.22

Use the application loader to load VPMAKR.LSP.

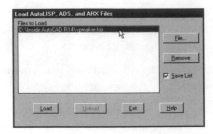

Figure 2.23

Select a window around a portion of the model.

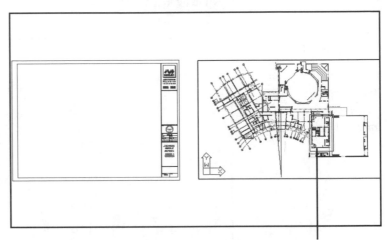

Place a window around a portion of the model

9. Enter a drawing scale, as shown in figure 2.24. You can click on the Settings button to change to a scale chart that suits your needs.

Figure 2.24

Select a drawing scale for the display of your model in a paper space viewport.

10. Drag the new viewport into position, as shown in figure 2.25. If your viewport is larger than the title block, you must change the drawing scale. In this case, place the viewport, erase it, and start over.

Figure 2.25

Place the new viewport within your title block.

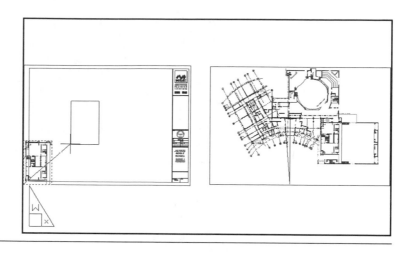

You can zoom in on the model in the large viewport during the selection of the window around the portion of the model that you want to display. This is helpful if you have a large model that is difficult to see in the viewport. You can also adjust the viewport to fine-tune the final view.

Setting Dimension Styles

Each discipline or industry has its own standards and preferences for dimensioning. AutoCAD enables you to store dimensioning standards as dimension styles. You can set the color of individual portions of a dimension, the text style the dimension uses, the arrow style, the way the dimension extension lines work, and the format of the dimension annotation. Each dimension feature, however, must be scaled appropriately for the scale that you use for the drawing. You can set dimensions to be scaled based upon paper space viewport scaling, and AutoCAD will adjust the dimension features for you. You should set up a generic dimension style for each type of dimension that you use (such as radial, leader, and linear) and save them in your template drawing. Figure 2.26 shows the Dimension Style dialog box that grants access to custom dimension styles and sets the dimension scale factor.

Note that you must set up your text style standards in your drawing before you set the dimension text style. You also can create custom blocks for use as arrows. Dimensions are made up from a complex set of options, and it will take some time and study on your part to tailor them for your needs and tastes. You will learn more about using dimension styles and the DDIM command in Chapter 18, "Productive Dimensioning," and Chapter 19, "Advanced Dimensioning."

Figure 2.26

Using the Dimension Styles dialog box enables you to set up custom dimension styles.

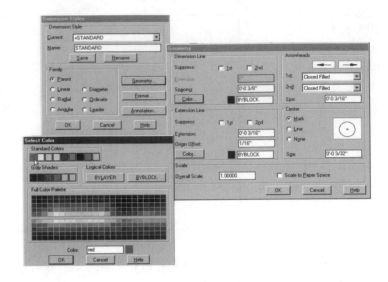

Using Xrefs

This chapter has already briefly discussed a variety of situations in which xrefs can be helpful in the delivery of a project. You should be aware of a few when using xrefs. First, xrefs must be located with the drawing so that AutoCAD can find them and include them in the drawing. If you send electronic drawings to consultants or clients, it is easy to forget the required xref—in such a case, the consultant or client could end up with an incomplete drawing. AutoCAD's XREF command has been enhanced to assist in listing attached xrefs in either List View or Tree View.

A second issue arises when problems are found in an xref drawing. In many situations, you will notice that something must be fixed in a drawing while you're working on an entirely different aspect of the drawing. For example, you could be dimensioning walls in a floor plan that is xref'd into the current drawing when you discover that a wall is drawn wrong. You then must open the xref'd drawing in another session of AutoCAD (if you're fortunate enough to have the memory and disk space required for opening multiple sessions of AutoCAD), or you must save your current drawing and open the xref'd drawing. As you might imagine, bouncing back and forth between the current drawing and the xref'd drawing can become quite tedious. If others are using the xref, too, then the problem is compounded because drawing access could be denied from time to time. Your other choice is to make notes to remind yourself that something must be fixed in the xref'd drawing.

If you need to use only part of an xref'd drawing, you can insert and clip the xref so that the desired portion of the drawing remains. You still have the advantages of current updates to the xref'd portion of the drawing, but you won't have the entire xref attached to the current drawing. If you don't anticipate changes to the xref'd drawing, you can attach the xref to make it a permanent part of the drawing. In this case, the xref'd drawing becomes an AutoCAD block that you can explode, modify, and clip as you desire. This chapter discusses blocks in a following section and points out the differences between using blocks and xrefs. You will learn more about xrefs in Chapter 13, "External References."

Creating Multiline Styles

AutoCAD enables you to draw multiple lines, offset at varying amounts from a guide line, at the same time. If you draw streets with curbs, multiple data lines, cavity walls, or other multiple-line objects, you might find it helpful to create standard multiline styles and save them for use in your projects. Multilines have limitations where editing is concerned, because the only changes you can make to the multiline components are via the MLEDIT command rather than standard AutoCAD editing and grip editing options. For example, if you use multilines to create walls, you cannot insert a door or a window into the wall by breaking the multiline except by using the MLEDIT command to break the multiline. If you grip-edit a multiline, you can edit only the outer boundary of the multiline. Because multilines behave as a single object, however, you can save considerable time in drawing creation and edits if you plan for their use. For example, if you must change a room configuration, editing a multiline changes all the wall lines at once.

INSIDER TIP

In general, any time that you have basic objects that are made up of multiple lines, you can make good use of multilines. If, however, multiple variations exist in the width, composition, and interruptions of the multilines, then you should carefully consider their use.

Figure 2.27 shows an example of creating a custom multiline.

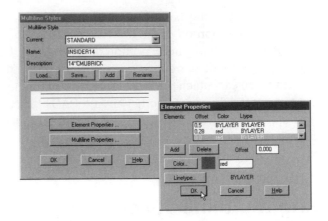

Figure 2.27

Creating custom multilines eases the editing process within a drawing.

Using Blocks

Blocks are primary components that contribute to time-saving in project delivery; they can be used in many ways. The importance of blocks cannot be overstated. Blocks can be used for symbols, components, details, standard text notation, and many other examples that are found in a good project-delivery system. The use of blocks also saves drawing disk space if multiple instances of their use exist because one definition of the block is saved in the drawing, and that definition is copied throughout the drawing without repeating all the block's components for each insertion. You should build a library of blocks that are used for repeating objects in your projects and keep them readily available for use. Or, you could purchase block libraries from third-party vendors.

Blocks can be created on Layer 0 so that they inherit the characteristics of the layer in which they are inserted, or they can contain multiple layer, color, and linetype definitions so that they maintain their appearance regardless of the layer on which they are inserted. Blocks also can be used with the AutoCAD ARRAY, MINSERT, DIVIDE, and MEASURE commands so that multiple copies can be created easily for such things as stair treads, elevations of fences and grilles, and flooring patterns. As with multilines, the use of blocks requires careful planning and repetitive standards for layer names, linetypes, block names, and component design. A sophisticated use of blocks also enables the assembly of projects from a kit of parts. For example, the U.S. Postal Service uses a kit of parts for the assembly of their new branch offices throughout the country. You will learn more about blocks in Chapter 12, "Creating and Using Blocks."

The use of xrefs has also been discussed in this chapter. As a general rule of thumb, you should address two prime considerations when deciding whether to use xrefs or blocks. First, if the need for continual updating isn't required, then blocks are more convenient to use than xrefs. You can update a block from time to time using the INSERT <resident block name>=<disk block name> technique. Second, and more important, if you want to freeze your drawings in time so that the electronic copy on disk matches the last version plotted, you should not use xrefs because they will be updated each time you open the drawing.

INSIDER TIP

A short AutoLISP routine is included on the accompanying CD that updates selected blocks in your drawing. Copy this file, blkupdt.lsp, to the R14\SUPPORT directory.

You must have the original block on your AutoCAD search path in order for the block on the disk to be found for updating. To run this routine, load the file and type **BLKUPDT** at the Command: prompt. For more information on using LISP, see Chapter 24, "Introduction to AutoLISP Programming."

The following exercise details the steps for creating a template drawing that you can use for your projects. The steps draw from all the topics discussed in this chapter.

INSIDER TIP

You will want to keep this drawing and refine it as you are able to more accurately predict key components that are duplicated from project to project.

CREATING A PROJECT TEMPLATE DRAWING

1. Based on previously discussed elements from this chapter, first create a title block for your needs containing as many of these elements as possible.

NOTE

No hard-and-fast rule for title block design exists, so you must start this exercise on your own. Don't worry if you think you might want to change something later. This exercise uses a method that enables you to change all your title blocks in a project at once.

2. Draw everything in the title block as real-world sizes; that is, so that the title block fits on the paper size that you want to use. Don't include any drawing-specific or

project-specific information in this drawing. Position the drawing so that (0,0) is placed in the lower left of your drawing sheet. Include an outline of the exact paper size that you will use. You can refer to figure 2.28 as an example.

Figure 2.28

This title block serves as a model for the title block you create in this exercise.

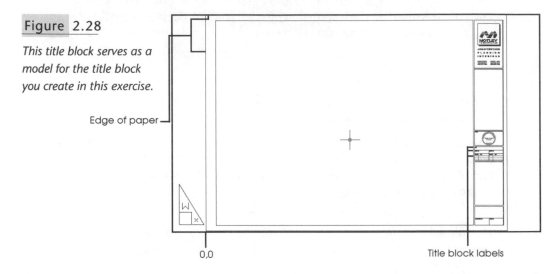

3. Use the LAYER command to create layer names for the title block linework, the title block labels, the drawing labels, and the project labels. Click on New from the Layer & Linetype Properties tab of the Linetype Properties dialog box to create the layers, as shown in figure 2.29.

Figure 2.29

Use the Layer & Linetype Properties dialog box to create a new layer.

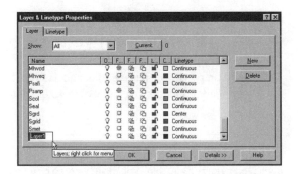

Choose an appropriate layer name for each object. Typing a comma after the layer name causes AutoCAD to create the previous layer (with default properties) and starts the next new layer. If you want, you can add any layers that you use throughout your projects. You can include redline layers, nonprinting layers, and layers from your layering standards, as discussed earlier in the chapter.

4. Set up your units and angles as noted earlier in the chapter. Use the DDUNITS command and establish appropriate settings for your work.

5. Use the STYLE command to bring up the Text Style dialog box, as shown in figure 2.30. Click on the New button and enter an appropriate style name to be used for labels within the title block. Click on OK to return to the Text Style dialog box. Type **0** inches in the Height edit box. This enables you to set the text height for each label as you go instead of setting preset text heights and naming a style for each one.

Figure 2.30

Creating a new text style involves selecting the height and style name for your drawing.

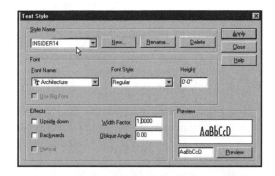

6. Put the labels in your title block using real-world text heights. If you always create your drawings using the same scale, you could consider creating your standard dimension styles in this drawing, too.

INSIDER TIP

Note that setting DIMSCALE to 0 is supposed to scale your dimensions based upon the model space viewport to paper space zoom factor, as well as to enable you to use a single dimension style. However, leaders and text don't have the same relationship to a paper space viewport. In the long run, you should find it simpler to create dimension families for each scale of drawing you will create.

7. Save the title block on your AutoCAD path so that it can easily be found by AutoCAD. You can place this drawing in the AutoCAD SUPPORT directory (if it will be applied to all projects) or in the temporary XREF directory (if it will be applied to specific projects). To determine the directory to use, you can check the Preferences dialog box, which can be accessed from the Tools pull-down menu. Select the Files tab and double-click on the Support File Search Path Folder or the Temporary External Reference File Location folder, as shown in figure 2.31.

NOTE

Note that the XREF directory might change from project to project depending upon how you choose to work. If you use this directory, you must copy your title block drawing to each project's XREF directory. Don't close the title block drawing because you will need it for the next step.

Figure 2.31

You can find AutoCAD's search paths through the Preferences dialog box.

8. If you want to use a different text style for drawing names and sheet numbers (known as drawing-specific labels), create another text style, as you did in step 4. Use the LAYER command to make the drawing-specific label layer (created in step 2) current. Now use the DDATTDEF command or the ATTDEF command to create attributes for each `drawing-specific` label. You will need your title block so that you can place the attributes in their proper location. If you find that you can use a default attribute value that generally saves you time, you should set defaults for your drawing-specific labels. (Follow this procedure if, for example, 90 percent of what you do is sprinkler plans.)

9. Use the LAYER command to bring up the Layer & Linetype Properties dialog box. In the Name column, right-click the mouse to bring up a pop-up menu and pick Select All. Select any light bulb icon in the O column to turn off all layers. A warning will be displayed that the current layer is off. Click on OK. Select the layer containing the attributes defined in step 6 and pick the light bulb icon in the O column to turn that layer back on. Now use the WBLOCK command to WBLOCK the attributes to a new drawing that is also on your AutoCAD search path.

10. Finally, use the NEW command to start a new drawing, click on the Start From Scratch button, and then click on the OK button, as shown in figure 2.32.

11. Double-click on the TILE button in the status bar to enable paper space. Use the XREF command and select the ATTACH button. Locate your title block drawing, highlight its name, and click on OK to get to the Attach Xref dialog box. Click on OK and insert your title block drawing at 0,0.

12. If you cannot see your entire drawing border, perform a ZOOM Extents. Now use the INSERT command to insert your drawing-specific attributes block at 0,0, leaving all the attributes blank.

13. Create a text style, if you want, for the project title. Then place the project title, project number, and other project-specific information in the proper title block area.

Figure 2.32

Start a new drawing from scratch to get an empty drawing.

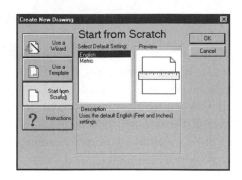

14. Use the MVIEW command to create a standard paper space viewport that will serve as a generic window on your model. At this point in time, the best choice is to create the viewport so that it matches the drawing area within your drawing border and also fills most of your screen.

15. Use the SAVEAS command from the File pull-down menu. Use the Save as type drop-down list to save the drawing as a template file, as shown in figure 2.33.

Figure 2.33

Save the drawing as a template file.

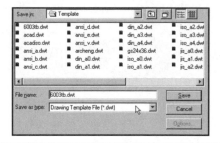

You should name the file using the file-naming conventions discussed earlier. This includes addressing the project number and adding appropriate extensions, such as TB for "title block." For example, 9701-1.00css-tb.dwt is for the first project created in 1997. It's revision 1 of the Title Block drawing created by css.

You should create a template drawing for each of your projects, but once you do, the information always will be formatted the same and you will save hours of drawing setup time.

Summary

In this chapter, you learned about the components of an effective project-delivery system. You also learned how to use AutoCAD features to help you in the management of project delivery. You learned the factors needed to get organized before creating a drawing, as well as how to use OLE to create a task list that is embedded in each drawing. You learned how to use a mock-up process to view your entire project as a whole for planning purposes based upon priorities, how much detail is necessary, how your drawings relate to other drawings and documents, and how to account for the people who work on the drawings.

Other sections discussed the use of repetitive elements and considerations for the number of different ways drawings can be displayed or published. You then reviewed the basic factors used in the initial drawing setup, such as paper, scale, units, angles, and precision. Finally, you learned about AutoCAD commands that can help in project delivery, including LAYER, LINETYPES, TEXT STYLE, VIEW, VIEWPORTS, DDIM, XREFS, MLINE, and BLOCK. Then you used some of these skills to set up a prototype drawing that you can use as a starting point for developing your own project-delivery methodology.

SETTING UP THE AUTOCAD 14 DRAWING ENVIRONMENT

by Michael E. Beall

Release 14 borrows an effective feature from the current release of AutoCAD LT for Windows 95: the Start Up dialog box. By responding to a series of questions, you can automate the configuration of your AutoCAD drawing session. This chapter presents the matrix of options available from this opening dialog box, as well as several other dialog boxes and tabs designed to make your drawing session more efficient. The exercises in this chapter will not only offer efficient solutions to the options presented, but will also help you to understand the alternatives that exist as you begin working with Release 14.

In Release 14, it is the intent of Autodesk to enable you to spend less time with settings, variables, and picking tools by providing you with a more efficient design and drafting tool. Chapter 1, "Exploring the New R14 Interface," reviewed the various tools, menus, and peripheral elements of the application window. This chapter picks up from there by covering the following topics:

- The Default Values
- Using Wizards to Automate Settings
- Using the Available Templates to Start a Drawing
- Configuring with Preferences

Starting from Scratch: The Default Values

After you have launched AutoCAD 14, you are presented with the Start Up dialog box shown in figure 3.1, which will assist you in beginning your drawing session.

Figure 3.1

The Start Up dialog box when launching Release 14.

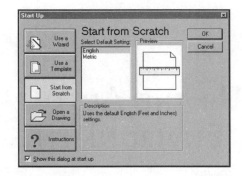

The following is the content of the instructions for the Start Up dialog box as it explains the purpose of the first four buttons:

```
Instructions

The buttons on the left determine how you
begin a drawing.

Choose "Use a Wizard" to be led through
setting up a drawing.

Choose "Use a Template" to start a drawing
based on a template.

Choose "Start from Scratch" to begin
drawing quickly using default English or Metric settings.

Choose "Open a Drawing" to open an
existing drawing.
```

In an effort to see if the default starting environment of Release 14 is what you need (units setting, drawing area, tools, and so on), the following exercise takes you into the AutoCAD drawing environment by starting from scratch.

BEGINNING AUTOCAD WITH THE DEFAULTS

1. Launch AutoCAD Release 14 from Windows 95/NT. The Start Up dialog box shown in figure 3.1 appears.

2. Click on the Start from Scratch button. You are given the option of using an English or metric default setting.

3. Use the English setting and click on OK to enter the AutoCAD drawing window.

4. Move the cursor in the drawing area. Notice on the status bar that the default value for the units is to 4 decimal point accuracy.

5. Choose Format, Units from the pull-down menus to display the Units Control dialog box shown in figure 3.2.

6. From the Precision drop-down list, select 0.000. Click on the Direction button to display the Direction Control dialog box shown in figure 3.3.

Figure 3.2

The Units Control dialog box.

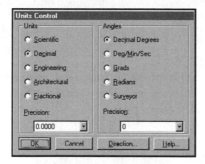

Figure 3.3

The Direction Control dialog box.

7. Click on OK to accept the default direction angle of East for 0.0 and default positive rotation of Counter-Clockwise. You return to the Units Control dialog box. Click on OK to close the Units Control dialog box.

8. Place the cursor in the lower-left corner of the drawing area and notice that the coordinates read very close to 0,0. Position the cursor in the upper-left corner of the drawing area to discover that the area currently displayed is roughly 15 inches × 9 inches.

9. Choose Format, Drawing Limits from the pull-down menus. The following prompt appears:

   `ON/OFF/<Lower left corner> <0.000,0.000>:`

10. Press Enter to accept the default position. The second prompt for the LIMITS command appears:

    `upper right corner <12.000,9.000>:`

11. Press Enter to accept the upper-right corner for the drawing limits and end the command. Although AutoCAD's currently displayed drawing area is wider than the 12 inches specified in the LIMITS command, the vertical dimension is used to quantify the area displayed in the drawing window.

12. Click on the Save tool from the Standard toolbar to open the Save Drawing As dialog box, then enter **03-START** as the drawing name.

NOTE

When considering the area for the drawing, keep in mind that objects in AutoCAD are always drawn full scale. It's not until you are ready to output the drawing to a printer or plotter that a plot scale is assigned.

The coordinate display on the status bar indicated the X,Y,Z position of the cursor from Absolute 0,0 (the location in the drawing where the X, Y, and Z axes cross). By moving the cursor in the previous exercise, you were able to determine that AutoCAD's default drawing area is essentially no bigger than a piece of paper. Specifying an area to start with by no means restricts you from drawing beyond that area. It is simply a point of departure that represents the general area in which you will be creating most of the geometry for your drawing. For projects and geometry smaller than a bread box, the default drawing area is perfect.

The Drawing Aids Dialog Box

Several other settings exist to help you in the creation of your drawing, many of which are found in the Drawing Aids dialog box shown in figure 3.4.

Figure 3.4

The Drawing Aids dialog box.

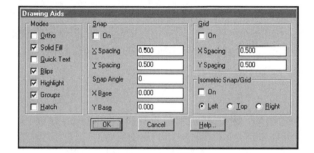

The Drawing Aids dialog box is divided into four areas: Modes, Snap, Grid, and Isometric Snap/Grid. Use the options in these areas to configure the current drawing session to your liking.

- **Modes.** Many of the items in this area enable you to specify the manner in which objects are displayed and selected. The treatment of solids, text, groups, and hatches can be specified in the Modes area. The highlighting of selected objects, placement of marker blips for every pick in the drawing, and the enabling of orthogonal cursor movement can also be set here.

- **Snap.** This area enables you to specify the incremental movement of the cursor in the X and Y direction as well as the setting of the base point for the snap and its rotation in the current X,Y plane. The increment snap can be toggled on and off by using the F9 function key or by double-clicking the SNAP tile on the status bar. The increment snap is applied to the entire coordinate system.

- **Grid.** The spacing of the grid dot pattern is specified in this area. The X and Y values need not be equal. The pattern of grid dots is toggled on and off by using the F7 function key or by double-clicking the GRID tile on the status bar. The grid pattern is displayed only within the bounding area of the drawing limits established with the LIMITS command.

- **Isometric Snap/Grid.** Use this area to specify the isometric angle rotation of the grid and snap based upon the view to be drawn. The Left radio button results in a 150 degree/90 degree axis pair, the Top setting results in a 30/150 axis pair, and with Right you will see a 30/90 axis pair.

INSIDER TIP

Choosing Help in the Drawing Aids dialog box invokes the context-sensitive Help window for the DDRMODES command (the command that opens the Drawing Aids dialog box). All selections for this dialog box are presented and cross-referenced to other Help files.

In the following exercise, you change some values in the Drawing Aids dialog box, and then use the Rectangle tool to understand how these features affect the process of creating objects.

DRAWING WITH THE GRID AND THE SNAP

1. Continuing from the previous exercise, choose Tools, Drawing Aids from the pull-down menus to open the Drawing Aids dialog box.

2. Change the X Spacing for the Snap to .250. Press Enter to automatically update the Y Spacing with the value of the X Spacing.

3. Click on OK to close the Drawing Aids dialog box. Press F9 to turn on the increment snap. Move your cursor to notice the updating of the coordinates in a .250 increment.

4. Press F7 to turn on the grid dot pattern. Notice that the pattern does not go all the way to the right side of the drawing screen but stops at 12.000 in the X axis. The grid pattern is displayed only within the bounding area of the drawing limits, although the increment snap is applied throughout the drawing.

5. With the grid and snap on, click on the Rectangle tool on the Draw toolbar. The following prompt appears:

    `First corner:`

6. Pick ① at the coordinate point 2.000,2.000 for the first corner as shown in figure 3.5. Then pick ② at the coordinate point 10.250,6.750 in response to the Other corner prompt.

7. The marker blips you see at each of the corners were created by AutoCAD because the current setting for the BLIPMODE variable is On. Click on the Redraw All tool from the Standard toolbar to refresh your screen, which will remove the display of the blips.

8. Choose Tools, Drawing Aids. In the Drawing Aids dialog box, toggle off the Blips setting in the Modes area. Click on OK to close the dialog box. Click on the Rectangle tool on the Draw toolbar.

Figure 3.5

Pick points for the rectangle.

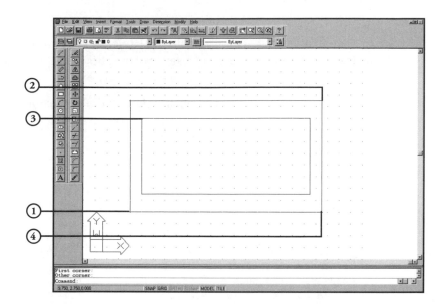

9. Pick ③ at the point 2.500,6.000 for the first corner and ④ at the point 9.750,2.750 for the other corner to create a rectangle. Notice that you do not see the marker blips at the corners this time.

10. Click on the Save tool on the Standard toolbar to save the 03-START drawing.

In the first exercise of this chapter you encountered the default settings by choosing the Start from Scratch button. Use this feature if you find that your project or geometry can be drawn with minimal changes to the defaults. If your drawing will require significant changes to the defaults, the sections in this chapter on templates and wizards will direct you in automating a start-up drawing more effectively.

NOTE

When using the Start from Scratch feature with metric default settings, the units are the same (0.0000) but the limits are set to 297.0000 × 210.0000, essentially the same size area (12 inches × 9 inches) where the millimeter is used as the base unit.

Using Wizards to Automate Settings

The wizard concept was developed by Microsoft. As you work with other Windows 95/NT software, you will find that many of the more powerful or complex programs provide "wizards" for everything from loading the software to automating your document or drawing. When you installed Release 14, a wizard guided you through the installation and consisted of a series of questions and options that enabled the software to be loaded to suit your operating environment.

When you select Use a Wizard from the Start Up dialog box or Create New Drawing dialog box, you can choose the Quick Setup or the Advanced Setup. The following are the Wizard Descriptions for each button:

```
(Quick Setup) Wizard Description
Sets unit of measurement style and drawing
area. Automatically adjusts settings such as
text height and grid. Based on the template
acad.dwt.

(Advanced Setup) Wizard Description
Expanded version of Quick Setup wizard.
Adds settings such as Layout and Title Block.
Based on the template acad.dwt.
```

Paper Space Defined

In the course of using the Advanced Setup wizard, you will encounter the concept of paper space. *Paper space* is a two-dimensional compositional tool. It provides you with a 2D environment (hence the word "paper") in which you can create viewports through which to see your objects in model space. *Model space*, conversely, is the three-dimensional environment in which you create the 2D or 3D objects, or "models," that comprise your drawing.

Imagine looking down at your desk in the morning, and then placing the desired title block (from your letterhead to an E-size pre-printed sheet) right in front of your face. It would appear as though your desk had disappeared. Blessing that it may be, if you cut a rectangular hole in the paper in front of your face, you would see your desk or a portion thereof. Your desk exists in model space; the paper is paper space. The rectangular hole in the paper represents a floating viewport in AutoCAD. Floating viewports can be created anywhere in paper space. After a floating viewport is created, it can be moved to another location, so essentially, the viewport just floats in paper space. You can "cut" several viewports in paper space to compose views of the object(s) in model space. Mystery solved.

Chapters 15, "Paper Space," and 20, "Productive Plotting," cover this powerful feature in detail. To help you understand the concepts until you get to those chapters, the following are a few handy facts that may help. The command alias appears in parentheses ( ), for example, TILEMODE (TM).

- **TILEMODE (TM) [Setting: 0 or 1].** This variable invokes or revokes the existence of the 2D paper space environment. It's the routine that causes the 2D paper to be placed between you and your objects in model space. If TILEMODE is On (1), any viewports you want to have will be "tiled" in three-dimensional model space using the VPORTS command; paper space doesn't exist for you to cut your own viewports into. The TILE tile on the status bar is black when TILEMODE is On. When starting AutoCAD from scratch, TILEMODE is set to 1 and you begin working in model space.

  When the TILE tile on the status bar is toggled off—TILEMODE is set to 0— paper space is invoked and you can create floating viewports through which to see your objects in model space.

  One of the steps in the Advanced Setup wizard automates the process of inserting a title block drawing into paper space and cutting a viewport. During this process, TILEMODE is set to 0, or turned Off, which invokes paper space. The area displayed in the floating viewport is the width and the length requested in the Step 5: Area tab.

- **MVIEW (MV).** Floating viewports are created in paper space using the MVIEW command. Chapter 15, "Paper Space," will discuss this command at length. When accepting the option to use paper space in Step 7 of the Advanced Setup wizard, a floating viewport is automatically created in paper space that displays the desired area.

- **MSPACE (MS).** This command switches the cursor from paper space to model space in a floating viewport. When the cursor is displayed in the floating viewport, you can work on the objects in model space. When the cursor is in a floating viewport, MODEL is displayed in the tile on the status bar.

- **PSPACE (PS).** This command switches you from the active floating viewport to paper space. Double-click on the MODEL tile to switch to paper space. If paper space has yet to be invoked, double-clicking on the MODEL tile will automatically turn off TILEMODE to invoke paper space and the tile will switch to PAPER.

Understanding the Wizard Selections

The template file acad.dwt contains the default values for units and the drawing limits encountered when starting from scratch. The wizards enable you to build upon and refine the default values loaded with the acad.dwt. The Quick Setup wizard only has two steps, Units and Area. The seven Advanced Setup steps and their uses are as follows:

- **Step 1: Units.** Choose the unit of measurement to be used in the drawing. The items in this tab are identical to those in the Units Control dialog box (DDUNITS), which you encountered in the previous exercise when starting from scratch. This step is also in the Quick Setup wizard.

- **Step 2: Angle.** Choose the unit of measurement for angles (Decimal, Deg/Min/Sec, and so on). This setting can also be made in the Units Control dialog box.

- **Step 3: Angle Measure.** Available also in the Direction Control dialog box (from DDUNITS), this step presents a graphical illustration of your selection for the desired direction from which angles will be measured. The default is East.

- **Step 4: Angle Direction.** Also included in the Direction Control dialog box, the Angle Direction step defaults to Counter-Clockwise.

- **Step 5: Area.** This is the other tab that is found with the Units tab in the Quick Setup wizard. The features in this tab automate the setting of the drawing limits by providing edit boxes for the Width and Length of the area in which you will create your drawing.

NOTE

The values entered for Width and Length are also used to define the area displayed in the floating viewport if you elect to use paper space in Step 7: Layout. If you will be using a title block without paper space, the values entered for Width and Length will be ignored.

- **Step 6: Title Block.** Several predefined title blocks come with AutoCAD Release 14. When you choose a Title Block Description from the drop-down list, you can see a preview of the title block and the file name. A copy of the selected file will be inserted as a block into the drawing. See Chapter 12, "Creating and Using Blocks," for a detailed discussion of the concept of blocks. If you do not use paper space (see Step 7: Layout), the selected title block will be inserted into the drawing without regard to the Width and Length values set in Step 5: Area. If paper space is used, the title block is inserted into paper space and a viewport is created with the dimensions specified in Step 5: Area.

■ **Step 7: Layout.** This tab enables you to use floating viewports to view your drawing. The "layout" name of this tab refers to the combination of a border and title block. If you decide not to have a border and title block in paper space, they are inserted into model space. If you decide to use neither paper space nor a layout, the area defined in Step 5 is used for the starting drawing area. In that case, you could have used Quick Setup.

When choosing to use paper space with a layout, the area specified in Step 5 defines the area of the floating viewport. The Layout tab then enables you to begin work on your drawing by choosing one of three configurations:

■ **Work on my drawing while viewing the layout.** Select this feature to begin creating the geometry in the floating viewport (model space) while viewing the title block and border layout in paper space. Because paper space is primarily a compositional tool, this may not be the most efficient configuration when starting a new drawing.

■ **Work on my drawing without the layout visible.** With this feature, you elect to work on the (new) drawing without the layout visible in paper space. AutoCAD will insert the desired title block and border into paper space, but will then toggle into model space in which you can begin creating the geometry for the drawing. When you are ready to see the layout in paper space, simply toggle the MODEL tile on the status bar to invoke paper space and see the drawing in the floating viewport. Keep in mind that the area defined in Step 5 determines the area initially displayed in the floating viewport. This option may be best when starting a new drawing.

■ **Work on the layout of my drawing.** Electing to work on the layout of the new drawing first sets paper space to be the current environment, where you can make edits to the title block and border before switching to the floating viewport to work on the geometry of your drawing in the model space.

In the following series of exercises, you use the Advanced Setup wizard to automate the configuration of a drawing for a small engineering project displaying two climate control units next to each other in a top view. You will use the Ansi_c title block with paper space. Although using a wizard may seem to be time-consuming initially, it is more efficient than going through the numerous dialog boxes to individually configure the drawing.

CONFIGURING AUTOCAD WITH THE ADVANCED SETUP WIZARD

1. Choose New from the Standard toolbar and save any changes to your current drawing. The Create New Drawing dialog box appears.

2. Click on Use a Wizard. You are presented with the options of Quick Setup or Advanced Setup.

3. Select Advanced Setup from the list. Click on OK to display the seven tabbed Advanced Setup dialog box shown in figure 3.6.

4. Change the Precision in the Step 1: Units tab from 0.0000 to 0.00. Click on Next to view the Step 2: Angle tab shown in figure 3.7.

Figure 3.6

The Step 1: Units tab of the Advanced Setup dialog box.

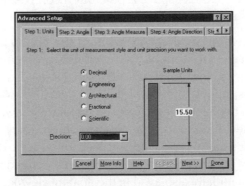

Figure 3.7

The Step 2: Angle tab of the Advanced Setup dialog box.

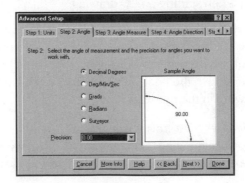

5. Change the Precision setting for the angle of measurement to 0.00. Click on More Info at the bottom of the Step 2: Angle tab to display the menu equivalent for changing the angle setting without using the wizard, then click on Next.

6. In the Step 3: Angle Measure tab shown in figure 3.8, click on Next to accept the default of East as the Angle Zero Direction.

7. The Step 4: Angle Direction tab shown in figure 3.9 displays the default of Counter-Clockwise. Click on the right arrow next to the tabs to scroll through tabs 5–7, and then click on Next.

Figure 3.8

The Step 3: Angle Measure tab of the Advanced Setup dialog box.

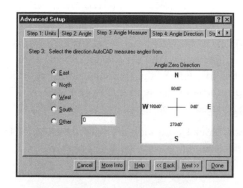

Figure 3.9

The Step 4: Angle Direction tab of the Advanced Setup dialog box.

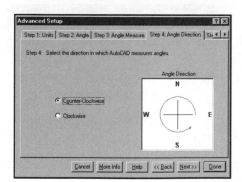

8. The Step 5: Area tab enables you to set the Drawing Limits by entering the desired Width and Length of your starting drawing area in model space. Enter **120** in the Width field and **72** in the Length field as shown in figure 3.10, and click on Next.

Figure 3.10

The Step 5: Area tab of the Advanced Setup dialog box.

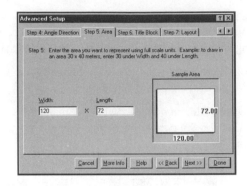

The last two tabs of the Advanced Setup wizard address the use of a predefined title block for the drawing and the use of paper space when laying out your drawing. Later in this chapter, you will use the Template wizard, at which time you will learn more about title blocks. For this exercise, however, you will elect to have a copy of the ansi_c.dwg inserted into paper space as the title block.

9. From the Title Block Description drop-down list of the Step 6: Title Block tab, scroll to the top of the list and choose ANSI C (in) as shown in figure 3.11. Click on Next to display the Step 7: Layout tab shown in figure 3.12.

Figure 3.11

The Step 6: Title Block tab of the Advanced Setup dialog box.

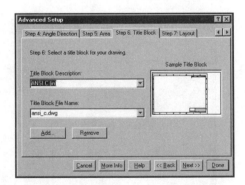

Figure 3.12

The Step 7: Layout tab of the Advanced Setup dialog box.

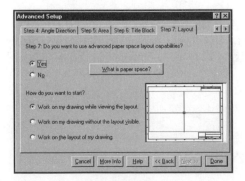

10. In the Layout tab, don't change the default settings. Click on Done to close the Advanced Setup dialog box and AutoCAD will configure your new drawing based on your responses to the wizard. Your drawing should look similar to that shown in figure 3.13.

11. Choose Save from the Standard toolbar and enter **03-Hpump** as the File name, then click on Save.

Figure 3.13

The new drawing configuration with a floating viewport in the title block.

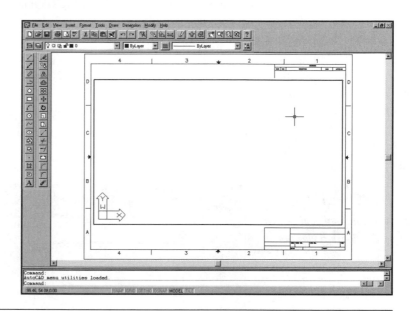

As you move your cursor within the floating viewport, notice that the coordinates are displayed at two decimal point accuracy. You will also see that TILEMODE is off, confirming the fact that paper space is displayed with a floating viewport (where your cursor is active in model space).

In the next exercise, after you become comfortable working with paper space and the toggles on the status bar, you create two 36 × 36 concrete pads for the heat pumps.

ADDING GEOMETRY TO MODEL SPACE

1. Place your cursor in the upper-right corner of the floating viewport. Notice that the area displayed is in the neighborhood of 120 × 72, which are the Width and Length values entered for Step 5: Area in the Setup wizard.

As you move out of the floating viewport, your cursor changes to a pointer, which means that you are no longer in a drawing environment within AutoCAD.

2. Switch to paper space by double-clicking the MODEL tile on the status bar, after which the tile will read PAPER and a crosshair will display across the entire application window. Another indication that paper space is current is the display of the paper space UCS icon in the lower-left corner of the drawing window.

3. Enter **MS** at the command line to issue the MSPACE command, which switches to model space in the floating viewport.

4. Choose Tools, Drawing Aids from the pull-down menus. In the Drawing Aids dialog box, set the X and Y Spacing for the Snap and Grid to 2.00 and turn them both on (by selecting the On check boxes in the dialog box, by using the status bar toggles, or by pressing F7 and F9).

5. To draw the first concrete pad for the heat pumps, choose the Rectangle tool from the Draw toolbar. Pick (1) at the point 14.00,10.00 and pick (2) at the point 50.00,46.00 (see fig. 3.14).

Figure 3.14

A rectangular pad drawn in the floating viewport.

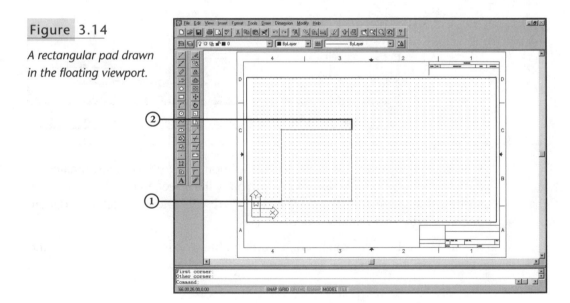

6. Revoke paper space by toggling on TILE on the status bar, effectively removing the paper space environment and leaving only the model space environment.

7. From the Zoom flyout on the Standard toolbar, choose Zoom All to display the drawing limits within the drawing area.

8. Turn on SNAP and GRID on the status bar. Choose the Rectangle tool again and place the first corner at ① at the point 62.00,10.00, and then pick 98.00,46.00 at ② as the other corner to draw the rectangle shown in figure 3.15.

Figure 3.15

Both concrete pads drawn in model space.

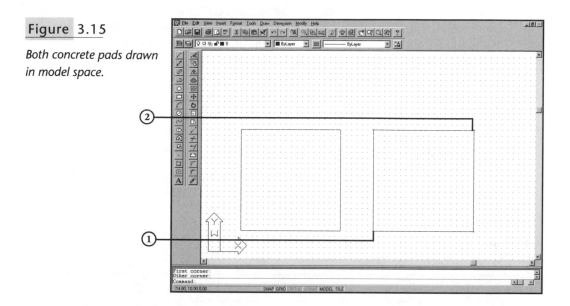

9. To confirm that the viewport in Paper space is still there, toggle off TILE on the status bar to see the two rectangles in model space through the floating viewport.

10. Choose Save to save the 03-Hpump drawing.

WARNING

If you elect to use the Advanced Setup wizard, make sure you confirm that the settings of all seven steps are the defaults; previous settings may not be what you want to use.

Using the Available Templates to Start a Drawing

Release 14 comes with 26 predefined template files. A *template file* is one that contains settings and/or geometry such as a title block that is used to begin your drawing. When you click on Start from Scratch in the Start Up dialog box, a copy of acad.dwt is loaded into the drawing editor under the temporary name Drawing.dwg. Click on the Save tool on the Standard toolbar to save any modifications to your drawing under a new name.

When using the Advanced Setup wizard and selecting a title block, the template files are inserted into the drawing as a block. When selecting the Use a Template button from the Create a New Drawing or Start Up dialog box, a copy of the template file (.dwt) is used to begin the drawing. In both cases, it is then up to you to save your drawing with a new name. When a template is selected from the list, a preview of the template is displayed in the Preview image area. For files containing a border and title block—whether inserted as a block in the Advanced Setup process or used as a template—a floating viewport is enabled when the drawing begins. All title blocks are attributed so you can easily modify the default text values.

Table 3.1 lists the name of the template file with the units used, the width and length of the drawing limits or the border, and whether a floating viewport is initialized when selected as the template for a new drawing.

Table 3.1

The Available Template Files

File Name	Units	$W \times L$	Tblock	Viewport	Notes
acad.dwt	0.0000	12×9	No	No	R14 default
acadiso.dwt	0.0000	420×297	No	No	Metric
ansi_a.dwt	0.0000	10.5×8	Yes	Yes	Landscape A
ansi_b.dwt	0.0000	16×10	Yes	Yes	
ansi_c.dwt	0.0000	21×16	Yes	Yes	
ansi_d.dwt	0.0000	32.5×21	Yes	Yes	
ansi_e.dwt	0.0000	42.5×33	Yes	Yes	
ansi_v.dwt	0.0000	8×10.5	Yes	Yes	Portrait A
archeng.dwt	0.0000	34.5×23	Yes	Yes	
din_a0.dwt	0.0000	1189×841	Yes	Yes	German metric
din_a1.dwt	0.0000	841×594	Yes	Yes	German metric
din_a2.dwt	0.0000	594×420	Yes	Yes	German metric
din_a3.dwt	0.0000	420×297	Yes	Yes	German metric

File Name	Units	W × L	Tblock	Viewport	Notes
din_a4.dwt	0.0000	210×297	Yes	Yes	Portrait A4 DIN
gs24x36.dwt	0.0000	34.5×23	Yes	Yes	Generic 24 × 36
iso_a0.dwt	0.0000	1189×840	Yes	Yes	English metric
iso_a1.dwt	0.0000	840×594	Yes	Yes	English metric
iso_a2.dwt	0.0000	594×420	Yes	Yes	English metric
iso_a3.dwt	0.0000	420×297	Yes	Yes	English metric
iso_a4.dwt	0.0000	210×297	Yes	Yes	Portrait A4 ISO
jis_a0.dwt	0.0000	1189×841	Yes	Yes	Japanese metric
jis_a1.dwt	0.0000	841×594	Yes	Yes	Japanese metric
jis_a2.dwt	0.0000	594×420	Yes	Yes	Japanese metric
jis_a3.dwt	0.0000	420×297	Yes	Yes	Japanese metric
jis_a4l.dwt	0.0000	210×297	Yes	Yes	Landscape A4 JIS
jis_a4r.dwt	0.0000	210×297	Yes	Yes	Portrait A4 JIS

In the following exercise, you start a new drawing and use iso_a4.dwt as the template. As a metric drawing, the units displayed in the status bar are millimeters. The default area of model space displayed in the floating viewport is the size equal to the dimensions within the border and title block. In this way you can begin with a 1:1 area for the drawing of a hollow metal door jamb.

BEGINNING A DRAWING WITH A METRIC TEMPLATE

1. Choose New from the Standard toolbar to display the Create New Drawing dialog box, and click on the Use a Template button.

2. Scroll down the list and choose iso_a4.dwt. A preview of the template will be displayed. Click on OK to display the drawing shown in figure 3.16.

3. Confirm that the SNAP is toggled on in the status bar (set to 5.0000 for this template). Choose the Polyline tool from the Draw toolbar. The following prompt appears:

   ```
   From point:
   ```

4. Pick ① at the point 70.0000, 200.0000 as shown in figure 3.17. The next prompt for the PLINE command appears:

```
Current line-width is 0.0000
```

```
Arc/Close/Halfwidth/Length/Undo/Width/<Endpoint of line>:
```

Figure 3.16

The new drawing using the iso_4.dwt template.

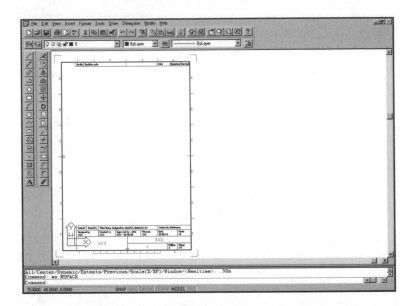

Figure 3.17

The polyline door frame in the floating viewport.

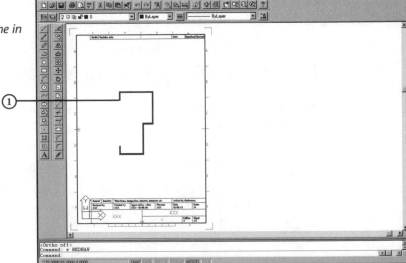

5. Enter **W** to change the width setting for the polyline. The following prompt appears:

   `Starting width <0.0000>:`

6. Enter **2** for the starting width value and press Enter to accept the default 2.0000 as the ending width value. The next prompt is as follows:

   `Arc/Close/Halfwidth/Length/Undo/Width/<Endpoint of line>:`

7. Toggle on ORTHO in the status bar (or press F8). Move the cursor north from the starting point and enter **13** to draw the polyline vertically 13mm.

8. Move the cursor to the right of the last point and enter **54** to draw the next segment 54mm.

9. Move the cursor down from there and enter **51**.

10. Move the cursor to the left and enter **16**.

11. Move the cursor down from the last point and enter **49**.

12. Move the cursor to the left and enter **38**.

13. The last segment goes up 13. Press Enter after the last segment has been drawn to end the command.

14. Choose the Save tool and enter **03-DRfrm** as the File name, then click on Save.

15. To confirm the door frame geometry was drawn in model space, toggle on TILE in the status bar. Paper space will be revoked, leaving you in the model space environment. Invoke paper space by toggling off TILE.

Release 14 automates the use of the provided templates very nicely by way of the Create New Drawing dialog box. Before plotting your drawing, refer to Chapter 20, "Productive Plotting," for specifics about plotting a drawing with a border and title block in paper space and a floating viewport.

INSIDER TIP

Many third-party software products load a modified version of the acad.dwt file during the installation of the product. When using any other product with AutoCAD, it's a good idea to have a backup copy of the acad.dwt. Also, some products may use the existing acad.dwt in its original configuration. For this reason, you should create your own template rather than modify the existing acad.dwt if you want to have a customized start-up template.

Customizing and Saving a Template File

Although Autodesk has made a considerable effort to provide a broad array of templates, many of you will probably want to customize your own by using one of the sample files or a previously created border and title block. Release 14 enables you to open any file and save it as a .dwt file similar to the creation of a template file in Word for Windows or other word processors you might have used.

In the following exercise, you will create a new drawing using the Advanced wizard to set the units, selecting Arch/Eng (in) as the title block in Step 6. The archeng.dwg inserted into the new drawing is the drawing file equivalent to the archeng.dwt template. Using the wizard enables you to easily set the units to Architectural at the outset.

CREATING AN ARCHITECTURAL TEMPLATE DRAWING

1. Choose New from the Standard toolbar and save any changes you may have made to the current drawing.

2. From the Create New Drawing dialog box, select Use a Wizard and Advanced Setup, and click on OK.

3. In Step 1: Units tab, select Architectural. Then scroll over and select Step 6: Title Block.

4. From the Title Block Description drop-down list, select Arch/Eng (in) and click on Done. AutoCAD will insert a copy of the archeng.dwg into the new drawing.

5. Choose File, Save As from the pull-down menus. Then double-click on the Template folder under Acadr14.

6. From the Save as type drop-down list, select Drawing Template File (*.dwt).

7. Change the name in the File name field to **ARCH-IN** and click on Save. The Template Description dialog box appears (see fig. 3.18).

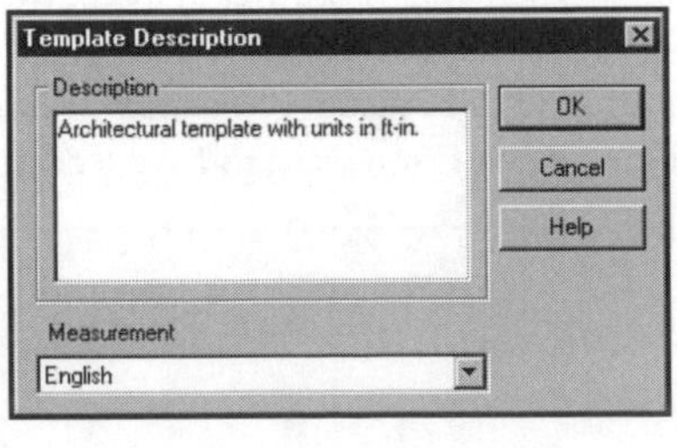

Figure 3.18

The Template Description dialog box.

8. Change the Description field to read:

    `Architectural template with units in ft-in.`

9. Click on OK. AutoCAD will set the current drawing to be arch-in.dwt.

10. To test this as a template file, choose New from the Standard toolbar. In the Create New Drawing dialog box, and click on Use a Template.

11. Scroll down the Select a Template list and select arch-in.dwt. Notice that the Template Description displays below the drop-down list. Click on OK.

12. Move the cursor around in model space in the floating viewport to confirm the architectural units setting.

In the next series of steps, you open the archeng.dwg drawing file, change the units to architectural, and save it as arch-in.dwg. This will make the file available both in the Advanced wizard as a title block drawing and as a template.

13. Choose Open from the Standard toolbar, and select archeng.dwg from the list of drawings in the Acadr14 folder, then click on Open.

14. Choose Format, Units from the pull-down menus and select Architectural from the Units Control dialog box, then click on OK.

15. Choose File, Save As and save the drawing as **arch-in.dwg** in the Acadr14 folder.

16. Choose the New tool. Select Use a Wizard with the Advanced Setup.

17. Scroll to Step 6: Title Block and click on the Add button to open the Select Title Block File dialog box.

18. Choose arch-in.dwg from the drawing list under Acadr14. Choose Open to return to the Title Block tab.

19. In the Title Block Description field, enter **Architectural Title Block in ft-in**, and click on Done.

You now have access to the customized drawing as a template file and as a drawing if you are using the Advanced Setup wizard. Note that it was not necessary to change the units in Step 1: Units of the wizard when creating a new drawing with the title block of arch-in.dwg because architectural units are part of the drawing file being inserted.

Any and all of the sample drawings can be further modified to suit your needs, but the general process of customizing your own template is very powerful. You could have templates for different drawing content such as a site plan sheet template using engineering units, a detail sheet with several floating viewports, a shop drawing sheet, and so on.

INSIDER TIP

The model space area displayed in the floating viewport is typically no larger than the actual area of the drawing title block in paper space. If you are going to customize your title blocks using the existing drawing or template files, you may want to read more about paper space in Chapter 15, "Paper Space," before refining your drawing.

Configuring the Drawing Environment with Preferences

Combine AutoCAD's increase in performance by virtue of new features and capabilities with the most current technology relating to interfaces with the Internet, networks, and third-party software and you have a pretty powerful mix. To help you configure AutoCAD to suit the way you use it, the Preferences dialog box (Tools, Preferences) presents you with an easy to understand group of eight categories: Files, Performance, Compatibility, General, Display, Pointer, Printer, and Profiles.

Specifying Search Paths and File Names

Networks are being used more and more where they were once only used for order entry, sales reporting, vendor communication, and customer tracking. The Files tab of the Preference dialog box, shown in figure 3.19, very effectively provides file- and folder-related tracking for nearly every application.

Figure 3.19

The Files tab of the Preferences dialog box.

The important thing to remember is that AutoCAD has default locations for all the search paths. As you select each item in the list, a description of the purpose is displayed in the description field under the list. The yellow items in the list specify folder or network drive locations for the item selected; the white items are the default files used for the items selected.

Table 3.2 lists the primary items listed in the Files tab and the default location for the folder or file.

Table 3.2

The Default Paths and Files from the Files Tab of Preferences

Item	Search paths, file names, and file locations
Support File Search Path	C:\ACADR14\support, C:\ACADR14\fonts, C:\ACADR14\help
Device Driver File Search Path	C:\ACADR14\drv
Project Files Search Path	Empty; no default
Menu, Help, Log, and Miscellaneous File Names Menu File	C:\ACADR14\support\acad
Alternate Table Menu File	Unspecified; no default
Help File	C:\ACADR14\help\acad.hlp
Automatic Save File	C:\WIN95\TEMP\auto.sv$
Log File	C:\ACADR14\acad.log
Default Internet Location	www.autodesk.com
Configuration File	C:\ACADR14\acad14.cfg
License Server	Licensed network server per Autodesk
Text Editor, Dictionary, and Font File Names	
Text Editor Application	Internal
Main Dictionary (Set Current)	American English, British English (ise), British English (ize)
Custom Dictionary File	C:\ACADR14\support\sample.cus
Alternate Font File	arial.ttf
Font Mapping File	C:\ACADR14\support\acad.fmp

continues

Table 3.2, continued

The Default Paths and Files from the Files Tab of Preferences

Item	Search paths, file names, and file locations
Print File, Spooler, and Prolog Section Names	
Print File Name	Current drawing name
Print Spool Executable	No default
PostScript Prolog Section Name	No default
Print Spooler File Location	C:\WIN95\temp
Template Drawing File Location	C:\ACADR14\template
Temporary Drawing File Location	C:\WIN95\temp
Temporary External Ref. File Location	Blank = Temp. Drawing File Loc.
Texture Maps Search Path	C:\ACADR14\maps

In the following exercise, you replace the current alternate font file setting, arial.ttf, with simplex.shx.

REPLACING THE DEFAULT ALTERNATE FONT FILE

1. Open the Preferences dialog box by choosing Tools, Preferences from the pull-down menus and select the Files tab.

2. Click on the plus sign (+) for Text Editor, Dictionary, and Font File Names to expand the listing.

3. Click on the plus sign (+) for Alternate Font File to display the current setting of arial.ttf.

4. Click on the Browse button to open the Alternate Font dialog box shown in figure 3.20.

Figure 3.20

The Alternate Font dialog box.

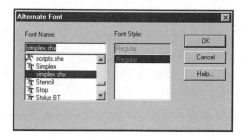

5. Select simplex.shx from the Font Name list, and click on OK to return to the Files tab.

6. Click on Apply to set simplex.shx as the alternative font file. Click on OK to close the Preferences dialog box and return to the drawing.

NOTE

Third-party products will frequently place their own menus and LISP routines in separate directories created during installation. Make sure the Support File Search Path and Device Driver File Search Path in the Files tab contain the proper path references for your third-party software if you find it is not performing properly.

Optimizing Release 14's Performance

As a graphics tool, AutoCAD implements many features that draw on the memory of your system such as circle smoothness, text display, and object dragging. The Performance tab shown in figure 3.21 enables you to fine-tune the optimization process AutoCAD uses to suit your application. If the visibility of every line of text in the drawing is not important to you, you may want to turn on Show text boundary frame only, which sets the QTEXT variable to Off.

Figure 3.21

The Performance tab of the Preferences dialog box.

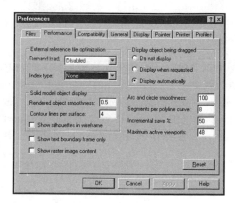

In the following content overview of the Performance tab, you may find some items that will provide improved performance for your system.

- **External reference file optimization.** This grouping gives you options on the extent to which AutoCAD loads external reference files. The new feature of external reference demand load has the following three options:

  - **Disabled.** If Demand load is disabled, AutoCAD will load more than just the elements of an external reference file that are necessary for the regeneration of the current drawing. Chapter 13, "External References," will explain the concept of this feature. Disabling Demand load can slow the performance of AutoCAD for that drawing.

  - **Enabled.** When enabled, AutoCAD only loads those elements of an external reference file necessary for the regeneration of the current drawing. This option will improve performance when working with external reference files. The downside to this feature is that other users who want to open the externally referenced file from your file server cannot do so while you are using it. For stand-alone installations of Release 14, this would be the best option.

  - **Enabled with Copy.** When the Enabled with Copy option is on, the externally referenced file can be opened and worked on by other users while you see only a copy in your drawing.

  The four index types on which the demand load acts, None, Layer, Spatial, and Layer & Spatial, are the sorting elements by which AutoCAD loads the external reference. Refer to Chapter 13, "External References," for a more complete definition of these features.

- **Solid model object display.** With the extensive solid modeling features of AutoCAD Release 14, optimizing the "number-crunching" during rendering and wireframe generation can be very important. This collection of items enables you to refine the impact each has on the performance of the system. Refer to the *AutoCAD Release 14 User Guide* for a more complete reference to these features.

- **Display object being dragged.** When objects are edited—that is, moved, copied, and so on—they are dynamically displayed and dragged to their new position. These three options—Do not display, Display when requested, and Display automatically—enable you to specify the mode in which AutoCAD displays the objects as they are being edited.

NOTE

The From object snap cannot be used if the display of the object is on when it is being dragged. Select Display when requested to enable the From object snap when moving or copying selected objects.

■ **Arc and circle smoothness (Range: 1–20,000; Default: 500).** The higher the value for this item, the longer it takes AutoCAD to display arcs and circles to your specification. This only affects the display of the objects on the screen. The smoothness of circles and arcs when they are plotted is determined by the capability of the output device. The default is just fine.

■ **Segments per polyline curve (Range: –32768–+32768; Default: 8).** Similar in rationale to the smoothness of circles and arcs, this value specifies the number of segments that comprise an arc in a polyline. The higher the number, the longer it will take to generate.

■ **Incremental save % (Range: 0–100; Default: 50).** A full save does not save wasted space, an incremental save does. The incremental save percentage setting specifies how much wasted space can be in the saved drawing before a full save kicks in. Optimum performance is realized at the default value of 50. At values below 20, AutoCAD incurs a full save every time, consuming more time than necessary.

■ **Maximum active viewports (Range: 2–48; Default: 48).** AutoCAD's sample title blocks and templates typically have one floating viewport. This setting enables you to have up to 48 viewports recognized in the current drawing. Because inactive viewports are blank and therefore their contents are not regenerated, set this to a value that is reasonable for your typical drawing needs to improve performance in your drawing.

■ **Show text boundary frame only.** When the location of text is more important than the content, turn on this item. A frame representing the boundary of the body of all text objects will be displayed to save on drawing regeneration time.

■ **Show raster image content.** Raster images are like faxes, which are essentially a lot of dots. When a raster image is imported into AutoCAD, you may elect to show the content or only the outline when it is moved.

■ **Reset.** If you have experimentally changed any of the values in the Performance tab, select Reset to reset the defaults.

Through the Performance settings in the Preferences dialog box you can more efficiently configure the operation of AutoCAD for your particular application.

Setting Internal and External Compatibility

With the number of people using AutoCAD these days, it has become increasingly important to maintain compatibility with earlier versions, not only in file types, but also in menu structure, keyboard entry, and especially the use of third-party products. The Compatibility tab shown in figure 3.22 contains four distinct groups addressing AutoCAD's compatibility with internal and external issues.

Figure 3.22

The Compatibility tab of the Preferences dialog box.

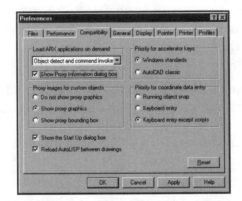

- **Load ARX applications on demand.** Third-party applications for Release 14 are written using the AutoCAD Runtime Extension programming tools. This grouping enables you to specify how AutoCAD treats objects created with third-party ARX programs. For more specific information regarding these features and other ADS issues, refer to the AutoCAD Help tool or the *Release 14 Customization Guide*.

- **Proxy images for custom objects.** This section continues with specifics on how third-party created images are to be handled. You can elect to have the custom objects displayed, not displayed, or have a box defining the boundary of the objects displayed in the drawing.

- **Priority for accelerator keys.** If you are upgrading to Release 14 from Release 12, this section enables you to retain Ctrl+C as *Cancel* (AutoCAD classic selection). When using the Windows standard selection, Ctrl+C issues the COPYCLIP command, enabling R13/R14 to be considered Windows-compliant products.

■ **Priority for coordinate data entry.** As you progress through this book, you will learn more about the many features in AutoCAD that enable you to accurately create the geometry for your drawing. This group gives you three options on which the accuracy method is dominant when more than one could be implemented. Chapter 6, "Creating Drawings with R14," will cover the use of object snaps and coordinate entry from the keyboard. Chapter 23, "Creating Scripts and Slide Libraries," will give you an idea how coordinate data entry can be used in script files. I would recommend you set the radio button in this area to Keyboard entry.

■ **Show the Start Up dialog box.** At the beginning of this chapter, you learned how to use the wizards and templates presented as options in the Start Up dialog box. If you deselect this feature, AutoCAD will begin with a copy of the acad.dwt drawing, essentially using the Start from Scratch option from the Start Up dialog box.

■ **Reload AutoLISP between drawings.** AutoLISP is a programming tool that enables users and third-party vendors to create programs similar to macros that run within AutoCAD. This feature in the Compatibility tab enables you to specify whether functions or variables established with an AutoLISP routine are to be retained as you go from drawing to drawing. Refer to the *Release 14 Customization Guide* or the Help files to learn more about AutoLISP. If you are interested in learning more about programming in AutoLISP, there are numerous resources such as the Authorized Training Centers or other New Riders titles that may help you in your efforts.

Efficient operation of the programming and objects available through third-party programs is the primary theme of the Compatibility tab. You are also given choices regarding your keyboard entry and AutoCAD's performance when specifying points.

General Operating Preferences

Drawing session features such as the creation of a log file, backup file, and the saving of the preview image seen for R13 and R14 drawings make up the content of the General tab of the Preferences dialog box shown in figure 3.23.

Figure 3.23

The General tab of the Preferences dialog box.

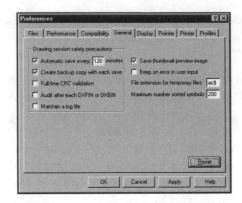

The following overview and short descriptions should help you to more clearly understand the choices available in the General tab:

■ **Drawing session safety precautions.** This grouping gives you options that will directly affect your drawings and any recovery necessary in the event your system, network, or power supply is compromised.

   ■ **Automatic save every *n* minutes.** Contrary to many user's beliefs, this feature does not create a drawing file (.dwg). It creates a file named auto.sv$, whose location and name can be specified in the Automatic Save File item in the Files tab of Preferences. There is only one auto.sv$, which is updated at the interval specified in this feature. In the event that you need to open this file as a drawing file, use Windows Explorer to rename the file with a .dwg extension.

   There is a basic CAD discipline that bears upon this setting—primarily the habit you have developed in the frequency of saving your drawing. If you habitually choose Save from the Standard toolbar (or the Windows-compliant Ctrl+S) every few minutes as you work in a drawing, the interval for this setting is of secondary importance. If, however, you are frequently amazed at the time that has elapsed since you last issued the SAVE command, set this interval to 30 minutes or less.

   The downside; a frequency of less than 30 minutes for the automatic save interval can be annoying as well as time-consuming, especially when working on what you may think is a slow system. Compounded with working on a drawing that is more than 2 MB, the interruption of your command sequence for the sake of an automatic save can give you second thoughts about using the feature at all. I would recommend an interval between 30 and 60 minutes.

■ **Create backup copy with each save.** In another effort to assist in providing a "safety net" for users, AutoCAD by default will automatically create a .bak file of the current drawing each time it is saved. Only one .bak file can exist for a drawing. This means this file is always one save away from containing the current geometry. This can potentially cause incredible amounts of backup files on a file server unless good CAD management techniques are implemented to "clean the refrigerator every Friday afternoon."

■ **Full-time CRC validation.** (Cyclic Redundancy Check) Occasionally users encounter corrupted files. Corrupted files may be created by your system or you may be given a corrupted file by a contractor or associate. Whatever the source, if you suspect a hardware or AutoCAD error, turn on this feature and AutoCAD will perform the CRC error-checking process each time an object is read into the current drawing.

■ **Audit after each DXFIN and DXBIN.** One method by which non-AutoCAD drawing files can be read by AutoCAD is for the originating program to create a DXF (Drawing Interchange File). Another file type readable by AutoCAD is the Binary version, the DXB. The DXFIN and DXBIN commands prompt for the .dxf or .dxb file to be loaded. This feature in the General tab lets you specify whether you want AutoCAD to perform an audit, or integrity check, on the geometry once it has been imported. For more specifics on DXF and DXB files, refer to the *Release 14 User Guide.*

■ **Maintain a log file.** Many applications would benefit from maintaining a log of commands for a project. This could be for internal tracking/audit purposes, confirmation of accuracy, and so on. One acad.log is maintained in the log file location specified in the Files tab. To give you an idea of the format and length of the log file, the following is the log file of the first exercise in this chapter, "Beginning AutoCAD with the Defaults":

```
[ AutoCAD - Wed Feb 19 12:41:02 1997 ]-- -- -- -- -- -- -- --
[ AutoCAD - Wed Feb 19 12:41:04 1997 ]-- -- -- -- -- -- -- --
Command:
AutoCAD menu utilities loaded.
Command: '_ddunits
Initializing... DDUNITS loaded.
Command: '_limits
Reset Model space limits:
ON/OFF/<Lower left corner> <0.000,0.000>:
Upper right corner <12.000,9.000>:
```

The acad.log file maintains dates of the AutoCAD session but does not record the names of the drawings loaded or saved. Therefore, when you have project-specific needs, you must either manually edit the log file (use the Windows Notepad), or keep a log beside your system to keep track of the drawings worked on.

■ **Save thumbnail preview image.** This feature requests that AutoCAD create a compressed BMP (bitmap) image of the drawing when saved. The image appears in several dialog boxes including the Advanced Setup wizard Title Block tab, using templates, and the Select File dialog box when opening a drawing.

■ **Beep on error in user input.** Veteran users can sometimes get ahead of themselves and not notice the command line, and new users will frequently overlook the next step of a sequence. For these and other reasons, Release 14 enables you to specify whether AutoCAD should beep when the user has not responded appropriately to the current prompt or command.

■ **File extension for temporary files.** Cross-referenced to the Files tab for Temporary Drawing File Location, the default ac$ indicates a temporary drawing file while an AutoCAD session is active. When using a network, the extension will be different for each node where this feature can be used to specify the unique network node name.

■ **Maximum number sorted symbols.** Many AutoCAD installations' Select File dialog box do not list the available files alphabetically. This can happen in a stand-alone or network environment. It is caused by having more files in the folder you are searching than the number specified in this feature for sorting. The default of 200 can easily be surpassed on network file servers that have only a couple busy users. To enable AutoCAD to alphabetize your files, enter a number greater than the number of files in the largest drawing folder. A value of 0 results in a chronological listing.

Preferences for the AutoCAD Display

The Display tab shown in figure 3.24 is one of the more gratifying tabs in that most of the changes made can be seen as soon as you return to the drawing window. The only feature in this tab that may adversely affect the performance of AutoCAD may be the elaborate nature of a font chosen for the graphics or Text windows.

Figure 3.24

The Display tab of the Preferences dialog box.

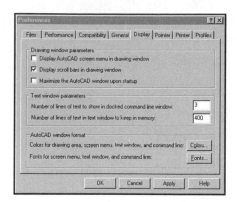

The following is an overview with short descriptions of the Display tab:

- **Drawing window parameters.** The features in this group enable you to specify the use of the side screen menu, display the scroll bars on the right side and bottom of the drawing window, and choose whether or not you want the AutoCAD application to be maximized when initially launched.

- **Text window parameters.** In Chapter 1, "Exploring the New R14 Interface," you encountered the ability to float or dock toolbars. The command-line window can also be floated or docked, as well as extended, to include as many or as few lines as you want. By default, the command-line window has three lines visible. Similar to a log file, AutoCAD defaults to maintaining up to 400 lines of the current drawing session in memory. The scroll bar on the side of the AutoCAD Text window enables you to scroll up or down to see the history of your current session.

INSIDER TIP

Lines from the AutoCAD Text window can be highlighted and copied to the Windows clipboard buffer and pasted into Notepad, Word, or other word processors.

- **AutoCAD window format.** The two selections in this group enable you to choose the color for several AutoCAD window elements as well as the fonts used in the screen menu, the Text window, and the command line. The initial colors for the AutoCAD window will default to the Windows 95/NT settings established in the Appearance tab of the Display item in the Windows Control Panel.

The Colors button of the Display tab opens the AutoCAD Window Colors dialog box shown in figure 3.25, which contains a list for the following window elements:

- Graphics window background
- Graphics text background
- Graphics text color
- Text window background
- Text window text color
- Crosshair color (XOR)

In addition to the Basic Colors displayed, you can create a custom color using the slide bars for red, green, and blue, based on your graphics card's capability and color palette. To return to the default color assignment, click on the Default Colors button.

Figure 3.25

The AutoCAD Window Colors dialog box.

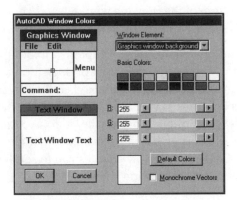

The Fonts button initially displays the Graphics Window Font dialog box shown in figure 3.26. The font selected in this dialog box specifies the look of the text in the screen menu. A scroll bar is provided for the extensive list of fonts. The default is MS Sans Serif, Regular, 8 point.

The Graphics and Text buttons provide the method by which you can toggle between the Graphics Window Font dialog box and the Text Window Font dialog box shown in figure 3.27. The list of fonts for use in the command line/Text Window is less extensive than that for the Graphics Window. The default setting is Courier, Regular, 10 point.

Figure 3.26

*The Graphics Window
Font dialog box.*

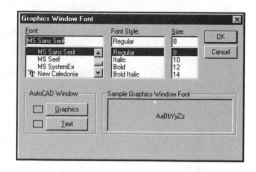

Figure 3.27

*The Text Window Font
dialog box.*

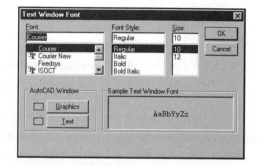

In the following exercise, you change several of the features presented in the Display tab.

CHANGING THE DISPLAY OF THE DRAWING AND TEXT WINDOWS

1. Begin a new drawing from scratch. Open the Preferences dialog box and select the Display tab.

2. Turn on the feature to display the screen menu, and change the number of docked lines in the command-line window to 2.

3. Click on the Colors button and select a color from the bottom row of the Basic Colors as the Graphics window background.

4. From the Window Element drop-down list, scroll down and select Crosshair (XOR). Then choose a color from the top row of Basic Colors, and click on OK to return to the Display tab.

5. Click on Apply to update the AutoCAD window under the Preferences dialog box with the side screen menu, two lines in the command window, and your background color.

6. Click on the Fonts button to display the Graphics Window Font dialog box. Select a unique font and the Italic Font Style.

7. Click on the Text button in the Graphics Window Font dialog box to switch to the Text Window dialog box. Select the Fixedsys font for the text to be displayed on the command line and in the AutoCAD Text window.

8. Click on Apply to apply the settings to the AutoCAD system registry. Click on OK to return to your AutoCAD application window.

INSIDER TIP

If you want a font size smaller than those listed in the Font dialog boxes (primarily for laptop applications), you can manually change the value in the Size box to a smaller point size such as 4 or 6.

In the next series of steps, you relocate the command-line window to the top of the drawing window and return the number of lines to three by dragging down the window size.

9. To relocate the command-line window, place your cursor anywhere along the top horizontal band of the command-line window frame. Pick and drag the bounding box image into the drawing window and release the cursor to see something similar to figure 3.28.

Figure 3.28

The floating Command Line window.

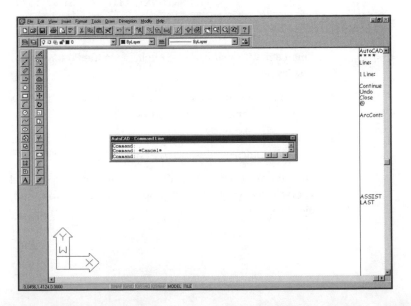

10. To dock the window at the top of the drawing window, pick anywhere in the AutoCAD - Command Line title bar. Then drag the bounding box image up to the bottom of the Object Properties toolbar and release the cursor when the image of the bounding box widens to the width of the drawing window.

11. To dynamically modify the Command Line window to display three lines, position your cursor on the thin window frame at the bottom of the Command Line window to display a vertical window sizing indicator for adjacent windows.

12. Drag the sizing indicator down just a bit to increase the depth of the docked Command Line window, and release the cursor. You may have to adjust it more than once to get the desired number of lines.

The settings selected from the Display tab, as well as all other settings in the Preferences dialog box are referred to as *system settings* and are saved to the AutoCAD registry and implemented with every session of AutoCAD. Some settings you have encountered in this chapter, such as drawing units, drawing limits, blips, and so on, are drawing settings and are only retained in the individual drawing in which they have been set.

The New Cursor Configuration Feature

Since day one, AutoCAD has had a full-screen cursor. While other competitive products came and went with their small or adjustable cursor size, Autodesk stayed with the full screen. Third-party programs for implementing a small cursor not withstanding, out-of-the-box AutoCAD was full screen. A new day is here and the faithful users are now given the opportunity to size the screen cursor from the Pointer tab shown in figure 3.29. The default of 5 percent of the screen size can be reset from 1 to 100. For three-view drawings and other projects requiring a full-screen cursor, at least it's nice to know you can modify the setting to suit the current drawing.

Figure 3.29

The Pointer tab of the Preferences dialog box.

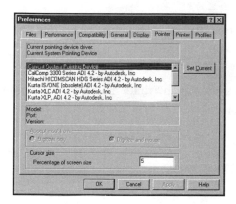

For digitizer users, install the input device driver per the vendor's installation guide, covering use with AutoCAD as well as Windows 95/NT. With proper installation, your driver will appear in the pointing device list. Select your digitizer driver from the list, and click on Set Current. You may then elect to use only the digitizer for input or both mouse and digitizer if this option is available for your device.

Adding and Configuring Plotters

Although the packaging has improved, the process by which a plotter or printer is added to the available output device list is relatively unchanged from earlier versions of AutoCAD. The Printer tab shown in figure 3.30 provides several features to make the addition of an output device as easy as possible.

Figure 3.30

The Printer tab of the Preferences dialog box.

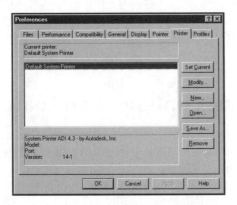

- ■ **Set Current.** When multiple devices are configured (local or networked), select the desired device in the list, and click on Set Current. The selection will be reflected in the Print/Plot Configuration dialog box as the current device.

- ■ **Modify.** Opens the Reconfigure a Printer dialog box shown in figure 3.31 in which you can modify the description or click on Reconfigure to go through the selection sequence for a new device.

- ■ **New.** Opens the Add a Printer dialog box shown in figure 3.32 from which you can select one of several existing drivers for various output devices.

Figure 3.31

The Reconfigure a Printer dialog box.

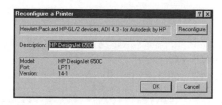

Figure 3.32

The Add a Printer dialog box.

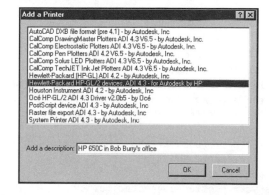

The following is the Text Window displayed after selecting the Hewlett-Packard HP/GL2 devices, ADI 4.3 - for Autodesk by HP in the listing:

```
Devices marked "NR" in the list below cannot print raster images
with this driver. Instead, if available, use a Windows System
Printer driver for your device (note that pen plotters cannot print
raster images).
Supported models:
1. HP DesignJet 755CM
2. HP DesignJet 750C Plus
3. HP DesignJet 750C
4. HP DesignJet 650C
5. HP DesignJet 350C
6. HP DesignJet 250C
7. HP DesignJet 700
8. HP DesignJet 600-NR
9. HP DesignJet 330
10. HP DesignJet 230
11. HP DesignJet 220
12. HP DesignJet 200
13. HP DraftMaster with Roll Feed-NR
14. HP DraftMaster Plus Sheet Feed-NR
15. HP DraftMaster Sheet Feed-NR
16. HP PaintJet XL300-NR
```

```
17. HP DraftPro Plus-NR
18. HP 7600 Color (obsolete)-NR
19. HP 7600 Monochrome (obsolete)-NR
20. HP LaserJet III-NR
21. HP LaserJet 4-NR
Enter selection, 1 to 21 <1>: 4
*********************************************************************
IMPORTANT: To change default values for settings like
==========
            - Print Quality
            - Media Orientation
            - Plotter memory
            - Annotations
         in your HP device, you should type HPCONFIG at
         the AutoCAD "Command:" prompt.
*********************************************************************
Specify port:
  <S>erial port (Local).
  <P>arallel port (Local).
  <N>etwork port.
What is your plotter connected to? <P>
Enter parallel port name for plotter or . for none <LPT1>:
Plot will NOT be written to a selected file
Sizes are in Inches and the style is landscape
Plot origin is at (0.00,0.00)
Plotting area is 43.00 wide by 33.00 high (E size)
Plot is NOT rotated
Hidden lines will NOT be removed
Plot will be scaled to fit available area
Do you want to change anything? (No/Yes/File) <N>:
```

If the port specified for the plotter connection is currently used, you see the following message:

AutoCAD Message

```
A Windows system printer is already configured for this port. Your
ADI driver's output will be rerouted to use the Windows spooler to
avoid conflict with this driver.
```

If your device is not on the list, refer to the vendor's installation guide for use with AutoCAD. An alternative would be to install the device as a Windows 95/NT system printer,and configure AutoCAD to use the current system printer. For further information regarding installation of your output device, refer to the *Release 14 Installation Guide*.

■ **Open.** Opens a .pc2 file created using the Save As feature from the Printer tab. See Chapter 20, "Productive Plotting," for more details on plotting your drawing in Release 14.

■ **Save As.** Saves the configuration of the selected plotter to a .pc2 file in the Acadr14 folder. The .pc2 file name defaults to the current drawing name.

■ **Remove.** Removes the selected printer from the listing.

Many of the features of the Printer tab are cross-referenced to the Print/Plot Configuration dialog box with regard to the device selected and the configuration settings set to current. With the use of the Profiles feature presented in the next section, Release 14 provides the method by which a user in a network environment can customize the system to meet his project needs.

Saving the Preferences to a Profile

Through the seven tabs of the Preferences dialog box, you have probably encountered numerous system settings you would no doubt like to adopt as your own. Using the Profiles tab shown in figure 3.33 you can save the current settings by name for retrieval later. The following list presents the features of this tab.

Figure 3.33

The Profiles tab of the Preferences dialog box.

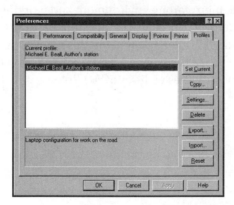

■ **Set Current.** Sets the profile selected in the listing to current.

■ **Copy.** Copies the selected profile to a new name, after which you may make modifications to the Preferences dialog box tabs. Click on Settings to save the changes to the new profile.

- **Settings.** Opens the Change Profile To dialog box with fields for Profile Name and Description. Click on Settings after making modifications to an existing profile.

- **Delete.** Deletes the selected profile from the list.

- **Export.** Opens the Export Profile As dialog box to create a .reg file in the Acadr14 folder. This is useful for taking your current profile settings from one office to another or for sharing optimum Release 14 settings with other users.

- **Import.** Imports the profile setting of a .reg file into the current AutoCAD session.

- **Reset.** Resets all defaults of the Preferences tabs.

Profiles enable AutoCAD users traveling between corporate offices to have the benefit of customized settings on any Release 14 station. Through the use of profiles, today's network AutoCAD user can experience a level of familiarity when working on Release 14 with little anxiety over the current system settings.

Summary

Release 14 now provides effective methods by which users can, with little time and effort, customize their starting environment and working environment, and ensure the integrity of AutoCAD in a networking configuration. Combined with the stability of the Windows 95/NT operating systems, this release can be easily adapted to meet the needs of the users. In essence, portability, functionality, and compatibility are three very real possibilities with AutoCAD Release 14.

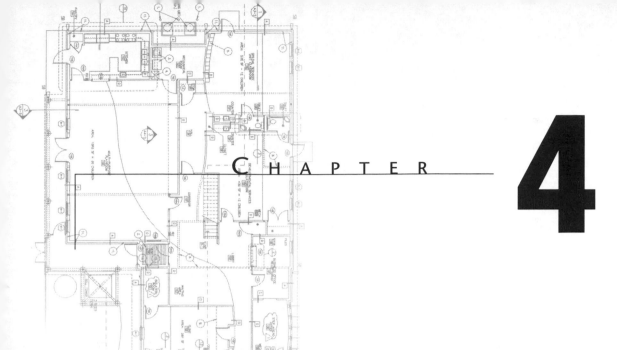

ORGANIZING DRAWINGS WITH LAYERS

by Michael E. Beall

Prior to the use of Computer Aided Design, projects consisted of dozens of mylar and vellum drawings that were ultimately printed or copied and then taken into the field or the shop where they were used in construction of a building project or fabrication of parts. Drawings are still necessary in the construction and fabrication process, but today, the person that initials the "Drawn by" box can more efficiently organize the information formerly drawn on those dozens of sheets by using layers.

Hardly anyone remembers the pin-registered drafting days, but layers essentially stem from the basic process of placing similar information on the same sheet. Multiple layers exist, including layers for the object geometry, dimensions, notes, and the border, among others. This chapter discusses the importance of layers through exercises designed to increase your efficiency in using Release 14. This chapter explores the following topics:

- Controlling the drawing's layer features
- Creating and assigning a color to new layers
- Locking layers
- Setting a layer filter
- Implementing layering standards

Controlling the Drawing's Layer Features

All objects in AutoCAD have at least three properties: color, layer, and linetype. When you create object geometry in AutoCAD—whether it's a rectangle, circle, text, or a dimension—all objects have a color, a layer assignment, and a linetype. Every drawing can have its own layer structure and configuration, or you can set up a layer configuration in a drawing template for consistency when creating new drawings.

NOTE

For more information on drawing templates, refer to Chapter 2, "Before the Drawing Begins: Planning and Organizing Projects." This chapter covers colors and layers. Linetypes are discussed in Chapter 5, "Using Linetypes Effectively."

Figure 4.1 displays the Layer tab of the Layer & Linetype Properties dialog box with the Details turned on.

Figure 4.1

The Layer tab of the Layer & Linetype Properties dialog box.

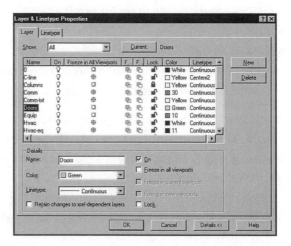

If you upgrade to Release 14, you will notice a distinct difference in this dialog box. As you encountered in Chapter 1, "Exploring the New R14 Interface," this dialog box has become totally Windows-compliant, in both the manner in which multiple layers are selected and the process by which layer names are changed. The Layer tab opens when you choose the Layers tool from the Object Properties toolbar.

NOTE

AutoCAD's default layer is 0. Geometry created on layer 0 has unique properties with respect to blocks. When creating new geometry for your project, it is best to create a new layer. For more information on the relationship of layers and blocks, refer to Chapter 12, "Creating and Using Blocks."

In the following exercise, you open 04-HOSP.DWG and use some of the features of the Layer tab. This exercise introduces you to the Layer drop-down list, a component of the Object Properties toolbar that displays the On/Off, Freeze/Thaw, Viewport Freeze/Thaw, and Lock/Unlock icons for controlling the layer display.

CHANGING LAYER VISIBILITY

1. Open the drawing 04-HOSP.DWG (see fig. 4.2) located in the folder containing the sample drawings from the accompanying CD.

Figure 4.2

The 04-HOSP drawing.

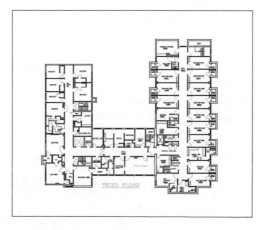

2. Click on the Layer drop-down list on the Object Properties toolbar displaying Walls as the current layer and turn on the layer Plumbing. Then press Enter and the drawing will redraw to display the objects on the Plumbing layer.

3. From the Layer drop-down list, freeze the Rm-name layer (pick the sun icon), and then press Enter.

4. Choose the Layers tool from the Object Properties toolbar to display the Layer tab of the Layer & Linetype Properties dialog box.

5. Select the Border layer and then drag the scroll box down, hold Ctrl, and select the Text layer to effectively select them both.

6. Freeze the Text layer and then scroll up to ensure that the Border layer has been frozen as well. Then click on OK.

7. Choose Erase from the top of the Modify toolbar, and then select the text Third Floor at ①, as shown in figure 4.3.

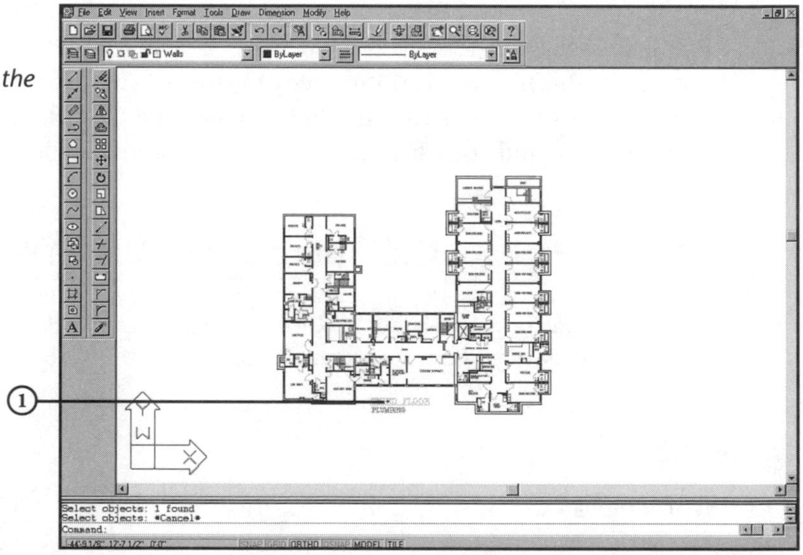

Figure 4.3

The pick point to select the text on the Title layer.

8. Enter **LA** at the command line to open the Layer tab. Then from the Show drop-down list, select All unused to display the Roof and Title layers.

9. Right-click (Enter button on the mouse) in an open area of the layer list to display the two-item selection menu shown in figure 4.4.

10. Click on Select All to select both layers, and then click on Delete to delete the unused layers from the list.

11. Select All from the Show drop-down list to display all remaining layers, and then click on OK.

12. Choose Save to save the drawing.

Figure 4.4

The selection menu available in the Layer tab.

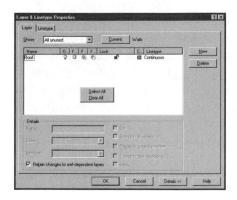

As you experienced in the previous exercise, it's very easy to control the various features of the drawing's layers. This flexibility is of critical importance as you work on drawings with a large amount of layers and AutoCAD has made some marked improvements in layer management tools with each new release. In the next section, you will learn more about specifying colors for new or existing layers.

Creating and Assigning a Color to New Layers

The process by which layers are created and manipulated gets easier with each release of AutoCAD. In Release 13, the color assignment of a layer was not editable within the layer list as it is in Release 14. The renaming of a layer has been enhanced by virtue of the Windows-compliant interface used within other applications for the renaming of files. And the most impressive layer feature is the ability to delete a layer with nothing on it, as you saw in the previous exercise.

Another advantage within the Layer tab is the Details section of features, which enables you to make selections for color and linetype from drop-down lists as presented in the following overview:

- **Name.** Using this edit field, you can enter a new layer name or rename an existing layer.

- **Color drop-down list/dialog box.** This feature enables you to choose one of the available seven named colors, or you can choose Other to select a pigment from your graphics card's color palette in the Select Color dialog box.

- **Linetype drop-down list.** This list provides the linetypes currently loaded in the drawing.

■ **Retain changes to xref-dependent layers.** If another drawing file has been externally referenced into the current drawing, you can elect to retain the layer settings (such as On, Off, and Locked) made to the xrefs in the current drawing by checking this box. Refer to Chapter 13, "External References," for more information on external reference files. Note, however, changes made to an xref's layers' visibility do not affect the original externally referenced drawing.

The remaining check boxes in the Details group are equivalent to the icon toggles found in the layer listing of the Layer tab and the Layer drop-down list in the Object Properties toolbar.

An Object's Color Property Assignment

When assigning a color property for objects, the most efficient and intuitive approach is to use the default setting of ByLayer. This simply means that the color of the geometry is determined by the layer on which it's drawn. Creating objects on a layer that's blue, for example, produces blue objects. To assign another color property would be to explicitly set the color of new objects without regard for the layer on which they are created. This leads to confusion for all involved in working on the drawing.

In the following exercise, you will rename an existing layer, create a new layer, and assign a color to that layer.

RENAMING AND CREATING LAYERS

1. Continue from the previous exercise and choose the Layers tool from the Object Properties toolbar to display the Layer tab of the Layer & Linetype Properties dialog box.

   Confirm the Layer tab displays the Details features.

2. Select the Border layer, and then scroll down and press Ctrl. Now select the Text layer.

3. Click off the Freeze in all viewports check box to thaw those two layers.

4. Click on New to add an edit box to the layer list and display Layer1 for the new layer name, as shown in figure 4.5.

Figure 4.5

The default new layer name is Layer1.

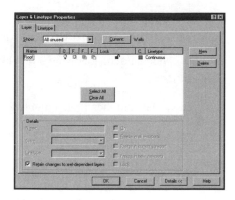

5. Type **EVAC** for the new layer name, and then press Enter.

6. From the Color drop-down list in the Details section, select one of the named colors for the Evac layer.

7. Scroll up and select the Border layer in the list, and then choose the magenta swatch under the Color column (yours may display C...) to open the Select Color dialog box shown in figure 4.6.

Figure 4.6

Select a new color for the Border layer in the Select Color dialog box.

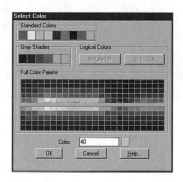

8. Select a new color from the Full Color Palette, and then click on OK.

9. Scroll down and select the Text layer. Double-click the Name layer in the Details section, and change the layer name to **Title_block_text**. Now click on OK.

10. Choose Named views from the Standard toolbar to display the View Control dialog box, and choose Evac from the list. Then choose Restore, OK to display the view shown in figure 4.7.

11. From the Layer Control drop-down list, scroll up and select the layer Evac to set this layer as the current layer.

12. Choose Draw, Polyline from the pull-down menus, and then pick ①, as shown in figure 4.7. You will see the following prompt for the PLINE command:

```
Current line-width is 0'-0"
Arc/Close/Halfwidth/Length/Undo/Width/<Endpoint of line>:
```

13. Enter **W** for the Width option, and the following prompt will appear:

```
Starting width <0'-0">:
```

14. Enter **12** for the starting width, and then press Enter to accept the default of <1'-0"> for the ending width.

Figure 4.7

The evacuation line appears in the restored EVAC view.

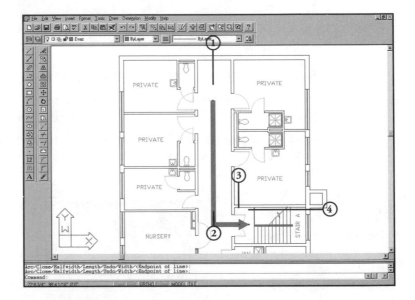

15. Pick the points at ② and ③, and then enter **W** to make an arrowhead by changing the width.

16. Enter **30** for the Starting width and enter **0** for the ending width.

17. Pick ④ and press Enter to end the command and complete the polyline.

18. Choose Save to save the drawing.

To more fully understand the importance of setting the color property for objects to ByLayer, in the following exercise you create another evacuation line. In this exercise, you create the object on the Walls layer in the color of the Evac layer. When you are finished, it will appear as though the new polyline is on the Evac layer, but you will then come to realize that it will not be frozen with the other evacuation line.

UNDERSTANDING THE LAYER COLOR PROPERTY

1. Continue from the previous exercise and use the Layer drop-down list to set Walls to be the current layer.

2. From the Color drop-down list, which currently displays ByLayer, select Red.

3. Choose Named views from the Standard toolbar to display the View Control dialog box and choose EAST-HALL from the list. Then choose Restore, OK to display the view shown in figure 4.8.

4. Choose Draw, Polyline from the pull-down menus. Then pick ① and enter **W** for the Width option.

5. Enter **12** for the starting width, and then press Enter to accept the default of <1'-0"> for the ending width.

Figure 4.8

The evacuation line in the east-hall view.

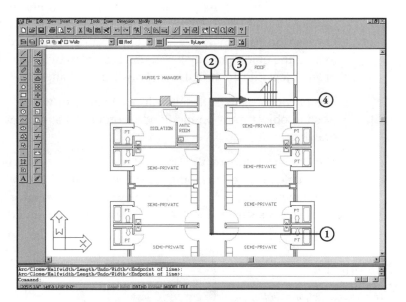

6. Pick the points at ② and ③. Then enter **W** to make an arrowhead by changing the width.

7. Enter **30** for the Starting width, and then enter **0** for the ending width.

8. Pick ④, and then press Enter to end the command and complete the polyline.

9. Use the Named view tool again to open the View Control dialog box and Restore the view ALL.

10. From the layer drop-down list, freeze the Evac layer, and then press Enter to see that the evacuation line drawn in the east hall is still visible.

The combination of a layer scheme with varying colors and the use of color ByLayer makes it easier for both the beginner and the veteran AutoCAD user to make sure new objects are being created on the proper layer.

NOTE

Objects take less storage space if the color is ByLayer because AutoCAD doesn't need to store the color with the object.

Modifying an Object's Properties

As stated at the beginning of this chapter, all objects contain three properties: layer, color, and linetype. As you have seen in the chapter exercises so far, the color assigned to the layer affects the color of the objects drawn on that layer. This is because the color value is set to ByLayer rather than an explicit color. To follow the logic, if the color property for an object is set to ByLayer and you change the layer of an object, the color of the object will also change.

The previous exercise resulted in a situation in which the color property of an existing object must be modified in order to have color consistency within the drawing.

The Properties tool on the Object Properties toolbar serves a dual function. If you select a single object to modify, an object-specific dialog box appears, much like the one shown in figure 4.9, which displays the properties for the evacuation Polyline. If you select a single object, AutoCAD provides edit and data fields specific to that object.

Figure 4.9

The Modify Polyline dialog box displays the properties for this object.

If two or more objects are selected when using the Properties tool, the Change Properties dialog box shown in figure 4.10 is displayed. In this case, only the common properties are displayed. The property changed in the Change Properties dialog box is applied to all objects selected, the selection set.

Figure 4.10

The Change Properties dialog box displays only common properties.

 Release 14 brings several new routines to the property-related assortment of features. Two of the new tools are Make Object's Layer Current and Match Properties. These tools intuitively automate the changing of the current layer and the modification of any of the object's existing properties. The Match Properties tool enables you to match some or all the properties from a source object and apply them to a destination object. If you want to match only some of the properties, you can select the desired properties from the Property Settings dialog box shown in figure 4.11.

Figure 4.11

The Property Settings dialog box enables you to match properties of two objects.

Two other less obvious approaches to changing object properties is that of editing an object's property from within the Layer Control and Color Control drop-down lists on the Object Properties toolbar. This method will be referred to as "toolbar editing" of the object properties. In the following exercise, you will use toolbar editing to economize the property modification processes.

UPDATING THE LAYER PROPERTY

1. Continue from the previous exercise and choose Zoom Previous from the Standard toolbar to return to the east-hall view.

2. Click on the edge of the evacuation polyline to display the object grips, as well as its layer property (Walls) in Layer Control.

3. From the Layer Control drop-down list, thaw the Evac layer, and then select the Evac layer name to change the layer property of the polyline. The drawing will regenerate because a layer was thawed.

4. While the polyline is still selected, select ByLayer from the Color Control drop-down list to change the color property for the polyline.

5. Restore the view WEST-HALL, and then change the color property back to ByLayer by using the Color drop-down list currently displaying Red.

In the next sequence of steps, you will use the Make Object's Layer Current tool to easily set the current layer. You also will use Match Properties to match the existing layer property to that of another object.

6. Choose the Match Properties tool from the Object Properties toolbar. The following prompt will appear:

   `Select Source Object:`

7. Pick a line on the stairs at ① in figure 4.12. This next prompt will appear:

   `Current active settings = color layer ltype ltscale thickness text dim hatch`

   `Settings/<Select Destination Object(s)>:`

8. Enter **S** to display the Property Settings dialog box and view the available properties that can be matched to the source object.

9. Click on OK to close the dialog box. Then select the elevator rectangle and press Enter to apply the properties from the selected source object.

Figure 4.12

Updating the current layer and adding the elevator lines.

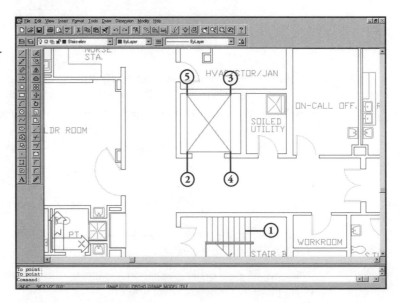

10. To quickly set the current layer to Stairs-elev, choose Make Object's Layer Current at the left end of the Object Properties toolbar. The following prompt will appear:

    `Select object whose layer will become current:`

11. Select the elevator rectangle. The Layer drop-down list will change to display the Stairs-elev as the current layer.

12. Choose Line from the Draw toolbar, and then double-click OSNAP on the Status bar to open the Osnap Settings dialog box.

13. Choose Endpoint from the Select Settings grouping, and then click on OK to return to the drawing.

14. Pick ② and ③ to create the first line, and then press Enter.

15. Press the spacebar to re-issue the LINE command. Pick ④ and ⑤ to add the second line, and then press Enter and save the drawing.

INSIDER TIP

For quick access to an extensive layer list in the Layer tab, the Home key instructs AutoCAD to go to and highlight the layer name at the top of the listing's available layer names. Press the End key and AutoCAD goes to and highlights the layer at the end of the listing. The Page Up key highlights the layer name at the top of the displayed list—continue pressing the Page Up key to scroll up one page at a time through the listing. Page Down acts in the same manner as Page Up, although this command highlights the layer at the bottom of the displayed list.

Locking Layers

When editing a drawing with multiple layers, you probably will mistakenly select objects that you don't want to edit. The ability to lock layers enables you to display the geometry on a critically relevant layer without selecting any objects created or inserted on that layer. Although objects on a locked layer are not selectable for edit commands, they can be snapped to using an object snap.

In the following exercise, you will lock several layers pertaining to the floorplan. You also will use the MOVE command to relocate the stairs in the EAST-HALL view.

LOCKING THE LAYER PROPERTY

1. Continue from the previous exercise and use the Named Views icon off the Standard toolbar to display the View Control dialog box to restore the EAST-HALL view.

2. Choose Layers from the Object Properties toolbar to display the Layer tab.

3. Select Doors from the layer list. Then press Ctrl and select Equip, Evac, and Walls at the bottom of the list.

4. From the Details grouping, select the Lock check box to lock the selected layers. Then click on OK to return to the drawing.

5. Choose Move from the Modify toolbar and pick ① and ②, as shown in figure 4.13. This places a crossing window around stair geometry. (Notice the prompt regarding locked layers.)

6. Press Enter to complete the selection. Then type **–12,0** and press Enter twice to move the stair geometry in the negative X direction 12 inches.

7. Choose Save to save the drawing.

Figure 4.13

Selecting an area containing locked layers.

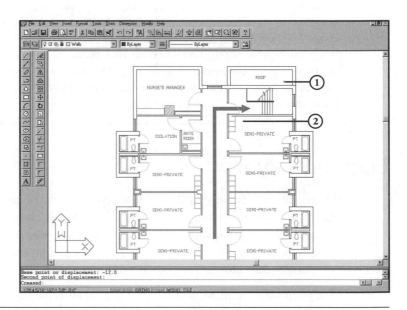

The locking of layers is most useful when working on drawings in which you simply need to see the geometry on a layer for reference with respect to any additional objects you may create, or in the case of the preceding exercise, edits on the existing drawing.

In the following section, you learn about another feature that enables you to specify the layer names displayed in the layer list from the Layer Control drop-down list, as well as in the Layer tab.

Setting a Layer Filter

As you have worked through this chapter, you have had the opportunity to scroll through a layer list to get to the layer you want to turn on or freeze. The 04-HOSP drawing that you have worked on is a relatively small drawing with only 24 layers. In this next section, you will encounter the concept of layer filters and the Release 14 Show drop-down list.

The layer filter features are particularly useful to those of you who would like to reduce the number of layers listed in the Layer Control drop-down list and the Layer tab. Although the power of these features is most evident when implemented with drawings that have dozens of layers, you can witness its capabilities with the hospital drawing.

Displaying a Filtered Layer List

Several items in the Show drop-down list at the top of the Layer tab enable you to shorten the displayed list of layers. Keep in mind that the selected layer filter does not turn layers off or freeze them; it simply removes them from the layer listing. The following list details the capabilities of the items on the Show drop-down list.

- **All.** The default setting displays all layers available in the current drawing.

- **All in Use.** This setting comes in handy when a template file contains various layers—such as objects, dimensions, and notes—that might not currently be in use. A layer "In Use" implies that geometry has been drawn on the layer. If you have not yet drawn anything on a layer, you can shorten the list displayed by choosing this option.

- **All Unused.** This feature displays only those layers on which you have not yet drawn.

- **All Xref dependent.** Only layers associated with a drawing that has been externally referenced into the current drawing are displayed in the layer list with this selection.

- **All not Xref dependent.** Layers that are not a part of an externally referenced drawing are displayed in the layer list with this selection. For a complete discussion on the XREF command and the concept of external reference files, refer to Chapter 13, "External References."

- **All that pass Filter.** This selection applies the criteria established in the Set Filter dialog box, which determines the layers displayed in the list. This item is automatically displayed after the criteria has been set in the Set Layer Filter dialog box.

- **Set Filter Dialog.** This selection opens the Set Layer Filters dialog box. This dialog box enables you to specify the criteria that the layer must match in order to be displayed in the layer list. This dialog box is presented later in this chapter.

In the following exercise, you will create a few new layers. You also will use the Show drop-down list to modify the display of the layer list using the available options.

USING THE SHOW DROP-DOWN LIST TO LIMIT THE DISPLAYED LAYERS

1. Continue from the previous exercise and use the Named Views tool from the Standard toolbar to display the View Control dialog box and restore the view named ALL.

2. Enter **-LAYER** to issue the command-line version of the LAYER command. The following prompt will appear:

   `-LAYER ?/Make/Set/New/ON/OFF/Color/Ltype/Freeze/Thaw/Lock/Unlock:`

3. Enter **N** for the New option to create several new layers at once. The following prompt will appear:

   `New layer name(s):`

4. Enter the following new layer names:

   Furn-existing, Furn-demo, Furn-new

5. Press Enter to return to the LAYER command options, and press Enter again to end the command.

6. Choose the Layers tool to open the Layer tab and view the addition of the three new layers to the layer listing.

7. Because nothing has been drawn on these layers, choose All in use from the Show drop-down listing to see the new layers removed from the listing.

8. To invert the alphabetic listing of layers, click once on the Name heading bar at the top of the listing. The list will begin with the Walls layer.

9. To display only those layers on which nothing has been drawn, choose All unused from the Show drop-down list to display the three new layers.

10. To display all layers in the hospital drawing, choose All from the Show drop-down list, and then click on OK.

As you can no doubt appreciate, abbreviated layer lists are very convenient for quick access to only those layers with which you will be working. In the following section, you review the more specific options of the Set Layer Filters dialog box.

Using a Layer Filter to Isolate Layer Display

For drawings with a more extensive layer list, the Show drop-down list may prove to be ineffective. The Set Layer Filters dialog box shown in figure 4.14 provides a more extensive toolset for specifying which layers will be displayed in the layer list.

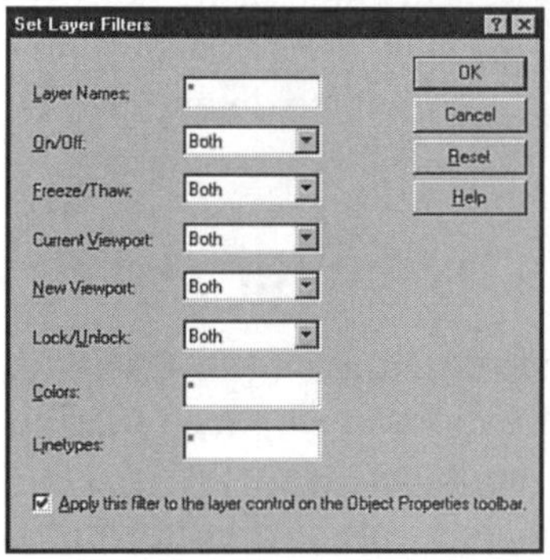

Figure 4.14

The Set Layer Filters dialog box offers more tools to specify the layers included in the layer list.

Contrary to the other features found in the Show drop-down list, the Set Layer Filters dialog box enables you to specify criteria for the layer names *seen in the list*, not the layer names you want to filter out of the list.

In the following exercise, you will change some layer names in order to create similar prefixes for similar layer content. You also will use the Set Layer Filter dialog box to configure the layer-name list for the hospital drawing.

SETTING A LAYER-NAME FILTER

1. Continue from the previous exercise and choose the Layers tool to open the Layer tab. Then choose Set Filter Dialog from the Show drop-down list.

2. Choose On from the On/Off drop-down list and Thawed from the Freeze/Thaw drop-down list. Then click on OK to display only those layers that are on or thawed in the layer-name list.

3. Open the Set Layer Filter dialog box again and choose Reset, then OK.

4. Select the Lights layer name. In the Details section, double-click on the Name edit box to change the layer name to **Lt-fixtures**. Perform the same operation for the Plumbing layer, changing it to **Pl-fixtures**. Then open the Set Layer Filters dialog box again.

5. Enter **pl*,lt*** in the Layer Names edit box, and click on OK to display only those groupings of layer names.

6. Select All from the Show drop-down list to display all the layer names, and then click on OK.

The setting of a layer filter is a different method of abbreviating the length of the layer list. The method you use, selections from the Show drop-down list, or the use of the Set Layer Filters dialog box will be determined by your application.

Selecting Objects by Layer Using an Object Filter

When presenting AutoCAD training to users across the country, instructors frequently encounter situations in which an outside contractor provides a company with a drawing that contains layers that aren't essential to the project. In these situations, certain objects within the drawing must be erased. To simplify the drawing, objects should be selected based upon the layer on which they exist before any layers are deleted from the listing.

NOTE

The object filter routine is covered more extensively in Chapter 10, "Basic Object Editing." However, the application in which objects are selected by layers will be immediately applicable to many readers when using Release 14.

By using a filter, you can specify criteria by which Release 14 filters the drawing objects to build the selection set. In the example just mentioned, a filter is built to enable AutoCAD to select objects that meet this criteria. The Object Selection Filters dialog box, shown in figure 4.15, displays the settings used in selecting objects based on the layers.

NOTE

Objects on layers that are locked or frozen will not be selected. However, it is not necessary for the layers to be on for objects on those layers to be selected.

Figure 4.15

The Object Selection Filters dialog box displays the settings used to select objects within layers.

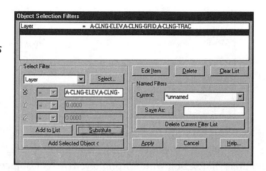

The drop-down list in the Select Filter area of the dialog box lists all AutoCAD's named objects and other criteria by which a filter can be built. In the previously mentioned scenario in which there are unwanted layers on a drawing, a filter would be built containing the layers having objects on them that are to be erased. In the following exercise, you open a drawing containing some of the layer names that adhere to the convention established by the task force. You then will apply a filter for the objects to be erased when prompted to select the objects.

APPLYING A FILTER

1. Open the drawing VLAYER-01.DWG, located in the sample directory of the accompanying CD.

2. Enter **-LA** to issue the command-line version of the LAYER command.

3. To quickly turn on all the layers of the drawing, enter **ON**. The following prompt will appear:

   ```
   Layer name(s) to turn On <>:
   ```

4. Enter ***** to select all layers and then press Enter twice. The drawing will redraw with all layers on, as shown in figure 4.16.

Figure 4.16

The VLAYER-01 drawing with all layers on.

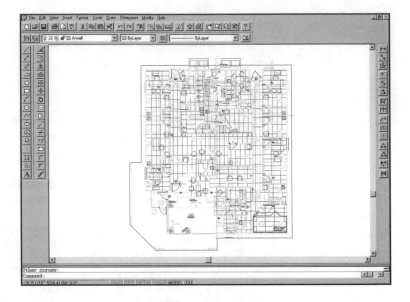

5. Choose Erase from the top of the Modify toolbar. Enter **FILTER** to open the Object Selection Filters dialog box when prompted to select objects.

6. From the drop-down list displaying Arc as the current item, scroll down and select Layer.

7. Click on the Select button to open the Select Layer(s) dialog box shown in figure 4.17.

Figure 4.17

The Select Layer(s) dialog box is used with object filters.

8. Choose the layers A-CLNG-ELEV, A-CLNG-GRID, and A-CLNG-TRAC. Then scroll down and select the layer A-ROOF-OTLN-NOTE and click on OK.

9. Choose Add to List.

10. Choose Apply to close the Object Selection Filters dialog box and return to the Select Objects: prompt.

11. Type **ALL** to select all objects on layers that are not locked or frozen. Then press Enter twice. The following message will appear:

     `2416 found`

     `2144 were filtered out`

12. Press Enter a third time to erase the selection set.

13. Now that no more objects exist on these four layers, choose the Layers tool to open the Layer tab.

14. Select A-CLNG-ELEV, then press and hold Shift and select A-CLNG-TRAC to select these three layers.

15. Scroll down, then press Ctrl and select the A-ROOF-OTLN-NOTE. Choose Delete to delete the layers from the list.

16. Choose Save to save the drawing.

The previous exercise instructed you on how to add a layer to the object selection filter criteria. In this example, if you did not know the names of the layers you wanted to include in the criteria, you simply used the LIST command (Tools, Inquiry, List) to ascertain the layer on which an object was created. Once that step was completed, you knew which layers to add to the criteria list.

Standardizing Layer Names

Whether you're the only person working on AutoCAD in your company or one of a few dozen, establishing standard layer names can increase your efficiency in layer management. As you might have encountered already, companies typically exchange CAD files to reduce duplication of work. In doing so, one of the first concerns checked is the presence of consistent layering. If layers are not consistent, the recipient might consider the drawing to be of poor quality based on the state of the layering alone.

The previous section on layer filters discussed the benefit of implementing a similar prefix for layers relating to the lighting and plumbing geometry. In the late 1980s, the Task Force on CAD-Layer Guidelines was formed to establish a consistent layer-naming convention and hierarchy. This task force is sponsored by several professional and government organizations, including American Consulting Engineers Council, American Institute of Architects, International Facility Management Association, American Society of Civil Engineers, Naval Facilities Engineering Command, United States Army Corps of Engineers, and the Department of Veterans Affairs. The task force is dedicated to improving layering consistency in CAD drawing production.

NOTE

To make these guidelines easily accessible to the AutoCAD user, Berry Systems, Inc., in Louisville, KY, has developed Visual LAYER, which enables you to implement this layering structure as well as integrate layering into existing drawings. The company's customers have found that Visual LAYER puts layer standards in a familiar and descriptive format and then makes them electronically transferable between companies. This ultimately makes business activities with these companies more productive and also ensures that the final CAD product is more consistent. A working version of the Visual LAYER product exists on the accompanying CD.

Release 14 does not provide a method by which the current layer properties and settings can be saved to a file. However, the Visual LAYER product found on the accompanying CD does enable you to save the current layer configuration to a file.

Summary

AutoCAD veterans who extensively utilize layering, even through recent versions of the software, will appreciate the improvements made in the layering tools of Release 14. Those of you just joining the ranks also will appreciate AutoCAD's compliance with the Windows 95/NT operating systems in the methods by which layers are selected, created, managed, and modified. The key concept to remember when working with layers is that the layer displayed in the drop-down list window on the Object Properties toolbar is the layer on which new geometry will be created. Also remember that you can see the objects that have been created on all the layers on the drawing if the layer(s) are on and thawed. In earlier versions of AutoCAD, the differences between freezing a layer and turning off a layer were rather significant. Release 14's treatment of these two layer settings is now virtually identical, so simply freezing a layer to render it invisible serves as the most effective method.

Companies interested in developing or implementing a consistent layer-naming convention should consider the Visual LAYER product introduced at Autodesk University in Chicago in 1996. This product efficiently automates an office standard and contains the layer-naming structure set forth by the Task Force on CAD-Layer Guidelines.

USING LINETYPES EFFECTIVELY

by Michael E. Beall

To add an object to your drawing that is drawn with something other than a continuous, solid line, you must change the linetype. This chapter explains how, when, and where to use the various linetypes provided with AutoCAD 14. The first section presents the basic concepts and applications of linetypes, and the second section covers the process of creating your own linetypes. The sections are subdivided as follows.

The section, "Working with Existing Linetypes," discusses the following:

- Assigning a linetype to a layer

- Working with the linetype scale factor

- Alternative settings for the linetype of new objects

- Setting an explicit linetype scale for objects

- Modifying the linetype and scale factor of existing objects

- Using the sample linetypes

The section, "Creating and Using Customized Linetypes," discusses the following:

- Creating new simple and complex linetypes
- The parts of a simple linetype pattern definition
- The parts of a complex linetype pattern definition
- Modifying an existing complex linetype

Working with Existing Linetypes

Each new release of AutoCAD provides you with an updated collection of linetypes to use in your drawings. Although you may need to create your own linetypes, 45 linetypes are at your disposal for immediate use. This section teaches you the basics, along with some effective methods of using linetypes, as well as a few tips and tricks.

Assigning a Linetype to a Layer

In Chapter 4, "Organizing Drawings with Layers," you learned that the layer and color values are two properties assigned to objects. The object's linetype is also property. Similar to assigning a color to a layer, a linetype value can be assigned to the layer on which the object will be drawn. Release 14 allows for on-the-fly linetype property assignment prior to drawing the object. You also can modify the linetype after the object has been drawn. All 45 default linetypes are stored in the acad.lin file, which is in the Acadr14\Support folder. Table 5.1 shows the linetypes available in Release 14.

Table 5.1

The Available AutoCAD 14 Linetypes

Linetype Name	Description
Acad_iso02w100	ISO dash __ __ __ __ __ __ __ __ __ __ __ __ __ __
Acad_iso03w100	ISO dash space __ __ __ __ __ __ __ __
Acad_iso04w100	ISO long-dash dot ____ . ____ . ____ . ____ . ____ .
Acad_iso05w100	ISO long-dash double-dot ____ .. ____ .. ____ .. ____ ..
Acad_iso06w100	ISO long-dash triple-dot ____ ... ____ ... ____ ... ____ ...
Acad_iso07w100	ISO dot . . . .

Linetype Name	Description
Acad_iso08w100	ISO long-dash short-dash___ _ ___ _ _ ___ _ _
Acad_iso09w100	ISO long-dash double–short-dash ___ _ _ ___ _ _
Acad_iso10w100	ISO dash dot _ . _ . _ . _ . _ . _ . _ . _
Acad_iso11w100	ISO double-dash dot _ _ . _ _ . _ _ . _ _ .
Acad_iso12w100	ISO dash double-dot _ .. _ .. _ .. _ .. _ .. _
Acad_iso13w100	ISO double-dash double-dot _ _ .. _ _ .. _ _ .. _ _ .
Acad_iso14w100	ISO dash triple-dot_ ... _ ... _ ... _ ... _ ...
Acad_iso15w100	ISO double-dash triple-dot _ _ ... _ _ ... _ _ ...
Batting	Batting SSSSSSSSSSSSSS
Border	Border _ _ . _ _ . _ _ . _ _ . _ _ . _ _ .
Border2	Border2 (.5x) _._._._._._._._._._._._
Borderx2	Borderx2 (2x) ___ ___ . ___ ___ . ___ ___ . _
Center	Center ___ _ ___ _ ___ _ ___ _ ___
Center2	Center2 (.5x) ___ _ ___ _ ___ _ ___ _ ___ _
Centerx2	Centerx2 (2x) _____ _ _____ _ _____ _ _____
Dashdot	Dashdot _ . _ . _ . _ . _ . _ . _
Dashdot2	Dashdot2 (.5x) _._._._._._._._._._._._._
Dashdotx2	Dashdotx2 (2x) ___ . ___ . ___ . ___ . ___ . _
Dashed	Dashed _ _ _ _ _ _ _ _ _ _ _ _ _
Dashed2	Dashed2 (.5x) _ _ _ _ _ _ _ _ _ _ _ _ _
Dashedx2	Dashedx2 (2x) ___ ___ ___ ___ ___ ___ ___ _
Divide	Divide ___ .. ___ .. ___ .. ___ .. ___ .. _
Divide2	Divide2 (.5x) _.._.._.._.._.._.._.._.._.
Dividex2	Dividex2 (2x) _____ . . _____ . . _____ . .
Dot	Dot ....
Dot2	Dot2 (.5x)................................

continues

Table 5.1, continued

The Available AutoCAD 14 Linetypes

Linetype Name	Description
Dotx2	Dotx2 (2x) . . . .
Fenceline1	Fenceline circle ——O——O——O——O——O——O——O——O
Fenceline2	Fenceline square ——[]——[]——[]——[]——[]——[]——
Gas_line	Gas line ——GAS——GAS——GAS——GAS——GAS——GAS
Hidden	Hidden _ _ _ _ _ _ _ _ _ _ _ _ _ _ _ _
Hidden2	Hidden2 (.5x) _ _ _ _ _ _ _ _ _ _ _ _ _ _ _ _ _ _ _
Hiddenx2	Hiddenx2 (2x) ___ ___ ___ ___ ___ ___ ___ ___
Hot_water_supply	Hot water supply —— HW —— HW —— HW —— HW —— HW
Phantom	Phantom ____ _ _ ____ _ _ ____ _ _
Phantom2	Phantom2 (.5x) ___ _ _ ___ _ _ ___ _ _ ___ _ _
Phantomx2	Phantomx2 (2x) _____ ___ ___ _____
Tracks	Tracks —I—I—I—I—I—I—I—I—I—I—I—I—I—I—I—I
Zigzag	Zig zag /\

As you can see from the preceding table, most linetypes are a collection of three, such as Border, Border2, and Borderx2; Center, Center2, and Centerx2; and so on. Notice that at the beginning of the description for these linetypes a factor is indicated. In essence you have a "standard," "half," and "double" scale arrangement, respectively. With the exception of the 14 Acad_iso linetypes, any linetype names without the "x2" or "2" suffix are the base linetypes, or the standard of the three.

NOTE

The sample ISO (International Standards Organization) linetypes found in the acad.lin file are designed for metric use with a pen width of 1 mm. To use them with the ISO predefined pen widths, the line has to be scaled with the appropriate value (for example, pen width 0.5 mm and LTSCALE 0.5).

One of the more common methods of using a linetype on your drawing is to assign it to a layer. In this case, the linetype property for new objects would be ByLayer. In an effort to conserve system memory, the Continuous linetype is the only linetype available when you start a new drawing. In the following exercise, you open an existing drawing and create a new layer, load the Hidden linetype, and assign it to the new layer.

SETTING THE LINETYPE PROPERTY TO BYLAYER

1. Open the drawing 05CAD-01.DWG and choose Layers from the Object Properties toolbar.

2. Create a new layer called Drawer, and then choose Continuous in the Linetype column to open the Select Linetype dialog box (see fig. 5.1).

Figure 5.1

The Select Linetype dialog box.

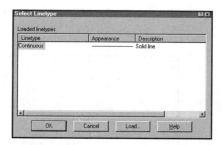

3. Because Continuous is the only loaded linetype in the drawing so far, click on the Load button to display the Load or Reload Linetypes dialog box (see fig. 5.2).

   The available linetypes from the default file of acad.lin are displayed in a list that has a vertical scroll bar.

4. Scroll down and select the Hidden linetype. Then click on OK to load the Hidden linetype and return to the Select Linetype dialog box.

Figure 5.2

The Load or Reload Linetypes dialog box.

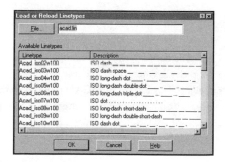

5. Select Hidden from the Loaded linetypes list. Then click on OK to return to the Layer tab and verify that Hidden is the linetype associated with the new Drawer layer.

6. Click on the Current button to set the Drawer layer to be current, and then click on OK to return to the drawing window.

7. With the Linetype drop-down list displaying the setting of ------- ByLayer, choose Rectangle from the Draw toolbar. The following prompt appears:

   `First corner:`

8. Pick ① at the point 10.50,10.50, as shown in figure 5.3. The following prompt appears:

   `Other corner:`

9. Pick ② at point 23.50,15.50 to place the other corner of the rectangle and complete the command.

10. Choose Save to issue the QSAVE command and save the drawing.

Figure 5.3

The drawer drawn in the Hidden linetype.

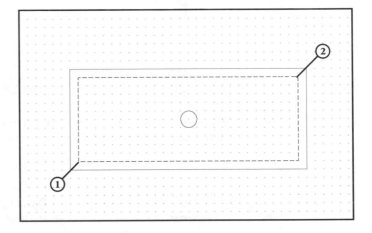

INSIDER TIP

Because AutoCAD is considered Windows-compliant, in most alphabetized listings throughout Release 14, pick anywhere in the listing, and then enter the first character of the file/item you are seeking. This causes AutoCAD to jump to the first item in the list that begins with that character. You can scroll from there to make your selection if needed.

On some of your screens, the dashed lines of the Hidden linetype may be difficult to distinguish, or might even be indiscernible. One alternative is to choose a different linetype for the Drawer layer. To help you more fully appreciate the benefits of having the linetype for new objects set to ByLayer, the following exercise changes the linetype associated with the Drawer layer. The drawing will automatically update all objects drawn on that layer with the new linetype.

CHANGING THE LINETYPE ASSOCIATED WITH THE LAYER

1. Continuing from the previous exercise, choose Layers from the Object Properties toolbar.

2. Choose Hidden in the Linetype column for the Drawer layer to open the Select Linetype dialog box.

3. Click on the Load button to open the Load or Reload Linetypes dialog box. Then scroll down and select the Hiddenx2 linetype. Click on OK to return to the Select Linetype dialog box.

4. Select Hiddenx2 from the list, and then click on OK to return to the Layer tab. Click on OK again to return to the drawing.

5. By changing the linetype associated with the Drawer layer, the drawing automatically regenerates to display the new rectangle in the Hiddenx2 linetype (see fig. 5.4). Choose Save to save the drawing.

Figure 5.4

The updated drawing with the Hiddenx2 linetype.

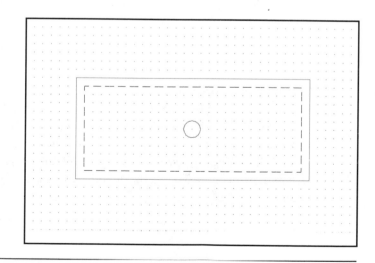

NOTE

If you feel that you will need several different linetypes in your drawing, choose the first linetype in the Load or Reload Linetypes dialog box. Scroll to the bottom of the list and, while holding down the Shift key, pick the last linetype. This will effectively select all items in the list. This method of selecting items in a list is a Windows 95/NT function of selecting a range of items.

Working with the Linetype Scale Factor

In the previous exercise, the linetype was changed to the Large size in order to get longer dashes on the rectangle representing the drawer behind the faceplate. For drawings in which even longer dashes are required, simply modify the linetype scale for the object. To establish a point of departure, figure 5.5 illustrates the dimensional relationship between the Dashed and Hidden linetypes. Knowing what the real distances are for the spaces and dashes of the different linetypes will help you understand how to modify their length.

Figure 5.5

Dimensional relationship between the Dashed and Hidden linetypes.

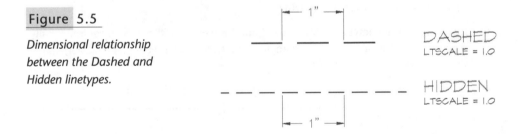

The most effective method of accommodating the need for longer (or shorter) increments of a non-Continuous linetype is to modify the LTSCALE (LineType SCALE) variable. This variable enables you to apply a factor to the scale of all non-Continuous linetypes in the drawing. It is a global setting within each drawing and should, therefore, be used wisely. The default value for LTSCALE is 1.0000. It is apparent from figure 5.5 that the default LTSCALE factor of 1.0000 is based upon the Dashed linetype.

In the following exercise, you change the LTSCALE factor to 1.5 using the Details options in the Linetype tab, as shown in figure 5.6. This will effectively result in a rectangle with dashes that are 50 percent longer.

Figure 5.6

The extended Linetype tab displaying the Details options.

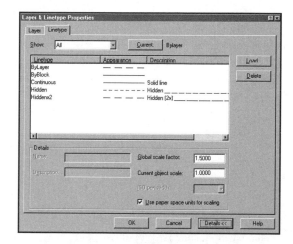

MODIFYING THE LTSCALE VARIABLE

1. Continuing from the previous exercise, choose Layers from the toolbar to open the Layer & Linetype Properties dialog box.

2. Select the Linetype tab, and then click on Details to display the available features.

3. Change the value for the Global scale factor to **1.5000**, and then press Enter. Your drawing will automatically regenerate to display the effect of the change.

4. Choose Save to save the drawing.

Alternative Settings for the Linetype of New Objects

In the previous series of exercises, the linetype setting for new objects was set to ByLayer. But suppose you want to draw a dashed line on a layer with a Continuous linetype? This is not uncommon in that it may not be necessary to create a separate layer only for a few objects that require hidden lines.

This section on alternative linetypes presents two methods that enable you to set the linetype property for new objects to something other than ByLayer. In doing so, you are essentially overriding the ByLayer linetype setting. In the following exercise, you set the linetype for new objects independent of the layer setting by using the Linetype tool on the Object Properties toolbar and the Linetype drop-down list.

INSIDER TIP

When creating or adding to multi-view drawings, it might be advantageous to set the size of the cursor to 100 percent of the screen in the Pointer tab of the Preferences dialog box. This will enable you to more easily confirm placement of lines in the different views.

SETTING THE LINETYPE FOR NEW OBJECTS

1. Open the drawing 05CAD-02.DWG and choose the Layers tool. Notice that the current linetype setting for the Objects layer is Continuous. Click on OK.

2. Choose the Linetype tool on the Object Properties toolbar to open the Linetype tab of the Layer & Linetype Properties dialog box.

3. Click on Load to open the Load or Reload Linetypes dialog box. Scroll down so you can see all three Dashed linetypes.

4. Holding the Shift key down, select Dashed, Dashed2, and Dashedx2 to highlight all three. Then release the Shift key and click on OK.

5. Select Dashed from the list, and then click on Current to set the linetype for the new objects you will create. This effectively overrides the ByLayer setting.

6. Click on OK to close the Layer & Linetype Properties dialog box. Pick the Line tool from the Draw toolbar. The following prompt appears:

   `_line From point:`

7. Pick ① at the point 3.25,12.50 to begin the line (see fig. 5.7). The following prompt appears:

   `To point:`

8. Pick ② at the point 3.25,11.00, and press Enter to complete the LINE command.

9. From the pull-down menus, choose Tools, Preferences. Select the Pointer tab of the Preferences dialog box.

10. In the Cursor size area at the bottom of the Pointer tab, change the Percentage of screen size value to 100. Press Enter to close the Preferences dialog box and apply the change.

11. Choose the Line tool again and pick points ③ and ④ to draw the second line for the hole. Press Enter to end the LINE command.

Figure 5.7

The dashed line locations in the three-view drawing.

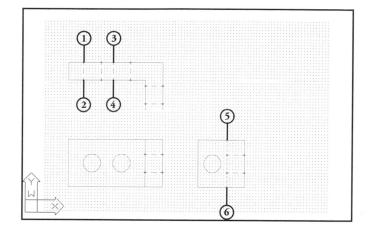

12. Select Dashed2 from the Linetype drop-down list to set the linetype for the next object you will create.

13. Use the LINE command again and pick ⑤ at the point 15.50,6.00, and ⑥ at the point 15.50,2.00. Then press Enter.

14. From the Linetype drop-down list, select the Dashed linetype again, and use the LINE command to draw the remaining dashed lines for the drawing (see fig. 5.7).

In the final few steps of this exercise you return to the ByLayer setting for the linetype and add the center lines for the holes in the bracket.

15. Choose the Layers tool, then choose the Center_lines layer in the list and set it to current.

16. Select Continuous in the Linetype column for the Center_lines layer. Click on Load from the Select Linetype dialog box.

17. From the Load or Reload Linetypes dialog box, choose Center, and then click on OK to return to the Select Linetype dialog box.

18. Choose Center from the Loaded linetypes list, and click on OK to assign the linetype. Click on OK again to return to the drawing.

19. Choose ByLayer from the Linetype drop-down list, and then choose the Line tool.

20. Draw the horizontal center line from ① to ② as shown in figure 5.8, and then press Enter to end the LINE command.

21. Add the two vertical center lines to the drawing, and then choose Save.

Figure 5.8

The three center lines for the circles.

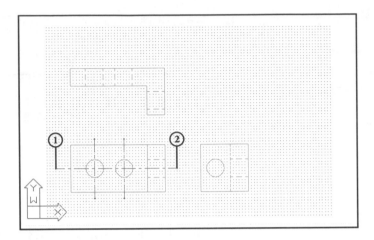

Figure 5.8

The three center lines for the circles.

Deleting Loaded Linetypes

It's pretty fair to say that the capabilities of the technology (hardware, memory, storage, and so on) can now adequately support the power of high-quality software, such as Release 14. Because of this, the importance of deleting extraneous linetypes (or layers) from a listing is not so much a system-saving issue as one of convenience and clarity. In Chapter 4, "Organizing Drawings with Layers," you learned how to delete a layer from the listing. The process of deleting a linetype from the Linetype tab of the Layers & Linetypes Properties dialog box is essentially similar to that of deleting layers. The single caveat to keep in mind is that all objects referencing any linetype(s) to be deleted must be erased first.

Setting an Explicit Linetype Scale for Objects

An object's linetype property can have the value of the layer (using the ByLayer setting), or it can be set explicitly by choosing a linetype to be used for new objects. Similarly, the object's linetype scale can be set independently of the current LTSCALE factor. This is where the waters can get a bit muddy. Bearing in mind that the LTSCALE value is applied globally to all non-Continuous linetypes in the drawing, it may be more advantageous to leave LTSCALE at the default factor of 1 and assign linetype scale factors to the objects individually. This can be done as they are being created or when they are modified later. To explicitly assign a scale factor to new objects, you set the CELTSCALE, which governs the Current object's LineType scale. Figure 5.9 illustrates the relationship between the Global scale factor (LTSCALE) and the Current object scale factor (CELTSCALE) applied to a Dashed linetype.

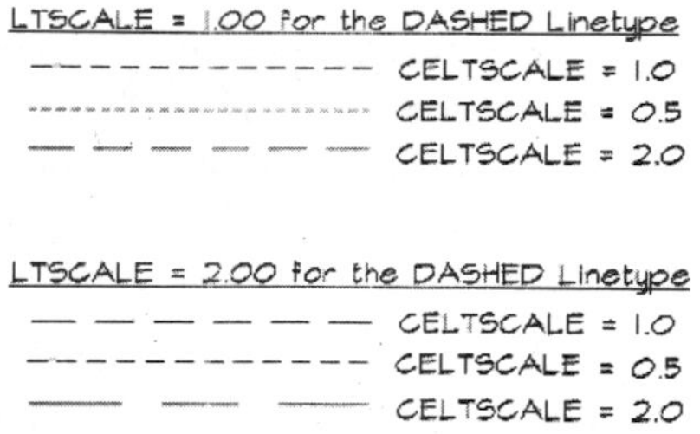

Figure 5.9

The LTSCALE and CELTSCALE relationship.

LTSCALE = 1.00 for the DASHED Linetype
— — — — — — — — — — — CELTSCALE = 1.0
···················· CELTSCALE = 0.5
— — — — — — — CELTSCALE = 2.0

LTSCALE = 2.00 for the DASHED Linetype
— — — — — — CELTSCALE = 1.0
— — — — — — — — — — CELTSCALE = 0.5
——— ——— ——— CELTSCALE = 2.0

In the following exercise, you set Current object scale factors in the Details area of the Linetype tab. The comparison will be made using different values for the CENTER2 linetype.

EXPLICITLY SETTING THE LINETYPE SCALE FOR NEW OBJECTS

1. Continuing from the previous exercise, choose the Linetype tool.

2. Change the Current object scale factor from 1.0000 to 1.5000, and click on OK. Because this is for objects yet to be drawn, the drawing has nothing to regenerate.

3. Use the LINE command to draw a new center line from ① to ② as shown in figure 5.10. Then press Enter.

Figure 5.10

The center lines with different Current object scale factors for the linetype.

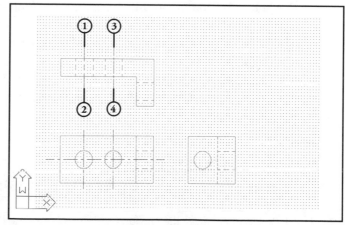

4. Choose the Linetype tool again. Change the Current object scale factor from 1.50 to 0.75, and click on OK.

5. Use the LINE command again to draw another center line from ③ to ④. Press Enter and save the drawing.

NOTE

The Current object scale factor (CELTSCALE) is not multiplied by the Global scale factor (LTSCALE). Only existing objects drawn in a non-Continuous linetype will be updated automatically when the Global scale factor is changed.

You can easily see the difference between the two scale factors. Also, remember that the current linetype property is ByLayer and that the lines were drawn on a layer with the linetype setting of Center. These are very powerful features and once you understand their relationship, your ability to quickly change how objects appear will increase dramatically.

Modifying the Linetype and Scale Factor of Existing Objects

You can easily modify an object's linetype or linetype scale by using the Properties tool introduced in Chapter 4, "Organizing Drawings with Layers." With this feature, you also can change the linetypes and/or linetype scales of one or more objects. When using the DDMODIFY or DDCHPROP commands to change the linetype scale of selected object(s), the change only applies to the object(s) selected; it does not change the current value displayed in the Current object scale (CELTSCALE) field of the Linetype tab.

The Match Properties tool, also introduced in Chapter 4, "Organizing Drawings with Layers," enables you to change geometrical properties by matching the properties of another object in the drawing. As is often the case, you may need to simply inquire existing geometry's properties or values prior to making a change. The LIST command will return information about the object(s) selected. In the following exercise, you use the Properties tool and the Match Properties tool to update the lines in the drawing.

MODIFYING THE LINETYPE AND LINETYPE SCALE OF EXISTING OBJECTS

1. Continuing from the previous exercise, choose the Properties tool from the Object Properties toolbar.

2. Select all the center lines you have drawn, and press Enter to display the Change Properties dialog box (see fig. 5.11).

Figure 5.11

The Change Properties dialog box.

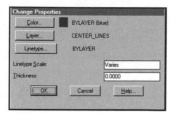

3. Change the Linetype Scale value from Varies to 0.75, and click on OK. The drawing will regenerate to update the selected lines.

4. From the pull-down menus, choose Tools, Inquire, List.

5. Select the vertical dashed line at ① as shown in figure 5.12, and then press Enter. Your screen will switch to the AutoCAD Text Window in which you will see the following display of properties and other information regarding the selected line:

```
LINE Layer: OBJECT
 Space: Model space
 Color: ByLayer Linetype: DASHED2
 Handle = 5D
 from point, X = 15.50 Y = 6.00 Z = 0.00
 to point, X = 15.50 Y = 2.00 Z = 0.00
 Length = 4.00, Angle in XY Plane = 270
 Delta X = 0.00, Delta Y = -4.00, Delta Z = 0.00
```

Figure 5.12

Selection of the dashed line to be modified.

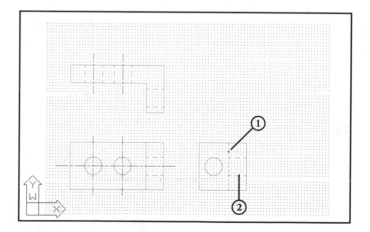

6. Press F2 to switch back to the drawing window. Choose the Match Properties tool on the Standard toolbar.

7. When prompted to Select Source Object, pick the dashed line at ②, and press Enter.

8. Pick the vertical dashed line at ① again as the destination for the source object's properties and press Enter. The drawing is updated with the new property assignments.

Creating and Using Customized Linetypes

This chapter is intended to bring you up to speed in not only using the simple linetypes provided with AutoCAD Release 14, but also in creating your own complex linetypes by building upon those that already exist. Although many applications can benefit from the array of available linetypes, you can customize or create an application-specific linetype with Release 14. This section takes you through the process of customizing linetypes and takes you through an exercise or two to illustrate their use.

Using Sample Complex Linetypes

In the first section of this chapter you learned how to load and use *simple* linetypes. A simple linetype is one that contains only dashes, dots, and spaces. A *complex* linetype, on the other hand, is a linetype that contains something other than the normal patterns of dashes and dots. It can contain text objects, angled or orthogonal lines, or other shapes you might create. As mentioned earlier in this chapter, the complex linetypes are found in the acad.lin file along with the other simple linetypes used in the exercises. The acad.lin file is an ascii text definition file that can be opened and modified to change the look of an existing linetype or to add a new one.

Table 5.2 lists and defines the seven sample customized linetypes and the three Center linetypes found in the acad.lin file to give you an idea of how simple linetype definitions appear.

Table 5.2

Comparing Complex Linetypes and Simple Center Linetypes

Linetype	Appearance	Definition
Fenceline1	——0——0——	A,.25,[CIRC1,ltypeshp.shx,s=.1],–.2,1
Fenceline2	——[]——[]——	A,.25,[BOX,ltypeshp.shx,s=.1],–.2,1
Tracks	-|-|-|-|-|-|-|-|-	A,.15,[TRACK1,ltypeshp.shx,s=.25],.15
Batting	SSSSSSSSSS	A,.0001,[BAT,ltypeshp.shx,s=.1],–.4

Linetype	Appearance	Definition
Hot_water_supply	— HW — HW	A,.5,–.2,["HW",STANDARD,S=.1, R=0.0,X=–0.1,Y=–.05],–.2
Gas_line	—GAS—GAS	A,.5,–.2,["GAS",STANDARD,S=.1, R=0.0,X=–0.1,Y=–.05],–.25
Zigzag	ΛΛΛΛΛΛΛΛ	A,.0001,[ZIG,ltypeshp.shx,s=.2],–.8
Center	— – — –	A,1.25,–.25,.25,–.25
Center2	— – — – —	A,.75,–.125,.125,–.125
Centerx2	——— —	A,2.5,–.5,.5,–.5

An observation is in order here regarding the default size of the linetype patterns. Throughout AutoCAD, you will encounter default settings in any number of commands and options. Historically speaking, AutoCAD's default values have always been small; they have been essentially designed for geometry-defining objects smaller than a breadbox. In the following exercise, you load the linetype definition file and use some sample linetypes in a site plan drawing—an application significantly larger than a breadbox. For that reason, the exercise also presents an excellent opportunity to increase the Global scale factor of all linetypes.

DRAWING WITH TWO SAMPLE LINETYPES

1. Open the drawing 05CAD-03.DWG located in the sample directory and choose the Linetype tool on the Object Properties toolbar.

2. Click on the Load button from the Linetype tab to open the Load or Reload Linetypes dialog box.

3. Scroll down the Linetype column and select Fenceline1. Scroll down further and press the Ctrl key on the keyboard and select the linetype Tracks.

4. Click on OK to load those two linetypes into the linetype list.

5. Change the Global scale factor in the Linetype tab from 1.0000 to 480.

6. Click on the Layer tab and select Continuous in the Linetype column for the Tracks layer to open the Select Linetype dialog box.

7. Select the Tracks linetype from the list, then click on OK to return to the Layer tab.

8. Click on OK. Select Continuous in the Linetype column for the Fencing layer to reopen the Select Linetype dialog box.

9. Select the Fenceline1 linetype from the Linetype list, and click on OK.

10. Confirm that the Tracks layer is current, and then click on OK to return to the drawing.

11. Choose the Line tool from the Draw toolbar and pick ①, then ②, as shown in figure 5.13. Press Enter to end the LINE command.

12. Set the layer FENCE1 to be Current in the Layer drop-down list, and choose the Linetype tool.

13. Change the Current object scale value to 0.5, and click on OK.

14. Use the LINE command to draw the fence line by picking points ③–⑥. Press Enter to end the command.

15. Choose Save to save the drawing.

Figure 5.13

Creating the railroad and fence lines.

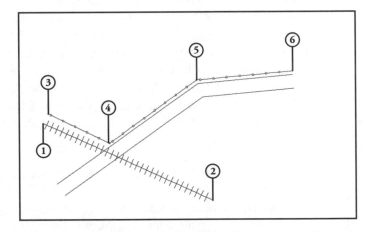

Inside the Simple Linetype Definition

Several terms are important to understand when creating your own linetype: Each linetype uses two lines of "code" to define the pattern of the linetype. The first line of code contains the name of the linetype and a description. The linetype name cannot contain spaces and begins with an asterisk, followed by a comma, after which you can add an optional description to help visualize the linetype. This is seen in the following guide and example for a linetype named INSIDE_DD:

*Linetype_name, optional description/appearance

*INSIDE_DD,__.__ · · __.__ · · __.__ · · __.__

The second line of the linetype definition is the code defining the pattern for the "pen motion" used in creating a line in this linetype. The pattern always begins with the alignment code of "A," followed immediately by a comma-delimited series of descriptors that define the first full sequence of the linetype pattern. No spaces are allowed in the linetype definition. For simple linetypes, use the following syntax to create the pattern definition:

- **Positive number:** The length of the dash in drawing units (pen down)

- **Negative number:** The length of the space in drawing units (pen up)

- **0 (zero):** A dot (pen down, pen up in one location)

The following linetype pattern definition is for the INSIDE_DD linetype:

A,.25,–.1,0,–.1,.25,–.125,0,–.125,0,–.125

NOTE

The description of the linetype may be a graphic representation of the pattern or a line of text such as Use this linetype for property lines. This description will be displayed in the Load or Reload Linetypes dialog box. If you elect to omit the description on the first line, do not follow the linetype name with a comma.

Creating a Simple Linetype

One of the great benefits of working in the Windows environment is the ability to switch to another application, create or edit the desired file or document, and then switch back to the original application. You can have several applications or programs open concurrently.

In the following exercise, you open the Windows Notepad application and create a new linetype definition file named inside14.lin from the existing acad.lin, and then add a linetype definition for the INSIDE_DD linetype.

CREATING AND ADDING A NEW LINETYPE

1. Continuing from the previous exercise, open Notepad. If you're using Windows 95 or Windows NT 4.x, choose Start, Programs, Accessories, Notepad.

2. Choose File, Open and open the folder Acadr14\support using the Look in drop-down list in the Open dialog box.

3. Change the pattern in the File name edit box to *.lin, select acad.lin from the list, and then click on Open to display the Notepad application as shown in figure 5.14.

4. Choose File, Save As. Enter **inside14.lin** in the File name edit box, and click on OK.

Figure 5.14

The bottom of the inside14.lin file in Notepad.

5. Scroll down and add a new linetype name and definition at the bottom of the file, below the pattern definition for the Zigzag linetype, by entering the following:

   `*INSIDE_DD,__.__  . .  __.__  . .  ___.__  . .`

6. On the second line, enter the following pattern definition (there are no spaces in this definition), and press Enter when finished:

   `A,.25,-.1,0,-.1,.25,-.125,0,-.125,0,-.125`

7. Choose File, Save to save the inside14.lin, then switch back to the current session of AutoCAD in the 05CAD-03 drawing.

8. To use the new linetype definition, choose the Linetype tool to display the Linetype tab of the Layer & Linetype Properties dialog box, then click on the Load button.

9. Click on the File button of the Load or Reload Linetypes dialog box, select inside14.lin from the Acadr14\Support folder, and click on Open.

10. Choose Inside_DD from the Available linetypes listing (it's now alphabetized) and click on OK.

11. From the linetypes list, select Inside_DD and set the Current object scale to 1.0000 in the Details area of the Linetype tab.

12. Click on the Current button to set the Inside_DD linetype to current, then click on OK.

13. Choose the Line tool from the Draw toolbar and pick the points ①–③ as shown in figure 5.15. Then press Enter and save the drawing.

Figure 5.15

Placing the INSIDE_DD linetype.

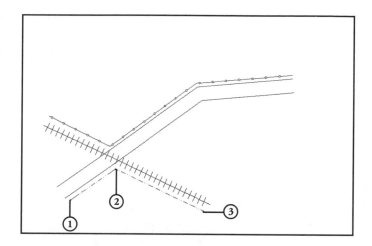

Inside the Complex Linetype Definition

Linetypes containing text objects or shapes are considered complex because their pattern definition is a bit more complex than those containing dots, dashes, and spaces. Complex linetype definitions, however, may also contain the elements used in creating simple linetype definitions. The complex pattern takes two lines of definition. The first line of the definition, which contains the name and optional description, is identical to that of the simple linetype. The second line of the complex definition contains transformation elements in brackets that define the text and shapes used. The following is an example of a complex linetype using a line of text in the pattern. Figure 5.16 illustrates where some of the values are applied.

A,1,["4 BOARD",Instyle,S=.25,R=30,X=0,Y=−.75],−1.50

The beginning A and the pen up, pen down values are identical to the syntax used in simple linetypes. The [bracketed transformation elements] are defined in the following list, each element being separated by a comma (no spaces):

■ **"text string":** Any text characters to be used in the complex linetype must be in quotes and can contain spaces.

- **textstyle:** The text style called for—the second element in the brackets—*must* exist in the drawing or the complex style will not be loaded. If no text style is specified, LT uses the current style.

- **S=value:** The scale factor to be used for the text height. If the height of the specified text style is preset (>0), this factor is multiplied by the height setting. If the height of the style is 0, the S value entered is the height of the text. This value will be multiplied by the current LTSCALE factor.

- **R=value:** The rotation value entered is from the default justification point of the text (lower left). When using an R value, the rotation is relative to the angle of the line. To force an absolute angle relative to the current UCS, replace the R= with A= and specify the Absolute angle for every instance of text.

- **X=value:** This value specifies the distance the text is shifted along the X-axis of the linetype. If this value is 0 or is omitted, the linetype is generated with no offset.

- **Y=value:** Enter a negative value for this element to cause the middle of the text string to be in line with the linetype, such as "text-." If left as 0, text will appear as "text."

- **Pen-up:** The trailing pen-up value is the distance the pen is up from the *insertion point* of the text.

Figure 5.16

The 4 BOARD linetype and the applied variables.

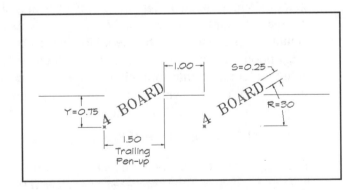

NOTE

Including text styles using non-standard AutoCAD fonts in customized linetypes is not recommended. If you send the drawing to others they must have the same font files in order to reload and use the customized linetype in other drawings. This also may violate copyright laws if you copy your custom fonts to distribute to others.

NOTE

After the alignment character of A, the first numeric entry is for the length of the first dash. Although common in simple linetype definitions, it is not necessary to follow the dash length with a pen-up negative value when creating complex linetypes with transformation variables in brackets, especially if the text is to be rotated.

Creating a Complex Linetype

Using the same method you used to create the simple linetype, in the following exercise you switch back to the Notepad and add a new complex linetype for a 4 BOARD fence to the inside14.lin linetype file, and then add it to the current drawing.

CREATING AND ADDING THE COMPLEX LINETYPE

1. Continuing from the previous exercise, switch back to Notepad and place your cursor at the bottom of the file.

2. Enter the following for the first line of the complex linetype:

   `*4_BOARD,  – –4 BOARD– –4 BOARD– –4 BOARD`

3. On the second line, enter the following pattern definition:

   `A,1,["4 BOARD",Instyle,S=.25,R=30,X=0,Y=-0.75],-1.50`

4. Choose File, Save to save the inside14.lin. Then switch back to the current session of AutoCAD.

5. Choose the Linetype tool. Click on the Load button.

6. Click on the File button, select inside14.lin from the Support folder, and click on OK to return to the Load or Reload Linetypes dialog box.

7. Select 4_board from the Available linetypes list and click on OK.

8. Choose 4_board from the list on the Linetype tab. Click on the Current button, and enter **0.50** in the Current object scale field.

9. Choose the Line tool and pick ①–④ to place the 4 BOARD fence line, as shown in figure 5.17. Press Enter.

Figure 5.17

The 4_BOARD linetype drawn on the site plan.

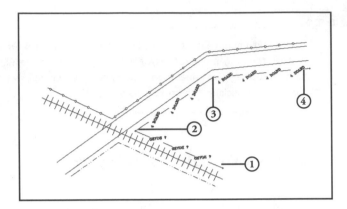

NOTE

Any shapes or text contained in complex linetypes are always drawn in their entirety. AutoCAD Release 14 always begins and ends the complex linetype with a dash by making minor adjustments in the lengths of the segments at either end. Text and shapes in the complex linetype, therefore, will not be trimmed.

Modifying an Existing Complex Linetype

When creating new linetype definitions, especially complex ones, the result of your efforts is not always desirable. In the previous exercise, the length of the text is a little too long and the frequency of the text in the line could be a bit less. The rotation of 30 degrees is probably unnecessary as well, but it was interesting to see the results of rotated text in the complex linetype.

In the following exercise you switch back to the Notepad window and modify the rotation angle setting, change the text from "4 BOARD" to "4-BD," and increase the spacing of the text along the line.

MODIFYING THE COMPLEX LINETYPE

1. Continuing from the previous exercise, switch back to the Windows 95 Notepad and change the linetype description in the first line of the linetype definition to ——**4-BD**——**4-BD**——**4-BD.**

2. In the second line, change rotation element from R=30 to **R=0** and change the text in quotes from "4_BOARD" to "**4-BD**."

3. Because the word is shorter now and is in-line, change the Y=value from Y=–0.75 to **Y=–0.1** (notice it is still negative).

4. Make the necessary dash and space changes at the beginning and end of the definition so your complex linetype definition for 4_BOARD looks like the following:

```
A,1.50,-.25,["4-BD",instyle,S=.25,R=0,X=0,Y=-0.1],-1.25
```

5. Choose File, Save to save the inside14.lin. Switch back to your drawing.

6. Choose the Linetype tool, then click on Load.

7. Click on the File button, select inside14.lin from the list, and click on OK to return to the Load or Reload Linetypes dialog box. The linetype description in the Available Linetypes list should display the new 4-BD text.

8. Choose 4_BOARD from the list, and click on OK.

9. A Reload Linetype alert box appears regarding the reloading of the 4_BOARD linetype. Click on Yes.

10. From the Linetype tab, click on OK to return to the drawing.

11. To force AutoCAD into regenerating the drawing with the new 4_BOARD linetype definition, choose View, Regen from the pull-down menus. Your drawing should look like that shown in figure 5.18.

Figure 5.18

The modified 4_BOARD linetype.

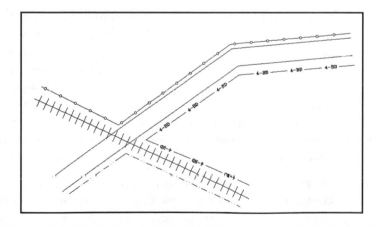

INSIDER TIP

Because the R=value is relative to the angle of the line drawn, to achieve right-reading text, draw your lines in from lower-left to upper-right or from upper-left to lower-right. Lines drawn in the other directions will result in the text of the linetype reading upside down.

Experiment further with the 4 board linetype by changing the R= variable to A= for an absolute angle of the text in the line. Figure 5.19 presents the application of the spacing variables used in the previous exercise so you can more fully understand the results.

Figure 5.19

The updated variables for the 4_BOARD linetype.

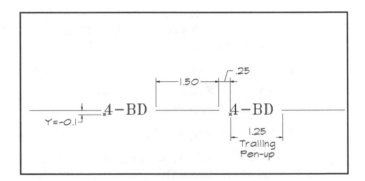

Summary

For the veteran user of AutoCAD, the improved interface for loading, assigning, and using linetypes is tremendous. The flexibility of the relationship between dialog boxes, tabs, and drop-down lists enables the newcomer to more quickly understand the manner in which linetypes are loaded and scaled. Release 14 has a wide assortment of linetypes—both simple and complex—available that can easily be implemented for nearly every discipline. For applications in which a linetype does not exist, the user can relatively quickly generate a new linetype. A more graphically dynamic drawing that can communicate the project clearly can now easily be generated using the substantial array of linetype features.

Because shape objects cannot be generated from within AutoCAD, adding text to a complex linetype is the most visually dynamic aspect of the complex linetype definition. For a more detailed account of how to create shapes that can be used in a complex linetype, refer to the *AutoCAD Release 14 User Guide*.

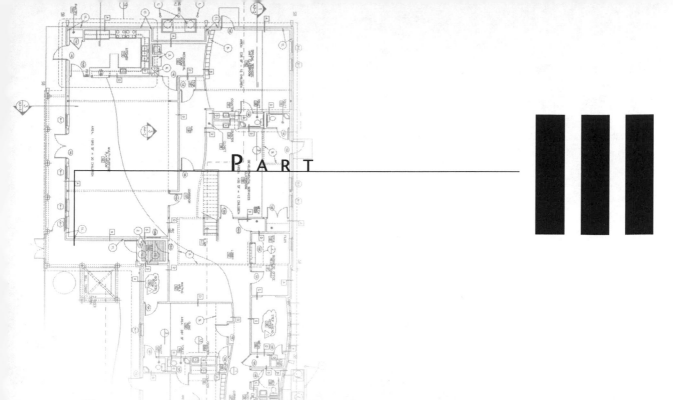

PART

III

CREATING AND EDITING DRAWINGS

Chapter 6: Creating Drawings with R14

Chapter 7: Creating Elementary Objects

Chapter 8: Creating Polylines and Splines

Chapter 9: Creating Complex Objects

Chapter 10: Basic Object Editing

Chapter 11: Advanced Geometry Editing

Chapter 12: Creating and Using Blocks

Chapter 13: External References

Chapter 14: Querying Objects

CHAPTER 6

CREATING DRAWINGS WITH R14

by David M. Pitzer

To create accurate drawings with AutoCAD, you must understand how to specify and enter coordinates, and understand the points that they are composed of. This, in turn, requires a knowledge of AutoCAD's basic coordinate display systems, the World Coordinate Systems (WCS) and User Coordinate Systems (UCS). AutoCAD is an extremely accurate design and drafting package with the capability of 16 decimal places of precision stored in its database. To actualize this amount of accuracy, AutoCAD supports several drawing aids that enable you to draw, place, and edit objects in your drawings. This chapter will discuss AutoCAD's coordinate systems and the methods you can use to make drawing with accuracy and precision easier.

This chapter covers the following topics:

■ Coordinate Systems

■ Coordinate Point Entry Methods

■ Changing Coordinate Systems

■ Setting Up Drawing Aids

■ Object Snapping

■ Construction Lines and Rays

Coordinate Systems

No matter what kind of drawing you do in AutoCAD, you need a systematic method of specifying points. Points define the beginnings, midpoints, and endpoints of lines, the center of circles and arcs, the axis points of an ellipse, and so on. The capability to place points accurately is important. When an AutoCAD command prompts you for a point, you can either specify a point on the screen with the mouse or pointing device or you can enter coordinates at the Command: line. When entering points, AutoCAD uses a three-dimensional Cartesian, or rectangular, coordinate system. Using this standard system, you locate a point in 3D space by specifying its distance and direction from an established origin measured along three mutually perpendicular axes: the X, Y, and Z axes. The origin is considered to be at 0,0,0. Figure 6.1 illustrates such a coordinate system. Only two dimensions are depicted with the Z axis projecting up, perpendicular to the page. If you are concerned only with two-dimensional drawings, this is the presentation of AutoCAD's coordinate system that will be seen.

In figure 6.1, the 4,6 coordinate indicates a point 4 units in the positive X direction and 6 units in the positive Y direction. Points to the left or below the origin have negative X and Y coordinate components, respectively. Figure 6.2 illustrates the same coordinate system, only now the third dimension and the Z axis are shown. To specify 3D points, you add a third element to the coordinate designation. The point 4,6,6 in figure 6.2 is located 4 units in the positive X direction, 6 units in the positive Y direction, and 6 units in the positive Z direction. The system of reckoning coordinates is independent of the units used so that distances can be in any measurement; for example, the X direction could be English feet or inches, or metric centimeters or kilometers.

Later in this chapter, you will learn about the various ways that you can change the origin as well as the orientation of the three axes of AutoCAD's rectangular coordinate system. No matter how the coordinate system is oriented, you must know how to enter points.

Figure 6.1

The X and Y axes in a 2D coordinate system.

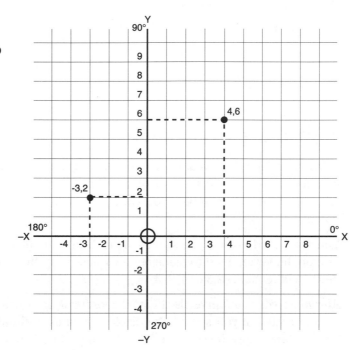

Figure 6.2

The 3D rectangular coordinate system.

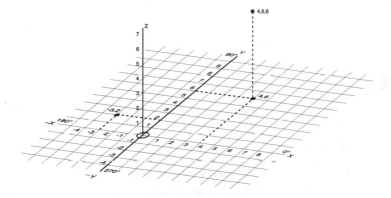

Coordinate Point Entry Methods

Many of the drawings you make in AutoCAD—regardless of their eventual complexity—consist of a few relatively basic AutoCAD objects such as lines, circles, or text elements. These objects require that you enter points that specify their location, size, and direction. Many editing operations also require that you specify points. There are four ways to enter points or coordinates in AutoCAD:

- Using absolute coordinates
- Using relative coordinates
- Using direct distance entry
- Using coordinate display

Using Absolute Coordinates

Absolute rectangular coordinates are always measured from the origin point, 0,0,0. In AutoCAD, you specify an absolute coordinate from the keyboard by typing in the X,Y,and Z axes values separated by a comma—X,Y for 2D points or X,Y,Z for 3D points.

You don't need to use a plus sign (+) if the displacement from the origin is positive. You do, however, need to place a minus sign (–) in front of displacements in the negative direction: –2,3 or 4,–6,3.

Absolute polar coordinates also treat 2D coordinate entry as a displacement from the origin or 0,0, but you specify the displacement as a distance and an angle. The distance and angle are separated by a left-angle bracket (<) with no spaces:

   distance<angle; for example, 25<135

Positive angles are measured counterclockwise from an assumed 0 degree that lies, by default, along the positive X axis as shown in figure 6.3.

NOTE

> When entering the angle portion of polar coordinates, you can specify the angle as either positive (counterclockwise) or negative (clockwise). Thus:
>
> 37<90 is equivalent to 37<–270
>
> This applies to both absolute and relative coordinate entry.

In the following exercise, you use both absolute rectangular and absolute polar coordinates to draw the outline of a fastener.

Figure 6.3

Default angle directions.

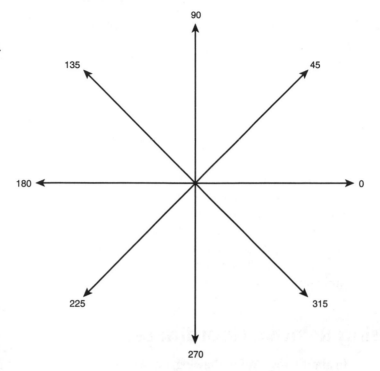

USING ABSOLUTE RECTANGULAR AND ABSOLUTE POLAR COORDINATE ENTRY

1. If necessary, start AutoCAD and begin a drawing using Wizard, Start from Scratch option.

2. Start the LINE command by either typing **L** or clicking on the Line tool on the Draw toolbar. Enter the following at the prompts:

```
From point: 4.5,4↵
To point: 6.5,5 ↵
To point: 9<38.34 ↵
To point: 7.8<25.36 ↵
To point: 6.5,4 ↵
To point: C ↵
```

3. Your drawing should look like figure 6.4.

Figure 6.4

*Outline drawn using
absolute coordinates.*

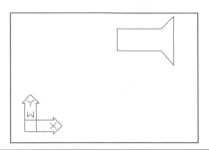

This exercise demonstrates the limitations of absolute coordinates. Although absolute coordinates are adequate for designating the beginning of a line, measuring subsequent points in relation to the drawing's origin is cumbersome and often inaccurate. When the lines outlining an object (such as the fastener in the preceding exercise) are not orthogonal, absolute coordinates are inadequate if any degree of accuracy and efficiency is desired. The use of relative coordinates solves this problem.

Using Relative Coordinates

In almost any kind of drawing, once you have established the beginning of a line, you usually know the X and Y displacement or the distance and angle of the next point. Relative coordinates do not reference the origin point but are reckoned relative to the last point. You can use this more straightforward method with either relative rectangular or relative polar coordinates. To distinguish relative coordinate entry from absolute entry, you precede relative coordinates with the "at" symbol (@); for example, @1.5,3 for relative rectangular entry or @2.6<45 for relative polar entry.

In the preceding relative rectangular entry, the point specified lies at a displacement of 1.5 units in the X axis direction and 3 units in the Y axis direction from the previous point; in the relative polar entry, the point lies 2.6 units at an angle of 45 degrees from the previous point. In the following exercise, the utility of relative coordinates is shown in drawing a fastener similar to the one in the previous exercise.

USING RELATIVE COORDINATES

1. Continue from the previous exercise.

2. Start the LINE command by typing **L** or clicking on the Line tool on the Draw toolbar. Enter the following at the prompts:

    ```
    From point: 9,5 ↵ (Note this is an absolute coordinate.)
    To point: @2<0 ↵ (Note this is a relative polar coordinate.)
    To point: @.8<46 ↵
    To point: @0,-2.2 ↵ (Note this is a relative rectangular coordinate.)
    To point: @.8<134 ↵
    To point: @2<180 ↵
    To point: C
    ```

3. Your drawing should now resemble figure 6.5.

Figure 6.5

Outline drawn using relative coordinates.

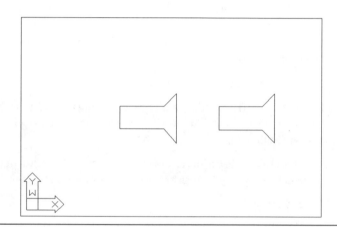

NOTE

The angles involved or the availability of distance information will usually determine whether it is easier to enter the next point using relative polar or relative rectangular coordinates.

As you can see, relative coordinate point entry is much easier to use and permits more accuracy. Even when your drawing involves purely orthogonal displacements, relative coordinate entry is the superior and usually the only accurate method.

Direct Distance Entry

A variation of relative coordinate entry, called *direct distance entry*, is supported in Release 14. In direct distance entry, instead of entering coordinate values, you can specify a point by moving the cursor to indicate a direction and then entering the distance from the first point. This is a good way to quickly specify a line length. This method is used primarily when the displacements involved are orthogonal and you can therefore have the ORTHO drawing aid turned on. The following exercise demonstrates the use of direct distance entry.

USING DIRECT DISTANCE COORDINATE ENTRY

1. Continue from the previous exercise by starting the LINE command. Respond to the first prompt as follows:

   From point: **7.5,7.5** ↵

2. Ensure that ORTHO mode is active by observing the ORTHO tile in the mode status bar at the bottom of the AutoCAD drawing window. If it is grayed-out (off), double-click it to turn it on.

3. With ORTHO mode on, move the crosshairs cursor any distance to the right of the point entered in step 1. Answer the current prompt as follows:

   To point: **2.3** ↵

4. Note that the first polyline segment is drawn 2 units orthogonally to the right of point 7.5,7.5. Also note that your coordinate entry, although "relative" to the preceding point, did not require the "@" prefix.

5. Now respond to the current prompt with a standard relative polar coordinate as follows:

   To point: **@.8<46** ↵

6. Enter the next polyline segment using direct distance entry by moving the crosshairs cursor any distance below the last point and entering the following at the current prompt:

   To point: **2.2** ↵

7. Note again that the preceding entry did not require the leading "@" symbol and that the line segment was drawn 2.2 units in the direction of the crosshairs cursor.

8. Again use standard relative polar coordinate entry for the next polyline segment:

   To point: **@.8<134** ↵

9. Respond to the current prompt by placing the crosshairs cursor to the left of the last point and entering:

   To point: **2.3** ↵

10. Complete the outline by typing **C** and pressing Enter. The outline should be similar to that completed in the previous exercise.

Direct distance entry provides a more direct and easier method of entering relative coordinates when the point lies in an orthogonal relationship to the previous point—a common situation in most drawings. Of course, if the point you want to designate lies on a snap point, whether orthogonal to the previous point or not, you can bypass keyboard entry by simply snapping the cursor to and clicking on the point. (The concept of "snapping" is covered later in this chapter.)

NOTE

Direct distance entry was actually introduced in AutoCAD midway through the Release 13 cycle in Release 13c4. It was not, however, well documented at that time and will be a "new" feature to many Release 14 users.

Coordinate Display

The coordinate display window located at the bottom-left end of the mode status bar is useful when entering coordinates, whether you type them at the Command: prompt or pick points on the screen with the screen cursor. Figure 6.6 shows this display with two concurrent sessions of AutoCAD active.

Figure 6.6

The coordinate display window shows coordinates in the current drawing units.

The upper display shows decimal units while the lower display is in architectural units. The coordinate display has three modes of operation and, depending on the mode selected and the command in progress, can display either absolute or relative coordinates. You can cycle through the various modes in three ways: by pressing either F6 or Ctrl+D or by double-clicking in the display area itself. The three modes of coordinate display are as follows:

- **Mode 0.** This mode displays the absolute coordinates of the last picked point. The display is updated whenever a new point is picked.

- **Mode 1.** This mode displays the absolute coordinates of the screen cursor and updates continuously as the cursor is moved. This is the default mode.

- **Mode 2.** This mode displays the distance and angle relative to the last point whenever a command prompt requesting either a distance or angle is active.

When Mode 0 is selected, the coordinate display appears grayed-out, although the coordinates of the last selected point are still visible. At an "empty" command prompt (no command in progress) or at an active prompt that does not accept either a distance or angle as input, you can only toggle between Mode 0 and Mode 1. At a prompt that does accept or require either a distance or angle as input, you can toggle among all three modes. Pay particular attention to the coordinate display window during the following exercise.

SWITCHING AMONG COORDINATE DISPLAY MODES

1. Continue from the previous exercise or open a new drawing. (Use the Wizard option, Start from Scratch if you are starting AutoCAD. You will not need to save this drawing.)

2. Ensure that SNAP mode is off by observing the SNAP tile in the mode status bar at the bottom of AutoCAD's application. If it is off, the window will be grayed-out. If necessary, double-click on the tile to make it appear grayed-out.

3. Ensure that the current mode setting of the coordinate display is "off" by pressing F6 until the display appears grayed-out.

4. Ensure that ORTHO mode is grayed-out (off) by pressing F8.

5. Now move the screen cursor within the drawing area. Note that the coordinate display remains static.

6. Double-click in the coordinate display area. Note that the display is no longer grayed-out.

7. Now move the screen cursor and notice that the coordinate display is continuously updated. The coordinate display is now in Mode 2.

8. Start the LINE command by typing **L** and pressing Enter. Because the From point: prompt does not accept distance or angle input, the display continues to update as you move the cursor.

9. Respond to the From point: prompt by typing in **4,7** and pressing Enter.

10. Notice that once a point has been specified, the coordinate display changes to show relative polar coordinates as you move the cursor. Type in the following absolute rectangular point:

    To point: **6,7** ↵

11. The line is drawn between the two points. Now press Ctrl+D. The display changes to Mode 1 (on) and the display is again in absolute rectangular format as you move the cursor.

12. Press F6. The display is now in Mode 0 (off). The display is grayed-out and static as you move the cursor. Enter the following at the prompt:

    To point: **2,3**

13. The next line is drawn. Now double-click in the coordinate display window. The display is now back in Mode 2 with the read-out once again in relative polar format.

14. Press the Esc key to end the LINE command. Then press the **U** key and press Enter to undo the line. Note that the display reverts to absolute rectangular because no command accepting distance or angle input is active.

In this exercise, you saw the three modes of coordinate display and how they can aid you in selecting points. You also manually used the three methods available to you for toggling among the three modes. Although the absolute rectangular read-out mode is of limited usefulness, it can, for example, be used to specify the starting point of an object such as a wall or to specify a set of known points in a surveying data context.

Changing Coordinate Systems

The beginning of this chapter looked at AutoCAD's rectangular or Cartesian coordinates system from the standpoint of entering coordinates representing points in your drawing (refer to fig. 6.1). You learned about absolute and relative coordinate entry in both rectangular and polar formats. When you begin a new AutoCAD drawing you are, by default, using a rectangular coordinate system that is called the World Coordinate System or WCS. This is, indeed, the familiar coordinate system with the origin at or near the bottom-left corner of the "page," or AutoCAD's drawing window.

This presentation of a standard rectangular coordinate layout is given a name because other coordinate systems and layouts are possible in AutoCAD. These coordinate systems are called Users Coordinate Systems, or UCS, because they may be defined in a number of ways by the user. UCSs make working in 3D space easier, although UCSs are frequently useful in 2D work as well.

World Coordinate System

The World Coordinate System is nothing more than a standard rectangular coordinate system with the origin in the lower-left corner of the screen, a horizontal X axis running left to right and a Y axis extending vertically from the top to the bottom of the screen. The Z axis is perpendicular to both the X and Y axes and is considered to extend in a direction perpendicular to the screen. To identify the WCS and establish its orientation, AutoCAD, by default, places the WCS icon at or near the origin. The WCS icon is shown in figure 6.7. Its defining characteristic is the "W" appearing on the icon; this tells you that you are in the World Coordinate System.

Figure 6.7

The World Coordinate System icon.

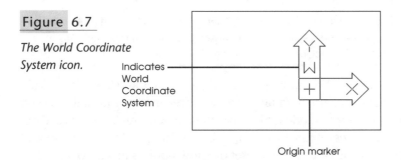

Indicates World Coordinate System

Origin marker

User Coordinate Systems

You can create your own coordinate systems called *User Coordinate Systems,* or UCSs. As the name suggests, a UCS is defined and controlled by you, the user. In a UCS, the origin as well as the direction of the X, Y, and Z axes can be made to move, rotate, and even align with drawing objects. Even though the three axes in a UCS remain mutually perpendicular, as they are in the WCS, a great deal of flexibility can be achieved in placing and orientating your UCS. The UCS command enables you to place a UCS origin anywhere in 3D space so that you can work relative to any point you want. You can also rotate the X,Y, and Z axes in 2D or 3D space. Figure 6.8 shows two UCS icons representing two different coordinate systems; one is the WCS, indicated by the "W" on the UCS icon; the other is a UCS defining a User Coordinate System. User Coordinate Systems are indispensable for working in 3D space.

The following exercise demonstrates how to create a User Coordinate System by aligning the UCS with two 2D points.

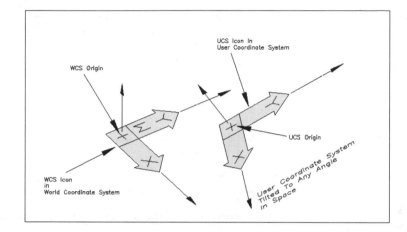

ALIGNING A UCS WITH A 2D OBJECT

1. Start a new drawing and name it CHAPTER6.DWG. Use the UCS.DWG from the accompanying CD as a prototype or template. (See Chapter 3, "Setting Up the AutoCAD 14 Drawing Environment," for information on using prototype drawings.)

2. Your drawing should resemble figure 6.9. Note that the W in the UCS icon indicates the World Coordinate System is current.

3. Choose Tools, UCS, 3point. The following prompt appears:

    ```
    Origin point <0,0,0>:
    ```

4. Shift+right-click to display the cursor menu and choose Endpoint. Then pick ① in figure 6.9. The following prompt appears (the points given as a default may differ in your drawing):

    ```
    Point on positive portion of the X-axis <6.58,2.04,0.00>:
    ```

5. Shift+right-click to display the cursor menu, choose Endpoint, and pick ②. The following prompt appears:

    ```
    Point on positive-Y portion of the UCS XY plane <5.19,2.96,0.00>:
    ```

6. Pick anywhere near ③. Note that the UCS icon changes orientation to align with the new UCS and that the W disappears, indicating you are no longer in the WCS (see fig. 6.10).

Figure 6.9

Pick a point to change the UCS.

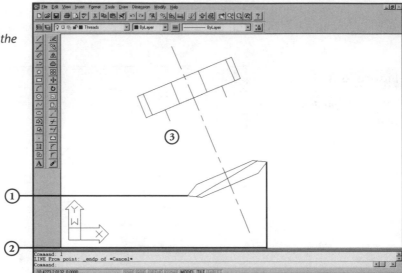

Figure 6.10

Arraying an object in the new UCS.

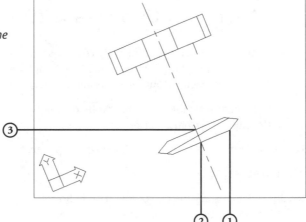

7. Choose Modify, Array. The following prompt appears:

    `Select objects:`

8. Pick anywhere on the object at ① and end the selection process by pressing Enter.

9. Answer the following prompts as shown:

    ```
    Rectangular or Polar array (<R>/P): R ↵
    Number of rows (---) <1>: 6 ↵
    Number of columns (|||) <1>: ↵
    ```

10. The following prompt appears:

    ```
    Unit cell or distance between rows (---):
    ```

11. Activate the cursor menu (Shift+right-click) and choose Intersection. Click at ②. Again activate the cursor menu, choose Intersection, and click at ③.

12. The array is carried out in a direction perpendicular to the X axis of the new UCS.

13. Return the UCS to the WCS with the USC command. Enter **UCS** and press Enter at the Command: prompt. When the following prompt appears, accept the default <World>:

    ```
    Origin/ZAxis/3point/OBject/View/X/Y/Z/Prev/
    Restore/Save/Del/?/<World>: ↵
    ```

    Your drawing should resemble figure 6.11.

14. Save this drawing by pressing Ctrl+S.

Figure 6.11

The completed array in the UCS.

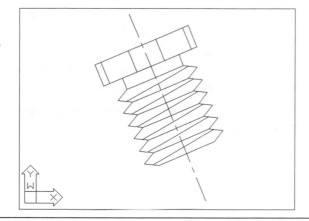

INSIDER **T**IP

It is possible to change the UCS to the position and orientation you want in two or more ways. In the preceding exercise, for example, you could have rotated the UCS about its Z axis instead of using the 3point option. I generally prefer to use the 3point option because it seems more positive and easier to use.

Although defining new UCSs is most frequently used in 3D drafting, the preceding exercise demonstrated that the capability to change the UCS is helpful in 2D work as well. By aligning the UCS with the horizontal axis of the thread object in the drawing, a simple 6-row array could be quickly carried out with the "axis" of the array perpendicular to the horizontal axis of the object. The following exercise demonstrates two more options of the UCS command, re-establishing the most previous UCS and controlling the display of the UCS icon.

DISPLAYING THE PREVIOUS UCS AND CONTROLLING THE POSITION OF THE UCS ICON

1. Continue in the drawing from the previous exercise or open CHAPTER6.DWG. The drawing will resemble figure 6.11.

2. Choose Tools, USC, Previous. Note that the UCS reverts back to the UCS defined in the previous exercise.

3. Now, choose View, Display, UCS Icon, Origin. Note that the UCS icon moves to the origin point of the currently defined UCS as shown in figure 6.12. This is the origin point you defined in step 4 of the previous exercise.

4. Now again, choose View, Display, UCS Icon, and notice that a check mark appears beside the Origin selection. Click on Origin to toggle the icon back to its former position at the lower-left corner of the screen.

5. Repeat the preceding step except choose ON to remove the check mark. Note that the UCS icon is no longer visible.

6. Save this drawing by pressing Ctrl+S.

Figure 6.12

Placing the UCS icon at the current origin.

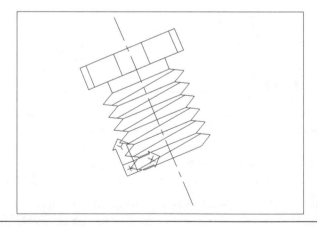

INSIDER TIP

Although the preceding exercise uses shortcuts from the main menu bar, I prefer to turn the UCS icon on and off by typing **UCSICON** at the Command: prompt, and then typing in either **On** or **Off**. This method seems faster. You can also move the UCS icon to and from the current origin with the UCSICON command and typing either **OR** for origin, or **N** for no origin. This seems faster than traversing across three levels of cascading pull-down menus.

The UCS Command

The UCS command is the key to placing, moving, rotating, and displaying User Coordinate Systems. When called from the Command: line, the UCS command presents the following options:

```
Origin/ZAxis/3point/OBject/View/X/Y/Z/Prev/Restore/Save/Del/?/
<World>:
```

You can use the following subset of these options for most 2D work:

- **Origin.** Specifies a new X,Y, or Z origin point relative to the current origin.

- **3point.** Enables you to set the X-Y axes by specifying the origin and a point on both the X and Y axes.

- **OBject.** Defines a new coordinate system based on a selected object.

- **Z.** Rotates the X-Y axes about the Z axis.

- **Prev.** Reverts back to the previous UCS. You can recall as many as the last 10 UCSs.

- **Restore.** Sets the UCS to a previously named UCS.

- **Save.** Enables you to store the current UCS with a name you specify.

- **Del.** Removes a stored UCS.

- **?.** Lists saved UCSs by name.

- **<World>.** The default option. Sets the current UCS to the WCS. You can choose this option by pressing Enter.

In addition to being able to recall the most immediate UCS using the Previous option, as you did in the preceding exercise, using the Save option of the UCS command enables you to name and save various UCSs as you define them. Then if you want to re-establish a UCS, choose Tools, USC, Named UCS to display the UCS Control dialog box. From there you can name, re-name, delete, and restore previously named UCSs.

The commands involved with controlling UCSs are also available as tools on the Standard toolbar as shown in figure 6.13. By resting the screen pointer on each tool momentarily, the name of the tool is displayed. In most cases, the displayed tooltips closely follow the names of the UCS command's options.

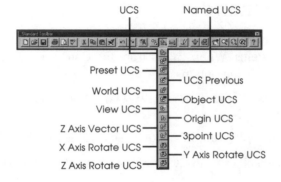

Figure 6.13

The UCS tools on the Standard toolbar.

INSIDER TIP

The tooltips displayed when you rest the screen pointer on a tool icon are, of course, rather short. As you work with toolbars, you will rely less and less on these tips. Keep in mind that for tools that you use less frequently, tooltips are also accompanied by a more extended "Help string" that is displayed at the lower-left portion of the screen. These Help strings are often more informative than the shorter tooltip.

The UCSICON Command

In the preceding exercise, you saw how the UCSICON command can be used to control the placement and visibility of the UCS icon. To round-out the discussion of User Coordinate Systems, here are the options for the UCSICON command. The UCSICON command displays the following prompt:

```
ON/OFF/All/Noorigin/ORigin <ON>:
```

- **ON.** Turns the UCS icon on.

- **OFF.** Turns the UCS icon off.

- **All.** Applies changes to the UCS icon in all displayed viewports; otherwise, changes affect only the current viewport.

- **Noorigin.** Displays the UCS icon at the lower-left corner of viewports.

- **ORigin.** Displays the UCS icon at the 0,0 origin of the current UCS if possible.

INSIDER TIP

Another capability of the UCS icon that you should know about is the system variable UCSFOLLOW. This variable controls whether or not a plan view will be automatically generated whenever you change the UCS. Setting this variable to 0 will not affect the view; setting it to 1 will cause the plan view to be generated. For 2D drafting, I find the automatic plan view setting to be helpful.

Setting Up Drawing Aids

AutoCAD has a number of Drawing Aids to help make your drawing more accurate and your work more efficient. These aids consist of a series of commands and system variables that you can use or set at the Command: prompt. You can also access them through the Drawing Aids dialog box. The Drawing Aids dialog box is shown in figure 6.14. It is accessed through Tools, Drawing Aids. This dialog box is also available from the Command: prompt by typing **DDRMODES**.

Figure 6.14

The Drawing Aids dialog box.

The Drawing Aids dialog box is divided into four sections: Modes, Snap, Grid, and Isometric Snap/Grid.

Modes

The Modes section contains the Ortho, Solid Fill, Quick Text, Blips, Highlight, Groups, and Hatch options. Each of these options is explained here:

- **Ortho.** The Ortho mode is useful when you are drawing orthogonal lines. It constrains the movement of the screen cursor to a horizontal or vertical movement relative to the current UCS and to the current Grid rotation angle. You can also control Ortho mode with the ORTHO command, by double-clicking the ORTHO tile on the mode status bar, or by pressing F8.

- **Solid Fill.** This option controls whether certain objects, such as polylines with width and solids, are displayed filled-in or in outline form. This setting can also be turned on and off with the FILL command.

- **Quick Text.** This option replaces text elements in your drawing with empty bounding boxes that indicate the outline of the text objects. Displaying text objects in this manner will decrease Regen and Redraw times. This feature is also controlled by the QTEXT command.

- **Blips.** This setting determines whether temporary "blips" or small screen markers are displayed when points are selected or entered. This feature is also controlled by the system variable BLIPMODE.

- **Highlight.** This option determines whether objects are highlighted when selected. You can also control highlights with the HIGHLIGHTS system variable.

- **Groups.** This option turns automatic Group selection on and off. With automatic Group selection, selecting an object that is a member of a group selects the entire group.

- **Hatch.** This option determines which objects will be selected when you select an associative hatch. With this option on, selecting an associative hatch also selects the boundary objects.

Snap

Options in this section of the Drawing Aids dialog box control the Snap grid (refer to fig. 6.14). When the Snap grid is enabled (a check mark, or "X," appears in the On check box), the movement of the crosshairs cursor is restricted to incremental displacements across a grid of invisible "snap" points. This enables you to snap to and select points on this grid with a high degree of precision. You can enter both X and Y spacing for your snap grid by typing in the input boxes in this section. The other options—Snap Angle, X Base, and Y Base—control the angle at which the grid is oriented with respect to the current UCS and the origin's coordinates of the snap's grid.

The Snap grid settings can also be controlled at the Command: prompt with the SNAP command. You can toggle the Snap feature on and off with the F9 key, by pressing Ctrl+B, or by double-clicking on the SNAP tile on the mode status bar.

By carefully selecting the spacing of the Snap grid, you can usually make the picking of points much easier because you bypass the need to enter points at the keyboard.

Grid

In addition to a grid of invisible snap points, you can apply a grid of visible points to the drawing area. This visible drawing aid is simply called Grid. The controls found in the Grid section of the Drawing Aids dialog box control the appearance of this grid of visible points.

When the On option is checked, grid points are made visible with the spacing specified by the values (in drawing units) that you type into the X Spacing and Y Spacing edit boxes (refer to fig. 6.14).

It is common to link the spacing of the grid of visible points (the Grid) to the grid of invisible snap points. To establish this link, the X and Y spacing of the Grid points is set to 0. AutoCAD will then use the X and Y spacing of the Snap points and automatically apply these to the visible Grid. You can, of course, override this 1:1 relationship by explicitly entering values other than 0 for the Grid spacing. Keep in mind that regardless of the setting(s) of the Grid points, the origin and angle of the Grid is always kept the same as the origin and angle of the Snap points.

You can also control the visible Grid with the GRID command and toggle the Grid on and off with the F7 key, by pressing Ctrl+G, or by double-clicking the GRID tile on the mode status bar.

INSIDER TIP

The Grid control section of the Drawing Aids dialog box largely duplicates functions available through the basic GRID command. Using the GRID command at the Command: prompt, however, offers an option, Grid spacing(X). Specifying a value followed by an "X" sets the Grid spacing to the specified value times the Snap interval. I often like to have my Snap spacing a fraction—say 1/4—of my Grid value. By using the "X" feature of the spacing setting available with the GRID command, this relationship between Grid and Snap remains in effect no matter how often I change the Grid setting.

Isometric Snap/Grid

You use the options in the Isometric Snap/Grid section of the Drawing Aids dialog box to draw a 2D isometric drawing. This section permits you to enable the isometric grid and set it to the standard Left, Top, or Right orientations.

INSIDER TIP

When entering values in X and Y spacing text edit boxes in both the Grid and Snap sections of the Drawing Aids dialog box, entering a value in the X Spacing box followed by the Enter key will automatically transfer the value to the Y Spacing box. Because I usually want both the X and Y values of both of these settings equal, this shortcut eliminates the need to type anything in the Y boxes.

Object Snapping

No matter how carefully you set your Snap interval or how often you change that interval, it is highly unlikely that all the points in your drawings will conveniently fall on these snap points. This becomes increasingly true as your drawing becomes populated with various objects that, themselves, have important geometric features, such as endpoints, centers, and tangent points, to which you will want to relate other drawing objects. Most modern CAD applications, including AutoCAD, therefore, provide some means of identifying these geometric points. These tools make the construction of new geometry easier, the objects created are drawn more accurately, and the results can be consistently maintained with far more precision than is possible in traditional manual drafting. In AutoCAD, this capability is called Object Snapping and the Object Snap or Osnap. In AutoCAD, these modes consist of a set of tools that permit this accurate geometric construction.

Osnaps are used to directly and easily identify key points either on or in relation to your drawing objects. Figure 6.15 shows the Object Snap toolbar and the pop-up cursor menu.

Figure 6.15

The Object Snap toolbar and the pop-up cursor menu.

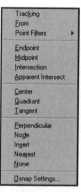

The Osnap toolbar and the Cursor menu contain the same Osnap modes presented in essentially the same order. You can display or activate the pop-up cursor menu by simultaneously holding down the Shift button and pressing the right mouse button, commonly called Shift+right-click, or simply Shift+Enter because the right mouse button serves as an Enter button. If you use a three-button mouse, the middle button can be configured to "pop up" the cursor menu.

The Osnap modes are also represented on the Standard toolbar by a "fly-out" toolbar. Figure 6.16 displays both the Osnap toolbar and the Osnap fly-out. As shown, the Osnap toolbar can be displayed in a vertical format and placed or moved to a convenient position in your drawing area. Figure 6.15 showed the same toolbar displayed horizontally.

Figure 6.16

The Object Snap toolbar and fly-out.

Object Snap fly-out

Object Snap toolbar

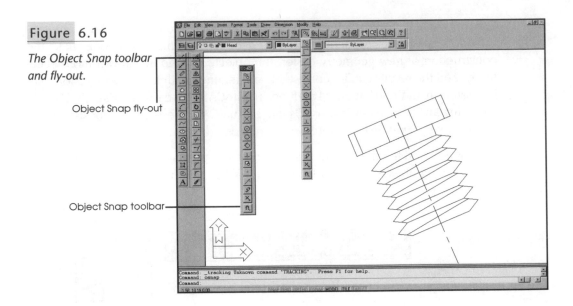

INSIDER TIP

Depending on personal preference and the type of drafting you are involved with, you can use the Osnap toolbar, in either a horizontal or vertical format (or a more compact rectangular arrangement), the Osnap fly-out from the Standard toolbar, or the pop-up cursor menu. The fly-out has the advantage of being present only during Osnap selections, the Osnap toolbar can be moved around and resized, and the cursor pop-up menu requires very little cursor movement. I almost always use the cursor menu because it seems to be the fastest means.

Osnap Modes

AutoCAD Release 14 has 13 Object Snap modes, including the new Tracking mode. Table 6.1 gives a description of each mode.

Table 6.1

AutoCAD Release 14 Object Snap Modes

Mode	Description
Center	Finds the center of a circle or an arc
Endpoint	Finds the endpoint of a line or an arc
From	Establishes a temporary reference point as a basis for specifying subsequent points
Insert	Finds the insertion point of text objects and block references
Intersection	Locates the intersection of two lines, arcs, or circles or the intersection of any combination of these
Midpoint	Finds the midpoint of a line or an arc
Nearest	Finds a point on an object that is nearest to the point you pick
Node	Locates the location of a Point object
None	Instructs AutoCAD not to use any Osnap modes
Perpendicular	Returns a point at the intersection of the object selected and a line perpendicular to that object from either the last or the next point picked
Quadrant	Finds the closest 0-, 90-, 180-, or 270-degree point relative to the current UCS on a circle or an arc
Tangent	Locates a point that is tangent to the selected circle or arc from either the last or the next point picked
Tracking	Specifies a point that is relative to other points, using orthogonal displacements

Running Osnap Toggle and Osnap Override

Running Osnap Toggle and Osnap Override are two new AutoCAD features. Although they were discussed in Chapter 1, "Exploring the New R14 Interface," they are important adjuncts to the overall operation of object snaps and are therefore briefly recapped here.

Running Object Snap Toggle

Running object toggle is an Osnap enhancement that enables you to toggle any running (continuing) Osnap off prior to selecting a point without losing the running Osnap settings. This feature is accessed by double-clicking the OSNAP tile on the mode status bar at the bottom of AutoCAD's screen. If this is done while no running Osnaps are in effect, the Osnap Settings dialog box is displayed, giving you the opportunity to set a running Osnap.

Object Snap Override

AutoCAD Release 14 provides an option that enables you to explicitly enter coordinate data that has priority over any running Osnaps that may be in effect. This enhances direct coordinate entry and you can be certain that such entries have precedence over any other settings.

AutoSnap

You saw AutoCAD Release 14's new AutoSnap feature in Chapter 1, "Exploring the New R14 Interface," and learned about controlling some of its features. This is an important new feature in AutoCAD and a closer look is taken in this chapter.

With AutoSnap, you can visually preview snap point candidates before picking a point. Depending on how you have AutoSnap's features set, AutoSnap will display a Snap Tip placard similar to the toolbar's Tool Tip feature. A marker distinctive to each Osnap mode can also be displayed in the color of your choice. You can also enable a "magnet" feature that snaps the marker into place much like the action of AutoCAD's Grips feature.

In the following exercise, you use some of AutoCAD's Osnap modes and the three methods of invoking them. In addition, you will see how the AutoSnap feature makes looking for and confirming Osnap points an unambiguous, efficient means of picking Osnap points.

BISECTING AN ANGLE USING OBJECT SNAPS WITH AUTOSNAP

1. Start a New drawing using the Wizard, Start from Scratch option. You will not need to name or save this drawing.

2. Choose View, Toolbars. The Toolbars dialog box appears.

3. In the Toolbars dialog box, scroll to and choose Object Snap. Note that the Object Snap toolbar appears (see fig. 6.17). Click on Close to dismiss the dialog box.

Figure 6.17

The Toolbars dialog box.

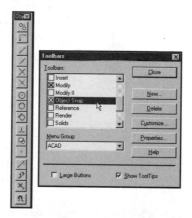

4. Use the DDOSNAP command to display the Osnap Settings dialog box and then choose the AutoSnap tab to display the AutoSnap page (see fig. 6.18). Ensure that the Marker, Magnet, and Snap Tip features are all enabled and that the Display aperture box is disabled as shown in figure 6.18. Click on OK to close the dialog box.

Figure 6.18

The Osnap Settings dialog box's AutoSnap tab.

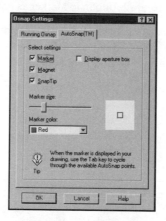

5. Use the LINE command to draw a line from ① to ② to ③ as shown in figure 6.19.

Figure 6.19

Creating an arc using AutoSnap modes.

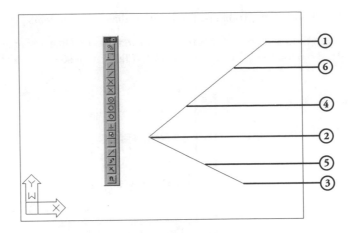

6. Choose Draw, Arc, the Center, Start, End. You see the following prompt:

   `arc Center/<Start point>: _c Center:`

7. Click on the Snap to Endpoint tool from the displayed Osnap toolbar. Then move and rest the screen cursor to a point near ④ in figure 6.19. Notice the AutoSnap marker displayed at ② and the Snap Tip identifying the lines endpoint.

8. Pick a point near ④. Then at the Start point: prompt, click and hold the Osnap fly-out on the Standard toolbar (see fig. 6.19) and then move to the Snap to Nearest tool and release the pick button. Move the cursor near to the lower line at ⑤. Note the appearance of the Nearest AutoSnap Marker as you approach ⑤.

9. Pick at ⑤. At the Angle/Length of chord/<End point>: prompt, Shift-Enter to display the screen pop-up menu. Then choose Endpoint and move the cursor toward ⑥. Note the appearance of the Endpoint Marker.

10. Pick the upper line at ⑥. AutoCAD draws the arc as shown in figure 6.20.

Figure 6.20

Bisecting an angle using Osnaps.

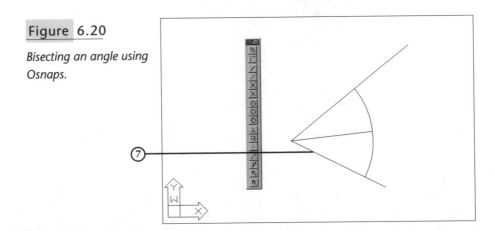

11. Type **L** and press Enter at the Command: prompt. At the From point: prompt, type **endp** and press Enter. Note the appearance of the Endpoint AutoSnap marker as you approach ⑦ in figure 6.20.

12. Click at ⑦. Then at the To point: prompt, click on the Midpoint tool on the Osnap toolbar and move the cursor to any point on the arc. Note the appearance of the Midpoint marker on the arc. With the marker showing, pick any point on the screen.

13. At the To point: prompt, press Enter to end the LINE command. The bisector line is drawn.

You do not need to save this drawing.

As seen in the preceding exercise, the use of Osnaps and the AutoSnap feature gives a definite, unambiguous indication of the geometry to which you are snapping. Even in crowded areas of a drawing, such as shown in figure 6.21, positive identification of which point is the current snap target is possible—out of several near the cursor.

Figure 6.21

AutoSnap provides positive identification of target geometry.

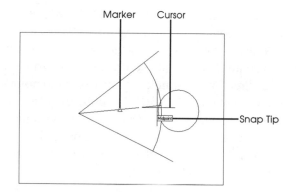

AutoSnap also supports a feature that enables stepping through the object snap points of objects lying within the target aperture when it is enabled. The Tab key is used to cycle from the closest to the furthest Osnap point from the center of the aperture box. The target geometry is highlighted to further aid in identification. This highlighting feature is shown in figure 6.22 where the midpoint of two objects lie very close together and both fall within the Osnap aperture box. Repeated pressing of the Tab key cycles among the objects, highlighting the target geometry so that you can snap to the correct object's midpoint.

Figure 6.22

In crowded areas, AutoSnap highlights target geometry.

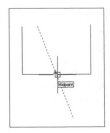

Tracking

 A new Osnap feature called *Tracking* is introduced in AutoCAD Release 14. As with many new AutoCAD features, this feature was first introduced in AutoCAD LT where it has been very popular. Although not an object snap in the strict sense, Tracking is used with standard Osnaps to enhance your ability to find points relative to another object's geometry.

You can use Tracking whenever AutoCAD prompts for a point. If you try to use Tracking at the Command: prompt, AutoCAD displays an error message. When you start Tracking and specify a point, AutoCAD constrains the next point selection to an orthogonal path that extends vertically or horizontally from the first point. The orthogonal direction determines which of the old point's values, X or Y, is replaced with the new point's X or Y value. If the rubber band is constrained to horizontal, then the X value is replaced. If the rubber band is constrained to the vertical, then the Y value is replaced. If you select a second point and press Enter to end Tracking, AutoCAD locates the new point at the intersection of an imaginary orthogonal path extending from the first two points.

In the following exercise, you use Tracking and Point Filters to find the center point of a rectangle.

FINDING THE CENTER OF A RECTANGLE USING TRACKING AND POINT FILTERS

1. Open TRACKING.DWG from the accompanying CD-ROM. You will use this drawing to practice the Tracking feature, but will not need to save your work. Your screen will resemble figure 6.23. Ensure that ORTHO mode is on.

Figure 6.23

Two rectangles.

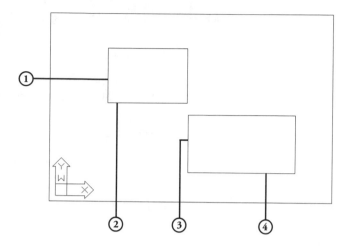

2. You will draw a line from the center of one rectangle to the center of the other rectangle. First, start the LINE command. Respond to the prompt by entering a point filter as follows:

   `From point: .y ↵`

   The following prompt appears:

   `Of:`

3. Invoke the Midpoint Osnap mode by typing **mid** and pressing Enter. Then move the cursor close to ① in figure 6.23. Note that the midpoint AutoSnap marker appears. Click at ①. Respond to the following prompt as shown:

   `mid of (need XZ): mid ↵`

4. At the mid of: prompt move the cursor near ②. Note the midpoint AutoSnap marker appears. Pick at ②. The from point of the lines is established at the intersection of the midpoints of the adjacent sides of the rectangle—the center on the rectangle. The following prompt appears:

   `To point:`

5. Respond to this prompt by invoking Tracking; type **tk** and press Enter. The following prompt appears:

   `First tracking point:`

6. Invoke the midpoint snap by using Shift+right-click to display the cursor menu, and then choose Midpoint. At the mid of: prompt, move the cursor near ③ and notice the AutoSnap midpoint marker. Pick at ③.

7. Move the cursor to the right to establish horizontal tracking. The following prompt appears:

    ```
    Next point (Press ENTER to end tracking):
    ```

8. Invoke the midpoint Osnap again and move the cursor toward ④ until the midpoint AutoSnap marker appears as shown in figure 6.24. Pick at ④ and respond to the following prompt as shown:

    ```
    Next point (Press ENTER to end tracking): ↵
    ```

9. AutoCAD draws the line between the two center points. End the LINE command by pressing Enter.

You will continue in this drawing in the next exercise.

Figure 6.24

A line between the center points of two rectangles.

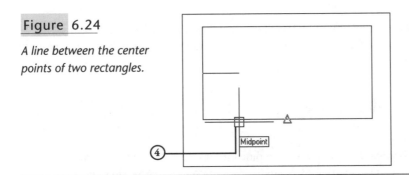

As you saw in the preceding exercise, object snaps are useful in identifying points on a drawing's object. You used the .Y Point Filter to temporarily store the Y coordinate value of the side of the first rectangle's midpoint, then you supplied the X coordinate value by snapping to the midpoint of the adjacent side. This established the intersection of the midpoints of the two sides, or the center of the rectangle. This point was then supplied to the LINE command as the initial From point. In this respect, Point Filters enable you to identify points that bear some relationship to other points, such as a common Y coordinate.

Next Tracking was turned on and the midpoint of one side (it would have made no difference which) was established as the first tracking point. With possible point selection now restrained to points orthogonal to this point, you established horizontal tracking by moving the cursor to the right and supplied the X point by choosing the midpoint of the adjacent side. When tracking was then turned off, the end of the first line segment was completed at the intersection of the midpoints of the two adjacent sides of the second rectangle or its center point.

Both Tracking and Point Filters must be invoked while a command requesting point entry is in progress. They each gather and store coordinate data, which is then fed to the suspended command.

From and Apparent Intersection Osnaps

Much like Point Filters and the Tracking feature, the "auxiliary" Osnaps From and Apparent Intersection supply data points that stand in some relationship to points on drawing objects. The From object snap establishes a temporary reference point as a basis for specifying subsequent points. From object snap is normally used in combination with other object snaps and relative coordinates. For example, at a prompt for the center point of an arc, you could enter **from endp**, select a line, and then enter **@4,5** to locate a point four units to the right and five units up from the endpoint of the line; the center of the circle would then be located at this point.

Apparent Intersection snaps to the apparent intersection of two objects that might or might not actually intersect in 3D space. In 2D drafting, Apparent Intersection is usually involved with the projected intersection of two line elements.

The following exercise demonstrates both the From and Apparent Intersection Osnaps as you center a circle at a distance from the apparent intersection of two lines.

BEGINNING A LINE AT A DISTANCE FROM AN APPARENT INTERSECTION

1. Continue from the previous exercise. Start the LINE command and enter the following at the prompt:

   From point: **from** ↵

2. At the Base point: prompt, invoke the mid Osnap:

   Base point: **mid** ↵

3. At the Of: prompt, move the cursor near to ① in figure 6.25 and click.

4. At the Offset: prompt, type the relative coordinate **@1.5,1** and press Enter. This establishes the starting point of the line.

5. At the To point: prompt, activate the Apparent Intersection Osnap as follows:

   To point: **appint** ↵

Figure 6.25

Using From to snap to relative geometry.

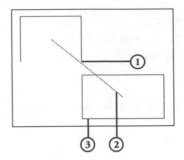

6. At the Of: prompt, move the cursor near to ②, note the appearance of the apparent intersection AutoSnap marker, and pick.

7. At the And: prompt, move the cursor near to ③, note the position of the intersection AutoSnap marker, and pick.

8. The end of the line segment is placed at the apparent intersection. Press Enter to end the LINE command. Your drawing should resemble figure 6.26.

Figure 6.26

A line drawn with the From and Apparent Intersection Osnaps.

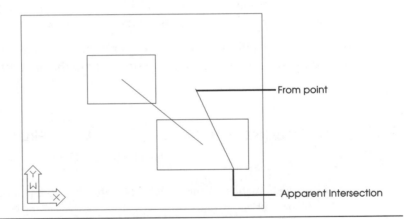

NOTE

Although you typed in the Osnap modes in the preceding exercise, you could, of course, use any of the three other methods of setting Osnaps—namely, the cursor pop-up menu, the Osnap toolbar, or the Osnap fly-out on the Standard toolbar.

When used in conjunction with the other Osnaps, the From and Apparent Intersection—as well as the Tracking and Point Filter features—provide a powerful set of tools that help you establish points and accurately place geometry in your drawing.

Construction Lines and Rays

With the existence of Point Filters, Apparent Intersection, From Osnaps, and the Tracking feature, little need exists for the "construction lines" used in traditional "pencil" drafting. Once you become competent with these drawing aids, the time and effort required to draw and subsequently erase traditional construction lines will seem inefficient.

There may be occasions, however, when the inclusion of construction lines may be indicated to assist in visually presenting the relationship among elements of a drawing. AutoCAD has two special line objects, xlines and rays, that function as traditional construction lines.

The XLINE command creates infinite lines, which are commonly used as construction lines. Xlines can be placed vertically, horizontally, at a specified angle, offset a specified distance, or as an angle bisector. Although xlines extend infinitely in both directions, they are ignored for the purpose of calculating the drawing's extents.

The RAY command creates "semi-infinite" lines commonly used as construction lines. A ray has a finite starting point and extends to infinity. As with the xline, the infinite length of a ray is ignored for the purpose of determining a drawing's extents.

In line with their use as a largely visual element, both xlines and rays are often placed on separate layers with a distinctive linetype and color assigned. Figure 6.27 shows a typical application of xlines.

Figure 6.27

Xlines and Rays serve as construction lines.

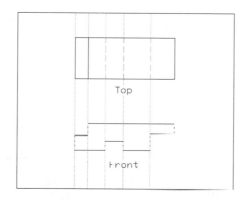

Summary

In this chapter, you learned about AutoCAD's coordinate system and the methods you can use to enter coordinate points in your drawings. Absolute coordinate entry enables you to specify points relative to the drawing's fixed 0,0 point, or origin. Relative coordinate entry, on the other hand, enables you to specify points relative to the previous point you entered. Relative coordinates are expressed either as an x and y distance or a distance and angle from the last point. You also learned how to change the orientation of AutoCAD's coordinate system and how to configure drawing aids such as Snap and Grid.

This chapter also covered the important concept of snapping to specific geometry in your drawings, such as a circle's center or the intersection of two lines. You learned that AutoCAD Release 14's new AutoSnap feature makes snapping to such points both easier and less ambiguous than in previous releases.

In the next chapter, you will learn how to draw the elementary objects that, taken together, comprise almost all of the drawings you will make in AutoCAD.

CREATING ELEMENTARY OBJECTS

by David M. Pitzer

No matter how complicated a drawing is, and no matter how many layers and linetypes it contains, almost all AutoCAD drawings are comprised of a few relatively basic shapes and forms. Circles, arcs, lines, rectangles, polygons, and ellipses are the basic elements from which both simple and complicated drawings are made. This chapter shows you the tools you will need to construct and control AutoCAD's basic drawing objects.

This chapter covers the following information:

- *Using the LINE command*

- *Using the ARC command*

- *Using the CIRCLE command*

- *Using the POLYGON command*

- *Drawing ellipses*

Using the LINE Command

Perhaps the most common object in a typical AutoCAD drawing is the line. In addition to representing the shortest distance between two points, lines serve a myriad of other useful purposes; centerlines locate other geometry, border lines indicate an area's constraints, and hidden lines represent objects or boundaries that are not visible from a given point of view. All these lines are usually further identified functionally by their linetype—the period pattern of interruptions in the line's continuity. Then, of course, "normal" continuous lines are representative of things such as walls or the sides of objects. Lines are very versatile. Drawing a line is one of the most basic operations in AutoCAD.

In the following exercise, you will learn the basics of using the LINE command as you begin drawing a fixture base.

NOTE

The exercises in this chapter use the templates IAC701.dwg and IAC702.dwg files found on the accompanying CD-ROM. These drawings have most settings, linetypes, and layers already set or defined for you. In the first part of the chapter, you learn about lines, circles, arcs, and polygons. When you finish this first section, your drawing will resemble figure 7.1. Later in the chapter, you will begin a new drawing in which you will practice constructing and accurately placing ellipses.

Figure 7.1

The completed fixture base.

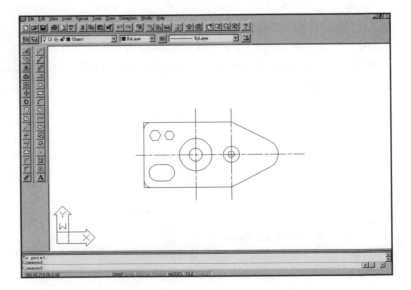

USING THE LINE COMMAND TO DRAW A FIXTURE BASE

1. Begin a new drawing called chap701.dwg using the IAC701.dwg as a template. Using template drawings is discussed in Chapter 3, "Setting Up the AutoCAD 14 Drawing Environment." Ensure that the current layer is Center.

2. Begin the LINE command by choosing Draw, Line. At the From point: prompt, type **38,88** and press Enter.

3. Use relative polar coordinate entry by typing **@208<0** and pressing Enter at the To point: prompt. Note that the line segment is drawn with a linetype of Hidden. End the LINE command by pressing Enter.

4. Restart the LINE command by pressing the spacebar. Answer the From point: prompt by typing **112,32** and pressing Enter. Ensure that the ORTHO mode is active by double-clicking the ORTHO button on the status bar.

5. Use direct distance entry by moving the cursor above the last point and answering the To point: prompt by typing **112** and pressing Enter. End the LINE command by pressing Enter. Note that the line segment is drawn 112 units at 90 degrees to the startpoint.

6. Ensure that SNAP mode is on and restart the LINE command by typing **L** and pressing Enter. Respond to the From point: prompt by pressing F6 until the Coordinate display on the status bar displays absolute coordinates. Then find and pick point 156,144.

NOTE

If you miss the point in the preceding step, press Esc to cancel the LINE command. Restart the command by pressing either Enter or the spacebar.

7. At the To point: prompt, type the relative rectangular coordinate **@0,–112** and press Enter. End the LINE command by pressing Enter. Your drawing should now resemble figure 7.2.

Figure 7.2

Setting up the centerlines for the fixture base.

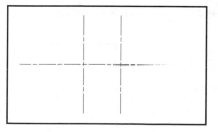

In the preceding exercise, you used several different methods of specifying coordinate point entry while using the LINE command. You also saw how the coordinate display, which is located on the status bar at the bottom of AutoCAD's display, can be helpful in locating both absolute and relative coordinate points. Keep in mind, depending on how your snap grid is set up and the value of the actual points, the snap feature can make finding many points much easier. For points that do not lie on your current snap grid, direct coordinate entry through the keyboard is the only practical method of having line segments begin and end where you want.

INSIDER TIP

In many situations, you will find yourself frequently changing the coordinate display mode as well as turning ORTHO and SNAP on and off. It is more convenient to use the function key shortcuts to control these functions. F6 controls the coordinate display, F8 toggles the ORTHO mode on and off, and F9 toggles the SNAP function.

In the following exercise, you will continue to use the LINE command as you outline the fixture base. After establishing the first corner of the base, you will use the efficient direct distance method of entering points that are orthogonal to the previous point.

USING THE LINE COMMAND TO DRAW THE FIXTURE BASE OUTLINE

1. Continue from the previous exercise. Change the current layer to OBJECT. Refer to figure 7.3 to help you identify the following points.

2. First, you will deliberately enter the wrong point to see how easy it is to recover from such a mistake. Begin the LINE command and specify the following From point: **150,48** and press Enter. Note that the point ① falls short of the right centerline.

Figure 7.3

Completing the fixture outline.

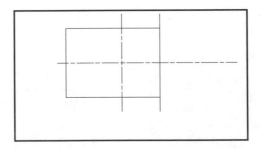

3. To recover from your mistake, use the LINE command's Undo option by typing **U** and pressing Enter, and then re-enter the point at ② by typing **156,48** and pressing Enter.

4. Now with ORTHO on and the cursor placed to the left of the previous point, use direct distance entry to specify the point at ③ by typing **108** and pressing Enter.

5. Move the cursor above the preceding point, enter **80**, and press Enter to draw a line segment to ④.

6. Move the cursor to the right of ④ and enter: **108** and press Enter. The line segment from ④ to ⑤ is drawn.

7. Now close the outline by using the Close option of the LINE command by typing **C** and pressing Enter at the To Point: prompt. This completes the LINE command.

8. The line segment from ⑤ to ② was drawn by mistake; it is not wanted. At the Command: prompt, issue the U command by typing **U** and pressing Enter. Note that all four line segments completed during the LINE command are erased. At the Command: prompt, issue the REDO command by typing **REDO** and pressing Enter. All four segments are redrawn.

9. To erase the last line segment, issue the ERASE command by typing **E** and pressing Enter at the Command: prompt. At the Select objects: prompt, type **L** and press Enter. Note that the last completed line segment is highlighted. Now, with the Select objects: prompt still current, press Enter. The line is erased. Your drawing should now resemble figure 7.4.

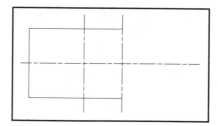

Figure 7.4

Three sides of the fixture base.

The LINE Command Options

The LINE command is straightforward and easy to use. It offers the following features:

- **From point.** At the From point: prompt, your input specifies the first point of the first line segment.

- **Continue.** If you press Enter at the From point: prompt, the line segment will start from the endpoint of the most recently drawn line or arc.

- **To point.** At the To point: prompt, your input specifies the point to which a line segment is drawn from the previous point.

- **Undo.** At any To point: prompt, you can enter U (undo) to undo the last line segment drawn. Repeating the U option will step back through line segments.

- **Close.** At the To point: prompt, you can enter C (close) to close a series of two or more line segments. A line is created from the last endpoint to the first point of the series.

Keep in mind that the LINE command draws line segments whose only connection is that the endpoint of one segment shares the same coordinate as the startpoint of the next segment.

INSIDER TIP

If you are constructing a long series of line segments using the LINE command, break the continuity of the chain occasionally by pressing Enter three times. This has the effect of ending the series, restarting the command, and beginning a new series from the end of the last. Then if you perform a U option at a Command: prompt, it will undo only the last LINE command's series of line segments, instead of all the segments.

You can end or exit the LINE command at any time by pressing Esc or by pressing Enter at any To point: prompt.

Using the ARC Command

The ARC command is used to draw circular arcs. Its several options make constructing an arc with a variety of known parameters such as center, startpoint, chord length, radius, and so on much easier than with traditional manual drafting methods.

In the following exercise, you will draw an arc by specifying three points on its circumference. After completing the arc, you will erase it and then draw two small arcs to round the corners of the fixture base. Use the coordinate display on the status bar and the Snap feature to identify points.

USING THE ARC COMMAND TO DRAW CIRCULAR ARCS

1. Continue with the drawing from the preceding exercise. If necessary, set the SNAP mode to on by pressing the F9 key. Begin the ARC command by clicking on the ARC tool on the Draw toolbar. Respond to the arc Center/<Start point>: prompt by picking the point at ① by typing **156,48** and pressing Enter.

2. At the prompt for the <Second point>:, pick the point at ② by typing **196,88** and pressing Enter. Note that the arc now drags as you move the cursor.

3. At the End point: prompt, pick the point at ③ by typing **156,128** and pressing Enter. The ARC command draws the arc and terminates. Your drawing should resemble figure 7.5.

Figure 7.5

Drawing an arc using the three-point method.

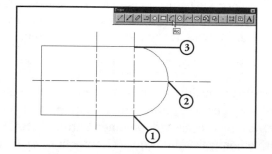

4. At the Command: prompt, issue the U command by typing **U** and pressing Enter, and note that the arc is deleted.

5. Start the ARC command again by typing **A** and pressing Enter. The following prompt appears:

```
Center/<Start point>:
```

6. Respond to this prompt by typing **56,128** and pressing Enter. See ④ in figure 7.6.

Figure 7.6

Creating rounded corners with the ARC command.

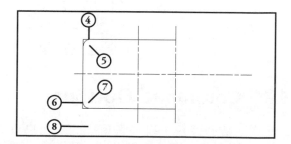

7. Respond to the next prompt by typing **C** and pressing Enter to select the Center option. Then, at the Center: prompt, pick the point at ⑤ by typing **56,120** and pressing Enter.

8. Make sure that ORTHO is on (press F8 if necessary) and note that as you move the cursor the arc snaps in 90-degree increments. Move the cursor to any point near 40,120 and pick. The ARC command draws the arc; ORTHO forces it up 90 degrees.

9. Restart the ARC command by pressing Enter. At the <Start point:> prompt, type **48,56** and press Enter. The arc starts at (6).

10. At the Center/End/<Second point:> prompt, type **C** and press Enter to start the center option, and then enter the relative rectangular coordinate **@8,0** and press Enter. This specifies the center of the arc at (7) and the Angle/Length of chord/<End point:> prompt appears.

11. Disable ORTHO mode by pressing F8 and notice that the arc drags with the cursor. Answer the current prompt by typing **A** and pressing Enter. Turn ORTHO back on with F8 and move the cursor anywhere above the center point. Note that the arc now snaps to 90-degree points. Pick any point directly above the center point near (8) to complete the arc and end the ARC command.

12. Save your drawing with the Quick Save option by pressing Ctrl+S.

Whenever you draw an arc, you know either its center or its startpoint and can supply the other necessary information from existing geometry in the drawing. Figure 7.7 shows the Arc cascade submenu from AutoCAD's Draw menu. This submenu conveniently lists the various choices that can be made depending on the information supplied. Starting the ARC command by using this submenu provides a shortcut through the longer prompt choices provided at the Command: prompt.

Figure 7.7

The Arc submenu offers 10 choices.

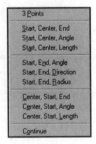

The ARC Command Options

The ARC command requires three pieces of information to complete an arc, one of which must be either the center or startpoint. The other required parameters can be supplied in various combinations. The following list explains these combinations:

■ **3-Points.** This method creates an arc that passes through three points that you supply. The first point is considered the startpoint, the second point is the endpoint, and the third point is any other point between these two. This is the default method of constructing arcs.

- **Start, Center.** This method requires the arc's starting and center points. The third piece of data can be the endpoint, an included angle, or the length of the chord. Counterclockwise arcs are drawn if the included angle is supplied as a positive angle; clockwise arcs are drawn if the angle is supplied as a negative angle. A positive chord length draws a minor arc (less than 180 degrees) and a negative chord length creates a major (greater than 180 degrees) arc.

- **Start, End.** This method enables you to supply the startpoint and endpoint of the arc and then to specify how to draw the arc. You define the arc with an angle, direction, radius, or center point. When supplied a positive angle, AutoCAD draws a counterclockwise arc; when supplied a negative angle, it draws a clockwise arc. If you choose the radius option, AutoCAD always draws the arc counterclockwise. A negative radius forces a major arc, and a positive radius forces a minor arc.

- **Center, Start.** This method enables you to first identify the center of the arc and then the startpoint. The arc is completed by supplying either the angle, length of chord, or endpoint. When you supply a length of chord, a negative length creates a major arc, and a positive length of chord creates a minor arc. If you supply an angle, a negative angle draws the arc clockwise; a positive angle draws the arc counterclockwise.

- **Continue.** This method is the built-in default. You invoke this option by pressing Enter at the first arc prompt. It begins a new arc tangent to the last line or arc drawn.

INSIDER TIP

There probably is no other AutoCAD command that seems at times to be as "uncontrollable" as the ARC command. The trick in drawing arcs with other than the basic and simple 3-point or start-center-end options is knowing how to force the arc in the direction you desire. Understanding that AutoCAD, by default, thinks of arcs as developing counterclockwise from the startpoint is the key. To force an arc to proceed clockwise requires you to input a negative angle, for example, or to supply a negative distance for a length of chord parameter. The same type of entries control whether an arc is drawn as a minor or major arc. Armed with this knowledge and a little practice, your arcs can come out correctly on the first try.

The ARC command's Continue option is often convenient when arcs are associated with line segments. The following exercise demonstrates this feature of the ARC command.

PUTTING LINES AND ARCS TOGETHER

1. Continue from the drawing in the preceding exercise. Make sure ORTHO mode is active. Refer to figure 7.8 for this exercise.

Figure 7.8

Use Continue options to draw slots.

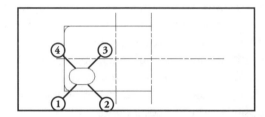

2. Start the LINE by typing **L** and pressing Enter, or clicking on the Line tool on the Draw toolbar. At the From point: prompt, pick at point ① by typing **64,56**. Then at the To point: prompt, type the relative coordinate **@12,0** and press Enter. See ② for reference.

3. Click on the Arc tool to cancel the LINE command and start the ARC command. Press Enter at the following prompt:

   `_Center/<Start point:>`

4. This activates the Continue option of the ARC command and starts an arc tangent to the line. Now pick the point at ③ by typing **76,76**.

5. Now restart the LINE command by clicking the Line tool again. Press Enter at the From point: prompt. This activates the Continue option and starts the line tangent to the arc. A new prompt appears. Respond as follows:

   `Length of line: 12 ↵`

6. Draw a line to ④. Now again choose the ARC command. Note that the LINE command is canceled. At the Center/<Start point:>, press Enter. The new arc starts tangent to the line. Pick the endpoint of the lower slot line at ①.

7. Your drawing should now resemble figure 7.8. Press Ctrl+S to save this drawing in its present form.

The drawing shows the fixture base with rounded corners on the left side. After the preceding exercise, you now have the tools to create such corners with the Continue options of the ARC and LINE commands.

NOTE

Chapter 11, "Advanced Geometry Editing," explains the use of the FILLET command, which provides an easy alternative way to create arcs tangent to lines.

Using the CIRCLE Command

Another basic AutoCAD shape is the circle. Circles are used to represent holes, wheels, shafts, columns, trees, and so on. Several methods of drawing circles exist and, unlike manual drafting, constructing circles in AutoCAD is quick and accurate. Circles have centers, diameters, radii, and tangent points. Providing a combination of these parameters will enable you to draw any circle anywhere you want.

In the following exercise, you construct a few basic circles as you add holes and sleeves to the fixture base.

ADDING HOLES AND SLEEVES BY DRAWING CIRCLES

1. Continue in the drawing from the previous exercise. Refer to figure 7.9 during this exercise.

Figure 7.9

Drawing and placing circles.

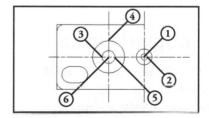

2. Start the CIRCLE command by typing **C** and pressing Enter, or picking the Circle tool from the Draw toolbar. The following prompt appears:

```
CIRCLE 3P/2P/TTR/<Center point>:
```

3. Respond to this prompt by picking a point at ① by typing **156,88**. Move the cursor and watch the radius and circle drag. The coordinate display should show changing

X,Y coordinates. If it doesn't, click on the display until it does. Now click twice in the coordinate display to change to a polar coordinate display. Slowly move the cursor and pick the point 4.00@<0.00 at ②. AutoCAD draws the circle.

4. Press Enter or the spacebar to restart the CIRCLE command. At the circle prompt, type @ and press Enter. Note that key combination re-enters the last point and establishes the center of a new circle. Respond to the next prompt as follows:

   `Diameter/<Radius> <4.00>: D ⏎`

5. This causes the command to prompt for a diameter. Type **20** and press Enter. This specifies the diameter and draws the circle.

6. Now choose Draw, Circle, 3 Points. The following prompt appears:

   `_circle 3P/2P/TTR/<Center point>: _3p First point:`

7. Respond to this prompt by picking the point **104,88** at ③. This sets the first of the three points at 8 units to the left of the centerlines. Respond to the prompts for the other two points as follows:

   `Second point:` pick the point 112,96 at ④

   `Third point:` pick the point 120,88 at ⑤

8. AutoCAD draws the circle with the three points you picked on the circumference. Now press Enter to restart the CIRCLE command with the default center-radius mode:

   `CIRCLE 3P/2P/TTR/<Center point>:`

9. At the preceding prompt, pick point 112,88 at ⑥. This sets the center point. Now experiment with the effects of ORTHO mode. Turn ORTHO mode off by pressing F8. Move the cursor around while watching the polar coordinate display. Pick when a radius of 20 displays. AutoCAD draws the circle with a radius of 20 units.

CIRCLE Command Options

The CIRCLE command provides you with several options to control the sequence in which you create circles. In addition to the default center-point, radius mode, you can create a circle by specifying three points on the circumference or by selecting two objects (lines, circles, or arcs) to which the circle is to be tangent and then specifying a radius. The CIRCLE command offers the following options:

■ **Center point.** Type or pick the center point and the CIRCLE command prompts for a radius or diameter. This is the default option.

■ **Radius.** If you choose Center point:, you then use the Radius option to enter a distance or pick two points to show a distance for the radius.

- **Diameter.** If you choose the Center point:, use the Diameter option to specify a radius. You can either enter a distance or pick two points to show a radius.

- **3P (3 Points).** Use this option to specify the circumference by entering or picking three points.

- **2P (2 Points).** Use this option to specify two diameter points on the circumference.

- **TTR (Tangent-Tangent-Radius).** Use this option to select two lines, arcs, or circles (any combination) that form tangents to the circle. Then specify the circle's radius.

NOTE

Note the difference between Center point/Diameter and the 2P option. Both options enable you to specify a diameter, but if you pick the second point with Center point/Diameter, it merely indicates the diameter's distance and the circle does not draw through the point. If you pick two points with 2P, a circle appears between those two points and the distance is the diameter. The 2P option enables you to draw a diameter circle the way most of us intuitively think about the term diameter.

In the following exercise, you practice using the TTR option of the CIRCLE command.

PRACTICING CIRCLES WITH THE TTR OPTION

1. Continue in the drawing from the preceding exercise. Refer to figures 7.10 and 7.11 during this exercise.

Figure 7.10

Placing circles using the Tangent-Tangent-Radius method.

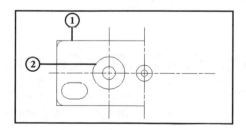

2. Start the CIRCLE command by clicking the Circle tool from the Draw toolbar. Respond to the prompt as follows:

```
_circle 3P/2P/TTR/<Center point>: T ⏎
```

3. This specifies the TTR option. The Enter Tangent spec: prompt appears.

4. Respond to this prompt by picking anywhere on the line ①. The Enter second Tangent spec: prompt appears.

5. Respond to this prompt by picking anywhere on the circumference of the circle at ②. Respond to the following prompt as shown:

    Radius: **20** ↵

6. AutoCAD draws the only circle ⑤ that is tangent to both the circle at ② and the line at ① having a radius of 20 units (see fig. 7.11). Issue the Undo command to delete the last circle. Note that the circle is deleted.

7. Now repeat steps 2 through 5, but at step 5 type **50** and press Enter. Once again, AutoCAD draws the only possible circle ⑥ tangent to both the circle at ③ and the line at ④ having a radius of 50 units (see fig. 7.11).

Figure 7.11

Drawing circles with the TTR option.

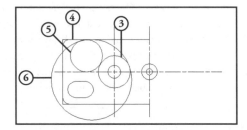

8. Issue the Undo command again to delete the last circle drawn.

9. Save your drawing by pressing Ctrl+S.

NOTE

When specifying the TTR option, you may encounter the message Circle does not exist. This indicates that no possible circle of the radius you specified or tangent to the two points you chose, or both, exists. Most often, the radius specified is too small.

Using the POLYGON Command

In AutoCAD, the POLYGON command is used to create regular polygons with sides of equal length. You can draw a polygon composed of from 3 to 1,024 sides. After you specify the number of sides, several options are available to complete the polygon.

■ **Number of sides:** At the number of sides prompt, you enter the number of sides (3 to 1,024).

■ **Edge/Center of polygon:** At this prompt, you choose whether you want to define the polygon by specifying its center or the endpoints of an edge.

■ **Inscribed in circle/Circumscribed about circle:** If you specify the center of the polygon, you have two options. If you choose Inscribe in circle, all vertices of the polygon fall on the circle; if you choose Circumscribe about circle, the radius equals the distance from the center of the polygon to the midpoints of the edges. If you use the pointing device to specify the radius, you dynamically determine the rotation and size of the polygon. If you specify the radius of the circle by typing a specific entry, the angle at the bottom edge of the polygon equals the current snap rotation angle (usually zero degrees).

■ **First endpoint of edge, Second endpoint of edge:** If you place the polygon by specifying its edge, these prompts enable you to specify the endpoint of one edge.

In the following exercise, you practice drawing a polygon representing a mounting hole on the fixture base.

ADDING A MOUNTING HOLE WITH THE POLYGON COMMAND

1. Continue in the drawing from the preceding exercise. Refer to figure 7.12 during this exercise.

Figure 7.12

Adding mounting holes with the POLYGON command.

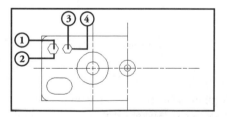

2. Start the POLYGON command. Choose Draw, Polygon. Answer the prompts as follows:

```
Polygon Number of sides <4>: 6 ↵
Edge/<Center of polygon>: 62,112 ↵ ①
Inscribed in circle/Circumscribed about circle (I/C) <I>: C ↵
Radius of circle: 6 ↵
```

3. AutoCAD draws the hexagon. Note that the bottom edge of the hexagon ② is drawn at 0 degrees.

4. Press the spacebar to restart the POLYGON command. Answer the prompts as follows:

```
Polygon Number of sides <6>: ↵
Edge/<Center of polygon>: 80,112 ↵ ③
Inscribed in circle/Circumscribed about circle (I/C) <I>: I ↵
Radius of circle: 6 ↵
```

5. AutoCAD draws the hexagon ④. Note that the default number of sides changed from 4 to 6 for the repeated command. Also note the difference in size between the inscribed and circumscribed figures (refer to fig. 7.12).

INSIDER TIP

AutoCAD's POLYGON command produces polygons that are composed of Light Weight Polylines. Light Weight Polylines are beneficial because they can be exploded into individual line segments for editing. Their width can be changed by using the PEDIT command. You'll learn about both of these techniques later in this book.

AutoCAD's POLYGON command provides a convenient way to draw regular (equilateral) multi-sided polygons, including triangles. Several options make sizing and placing of the final polygon relatively easy.

The fixture base drawing that has gradually grown during this chapter is almost complete. In the following exercise, you will use the line/arc continue method of "rounding corners" that you learned earlier in this chapter to complete the drawing.

COMPLETING THE FIXTURE BASE WITH A ROUNDED CORNER

1. Continue with the drawing from the preceding exercise. Refer to figure 7.13 during this exercise. Make sure that coordinate readout is active. If necessary, press F6 to make it active.

2. Start the LINE command by typing **L** and pressing Enter. At the From point: prompt, find and pick the point 156,128 ①.

3. At the To point prompt:, type the relative coordinate: **@48,–24** and press Enter. A line is drawn to ②.

Figure 7.13

Finishing the fixture base with a rounded end.

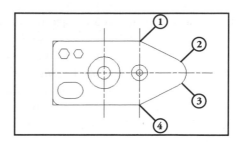

4. End the LINE command by pressing Enter. Start the ARC command by typing **A** and pressing Enter. Press Enter again to use the Continue option. At the End point: prompt, type the relative polar coordinate: **@32<270**. AutoCAD draws the arc ③.

5. Now start the LINE command again and press Enter to activate the Continue option. At the Length of line: prompt, find and pick point 156,48 ④. (If necessary, press F6 until the coordinate display shows absolute coordinates.) Press Enter to end the LINE command.

6. This completes the fixture base and your drawing should look like figure 7.1 at the beginning of this chapter. You are now finished with this drawing.

So far in this chapter you have learned about the basic AutoCAD drawing elements of lines, circles, arcs, and polygons. You will use these elements over and over again in most of your drawings. You have also learned how AutoCAD gives you a large amount of flexibility in constructing and placing these basic elements. Next you will learn how to draw ellipses.

Drawing Ellipses

Until AutoCAD Release 13, AutoCAD constructed ellipses using a special line object called a polyline. *Polylines* are very versatile drawing elements, and you will learn about them in Chapter 8, "Creating Polylines and Splines," but they do not make true ellipses. In Release 14, AutoCAD can draw mathematically true ellipses with geometric centers and accurate quadrant points.

AutoCAD is still capable of constructing elliptical representations of ellipses using polylines; however, now the system variable PELLIPSE determines the type of ellipse drawn. A value of 1 creates a polyline representation; a value of 0 creates a true ellipse.

INSIDER TIP

In Release 14, the default method of drawing ellipses is to draw true ellipses. Unless you have a specific reason to use the less-accurate polygon approximation, leave the system variable PELLIPSE set to 0 and draw true ellipses. Polygon ellipses offer little, if any, advantage.

Ellipses are somewhat complicated geometric figures, but if you have a basic understanding of the geometry of an ellipse, AutoCAD enables you to draw them easily. Ellipses have both a *major axis* and a *minor axis,* as shown in figure 7.14. Although from a mathematical point of view an ellipse has two "centers" or foci, AutoCAD considers the geometric center to be the intersection of the two axes. The quadrants of an ellipse are the points of intersection between the axes and the ellipse. In AutoCAD, you can use both the quadrants and center of an ellipse as object snap points.

Figure 7.14

The geometry of an ellipse.

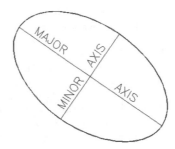

AutoCAD offers you several ways to specify the various parameters of an ellipse.

ELLIPSE Command Options

When you issue the ELLIPSE command, the following prompt appears:

```
Arc/Center/<Axis endpoint 1>:
```

- **Axis endpoint 1.** You specify an axis (major or minor) endpoint. The Axis endpoint 2: prompt will appear, at which you specify the second axis endpoint. The <Other axis distance>/Rotation: prompt appears. If you specify the other axis distance, AutoCAD draws the ellipse. If you specify Rotation (by typing **R** and pressing Enter), AutoCAD prompts for an angle.

- **Center.** If you choose the Center option, the Center of ellipse: prompt appears, at which you specify the center point. The Axis endpoint: prompt appears. Specify an endpoint. The <Other axis distance>/Rotation: prompt appears. If you specify the other axis distance, AutoCAD draws the ellipse. If you specify Rotation (by typing **R** and pressing Enter), AutoCAD prompts for an angle. The angle specifies the ratio of the major axis to minor axis. An angle of 0 defines a circle. The maximum angle acceptable is 89.4, which yields a "flat" ellipse.

■ **Arc.** If you choose the arc option (by typing **A** and pressing Enter), the <Axis endpoint 1>/Center: prompt appears, which requests the same information as the prompt for a full ellipse. After answering the prompt sequence for the full ellipse, the Parameter/<start angle>: prompt appears. Specifying a point defines the start angle of the arc and the Parameter/Included/<end angle>: prompt appears. Specifying an end angle draws the arc. Specifying I, for Included, enables you to specify an included angle for the arc, beginning with the start angle.

NOTE

In reckoning angles for elliptical arcs, the direction of the first point of the major axis is considered 0 degrees. If the system variable ANGDIR is set to 0 (the default), angles for the elliptical arc are measured counterclockwise; if set to 1, they are measured clockwise. If the minor axis is defined first, the major axis zero point is 90 degrees in a counterclockwise direction. If you choose the Included angle option, the angle is measured from the startpoint, not the 0 degree point.

INSIDER **T**IP

When specifying elliptical arc angles, it is helpful to set the coordinate display on the status bar to indicate polar coordinates. Cycling through the coordinate display modes by pressing the F6 key enables you to do this.

In the following exercises, you practice drawing ellipses in a typical 3-view mechanical drawing. During the exercises, you will utilize the object snap techniques learned in Chapter 6, "Creating Drawings with R14." In this exercise, you first use a full set of construction lines to draw an ellipse in one view, then a reduced set of construction lines provides the information you need to draw an ellipse in another view.

DRAWING ELLIPSES IN A 3-VIEW DRAWING

1. Begin a new drawing called CHAP7-2.dwg. Use the IAC702.dwg template found on the accompanying CD-ROM. Your drawing will initially resemble figure 7.15. Your first step will be to add an ellipse to the top view.

Figure 7.15

You will add ellipses to this 3-view drawing.

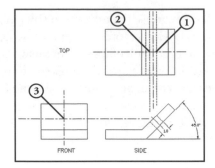

2. Start the ELLIPSE command by clicking on the Ellipse tool on the Draw toolbar. The following prompt appears:

   `Arc/Center/<Axis endpoint 1>:`

3. Choose the default endpoint option by typing **int** and pressing Enter to activate the Intersection osnap mode. Move the osnap box over the intersection at ① of figure 7.15 and pick. When the following prompt appears, type the following:

   `Axis endpoint 2: int ⏎`

4. Move the osnap box over the intersection at ② and pick. These two picks establish one axis of the ellipse. The following prompt appears:

   `<Other axis distance>/Rotation:`

5. Note that the hole you are representing is 1 unit in diameter and that the "other" axis distance is half that distance from the center of the ellipse. Therefore, respond to the above prompt by entering: **.5** and pressing Enter. AutoCAD draws the ellipse.

   Ensure that the ORTHO mode is active before beginning the next step.

6. Restart the ELLIPSE command by pressing Enter. This time, choose the Center option by answering the initial prompt as follows:

   `Arc/Center/<Axis endpoint 1>: C ⏎`

7. Respond to the Center of ellipse: prompt by invoking the Intersection osnap again (**int** and press Enter) and picking the intersection at ③.

8. Respond to the Axis endpoint: prompt using direct distance entry. Drag the cursor to the left or right of the center point established in step 7 and enter **.5** and press Enter. The ellipse is started and the following prompt appears:

   `<Other axis distance>/Rotation:`

9. Note that you do not have the information immediately available to establish the other axis distance in this view. Therefore, select the Rotation option by entering **r** and pressing Enter at the current prompt. The following prompt appears:

   `Rotation around major axis:`

10. Notice that the hole you are representing is at an angle of 45 degrees to this view. Therefore, respond to the current prompt by entering: **45** and pressing Enter. AutoCAD draws the ellipse. You are finished with this drawing.

In the preceding exercise, you constructed an ellipse by specifying the axes and then by specifying the center and a rotation about the major axis.

NOTE

Although construction lines were used in the preceding exercise to assist in visualizing the geometry of the ellipses, both of the ellipses could have been constructed utilizing only point filters and object snaps methods.

Summary

In this chapter, you have learned to use the commands AutoCAD provides for drawing basic objects, from simple lines to complicated arc segments. Mastering their use forms the basis of the range of skills required to use AutoCAD effectively.

Although the LINE command involves few options, used in combination with the other basic objects and drawing aids, such as ORTHO and object snaps, it is a fundamental component of most AutoCAD drawings.

When drawing circles and arcs, several methods are available. The method you select depends on the information that you have available. You can often use more than one of the methods to accomplish the task. Understanding how and when to use each method enables you to quickly construct complex designs.

Polygon objects are common figures found in many AutoCAD drawings. Knowing how to construct them quickly and accurately increases your efficiency.

True mathematical ellipses and elliptical arcs are possible in AutoCAD. Ellipses have true center and quadrant points to which you can snap. These objects are also frequently used to represent circular objects viewed in axonometric views.

CREATING POLYLINES AND SPLINES

by David M. Pitzer

In the previous chapter, you learned about lines and arcs and how to use them to draw straight line segments and circular arcs. Lines and arcs are separate entities, even if they are connected end-to-end. A box drawn with the LINE command, for example, is really four separate line segments whose endpoints share an endpoint with another line segment. Polylines, however, are multi-segmented objects; they can be composed of multiple straight or curved segments. A polyline, no matter how many segments it is composed of, acts as a single, multi-segmented line.

In most AutoCAD drawings, you use traditional elements, such as lines, arcs, polylines, and circles. Sometimes, however, you may want to draw smooth, irregular curves. AutoCAD provides the spline object for drawing free-form irregular curves. Splines are useful when you need to draw map contours, roads, walkways, or other smooth, flowing objects.

This chapter covers the following topics on polylines and splines:

- Polylines versus lines
- Creating polylines
- Lightweight polylines
- Editing polylines
- Creating true splines
- Controlling splines with SPLINEDIT

Polylines versus Lines

Polylines are different from the line segments created by AutoCAD's LINE command. Polylines are treated as single objects and can include both line and arc segments connected at their vertices. AutoCAD stores information about the vertices and you can access this information and edit the appearance of the polyline.

Polylines offer two advantages over lines. First, polylines are versatile; they can be straight or curved, thin or wide, and even tapered. Figure 8.1 shows some of the various forms a polyline can take.

Figure 8.1

Polylines can assume various forms.

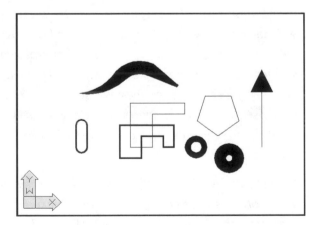

Second, editing polylines is easier; you can select any segment of a polyline because all segments are connected. This makes editing operations, such as moving or copying, faster and more accurate. Objects drawn with lines and arcs may appear to be connected but, depending on how they were drawn, may actually have gaps or discontinuities that make using them as boundaries for cross hatching difficult.

Creating Polylines

Polylines are created using the PLINE command. The PLINE command enables you to draw two basic kinds of polyline segments, straight lines and arcs, so some PLINE prompts are the same as those you find in the LINE and ARC command prompts. If, for example, you draw straight polyline segments, you will find options such as Endpoint, Close, and Undo. You see these options in the standard polyline prompt for line segments:

```
Arc/Close/Halfwidth/Length/Undo/Width/<Endpoint of line>:
```

In addition, certain prompts are specific to polylines:

- **Arc.** Switches from drawing polylines to drawing polyarcs and issues the polyarc options prompt.

- **Close.** Closes the polyline by drawing a segment from the last endpoint to the initial start point and exits the PLINE command.

- **Halfwidth.** Prompts for the distance from the center to the polyline's edge (half the actual width). See the Width option.

- **Length.** Prompts for the length of a new polyline segment. AutoCAD draws the segment at the same angle as the last line segment or tangent to the last arc segment. The last line or arc segment can be that of a previous polyline, line, or arc object.

- **Undo.** Undoes the last drawn segment. It also undoes any arc or line option that immediately preceded drawing the segment. It does not undo width options.

- **Width.** Prompts you to enter a width (default 0) for the next segment. Enables you to taper a segment by defining different starting and ending widths. AutoCAD draws the next segment with the ending width of the previous segment. Unless you cancel the PLINE command prior to drawing a segment, the ending width is stored as the new default width.

- **Endpoint of line.** Prompts for the endpoint of the current line segment. This is the default option.

If, at the prompt for a new straight line segment, you select the Arc option, the Arc mode options prompt appears:

```
Angle/CEnter/CLose/Direction/Halfwidth/Line/Radius/Second pt/Undo/
Width/<Endpoint of arc>:
```

This prompt contains some of the same options as the ARC command. The options include the following:

- **Angle.** Prompts for an included angle. A negative angle draws the arc clockwise.

- **CEnter.** Prompts you to specify the arc's center.

- **CLose.** Closes the polyline by using an arc segment to connect the initial start point to the last endpoint, and then exits the PLINE command.

- **Direction.** Prompts you to specify a tangent direction for the segment.

- **Halfwidth.** Prompts for a halfwidth, the same as for the Line option.

- **Line.** Switches back to the line mode.

- **Radius.** Prompts for the polyarc's radius.

- **Second pt.** Selects the second point of a three-point polyarc.

- **Undo.** Undoes the last drawn segment.

- **Width.** Prompts you to enter a width, the same as in line mode.

- **Endpoint of arc.** Prompts for the endpoint of the current arc segment. This is the default option.

INSIDER TIP

You can close a polyline of two or more segments after the fact; use the PEDIT command's Close option. Using the PEDIT Close option draws a line between the last point of the polyline and the first. The PEDIT command is covered later in this chapter.

Although using the PLINE command to draw lines and arcs is similar to using the LINE and ARC commands to draw similar objects, there are several important differences.

- You get all the line or arc mode prompts every time you enter a new polyline vertex.

- Additional prompts, such as for the Halfwidth and Width, control the width of the segment.

- You can switch back and forth from line segments to arc segments as you add additional segments to the polyline.

■ You can apply linetypes continuously across vertices.

■ You can apply the MEASURE and DIVIDE commands to polyline paths.

■ You can use the AREA command to report the total length of a polyline and to calculate the area enclosed by certain polylines.

In the following exercise, you practice drawing a single polyline using many of the options for both the Line and Arc mode options of the POLYLINE command.

PRACTICING WITH THE POLYLINE COMMAND OPTIONS

1. Begin a new drawing named **chap08.dwg** using this chapter's IAC801.DWG on the accompanying CD as a template (see fig. 8.2).

2. Start the POLYLINE command by typing **PL** and pressing Enter. The initial polyline prompt From point: appears. Respond by entering the point **2.5,1.0** and pressing Enter. The line mode options prompt appears.

Figure 8.2

Drawing a multi-segment polyline.

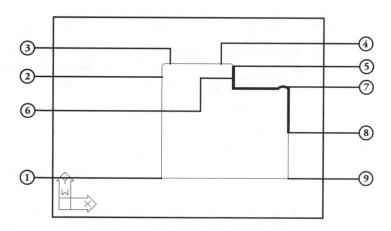

3. Use the default endpoint option by entering the relative polar coordinate **@5<90** and pressing Enter. AutoCAD draws the first segment of the polyline from ① to ②. The Line options prompt re-appears.

4. Switch to the Polyarc mode by typing **A** and pressing Enter. The Arc mode options prompt appears.

5. Use the default Endpoint of arc: option by typing **@.25<45** and pressing Enter. AutoCAD draws the polyarc to ③. The Arc mode options prompt re-appears, as in step 4.

6. Switch back to the Line mode by typing **L** and pressing Enter. The Line mode options appear. Choose the Length option by entering **L** and pressing Enter. Then at the Length of line: prompt, type **3** and press Enter for the length. AutoCAD draws the next segment 3 units long, to ④. Now switch back to the Arc mode.

7. Choose the angle option by typing **A** and pressing Enter. Type **–90** and press Enter at the Included angle: prompt. This specifies a 90 degree clockwise angle at ⑤. The Center/Radius/<Endpoint>: prompt appears.

8. Choose the Radius option by typing **R** and pressing Enter. Then enter the value **.125** and press Enter. Respond to the Direction of chord <0>: prompt by typing **315** and pressing Enter.

9. Switch to the line mode again and choose the Width option by entering **W** and pressing Enter at the Line mode prompt.

10. Respond to the Starting width <0.0>: prompt by typing **0.1** and pressing Enter. Accept the Ending width <0.1>: prompt by pressing Enter. Respond to the Line mode prompt by entering **@1<–90** and pressing Enter.

11. AutoCAD draws the next segment with a uniform width of 0.1 units ⑥. At the Endpoint of line: prompt, enter the relative coordinate **@2,0** and press Enter. AutoCAD draws the next segment at the current width of 0.1 units.

12. Switch to the Arc mode by typing **A** and pressing Enter at the Line mode prompt. Respond to the Arc mode prompt by typing **CE** and pressing Enter. Then type **@.25, –.25** and press Enter to specify the center of the next arc section.

13. Respond to the next two prompts as follows:

    ```
    Angle/Length/<End point>: A↵
    Included angle: –90↵ (see ⑦)
    ```

14. Switch to the line mode (type **L** and press Enter) and enter the relative polar coordinate; type **@2<270** and press Enter in response to the endpoint: prompt.

15. AutoCAD draws the next line segment at the current 0.1 width ⑧. Now change the width for the next segment by typing **W** and pressing Enter. Respond to the width prompts as follows:

    ```
    Starting width <0.1>: 0 ↵
    Ending Width <0.0>: ↵
    ```

16. Now respond to the Line mode prompt by typing **L** and pressing Enter to select the Length option. Respond to the Length of line: prompt by typing **2.05** and pressing Enter. AutoCAD draws the next segment at 0 width to ⑨.

17. At the next Line mode prompt, choose the Close option by typing **C** and pressing Enter. AutoCAD closes the polyline by drawing the next segment to ① and exits the POLYLINE command.

18. Your drawing should now resemble figure 8.2. You continue using this drawing in the next exercise. For now, press Ctrl+S to save the drawing.

Note

Polylines can consist of a number of segments, with the possibility of significant changes in the polyline's characteristics taking place from segment to segment. The endpoint of one segment is the start point of the next. Later, when we discuss editing polylines, we refer to these points collectively as *vertices* or singly as a *vertex*.

As you saw in the preceding exercise, you can easily switch back and forth between the Line mode and the Arc mode in the POLYLINE command. Each mode has its own set of prompts that repeat after you draw each segment. You also noticed that both line and arc segments can have widths other than zero, and that when you specify a new width, it becomes the default width for the next segment. In other words, both the mode (Line versus Arc) and the width remain in effect unless and until you explicitly change them.

In the following exercise, you construct an arc leader using both the Line and Arc modes as well as the capability to vary the width of a single polyline segment.

Drawing an Arc Leader with a Polyline

1. Continue in the drawing from the preceding exercise. Refer to figure 8.3 for this exercise.

Figure 8.3

Picking the point for an arc-leader.

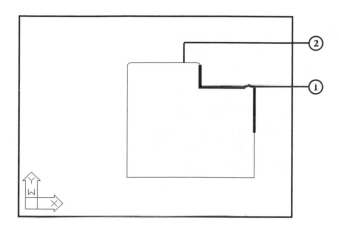

2. Begin the POLYLINE command by choosing the Polyline tool from the Draw menu. The From point: prompt appears.

3. Pick a point near ① in figure 8.3, and then choose the Width option by typing **W** and pressing Enter.

4. Respond to the two width prompts as follows:

```
Starting width <0.0>: ↵
Ending width <0.0>: .1↵
```

5. The Line mode prompts appear. Respond to the default Endpoint of line: prompt by typing **@.2<115** and pressing Enter.

6. AutoCAD draws the first segment with a tapered width and the prompt returns. Type **W** and press Enter.

7. Respond to the width prompts as follows:

```
Starting width <0.1>: 0↵
Ending width <0.0>: ↵
```

8. Now respond to the Line mode prompt by choosing the Arc option by typing **A** and pressing Enter.

9. The Arc mode prompts appear. Respond to the default <Endpoint of arc>: prompt by moving your cursor to a point near ② and picking. AutoCAD draws the arc and exits the POLYLINE command.

Your drawing should now resemble figure 8.4.

Figure 8.4

Constructing an arc-leader with a polyline.

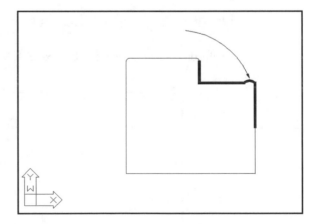

10. Save this drawing.

The preceding exercise emphasizes the versatility of polylines. Not only can polylines have varying width, but each segment can have different starting and ending widths. The current polyline width is stored in the system variable PLINEWID.

Controlling Polyline Appearance with FILL

A drawing that consists of a large number of polylines with widths other than zero can severely increase the time AutoCAD takes to redraw the screen or to plot the drawing. AutoCAD provides the FILL command to enable you to control the visibility of the filled portion of wide polylines. When you turn FILL off, AutoCAD displays or plots only the outline of filled polylines. You must regenerate the drawing before you can see the effect of the FILL command. Figure 8.5 shows the effect of having FILL on and off.

Figure 8.5

Fill can be turned on or off.

NOTE

The FILL command actually controls the setting of the system variable FILLMODE. A setting of 1 is the same as having FILL on; a setting of 0 is the same as having FILL off.

In addition to polylines, the FILL command controls the appearance of solid fill hatches and of objects created using the SOLID, TRACE, and MLINE commands.

Lightweight Polylines

 In AutoCAD Release 14, there is a new polyline object, called a *lightweight polyline*, that serves as a replacement for the 2D polyline found in earlier releases. Lightweight polylines provide most of the functionality of the older 2D polyline, but also offer substantially improved performance and reduced storage requirements in the AutoCAD database. Briefly, lightweight polylines do not store their vertex data as separate entities like 2D polylines do. Instead, they store this data as an array along with the lightweight polyline object data. The "behind-the-scenes" result is a "lighter," more efficient polyline object.

All polylines created using the POLYLINE command are, by default, lightweight polylines, although you can override that rule by using the system variable PLINETYPE, described in the next section, "PLINETYPE System Variable."

A lightweight polyline can have the following characteristics:

- Straight line segments
- Arc segments
- Constant and variable width
- Thickness

Some of the functionality and control available in the older 2D polyline objects are not available in lightweight polylines, including arc fit curve data, spline fit data, and curve fit tangent direction data.

PLINETYPE System Variable

To provide compatibility with the older 2D polyline object of previous AutoCAD releases (Release 13 and before), the system variable PLINETYPE is provided in AutoCAD Release 14. PLINETYPE specifies whether AutoCAD uses optimized, lightweight polylines. It controls both the creation of new polylines with the PLINE command and the conversion of existing polylines in drawings from previous releases. PLINETYPE can have one of three settings, with the following meanings:

0   Polylines in older drawings are not converted on open; PLINE creates old-format (2D) polylines.

1   Polylines in older drawings are not converted on open; PLINE creates lightweight (optimized) polylines.

2   Polylines in older drawings are converted on open; PLINE creates lightweight (optimized) polylines.

NOTE

> PLINETYPE also controls the polyline type created by using the following commands: BOUNDARY (when object type is set to Polyline); DONUT; ELLIPSE (when PELLIPSE is set to 1); PEDIT (when selecting a line or arc); POLYGON; and SKETCH (when SKPOLY is set to 1).

You also can manually convert the older 2D polylines by using the new Release 14 CONVERT command, which is described next.

CONVERT Command

Because old-style polylines are not necessarily automatically converted to the newer optimized polylines in Release 14, and because old-style polylines may be created in Release 14 drawings either by the user (by inserting an exploding block containing old-style polylines) or by third-party applications (depending on how the system variable PLINETYPE is set), AutoCAD Release 14 provides the CONVERT command, which enables you to explicitly convert 2D polylines (or associative hatch objects, covered in Chapter 17, "Drawing Hatch Patterns") to the optimized, lightweight polyline format. The prompts for the CONVERT command are as follows:

```
Hatch/Polyline/<All>:
```

You may enter **H** for hatches, **P** for polylines, or **A** for both. The next prompt appears:

```
Select/<All>:
```

Enter **S** to select objects or **A** to convert all candidate objects in the drawing. Depending on your response to these two prompts, AutoCAD displays one or both of the following messages:

```
number hatch objects converted.
number 2d polyline objects converted.
Where number is the number of polylines actually converted.
```

NOTE

> Polylines that contain curve fit or splined segments always retain the old-style format, as do polylines that contain extended entity data.

The new lightweight polyline object offers increased efficiency because it requires less memory to store its data and because it decreases the drawing file storage space requirements. Except for lightweight polylines' inability to handle curve fit and spline fit data, optimized, they behave exactly like the old-style 2D polylines.

The 3DPLOY Command

The 3DPOLY command produces three-dimensional polylines. 3D polylines in some respects are not as versatile as either lightweight polylines or 2D polylines because they can only contain straight line segments with no width information. They are more versatile than lightweight or 2D polylines, however, because you can draw them with a 3D, Z coordinate, in addition to the required X and Y coordinates.

Editing Polylines

As you have seen so far in this chapter, polylines are complex objects, capable of consisting of a collection of arc and line segments, each possessing the additional capability of containing width information. AutoCAD, therefore, provides the PEDIT command, a command devoted to editing these complex entities. As with 2D polylines, 3D polylines, meshes, and pface meshes, lightweight polylines are edited with the PEDIT command. PEDIT does not differentiate between the new lightweight and the old-style polylines.

Editing Entire Polylines with PEDIT

PEDIT contains a large number of subcommands or options for the various polyline properties. To manage this large number of options, AutoCAD divides them into two groups of editing functions. The primary group operates on the polyline as a whole, while a secondary group is devoted to the vertices that mark the beginnings and ends of polyline segments. The primary group of PEDIT options are as follows:

- **Close/Open.** Adds a segment (if required) and joins the first and last vertices to create a continuous polyline. If the polyline is open, the prompt shows Close; if the polyline is closed, the prompt shows Open. A polyline can be open, even if the first and last points share the same coordinates. A polyline is open unless the polyline Close option is used when you draw it or you later use the Close option to close it.

- **Join.** (2D only) Enables you to add selected arcs, lines, and other polylines to an existing polyline. Endpoints must be exactly coincident before you can join them. You can join lines, arcs, 2D polylines, and lightweight polylines to lightweight polylines or 2D polylines. Specifically:

- If you are editing a lightweight polyline, AutoCAD converts all joined segments to a single lightweight polyline at the end of the command.

- If you are editing an old-style 2D polyline, AutoCAD converts all joined segments, as in previous releases. This would be the case for 2D polylines that were not converted when the drawing was opened.

■ **Width.** (2D only) Prompts you to specify a single width for all segments of a polyline. The new width overrides any individual segment widths already stored. You can edit widths of individual segments by using a suboption of the Edit vertex option.

■ **Edit vertex.** Presents a prompt for a set of options that enable you to edit vertices and their adjoining segments.

■ **Fit.** (2D only) Creates a smooth curve through the polyline vertices. AutoCAD converts lightweight polylines to 2D polylines before computing the curve.

■ **Spline curve.** Creates a curve controlled by, but not necessarily passing through, a framework of polyline vertices. AutoCAD converts lightweight polylines to 2D polylines before computing the curve.

■ **Decurve.** Undoes a Fit or Spline curve, restoring it back to its original definition. Selecting the Decurve option has no effect on lightweight polylines because they do not support curve or spline fitting.

■ **Ltype gen.** (2D only) Controls whether linetypes are generated between vertices (Ltype gen OFF) or between the polyline's endpoints (Ltypes gen ON), spanning vertices. AutoCAD ignores this option for polylines that have tapered segments (see fig. 8.6).

■ **Undo.** Undoes the most recent PEDIT function.

■ **eXit.** (the default <X>) Exits the PEDIT command.

Figure 8.6

The effect of turning Ltype Gen on and off.

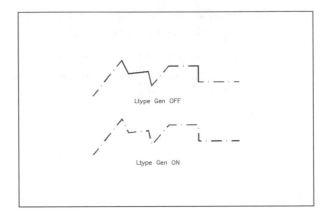

When PEDIT prompts Select polyline:, you can pick a polyline line, arc, or other polyline object. The PEDIT command operates on only one object at a time. PEDIT does not support noun/verb selection. Before you select a wide polyline, you must select either an edge or at a vertex. You can use a Window or Crossing selection, but you must first enter **W** or **C** because PEDIT does not support the implied windowing selection feature. For convenience, you also can use the Last, Box, Fence, All, Wpolygon, and Cpolygon (but not Previous) selection methods. Selection ends as soon as PEDIT finds a line, arc, or polyline. If your selection method includes more than one, PEDIT selects only one, usually the youngest, or most recently created, one. If the first object you select is not a polyline, AutoCAD asks if you want to turn it into one.

In the following exercise, you practice using some of the options of the primary PEDIT command options.

USING THE PRIMARY OPTIONS OF THE PEDIT COMMAND

1. Start a new drawing called **Parking.dwg**, using the CH08b.DWG on the accompanying CD as a template (see fig. 8.7).

2. Start the PEDIT command by typing **PE** and pressing Enter. You will first join two separate polylines. At the Select polyline: prompt, pick the line at ①. The primary PEDIT prompt appears.

Figure 8.7

Editing entire polylines.

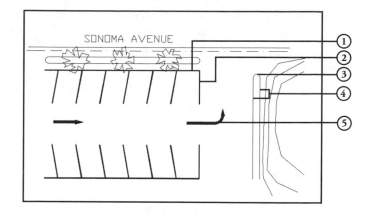

3. Choose the Join option by entering **J** and pressing Enter. Then at the Select objects: prompt, pick the polyline at ② and close the selection process by pressing Enter. AutoCAD joins the two lines into a single polyline and the primary prompt returns.

4. Next, use the Width option to change the width of the new polyline. Choose the Width option by typing **W** and pressing Enter. Answer the Enter new width for all segments: prompt by typing **9** and pressing Enter.

5. Note that the polyline changes to a new width of 9 inches and the prompt returns. The line is too wide. Type **U** and press Enter to undo the previous edit. The prompt returns. Type **W** and press Enter again. At the Enter new width for all segments: prompt, enter **3** and press Enter. The line changes width, and then the prompt returns. Note that the default option is eXit <X>. Accept this option by pressing Enter. The PEDIT command ends.

6. Next, you convert an arc object into a polyarc and join it to two polylines. Press Enter or the spacebar to restart the PEDIT command. At the Select polyline: prompt, pick the arc object at ③. The following prompts appear:

   ```
   Object selected is not a polyline
   Do you want to turn it into one? <Y>
   ```

7. Accept the default, <Y>, yes option by pressing Enter. The primary PEDIT prompt appears. Choose the Join option by typing **J** and pressing Enter. At the Select objects: prompt, pick the two polylines at ④. AutoCAD joins the three polylines. Press Enter to end the PEDIT command.

8. Next, you will explode a polyline, using AutoCAD's EXPLODE command. To start the EXPLODE command, type **EXPLODE** and press Enter at the Command: prompt. The Select objects: prompt appears.

9. Pick the arrow at ⑤ and press Enter. Note that the width information for this polyline disappears. Actually, AutoCAD destroys the polyline, demoting it to a Line object.

10. Restore the polyline arrow with the U command by entering **U** and pressing Enter. AutoCAD restores the polyline object.

11. You will use this drawing in the next exercise. For now, press Ctrl+S to save it.

In the preceding exercise, you saw that you can work with one polyline at a time. The primary PEDIT prompt with its several options returns after each edit operation, on the assumption that you may want to edit another polyline parameter. You must specifically dismiss the prompt by either accepting the default eXit option or pressing Esc to cancel the command. Also note that several of the options in the primary prompt undo other options. For example, after performing a Fit (curve) edit, you can undo the operation with the Decurve option. The Undo option undoes the last edit operation and returns the primary prompt. The EXPLODE command destroys a polyline and reduces it to a lower order object, either a line or arc.

INSIDER TIP

You can produce a wide polyline with an apparent mitered end by using a trick. After specifying the last vertex, set the width to taper from the current full width to zero, and then draw another very short segment using a typed relative polar coordinate. The "miter" will appear perpendicular to the angle you type.

For example, enter **@0.00001<45** to miter the top of a vertical wide polyline to an angle of 135 degrees (45 + 90). The end of the last segment is actually pointed, but the extremely short length has the effect of ending the previous segment with a miter.

Using the PEDIT Fit and Spline Options

PEDIT provides two options for making a polyline that passes through or is influenced by control points (see fig. 8.8). A *fit curve* actually passes through vertex points and consists of two arc segments between each pair of vertices. A *spline-fit curve* interpolates between control points, but the curve doesn't necessarily pass through the points.

Figure 8.8

Creating curves from polylines.

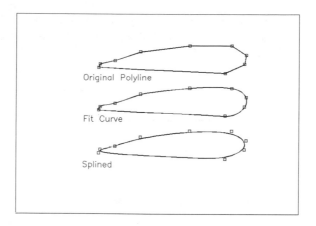

To help you visualize a spline-fit curve, AutoCAD provides the system variable SPLFRAME. If you set SPLFRAME to a value of 1, the reference frame with control points appears. Figure 8.8 shows only the control points. In the case of the original polyline, the control points are coincident with the polyline's vertices. In the instance of the fit curve example, the straight line segments between control points (vertices) have been replaced with arc segments, but still pass through the control points. The spline-fit curve uses the control points as guides to influence the shape of curve.

AutoCAD can generate two types of spline-fit polylines: a quadric b-spline and a cubic b-spline. The system variable SPLINETYPE controls the type of curve generated. A SPLINETYPE value of 5 approximates a true quadric b-spline; a value of 6 approximates a true cubic b-spline. In addition, the system variable SPLINESEGS controls the fineness of the b-spline. The numeric value of SLINESEGS sets the number of line segments in the control frame.

In the following exercise, you use both the Fit and Spline options of PEDIT to generate curves from polylines.

GENERATING CURVES WITH PEDIT

1. Continue in the drawing from the previous exercise (see fig. 8.9).

2. First, zoom in to the contour lines area of the parking lot. Start the ZOOM command by typing **Z** and pressing Enter. The Zoom prompt appears.

3. Choose the Center option from the Zoom prompt by typing **C** and pressing Enter.

4. Respond to the Center point: prompt by typing **70',68'** and pressing Enter. At the Magnification or height <0'-0">: prompt, type **1.5x** and press Enter. Your drawing should resemble figure 8.9.

Figure 8.9

Creating smooth curves with PEDIT.

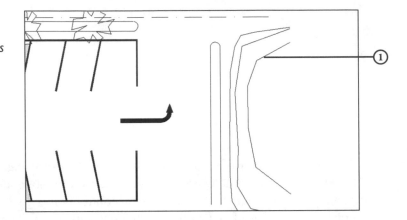

5. You will smooth the contour line at ① first. Start the PEDIT command by typing **PE** and pressing Enter. Pick the polyline at ① at the Select polyline: prompt. The primary PEDIT options appear. Type **F** (for Fit) and press Enter.

6. AutoCAD performs a fit curve smoothing on the polyline and the prompt returns. This does not smooth the curve as you want, so select the Undo option by typing **U** and pressing Enter. AutoCAD undoes the fit curve operation. The PEDIT prompt returns.

7. Now choose the Spline option by typing **S** and pressing Enter. AutoCAD spline-fits the polyline. Note that this curve more closely approximates the contour. Exit the PEDIT command by pressing Enter.

8. By turning on the spline frame, you can examine the original data points for this new curve. At the Command: prompt, enter **SPLFRAME** and press Enter. Respond to the SPLFRAME prompt by typing **1** and pressing Enter.

9. For the spline frame to display, you must regenerate the drawing. At the Command: prompt, type **REGEN** and press Enter. The spline frame displays. Note that with an open polyline such as this contour line, the spline-fit curve passes through the spline frame at the start and end points.

10. Turn the spline frame off by repeating step 8, but setting the SPLFRAME variable to **0**. Then perform another regen to clear the frame.

11. You will use this drawing and view in the next exercise. For now, save the drawing by pressing Ctrl+S.

In the preceding exercise, you saw how the PEDIT command takes data points in the form of polyline vertices and transforms them into a close approximation of a true b-spline curve. In many instances, these polyline spline-fit curves are adequate for representing data such as contour lines. At other times, the smoothing procedure of the fit-curve procedure will suffice to remove the angles present at polyline vertices.

NOTE

Lightweight polylines do not support either the fit-curve or spline-fit options of the PEDIT command. Whenever you choose either of these options, AutoCAD, if necessary, converts lightweight polylines into the old-style 2D polyline, and then carries out the transformation to a curve. If the curve is subsequently changed back to its original shape using the Decurve option of the PEDIT Command, AutoCAD converts the 2D polyline back into a lightweight polyline.

Editing Polyline Vertices with PEDIT

Each polyline segment belongs to and is controlled by the preceding vertex. The Edit vertex option of the primary PEDIT set of options displays another prompt with a separate set of options. When you use these options, AutoCAD marks the current vertex of the polyline with an X to show the vertex you are editing. Move the X (by pressing Enter to accept the <N>, next, prompt) until the X marks the vertex you want to edit.

Options for the Edit vertex option of the PEDIT command are as follows:

- **Next/Previous.** Moves the X marker to a new current vertex. Next is the initial default.

- **Break.** Splits the polyline in two or removes segments of a polyline at existing vertices. The first break point is the vertex on which you invoke the Break option. Use Next/Previous to access another vertex for the second break point. The Go option performs the actual break.

- **Insert.** Adds a vertex at a point you specify, following the vertex currently marked with an X. You can combine this option with the Break option to break between existing vertices.

- **Move.** Changes the location of the current (X-marked) vertex to a point you specify.

- **Straighten.** Removes all intervening vertices from between the two you select and replaces them with one straight segment. This option also uses the Next/Previous and Go options.

- **Tangent.** Sets a tangent to the direction you specify at the currently marked vertex to control curve fitting. You can see the angle of the tangent at the vertex with an arrow and you can drag it with the screen cursor or enter the angle at the keyboard.

- **Width.** Sets the starting and ending width of an individual polyline segment to the values you specify.

- **eXit.** Exits vertex editing and returns to the primary PEDIT prompt.

INSIDER TIP

It is usually easier to edit the position of a polyline vertex by using AutoCAD's Grips feature. This is especially true for spline-fit polylines. Chapter 10, "Basic Object Editing," covers grips editing.

In the following exercise, you perform vertex editing on polylines in the current exercise drawing.

EDITING POLYLINE VERTICES WITH PEDIT

1. Continue in the drawing from the previous exercise (see fig. 8.10). You first move the first vertex of the polyline contour at ①. Begin by starting the PEDIT command and pick the contour line at ①.

Figure 8.10

Moving a polyline vertex.

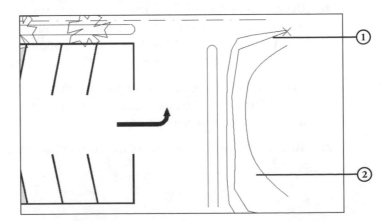

2. At the primary PEDIT prompt, choose the Edit vertex option by typing **E** and pressing Enter. Note that an X appears at the endpoint and first vertex of the line and the Edit vertex: prompt appears.

3. If the vertex you want to move is already selected (marked with an X), respond to this prompt by typing **M** and pressing Enter. Respond to the Enter new location: prompt by typing **@0,–12** and pressing Enter. (Note: Watch the vertex as you press Enter.)

4. Move the vertex down 12 units in the –Y direction. The Edit vertex prompt returns.

INSIDER TIP

In the next step, if you go too far, type **P** and press Enter to return to the previous vertex.

5. For the purposes of this exercise, assume you want to insert a new vertex between the current fourth and fifth vertices, as shown at ②. "Walk" the current vertex down the line by pressing Enter to accept the default Next (vertex) option. You need to press Enter three times. The X is now at vertex 4 at ③ (see fig. 8.11).

Figure 8.11

Inserting a new vertex.

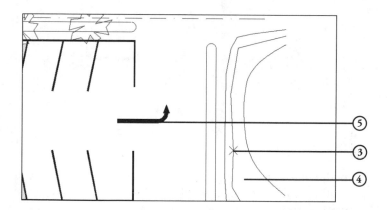

6. Now choose the Insert option by typing **I** and pressing Enter. Answer the Enter location of new vertex: prompt by picking a point near ④, as shown in figure 8.11. AutoCAD inserts a new vertex and the prompt returns.

7. Select the Edit vertex mode by typing **X** and pressing Enter. The primary PEDIT prompt returns. Select the Spline option by typing **S** and pressing Enter. AutoCAD spline-fits the curve.

8. Close the PEDIT command by accepting the default <X> (eXit) option.

9. Re-start the PEDIT command by pressing the spacebar. At the PEDIT prompt, pick the polyline at ⑤. You will change the width of the vertex at the base of the arrowhead.

10. Choose the Edit vertex option of the primary PEDIT prompt and choose Next until the active vertex is at the base of the arrowhead. This is the third vertex.

NOTE

In the next step, watch the width of the arrowhead as you press Enter.

11. Choose the Width option by typing **W** and pressing Enter. At the Enter starting width <1'-4">: prompt, enter the new value by typing **20** and pressing Enter. AutoCAD changes the width of the arrowhead base. At the Enter ending width <1'-8">: prompt, type **0** and press Enter.

12. Exit the Edit vertex prompt by typing **X** and pressing Enter. Then exit the PEDIT command. Your drawing should now resemble figure 8.12.

Figure 8.12

The finished parking lot drawing.

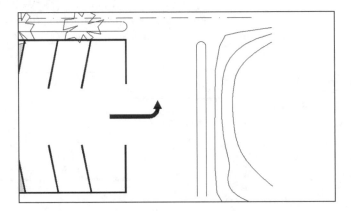

In the preceding exercise, you saw how to make changes to an existing polyline by editing parameters at its vertices. When combined with the primary editing option, the Edit vertex option provides a great degree of editing capability for polylines.

Creating True Splines

To create true spline curves in AutoCAD Release 14, you use the SPLINE command. Splines can be either 2D or 3D objects. You draw splines by specifying a series of fit-data points (vertices) through which the curve passes. The fit-data points determine the location of the spline's control points. Control points contain the curve information for the spline. AutoCAD's spline objects are true splines, unlike the spline approximations formed by spline-fit polylines. AutoCAD's SPLINE command draws non-uniform rational B-splines (NURBS). AutoCAD NURBS are mathematically more accurate than spline-fit polylines. Even though spline objects are more accurate than spline-fit polylines, they actually require less memory for storage and result in smaller drawings, other factors being equal.

You can use the SPLINE command to convert 2D and 3D spline-fit polylines into true splines. Unlike spline-fit polylines, which may be either quadric or cubic spline approximations depending on how the SPLINETYPE system variable is set, the SPLINETYPE system variable does not affect the true spline objects produced by the SPLINE command.

The SPLINE command offers the following options:

- **Object/<Enter first point>.** The default option of the main prompt specifies the starting point of the spline. After you specify a starting point, AutoCAD prompts you to specify a second point. Spline objects must consist of a minimum of three points.

- **Object.** This option enables you to convert existing spline-fit polylines to true spline objects. After you specify this option, AutoCAD asks you to specify a spline-fit polyline.

- **Close/Fit Tolerance/<Enter point>.** After you specify a second point for the spline, AutoCAD displays this prompt. The default option is to continue to specify additional data points for the spline you are drawing. If you press Enter, AutoCAD prompts you to specify the tangent information for the start and endpoints, and then ends the command.

- **Close.** This option causes the start and end of the spline to be coincident and to share vertex and tangent information. When you close a spline, AutoCAD prompts only once for tangent information.

- **Fit Tolerance.** This option controls how closely the spline curve follows the data points. The distance of the Fit Tolerance is expressed in current drawing units. The smaller the tolerance, the closer the spline fits the data points. A value of 0 causes the spline to follow the data points exactly.

- **(Undo).** Although this option does not appear in the prompt, you can enter **U** after any point to undo the last segment.

In the following exercise, you use the SPLINE command to draw the outline of a mechanical part.

CONSTRUCTING A SPLINE

1. Begin a new drawing called **Spline.dwg** using the book's IAC803. DWG on the accompanying CD as a template (see fig. 8.13).

Figure 8.13

Fitting a spline to data points.

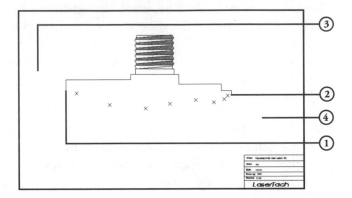

In the next step, you use the pre-positioned data points shown in the drawing by X points. A node running Osnap has been set so you can easily snap to these data points.

2. Start the SPLINE command by either entering **SPL** and pressing Enter or by choosing the Spline tool from the Draw toolbar. The Object/<Enter first point>: prompt appears.

3. Use the default option by setting an Endpoint Osnap and snapping to the endpoint at ①. The Enter point: prompt appears.

4. Continue to specify points, snapping to each successive X node at each Enter point: prompt. Finally, invoke another Endpoint Osnap and snap to the point at ②.

5. Press Enter to end the Enter point: prompt. The Enter start tangent: prompt appears.

6. A rubber band line stretches from the first spline point. Invoke the ORTHO mode (press F8) and pick a point near ③. At the Enter end tangent: prompt, pick a point near ④. AutoCAD completes the spline.

7. Turn ORTHO mode off by pressing F8 again. Your drawing should now resemble figure 8.14.

Figure 8.14

The completed spline curve.

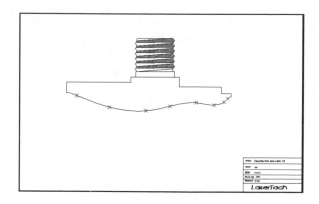

8. You will use this drawing in the next exercise, but for now save your work by pressing Ctrl+S.

In the preceding exercise, you used pre-positioned points to help construct the spline. Depending on the type of work you want to do, you usually base splines on some form of preliminary data points rather than just draw the curve in free-form style, although both methods are available with AutoCAD. At best, splines are "tricky" objects to construct, and once drawn, you frequently need to alter or refine them.

Controlling Splines with SPLINEDIT

The SPLINEDIT command enables you to edit a spline's control points and, if present, fit-data points. When you draw a spline, you pick fit-data points. AutoCAD uses these points to calculate the location of the spline's control points. You can add additional control or fit-data points or move points already present. You can change the *weight,* or influence of control points, as well as the tolerance of the spline. You also can close or open a spline and adjust the tangent information of the start and endpoints.

Control points usually are not located on the spline curve (except at the start and endpoints), but they control the shape of the spline. AutoCAD uses the fit-data points to calculate the position of the control points. After AutoCAD determines the control points, it no longer needs the fit-data points. If you remove the fit-data from a spline, though, you cannot use any of the fit-data editing options of the SPLINEDIT command to further edit the shape of the spline.

When you select a spline for editing, AutoCAD displays its control points just as it does if you use grips editing, although grips editing is not available through the SPLINEDIT command. The SPLINEDIT command works on only one spline object at a time. The Noun/Verb selection method is not available with SPLINEDIT.

The SPLINEDIT command has the following options:

■ **Fit Data.** Enables you to edit the fit-data points for spline objects that have them, in which case, AutoCAD displays another prompt of Fit Data options described following this list.

■ **Close.** Closes an open spline. Adds a curve that is tangent between the start and end vertices for splines that do not have the same start and endpoints. If the spline does have the same start and endpoints, the Close option makes the tangent information for each point continuous. If the spline is already closed, the Close option is replaced by the Open option.

■ **Open.** Opens a closed spline. If the spline did not have the same start and endpoints prior to being closed, this option removes the tangent curve and removes tangent information from the start and endpoints. If the spline shares the same start and endpoint before you close it, the Open option removes the tangent information from the points.

■ **Move Vertex.** Enables you to move the control vertices of a spline. You specify a vertex to edit by moving the current vertex to the next or previous vertex.

■ **Refine.** Displays suboptions that enable you to add control points and adjust the weight of control points. You can add individual control points in areas where you want finer control of the curve. Performing any refine operation on a spline removes fit-data from the spline. You can reverse the effect of the Refine option and restore the fit-data with the Undo option before ending the SPLINEDIT command. The following list describes the Refine options.

  ■ **Add control point.** Enables you to add a sing le control point to a spline. AutoCAD locates the new control point as close as possible to the point you pick on the spline. Adding a control point does not change the shape of the spline.

  ■ **Elevate Order.** Elevates the order of the spline's polynomial, which adds control points evenly over the spline. This option does not change the shape of the spline. The order of the polynomial cannot be reduced once increased.

- **Weight.** Controls the amount of tension that pulls a spline toward a control point.

- **eXit.** Returns to the main SPLINEDIT prompt.

- **rEverse.** Changes the direction of the spline.

- **Undo.** Undoes the most recently performed SPLINEDIT option.

- **eXit.** Ends the SPLINEDIT command.

The following are the suboptions of the Fit Data option for editing spline object fit-data. When you choose the Fit Data option, the grips-like boxes change to highlight the fit-data points.

- **Add.** Adds additional fit-data points to the curve. Adding fit-data points changes the shape of the spline curve. Added fit-data points obey the current tolerance of the spline.

- **Close.** Performs the same function as the control point Close option using fit-data points.

- **Open.** Performs the same function as the control point Open option using fit-data points. The Open option replaces the Close option if the spline is already closed.

- **Delete.** Removes fit-data points and redraws the spline to fit the fit-data points that remain.

- **Move.** Enables you to move fit-data point vertices of a spline. You specify a vertex to edit by moving the current vertex to the next or previous vertex. You cannot edit fit data information with AutoCAD's grips editing feature.

- **Purge.** Removes all fit data from the spline.

- **Tangents.** Enables you to change the tangent information of the start and endpoints of a spline.

- **toLerance.** Changes the tolerance of the spline's fit-data points and redraws the spline. A spline loses its fit data if you change the tolerance and move a control point or open or close the spline.

- **eXit.** Returns to the control point editing prompt.

In the following exercise, you edit the spline you drew in the preceding exercise using some of the options of the SPLINEDIT command. First, you reduce the number of fit-data points, and then you add additional control points to the spline by changing its order.

EDITING A SPLINE

1. Continue from the previous exercise. Remove the running node osnap.

2. Start the SPLINEDIT command by either clicking on the Splinedit tool on the Modify II toolbar, or from the Modify menu, choose Object, Spline. Select the spline you drew in the preceding exercise. The control points appear (see fig. 8.15) and the following prompt appears:

   ```
   Fit Data/Close/Move Vertex/Refine/rEverse/Undo/eXit <X>:
   ```

Figure 8.15

The Fit Data option displays a spline's control points.

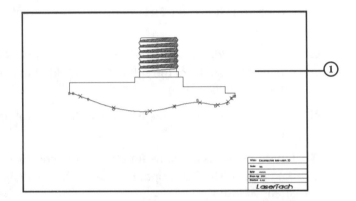

3. Choose the Fit Data option by typing either **F** or **D** and then pressing Enter. AutoCAD changes the control points to show the fit data points. Notice that the fit data points are not the same as the control points. The Fit Data prompt appears.

4. Choose the Delete option and then pick a couple of points. Note that the points disappear as you pick them. Press Enter after you remove the points. The prompt returns. Choose the Tangents option. The System default/<Enter start tangent>: prompt appears.

5. Press Enter to keep the current tangent. Then at the System default/<Enter end tangent>: prompt, pick a point near ①, as shown in figure 8.15.

6. When the prompt returns, press Enter to return to the main control point prompt. The control points are displayed and the control point prompt appears.

7. Choose the Refine option, and then at the new prompt, choose the Elevate option.

8. At the Enter new order <4>: prompt, type **6** and press Enter. This elevates the order of the polynomial and adds control points. The prompt returns. Respond by pressing Enter to exit to the main prompt.

9. Press Enter again to exit the PLINEDIT command.

10. From the layer control box on the Object Properties toolbar, turn off the layer Frame. Your drawing should now resemble figure 8.16. You are finished with this drawing.

Figure 8.16

Completed spline-fit curve.

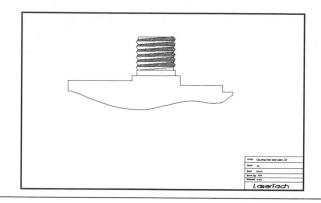

The options and sub-options of the SPLINEDIT command offer a great deal of control. In this exercise, you had the opportunity to investigate several ways you can modify and "tweak" a spline object. Splines are quite complex, but offer the advantage of also being quite accurate and flexible.

INSIDER **T**IP

As with polylines, the most efficient way to edit true splines often is to use AutoCAD's grips editing feature. Chapter 10, "Basic Object Editing," tells more about grips editing.

Summary

In this chapter, you explored the versatility of polylines. You learned about AutoCAD Release 14's new lightweight polyline and saw how you can edit polylines in a variety of ways. You also saw how to convert polylines into two different types of curves. You learned about the versatility and accuracy of true NURB splines and the many ways of editing and shaping them into complex smooth curves. Many of the shapes you may be required to draw in AutoCAD are not composed of straight lines, and being able to fit polylines to complex curves is an important skill to have.

CREATING COMPLEX OBJECTS

by David M. Pitzer

This chapter tells you about two complex AutoCAD objects: regions and multilines. Regions are rather esoteric in that they are 2D objects that behave in many ways like solids; you can place holes in regions, for example. Multilines, on the other hand, are very practical AutoCAD objects that consist of sets of parallel lines that behave as a single line. They are useful as drawing objects representing walls. Specifically, this chapter will cover the following topics:

- *Creating Regions*

- *Understanding Boolean Operations*

- *Extracting Data from a Region Model*

- *Creating Multiple Lines*

Creating Regions

An AutoCAD *region* is a two-dimensional enclosed area formed from closed shapes called loops. The term *loops* is perhaps a little misleading because loops can be composed of straight lines. Specifically, a loop is a curve or a sequence of connected curves that forms an area on a plane that has a boundary that does not intersect itself. Loops can be combinations of lines, polylines, circles, arcs, ellipses, elliptical arcs, 3D faces, traces, and solids. Loops can be composed of several such objects, as long as the objects themselves are closed or form closed areas by sharing endpoints with other objects. Although you use regions primarily in three-dimensional models, they are also useful in two-dimensional drawing since they allow the construction of shapes that would be difficult to create using standard editing commands.

You can create regions from multiple loops and out of open curves whose endpoints are connected to form loops. Open curves that intersect in their interior, for example, arcs or self-intersecting curves, cannot form regions. You use the REGION and BOUNDARY commands to create regions.

 NOTE

The term *closed* as used here does not mean that the Close option of the LINE or PLINE command was used to close a series of such lines, but rather, that the coordinates of the beginning line segment and the last line segment are coincident.

The REGION Command

The REGION command prompts you to select objects that you want to convert to regions. You can use any standard selection method. Valid selections are closed lines, polylines, splines, circles, or any group of objects whose endpoints connect to form a closed loop. Self-intersecting objects or objects whose endpoints do not connect do not qualify. Figure 9.1 shows some examples of valid and invalid selections for the REGION command. The REGION command converts valid selections into regions, reporting the number of loops extracted and the number of regions created on the command line.

INSIDER **T**IP

By default, the REGION command "consumes" the selected object(s) in making the regions. That is, it replaces the selected objects with regions and deletes the original objects. You may sometimes use the loop objects as a template for several regions and may, therefore, want to keep the original objects. The system variable DELOBJ controls whether objects are retained. If you want to keep the original objects, set the DELOBJ system variable to 0 (off).

Figure 9.1

Examples of valid and invalid selections for the REGION command.

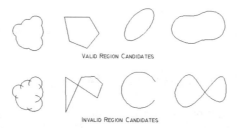

In the following exercise, you create various regions from pre-drawn closed loops.

CREATING REGIONS

1. Begin a new drawing called **CHAP9.dwg** using this book's IAC901.dwg as a template (it should resemble figure 9.2). The layer LOOPS should be current. This drawing is included on the accompanying CD.

Figure 9.2

Creating regions from closed loops.

2. The LOOPS layer contains 10 closed curves or loops. The curves represent polylines, circles, lines, and splines. You will convert these into regions.

3. Start the REGION command by clicking on the Region tool on the Draw toolbar, or by choosing Region from the Draw pull-down menu. After the Modeler DLL loads, the Select objects: prompt appears.

4. Select all the curves by typing **all** and pressing Enter. AutoCAD should find 25 objects. Press Enter. AutoCAD responds:

```
10 loops extracted.
10 regions created.
```

5. Note that although 25 objects were selected, AutoCAD found 10 closed loops and created 10 regions.

6. You will use this drawing in the next exercise. For now, press Ctrl+S to save your regions.

The 10 regions you created in the preceding exercise do not look any different from the original closed loops. Later, however, you see how differently they act.

Creating Regions with BOUNDARY

You can create regions another way. The BOUNDARY command can create either a polyline boundary or a region from an *enclosed* area. An enclosed area differs from a closed area (required by the REGION command) in that the curves that the BOUNDARY command considers need not have their endpoints coincident or connected. For example, referring to figure 9.1, the first set of overlapping arcs on the lower line are not closed but they do *enclose* an area. The BOUNDARY command can form a region from these arcs; the REGION command cannot. In such cases, the region that BOUNDARY creates takes the same shape as it would were the curves closed.

NOTE

Unlike the REGION command, BOUNDARY creates new regions from objects but leaves the original objects in place regardless of the setting of the DELOBJ system variable. You can, of course, delete these objects using the ERASE command.

In the following exercise, you create a region from curves that enclose an area but do not themselves form a closed loop. You use the Region object type option of the BOUNDARY command. Figure 9.3 shows the Boundary Creation dialog box with the Region option selected in the Object Type drop-down list.

Figure 9.3

*The Boundary Creation
dialog box.*

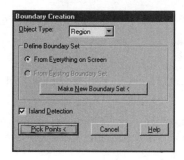

CREATING REGIONS WITH BOUNDARY

1. Continue in the drawing from the previous exercise. Thaw the SHIELD layer and make it the current layer. Refer to figure 9.4 for this exercise.

Figure 9.4

*Creating a boundary from
an enclosed area.*

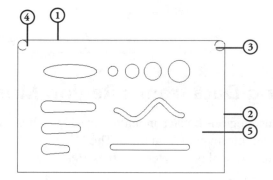

The objects on the SHIELD layer consist of a line ①, a polyline ②, and two arcs ③ and ④. These objects enclose an area.

2. From the Draw pull-down menu, choose Boundary to start the BOUNDARY command. The Boundary Creation dialog box appears (refer to figure 9.3). Select Region from the Object Type drop-down list.

3. Still in the Boundary Creation dialog box, choose Pick Points and pick anywhere near ⑤ in figure 9.4. The following prompts appear. Press Enter in response to the final prompt.

```
Select internal point: Selecting everything...
Selecting everything visible...
Analyzing the selected data...
Analyzing internal islands...
Select internal point: ↵
```

4. AutoCAD creates the region and displays the following two prompts:

```
11 loops extracted.
11 regions created.
```

5. AutoCAD has created a new region in addition to the 10 regions created in the previous exercise.

6. Use the ERASE command (type **E** and press Enter) to erase the arcs at ③ and ④. Your drawing should now resemble figure 9.5. Save your work.

Figure 9.5

The completed regions.

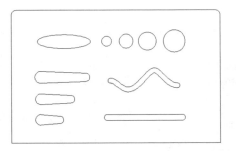

Extracting Data from a Region Model

Because regions behave in many ways like solids, you can extract a great deal of physical information from them. The MASSPROP command allows you to display certain physical parameters, such as area.

The MASSPROP command prompts you to select a region or regions. AutoCAD then displays a list of physical properties on the text screen. The following is the data that AutoCAD displays for the shield model you constructed in the exercises for this chapter.

```
--------------      REGIONS    ---------------
Area:                   61.0053
Perimeter:              80.9890
Bounding box:       X: 1.5000  --  12.0000
                    Y: 1.2500  --  7.8750
Centroid:           X: 6.8334
                    Y: 4.5380
Moments of inertia: X: 1490.2179
                    Y: 3432.9384
Product of inertia: XY: 1887.8823
Radii of gyration:  X: 4.9424
                    Y: 7.5015
```

```
Principal moments and X-Y directions about centroid:
            I: 233.8782 along [0.9999 -0.0110]
            J: 584.3485 along [0.0110 0.9999]
```

After AutoCAD displays this information, a prompt appears that allows you to save the information to a file. Note that, because regions are actually 2D areas, the information includes such parameters as Area and Perimeter rather than Mass and Volume. In many ways, regions are mathematical "fictions" because any true object—or a computer model of any true object—would have both mass and volume. Nonetheless, regions are useful AutoCAD objects, or models, that may be manipulated in real-world ways.

Understanding Boolean Operations

Regions are interesting objects. Although they have no thickness, they behave in many ways like solids. In AutoCAD, you can act on regions as you would if they were actual 3D solids. For example, if you have a region, you may want to place holes in it or attach another region to it or trim it in some manner. In true solids, you can perform such operations by performing mathematical operations collectively known as *Boolean operations*. Three Boolean operations and commands exist in AutoCAD: UNION, SUBTRACT, and INTERSECT.

The UNION command enables you to mathematically join two or more regions into a single region of their combined areas. Interestingly, the regions do not have to touch (much less overlap) to be joined. Figure 9.6 shows the result of using the UNION command.

Figure 9.6

The results obtained with the UNION, SUBTRACT, and INTERSECT commands.

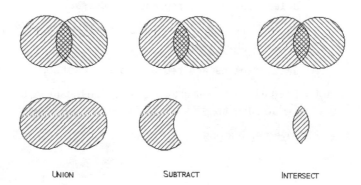

UNION   SUBTRACT   INTERSECT

The SUBTRACT command allows you to cut holes into or areas out of regions. These holes and cutouts become a part of the region; if you move the region, the holes also move. Figure 9.6 illustrates the effect of using the SUBTRACT command. AutoCAD prompts you for the region to subtract from and then asks for the regions you want to subtract.

The INTERSECT command creates a new region from the area common to two or more overlapping regions. Figure 9.6 depicts the effect of using the INTERSECT command.

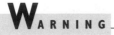

WARNING

Using the INTERSECT command on regions that do not intersect or overlap creates a region that has no area, called a *null* region. Essentially, AutoCAD deletes the regions you selected. If this occurs, you can use UNDO to restore the regions.

In the following exercise, you will create some Boolean holes in the shield region you created in the preceding exercise. You use the regions you created from closed loops earlier with the REGION command.

CUTTING HOLES IN REGIONS WITH SUBTRACT

1. Continue from the preceding exercise. The layer SHIELD should remain current.

2. Start the SUBTRACT command by choosing Modify, Boolean, Subtract. The following prompt appears:

   ```
   Select solids and regions to subtract from...
   ```

3. Pick the shield region at a point such as ① in figure 9.7 and then press Enter. The following prompt appears:

   ```
   Select solids and regions to subtract...
   ```

4. Use a window to select the regions within the shield, as shown in figure 9.7, at ② and ③, and then press Enter. AutoCAD subtracts the regions.

5. Save your drawing.

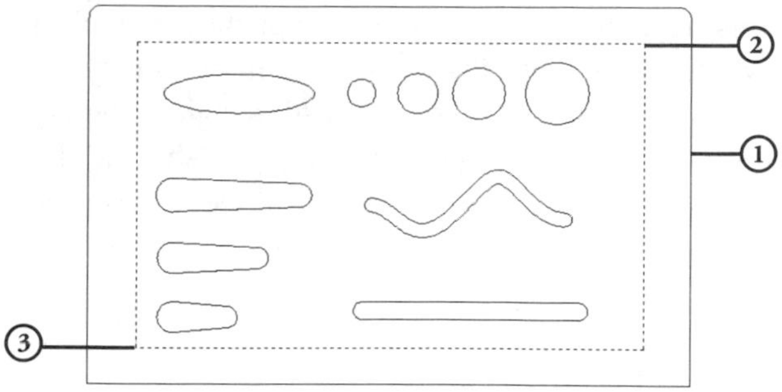

Figure 9.7

Select the interior regions to create holes.

Although your drawing now looks exactly as it did when you began the preceding exercise, you actually cut 10 holes into the larger shield region. Figure 9.8 shows a rendered, perspective view of your drawing in its present state. As you can see, there are holes in the shield.

Figure 9.8

A rendered view of the shield drawing.

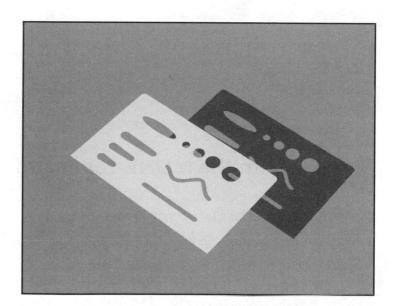

INSIDER TIP

Because regions act much like solids, you can change their shape only by using Boolean operations. If you want to change regions back into their constituent lines, circles, and arcs, you must use the EXPLODE command.

Regions are interesting objects. Although they are technically two-dimensional, they behave in many ways like real-world, three-dimensional objects. Boolean operations allow you to easily alter AutoCAD's region objects in ways not available using conventional editing methods, resulting in "shapes" that would be difficult to draw otherwise. In the next section, you will learn about another interesting AutoCAD object: multiple parallel lines, or mlines.

Creating Multiple Lines

Multilines (mlines) are objects that contain multiple parallel lines called *elements*. Multilines are convenient when drawing objects such as walls in floor plans, which are often represented by two or more parallel lines. Each element of a multiline is defined, in part, by its distance or *offset* from a center, where the center is considered *zero offset*. Figure 9.9 shows the parts of a typical mline object.

Figure 9.9

Multiline elements.

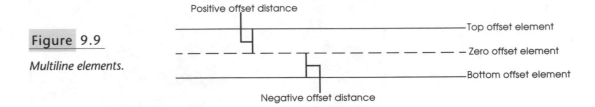

Drawing with the MLINE Command

Multilines are created using the MLINE command, which returns the Justification/ Scale/STyle/<From point>: prompt.

- **Justification.** Enables you to control whether AutoCAD draws the mline from the top offset, the zero offset, or the bottom offset.

- **Scale.** Enables you to control the scale at which AutoCAD draws the mline. AutoCAD multiplies the offset distances by this scale factor.

- **STyle.** Allows you to set the current mline style. You use the MLSTYLE command to define mline styles. Entering **Z ?** at this prompt displays a list of currently defined mline styles.

- **From point.** Prompts you for the starting point of the mline. (From point is the default option.) After you pick a starting point, AutoCAD prompts for the To point:. You can use an Undo option to undo the last drawn mline segment. After you pick two points, you can use a Close option to close the mline and clean up the last corner.

By default, AutoCAD draws multilines with two elements, one having an offset of 0.5 and the other with an offset of –0.5, resulting in a default mline of two elements, 1 unit apart. By adjusting the mline scale, you can control the distance between elements. For example, setting the mline scale to 6 produces two parallel lines, 6 units apart.

In the following exercise, you begin to create a floor plan for a house using the default multiline style.

CREATING EXTERIOR WALLS WITH MULTILINES

1. Begin a new drawing called **FLOORPLN.dwg,** using this book's IAC902.dwg on the accompanying CD as a template. If necessary, set the PLAN layer current.

2. Start the MLINE command by clicking on the Multiline tool on the Draw toolbar, or by choosing Draw, Multiline. Respond to the MLINE prompts as shown:

```
Justification/Scale/STyle/<From point>: S↵
Set Mline scale <1.00>: 6↵
Justification/Scale/STyle/<From point>: 30',30'↵
<To point>: @22'<0↵
```

3. AutoCAD starts the mline and draws the first segment. Note that since you set the scale to 6, the distance between the two lines is 6 units (inches in your drawing) apart. Since the floor plan lines are orthogonal to each other, you can reduce your typing by using Direct Distance entry. Press F8 to turn ORTHO mode on. The Undo/<To point>: prompt is current.

4. Respond to this prompt by moving your cursor above the last point and typing **26'** and pressing Enter. ORTHO mode forces the new segment to a point @26'<90 from the previous point. The Close/Undo/<To point>: prompt appears.

5. Move the cursor to the left of the last point and type **22'** and press Enter. Direct Distance entry draws the next segment @22'<90 to the last point. The Close/Undo/<To point>: prompt returns. Respond by typing **C** and pressing Enter.

6. AutoCAD closes the mline by drawing a segment from the last point to the start point. Your drawing should now resemble figure 9.10.

7. Save your work.

Figure 9.10

Floor plan outline using mlines.

Defining Mline Styles with MLSTYLE

The default multiline style consists of two lines, each 0.5 units from the zero offset. It is called the *Standard mline style*. By adjusting the scale and justification, the Standard mline style can serve many purposes—but still is limited to only two lines. The MLSTYLE command allows you to create more complex multiline styles.

Issuing the MLSTYLE command opens the Multiline Styles dialog box, shown in figure 9.11. The Multiline Style area of the dialog box gives you information about the multiline styles available in the drawing and offers options for loading, saving, adding, and renaming multiline style definitions. Unless you save them to a file, multiline styles exist only in the current drawing. To share multiline styles among drawings, you must save the multiline style definition to a file. Multiline styles are stored in MLN files. The Standard multiline style is stored in ACAD.MLN, usually found in the \SUPPORT directory or folder of your Release 14 installation.

Figure 9.11

The Multiline Styles dialog box.

Clicking on the Element Properties button displays the Element Properties dialog box shown in figure 9.12. The Element Properties dialog box enables you to define the elements of a multiline style. Each element is defined as a distance from the zero offset. AutoCAD draws elements that have a positive offset above the zero offset and elements that have a negative offset below the zero offset. The elements that have the greatest absolute offsets become the top and bottom justification elements.

Figure 9.12

The Element Properties dialog box.

You can define as many as 16 elements in a single multiline style. In addition to an offset distance, you can assign each element a linetype and color, which enables you to create very complex multiline styles.

NOTE

Although you can assign a separate linetype and color to each element of a multiline, the multiline itself resides on a single layer. If you freeze a layer that contains a multiline, you freeze the entire multiline.

Clicking on the Multiline Properties button opens the Multiline Properties dialog box (see fig. 9.13). The Multiline Properties dialog box presents you with some options for the display and generation of multilines. The Display joints check box provides you with the means to control the display of corner joints, as shown in figure 9.14.

Figure 9.13

The Multiline Properties dialog box.

The Caps area of the dialog box enables you to control the creation of the start and end of multilines. The Angle option enables you to control the miter angles of the end cap. Figure 9.15 shows the various capping effects.

Figure 9.14

Multilines with and without joint display.

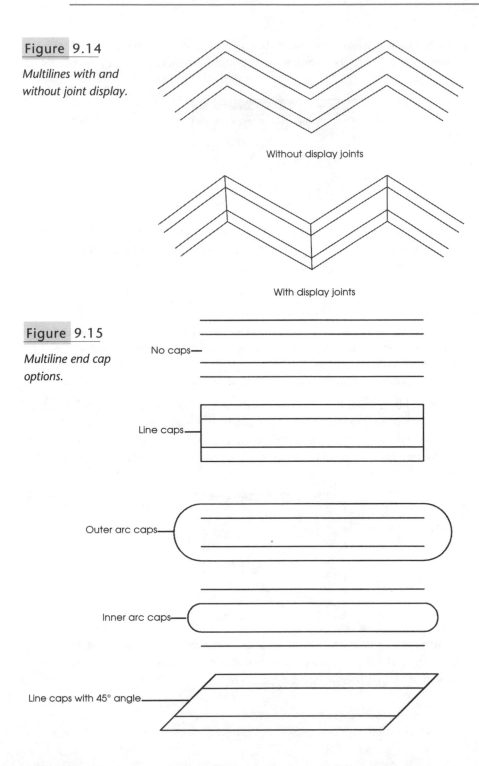

Without display joints

With display joints

Figure 9.15

Multiline end cap options.

No caps—

Line caps—

Outer arc caps—

Inner arc caps—

Line caps with 45° angle—

The options in the Fill area of the Multiline Properties dialog box enable you to fill in the multiline with a solid color. If you set the Fill option to on (mark the On check box), AutoCAD fills in the area between the outermost offset elements with the color you specify in the multiline style.

In the following exercise, you create two new multiline styles for the interior walls and closet shelves of your floor plan drawing.

CREATING MULTILINE STYLES

1. Continue from the preceding exercise. Layer PLAN should still be current.

2. Choose Format, Multiline Style. The Multiline Style dialog box appears. Click on the Element Properties button. The Element Properties dialog box appears.

3. In the Elements list, select the 0.5 element and type **2** in the Offset edit box. Now, select and highlight the –0.5 element and enter **–2** in the Offset edit box. Click on OK to dismiss the dialog box.

4. Back in the Multiline Styles dialog box, click on the Multiline Properties button and in the Multiline Properties dialog box, place an X in the Start and End Line check boxes. Click on OK to close the dialog box.

5. In the Multiline Styles dialog box, type **WALL_4** in the Name box and **4"WALL** in the Description box. Click on the Add button. Next, you create another multiline style for the closet shelving.

6. While still in the Multiline Styles dialog box, click on Element Properties. In the Element Properties dialog box, select the 2.0 element in the elements list and enter a new value of **20** in the Offset edit box. Then select the –2.0 element and enter **16** in the Offset edit box.

7. Now click on Linetype, and then in the Select Linetype dialog box, select Dashed from the list of available linetypes. Click on OK to close the Select Linetype dialog box and OK again to close the Element Properties dialog box.

8. In the Multiline Styles dialog box, click on Multiline Properties and clear the Xs from the Start and End Line check boxes, and then click on OK.

9. In the Multiline Styles dialog box, type **Shelf** in the Name box and **20"Closet-shelf** in the Description box, and then click on the Add button. Click on OK to close the dialog box.

10. Save your drawing.

Now, in addition to the Standard multiline style, you have two additional styles. In the following exercise, you use these multiline styles to create the interior walls of the floor plan.

CREATING ADDITIONAL MULTILINE STYLES

1. Continue from the preceding exercise. Make sure ORTHO mode is on. First, perform a ZOOM with Center option.

    ```
    Command: Z↵
    All/Center/Dynamic/Extents/Previous/Scale(X/XP)/Window/
    <Realtime>: C↵
    Center point: 41',43'↵
    Magnification or Height <1.00> : 1.5x↵
    ```

2. Start the MLINE command by typing **MLINE** and pressing Enter at the Command: prompt. Respond to the prompts as follows:

    ```
    Justification/Scale/STyle/<From point>: S↵
    Set Mline scale <6.00>: 1↵
    Justification/Scale/STyle/<From point>: ST↵
    Mstyle name (or ?): WALL_4↵
    Justification/Scale/STyle/<From point>:
    ```

Figure 9.16

Floor plan with interior walls and shelf.

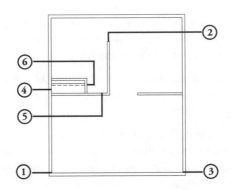

3. To respond to the current <From point>: prompt, refer to figure 9.16. Using the FROM and the ENDPoint object snap, pick at ①.

    ```
    <Offset>: @13'<90↵
    <To point>: @9'6<0↵
    ```

4. At the Undo/<To point>: prompt, pick a point near ②. This segment is too short right now, but you will clean it up later. For now, just press Enter to end the command.

5. Restart the MLINE command by pressing Enter again.

6. Use the FROM and ENDPoint combination again and pick at ③.

    ```
    <Offset>: @13'<90↵
    <To point>: @7'6<180↵
    <To point>: ↵ (Note the end cap on the wall.)
    Command: ↵
    ```

Justification/Scale/STyle/<From point>: *Use the FROM and ENDPoint combination and pick at* ④.
<Offset>: **@30<90**↵
<To point>: **@6'<0**↵
Undo/<To point>: *Using the PERPendicular osnap, pick* ⑤.
Close/Undo/<To point>: ↵
Command: ↵ *to repeat the MLINE command.*
Justification/Scale/STyle/<From point>: **ST**↵

7. You will now pick a new multiline style and justification.

Mstyle name (or ?): **SHELF**↵
Justification/Scale/STyle/<From point>: **J**↵
Top/Zero/Bottom <top>: **Z**↵

8. At the Justification/Scale/STyle/<From point>: prompt, pick at ④ using the ENDPoint osnap.

9. At the <To point>: prompt, pick at ⑥ using the PERPendicular osnap, and then press Enter to end the command.

10. Save your drawing.

NOTE

You currently cannot redefine or reload a multiline style after you create it. If you need to make changes to a multiline style, you must EXPLODE or ERASE all multilines that have that style, PURGE the multiline style from the drawing, re-create the multiline, and re-create any multilines that use the new style.

If you have saved the multiline style to a MLN file, you can redefine the style by changing the DXF codes in the style definition file. The changes affect only new multilines drawn with that style, however; existing multilines do not change. See *The AutoCAD Customization Guide* for information about DXF codes.

Editing Multilines with MLEDIT

Because multilines are rather unique, they have a unique set of editing tools. The MLEDIT command gives you a set of tools for cleaning up and editing multilines.

MLEDIT does not actually "cut" or break the multilines, but simply suppresses the display of the various multiline cut segments. This is done so that you can later redisplay (or "heal") the cut segments.

INSIDER TIP

To tell whether a multiline has cut segments, simply pick on any portion of the multiline. The entire multiline segment highlights, and grips (if enabled) appear at each multiline vertex.

When you issue the MLEDIT command, the Multiline Edit Tools dialog box opens (see fig. 9.17). This dialog box provides 12 tools for editing multilines. You can divide the MLEDIT tools into four categories: crosses, tees, corners, and cuts.

Figure 9.17

The Multiline Edit Tools dialog box.

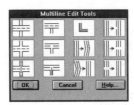

Crosses

The MLEDIT command's three cross tools (Closed Cross, Open Cross, and Merged Cross) enable you to clean up various crossing intersections. Figure 9.18 shows the various effects of these tools.

Figure 9.18

Closed, open, and merged crosses.

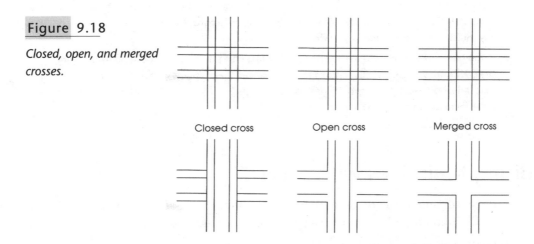

When you choose one of the cross tools, AutoCAD prompts you to select two mlines. AutoCAD always cuts the first mline you choose. AutoCAD cuts the second mline according to the tool you use.

For merged crosses, AutoCAD creates a corner out of matching pairs of mline elements. In other words, the outermost elements of the first mline create a corner with the outermost elements of the second mline, the second pair of elements in the first mline creates a corner with the second pair of elements in the second mline, and so on. If you leave an unmatched element in one of the mlines, AutoCAD leaves it uncut.

Tees

You use the next three multiline editing tools to clean up intersections. The tools behave in much the same way as the crossing tools. Figure 9.19 shows the effects of using the various tee tools.

Figure 9.19

Closed, open, and merged tees.

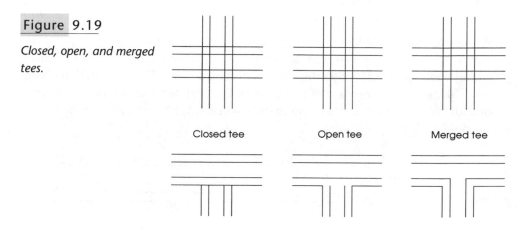

As with the cross tools, AutoCAD prompts you to select two mlines. AutoCAD cuts the first mline to make the base of the tee and cuts the second mline according to the tool you use.

Corners

The MLEDIT command's corner tools enable you to clean up corner intersections between two multilines as well as add and remove vertices from multilines. The corner joint tool creates a clean corner joint from two multilines. Figure 9.20 shows the effect of the corner joint.

Figure 9.20

A corner joint.

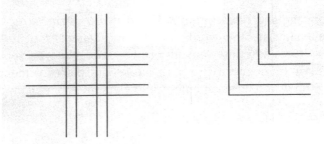

I NSIDER TIP

When you make a corner joint, make sure that each mline has the same number of elements; that's a good way to ensure that the corners miter properly. Doing otherwise can lead to unpredictable results.

When you create a multiline, AutoCAD places a vertex at each point you pick. The Add Vertex and Delete Vertex tools enable you to create and remove vertices from a multiline. Figure 9.21 shows the effect of adding a vertex. The top multiline is the original mline with a vertex at each endpoint. The middle multiline shows the effect of adding a new vertex and the bottom shows the mline after you use grips to stretch the mline.

Figure 9.21

Adding a vertex to a multiline.

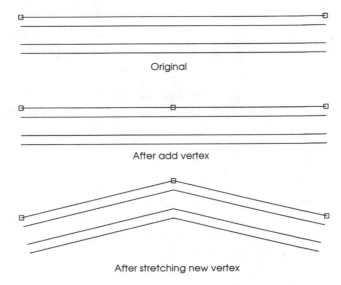

Original

After add vertex

After stretching new vertex

You can use the Delete Vertex tool to remove a vertex from multilines that have three or more vertices. If you select an mline that has only two vertices, AutoCAD simply ignores the pick and allows you to try again.

Cuts

The cut tools enable you to break sections out of the individual elements of a multiline. You can use the Cut Single tool to break a section out of a single element of a multiline. You simply pick two points on the element and AutoCAD cuts the portion of the element between the two points. The Cut All tool works similarly but cuts all the elements. Figure 9.22 shows the effects of using the Cut Element and Cut All tools.

Figure 9.22

The multiline cut tools.

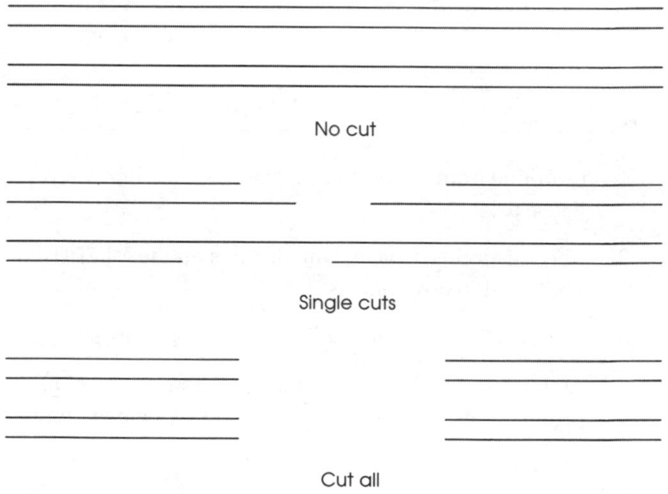

No cut

Single cuts

Cut all

AutoCAD doesn't actually cut the multiline itself—it simply suppresses the display of those sections. The multilines are still a single object. The Weld All tool prompts you to pick two points on a multiline. AutoCAD redisplays any cut sections between the two points you pick. The fact that AutoCAD doesn't break the multiline enables you to reverse the effects of the cut tools, using the Weld All tool. Figure 9.23 shows the effect of using the Weld All tool.

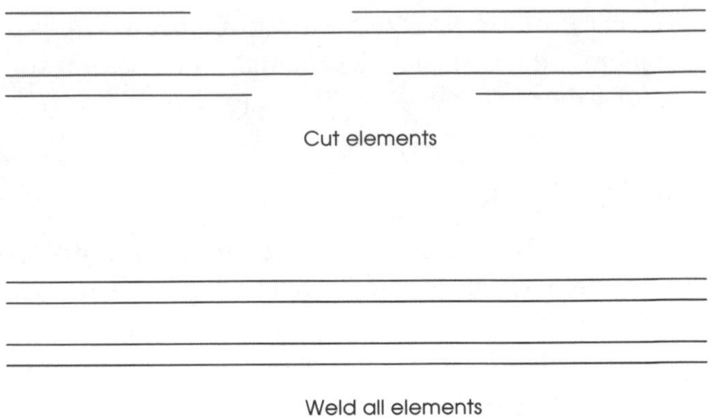

Figure 9.23

Welding a cut mline.

Cut elements

Weld all elements

In the following exercise, you use some of the multiline editing tools to create door openings in the walls of your floor plan.

EDITING MULTILINES

1. Continue from the preceding exercise. The PLAN layer should still be current. Refer to figure 9.24.

2. Choose Modify, Object, Multiline to start the MLEDIT command. The Multiline Edit Tools dialog box appears.

3. Double-click on the Closed Tee icon (top icon, second column).

4. At the Select first mline: prompt, pick the mline at ①. At the Select second mline: prompt, pick the mline at ②. Press Enter twice to end the command.

Figure 9.24

Editing with MLEDIT.

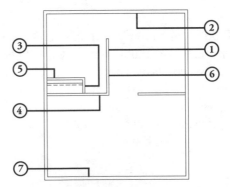

5. Restart the MLEDIT command and double-click on the Merged Tee icon (middle icon). At the Select first mline: prompt, pick the mline at ③. At the Select second

mline: prompt, pick the mline at ④. At the next Select first mline (or Undo): prompt, press Enter.

6. Next you use the Cut All tool to create some door openings. At the Command: prompt, press Enter.

7. Double-click on the Cut All icon (middle icon, last column).

8. Using the FROM and ENDPoint object snap, pick at ⑤.

```
Offset: @6<0↵
Select second point: @4'8<0↵
```

9. Using the FROM and ENDPoint object snaps, pick ⑥.

```
Offset: @6<90↵
Select second point: @30<90↵
```

10. Using the FROM and MIDpoint object snaps, pick at ⑦.

```
Offset: @3'<180↵
Select second point: @6'<0↵
Select mline(or Undo): ↵
```

11. You have completed making the opening in your mlines. If you want, you can cap the open lines using a running ENDPoint osnap and the LINE command. When you finish, your drawing should resemble figure 9.25.

This completes your work in this drawing.

Figure 9.25

Completed floor plan with capped openings.

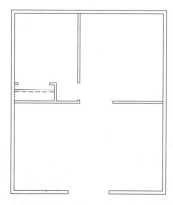

Mlines make it very easy to draw sets of two or more parallel lines, a frequent requirement when making drawings such as floor plans. The ability to set the distances between Mline elements and to assign various linetypes to the individual elements make Mlines very flexible. Mlines can be edited in a number of ways and their styles can be saved and recalled as needed. They are one of the most flexible elements in AutoCAD.

Summary

The complex objects that this chapter has discussed extend your AutoCAD drawing capabilities. Regions enable you to model real objects in 2D space and Boolean operations enable you to modify regions in ways you cannot edit other enclosed two-dimensional geometry. The resulting geometry would be difficult to achieve using standard, non-Boolean, editing commands. Multilines enable you to draw and edit sets of customizable parallel lines and make it easy to present parallel sets of lines in visually effective ways. They enable you to save significant amounts of time in the many drawing situations that require drawing and editing parallel lines.

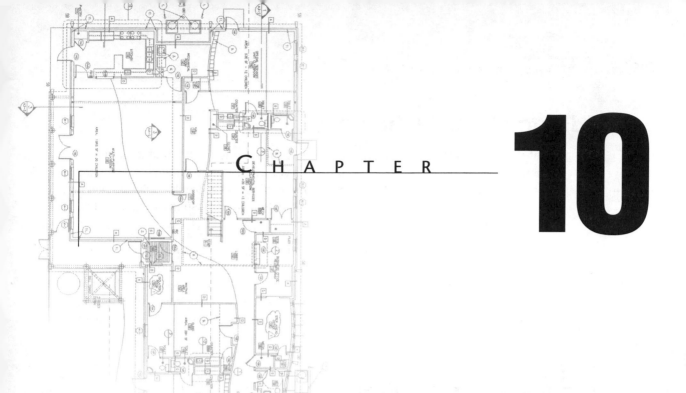

CHAPTER 10

BASIC OBJECT EDITING

by Francis Soen

Part of the normal drawing process involves modifying, or editing, what has already been drawn. Two broad classes of editing commands are available to you: editing commands that can be used on a variety of objects and editing commands that are designed for a specific type of object. This chapter concentrates on the general editing commands and processes, while Chapter 11, "Advanced Geometry Editing," concentrates on object-specific types of editing commands. This chapter discusses the following skills:

- *Renaming and purging named objects*

- *Selecting objects for editing*

- *Defining and using groups*

- *Changing an object's properties*

- *Erasing objects*

- *Invoking grip modes*

- *Undoing changes*

- *Resizing objects*

- *Duplicating objects*

Editing Named Objects

AutoCAD objects fall into two expansive categories: named and unnamed objects. Named objects are items that you name when you create them—named objects are referred to by their assigned names. Examples of named objects include layers, block definitions, and text styles. Unnamed objects are objects such as lines, circles, and arcs that cannot be assigned names.

Named objects can be physical objects, such as blocks, that can be edited with multiple commands covered in this chapter. Named objects also can be non-physical objects, such as named views or User Coordinate Systems (UCSs), that can be edited only with the specific commands covered in this section. In this portion of the chapter, you will be introduced to the editing operations used to manipulate named objects.

Renaming Named Objects

Sometimes you need to rename a layer or a block because of changing conditions or simple typographic errors committed when you initially created the objects.

To rename a named object, you can use the Rename dialog box (see fig. 10.1), which is invoked by choosing Rename from the Format pull-down menu.

Figure 10.1

The Rename dialog box of DDRENAME can be used to rename a named object.

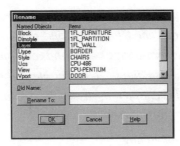

After you choose the type of named object to be renamed, a list of the existing objects of that type are displayed. You select the specific object to be renamed, type the new name in the text-edit box next to the Rename To button, and press the Rename To button to implement the name change.

NOTE

Layer 0 is the only layer that cannot be renamed, which accounts for why this layer is never displayed as part of the list of layers that can be renamed.

Deleting Named Objects

Sometimes you end up with unneeded layers or linetypes and want to delete the objects from the drawing.

The act of deleting a named object is referred to as *purging* the object. This action is performed with the PURGE command, which is invoked by choosing Purge from the Drawing Utilities submenu of the File menu. You can choose to purge all named objects or limit the command to a specific type of named object, such as text styles. Named objects that are not used, such as a layer with no objects drawn on it, are referred to as unreferenced objects. Only unreferenced objects can be purged from a drawing. Whenever PURGE finds a NAMED object suitable for deletion, you are asked to confirm the deletion prior to the object being deleted.

NOTE

Layer 0 can never be deleted, even if it is unreferenced.

Although saved Users Coordinate Systems, UCSs, views, and viewport configurations are named objects and can be renamed with the Rename dialog box, PURGE does not give you the option of deleting these types of objects. Instead, if you want to delete the objects, you must employ the command used to manage them. For example, you cannot use the PURGE command to delete a named view. Instead, you must use the Delete button of the View Control dialog box to delete a named view. Use DDUCS to delete UCSs and use VPORTS to delete named viewport configurations.

INSIDER **T**IP

If you have many unreferenced objects to be purged, the PURGE command could prove to be annoying because the system asks you to confirm the deletion of each object before the deletion is actually processed. A quicker way to purge a drawing of all unreferenced objects (except saved UCSs, views, and viewport configurations) is to use the EXPORT command (see Chapter 27, "Publishing on the Web"). The EXPORT command enables you to create a new drawing file and specify the "*" wild-card character as the block name to be exported. The "*" option specifies both that the entire drawing should be exported to the new drawing file and that all unreferenced named objects should be purged from the new drawing. The name of the new drawing created can be the same as the current drawing. In this case, you essentially replace the current version of the drawing with a new purged version.

In the following exercise, you will purge an unreferenced layer and rename another.

PURGING AND RENAMING LAYERS

1. Open the drawing MODIFY.DWG. From the File menu, choose Drawing Utilities, Purge, and Layers. When prompted for layer names to purge, enter an *. When prompted for `Verify each name to be purged?`, enter **Y**. Purge the BORDER and 1FL_FURNITURE layers, but *do not* purge the CPU-PENTIUM layer.

2. Choose Rename from the Format menu, and choose Layer from the Named Objects list (see fig. 10.2). Then choose CHAIRS from the items list. Enter **EXEC-CHAIRS** in the Rename To text-edit box, and then click on the Rename To button. Click on the OK button to exit the Rename dialog box.

3. Save the drawing.

Figure 10.2

Renaming layer CHAIRS to EXEC-CHAIRS.

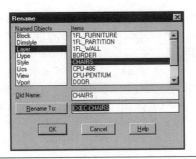

Modifying Named Objects

Some named objects, specifically text styles, dimension styles, and multiline styles, are also known as *named styles*. A style is really nothing more than a collection of settings that affects a particular type of object. In addition to being renamed and purged, named styles can be modified in other ways. Specific information on modifying each type of named style is discussed in detail in the various sections of this book that discuss defining and using the different objects. For example, Chapter 16, "Text Annotation," details the creation and subsequent modification of text styles.

The remainder of this chapter concentrates on commands that you use to edit the objects in your drawing such as lines, circles, and block insertions. Before you can learn to use specific editing commands, you must first lean how to select the objects you want to change, which is the subject of the next section.

Selecting Objects to Edit

When you edit objects, a variety of options exist when it comes to selecting objects for specific commands. Some commands, such as the DDEDIT command, prompt you to select a specific type of object or, as with the FILLET command, a specific number of objects. Other commands, such as the ERASE command, enable you to perform a general selection process that invites you to select as many different objects as you want using a variety of techniques. Any command, such as ERASE, that starts with the Select Objects: prompt enables you to use the general selection process, which is the topic of the next section.

Assembling a Selection Set

Many of the editing commands start by displaying the Select Objects: prompt. The Select Objects: prompt signals the beginning of the open process used to assemble a selection set. This process enables you to select the desired objects with a variety of methods, all of which are defined in the following list. Most of the selection options covered in the following list are invoked by typing a key letter or two at the Select Objects: prompt—the necessary key letters are capitalized in the option word itself. The general selection process is open-ended, which means that you can invoke any of the options listed as many times as you want and in any order that you want. All selected objects are highlighted on the screen as a visual confirmation. The highlighting of objects is enabled (default setting) with the Highlight option in the Drawing Aids dialog box (DDRMODES command). To signal that the selection set is complete, and to move on with the rest of the editing command you are using, press the Enter key or the spacebar at the Select Objects: prompt.

The general selection process provides you with a variety of options with which to select the desired objects:

- Picking the objects directly

- Using an implied window

- Using an explicit window or crossing windows

- Selecting the last object

- Selecting all objects

- Using a fence

- Using a window or crossing polygon

- Selecting the previously selected objects

- Using the multiple option

- Selecting groups

- Undoing the last selection option

- Removing previously selected objects

- Using Object Cycling

All of the preceding options are discussed in detail in the following sections.

Picking the Object

As you are prompted to directly select objects, the normal pointer is replaced with a box cursor, which is referred to as the *pickbox*. To select an object directly, position the pickbox over the object and select it. The size of the pickbox is controlled through the Object Selection Settings dialog box (see fig. 10.3).

Figure 10.3

The Object Selection Settings dialog box of DDSELECT enables you to control various aspects of the selection process.

Using Implied Windowing

When you position the pickbox over an empty portion of the drawing and pick a point, the system assumes that you want to anchor a rectangular window at that point. You determine its size by dragging its outline and then picking a second point (the opposing diagonal corner point relative to the anchor point). When the window is defined from left to right, then all objects completely enclosed in the window are selected. As shown in figure 10.4, using a window would result in just the circle being selected. When the window is defined right to left, it is referred to as a crossing window. In a crossing window, all objects that are completely enclosed in the window or that merely cross the boundaries of the window are selected. A crossing window is drawn with a dashed linetype, whereas a window is drawn with a continuous linetype. As shown in figure 10.4, using a crossing window would result in the circle and the three lines being selected. If you disable the Implied Windowing setting in the Object Selection Settings dialog box, then this facility is disabled.

Figure 10.4

Using a window versus a crossing window to select objects.

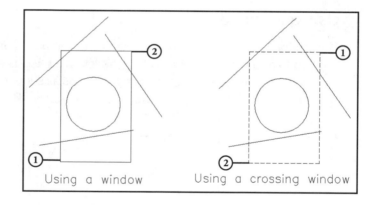

Using a window   Using a crossing window

Using a Window

With the Window option, you are explicitly defining a window with which to select objects. With a window, you pick two points to define the size and location of a rectangular window. All objects completely enclosed in the window are selected. Unlike an implied window, the first point selected need not be located in an empty portion of the drawing. Furthermore, it does not matter whether the window is defined left to right or right to left. The Window option is superior over an implied window when you deal with a crowded drawing and encounter difficulties finding an empty area of the drawing in which to anchor the implied window.

Using a Crossing Window

The Crossing option is similar to the Window option, except that, in this case, all objects that are completely enclosed in the window or that cross the window's boundaries are selected.

Selecting the Last Object

The Last option automatically selects the last object drawn.

Selecting ALL Objects

The ALL option selects all objects not residing on a locked or frozen layer. This option will select objects even if they are not visible in the current view. Be careful in using this option with the ERASE command.

Using a Fence

This option enables you to define a series of temporary line segments, which is referred to as a fence. All objects that the fence intersects are selected. The fence segments themselves are drawn as dashed lines as shown in figure 10.5. In figure 10.5, only the lines and not the circle would be selected.

Figure 10.5

Using the Fence option to select the lines.

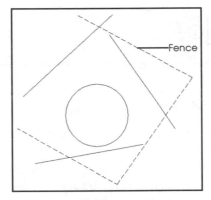

Using a Window Polygon

The Wpolygon (Window Polygon) option is similar to the Window option, except that, in this case, you define an irregular polygon-shaped window rather than a rectangular window. Figure 10.6 illustrates using the polygon option to select just the circle and bottom line. You may define the window polygon with as many points as necessary. The Wpolygon option automatically draws the closing segment back to the beginning point.

Figure 10.6

Using the Wpolygon option.

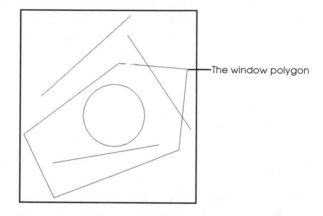

The window polygon

Using a Crossing Polygon

The Cpolygon option is similar to the Crossing option, except that, in this case, you define an irregular polygon-shaped window rather than a rectangular window. Figure 10.7 illustrates using the Cpolygon option to select the circle and two of the three lines.

Figure 10.7

Using the Cpolygon option.

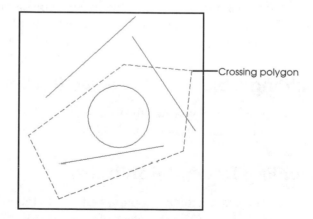

Crossing polygon

Previous

This option enables you to select the selection set assembled in the previous command.

Picking Multiple Objects Directly

Generally, as you select each object directly, the point is processed and any object that is found in the area covered by the pickbox is highlighted and selected. Then another Select objects prompt is displayed. With the Multiple option invoked, however, the pick points are not processed and the selected objects are not highlighted until you press the Enter key or the spacebar.

Selecting Groups

The Group option enables you to specify the name of a defined group. Groups are discussed later in this chapter, in the section entitled "Creating and Editing Groups."

Undo Option

The Undo option undoes the last option performed. Rather than typing the letter U, you can invoke this option with the Undo tool, located on the Standard toolbar.

Removing Objects from the Selection Set

By default, you work in the Add mode, so that any objects selected automatically are added to the selection set. The Remove option switches you to the Remove mode. In this mode, all objects selected are removed from the selection set. Undo is often used to remove the objects just selected from the selection set, but the Remove option enables you to select only the specific objects you want to remove from the selection set. You remain in the Remove mode until you either end the selection process (by pressing the Enter key or the spacebar) or by invoking the Add option.

Adding Objects to the Selection Set

This option switches you from the Remove mode back to the Add mode. By default, the general selection process starts off in the Add mode.

Holding Down the Shift Key

Instead of using the Remove option switch into the Remove mode, you can hold down the Shift key as you select objects already in the selection set (already highlighted). This action also causes the objects to be removed from the selection set. You can hold down the Shift key in combination with any of the aforementioned methods of selecting objects. Once you let go of the Shift key, you immediately are placed back into the Add mode, and all subsequently selected objects are added to the selection set.

Using Object Cycling

In a crowded drawing, it is sometimes difficult to select an object directly without inadvertently picking another nearby object. In such situations, you can magnify the view of the area, making it easier to select the required object. You also can use object cycling to ease this process.

To use object cycling, position the pickbox over the desired object once you are at the Select Objects: prompt. While holding down the Ctrl key, pick that point. Holding down the Ctrl key initiates object cycling, so an object occupying the area of the pickbox is highlighted. The next time you left-click (without holding down the Ctrl key), another object occupying the area of the pickbox is highlighted. If the highlighted object is not the required object, however, simply left-click again and the next object residing in the area of the original pick location is highlighted. Every time you left-click, the next object found in the area of the original pick location is highlighted until you cycle back to the first highlighted object. When the desired object is highlighted, you can end the cycling by pressing the Enter key or the spacebar, or by right-clicking.

As you continue to left-click and highlight the various objects, the actual physical location of the pickbox is immaterial. The location of the pickbox at the time you initiate object cycling is what defines the area that is searched.

So far, this chapter has discussed how to select objects for editing. The next section discusses how to search for objects that have certain like attributes. This process is called object filtering.

In addition to the options listed earlier, you can use several other options, including BOX, AUto, and Single. These options are commonly used by programmers defining new AutoLISP and ARX-based commands or new menu macros.

The selection options previously discussed are only usable if you choose the command first and respond to the command's prompt to select objects.

INSIDER TIP

Highlighting selected objects is enabled by the Highlight setting in the Drawing Aids dialog box, accessed via the Tools menu. Generally, highlighting is enabled, but it can be disabled inadvertently when you interrupt a macro or a program that manipulates the setting. If you see that objects are not being highlighted as you select them, check this setting.

The Object Selection Settings dialog box (refer to fig. 10.3) is displayed by choosing Selection from the Tools menu. In this dialog box, you can find the settings to control various aspects of the selection process. The following sections discuss these settings in more detail.

Dealing with Noun/Verb Selecting

The first option in the Object Selection Settings dialog box is Noun/Verb Selection, which is enabled by default. With this setting enabled, you have the option to select the objects to be manipulated prior to invoking the command you want to use. When the Noun/Verb option is disabled, you must invoke the command first and then select the objects to be modified. This option affects only commands that start with the Select Objects: prompt (such as the ERASE or LIST commands), which, as discussed in the previous section, signals the beginning of the general selection process.

INSIDER TIP

Working with the enabled Noun/Verb option can be confusing. You might consider turning the option off until you are comfortable with the process of selecting objects and using the various editing commands themselves. If you leave Noun/Verb enabled and accidentally select objects before choosing a command, simply press the Esc key to deselect the objects. Press the Esc key once more to get rid of the blue grip boxes. (These boxes are discussed in more detail later in the chapter.)

If you choose to select objects and then select the command, you are limited to picking objects directly, or using an implied window, both of which are discussed in detail in the next section.

Replacing and Adding Additional Selected Objects with the Use Shift to Add Option

The Use Shift to Add setting in the Object Selection Settings dialog box is disabled by default. As such, when you select additional objects in the Add mode of the general selection process, the objects automatically are added to previously selected objects. If you enable the Use Shift to Add option, any selection of objects after the initial selection process replaces the previously selected objects rather than adding to them. To add more objects to those previously selected, you must hold down the Shift key as you select the additional objects.

INSIDER TIP

This option is provided for compatibility with the way other Windows 95 applications deal with selecting objects. With AutoCAD, having to press the Shift key to select additional objects is just another unneeded step. As such, leave this option disabled.

The Press and Drag option is the next setting in the Object Selection Settings dialog box and is discussed in the next section.

Using Press and Drag

Generally, the Press and Drag option in the Object Selection Settings dialog box is disabled. Consequently, when you define a rectangular window—(whether it be an implied window, window, or crossing window)—you do so by picking an initial point to anchor one corner of the window. You then pick another point as the location of the opposing corner point. With Press and Drag enabled, you first pick the initial corner point and then must continue to depress the pick button as you drag the shape of the rectangular window on your screen. You define the location of the second corner point by releasing the pick button. Enabling this option makes the process of selecting objects with a rectangular window in AutoCAD compatible with the process of using a window to select objects in Windows NT or Windows 95 itself. Whether you enable this option or not is a matter of user preference.

Using Implied Windowing

By default, the Implied Windowing option in the Object Selection settings dialog box is enabled. If you disable this setting, the only way you can define a window or a crossing window in the general selection process is to choose to use the Window or Crossing window options. Implied Windowing is very useful and the option to disable it is provided simply for backward-compatibility with previous versions of AutoCAD. The Implied Windowing setting only affects the general object selection process. Even with this setting disabled, you will still be able to select objects with an implied window at the Command: prompt for use with the grip commands or with the Noun/Verb setting. Grips are discussed in detail in the section titled "Using Grip Editing Commands." This ends the discussion of the Object Selection Settings dialog box. In the next section, the usage of object filters is discussed.

Using Object Selection Filters

Object filtering enables you to search for objects based on certain attributes. For example, you could use object filtering to select all circles in a drawing with a specific radius. To invoke object filtering, type the command **FILTER** at the Select Objects: prompt. This displays the Object Selection Filters dialog box (see fig. 10.8).

Figure 10.8

The Object Selection Filters dialog box of FILTER initiates object filtering.

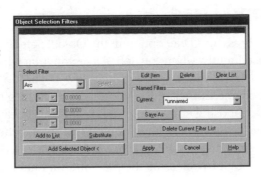

You can then assemble a list of the properties, also known as filters, with which you want to conduct the search. Then, by clicking on the Apply button, you can select a group of objects within which you want to find those objects that meet your list of characteristics. The following sections discuss how to define your list of filters.

Defining a Simple Selection Criteria for Filters

A filter can be a type of object or a characteristic of that type of object. For example, you can search for arcs in general or arcs that have a specific radius. The list of available filters is extensive and is displayed by choosing the Filters drop-down list. If you choose a characteristic of an object, you also must supply the specific value of that characteristic that you seek with the text-edit box, located below the filter list. For some properties, you can use the Select button to choose the specific value from a list of valid values. For other properties, you must type that value in the text-edit box.

After you select the property and its associated value (if any), click on the Add to List button to add the property to the list of filters. You then should select the objects you want to search by clicking on the Apply button.

To remove a filter from the list, choose the filter and press the Delete button. To edit the specific value of a filter on the list, select the filter and click on the Edit Item button. After changing the value of the property, click on the Substitute button to replace the old property with the revised property.

Defining a Complex Selection Criteria for Filters

The search criteria employed can be a complex set consisting of multiple filters. By default, when you assemble a list of filters, only objects that meet all the individual filters are selected. For example, you could choose to select only arcs that reside on the layer CURVES by choosing the Arc and Layer filters. In doing so, you assemble a list of properties that must be met; this is referred to as an AND conditional. When you assemble a list of properties, the system assumes that you are assembling an AND conditional. Other options do exist, however.

The most common option is to create an OR conditional. In an OR conditional, the objects must meet only one of the conditions, not all of them. For example, you could assemble a list of properties such that any object that is an arc or that resides on the CURVES layer is selected. You begin an OR conditional by choosing the **Begin OR filter. Then you assemble the various properties in which you are interested. You end the list of properties with the **End OR filter.

The list of filters can consist of AND and OR conditionals nested within each other, but for most users a simple search criteria consisting of a single filter is enough.

INSIDER TIP

To gain an idea of the properties that are available for a particular object, click on the Add Selected Object button and choose a single object. All the relevant filters and their specific values for the selected object automatically are assembled into a list. You then can delete the filters you do not need, leaving only the properties for which you want to search.

Saving and Restoring the Criteria for Filters

To save a list of properties you have assembled so that the list can be reused at a later date or in another drawing, type a name in the Save As text-edit box and click on the Save As button. The next time you want to use that filter, simply select its name from the Current drop-down list. To delete a named filter list, select the name from the Current drop-down list and click on the Delete Current Filter List button. Named filter lists are saved in the file FILTER.NFL, which is created in the working directory when you initially click on the Save As button.

In addition to searching for objects that share certain properties, you can link disparate objects together in order to select them as a group. This process is discussed in the following section.

Creating and Editing Groups

You can link disparate objects on different layers into what is referred to as a group. Once a group is created, all the member objects of the group can be selected by selecting one member of the group or by naming the group. Assembling the objects into a group, however, does not prevent you from editing the member objects individually. To create and edit a group, you can use the GROUP command, which you initiate by choosing Object Group from the Tools menu (see fig. 10.9).

The following sections discuss how to use the GROUP command for specific tasks.

Figure 10.9

The Object Grouping dialog box of GROUP enables you to create and edit a group.

Creating a Group

Every group must have a name. To create a group, you first type a name in the Group Name text-edit box. Then, click on the New button and select the objects you want to include in the group. To complete the creation of the group within the drawing you must click on the OK button in the Object Grouping dialog box. If you do not want to name the group, enable the Unnamed option, and AutoCAD will give the group an arbitrary name that begins with an asterisk. Unnamed groups also are created when you duplicate a group using commands such as COPY or ARRAY. To include unnamed groups in the list of groups displayed in the dialog box, enable the Include Unnamed option.

By default, any group you create is selectable. This means that the group of objects can be selected by name or by selecting a member. If you turn off the Selectable option before you create a group, the group will not be selectable. The individual group members still will be listed as members of the group, but they will be selectable only as individual objects. One reason you might want to create a non-selectable group is that you want to associate various objects together for use with custom programs (created by you or a third-party developer) that interact with the drawing database but are not for use with AutoCAD editing commands. The use of non-selectable groups is generally not done by typical users; so as a rule, always make your groups selectable.

A group can have as many members as you desire, and an individual object can be a member of more than one group. The group description is an optional piece of information that you use to better describe the contents of the group or the relationship between the member objects.

Selecting a Group to Edit

After you create a selectable group, you can select all members of the group simply by selecting any one group member or by naming the group. Whether all members of a selectable group also are selected when one member is selected is controlled by the Object Grouping setting in the Object Selection Settings dialog box. The Object Grouping setting can be enabled or disabled with the Ctrl+A key sequence. Even with the Object Grouping setting disabled, the members of a selectable group always can be selected simply by naming the group at the Select Objects: prompt.

To select a group by name, specify the Group option at the Select Objects: prompt (type **G** at the prompt).

Inquiring About a Group's Membership

If you ever forget whether an object is a member of a group or which objects are members of a particular group, you can use several buttons to find this information. Use the Find Name button to determine the group, if any, to which a selected object belongs. Select a group name from the list of group names, and choose the Highlight button to show all the members of the selected group highlighted on-screen. You also can use the LIST command to see the groups, if any, to which selected objects belong.

Modifying an Existing Group

To modify the makeup of a particular group, first select the group name from the list of groups. The following list shows the buttons you use to modify the group you select (refer to fig. 10.9):

- **Remove and Add buttons.** You can use these buttons to remove an object from or add an object to an existing group.

- **Rename or Description buttons.** You can rename a group or change the group's description by selecting the group name, typing in the new name or description, and then selecting either of these buttons.

- **Selectable button.** Use this button to change the selectable status of the selected group.

- **Re-order button.** Selecting this button displays the Order Group dialog box, which enables you to change the order in which the member objects are arranged in a group.

Deleting a Group

To remove or undefine a group, use the Explode button (not the EXPLODE command) of the Object Grouping dialog box (refer to fig. 10.9). Exploding a group dissolves the associations between the member objects but does not erase the member objects.

The previous sections have discussed the various ways to select an object or objects for editing. After you have selected the object, you can change its properties, as discussed in the following section.

Changing an Object's Properties

The properties of an object are defined as its layer, color, and linetype and, for most objects, also include its object linetype scale and/or thickness. You can use the Object Properties toolbar, the Properties tool off the Object Properties toolbar, or the Match Properties tool off the Standard toolbar to change an object's properties (see fig. 10.10).

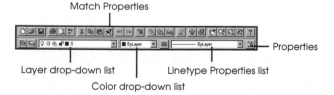

Figure 10.10

The Standard and Object Properties toolbar.

Match Properties · Properties · Layer drop-down list · Linetype Properties list · Color drop-down list

Editing with the Object Properties Toolbar

The Object Properties toolbar is used to change the layer, color, and linetype of selected objects. At the Command: prompt, select the object or objects you want to change. The layer, color, and linetype drop-down lists display the current settings of the selected objects. If you have selected multiple objects for editing, and a particular property varies for the selected objects, the corresponding drop-down list displays a blank value. To change a specific property of the selected objects, choose the appropriate drop-down list and choose a new setting.

NOTE

To use the Object Properties toolbar to change the properties of selected objects, you must have the Noun/Verb setting in the Object Selection Settings dialog box enabled.

Using the Properties Tool

You can use the Properties tool from the Object Properties toolbar or the Modify menu to change the properties of selected objects. If you select a single object, the Modify dialog box is displayed (see fig. 10.11).

Figure 10.11

The Modify Line dialog box of DDMODIFY is displayed if a single line is selected.

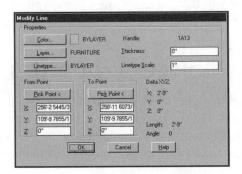

If you select more than one object, the Change Properties dialog box is displayed (see fig. 10.12).

Figure 10.12

The Change Properties dialog box of DDCHROP is displayed if multiple objects are selected.

The appearance of the Modify dialog box is adjusted for the type of object displayed. The top portion of the dialog box contains the general properties of the object, while the bottom portion contains the properties specific to that type of object. The lower portion changes depending on the type of object selected.

The Change Properties dialog box is, in effect, just the top portion of the Modify dialog box.

Using the Match Properties Tool

 The Match Properties command can be chosen from the Standard toolbar or the Modify menu. The Match Properties command enables you to change specific properties of selected objects to match the corresponding properties of a source object. The following steps are necessary to use this command:

1. Choose the source property, the object you want to emulate.

2. Using the Settings option, choose the properties of the destination objects to be changed. The default changes all properties.

3. Select the destination objects, the properties of which are changed to match the properties of the source object.

In the next exercise, you will create a group and change the layer property of one of the computers in the drawing.

CREATING GROUPS AND MODIFYING THE PROPERTIES OF OBJECTS

1. Continue to use the drawing MODIFY.DWG. Choose Named Views from the View pull-down menu, select the view named OFFICE-A. Click on the Restore button on the View Control dialog and then click on the OK button to restore the view OFFICE-A.

2. Select the computer on the desk by picking ① (see fig. 10.13) at the Command: prompt. The computer is drawn with a block, which is discussed in Chapter 12, "Creating and Using Blocks."

3. Note that the layer displayed in the Layer drop-down list is the CPU-486 layer on which the computer is inserted. Choose the Layer drop-down list and select the layer CPU-PENTIUM. You have just moved the computer to a different layer.

4. Press the Esc key twice. This de-selects the computer and shuts off the display of the grip points.

Figure 10.13

Modifying the layer of the computer in Office-A.

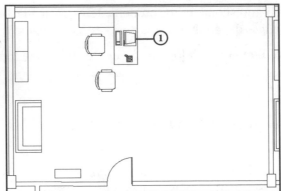

5. Restore the view OFFICE-D. Choose Named Views from the View pull-down menu, select the view named OFFICE-D. Click on the Restore button on the View Control dialog box and then the OK button to restore the view. Choose Object Group from the Tools menu. Enter PENTIUM COMPUTERS into the Group Name text-edit box and click on the New button. Pick ① and ② (see fig. 10.14) to select those two computers to include in the new group. Press the Enter key to exit object selection—the Object Grouping dialog box is re-displayed. Click on the OK button.

Figure 10.14

Creating a group consisting of two computers.

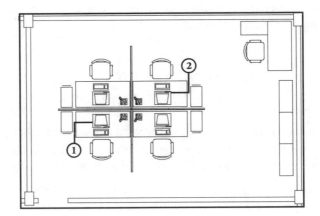

6. Choose Selection from the Tools pull-down menu. Make sure that the Object Grouping setting is enabled in the Object Selection Settings dialog box. Click on the OK button.

7. Pick ① again. Notice that both computers were selected. Choose the Layer drop-down list and select the CPU-PENTIUM layer. Press Esc twice.

8. Save the drawing.

Sometimes you might want to modify existing objects, as discussed in the previous sections. At other times, you might want to remove selected objects from a drawing entirely. The following section explains how to do so.

Erasing Objects

You can use the ERASE command to remove selected objects from a drawing. The ERASE command is found on both the Modify toolbar and the Modify menu. The command starts with the Select Objects: prompt, signaling the start of the general selection process. After selecting the desired objects, press the Enter key or the spacebar, or right-click to end the general selection process. Because the ERASE command does not require any further information, the objects then are erased. If Noun/Verb is enabled, you can select the objects first and then choose the ERASE command.

If you erase any objects by accident, you can undo the ERASE command. A specific command also can be used to retrieve erased objects. Type the OOPS command whenever you want to retrieve the objects removed with the last ERASE command without affecting any other editing performed since the last ERASE command.

In addition to erasing objects, we have a group of editing commands referred to as grip editing commands. These grip commands are the topic of the next section.

Using Grip Editing Commands

Grip editing is a facility that integrates object snap points with the most commonly used editing commands and then places the combined capabilities literally at your fingertips. With grips, it is possible to edit objects and select specific object snap points without ever having to pick a tool, use a menu command, or type a command. In the following sections, you will learn how to enable grip modes, activate grips, and make use of the various options available with grips.

Enabling Grip Modes

Grip modes are an optional facility that you can choose to use. By default, grips are enabled, but if you want, you can disable grips by disabling the Enable Grips setting in the Grips dialog box (see fig. 10.15), which is displayed by choosing Grips from the Tools menu.

Figure 10.15

The Grips dialog box of DDGRIPS controls how grips behave.

With grips enabled, you start the process of using grip modes by selecting the objects you want to edit at the Command: prompt. In other words, you do not initiate any commands. Instead, you simply select the objects by picking them or by using implied windowing. After you have selected the objects, the objects' grip points are displayed as blue squares. The color and size of these "unselected grip points" are set with the Unselected button in the Grips dialog box. The displayed grip points correspond to the control points of the objects, and for the most part, these points are the same as the object snap points for the various types of objects. The major exceptions to this rule are discussed in table 10.1.

Table 10.1

Specific Grip and Object Snap Discrepancies

Object	Description
Arc	Only three grip points exist for an arc: its endpoints and its midpoint. In contrast, object snap points include the center point and visible quadrant points.
Block Insertion	By default, only one grip point is displayed at the insertion point of each block insertion. However, if you enable the Enable Grips Within Blocks setting of the Grips dialog box, then the grip points of all the component objects are also displayed.
Elliptical arc	Grip points correspond to the arc's endpoints, midpoint, and center points but not to its visible quadrant points.
Mline	Grip points exist at the points used to locate the mline object. In contrast, endpoint and midpoint object snap points exist on each visible segment.
Mtext	Four grip points exist per mtext object, one at each corner of the imaginary box that surrounds each mtext object. In contrast, only one insertion object snap point exists per mtext object.

Object	Description
Spline	A grip point exists at every point used to define the spline, known as the spline's control points. Object snap points include only the endpoints.

As with object snap, grip points enable you to easily choose a very specific point on an object. After the grip points are displayed, you must choose one point to activate grip modes.

Activating Grip Modes

After you have selected the objects to be edited, and after the grip points are displayed, you initiate the grip mode commands by picking one of the grip points. The grip points affect the cursor much like object snap points do—the grip points act as magnets and pull the cursor into the box.

After a grip point is selected, it is displayed as a red box and is referred to as a *selected grip point*. The color used to fill in the grip box is set with the Selected button in the Grips dialog box. The selected grip point subsequently is used as the base point for the various grip mode commands: stretch, move, rotate, scale, and mirror. Initially, the Stretch grip command is activated, but you can press the spacebar to cycle through the other grip commands. Alternatively, right-click and pick the desired grip command from the menu that appears. The various mode options are discussed in the following sections.

Deactivating Grip Points and Commands

When you select objects at the Command: prompt, the grip points of the objects are displayed and the objects are highlighted. The highlighting indicates the objects have been selected. If you press the Esc key once, the objects will be de-selected (no longer highlighted) but the grip points will still be displayed. To erase the display of the grip points, you need to press the Esc key one more time. In previous versions of AutoCAD, a common procedure that was employed was to select objects and press the Esc key once so that the objects' grip points could be selected (much like snap points) during a grip command but not affect the objects themselves. You could also selectively de-select highlighted objects by pressing the Shift key and selecting the highlighted objects thereby leaving the grip points displayed. These two procedures still work in R14, but the new Autosnap feature makes them irrelevant because Autosnap automatically displays the snap points on nearby objects.

Another common problem that users run into using grips is that they accidentally select objects and activate the grip command mode by selecting one of the grip points. To exit grip command mode, just press the Esc key. Remember, in AutoCAD, pressing the Esc key always cancels the current operation. To de-select the objects and erase the display of the grip points, press the Esc key two more times.

Using the Stretch Mode

The default grip command is Stretch, which enables you to relocate the selected grip point. This in turn affects only the object or objects that are defined by the selected grip point. For example, if the selected grip point is the endpoint of a line (as shown in figure 10.16), then that endpoint of the line is moved to the new position.

Figure 10.16

Using Grips to stretch two lines.

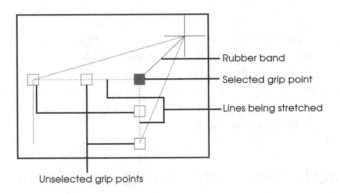

If the selected grip point is the endpoint at which two lines meet, then both lines are stretched to the new endpoint location. As you decide on the new location of the selected grip point, notice that the rubber band is anchored at the selected grip point. Thus, the selected grip point is referred to as the *base point* of the stretch.

Stretching Multiple Points at the Same Time

If you want to stretch more than one point at a time, you must initiate a modified procedure to activate grips. First, you must select all the grip points that you want to move during the stretching procedure while holding down the Shift key. Then, after releasing Shift, pick the grip point that you want to use as the base point of the stretching. This last pick activates the grip commands.

Using Relative Coordinates

If you know the exact delta-X, delta-Y, delta-Z, or distance and angle you want to apply to the selected grip point, you can use relative coordinates rather than picking the new location. You also can define the distance and direction of the stretch with direct distance entry.

The next grip command to be discussed is the Move mode.

Using the Move Mode

Use the Move grip command simply to move the selected objects to the new location. Unlike the Stretch grip command—in which only the selected objects that are controlled by the selected grip point are affected—all selected objects are moved with the Move command (see fig. 10.17).

Figure 10.17

The Move grip command moves all selected objects.

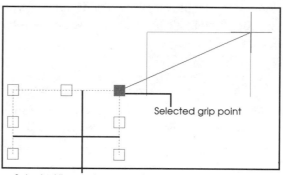

Selected grip point

Selected lines being moved

As with the Stretch grip command, the selected grip point is used as the base point for the move. If you know the exact delta-X, delta-Y, delta-Z, or distance and angle you want to apply to the selected grip point, you can use relative coordinates rather than picking the new location. You also can define the distance and direction of the move with direct distance entry.

Using the Rotate Mode

The Rotate grip command enables you to rotate the selected objects about the selected grip point (see fig. 10.18).

Figure 10.18

Grips can be used to rotate selected objects.

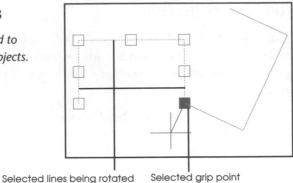

Selected lines being rotated   Selected grip point

You can specify the amount of rotation to apply to the selected objects graphically by using the rubber band or by typing the specific value. Alternatively, you can specify the Reference option.

To use the Reference option, you first must define a reference angle—either a real or imaginary line—by picking its two endpoints or typing an angular value. Then, you must specify the angle to which you want the reference line to be rotated by dragging or typing the angle.

INSIDER TIP

The Reference option is useful when you know the angle to which you want to rotate a known reference line but do not know the exact amount of rotation needed.

Using the Scale Mode

The Scale grip command enables you to scale the selected objects about the selected grip point. You can either type the scale factor or pick a point. Picking a point defines the length of the rubber band, which is subsequently used as the scale factor. The grip point is the static point about which the objects expand or contract. Just as with the Rotate grip command, the Scale grip command has a Reference option.

To use the Reference option, you first must define a reference length—either a real or imaginary line—by picking its endpoints or typing a known length value. Then, you must specify the length to which you want the reference line to be scaled. The second length can be defined by typing the new length or picking a point, in which case the length is the length of the rubber band.

Using the Mirror Mode

The Mirror grip command enables you to mirror the selected objects about the mirror line that is anchored at the selected grip point (see fig. 10.19).

Figure 10.19

The Mirror grip command enables you to mirror objects.

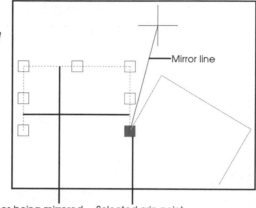

The mirror line is the line about which all the selected objects are flipped. Text and mtext objects also are flipped so that they appear backward. If you want the text and mtext objects to remain readable, type **MIRRTEXT** at the Command: prompt, and set the system variable to 0.

Invoking the Base Point Option

The Base point option enables you to relocate the anchor point of the rubber band. For the Stretch grip command, relocating the base point does not affect the grip point that is stretched. A Base point option exists in each grip mode command prompt.

Invoking the Copy Option

A Copy option also exists in each grip mode command prompt. When this option is invoked, the original objects are left untouched and the changes are made to copies of the originals. Invoking the Copy option also enables you to make multiple copies for each of the grip commands.

An alternative to specifying the Copy option is to hold down the Shift key as you pick the point to complete the command. Be aware, however, that if you continue to press the Shift key, the system uses the distance and direction from the original object to the first copy point to overlay a set of invisible snap points. (This process works in a manner similar to the SNAP command.) For the Stretch, Move, and Scale commands, the snap points are arranged into a grid, with one of the grid axes running from the base point to the first selected point (see fig. 10.20).

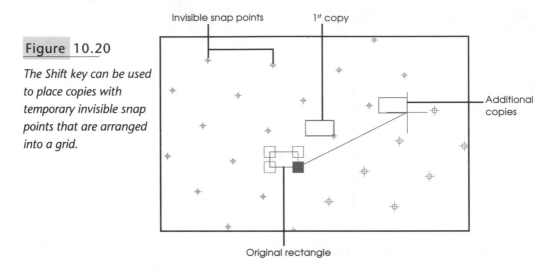

Figure 10.20

The Shift key can be used to place copies with temporary invisible snap points that are arranged into a grid.

For the Rotate and Mirror grip commands, the snap points are arranged into a circular arrangement such that the angular displacement between adjacent snap points is equal (see fig. 10.21).

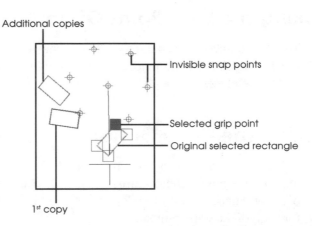

Figure 10.21

The Shift key also can be used to place copies with temporary snap points that are arranged into a polar configuration.

In the next exercise, you will use grips to make changes and additions to the office layout in the drawing MODIFY. These changes include rotating and duplicating a chair in the office layout and stretching the cabinet.

USING GRIPS TO MAKE CHANGES AND ADDITIONS

1. Continue to use the drawing MODIFY.DWG. Choose Named Views from the View pull-down menu, select the view named OFFICE-A. Click on the Restore button on the View Control dialog box and then the OK button to restore the view OFFICE-A. At the Command: prompt, pick the chair located below the desk and the other chair (see fig. 10.22). This chair is a block insertion, which explains why only one grip point is displayed.

Figure 10.22

Grips can be used to stretch the cabinet and rotate and duplicate a chair in this drawing.

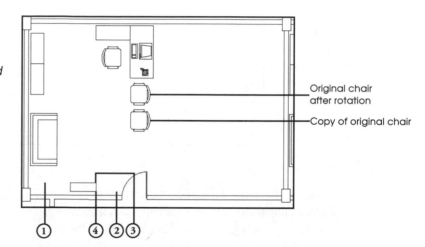

Original chair after rotation

Copy of original chair

2. Select the grip point. You have just activated the grip commands and the default command, Stretch. Right-click and a menu should appear on the screen. Choose Rotate from the menu, and type **180**. You have just rotated the chair 180 degrees.

3. Select the same grip point, and press the spacebar once. You have just cycled to the Move grip command. Now type **C** to specify the Copy option. Now type **@3'<270**. You have just made a duplicate, which is located 3' below the original chair. Press the Enter key to exit the Move grip command, and press Esc twice.

4. At the Command: prompt, use Implied Windowing to pick ① and ② to select the cabinet. Because the cabinet was drawn with four lines, it has grip points at the endpoints and midpoints.

5. While holding down the Shift key, pick ③ and ④. Holding down the Shift key enables you to select multiple points to stretch. Release Shift, and pick ① to activate the grip commands and the default grip command, Stretch. Type **@2'<0** to stretch the rectangle 2' to the right, and press Esc twice.

6. Refer to step 1 and restore the view OFFICE-B. At the Command: prompt, select the chair (see fig. 10.23), and pick the grip point to enable the grip commands. Right-click and choose Rotate, and then right-click and choose Basepoint. Holding the Shift key, right-click the mouse and select CENter from the Object Snap pop-up menu, pick ①. Right-click and choose Copy. Then type **90**, **180**, and **270** to make three copies. Press the Enter key once to exit the Rotate grip command. Press the Esc key twice.

Figure 10.23

The Rotate and Copy commands enable you to make duplicates in a polar (or circular) arrangement.

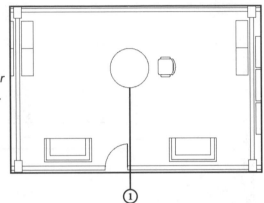

7. Refer to step 1 and restore the view OFFICE-E. At the Command: prompt, select the office cubicles on the left side of the room with an implied crossing window by picking ① and ② (see fig. 10.24). Pick one of the displayed grip points. Right-click and pick Mirror, and then right-click and pick Copy. Now right-click and choose Base Point. Then, using Midpoint object snap, pick ③. Enable Ortho mode and pick ④. By enabling Ortho mode, you ensure that you create a horizontal or vertical mirror line. Press the Enter key to exit Mirror grip command. Press the Esc key twice.

8. Save your drawing.

Figure 10.24

The Mirror and Copy commands enable you to create a mirrored copy.

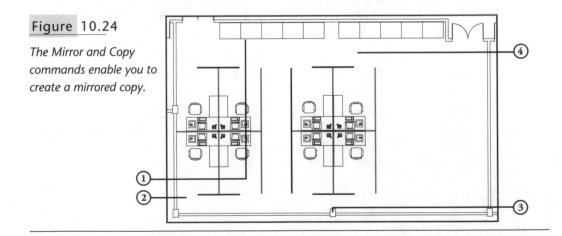

Undoing Changes

In previous sections, you learned to use the Undo tool on the Standard toolbar to undo the effects of the last command or to specify the Undo option of a specific command (such as the LINE command). The Undo tool subsequently issued the U command or option. A more powerful version of the U command also exists: the UNDO command, issued by typing UNDO: at the Command: prompt. The various options of the UNDO command are discussed in the following sections.

Undoing Multiple Commands

The U command is used to undo the effects of a command one command at a time. With UNDO, you can specify the number of commands to be undone by typing the number of commands you want to undo at the UNDO: command prompt. The REDO command undoes the effects of the UNDO command regardless of the number of options that you specify within a single UNDO. Often, however, you will not know exactly how many commands you must undo to revert the drawing to a previous state. In these cases, markers prove handy.

Leaving and Using Markers

When you specify the Mark option of the UNDO command, a mark (a device much like a bookmark) is placed in the Undo information file that is maintained by AutoCAD. Later, during the drawing session, specifying the Back option instructs the UNDO command to undo all the commands issued since the last time the Mark option was specified. In addition to undoing the commands, the Back option also removes the last mark. You can issue the Mark option of the UNDO command as many times as you want during a drawing session.

INSIDER TIP

Issue the Mark option when you think that you will make changes to the drawing that you are not certain you will want to keep. Then, if you decide to discard the changes, simply issue the Back option. Alternatively, you can save the drawing before you make the changes, and if you want to discard the changes, you can issue the OPEN command, discard the changes, and open the same drawing once again.

UNDO also enables you to control the scope of the UNDO facility and is discussed in the next section.

Controlling UNDO

The Control option enables you to specify how powerful the UNDO and U commands are. By default, AutoCAD keeps track of all the commands issued in a drawing session, which enables you to undo any number of commands you want. You can, however, choose to disable the ability to undo commands by choosing the None option. You also can limit AutoCAD's ability to undo commands to just one command. Typically, the only time you must deal with the options available through Control is when you are critically short of drive space—this is because keeping track of commands issued takes up drive space. In such situations, it is better to allocate more free drive space than to limit the ability of AutoCAD to undo commands.

Resizing Objects

In addition to the grip editing commands, a number of other commands can be used to modify existing objects. Two of these grip editing commands—Stretch and Scale—are used to resize objects. Other commands that can be used to resize objects are SCALE, STRETCH, LENGTHEN, TRIM, EXTEND, and BREAK, all of which are covered in this section. These commands can be found on both the Modify toolbar and menu.

Scaling Objects

As with the Scale grip command, the SCALE command is used to scale objects up or down in size. The major difference between the two scaling commands is that with grips, the options that you have for selecting objects are limited to picking the objects directly and using an implied window. The SCALE command employs the general selection process, which gives you more options for selecting the objects. After selecting the objects to be scaled, you are prompted to select a base point that is the equivalent to the grip point that you select when you edit objects with the grip commands. You then can enter a scaling factor by typing or picking a point, or you can specify the Reference option. If you pick a point, the length of the rubber band is used as the scaling factor.

INSIDER TIP

One advantage that the Scale grip command has over the SCALE command is that this command enables you to use the Copy option to scale and make copies of the selected objects simultaneously.

The next section discusses the STRETCH command.

Stretching Objects

As with the Stretch grip command, the STRETCH command is used to stretch an object's length by moving a portion of the object. Although the command does issue the general Select Objects: prompt, you must select the desired objects in a specific manner by using an implied crossing window, the Crossing window, or Cpolygon options. This is because the objects to be stretched must be selected with a crossing window of some sort. You can use only one crossing window per occurrence of the STRETCH command. If you define more than one crossing window in selecting the objects, only the objects selected with the last crossing window are stretched.

After completing the selection of the objects, you are prompted to select a base point or enter a displacement. The base point is the equivalent of the selected grip point in grip editing. If you choose to pick a base point, you also must specify a second point for the new location of the base point. As an alternative to picking a base point, you can specify a displacement.

The displacement is defined as the delta-X, delta-Y, and delta-Z—or the distance and angle from the base point to the second point, which is essentially the amount of stretching you want to apply to the objects. If you know the exact displacement desired, you can enter the displacement at the prompt for the base point. The displacement is entered as an absolute Cartesian coordinate or polar coordinate. Initially, the STRETCH command interprets the displacement as a point and anchors the rubber band at that point. You force the STRETCH command to interpret the numbers as a displacement by pressing the Enter key or the spacebar at the prompt for the second point. (In other words, do not define a second point.)

The STRETCH command moves all objects that are completely enclosed in the crossing window. Any objects not completely enclosed are stretched by moving the endpoints in the crossing window while keeping the endpoints outside the crossing window immobile.

INSIDER TIP

The Stretch grip command offers two advantages over the STRETCH command. The Copy option of the Stretch grip command enables you to scale and make copies of the selected objects simultaneously. In addition, STRETCH cannot be used to stretch circles or ellipses, and the Stretch grip command can.

The next section deals with the LENGTHEN command, for which there is no equivalent grip command.

Lengthening and Shortening Objects

Any open object, such as a line or an arc, can be lengthened or shortened with the LENGTHEN command. Table 10.2 details the options at the initial prompt.

Table 10.2

The LENGTHEN Options

Option	Description
Select object	The default option involves selecting an object. When an object is selected, its length is displayed and the initial prompt is re-displayed.
DElta	Use this option to specify the length by which the object is to be lengthened or shortened. Enter a positive value to lengthen the object, and enter a negative value to shorten the object. If the object to be affected is an arc, you have the option of entering a change in the arc length (the default) or a change in the included angle.
Percent	Use this option to define the change as a percentage, where 100 percent is the original length. Enter a percentage greater than 100 percent to lengthen the object and a percentage less than 100 percent to shorten the object.
Total	Use this option when you know the final length you want to the object to have.
Dynamic	Use this option to drag the endpoint to the desired location. In dragging the endpoint of the object, the alignment of the object does not change.

After defining the amount of change to be applied, pick the object to be affected. The endpoint nearest the point used to select the object is the endpoint that is moved, so favor the endpoint that you want to affect in selecting the object. Although the prompt indicates that you can select only one object to lengthen at a time, you can select multiple objects with the Fence selection option. Simply type **F** at the <Select Object To Change>/Undo: prompt, and define the fence.

In addition to LENGTHEN, another command you can use to shorten objects is TRIM. TRIM is the topic of the next section.

Trimming Objects

Use the TRIM command to trim an object to an existing boundary. You begin the trimming process by selecting the object that defines the boundary, the cutting edge. You can select multiple cutting edges. You then select the object to be trimmed to the selected cutting edge. If you want to select more than one object at a time, use the Fence option to select multiple cutting edges or multiple objects to be trimmed.

Any edge object, such as a line or a circle, can be used as a cutting edge or can be the object being trimmed. An mline object, however, can be selected as a cutting edge, but cannot be trimmed.

With the TRIM command, the result is dependent on the point you use to select the object being trimmed (see fig. 10.25).

Figure 10.25

The result of TRIM varies with the point you pick.

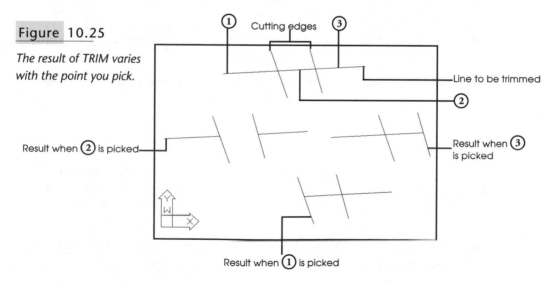

Starting from the point that is used to select the object, the TRIM command proceeds in one direction along the object until it encounters either an endpoint or a cutting edge. Then the TRIM command proceeds from the original pick point in the opposite direction until it encounters either an endpoint or another cutting edge. The resulting portion of the object is then removed. Under no circumstances can an object be trimmed in such a way that nothing is left of the object.

Using the Edge Option to Extend the Cutting Edges

By default, the object to be trimmed must actually intersect with the cutting-edge object to which it is being trimmed. If you want, you can bypass this requirement with the Edge option. Choosing the Extend setting of the Edge option extends the cutting edges, if necessary, so the object being trimmed no longer must intersect the cutting edge.

Using the Project Option to Trim Objects in 3D Work

The Project option is used exclusively for 3D work in which the object being trimmed lies at a different elevation (Z coordinate) than the cutting edge. In such cases, the two objects can never actually intersect, but they can appear to intersect in a particular view. Using the Project option, you can instruct the TRIM command to initiate one of three actions:

- Using the None setting, you can force TRIM to trim only objects that actually intersect with a cutting edge.

- The UCS option causes the objects to be projected to the current XY plane of the current UCS before trimming occurs.

- The View option also causes the objects to be projected but onto a plane perpendicular to the current viewing direction.

INSIDER TIP

If you press the Enter key without selecting any cutting edges, then all edge objects on the screen are automatically selected as valid cutting edges. In addition, an object that is selected as a cutting edge can itself be trimmed with the same TRIM command.

Not only can you trim objects but you can also extend objects and that is the topic of the next section.

Extending Objects

The EXTEND command is used to elongate an edge object to an existing boundary (see fig. 10.26).

Figure 10.26

You can extend a line by using the EXTEND command.

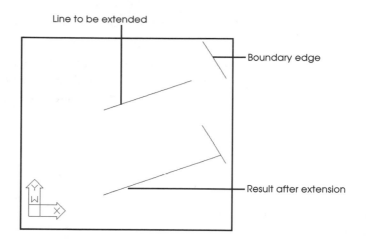

EXTEND is the complement to the TRIM command, so it has the same options. Instead of prompting you to select cutting edges, however, the EXTEND command prompts you to select boundary edges. The Project and Edge options are settings shared by the TRIM and EXTEND commands. This means that whenever you change the Edge and Project settings in the TRIM command, the EXTEND command also is affected.

Another command that can be used to trim an object is the BREAK command, which is discussed in the next section.

Breaking Objects

To remove a portion of an object, you can use the TRIM command or another command, the BREAK command. BREAK offers two advantages over TRIM for removing a portion of an object. First, you do not need any cutting objects to use BREAK. Second, the BREAK command can be used to break an object into two objects without removing any part of the two resulting objects.

After you select the object to be broken, the default option selects a second point on the object. Then the portion of the object between the point used to select the object and the second point is removed. In the case of curved edge objects, such as a circle, the removal process proceeds from the first point to the second point in a counter-clockwise direction. Sometimes, however, the point used to select the object is not where you want to begin the break. In this instance, you can use the First option to redefine the beginning point of the break and then choose the endpoint of the break.

If the second point (or the two points you pick for the First option) that you selected for the end of the break does not actually lie on the object to be broken, the point is projected back to the object and the projected point is used as the end of the break (see fig. 10.27).

If you simply want to break an object into two objects without actually removing a portion of the object, define the second point at the same location as the first point of the break. The easiest way to do this is to enter the relative coordinates @0,0 (or @ for short) as the second point.

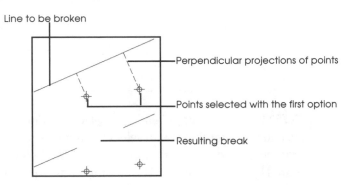

Figure 10.27

The first option of the BREAK command enables you to determine the starting point of the break.

Relocating Objects Using MOVE, ROTATE, and ALIGN

In addition to the Move and Rotate grip commands, the MOVE, ROTATE, and ALIGN commands can be used to relocate and/or re-orient selected objects. MOVE and ROTATE are found on both the Modify menu and the toolbar. The ALIGN command is only found on the 3D Operations submenu under the Modify pull-down menu.

Moving Objects

As with the Move grip command, you use the MOVE command to move selected objects to a new location. After selecting the objects, select the base point for the move. The base point typically is chosen as a point on one of the objects being moved. You then pick a second point, which is the new location of the base point.

In reality, the MOVE command simply calculates the distance and direction from the first point to the second point and then uses that information for the move. Picking the base point such that it is on one of the objects being moved simply makes it easier for you to visualize the end result of the MOVE command. As an alternative to picking a base point, you can specify a displacement.

Specifying Displacement

The displacement is defined as the delta-X, delta-Y, and delta-Z—or the distance and angle from the base point to the second point. Essentially, this is the amount of movement you want to apply to the objects. If you know the exact displacement desired, you can enter the displacement at the prompt for the base point. The displacement is entered as an absolute Cartesian coordinate or polar coordinate. Initially, the MOVE command interprets the displacement as a point and anchors the rubber band at that point. You force the MOVE command to interpret the numbers as a displacement by pressing the Enter key or the spacebar at the prompt for the second point. (In other words, do not define a second point.)

INSIDER TIP

The advantage of using MOVE over the Move grip command is the extra flexibility you gain with the general selection process employed by MOVE.

Rotating Objects

You can use the ROTATE command to rotate selected objects about a particular point, the base point of the rotation. After you pick the base point, the default option enables you to specify a rotation angle by typing the rotation angle, picking a point, or specifying the reference option. If you pick a point, the angle of the rubber band is used as the rotation angle.

INSIDER TIP

One advantage of using the Rotate grip command is that with the Copy option, you can make copies and rotate the copies simultaneously. Another advantage of the Rotate grip command is that by pressing the Shift key, you can make evenly spaced copies arranged in a polar configuration. On the other hand, the ROTATE command gives you added flexibility in selecting the objects to be moved by employing the general selection process.

Aligning Objects

The ALIGN command initially was conceived as a 3D editing command, which explains why it is found in the 3D Operation submenu of the Modify menu. In 2D work, however, ALIGN can be very useful. In effect, it is a combination of the MOVE,

ROTATE, and SCALE commands. ALIGN typically is used to align one object with another object (see fig. 10.28).

Figure 10.28

Using ALIGN enables you to move and rotate selected objects.

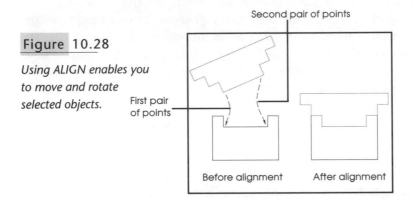

After selecting the objects to be aligned, you are prompted to specify up to three pairs of points. Each pair consists of a source point and a destination point. The source point is a point on the object to be aligned, and the destination point is the corresponding point on the object to which you want to align.

As you can see in figure 10.28, you must specify only two pairs of points in 2D work—simply press the Enter key when prompted for the third pair. The selected objects are moved from the first source point to the first destination point. Then the objects are rotated such that the edge defined by the first and second source points are aligned with the edge defined by the first and second destination points.

Finally, you have the option to scale the objects such that the length defined by the first and second source points is adjusted to be equal to the length defined by the first and second destination points. In effect, this scaling option serves the same function as the Reference option of the SCALE command.

Duplicating Objects

With the grip editing commands, you can use the Copy option to make copies of the selected objects. Depending on the specific grip command you use, you can create exact duplicates or mirrored, rotated, scaled, or stretched duplicates. You also can use the COPY, OFFSET, MIRROR, and ARRAY commands—and even the Clipboard—to make copies of selected objects.

Copying Objects

The COPY command is used to make exact duplicates of selected objects. After you select the objects to be duplicated, you are prompted to specify the base point of the displacement and a second point. The distance and direction from the first point to the second point is calculated and used to locate the duplicate objects. To aid you in visualizing the results, pick a base point on one of the objects to be duplicated (for example, the center of a circle). The second point then becomes the point on the duplicates that corresponds to the first point on the originals.

Defining a Displacement

The displacement is defined as the delta-X, delta-Y, and delta-Z—or the distance and angle from the base point to the second point. If you know the exact displacement, you can enter the displacement at the prompt for the base point. The displacement is entered in an absolute Cartesian coordinate or polar coordinate form. Initially, the COPY command interprets the displacement as a point and anchors the rubber band at that point. You force the COPY command to interpret the numbers as a displacement by pressing the Enter key or the spacebar at the prompt for the second point. (In other words, do not define a second point.)

Making Multiple Copies

Generally, COPY makes a single set of the duplicates of the selected objects. You can, however, use the Multiple option to make multiple duplicates of the selected objects. After you specify the Multiple option and choose an initial base point, the COPY command repeatedly prompts you to select a second displacement point to locate the duplicates. The Multiple COPY command is ended by pressing the Enter key.

Copying with Offsets

With the OFFSET command, you can create a copy offset a certain distance from the original object. At the initial prompt, you have the choice of entering the offset distance or using the Through option. To enter a specific offset distance, simply type the distance (or pick two points on the screen) at the initial prompt. Thereafter, you can select one object at a time to create an offset from the duplicate and choose the side of the original on which you want the duplicate made.

If you choose the Through option, then you must pick a point after you select the object you want to copy. The distance along a perpendicular from the point that you pick to the original object serves as the offset distance. The pick point also is used to control the side of the original on which the duplicate is made.

The copy made by the OFFSET command might or might not be an exact duplicate of the original. Table 10.3 lists the various types of objects you can choose with the OFFSET command and the shape of the resulting copy.

Table 10.3

Objects and Resulting Duplicate with OFFSET

Original Object	Resulting Duplicate
arc	The new arc is created so that it has the same included angle and center point as the original arc, but the arc length will change.
circle, ellipse	The new circle or ellipse is created so that it has the same center point as the original circle or ellipse. The radius of the new circle on the axis lengths of the new ellipse will be different from the original object's radius on axis lengths.
line, ray, xline	The new line, ray, or xline is an exact duplicate of the original.
lwpolyline	The lengths of the line and arc segments of the new lwpolyline are adjusted such that the endpoints of the new polyline are located along a direction perpendicular to the corresponding endpoints on the original open lwpolyline. For an intermediate vertex point, the new vertex points are located along a direction that bisects the angle between the segments on either side of the vertex point.
spline	The length and shape of the new spline are adjusted so that the endpoints of the new spline are located along a direction perpendicular to the corresponding endpoints on the original open spline.

Figure 10.29

Making copies of a circle, an arc, and an ellipse with OFFSET.

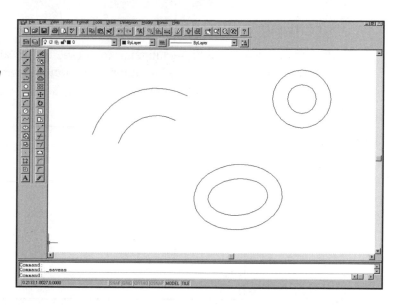

Creating a Mirror Image

With the MIRROR command, you can create a mirror image copy of the selected objects. After you select the objects to be mirrored, you are prompted to pick two points to define the location of the mirror line. The mirror line is the line, or axis, about which the mirror image is created. The mirror line itself does not have to be a real line.

The only option you have with the MIRROR command is whether or not the original objects should be deleted. The default is to not delete the original objects.

As with the MIRROR grip command, the copy of text and mtext objects will appear backward, like if you held a page of text up to a mirror. To prevent text from being flipped in the copy, set the system variable MIRRTEXT to 0 at the Command: prompt.

Creating Arrays of Objects

The ARRAY command is used to make multiple copies of selected objects such that the copies are arranged in rows and columns (a rectangular array) or in a circular arrangement (a polar array).

Creating a Rectangular Array

If you choose to create a rectangular array (see fig. 10.30), you are prompted to supply the number of rows and columns, the distance separating adjacent rows, and the distance separating adjacent columns.

Figure 10.30

Creating a rectangular array consisting of rows and four columns of copies.

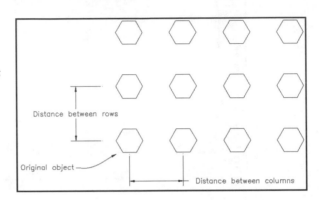

Generally, you type the row and column distances. You can, however, specify the distances with a window (referred to as a unit cell) by picking the two corner points of the window at the Unit cell or distance between rows (- - -): prompt. The height of the window is used as the distance between rows, and the width of the window is used as the distance between columns.

If you type a negative distance for the distance between the columns, the columns are propagated in the negative direction along the X axis; otherwise, they are created in the positive X direction. If you type a negative distance for the distance between the rows, the rows are propagated in the negative direction along the Y axis; otherwise, they are created in the positive Y direction. If you choose to use a unit cell to specify the distances, then the direction in which the rows and columns are propagated is determined by the direction from the first window point to the second window point.

Creating a Polar Array

If you choose to create a polar array, you are prompted to specify the center point about which the copies are made, the number of items (or copies) you want to create (include the original as one item), and the angle to fill (see fig. 10.31).

The angle to fill is the angle that you want to occupy with your copies. The angle fill is used to determine the angular separation between adjacent items. For example, if you specify 6 items and 180 degrees as the fill angle, then the angular separation between adjacent items is 180 divided by 6, or 30 degrees. If a positive fill angle is specified, then the copies are made in a counterclockwise direction; otherwise, the copies are made in a clockwise direction.

Figure 10.31

Creating a polar array of copies creates a circular arrangement.

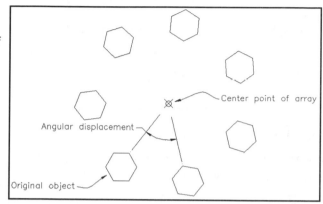

If you fail to supply the number of items (if you press Enter without typing the number of items) or the angle to fill (if you type 0 as the angle), then you are prompted to define the angle to be used as the angular separation between adjacent items in the array.

The final prompt gives you the choice of rotating or not rotating the copies. If you answer "Y," the default setting, then the copies are rotated about the single reference point of the selected objects as the copies are made. If you answer "N," then the copies are not rotated about the reference point of the selection set. The reference point of the selection set is determined from the last object selected. If a window of some type is used to select the objects, then the last object in the selection set is picked arbitrarily. The reference point selected is based on the type of object (see table 10.4).

Table 10.4

Point on Object Used as the Reference Point for a Polar Array

Object	Reference Point Used
block insertion, text, mtext	Insertion point
dimension objects	One of the definition points of the dimension object
lines, rays, traces, mlines	One of the endpoints
arcs, circles, ellipses	The center point

continues

Table 10.4, continued

Point on Object Used as the Reference Point for a Polar Array

Object	Reference Point Used
lwpolylines, splines	The first vertex point
xlines	The point connecting an imaginary line perpendicular to the xline to the center point of the polar array

INSIDER TIP

As long as you use the default setting of rotating the copies, the resulting polar array will appear to be symmetrical regardless of the objects selected.

Copying with the Clipboard

To copy using the clipboard, choose Copy from the Edit pull-down menu. This copies selected objects to the clipboard. Choose Copylink to copy the current view to the clipboard. Copylink copies all objects in the drawing but also preserves the current view of the drawing. As an alternative, you can use the Cut command to copy objects to the clipboard and remove them from the drawing.

If you choose Paste from the Edit menu in an AutoCAD drawing, the contents of the clipboard are inserted as a block with an arbitrary name. You will want to explode the insertion so that you do not have to deal with the arbitrary block name assigned by the Paste command. You cannot use Paste Special when the contents you want to paste are taken from another AutoCAD drawing.

You also can paste an entire drawing into the current drawing by dragging the icon of the file to be pasted into the current drawing.

See Chapter 25, "ActiveX Automation," for a more detailed discussion on how to use the clipboard to cut/copy and paste between AutoCAD and other applications. In the next exercise, you will create some duplicates using the ARRAY command.

CREATING A RECTANGULAR ARRAY OF DUPLICATES

1. Continue to use the drawing MODIFY.DWG. Choose Named Views from the View pull-down menu, select the view named OFFICE-C. Click on the Restore button on the View Control dialog box and then the OK button. Choose Array from the Modify tool-bar or the menu. Select the desk and chair, and choose the R (rectangular) option.

2. Type **3** for the number of columns and **4** for the number of rows (see fig. 10.32).

3. Type **10'** for the distance between rows and **–12'** for the distance between columns.

We are now finished with this drawing, so you may exit the drawing.

Figure 10.32

Creating a three row by four column array of copies with ARRAY.

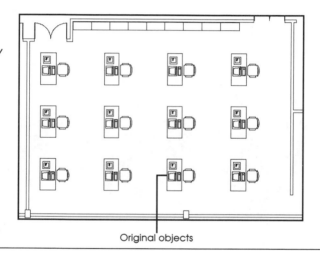

Original objects

Summary

In this chapter, you learned the general commands and tools used to select objects and then edit them. Grip commands give you access to the most common editing operations simply by selecting the objects to be edited and then activating one of the grip points. If you want more flexibility in selecting objects, you can use the command-line version of the various grip commands. For example, you can use the command-line command STRETCH or the grip command Stretch. In addition to the editing operations you can carry out with grips, there are quite a number of other editing commands, such as TRIM or EXTEND, that are available. The next chapter covers the other remaining editing commands not covered in this chapter and some additional bonus editing tools supplied with AutoCAD.

ADVANCED GEOMETRY EDITING

by Francis Soen

In the previous chapter, "Basic Object Editing," you learned the basic commands and tools needed to make changes to existing objects. In this chapter, you build on that foundation and learn about the following topics:

- *How to create chamfers from existing line objects*

- *How to create fillets from existing objects*

- *How to explode, or break apart, compound objects*

- *How to install and use the bonus editing commands supplied with AutoCAD*

- *What other object-specific editing commands are available and what parts of this book cover them*

Beveling Corners

If your design requires you to draw a beveled corner, use the CHAMFER command. The CHAMFER command is used to bevel corners formed by two nonparallel lines, rays, xlines, or line segments of a polyline. The command is issued by choosing Chamfer from the Modify pull-down menu or toolbar. To use the CHAMFER command, you first set the parameters defining the bevel to be generated, and then select the two line segments that form the corner.

Defining the Bevel

To obtain the desired bevel, you first define one of two sets of parameters. One set of parameters, accessed with the Distances option, enables you to define the beveling operation with two distances, one along the first selected line and the other along the second selected line. Both distances are measured from the corner, or intersection, of the two lines (see fig. 11.1).

Figure 11.1

The Distance option enables you to define the bevel with distances measured from the intersection of two selected lines.

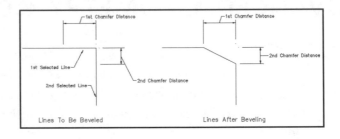

The other set of parameters, accessed with the Angle option, consists of a distance measured from the corner point along the first selected line and the angle of the new line relative to the first selected line (see fig. 11.2).

Figure 11.2

The Angle option enables you to define the bevel with a distance and an angle.

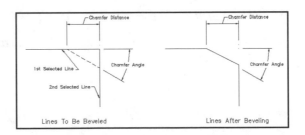

You can use either or both of the Distances and Angle options, depending on what design information is available to you. The CHAMFER command utilizes the most recently defined set of parameters. If both sets of parameters are defined, you can switch between them by using the Method option.

INSIDER TIP

When you select either the Distances or the Angle option and set the parameters, the CHAMFER command ends. You must repeat the command and select the two line segments to produce the bevel. Remember, a quick way to repeat the last command issued is to press the spacebar or the Enter key at the Command: prompt.

The two lines you bevel do not have to intersect at a corner point. CHAMFER automatically trims or extends the two lines to a corner point before generating the bevel line. A quick way to trim or extend two lines to a corner point is to use the CHAMFER command with the distances set to zero (see fig. 11.3).

Figure 11.3

Using CHAMFER with zero distances trims or extends two lines to a corner point.

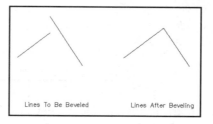

Lines To Be Beveled   Lines After Beveling

If the two lines selected are on the same layer and have identical color and linetype properties, the new bevel line is drawn with the same properties. If there is a difference in a particular property of the two selected objects, then the bevel line takes on the current value of that object property. For example, if the two selected lines are drawn on different layers, then the new bevel line is drawn on the current layer. If the two selected lines are drawn with a different color, then the bevel line is drawn with the current color property. If the two selected lines are drawn with a different linetype, then the bevel line is drawn with the current linetype property.

NOTE

If two objects are drawn on two different layers and are displayed in two different colors, it does not mean that the color property of the two objects is different. If the two layers have different colors assigned to them and the color property of the two objects is BYLAYER, then the two objects are drawn with the color assigned to the layer the objects reside on. Obviously, if the two layers have different assigned colors, the BYLAYER color setting results in the objects being drawn in two different colors; however, both objects have the identical BYLAYER color property. The BYLAYER setting also affects the linetype used to display objects in the same manner.

Dealing with Polylines

To bevel all the corners of a polyline simultaneously, specify the Polyline option and select the target polyline. Be aware, however, that when you generate a bevel line at any angle other than 45° relative to the selected lines, the result will not be symmetrical (see fig. 11.4).

Figure 11.4

Using the Polyline option simultaneously bevels all the corners of a rectangle drawn with RECTANG, but the result can be asymmetric.

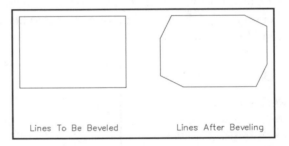

Lines To Be Beveled   Lines After Beveling

This asymmetric result is produced because the polyline segments are processed in the order in which they are drawn. To produce a symmetrical beveled shape, you must bevel one corner at a time. By explicitly selecting the first and second line segments, you control how much each segment is trimmed.

To Trim or Not to Trim

As previously stated, by default, CHAMFER extends or trims the lines to a corner point before applying the chamfer distances and/or angle. If, however, you want to draw the bevel line without any modifications to the original lines, choose the Trim option. At this point, you may choose between either the Trim or No trim settings. If you do not want the original lines modified, then choose the No trim setting. In the following exercise, you use the CHAMFER command to bevel the corners of a rectangle.

BEVELING THE CORNERS WITH CHAMFER

1. Open the drawing MODIFY2.DWG in the Chapter 11 Exercise folder on the accompanying CD. This drawing contains Plan and Elevation views of a part. Using CHAMFER, you are going to bevel the corners in the Plan view.

2. Choose Chamfer from the Modify toolbar or drop-down list, choose Angle, and set the chamfer distance to 1 and the chamfer angle to 45 degrees.

3. Repeat the CHAMFER command, this time choosing the Polyline option and selecting the rectangle in the Plan view. Note how all the corners are beveled in one operation.

4. Choose Undo from the Standard toolbar to undo the CHAMFER command. The rectangle is restored to its original shape.

5. Repeat the CHAMFER command. Select the two lines that form the upper-left corner of the rectangle (see fig. 11.5). Repeat the CHAMFER command, and then select the two lines that form its upper-right corner. The two top corners are now beveled at a 45° angle.

6. Repeat the CHAMFER command, this time specifying the Distances option. Then set the first distance to 1.0 and the second distance to 0.5.

7. Repeat the CHAMFER command, and select the lines that form the lower-left corner with ① and ②. Then repeat the CHAMFER command, and select the lines that form the lower-right corner with ③ and ④. Remember—the order in which you select the lines is important.

8. Save the drawing. Your rectangle should resemble the one in figure 11.5. (This drawing is used in the next exercise so keep it open.)

Figure 11.5

Beveling the corners of the rectangle.

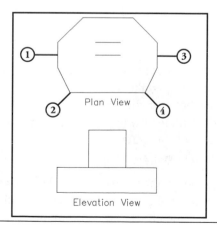

Filleting Objects

If your design requires that you draw a rounded corner, then use the FILLET command. FILLET is issued by choosing Fillet from the Modify pull-down menu or toolbar. With FILLET, you not only can create rounded corners between two lines, rays, xlines, or line segments of a polyline, but also simply draw an arc segment between any combination of two lines, rays, xlines, circles, ellipses, arcs, elliptical arcs, or splines. The generated arc is always drawn such that it starts and ends tangent to the two selected objects.

Controlling the Operation

To draw the arc, you first use the Radius option to set the radius, and then you select the two objects. As with CHAMFER, if the two objects are nonparallel lines, the lines are trimmed or extended to a corner point, and the arc is drawn such that the tangent lengths are equal (see fig. 11.6).

Figure 11.6

FILLET draws an arc joining two nonparallel lines.

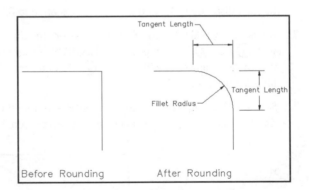

With the FILLET command (unlike the CHAMFER command), the two lines do not have to be nonparallel lines. If the lines are parallel, FILLET automatically draws a semicircle between the ends of the two lines, using the endpoint of the first selected line to determine how far to trim or extend the second selected line (see fig. 11.7). The radius of the generated semicircle is set automatically to half the distance between the two parallel lines.

As mentioned earlier, you can use FILLET for more than just working on lines. Figure 11.8 shows some of the possible combinations of objects on which you can use FILLET, and the effect of the command.

Figure 11.7

FILLET draws a semicircle between the ends of two parallel lines, using the endpoint of the first line to determine where to trim the second line.

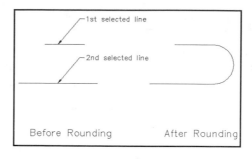

Figure 11.8

FILLET can be used with many objects other than lines.

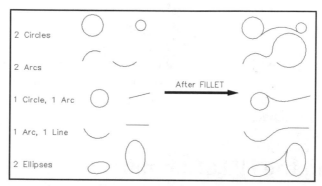

Using FILLET with any objects other than line objects (such as arcs) can produce surprising results (see the two arcs in fig. 11.8). The governing rule is that the generated arc must be drawn in such a way as to start and end tangent to the two selected objects.

If the two selected objects reside on the same layer and have identical color and linetype properties, the new arc is drawn with those properties. If there is a difference in a particular property of the two selected objects, then the arc takes on the current value of that object property. For example, if the two selected objects are drawn on different layers, then the new arc is drawn on the current layer. If the two selected objects are drawn with a different color, then the arc is drawn with the current color property. If the two selected objects are drawn with a different linetype, then the arc is drawn with the current linetype property.

INSIDER TIP

After you choose the Radius option and set the radius, the FILLET command (like the CHAMFER command) ends. To select the objects, you must repeat FILLET. An easy way to do this is by pressing the spacebar or the Enter key.

A quick and easy way to extend or trim two lines to a corner point is to use FILLET with a zero radius.

Working with Polylines

If you want to round all the corners of a polyline simultaneously, first choose the Polyline option and then select the polyline. If an arc segment separates two line segments, the arc segment is automatically removed and then replaced by the new arc generated by FILLET.

Using the FILLET Command

Generally, if you use FILLET on two objects that are not closed (such as on any object other than a circle or ellipse), the two objects are trimmed or extended as necessary so that the arc can be drawn correctly. If you do not want the original objects to be trimmed, choose the Trim option, and then choose No Trim. This Trim option is the same as the Trim option in the CHAMFER command. This setting is common to both commands, so setting Trim in FILLET affects CHAMFER, and vice versa.

In the following exercise, you use the FILLET command to round off the sharp corners in the drawing MODIFY2.

USING FILLET TO ROUND OFF SHARP CORNERS

1. Continue to use the drawing MODIFY2.DWG. Choose FILLET from the Modify toolbar or pull-down menu.

2. Specify the Radius option, and type **0.5**.

3. Repeat the FILLET command. Specify the Polyline option and pick ① (see fig. 11.9).

4. Repeat the FILLET command, and pick ② and ③. Repeat the FILLET command, this time picking ④ and ⑤.

5. Repeat the FILLET command. Specify the Trim option, choose the No Trim setting, and pick ⑥ and ⑦.

6. Repeat the FILLET command, this time picking ⑧ and ⑨.

7. Choose Trim from the Modify toolbar or pull-down menu. Select (as the cutting edges) the last two arcs you drew with the FILLET command. Trim the two vertical lines by picking ⑩ and ⑪.

8. Save the drawing, and close the file. You have finished rounding the corners and modifying this drawing. (You are done modifying this drawing so go ahead and close it.)

Figure 11.9

Rounding the corners with FILLET.

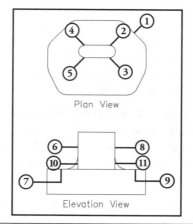

Exploding Objects

Several objects are considered *compound* objects—the objects themselves are composed of other AutoCAD objects. Compound objects can be *exploded*, or broken down, into their constituent parts with the EXPLODE command. You usually explode a compound object in order to modify one or more of its constituent objects in a way that you cannot do with the compound object itself.

EXPLODE is issued by choosing Explode from the Modify pull-down menu or toolbar. Table 11.1 lists the types of 2D compound objects covered in this book (with appropriate chapter references), and describes briefly how EXPLODE affects the objects, and some reasons why you would consider exploding the object.

Table 11.1

2D Compound Objects and EXPLODE

Object Type	Result of EXPLODE
Block insertions	An insertion of a block is replaced with duplicates of the block's component objects. Component objects originally drawn on Layer 0 are redrawn onto Layer 0.
	A block insertion is usually exploded because you want to modify the component objects themselves. This is usually, but not always, done in the context of redefining the block definition. See Chapter 12, "Creating and Using Blocks," for more information.
Dimensions	A dimension is replaced by a combination of lines, mtext, points, solids, and block insertions. Dimensions usually are exploded so that you can further manipulate their component objects. Generally, because exploded dimensions are no longer associative, you should avoid exploding dimensions. For information about dimensions, see Chapter 18, "Productive Dimensioning," and Chapter 19, "Advanced Dimensioning."
Hatch	Hatch is replaced by its component lines. An exploded hatch is no longer associative. Again, because of the loss of associativity, exploding a hatch is normally not a good idea. Hatching is covered in Chapter 17, "Drawing Hatch Patterns."
Mline	An mline is replaced by its component lines. In this way, you can work around editing commands, such as Extend and Trim, that don't work with mlines. By replacing the Mline object with its component lines, you then can trim or extend those lines. Mlines are covered in Chapter 9, "Creating Complex Objects."
Polylines	A polyline is replaced by a series of lines and arcs. If the polyline has a width, the replacement lines and arcs will have no width. Polylines are drawn with the PLINE, POLYGON, RECTANG, and DONUT commands, which are covered in Chapters 7, "Creating Elementary Objects," and 8, "Creating Polylines and Splines."
Region	A region is replaced by the edge objects (such as lines and circles) that define the loops (closed shapes) in the region. Regions are covered in Chapter 9, "Creating Complex Objects."

INSIDER TIP

An exploded object can only be returned to its original unexploded form by using the U or the UNDO commands.

Using Bonus Tools

In addition to the standard editing commands discussed in this chapter and the last, AutoCAD provides a group of "bonus" commands, some of which are useful for modifying existing objects. The bonus tools are automatically installed when you choose the Full install option when you initially install AutoCAD. You can add the Bonus tools by running the install procedure, choosing the Custom install option, and Selecting the Bonus tools.

All the commands covered in this section are located in the Modify submenu of the Bonus pull-down menu, or on the Bonus standard toolbar.

Extended Change Properties

To change the properties of objects, you usually select the objects at the Command: prompt, and then set the desired layer, color, and linetype properties through the Properties toolbar. The DDCHPROP2 command comes in handy for setting other properties. To use this command, choose Extended Change Properties on the Properties toolbar to display the Change Properties dialog box (see fig. 11.10).

Using the Change Properties dialog box, you can change not only the layer, color, and linetype properties, but also the object's linetype scale and thickness (for 3D work only). You can also change a polyline's width and elevation, and the height and style of text, mtext, or an attribute definition.

Figure 11.10

The Change Properties dialog box is displayed by the DDCHPROP2 command.

Multiple Entity Stretch

 The standard STRETCH command (not the Grip Stretch command) affects only the objects selected with the last crossing window or polygon. MSTRETCH, which is issued by choosing Multiple Entity Stretch, enables you to select the objects to be stretched with more than one crossing window or polygon. This command is designed to use only a crossing window (the default option) or a crossing polygon to select the objects. Another difference between STRETCH and MSTRETCH is that MSTRETCH does not offer a displacement option; you must specify two points to define the distance and the direction of the stretch.

Move Copy Rotate

You have the grip commands Move and Rotate, and by using the Copy option, you also can make copies with grips. If you need more flexibility in selecting the objects to edit, you can use the MOVE, COPY, and ROTATE commands. The MOCORO command, which is issued by choosing Move Copy Rotate, enables you to perform all three editing operations on the selected objects. After selecting the objects you want to edit, you are prompted to select a base point. This base point is the base point that is used in the Move, Copy, and Rotate operations. After picking a base point, the following prompt is displayed:

```
Move/Copy/Rotate/Scale/Base pt/Undo/<eXit>:
```

Choose the option corresponding to the operation you want to carry out. After the selected operation is carried out, the Command: prompt is re-displayed, enabling you to choose another option. To exit the command, choose the default option, eXit.

Cookie Cutter Trim

 To issue the EXTRIM command, choose Cookie Cutter Trim. This command is different from the TRIM command in that you need not select the objects to be trimmed. Instead, you simply select the object (a line, circle, arc, or polyline) to be used as the cutting edge when EXTRIM prompts you to do so. Thereafter, all you have to do is pick a point to indicate on which side of the cutting edge you want to trim. EXTRIM then automatically trims the objects that intersect with the cutting edge, removing the portion that resides on the side of the cutting edge you indicated with your pick point.

EXTRIM is especially useful when you have a closed or almost closed cutting edge defined (such as a circle or a closed polyline). In such situations, the point you pick to indicate which side of the cutting edge to trim really indicates whether you want the portions outside or inside the cutting edge trimmed. In the example shown in figure 11.11, the circle is used as the cutting edge. When you pick inside the circle ① as the side of the cutting edge to trim, you get result A. When you pick outside the circle ② as the side of the cutting edge to trim, you get result B.

Figure 11.11

When you use EXTRIM with a closed cutting edge, of the edge to trim, you can specify which side of the edge to trim.

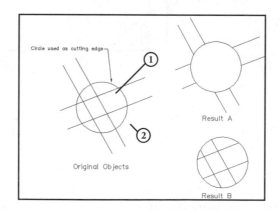

Extended XCLIP

 CLIPIT is issued by choosing Extended Xclip. Generally, you use IMAGECLIP to clip an image and XCLIP to clip an external reference or block insertion.

With both the IMAGECLIP and the XCLIP commands, the clipping boundary is restricted to a rectangular area or an irregular area defined by a polyline comprising line segments (no arc segments). CLIPIT combines IMAGECLIP and XCLIP into one command, enabling you to clip an external reference, a block insertion, or an image. Additionally, CLIPIT enables you to define the clip boundary with an arc or a circle.

NOTE

Blocks are covered in Chapter 12, "Creating and Using Blocks," and in Chapter 13, "External References."

Actually, CLIPIT approximates the shape of the arc or circle with a polyline that consists of a finite number of segments (see fig. 11.12). The number of segments is set when you enter a value in response to the prompt `Resolution for segmentation of arcs (large val = smooth):`. The higher the number, the more segments used to approximate the curve.

Figure 11.12

Approximating a curve with a polyline.

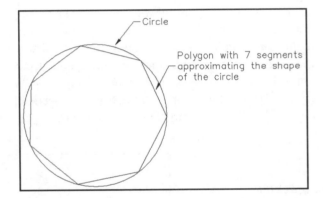

INSIDER **T**IP

If you simply press Enter, instead of typing a number for the resolution, CLIPIT uses a number based on the resolution of your display. This default number usually is adequate for acceptable results.

CLIPIT simply invokes the clipping option for images, blocks, and external references. This command does not change the object in any way. To restore the unclipped display of the object, you must use the Off option in either IMAGECLIP or XCLIP, whichever is appropriate.

Multiple PEDIT

  MPEDIT is issued by choosing Multiple Pedit. The difference between MPEDIT and PEDIT is that with MPEDIT, you can affect more than one polyline at a time for certain options. With MPEDIT, you can perform the following actions:

- Open closed polylines.

- Close open polylines.

- Change the width of the polylines.

- Fit curves through the polylines.

- Spline the polylines.

- Decurve the curved or splined polylines.

- Set the linetype-generation setting for the polylines.

The major omission in MPEDIT (compared to PEDIT) is the Vertex option, which enables you to edit, add, or delete specific vertex points. If you want to edit the vertex points of a polyline, use grips or the PEDIT command. For a thorough coverage of PEDIT, see Chapter 8, "Creating Polylines and Splines."

Trim to Block Entities

You cannot use the standard TRIM command to trim objects to component objects of an insertion of a block. The bonus command TRMBLK, which is issued by choosing Trim to Block Entities, enables you to select certain types of objects within an insertion of a block, as the cutting objects for the TRIM command. As with the EXTBLK command, some limitations exist as to the types of component objects of an insertion that you can select to use as cutting edges. If you are dealing with a uniformly scaled block insertion (X, Y, and Z scales are equal), you only can select lines, circles, arcs, text, and mtext objects. With non-uniformly scaled block insertions, you only can select lines. Unlike the TRIM command, TRMBLK does not have the Edge or Project options.

Extend to Block Entities

You cannot use the standard EXTEND command to extend objects to component objects of an insertion of a block. The bonus command EXTBLK, which is issued by choosing Extend to Block Entities, enables you to select certain types of objects within an insertion of a block, as the boundary objects for the EXTEND command. There are, however, some limitations as to the types of component objects of an insertion that you can select to use as boundary objects. If you are dealing with a uniformly scaled block insertion (X, Y, and Z scales are equal), you only can select lines, circles, arcs, text, and mtext objects. With non-uniformly scaled block insertions, you only can select lines. Unlike the EXTEND command, EXTBLK does not have the Edge or Project options.

Modifying Specific Types of Objects

Some objects have an associated editing command to enable you to perform certain modifications to that specific type of object. This section covers these object-specific editing commands, which are issued from the Objects submenu of the Modify pull-down menu. To fully understand how or when each editing command is used, you might need to read the chapter in which the specific object type is covered in detail.

Editing a Hatch

The HATCHEDIT command enables you to modify the parameters of an associative hatch object. Choosing Hatch from the Objects submenu issues the HATCHEDIT command and displays the Hatchedit dialog box (see fig. 11.13).

Figure 11.13

The dialog box of HATCHEDIT.

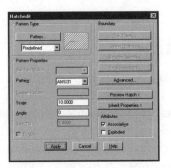

Using the Hatchedit dialog box, you can change the pattern or any of the other parameters that govern the generation of the hatch. You can even remove the associativity or even explode the hatch object (though neither is recommended). Drawing and editing hatch objects are covered in detail in Chapter 17, "Drawing Hatch Patterns."

In the following exercise, you use some of the bonus commands to complete the landscaping design for a building.

EDITING LANDSCAPE WITH THE BONUS COMMANDS

1. Open the drawing LANDSCAPE.DWG found in the Chapter 11 Exercise folder of the accompanying CD. Choose Named Views from the View menu. Restore the view ENTRANCE.

2. Choose Cookie Cutter Trim from the Modify submenu of the Bonus menu. Pick ① (see fig. 11.14) to select the rectangular polyline as the cutting edge. Pick ② as the side to trim on. All the lines are then trimmed back to the polyline (see fig. 11.15).

Figure 11.14

The pick points needed for the various bonus commands to trim lines, make copies, and stretch objects.

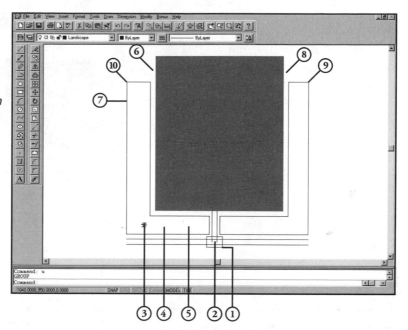

3. Choose Named Views from the View menu. Restore the view FRONT-LAWN. Choose Move Copy Rotate from the Modify submenu of the Bonus menu. Pick ③ to select the tree as the object to be edited. The tree is a block insertion and as such, is a single object, not a collection of lines. You will learn about blocks in Chapter 12. Press the Enter key to end the selection process. Right-click and choose Intersection and pick the center of the tree as the base point.

4. Specify the Copy option and pick ④ as the second point of displacement. Pick ⑤ as the second point of displacement to make a second copy. Press the Enter key to exit the Copy option.

5. Specify the Scale option. Enlarge the tree to approximately twice its original size by dragging its shape. Figure 11.15 shows what the trees should look like. Press the Enter key to end the command.

6. Choose Named Views from the View menu and restore the view ALL. Choose Multiple Entity Stretch from the Modify submenu of the Bonus menu.

7. Pick ⑥ and ⑦ to define the first crossing window. Pick ⑧ and ⑨ to define the second crossing window. Press the Enter key to end the selection process.

8. Right-click and choose Intersection. Pick ⑩ to select the endpoint of the line. Type @90<90 to define the second point of the stretch. Figure 11.15 shows the end result of the Multiple Entity Stretch command.

9. Save the drawing. You are done editing the drawing so you may exit the drawing.

Figure 11.15

The results of applying the Cookie Cutter Trim, Move Copy Rotate, and Multiple Entity Stretch commands.

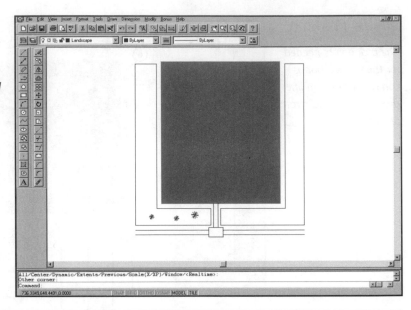

Editing Attribute Values

There are two editing commands available that are to be used specifically on attribute objects within an insertion of a block. The commands are DDATTE and ATTEDIT, both of which are discussed in the following sections.

Using DDATTE on Attributes

If you want to change the text values of variable attributes that are part of an inserted block, use the DDATTE command, which is issued by choosing Single from the Attribute submenu. After selecting the block insertion, the Edit Attributes dialog box is displayed. It shows the attribute prompts and the current text values of the attributes (see fig. 11.16).

Figure 11.16

The Edit Attributes dialog box is displayed by the DDATTE command.

If more attributes exist than can be displayed in the dialog box, use the Next and Previous buttons to display the additional sets of attributes.

Using ATTEDIT on Attributes

Whereas DDATTE enables you to change the text values of attributes, the ATTEDIT command enables you to change other properties of inserted attributes. ATTEDIT is issued by selecting Global from the Attribute submenu. You are asked whether you want to edit attributes one at a time. If you answer No, you can perform a text search-and-replace on the selected attributes. If you answer Yes to editing attributes one at a time, you can change the value, position, height, rotation angle, style, and color of the selected attributes.

Whether you answer Yes or No, you also have the option of filtering the selected attributes by block name, attribute tag name, or attribute value. The default value for all three filters is an asterisk (*), which indicates that no filters should be used and that the attributes the user selects are to be accepted.

If you are not familiar with attributes, see Chapter 12, "Creating and Using Blocks," for complete coverage of attributes and their use in block insertions.

Editing External References

There are two editing commands available that are to be used specifically on external references. The commands are XBIND and XCLIP, both of which are discussed in the following sections.

Binding External References

To import or bind a block, dimension style, layer, linetype, or text style defined in an external reference, use the XBIND command. XBIND is issued by choosing Bind from the External Reference submenu. The Xbind dialog box (see fig. 11.17) displays all external references and the objects that can be imported from each external reference.

To clip (or hide) a portion of an inserted block or external reference, issue the XCLIP command by choosing Clip from the Object submenu. With XCLIP, you define a rectangular or irregular polyline clipping boundary for the selected block insertion or external reference. The portion of the block insertion and external reference outside the clipping boundary then becomes invisible. XCLIP also enables you to turn clipping on or off, or display or delete the clipping boundary of the selected object. One option, Clipdepth, is designed for use in 3D drawings.

Figure 11.17

*A typical Xbind dialog box
displays the external
references and the objects
that can be imported from
them.*

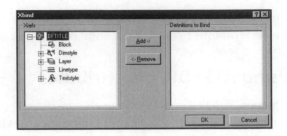

You can display the clipping boundaries of all block insertions and external references by turning on the system variable XCLIPFRAME. XCLIPFRAME is accessed by choosing Frame from the External Reference submenu.

For additional information about blocks and external references, see Chapters 12 and 13, respectively.

Editing Images

There are three editing commands available that are to be used specifically on images. The commands are IMAGECLIP, IMAGEADJUST, and TRANSPARENCY. In addition to the commands, the system variables IMAGEFRAME and IMAGEQUALITY affects images. The commands and system variable are discussed in the following sections.

Clipping Images

You can clip portions of an image also. The equivalent of XCLIP for images is IMAGECLIP, which is issued by choosing Image Clip from the Object submenu. With IMAGECLIP, you define a new rectangular or irregular polyline clipping boundary, or turn on or off the clipping boundary, to delete the clipping boundary. To display the clipping frame of all images, turn on the system variable IMAGEFRAME by choosing Frame from the Image submenu.

Adjusting the Image

Several additional editing commands are available in the Image submenu. Choosing Adjust issues the IMAGEADJUST command and displays the Image Adjust dialog box (see fig. 11.18), in which you can adjust the brightness, contrast, and fade settings of the selected image.

Figure 11.18

The Image Adjust dialog box is displayed by the IMAGEADJUST command.

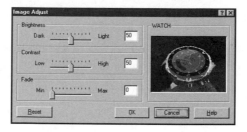

You can accelerate the display of images by setting the system variable IMAGEQUALITY to the Draft setting. IMAGEQUALITY, accessed by choosing Quality from the Image submenu, affects only the display of images, not the plotting of images; images are always plotted at the High quality setting.

Controlling Transparency

Some image file formats support a transparency setting for pixels. When transparency is enabled, the graphics on the display show through the transparent pixels of the overlaid image. By default, images are inserted with transparency off. You can turn this setting on or off for the selected images by using the TRANSPARENCY command, issued by choosing Transparency from the Image submenu.

Editing Multilines

The MLEDIT command is designed specifically to enable you to perform specialized editing operations on mline objects. To issue the MLEDIT command, choose Multiline from the Objects submenu. Figure 11.19 shows the Multiline Edit Tools dialog box.

Figure 11.19

The Multiline Edit Tools dialog box is displayed by the MLEDIT command.

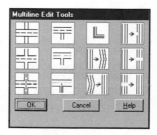

With MLEDIT, you can clean up various types of intersections of two mlines, remove or add a vertex point in an mline, and insert or heal breaks in an mline. Mlines are covered in detail in Chapter 9, "Creating Complex Objects."

Editing Polylines

PEDIT is designed for polylines and is issued by choosing Polyline from the Object submenu. With PEDIT, you can accomplish the following tasks:

- Create a polyline from a selected line or arc.
- Close an open polyline (Close option) or open a closed polyline (Open option).
- Join additional segments to the selected polyline (Join option).
- Change the polyline's width (Width option).
- Set the polyline's Ltype generation setting (Ltype gen option).
- Fit a curve to the polyline (Fit option).
- Fit a spline to the polyline (Spline option).
- Delete the curve or spline fitted to the polyline (Decurve option).
- Move, delete, or add vertex points in the polyline (Vertex option).

Polylines are covered in detail in Chapter 8, "Creating Polylines and Splines."

Editing Splines

SPLINEDIT is designed for splines and is issued by choosing Spline from the Objects submenu. With SPLINEDIT, you can accomplish the following tasks:

- Edit the fit points of the spline (Fit Data option).
- Open or close a spline (Open and Close options).
- Move the vertex points of the spline (Move option).
- Control the number or weighting of the control points (Refine option).
- Reverse the direction of the spline (Reverse option).

Splines are covered in detail in Chapter 8, "Creating Polylines and Splines."

Editing Text and Mtext

DDEDIT, designed to edit text and mtext objects, is issued by choosing Text from the Objects submenu. If a text object is selected, a line text editor is displayed. If an mtext object is selected, the Multiline Text Editor dialog box is displayed. The drawing and editing of text is covered in detail in Chapter 16, "Text Annotation."

Summary

This completes the discussion of the general editing commands available to you. This chapter also introduced you to the available object-specific editing commands. To learn more about how and when to create and edit the objects discussed with the object-specific editing commands, please refer to the chapters cited in the text. In the next chapter, you learn how to create and use blocks, an important productivity tool.

CREATING AND USING BLOCKS

by Bill Burchard

Blocks are a very powerful feature of AutoCAD. They enable you to define an object or collection of objects that can be inserted into a drawing over and over, without having to redraw the objects again from scratch. They provide the capability to significantly reduce a drawing's file size. More importantly, although a drawing may contain hundreds of insertions of a particular block, if it becomes necessary to edit the blocks, AutoCAD requires only that you edit the original block definition. Once redefined, the hundreds of instances of the inserted block will automatically be updated. The new changes will appear instantly. Additionally, attributes can be attached to a block, providing a means to create, and then extract, useful data unique to a particular block insertion.

To use the power of blocks to their fullest capabilities, it is necessary to first understand the nature of blocks. By understanding how blocks work, and how to properly manage blocks, you will learn how to make AutoCAD do tedious, repetitious tasks automatically, thereby increasing your productivity.

This chapter discusses the following subjects:

- The importance of understanding block concepts
- What happens to AutoCAD's database when a block is defined
- The importance of current UCS when defining a block
- Various methods of inserting blocks
- How AutoCAD uses the block table to create the insert object
- The effect of creating blocks on a normal layer
- The effect of creating blocks on layer 0
- The advantage of creating complex blocks from simpler blocks
- The problem of redefining nested blocks with INSERT=
- The importance of managing blocks in block libraries
- Creating a block library from existing block definitions
- Inserting blocks from a block library using drag and drop
- Creating an Image Tile Menu for graphically selecting objects from block libraries

Understanding Blocks

A *block* is a collection of individual objects combined into a larger single object. Think of the block as the parent of a family, and the individual objects as the parent's children. Although the children have identities of their own (color, layer, and linetype), they are also under the control of their parent, which also has its own color, layer, and linetype properties.

The fact that both the block (parent) and its individual objects (children) have their own color, layer, and linetype properties makes it important to understand how these properties are affected by certain conditions. For example, assume that a block has been created from several child objects, and that each child object was originally created on its own layer. The layers on which the child objects were created can be frozen individually. If one of these layers is frozen, the child object that was created on that layer will also be frozen and become invisible. However, the other child objects will still be visible because the layers they are on are still thawed. In contrast, if the parent block is inserted on its own layer, and that layer is then frozen, all its child objects will also be frozen. This is true even though the layers of the child objects are thawed.

For example, figure 12.1 shows an inserted block made up of three child objects. The parent block is inserted on layer Parent. The rectangle, triangle, and circle were on layers of Rectangle, Triangle, and Circle, respectively, when they were selected to define the block.

Figure 12.1

The parent block with its three child objects.

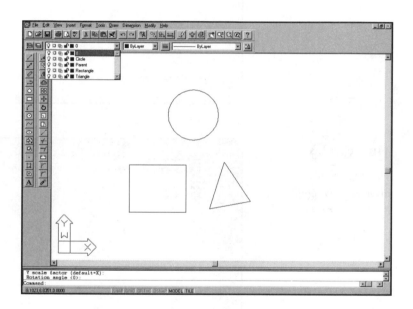

When the Triangle layer is frozen, as shown in figure 12.2, only the triangle child object disappears. This is true even though the triangle is part of another object—the inserted block object.

In contrast, all the child objects disappear when the Parent layer is frozen, as shown in figure 12.3. This demonstrates the difference between freezing a child object's layer versus its parent's layer.

Figure 12.2

The parent block with the Triangle layer frozen.

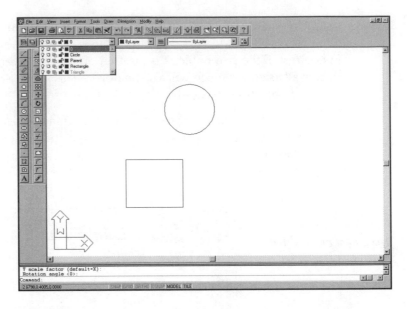

Figure 12.3

The inserted block disappears when the Parent layer is frozen.

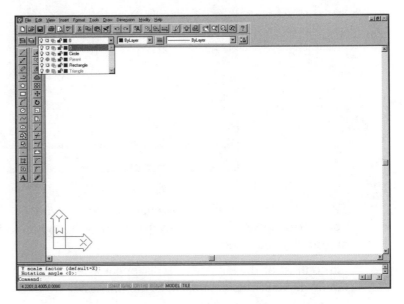

This example is just one of several different conditions that can influence the behavior and appearance of a block. Understanding the rules that govern these conditions is essential to extracting the power of blocks and to increasing your productivity.

Defining Blocks

What happens inside a drawing when a new block is defined? If you have created blocks before, you know that once you select the child objects that make up the block, they all disappear from the screen. This happens because AutoCAD automatically erases them once they have been used to define a block.

INSIDER TIP

Use the OOPS command to unerase the objects. The OOPS command can always be used to unerase the last object erased. This is true even if several other commands have been executed after an object is erased.

NOTE

I always thought it silly that AutoCAD erased the objects. After all, I typically created the objects where I needed them in the first place. I was only trying to make a copy of the objects to put someplace else in my drawing. Why, then, would it erase them? The following paragraph explains.

There is a logical reason why AutoCAD erases the objects. The block command is more than another COPY command. Instead, it is a way of making copies of a collection of child objects that uses less file space. It keeps the file size of an AutoCAD drawing smaller by storing each child object's property data in a place AutoCAD calls the Block Table. It stores this information under the name of the parent block. When a block is inserted into AutoCAD, instead of duplicating the property data of each child object (as the COPY command does), AutoCAD simply refers back to the property data stored in the Block Table. It then draws the child objects based upon this data. This enables AutoCAD to store each child object's property data in just one place, the Block Table. You can therefore insert multiple copies of a block, duplicating the child objects where needed. In each case, AutoCAD refers back to the Block Table for the data it needs to draw the child objects. Consequently, AutoCAD erases the original objects once they are used to define a block because it assumes you will want to reinsert those objects as a block, reducing the file size of your drawing.

NOTE

AutoCAD R14 has a new command called BMAKE. This command opens the Block Definition dialog box shown in figure 12.4. Its features enable you to do the following:

■ Specify the name of the block

■ Specify the insertion base point for the block

■ Specify the objects to include in the new block

■ List block names in a separate dialog box

■ Prevent objects used to define the block from being erased

Figure 12.4

The Block Definition dialog box displayed with the BMAKE command.

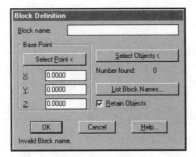

The following exercise shows how AutoCAD stores block data in the Block Table, and refers to the Block Table to draw instances of child objects.

VIEWING THE BLOCK TABLE'S DATA

1. Open the 12DWG01.DWG drawing file on the accompanying CD.

   This drawing consists of five objects: the circle, triangle, and rectangle objects along the top of the screen, and the two inserted block objects along the bottom of the screen. The child objects of both block insertions are made from the three objects along the top of the screen.

2. Next, choose Tools, Inquiry, List to list the database information for the circle object and the inserted block object on the lower left.

3. Select the circle object in the upper-left corner.

4. Select the circle child object of the inserted block in the lower-left corner, and then end object selection.

5. The AutoCAD Text Window displays the data list, as shown in figure 12.5. The circle object's data list starts with the title CIRCLE. This indicates what type of AutoCAD object it is. Notice that the inserted block's data list starts with BLOCK REFERENCE. Even though you selected the circle child object, the data list describes its parent's data.

Figure 12.5

The AutoCAD Text Window displays the selected object's data list.

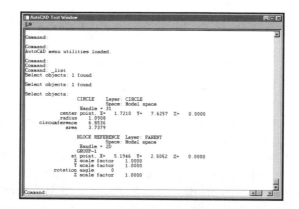

Next, you will use an AutoLISP function to select the three circle objects. This function selects objects, including child objects nested in blocks or xrefs. It then displays the stored data AutoCAD uses to draw the objects on-screen.

6. At the command prompt, type **(nentsel)**, including the parenthesis.

7. Select the circle child object in the inserted block on the lower left.

8. At the command prompt, type **(nentsel)** again.

9. Select the circle child object in the inserted block on the lower right.

10. At the command prompt, type **(nentsel)** again.

11. Select the circle object in the upper-left corner.

12. Press F2 to display the AutoCAD Text Window.

The AutoCAD Text Window displays the object's data list. An example of this is shown in figure 12.6. In each data list, AutoCAD displays different types of data in several groups separated by parenthesis. Each data list begins with the entity's name. This name is created by AutoCAD and is saved with the drawing. Each entity name represents a unique object identifier. The same name is never used twice during the life of a drawing. If an entity is erased, AutoCAD retires its entity name.

Figure 12.6

*The object data list of the
selected circle objects.*

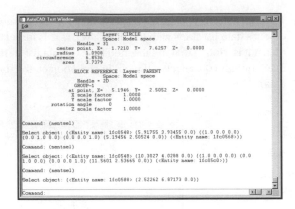

Note the entity names at the beginning of each list in figure 12.6. The first two lists display the same entity name, 1fc0548. If AutoCAD never uses the same entity name twice, why does this same name appear twice with two different entities? This occurs because the circle child object chosen in each inserted block refers to the same block of data in the Block Table. Also note that, even though the circle child object was defined with the circle in the upper-left corner, AutoCAD created a new set of circle data for the block definition. That's why the data list for the circle object starts with a different entity name, 1fc0588.

This example demonstrates how block definitions reduce a drawing's file size. By referring to the same object data in the Block Table when drawing the child object, AutoCAD avoids duplicating the object data it would otherwise create using the COPY command.

This example also demonstrates how AutoCAD automatically updates hundreds of block insertions instantly. When an existing block is redefined, the object data in the Block Table that each inserted block object refers to is changed. Consequently, when AutoCAD redraws the inserted block objects, it uses the new data as the guide to draw the child objects.

The Effect of the Current UCS on Block Definitions

When you create a block, you must define its insertion base point. This point's coordinates are relative to the block object, and are set to 0,0,0. Consequently, when defining a block's insertion base point, even though the current UCS (User-defined Coordinate System) coordinates may be 100,100,100 when you pick them, AutoCAD ignores these values and stores the block's insertion base point as 0,0,0. This is true in both paper space and model space. If this block is then exported out as its own drawing using the WBLOCK command, the insertion base point will be at 0,0,0 of the

WCS (World Coordinate System) in the new drawing. This feature enables predictable insertion of blocks.

To demonstrate that AutoCAD redefines a block's insertion base point to 0,0,0, the following exercise lists the data values for two different objects. The first object is a circle whose center is at 100,100,100. The second object is a block inserted at 95,100,0. The block definition is made from the same circle. Its insertion base point was defined as the center of the circle.

COMPARING THE CIRCLES' CENTER COORDINATE VALUES

1. Open the 12DWG02.DWG drawing file, which can be found on the accompanying CD.

    The drawing contains the two circles. The circle on the right has a center coordinate value of 100,100,100.

Next, you will view the objects data values using AutoLISP functions.

2. At the command prompt, type **(entget (car (entsel)))**.

3. Select the circle on the right.

4. Press F2.

The AutoCAD Text Window opens and displays the data values of the circle object. Inside each set of parenthesis are data values. Each set of parenthesis typically holds two values separated by a period. These represent data pairs. The number on the left is the group code, which indicates the type of data contained in the data pair. The right value is either a number or a text string that indicates the value for the group code.

For example, the 0 group code represents the type of object. In this case, the data is for a CIRCLE object. There exists one set of parenthesis that contain more than a pair of data. Its group code is 10, which indicates this data contains the coordinate values for the object. These are listed in X,Y,Z order, and the coordinate values indicate that the center of this circle is at 100.0,100.0,100.0.

For comparison, you will now use another set of AutoLISP functions to view the data values for the inserted block object.

5. At the command prompt, type **(entget (car (entsel)))**.

6. Select the circle on the left.

7. Press F2.

In this case, the 0 group code indicates that this is an INSERT object, which is a block reference. The 2 group code indicates the name of the block definition used to draw this block. In this case, when the block was defined, it was named C1. Notice the coordinate values of the 10 group code. They are 95.0,100.0,100.0, which is where the block was inserted in model space.

Finally, you are ready to view the child object's coordinate values.

8. At the command prompt, type **(entget (car (nentsel)))**. Note the n character in front of entsel.

    The function nentsel stands for nested entity selection. This function can be used to select the child (or nested) objects of blocks. In contrast, the entsel function stands for entity selection, and can be used to select the insert (or parent) object.

9. Select the circle on the left.

10. Press F2.

NOTE

AutoCAD ignores the current UCS coordinate values in paper space and model space when defining a block's insertion base point.

Notice, in this case, the 10 group code coordinate values are 0.0,0.0,0.0. This is because AutoCAD redefines a block's insertion coordinates as 0,0,0. This is true, even though the original circle used to define this block (the circle on the right) has its center coordinates' values defined as 100.0,100.0,100.0. Figure 12.7 shows the results of the previous exercise.

Figure 12.7

The data pairs of the selected objects.

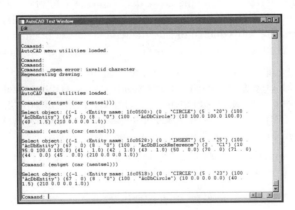

INSIDER TIP

When defining the insertion base point of a new block, simply imagine that AutoCAD is temporarily redefining the UCS origin to the point you pick.

In addition to understanding how AutoCAD deals with the current UCS's coordinates when defining a block, you must also understand the effect that the current UCS's X axis orientation has on the angle a block assumes when it is inserted into a drawing.

When creating a block, AutoCAD uses the current UCS to determine its insertion angle. This angle is oriented relative to the current UCS's X axis. It then assigns this angle to the block as a WCS X axis. This means that when you define a block, you are assigning its own WCS value. If this block is then exported out as its own drawing using the WBLOCK command, the WCS's X axis direction in the new drawing is the same as the UCS's X axis direction used to define the block. Understanding this property will ensure the proper insertion of blocks you create. Even though you can define a block's rotation upon insertion, commands exist that will automatically insert multiple copies of a block, but do not give the opportunity to set the rotation. In these cases, if the rotation is not set properly when the block is created, you will be forced to edit the rotation of each block individually. Correctly setting the UCS's X axis relative to the block you are creating is important in enabling quick insertion of blocks with minimal input from the user, therefore maintaining a high level of productivity.

To demonstrate the effect of the current UCS's orientation, you will insert two different arrowhead blocks into an existing drawing.

EXAMINING THE EFFECT OF THE CURRENT UCS' ORIENTATION

1. Open the 12DWG03.DWG drawing file on the accompanying CD.

   The drawing contains two sets of objects that appear on the right side of your screen. Both sets are made up of a closed polygon in the shape of an arrowhead with a text object inside. The first set was used to create a block definition called AR1. The second set was used to create a block definition called AR2.

It is important to note the X axis orientation relative to the two arrowheads. Both arrowheads were defined as blocks with the same UCS orientation. As a consequence, when you insert each block during this exercise, you will see the effect the current UCS orientation has on the insert objects.

Now, you will insert AR1.

2. From the Insert menu, choose Block. The Insert dialog box opens.

3. Click on the Block button. The Defined Blocks dialog box opens.

4. Select the AR1 block.

5. Click on OK to close the Defined Blocks dialog box, then click on OK to close the Insert dialog box.

   The dialog boxes close and the AR1 insert object appears. Notice that the arrowhead is oriented in the same direction as the original AR1 object set that appears in the lower-right side of your screen.

6. Choose a location to insert the arrowhead and accept the default values for scale and rotation.

Now, you will insert AR2.

7. From the Insert menu, choose Block to open the Insert dialog box.

8. Click on the Block button to open the Defined Blocks dialog box.

9. Select the AR2 block.

10. Click on OK to close the Defined Blocks dialog box, then click on OK to close the Insert dialog box.

    The dialog boxes close and the AR2 insert object appears. Notice that the arrowhead is oriented in the same direction as the original AR2 object set that appears in the upper-right side of your screen.

11. Choose a location to insert the arrowhead and accept the default values for scale and rotation.

Your drawing should look similar to figure 12.8.

Figure 12.8

The two arrowhead blocks are inserted.

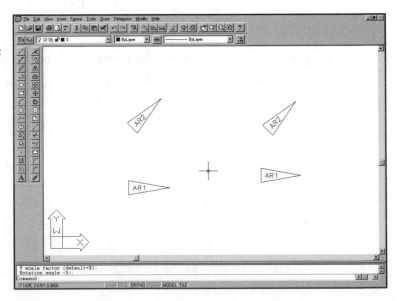

Now you will change the rotation of the WCS about the Z axis. Then, you will redefine the AR2 block.

12. From the Tools menu, choose UCS, Z Axis Rotate.

13. At the prompt, enter **45**.

    Notice that the X axis arrow is now rotated parallel to the AR2 object set.

14. From the Draw menu, choose Block, Make. The Block Definition dialog box opens.

15. In the Block Name text box, enter **AR2**.

16. Click on the Select Point button.

17. Using End Point snap, select the arrowhead tip of the AR2 object set.

18. Click on the Select Objects button.

19. Select the two AR2 objects.

20. Click on OK.

21. Click on the Redefine button to close the Warning dialog box.

    AutoCAD redefines the AR2 block definition using the current UCS's X axis orientation, and regenerates the drawing. If the AR2 object set was erased from your screen, enter **OOPS** at the command prompt to unerase it.

Next, you will set the UCS back to the WCS, and insert the AR2 block.

22. From the Tools menu, choose, UCS, World.

23. From the Insert menu, choose, Block to open the Insert dialog box.

24. Click on the Block button to open the Defined Blocks dialog box.

25. Select the AR2 block.

26. Click on OK to close the Defined Blocks dialog box; then click on OK to close the Insert dialog box.

    The dialog boxes close and the AR2 Insert object appears. Notice that the arrowhead is now oriented in the same direction as the WCS X axis.

27. Choose a location to insert the arrowhead and accept the default values for scale and rotation.

Your drawing should look similar to figure 12.9.

Figure 12.9

The redefined AR2 block is inserted.

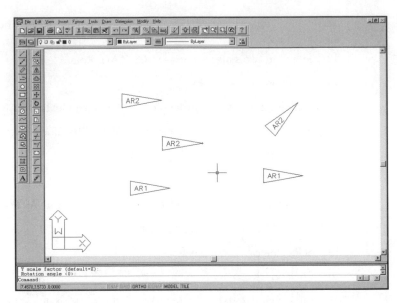

The previous two exercises demonstrate how AutoCAD deals with the current UCS when defining a block. Both the block's Insertion Base Point and the current UCS's X axis affect the way a block will first appear when being inserted. By understanding these two factors, you can control the way a block inserts into your drawing, minimizing user input, while maximizing productivity.

INSIDER TIP

You can preset the scale and rotation of a block before it is inserted. This feature is useful when you want to see the effect of a scale or rotation angle prior to inserting the block. To take advantage of this feature, type -I at the command prompt to start the command-line version of the Insert command. Select the block to be inserted. When AutoCAD prompts for the insertion point, type **S** to preset the scale or **R** to preset the rotation. AutoCAD prompts for the appropriate values, and then continues with the INSERT command's normal prompts. This is useful because you can preview the block after adjustments in scale and/or rotation, and if the scale and/or rotation are not correct, cancel the command and use the S and R sequence again.

Inserting Blocks

Several commands can be used to insert blocks. Understanding the unique features of these commands is important in selecting the right tool for a particular task.

INSERT and DDINSERT

The INSERT and DDINSERT commands are used to insert blocks. The INSERT command prompts for insertion information at the command line, whereas DDINSERT prompts for the same information through dialog boxes. The DDINSERT dialog box interface makes it easy to select blocks already stored in the current drawing's Block Table. DDINSERT also makes it easy to search for blocks stored outside the current drawing by path and drawing name.

INSIDER TIP

When using script files to perform repetitive tasks, you should use the INSERT command, because script file instructions cannot be passed to a dialog box. This is also true for AutoLISP routines. When inserting blocks during a normal drawing session, you may prefer to use the DDINSERT command.

NOTE

AutoCAD R14 has assigned a new command alias to the DDINSERT command. To open the Insert dialog box, simply type **I** at the command prompt. To start the INSERT command at the command-line prompt, type **-I**.

MINSERT versus ARRAY

Sometimes it may be necessary to insert a block as a rectangular array. Two options exist to accomplish this.

MINSERT Command

First, the MINSERT command combines the INSERT and ARRAY commands. When executed, the first command-line prompts are the typical ones for inserting a block.

Next appear the typical command-line prompts for creating an array. The exception is MINSERT can only create rectangular arrays. Therefore, no option is available to select a rectangular or polar array.

One drawback to this command is that the MINSERT object cannot be exploded. If the position of its child objects needs to be edited, the MINSERT object must be erased and then reinserted. The advantage to using this command, however, is that the MINSERT object requires less file space to define it, thereby reducing the file size of your drawing. It is important to note that the reduction in file size can be dramatic. For example, a simple block inserted as an array of 100×100 using the MINSERT command will have little impact, if any, on increasing the file's size. In contrast, the block inserted using the ARRAY command can increase the file's size by $\frac{1}{2}$ MB or more.

If you have a situation in which you need to insert an array of blocks, and you will not need to explode the objects, I suggest using the MINSERT command. Otherwise, use the ARRAY command discussed in the next section.

ARRAY Command

The ARRAY command accomplishes the same thing as the MINSERT command, only with more capabilities. With the ARRAY command, you have the option of rectangular or polar arrays. Also, once the array is created, you can explode the inserted objects individually, or move them independently of the other Insert objects. To use the ARRAY command with a block, however, you must first use the INSERT command to create the first object, and then use the ARRAY command to create the desired array.

The disadvantage of using the ARRAY command is that multiple insertions of the block object are made, which therefore increases your drawing's file size.

MEASURE and DIVIDE

The MEASURE and DIVIDE commands provide a method of inserting a block along a path.

MEASURE Command

The MEASURE command enables multiple insertions of a block along a line, arc, or polyline at a given distance. To demonstrate, the next exercise will create a series of rectangles along the centerline of a street design. By creating a block of a rectangle and inserting it at the appropriate distances along the centerline path, a series of templates can quickly be created. These templates can be used to define the various Plan View sections for the street design.

USING MEASURE TO SET A SERIES OF BLOCKS ALONG A PATH

1. Open the 12DWG04.DWG drawing file on the accompanying CD.

   This file contains a typical street centerline with right-of-way lines. A block called Viewport exists in the Block Table. This block consists of a rectangle with an insertion base point located in the center of the rectangle. The rectangle is 400 feet wide by 1000 feet long.

   You will use the MEASURE command to insert a series of this block every 800 feet along the centerline.

2. Type **MEASURE** at the command prompt.

3. Select the red centerline.

4. Type **B** to select block.

5. Type the block name **Viewport**.

6. Type **Y** to align the block with the selected object.

7. Enter a segment length of **800**.

   AutoCAD draws the Viewport block along the centerline path, placing one every 800 feet, as shown in figure 12.10.

Figure 12.10

The MEASURE command places the Viewport block along a path.

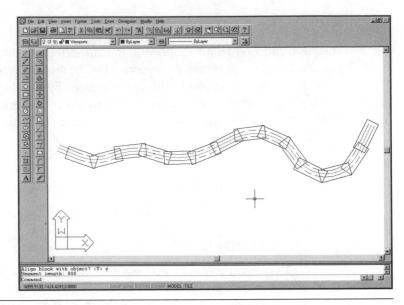

DIVIDE Command

The DIVIDE command allows multiple insertions of a block along a line, arc, or polyline any given number of times. Suppose you must draw a series of manholes along the street centerline in the previous example. With the Manhole block already created, you can use the DIVIDE command to insert 30 copies of it along the centerline path.

USING DIVIDE TO INSERT 30 MANHOLE BLOCKS ALONG A PATH

1. Continue with the previous drawing.

2. Type **DIVIDE** at the command prompt.

3. Select the red centerline.

4. Type **B** to select block.

5. Type the block name **Manhole**.

6. Type **Y** to align the block with the selected object.

7. Enter a segment number of **30**.

   AutoCAD draws 30 evenly spaced Manhole blocks along the centerline path, as shown in figure 12.11.

Figure 12.11

The DIVIDE command evenly spaces the Manhole block along a path.

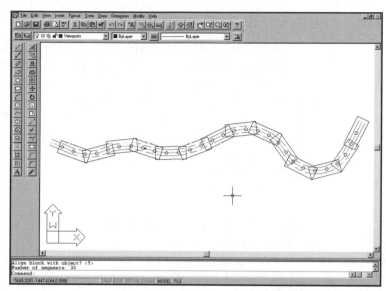

NOTE

When inserting blocks into a drawing, it is important to remember that AutoCAD aligns the block's WCS parallel to the current UCS. This feature not only affects the insertion angle of the block, but also affects the rotation angle. If the rotation angle is assigned when a block is inserted, the rotation angle is relative to the current UCS. This is true in both paper space and model space.

Block Reference

Typically, when CAD technicians insert a block, they believe they have created a Block object. Although referring to the inserted object as a block is common, technically it's incorrect. Blocks only reside in the Block Table. When you insert a block, you are actually creating an Insert object. The Insert object references a particular set of block data in the Block Table. This is called a Block reference. AutoCAD uses the Block reference to find the data stored in the Block Table. It uses this data to draw the child objects that make up the Insert object.

Although only one set of data in the Block Table is used to define a block, there can be multiple block references referring to that data. In fact, there is no limit to the number of Insert objects that can be created. In each case, AutoCAD uses the Block reference to find the data it needs to draw the Insert object.

Behavior of Block Properties

There are two properties of blocks that behave in different ways depending on their settings when the block is defined. The color and linetype properties can behave in different but predictable ways when defined on the 0 layer as opposed to other layers. Also, the color and linetypes can be defined explicitly by selecting particular values, or implicitly by defining them as BYLAYER or BYBLOCK.

The Effect of Creating Blocks on a Normal Layer

The simplest way to control the appearance of a block is to define it on a particular layer and explicitly define its color and linetype. For example, suppose you have created a circle object on a layer called circles. To explicitly define its color and linetype, choose Modify, Properties, select the circle, and press Enter. In the Modify Circle dialog box, click on the Color button and select a color from the Select Color dialog box, then click on OK. Then click on the Linetype button and select a linetype from the Select Linetype dialog box, then click on OK. The Modify Circle dialog box now lists the color and linetype you chose as the properties of the circle. You have defined these two values explicitly. As a consequence, if the circle object is used to define a block and the block is inserted into the drawing, its color and linetype will be constant. It will always be the color and linetype you explicitly defined.

In contrast, if the color and linetype are defined implicitly by choosing BYLAYER, these values can be changed by altering the original layer's color and linetype values. For example, suppose the circle object in the previous example has its color and linetype defined as BYLAYER, and the circle object is on the circle's layer when it is used to define a block. When the block is inserted into the drawing, the color and linetype of the circle can be changed by altering the color or linetype of the circle's layer. This is true even if the block is inserted onto a different layer. A child object with its color and linetype properties set to BYLAYER has those properties determined by the values of its original layer.

The Effect of Creating Blocks on Layer 0

The layer 0 has a unique feature. When a block is defined from child objects created on the 0 layer, AutoCAD assigns special properties to that block if its color and linetype properties are set to BYLAYER or BYBLOCK. This feature is powerful.

If BYLAYER is used to define a child object's color and linetype, the layer the block is inserted on controls the child object's color and linetype values.

The following exercise demonstrates how to insert a block whose color and linetype properties have been set to BYLAYER.

INSERTING A BLOCK WITH BYLAYER PROPERTIES

1. Open the 12DWG05.DWG drawing file on the accompanying CD.

    The screen is blank, containing no objects. In this drawing file, two blocks are already defined. The block C1 is a circle created on layer 0 with its color and linetype properties set to BYLAYER. The block C2 is a circle created on layer 0 with its color and linetype properties set to BYBLOCK.

    Note that on the Object Properties toolbar, the current layer is BLUE, and both color and linetype values are set to BYLAYER.

2. From the Insert menu, choose Block.

3. Click on the Block button.

4. Select the C1 block.

5. Click on OK to close the Defined Blocks dialog box, and click on OK to close the Insert dialog box.

6. Choose a location on the left side of the screen to insert the block. Accept the default values for scale and rotation.

The C1 block is inserted and assumes the color and linetype of the BLUE layer's values.

If BYBLOCK is used to define a child object's color and linetype, the current object's creation values control the child object's color and linetype values. This is true no matter what layer the block is inserted on. These values are controlled from the Object Properties toolbar.

The following exercise demonstrates how to insert the C2 block whose color and linetype properties have been set to BYBLOCK.

INSERTING A BLOCK WITH BYBLOCK PROPERTIES

1. Continue with the 12DWG05.DWG drawing file. From the Object Properties toolbar, change the color property to Magenta and change the linetype property to Hidden2.

2. From the Insert menu, choose Block. The Insert dialog box opens.

3. Click on the Block button. The Defined Blocks dialog box opens.

4. Select the C2 block.

5. Click on OK to close the Defined Blocks dialog box, and click on OK to close the Insert dialog box.

6. Choose a location on the right side of the screen to insert the block and accept the default values for scale and rotation.

Your screen should look similar to figure 12.12. Notice that the C1 block acquired the color and linetype values based on the layers values, while the C2 block acquired the color and linetype values set by the Object Properties toolbar.

Figure 12.12

The effect of BYLAYER versus BYBLOCK.

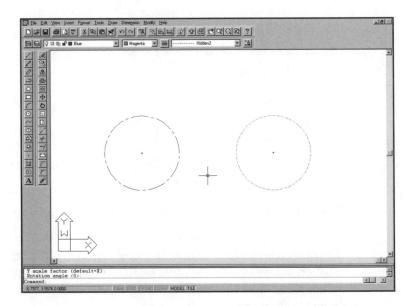

NOTE

DEFPOINTS is another layer that AutoCAD deals with uniquely. AutoCAD automatically creates this layer any time you draw associative dimensions. The unique property of this layer is that any objects residing on this layer will not be plotted. This is useful because the point objects that AutoCAD uses to control a dimension's value do not need to be plotted, but they are necessary to determine a dimension's value. As a dimension is resized using these point objects, its dimension value is adjusted accordingly. Because these point objects are only necessary to extract a dimension's value, it inserts them on the DEFPOINTS layer, so they won't plot.

WARNING

I have occasionally been frustrated by objects that would not plot, even though I could see them on-screen. The problem was that the objects, including blocks, were accidentally placed on the DEFPOINTS layer.

Understanding Block Attributes

Block attributes are an additional feature of blocks that is very useful. Block attributes store informational data. This data can be defined as a constant value, or can be input by a user at the moment the block is inserted, or edited afterward.

INSIDER TIP

There is no limit to the number of attributes that can be associated with a block. I have attached 20 or 30 attributes to title sheets. When the title sheet block is inserted into the current drawing, the user is prompted for various values. Sheet number, title, the project engineer's name, the CAD technician's name, and so on. This is useful for guaranteeing that appropriate data is created in a drawing and not accidentally overlooked.

When creating attributes for a block, it is important to control the sequence by which a user is prompted for data. For example, if a block will prompt for a series of data, and this data appears on-screen in alphabetical order, it makes sense to prompt the user for the data in the same order in which it appears on-screen. If you are accustomed to reading from left to right, top to bottom, this is the way you should have attributes prompt for data.

To demonstrate, the following exercise will create two block definitions from a circle object that has five attributes. For the first block, the attributes will be selected from top to bottom. For the second, the attributes will be selected from bottom to top. Finally, the two blocks will be inserted so that you can observe the order in which you are prompted to define values for the attributes.

DETERMINING THE ORDER ATTRIBUTES PROMPT FOR VALUES

1. Open the 12DWG06.DWG drawing file on the accompanying CD.

    The drawing already contains the circle and five attributes you will use to define the two blocks.

2. From the Draw menu, choose Block, Make.

3. In the Block Name text box, enter **C1**.

4. Click on the Select Point button.

5. Use Center osnap, and then select the circle.

6. Click on the Select Objects button.

7. Select the circle object first, and then select each attribute from the top down.

8. Press Enter after you have selected all of the objects.

9. Be sure the Retain Objects box is checked, and then click on OK.

10. From Draw, choose Block, Make.

11. In the Block Name text box, enter **C2**.

12. Click on the Select Point button.

13. Use Center osnap, and then select the circle.

14. Click on the Select Objects button.

15. Select the circle object first, and then select each attribute from the bottom up.

16. Press Enter after you have selected all of the objects.

17. Be sure the Retain Objects box is not checked, and then click on OK.

Now you will insert the two blocks that were defined to observe the order. You will be prompted to fill in the attributes.

18. From the Insert menu, choose Block.

19. Click on the Block button.

20. Select the C1 block.

21. Click on OK, and OK again.

22. Choose a location near the center of the screen to insert the block and accept the default values for scale and rotation.

23. Enter the numbers **1**, **2**, **3**, **4**, and **5** in order when prompted for a value.

   AutoCAD inserts the block. The numbers 1, 2, 3, 4, and 5 appear in numerical order from top to bottom.

24. From the Insert menu, choose Block.

25. Click on the Block button.

26. Select the C2 block.

27. Click on OK, and OK again.

28. Choose a location on the right side of the screen to insert the block and accept the default values for scale and rotation.

29. Enter the numbers **1**, **2**, **3**, **4**, and **5** in order when prompted for a value.

   AutoCAD inserts the block. The numbers 1, 2, 3, 4, and 5 appear in reverse order, as shown in figure 12.13.

Figure 12.13

The effect of the order in which attributes are selected.

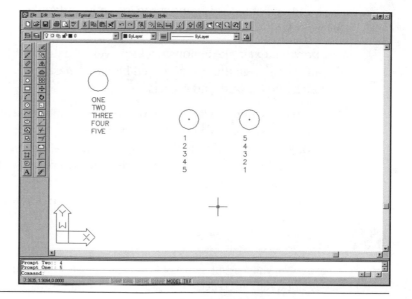

NOTE

The order in which attributes prompt for data is affected by the order in which they are selected when being defined. Therefore, their originally defined order is important when using the ATTREDEF command to redefine blocks with attributes.

INSIDER TIP

To determine the proper order to select attributes when redefining a block, use the LIST command to list one of the block insertions. The order the attributes appear in the list is the order in which they should be selected when redefining the block because this is the order in which they were originally defined.

Using Nested Blocks

As indicated earlier in this chapter, two significant reasons exist for using blocks. The first is to reduce a drawing's file size. The second is to quickly update all the insertions of a particular block. For example, suppose you have a block that is made up of a circle with a text object in its center, and you have inserted this particular block hundreds of times. If the text value is currently the letter M, but needs to be changed to S, you can simply redefine the block with the correct letter. Once it is redefined, the hundreds of block insertions are instantly updated with the S text value. This is a very valuable feature that will dramatically increase your productivity.

The previous example demonstrates a powerful feature of blocks. This power can be expanded through the use of nested blocks. A *nested block* is simply a block that contains other blocks and objects.

Nested blocks increase the power of blocks by making it easier to redefine blocks. For example, suppose you have a block that is made up of 35 objects. If only one of these objects may occasionally change, you can define that object as its own block. Then insert the block and use it to define the complex block, along with the other 34 objects. If it becomes necessary to change that object, you can simply redefine the nested block. Once redefined, the complex block is automatically updated.

WARNING

One problem you must be aware of exists when redefining nested blocks. To redefine a nested block, you must redefine it explicitly in the current drawing. If you redefine a nested block in its parent block outside of the current drawing and then use the INSERT= command to redefine the parent block in the current drawing, the nested blocks won't be updated. AutoCAD only redefines the parent block when you use the INSERT= command. The nested block definitions in the current drawing always take precedence over nested block definitions inserted from another drawing.

INSIDER TIP

The INSERT= command is a technique that enables you to redefine a nested block. Simply WBLOCK the updated nested block to its own drawing, and use the INSERT= command to redefine the nested block in the necessary drawing.

Managing Blocks Effectively

As you learn how to take advantage of the power of blocks, you will eventually develop hundreds of blocks, possibly more. You can further enhance the power of blocks, by managing those blocks in a fashion that enables you and other users to quickly find the desired block definition. If this is not done, productivity will be lost in one of two ways: First, significant time will be spent trying to simply find the appropriate block. Second, if the block can't be found, time will be spent re-creating the block from scratch. It is therefore necessary to establish criteria that everyone follows to properly create and store blocks for future use.

WBLOCK Command

When creating a block library, the most important component is the block itself. Using the WBLOCK command is a convenient way to quickly extract blocks that have already been defined in existing drawings. Existing drawing files are the first place you should go to develop your block library because they contain the blocks that your organization frequently uses.

NOTE

When inserting a block from outside the current drawing, the Select Drawing File dialog box appears. This dialog box displays the preview image of the highlighted drawing. When a drawing file is made using the WBLOCK command, however, the preview image is not created.

When creating blocks with the WBLOCK command, avoid using characters that AutoCAD doesn't accept for blocks. For example, it may be tempting to use spaces in long file names because of their easy-to-read nature, but AutoCAD will not enable you to insert the block into your current drawing with that name. This occurs because the block's name contains characters acceptable to long file names, but unacceptable to AutoCAD. In this particular case, AutoCAD displays a warning noting that a block name must be less than 32 characters long and contain no spaces. It requires you to rename the block before it will be inserted into the current drawing. These setbacks begin to degrade the efficiency of managing your blocks.

INSIDER TIP

To create a viewable preview image for the block, open the block's drawing file and then save it. AutoCAD will create the image file and display it when the block's drawing file is highlighted.

Organizing Blocks

The key to managing your block library is to organize the block locations using a well thought out path structure. Store blocks in a standard location on each computer, such as on the C drive under a subdirectory called WORK\BLOCKS. You can further organize blocks into classes and subclasses. The organizational structure should reflect a class structure used in your industry. For example, in civil engineering, it may be useful to organize standard storm drain junction structures using the following path structure:

```
C:\WORK\BLOCKS\STANDARDS\ORANGE_COUNTY\STORM_DRAIN\
JUNCTION_STRUCTURE-201A\STD-OC-SD-JS-201A.DWG
```

Following this type of structure, a CAD technician could easily follow the path to find a particular block. If the block was not found with this path structure, it indicates that the block was probably not created yet. Therefore, it can be created in the current drawing, and then WBLOCKed out to the appropriate path location.

Drag and Drop Insertion

By organizing your blocks appropriately, you can easily find blocks using Windows Explorer. You can then insert the block using Windows Drag and Drop feature. For example, simply choose the drawing file's name in Explorer and drag the file name onto the AutoCAD icon in the Windows taskbar. The AutoCAD window will open, and you can insert the block.

NOTE

If the block name contains characters that AutoCAD does not accept for blocks or xrefs, AutoCAD will display the Substitute Block Name dialog box. You must then provide a new name for the block using the appropriate characters.

Image Tile Menus

AutoCAD provides a fairly simple way to create preview images of blocks. By using Image Tile Menus, you can visually display previews of hundreds of blocks, 20 images at a time. The Image Tile Menu dialog box can be easily customized for use with blocks. When the Image Tile Menu is displayed, the user simply chooses the desired block. Once selected, the INSERT command is automatically executed with the selected block.

For example, figure 12.14 shows an Image Tile Menu that took only a few minutes to create. The images are from the six ANSI drawing files that come with AutoCAD. They are found in Release 14's parent directory. The ACAD.MNU file was modified as follows by adding the following text:

```
**image_Borders
[Standard Sheet Borders]
[borders(ansi_a,ANSI A Border)]^C^C_insert "ansi_a"
[borders(ansi_b,ANSI B Border)]^C^C_insert "ansi_b"
[borders(ansi_c,ANSI C Border)]^C^C_insert "ansi_c"
[borders(ansi_d,ANSI D Border)]^C^C_insert "ansi_d"
[borders(ansi_e,ANSI E Border)]^C^C_insert "ansi_e"
[borders(ansi_v,ANSI V Border)]^C^C_insert "ansi_v"
```

This text simply tells AutoCAD where to find the images to display in the menu's tiles, and the command to execute when one of the tiles is selected. In this case, the INSERT command will be selected and the appropriate drawing file will be used. You will find a detailed discussion of Image Tile Menus in Chapter 23, "Creating Scripts and Slide Libraries."

Figure 12.14

The customized Image Tile Menu.

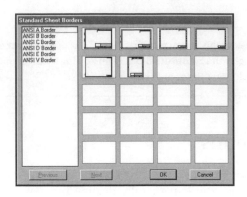

Summary

Blocks are a very powerful feature of AutoCAD. This chapter has shown you how to extract the power of blocks by explaining the nature of blocks. You learned what happens to AutoCAD's database when a block is defined, and how the current UCS affects a block when it's being defined or inserted. You learned how AutoCAD stores a block definition in the block table, and how it references the block table to create the insert object. You saw the effects of defining blocks on a normal layer and on layer 0, and the difference between explicitly and implicitly defining the color and linetype properties of a block. The advantages of creating complex blocks from simpler blocks were discussed, and the steps necessary to redefine nested blocks with the INSERT= command were explained. Several techniques for managing block libraries, which enable you to quickly find the block you need, were presented.

By understanding how blocks work, and how to properly manage blocks, you have learned how to make AutoCAD do tedious, repetitious drafting work automatically to increase your productivity.

EXTERNAL REFERENCES

by Bill Burchard

External references, or xrefs, are a powerful feature of AutoCAD. They provide the capability to create composite drawings from other drawings, even while those other drawings are being edited. In a multidisciplinary work environment, you can attach another discipline's drawings to see the impact their design will have on your design. The drawings can be attached temporarily, or inserted permanently as a block. You can permanently insert the entire xref, or just its dependent symbols. With Release 14's new xref features, you can attach an entire xref or just the portions you need to review. You can even define an irregularly shaped polygon as the clipping boundary for the portion of the xref you want to attach. By attaching small portions of an xref, you can dramatically reduce regen times. Other new features include the new External Reference dialog box and the capability to temporarily unload an xref while maintaining its path in the current drawing. These new features make AutoCAD's xref capabilities even more powerful and versatile and can dramatically increase your productivity.

This chapter discusses the following subjects:

- Attaching versus overlaying xrefs
- Binding versus xbinding xrefs
- Creating clipping boundaries
- The new XCLIP command
- Demand loading
- Spatial and layer indexes
- The improved way AutoCAD deals with circular xrefs
- The new PROJECTNAME system variable
- The new xref UNLOAD feature
- The new External Reference dialog box
- The new Tree View feature
- The special properties of xref objects created on layer 0

Introducing General XREF Features

External references are similar in behavior to blocks. The major difference is that blocks are inserted permanently into the current drawing, whereas xrefs are only attached to a drawing. Consequently, xrefs can be easily unattached when they are no longer needed.

When Should You Use Xrefs?

Use xrefs when the objects in external drawings that you need to view are undergoing change. Blocks should be used to insert small static, or unchanging, external drawings, whereas xrefs should be used to attach dynamic or changing drawings. The latest copy of an xreffed drawing is inserted automatically when you open a drawing; to update blocks, however, you must redefine them. During an editing session, you can reload the xref to update the reference to reflect the most recent condition of the xref. Also, use xrefs instead of blocks when the attached drawing is large. By using new features described later in this chapter, you can insert only the small portion of an xref you need, thereby reducing regen time.

Inserting an Xref: Attach versus Overlay

You can xref a drawing two different ways. You can attach it to the current drawing, or you can overlay it. Both methods enable you to turn layers on and off or to freeze and thaw layers. Both enable you to change the color and linetypes of layers of xreffed drawings. What's the difference?

Advantages and Disadvantages of Attaching Xrefs

Originally, the only way an xref could be loaded into a drawing was by attaching it. This feature was very useful when you wanted to view an existing drawing in the current drawing without actually making it a permanent part of the current drawing, and it gave xrefs an advantage over blocks.

In a typical civil engineering firm, for example, the architectural department is responsible for a building's layout, and the engineering department is responsible for the grading plan layout. Each department needs to insert the other's drawings from time to time to make sure that the architect's building layout matches the grading plan's building pad. By temporarily attaching the drawing as an xref, each department can view the latest design of the other department, and each can determine the effect on its drawing of any new modifications to the design. This feature is very useful.

Unfortunately, inconveniences can occur with attaching xrefs. A typical grading plan, for example, must show the existing conditions as well as the new design's contours and elevations. The existing buildings and roads to be removed and the existing contours and elevations are all necessary to the design of the project and must be part of the grading plan. The architect does not need to view the existing conditions along with the proposed design, however. Not only does the additional xref data make the proposed grading design more difficult for the architect to discern, but it also increases regen time.

Overlaying Xrefs

Overlaying is useful in reducing the amount of xref data loaded into a drawing. In the preceding example, by creating a drawing of the existing conditions only and loading it into the grading plan, overlayed as an xref, the needs of the engineer are met. The engineer can view the existing conditions and design the grading plan. More important, when the architect inserts the grading plan by attaching it as an xref, only the grading plan is visible. Even though the existing-condition drawing is technically a nested xref in the grading plan, it is not inserted into the architect's drawing because it was overlayed in the grading plan. As a consequence, the architect can view only the new grading design and, at the same time, the engineer can view the existing conditions.

If you need to load an xref drawing into your current drawing, and there is a chance that another person may load your drawing into his or hers, consider loading the xref you need as an overlay. This overlay enables you to view the xref and enables other people to load your drawing and avoid loading unwanted nested xrefs.

The following exercise demonstrates the difference between attaching and overlaying an xref.

ATTACHING VERSUS OVERLAYING AN XREF

1. Open the 13DWG01c.DWG drawing file on the accompanying CD to display a tentative tract map consisting of right-of-way lines, property lines, street centerlines, and proposed building pads.

Next, you insert two xrefs. One is attached, and the other is overlayed.

2. From the Insert menu, choose External Reference and then click on Attach.

   The Select File to Attach dialog box opens.

3. From the Select File to Attach dialog box, open the 13DWG01a.DWG drawing file.

4. In the Attach Xref dialog box, under Reference Type, choose Overlay.

5. Under Parameters, clear any checked Specify On-screen check boxes.

6. Click on OK.

   AutoCAD displays the existing contours.

7. From the Insert menu, choose External Reference and then click on the Attach button.

   The Attach Xref dialog box opens.

8. Click on the Browse button.

9. From the Select File to Attach dialog box, open the 13DWG01b.DWG drawing file.

10. In the Attach Xref dialog box, under Reference Type, choose Attachment.

11. Under Parameters, clear any checked Specify On-screen check boxes.

12. Click on OK.

    AutoCAD displays the existing trees. Your drawing should now look like figure 13.1.

Figure 13.1

The two xrefs, attached and overlayed in the current drawing.

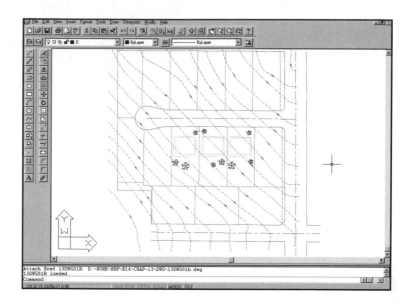

13. Save the file in the ACADR14\SAMPLE directory.

14. Open the 13DWG01d.DWG drawing file on the accompanying CD to display the building footprints of the architect's drawing.

Next, you insert the tentative tract map drawing, with its two xrefs.

15. From the Insert menu, choose External Reference and then click on the Attach button.

    The Select File to Attach dialog box opens.

16. From the Select File to Attach dialog box, open the 13DWG01c.DWG drawing file from the ACACR14\SAMPLE directory.

17. In the Attach Xref dialog box, under Reference Type, choose Attachment.

18. Under Parameters, clear any checked Specify On-screen check boxes.

19. Click on OK.

    AutoCAD displays the xreffed drawing. Note that the nested tree xref displays, but that the nested contour xref does not. This occurs because the contour drawing was overlayed, whereas the tree drawing was attached to the tentative tract map drawing. Your drawing should resemble figure 13.2.

Figure 13.2

The nested tree xref displays, but the nested contour xref does not.

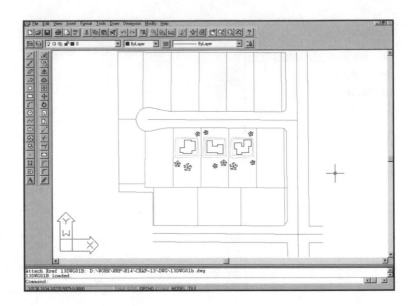

20. Save the file in the ACADR14\SAMPLE directory.

By using the attach and overlay features as shown in the preceding exercise, you can easily manage the visibility of xreffed drawings.

Permanently Inserting an Xref: Bind versus Xbind

Occasionally, you must make an xref drawing a permanent part of the current drawing so that you can edit its objects. This can be accomplished by *binding* the xref to the current drawing (inserting the entire xref into the drawing as a block). Then you can explode the block and manipulate its individual objects.

For example, during the life cycle of a project, your office may use xrefs to manage a project's drawing files. When the project is finished, however, if you are required to deliver the drawing files to the client, the client may not accept any drawings that have xrefs attached. Consequently, you will be required to bind the xrefs permanently to the drawing files.

New to Release 14 is the Bind Type feature. When an xref is bound to a drawing, AutoCAD places the xref's objects on existing layers of the same name in the current drawing. This feature eliminates the redundancy of duplicate layer names.

On certain occasions, however, it is useful to only bind an xref's *dependent symbols* (blocks, dimension styles, layers, linetypes, and text styles) without also permanently binding all the xref's objects. You can accomplish this with the XBIND command.

Suppose, for example, that you have attached an xref to a current drawing. You intend to leave the xref attached for a short time only and then detach it. After the xref is attached, you notice that some of its text objects are using a text style that you want to use in the current drawing. This can be accomplished easily with the XBIND command.

The following exercise demonstrates how to use XBIND to attach an xrefs-dependent text style.

XBINDING A DEPENDENT TEXT STYLE

1. Start a new drawing.

Next, you attach an xref drawing that contains the Simplex text style.

2. From the Insert menu, choose External Reference, and then click on the Attach button.

   The Select File to Attach dialog box opens.

3. From the Select File to Attach dialog box, open the 13DWG02.DWG drawing file on the accompanying CD.

4. In the Attach Xref dialog box, under Reference Type, choose Attachment.

5. Under Parameters, clear any checked Specify On-screen check boxes.

6. Click on OK.

AutoCAD attaches the xref, and the text appears in the current drawing.

Next, you use XBIND to insert the dependent text style.

7. From the Modify menu, choose Object, External Reference, Bind. The Xbind dialog box appears (see fig. 13.3).

8. Double-click on the highlighted xref name.

Figure 13.3

The Xbind dialog box.

AutoCAD displays the five dependent symbol headings in the xreffed drawing's symbol table. Notice that a small box containing a plus sign is next to two of the symbol headings.

9. Click on the box with the plus sign next to the Textstyle heading.

   AutoCAD displays two dependent text style symbols.

10. Choose the 13DWG02|SIMPLEX text style symbol.

    The selected text style symbol is highlighted.

11. Click on the Add button.

    The highlighted text style symbol appears in the Definitions to Bind text box.

12. Click on OK.

13. From the Format menu, choose Text Style. The Text Style dialog box opens.

14. Under Style Name, open the drop-down list and look at the available style names.

Notice that the text style 13DWG02$0$SIMPLEX is listed as a selection, as shown in figure 13.4. This is the standard way AutoCAD names a dependent symbol that it binds to the current drawing.

Figure 13.4

The dependent text style symbol is now inserted into the current drawing.

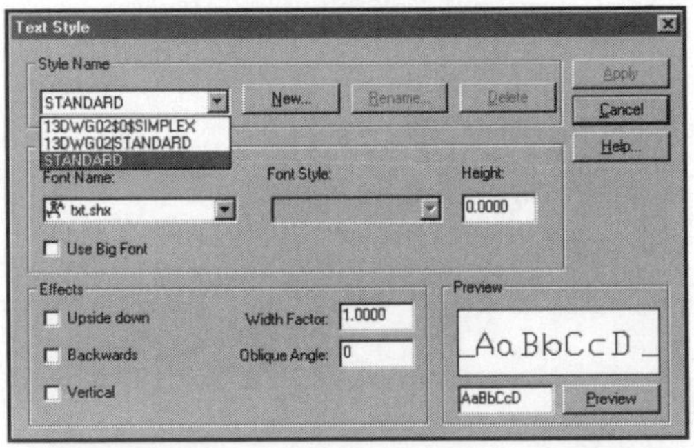

NOTE

XBIND does not permit you to load dependent data from the view table into the current drawing.

By using AutoCAD's Bind and Xbind features, you can permanently insert the entire xref, or just insert specific dependent symbols, such as text style and linetypes.

Using Release 14's XREF Enhancements

 The newest release of AutoCAD offers some welcome enhancements for working with xrefs. The following are among the improvements you will find in dealing with xrefs in Release 14:

- **Clip Boundaries.** The new XCLIP command enables you to use irregularly shaped polygons as xref clip boundaries.

- **Improved performance with demand loading, and layer and spatial indexing.** The new demand loading feature used in conjunction with layer and spatial indexing for xrefs reduces the number of xref objects loaded into a drawing, which improves performance.

- **Circular xrefs.** AutoCAD R14 deals differently with the problem of circular xrefs than previous releases. Now it loads an xref drawing up to the point at which circularity is encountered.

- **PROJECTNAME.** AutoCAD R14 enables you to define search paths and store them in a project name. AutoCAD uses these search paths to find xref files. The PROJECTNAME system variable points to a section in AutoCAD's registry that can contain one or more project names.

- **Unloading and reloading.** Now you can temporarily unload an xref from the drawing to increase performance, while maintaining the xref's path.

With these new features, AutoCAD's improved external referencing capabilities will increase your productivity.

Clipping Boundaries

AutoCAD has a new command called XCLIP. With this command, you can use rectangles and irregularly shaped polygons to define clipping boundaries for xrefs. The polygons can be created on the fly or by selecting an existing 2D polyline. After the clipping boundary has been chosen, AutoCAD removes from display that portion of the xref that lies outside the clipping boundary.

NOTE

The XCLIP command replaces the XREFCLIP command.

The following exercise demonstrates how to use the Select Polyline feature of the XCLIP command to define the xref clipping boundaries with a polygon.

USING THE SELECT POLYLINE FEATURE OF THE XCLIP COMMAND

1. Open the 13DWG03b.DWG drawing file on the accompanying CD.

   The 13DWG03a.DWG drawing file is already attached as an xref. It is the drawing with the contours (the wavy lines).

   In the following steps, you use the Select Polyline feature of the XCLIP command to clip the xref with an irregular polygon.

2. From the Modify menu, choose Object, Clip.

3. Select the xref and then press Enter.

4. Press Enter to accept the New boundary default.

5. Enter **S** to choose Select polyline.

6. Select the large, green polyline.

AutoCAD determines the limits of the clipping boundary and then redisplays only the portion of the xref that is inside the clipping boundary (see fig. 13.5).

Figure 13.5

The clipped xref with boundaries determined by the chosen polyline.

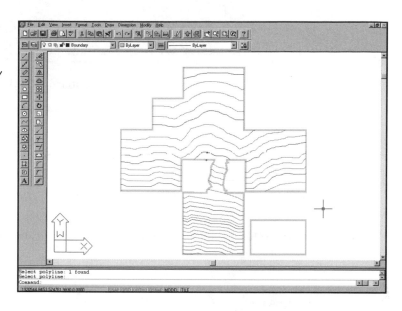

7. Save the file in the ACADR14\SAMPLE directory.

The preceding exercise demonstrated how to use the Select Polyline feature of the XCLIP command. In some cases, however, defining only one clipping boundary for the xref may not be enough. The following section leads you through the necessary steps to create multiple boundaries.

Creating Multiple Clipping Boundaries

One limitation of the XCLIP feature is that an xref can have only one clipping boundary. But what if you want to clip the same xref with more than one polygon? How do you create multiple clipping boundaries? One answer is to insert the same xref more than once.

The following exercise demonstrates how to use two separate polygons to create two clipping boundaries for the same xref.

USING TWO SEPARATE POLYGONS TO CREATE MULTIPLE CLIPPING BOUNDARIES FOR THE SAME XREF

1. Continue with the 13DWG03b.DWG drawing from the previous exercise.

2. From the Format menu, choose Rename. The Rename dialog box appears.

3. In the Named Object text box, choose Block.

   The xref drawing name 13DWG03a should appear in the Items text box. AutoCAD enables you to change this name.

4. Select the xref name 13DWG03a in the Items text box. The name now appears in the Old Name text box.

5. In the text box below the Old Name text box, type **BIG-POLY**.

6. Click on the Rename To button. The new xref name BIG-POLY appears in the Items text box.

7. Click on OK.

Next, attach the same xref drawing, as follows:

8. From the Insert menu, choose External Reference and then click on the Attach button.

The Attach Xref dialog box opens.

9. Click on the Browse button.

The Select File to Attach dialog box opens.

10. From the Select File to Attach dialog box, open the 13DWG03a.DWG drawing file on the accompanying CD.

11. In the Attach Xref dialog box, under Reference Type, choose Attachment.

12. Under Parameters, clear any checked Specify On-screen check boxes.

13. Click on OK. AutoCAD attaches the xref again.

Next, use the Select Polyline feature of the XCLIP command to clip the xref by selecting the small rectangular polygon, as shown in the following steps:

14. From the Modify menu, choose Object, Clip.

15. Select the xref in the area inside the small, green rectangle and then press Enter.

Because the first xref has been clipped and can be selected only from inside the large polygon, you guarantee that you are choosing the correct xref to clip by selecting inside the small rectangle.

16. Press Enter to accept the New boundary default.

17. Enter **S** to choose Select polyline.

18. Select the small, green rectangle.

AutoCAD determines the limits of the clipping boundary and then redisplays only the portion of the xref that is inside the clipping boundary (see fig. 13.6).

Figure 13.6

The same xref is inserted and clipped twice.

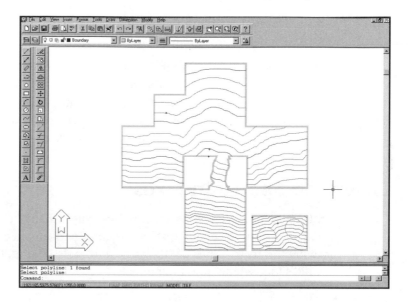

19. Save the drawing.

INSIDER **T**IP

As an alternative to reinserting the xref under a different name, you can make a copy of it with the COPY command. Just insert the copy in the same X,Y,Z position as the original. If you use this method, the xref should be copied before using the XCLIP command the first time. Note the display will not change until both areas have been clipped.

INSIDER **T**IP

The xref can be renamed from the External Reference dialog box. Simply highlight the xref to be renamed and then hold down the left mouse button for a couple of seconds. When you release the left mouse button, the highlighted name will appear as a boxed area and the name can be changed.

NOTE

The XCLIP command also clips blocks.

Demand Loading

Demand Loading, a feature new with Release 14, works in conjunction with layer and spatial indexes and enhances AutoCAD's performance by reducing regen times.

Demand Loading is a system variable, named XLOADCTL, that instructs AutoCAD to take advantage of layer and spatial indexes that exist in xrefs. By enabling Demand Loading (setting XLOADCTL to either 1 or 2), AutoCAD loads only objects on layers that are thawed when the xref has layer indexes and loads only objects within the clipping boundary when the xref has spatial indexes.

Layer and Spatial Indexes

AutoCAD has another new system variable, called INDEXCTL, that controls layer and spatial indexing. By enabling this variable, performance can be enhanced by reducing the regen times of drawings with xrefs. The following table shows the variable's four settings and their effects.

Setting	Effect
0	Both layer and spatial indexing disabled
1	Only layer indexing enabled
2	Only spatial indexing enabled
3	Both layer and spatial indexing enabled

NOTE

Setting the INDEXCTL system variable to a value other than 0 enables layer or spatial indexing (or both). Consequently, when the drawing is saved, AutoCAD adds to it the additional layer and spatial index data, thereby increasing the drawing file's size.

When layer indexing is enabled, AutoCAD does not load an xref's objects residing on layers that are frozen in the current drawing. When spatial indexing is enabled, AutoCAD will not load an xref's objects that reside outside the clip boundary. In both cases, fewer objects are brought into the current drawing, and regen times are reduced.

Spatial indexes work three dimensionally by defining a front and back clipping plane. The front and back clipping plane is defined via the XCLIP's commands Clipdepth feature. By creating a clipping boundary and specifying the Clipdepth, you can greatly limit the xref objects that AutoCAD loads into the current drawing session.

Layer and spatial indexes are created in a drawing when the INDEXCTL system variable is set to the desired value and the drawing is then saved. If INDEXCTL is set to 3, for example, both layer and spatial indexes are created when the current drawing is saved. The indexes are saved with the drawing. Consequently, if you attach the drawing as an xref to a new drawing that has demand loading enabled, AutoCAD uses the xref's layer and spatial indexes to load only those objects that are on thawed layers and lie inside the clipping boundary.

NOTE

Layer and spatial indexes are available only with Release 14 drawings. Previous releases of AutoCAD do not create layer and spatial indexes when drawings are saved.

INSIDER TIP

Leave the INDEXCTL system variable set to its default value of 0. Set the variable to a value other than 0 only when the file you are saving is to be used as an xref; then, after saving the file, reset the variable to a value of 0. This process ensures that other drawings you open will not be saved with layer and spatial indexing, and thereby reduces the file's size.

Circular Xrefs

With Release 14, AutoCAD now has the capability to handle *circular xrefs*. This means that an xref that has the current drawing attached to it as an xref can also be attached to the current drawing as an xref. In earlier releases, AutoCAD would issue a warning and abort the XREF command. Now, AutoCAD loads the xref up to the point where the circularity exists. It stops at the point of circularity because a drawing cannot load itself as an xref into itself.

In a previous exercise, for example, you attached a tentative tract map to an architect's building plan so that you could compare the building pad sizes with the building footprints. With Release 14's new circular xref enhancements, the tentative tract map drawing can xref the building footprint drawing at the same time the building footprint drawing xrefs the tentative tract map.

The following exercise demonstrates the new circular xref feature.

CREATING A CIRCULAR EXTERNAL REFERENCE

1. Open the 13DWG01c.DWG drawing file from the ACADR14\SAMPLE directory.

   The drawing opens and displays a tentative tract map.

The next step is to insert the building footprints drawing.

2. From the Insert menu, choose External Reference, and then click on the Attach button.

   The Attach Xref dialog box opens.

3. Click on the Browse button.

4. From the Select File to Attach dialog box, open the 13DWG01d.DWG drawing file from the ACADR14\SAMPLE directory.

5. In the Attach Xref dialog box, under Reference Type, choose Attachment.

6. Under Parameters, clear any checked Specify On-screen check boxes.

7. Click on OK.

   AutoCAD displays the AutoCAD Alert warning box (see fig. 13.7), which indicates that you are about to create a circular external reference and asks whether you want to continue.

Figure 13.7

The AutoCAD Alert warning box.

8. Click on Yes.

AutoCAD attaches the circular xref, as shown in figure 13.8. Notice that AutoCAD displays the following message: `Breaking circular reference from 13DWG01D to current drawing`. AutoCAD stops loading a circular xref at the point at which it becomes circular. Consequently, if the newly attached drawing contains any xrefs of its own, those xrefs will not be loaded. In the case of circular references, AutoCAD will not load any nested xrefs past the point of circularity.

Figure 13.8

The circular xref.

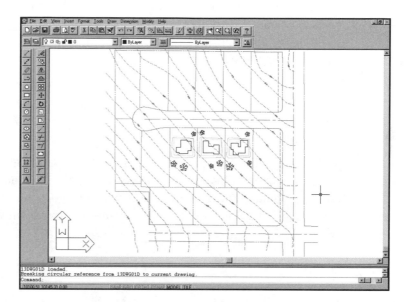

9. Save the file in the ACADR14\SAMPLE directory.

So far, this section has discussed several improved features of Release 14 relating to xrefs. Another new system variable, PROJECTNAME, enables you to create multiple project names with different xref search paths.

Using PROJECTNAME to Specify Xref Search Paths

Release 14 has a new system variable, called PROJECTNAME, that stores the current project name. The project name file contains search paths for xrefs. You can create multiple project names, each of which contains a specific set of xref search paths. When you type **PROJECTNAME** at the Command: prompt, AutoCAD displays the current project name and enables you to enter a new name. AutoCAD then makes the search paths contained in the new project name file current. Consequently, when AutoCAD searches for an xref, it includes the paths listed in the current project name file.

AutoCAD saves the project name with the drawing, but does not save the search paths contained in the project name file with the drawing. These search paths must be explicitly defined in AutoCAD by using the Preferences dialog box. Therefore, a drawing can be loaded with a PROJECTNAME variable that is not explicitly defined. AutoCAD does not issue a warning that the folder name is not defined and that no xref search paths exist. Users are responsible for creating the project name file and for defining the search paths in the Preferences dialog box so that AutoCAD can take advantage of this feature.

This feature provides the ability to have multiple paths stored in different project name files. When a particular set of search paths is needed, just those paths are loaded and used for the current drawing. This avoids having to define all possible paths and have them all load for each drawing.

Additionally, all search paths are organized in separate files. This includes search paths for support files, device drivers, and print spoolers. Instead of searching through potentially hundreds of search paths to determine if the correct path already exists, existing paths can easily be determined by viewing the appropriate path folder.

NOTE

When AutoCAD searches for xrefs, it searches first for hard-coded paths, then PROJECTNAME search paths, and finally AutoCAD's default search paths.

The following exercise demonstrates how to add, remove, and modify project name search paths.

ADDING, REMOVING, AND MODIFYING PROJECT NAME SEARCH PATHS

1. Start a new drawing.

2. From the Tools menu, choose Preferences, and then select the Files tab.

3. Double-click on the Project Files Search Path title. A subdirectory appears beneath the title. If you have not yet defined any project names, the only subdirectory listed is empty.

4. To create a project name, choose the Project Files Search Path folder and then click on the Add button. AutoCAD creates a new folder with the title Project1. This name is ready to be edited.

5. Type the new project name, **Path One**, and press Enter. AutoCAD creates the new project name (see fig. 13.9).

Figure 13.9

The new project name, Path One, is displayed.

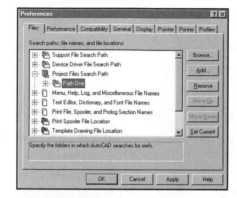

6. With the Path One project name still highlighted, click on the Add button. AutoCAD creates a new search path directory. You can either type a search path or browse for a search path.

7. Click on the Browse button. The Browse for Folder dialog box appears.

8. Browse for any folder in your list and then click on OK. AutoCAD returns to the Preferences dialog box and displays the selected path.

9. To save the project name and its search paths, click on the OK or Apply button.

You can add as many paths as necessary to each project name, and you can create as many project names as necessary.

The Move Up and Move Down buttons enable you to control the order in which the search paths appear under the project name; when AutoCAD uses the project name to search for xrefs, it follows this order.

The Remove button removes project names and their search paths.

When a project name is highlighted, click on the Set Current button to set the PROJECTNAME variable to the highlighted name. The highlighted project name's search paths then become the current paths AutoCAD uses to find xrefs.

The last new xref-related feature discussed here is the UNLOAD command, which is used in conjunction with RELOAD to remove an xref from or reload it into the current drawing.

The UNLOAD and RELOAD Commands

With Release 14, the XREF command has a new feature called UNLOAD, which removes an xref from the current drawing, but leaves its path. To insert the drawing again, use the XREF command's RELOAD feature. RELOAD reinserts an unloaded xref or updates a loaded xref.

INSIDER TIP

Loaded xrefs can significantly increase regen times. If you are editing a drawing and do not need to see a loaded xref, use the UNLOAD command to remove it temporarily from the drawing. This will increase your productivity.

Managing Xrefs

The advantage of using xrefs is that they provide the capability to create composite drawings that have relatively small file sizes and are easily updated. Unfortunately, on large projects involving multiple disciplines, keeping track of xref drawings can be difficult. Proper xref management is critical to ensure that composite drawings can find the latest versions of xrefs on stand-alone stations or over networks. Features available in AutoCAD can make managing xrefs easier to do. By using these features, you save time and reduce errors on your project.

The New Release 14 Xref Dialog Box

With the latest release of AutoCAD comes the new External Reference dialog box. This new feature is a welcome improvement for anyone who uses xrefs daily. Previously, xref manipulations could take place only from the command line. The command line version is still available, but the new External Reference dialog box makes the task of managing xrefs easier. The dialog box's diagrams and intuitive button commands are great visual aids, as is its display of such pertinent data as the xref's name, current load status, whether the xref is attached or overlayed, and the xref's file size and last modification date.

Displaying Xrefs with List View versus Tree View

When the new Tree View feature is selected, it displays any nested xrefs that may exist and a diagram of the hierarchy of xrefs. This capability makes it easy to see which xrefs have been attached and how they relate to one another.

NOTE

The Tree View feature is one of the features I like most. It instantly displays a visual diagram of xrefs and any nested xrefs. More importantly, the nested xrefs are actually shown attached to their parent xref. This enhancement is a welcome improvement over how previous releases of AutoCAD simply listed nested xrefs as being attached to the current drawing, when in reality they were attached to another xref drawing.

The following exercise demonstrates the new Tree View feature.

ACCESSING TREE VIEW DISPLAY

1. Open the 13DWG04a.DWG drawing file on the accompanying CD.

    The drawing contains two xrefs, each of which also contains two xrefs. When the drawing opens, the hierarchy of the xrefs and nested xrefs displays.

2. From the Insert menu, choose External Reference. The External Reference dialog box opens. Initially, it opens in List View mode. Two buttons appear in the upper-left corner of the dialog box. The one on the left, the List View button, is grayed. The one on the right is the Tree View button.

INSIDER TIP

In List View mode, you can sort the xrefs in the display box in ascending or descending order. This is true for any of the displayed data. To sort, choose a column's title bar. AutoCAD sorts the data in ascending order based on the selected column. Select the column's bar again to sort the data in descending order.

3. Click on the Tree View button.

The text box below the buttons changes and now displays the hierarchy of the xrefs (see fig. 13.10). From this display, you can easily manage the xrefs. For example, you can unload a nested xref that is no longer needed.

4. In the External Reference dialog box, choose XREF1A.

Figure 13.10

The External Reference dialog box for the Tree View display.

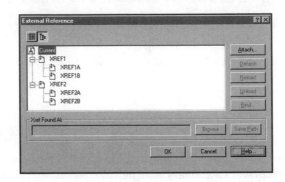

Several buttons in the External Reference dialog box become active, and the xrefs path and drawing file name appear (see fig. 13.11).

5. Click on the Unload button.

Figure 13.11

The dialog box's buttons become active when XREF1A is selected.

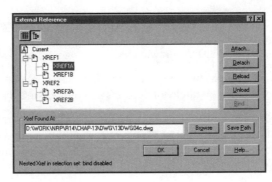

6. Click on OK.

AutoCAD unloads the nested xref XREF1A and redisplays the drawing (see fig. 13.12).

Figure 13.12

The drawing's display after the nested xref XREF1A is unloaded.

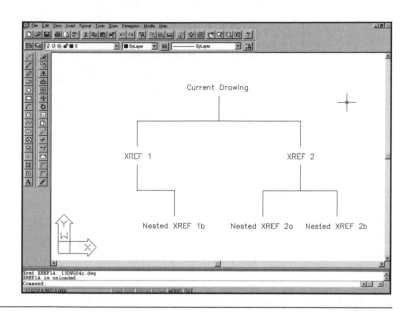

NOTE

The best way to eliminate display of unwanted nested xrefs is to overlay an xref, but you can achieve the same effect—reducing regen time—by unloading an unwanted nested xref.

WARNING

Xref-dependent symbol names in the current drawing can be only 31 characters long. This can cause problems when you are using long file names for drawings to be used as xrefs.

Explicit and Implicit XREF Paths

An xref's path can be defined explicitly or implicitly. *Explicit paths* typically refer to a particular hard drive and include all the subdirectories that indicate the location of the xref file. *Implicit paths* contain only a partial subdirectory path and end with the xref's file name.

The advantage of implicit paths is that the partial path data is saved with the drawing. If the drawing is opened on another workstation, AutoCAD will successfully resolve the xref as long as the implicit path hierarchy exists at the new workstation.

For example, suppose that a drawing lies in the following directory:

```
D:\WORK\JOB-ONE\13DWG05A.DWG
```

Also suppose that this drawing has an xref attached that lies in the following directory:

```
D:\WORK\JOB-ONE\XREFS\13DWG05B.DWGT
```

This xref path is explicitly defined. While you edit the 13DWG05A.DWG file at the original workstation, AutoCAD can successfully resolve the xref because it will find it in the explicit path.

But what happens if the drawing and xref are moved to another workstation? Suppose that the files are moved to the following hard drive and directory:

```
D:\ACADR14\SAMPLE\13DWG05A.DWG
D:\ACADR14\SAMPLE\XREFS\13DWG05B.DWG
```

The 13DWG05A.DWG file can still be opened in AutoCAD on the new workstation, but if the xref's path is not in a normal search path, AutoCAD issues the following error message:

```
Resolve Xref XREF1: D:\WORK\JOB-ONE\XREFS\13DWG05b.dwg
Can't find D:\WORK\JOB-ONE\XREFS\13DWG05b.dwg
```

AutoCAD opens the 13DWG05B.DWG drawing without the xref (which it could not find). To avoid this problem, you can redefine the xref's path implicitly.

IMPLICITLY DEFINING AN XREF'S PATH

1. Create a new directory folder called XREFS in the ACADR14\SAMPLE subdirectory.

2. Copy the 13DWG05A.DWG drawing file on the accompanying CD into the ACADR14\SAMPLE subdirectory.

3. Copy the 13DWG05B.DWG drawing file on the accompanying CD into the ACADR14\SAMPLE\XREFS subdirectory.

4. Open the 13DWG05A.DWG drawing file from the ACADR14\SAMPLE directory.

   The drawing opens, and then issues the warning that it can't find the xref.

5. From the Insert pull-down menu, choose External Reference. The External Reference dialog box appears (see fig. 13.13). Notice that the XREF1 drawing file is listed as an xref, but its status is Not Found.

Figure 13.13

AutoCAD does not find the XREF1 file.

6. Select the Reference Name XREF1. The Xref Found At text box becomes active.

7. Choose the Browse button next to Xref Found At. The Select new path dialog box opens.

8. Open the 13DWG05B.DWG drawing file from the ACADR14\SAMPLE\XREFS directory.

   The display returns to the External Reference dialog box and the xref's path is now displayed in the Xref Found At text box (see fig. 13.14).

Figure 13.14

The XREF1 file is now displayed in the Xref Found At text box.

Notice that the XREF1 status is still Not Found.

9. Click on the Reload button. The XREF1 status changes to Reload (see fig. 13.15). It is important to note that the xref has not yet been reloaded.

Figure 13.15

The XREF1 file status is now listed as Reload.

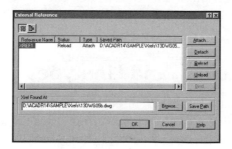

10. Click on the OK button.

    AutoCAD reloads the xref. While this accomplished the task of finding and loading the xref, the method just used will need to be repeated on every workstation the files are moved to. To avoid redefining the path, use the XREF command from the Command: line to create an implicit search path, as follows:

11. Type **–XREF** at the Command: prompt, and press Enter.

12. Next, type **P** to change the xref's path, and press Enter.

13. Then, type the name of the xref, **XREF1**, and press Enter.

    AutoCAD displays the xref's old path and prompts for the new path.

14. Type the partial path where the xref is located, as follows: **XREFS\13DWG05B.DWG**, and then press Enter.

    AutoCAD redefines the explicit path as implicit, and then reloads the xref.

15. From the Insert pull-down menu, choose External Reference.

    The External Reference dialog box appears (see fig. 13.16). Notice that the XREF1 drawing file status is Loaded, and the Saved Path is implicitly defined as XREF\13DWG05B.DWG.

Figure 13.16

The XREF1 file status is now listed as Loaded and its saved path is defined implicitly.

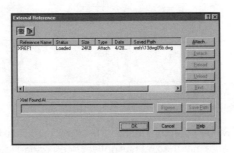

By using the preceding technique to define xref paths implicitly, you can avoid the problem of unresolved xrefs when transferring drawing files from one workstation to another.

Xref Layers, Colors, and Linetypes

When an xref is attached to the current drawing, AutoCAD duplicates the xref's layer names in the current drawing. AutoCAD prefixes the layer names with the xref's name, followed by the pipe symbol (|). Then, AutoCAD assigns these new layers the same colors and linetypes as those in the xref drawing.

The only time AutoCAD does not assign the same colors and linetypes as those in the xref is when the objects are created on layer 0 in the xref. Just like blocks, these xref objects have special properties. If their color and linetype properties are set to BYLAYER, they assume the color and linetype of the layer on which the xref is inserted. If their color and linetype properties are set to BYBLOCK, they assume the color and linetype properties that are currently defined for the creation of new objects in the current drawing. Finally, if their color and linetype properties are explicitly defined, those properties remain fixed.

You can change the color and linetypes of an xref. These changes appear in the current drawing and do not affect the color and linetypes in the original xref file. After you exit the drawing, however, any changes to the color and linetype properties are lost. When the drawing is opened again, the color and linetypes assume the settings in the original xref.

INSIDER TIP

To save any changes you make to an xref layer's color and linetype properties with the current drawing, set the system variable VISRETAIN to 1. This enables the current drawing to restore the changes you made to the xref layer's color and linetype properties in a previous editing session.

Summary

In this chapter, you learned about the differences between attaching and overlaying xrefs and about the differences between binding and xbinding xrefs. The new xref-related features of Release 14, including how to create clipping boundaries with the new XCLIP command, were discussed. You learned how to increase productivity with demand loading and spatial and layer indexes. The improved way AutoCAD deals with circular xrefs was covered, as was the new PROJECTNAME system variable, and the way it stores xref's paths. You also learned about the new External Reference dialog box and its Tree View and new xref UNLOAD features.

AutoCAD 14's new xref capabilities are a powerful tool. You can save regen time and increase your productivity by using these new xref features to reduce the number of xref objects loaded into a drawing and to better manage xrefs and nested xrefs.

QUERYING OBJECTS

by Bill Burchard

To use the power of AutoCAD, you must be able to extract information from AutoCAD objects. When an object is created, AutoCAD does more than just draw the object on the computer screen. It creates a list of object data and stores this data in the drawing's database. This data includes not only the layer, color, and linetype of an object, but also the X,Y,Z coordinate values of an object's critical elements, such as the center of a circle, or the endpoint of a line. The data can include the names of blocks, as well as their X,Y,Z scale and rotation angles. Information about block attributes and their text values can be extracted. The two-dimensional area of closed polygons, as well as three-dimensional volumes of objects can be determined. By querying AutoCAD's objects, you can extract a wealth of information pertinent to your work, and you can query important data that AutoCAD creates automatically.

This chapter discusses the following topics:

- Block and attribute data extraction
- The DDATTEXT/ATTEXT commands
- Block and attribute extraction formats
- Report templates
- Controlling the CDF file delimiters
- Specifying field width and numeric precision
- Extraction data types
- Querying information from the Object Properties toolbar
- Querying for 2D and 3D distances
- Querying for areas in blocks and xrefs
- Querying with AutoLISP

Extracting Block and Attribute Data

Blocks and attribute object definitions contain a great deal of data. AutoCAD automatically creates some of the data, including data that defines the block, such as the block's name, its insertion coordinates, its insertion layer's name, its X,Y,Z scale factors, and its X,Y,Z extrusion direction. This wealth of information can easily be extracted into a text file.

Attribute data is user-defined. The data that AutoCAD extracts consists of one element, which is either a character string or a numeric value. The attribute value can be anything the user wants it to be, and the number of attributes that can be attached to a block is unlimited.

By choosing the particular data records of blocks and attributes you need, you can easily extract a wealth of important information from your drawing.

Using DDATTEXT/ATTEXT Commands

The commands used to extract block and attribute data have been around for several releases of AutoCAD and have not changed. The ATTEXT command, the command-line version, prompts you line-by-line for the information needed to extract data. The DDATTEXT is its dialog box counterpart, and is shown in figure 14.1. Both commands create an ASCII text file (by default, a TXT file) containing the extracted information.

Figure 14.1

The Attribute Extraction dialog box.

INSIDER **T**IP

I use the DDATTEXT command to extract block and attribute data, preferring it simply because it is intuitive. To extract block and attribute data from script files or AutoLISP routines, however, I use the command-line version, ATTEXT, because script files and AutoLISP routines cannot pass information to a dialog box.

Either of these commands tell AutoCAD which block and attribute information to extract and how the extracted information will be arranged. The arrangement of the information is determined by a template file (discussed later in this chapter) and the file format you select, as discussed in the following section.

Extraction Formats

The first item AutoCAD requests via the Attribute Extraction dialog box or the ATTEXT command controls the extraction file format. The selected format determines the way each field within each record is separated and stored in the ASCII text file. AutoCAD provides three types of extraction file formats:

- CDF, or Comma Delimited File
- SDF, or Space Delimited File
- DXF, or Drawing Interchange File

Figure 14.2 shows a drawing with several block insertions. Each insertion has three attributes. In the following three sections, the attribute data is extracted and the data is displayed in each format.

Figure 14.2

*Inserted block objects,
each with three attributes.*

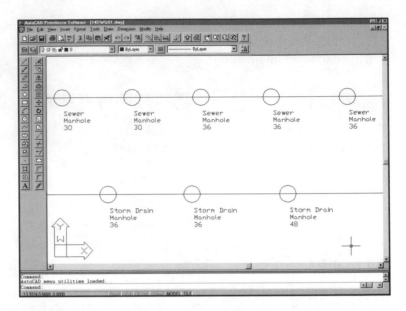

CDF File Format

The CDF file format writes one record for each block on a separate line. Each data value in a record is separated from the next by a comma, with text strings enclosed in apostrophes, as follows:

```
'Sewer','Manhole', 36
'Storm Drain','Manhole', 48
'Storm Drain','Manhole', 36
'Sewer','Manhole', 36
'Sewer','Manhole', 36
'Storm Drain','Manhole', 36
'Sewer','Manhole', 30
'Sewer','Manhole', 30
```

Notice that no spaces are between the fields separated by commas, with the exception of fields that contain numeric data. A single space precedes each number. If the number were negative, this space would be occupied by a minus sign. Note also that spaces are allowed in text strings enclosed in apostrophes.

SDF File Format

The SDF file format also writes one record for each block on a separate line; in this format, however, each data value in a record occupies a predefined field width. If the string or numeric value does not use the entire space allotted, AutoCAD fills the remainder of the field with spaces, as follows:

```
Sewer          Manhole        36
Storm Drain    Manhole        48
Storm Drain    Manhole        36
Sewer          Manhole        36
Sewer          Manhole        36
Storm Drain    Manhole        36
Sewer          Manhole        30
Sewer          Manhole        30
```

Note that no commas or apostrophes are used in this file format. Note also that the data values are aligned in easy-to-read columns. In each column, all string values are left-justified, and numeric values are right-justified.

DXF File Format

The DXF file format writes block data in AutoCAD's standard drawing interchange file format. An excerpt from a DXF file created with the DDATTEXT command follows:

```
  0
INSERT
  2
MANHOLE
 10
5.115973
 20
5.442408
 30
0.0
  0
ATTRIB
  1
Sewer
  2
OBJECT_CATEGORY
  0
ATTRIB
  1
Manhole
  2
OBJECT_TYPE
  0
```

```
ATTRIB
  1
36
  2
OBJECT_SIZE
  0
SEQEND
  0
EOF
```

This portion of the DXF output file is fragmented and represents attribute data from only one inserted block object. The entire DXF file created from the selected block insertions would fill about 30 pages of this book and be pretty boring to read. If you are familiar with DXF group codes, you may be able to decipher this fragment.

The CDF, SDF, and DXF file formats provide the capability for extracting block and attribute data into an ASCII text file. The CDF and SDF file formats are the most useful, enabling you to extract just the data you need, arranged in the order you want. The DXF file format, in contrast, is useful only when you need a copy of the DXF group code of the selected block objects.

Report Templates

To extract block and attribute data, the ATTEXT and DDATTEXT commands request the name of a template file. *Template files* are simple ASCII text files that list the data you want AutoCAD to extract. For example, a particular block may have 25 attributes attached to it. If you need only three, the template file would indicate which three to extract.

The following exercise demonstrates how to create a template file and then use it to write specific block and attribute data out to a text file in the CDF file format.

INSIDER TIP

> In the following exercise, I use the WordPad program, which comes with both Windows 95 and Windows NT. You can also use another text editor called NotePad, which automatically saves files as ASCII text files.

CREATING AND USING A TEMPLATE FILE TO EXTRACT BLOCK AND ATTRIBUTE DATA

1. Open the 14DWG01.DWG drawing file found on the accompanying CD-ROM.

   The drawing opens, displaying several blocks. Each block represents a manhole, and also has attributes attached that uniquely describe it. For this exercise, you will extract each block's X,Y,Z insertion coordinates. You will also extract the attributes that indicate the block's diameter, and whether this is a sewer or storm drain manhole.

2. From the Start button on the Windows Taskbar, choose Programs, Accessories, WordPad. This opens WordPad.

3. In WordPad, enter the following lines, using spaces to align the columns:

   ```
   BL:X               N010004

   BL:Y               N010004

   BL:Z               N010004

   OBJECT_CATEGORY    C015000

   OBJECT_SIZE        N004000
   ```

   In the previous step, the first column contains the field name. In the field name column, block data to be extracted begins with BL:, and is followed by the descriptor that indicates the data to extract. In this example, the block's X, Y, Z insertion coordinates are being extracted. Attribute data is extracted by specifying the attribute's tag in the field name column. In this example, the tag names are OBJECT_CATEGORY and OBJECT_SIZE, and were defined when the attribute was created.

   The second column contains data that specifies whether the field will contain numeric or character values. This is discussed in detail later in the chapter.

4. In WordPad, choose File, Save. The Save As dialog box opens.

5. From the Save as type drop-down list, select Text Document, as shown in figure 14.3. This saves the file as an ASCII text file.

Figure 14.3

Choose Text Document to save the file in ACSII format.

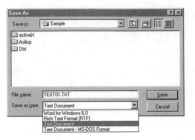

6. Save the file in the ACADR14\SAMPLE directory and name it **TEST01.TXT**, as shown in figure 14.3.

7. Close WordPad.

   Now that the template file is created, you will return to the AutoCAD drawing you already opened to extract its data.

WARNING

When you create a template file, it is important to ensure that the file is saved as an ASCII text file with the file extension .TXT. This is the file type and extension that AutoCAD looks for.

8. Return to AutoCAD and enter **DDATTEXT** at the Command: prompt. The Attribute Extraction dialog box opens.

9. In the File Format area, select Comma Delimited File (CDF).

10. Click on the Select Objects button, and then select the blocks individually. Start at the upper-left corner of the top row, and highlight across from left to right. Then continue with the bottom row, highlighting from left to right. After selecting all the blocks, press the Enter key to exit object selection and return to the Attribute Extraction dialog box.

11. Click on the Template File button, and open the TEST01.TXT file you saved in the ACADR14\SAMPLE directory.

    The TEST01.TXT file name and its path appear in the text box, as shown in figure 14.4.

Figure 14.4

The Attribute Extraction dialog box.

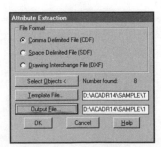

12. Click on the Output File button and go to the ACADR14\SAMPLE directory. Then choose Save.

    The 14DWG01.TXT file name and its path appear in the text box, as shown in figure 14.4.

13. Click on OK. AutoCAD creates the file and indicates that eight records exist in the extract file.

Next, you will open the 14DWG01.TXT extract file in WordPad and view it.

14. From the Start button on the Windows Taskbar, choose Programs, Accessories, WordPad.

15. Choose File, Open to display the Open dialog box.

16. From the Files of type drop-down list, select Text Documents (*.txt), as shown in figure 14.5.

Figure 14.5

The Open dialog box.

17. From the ACADR14\SAMPLE directory, open the 14DWG01.TXT extract file.

The extract file should contain the following data, in the order shown:

```
67.8188, 111.6738, 0.0000,'Sewer', 30
101.1619, 111.6738, 0.0000,'Sewer', 30
134.0559, 111.6738, 0.0000,'Sewer', 36
167.7358, 111.6738, 0.0000,'Sewer', 36
203.8855, 111.6738, 0.0000,'Sewer', 36
89.4862, 65.2266, 0.0000,'Storm Drain', 36
129.5653, 65.2266, 0.0000,'Storm Drain', 36
175.3699, 65.2266, 0.0000,'Storm Drain', 48
```

The first three fields represent the X,Y,Z insertion coordinates of the block insertions. The last two fields are extracted from the Object_Category and Object_Size attributes, respectively.

Controlling the CDF File Delimiters

The previous exercise created a Comma Delimited File (CDF). In this format, commas separate the fields and text strings are enclosed in apostrophes. Although this is very useful, commas and apostrophes might not be the delimiters you need. Fortunately, AutoCAD provides the capability to specify the characters used to delimit CDF files.

The C:DELIM template field indicates to AutoCAD which character to use as the field delimiter. The C:QUOTE template field indicates to AutoCAD which character to use to enclose text strings. Both of these template fields must be entered at the beginning of the template file.

For example, in the previous exercise, you could have indicated to AutoCAD that you wanted the extract file's fields separated by semicolons, with text strings enclosed in quotation marks. To do this, you would add the following lines to the template file:

```
C:DELIM            ;
C:QUOTE            "
BL:X               N010004
BL:Y               N010004
BL:Z               N010004
OBJECT_CATEGORY    C015000
OBJECT_SIZE        N004000
```

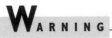

WARNING

To specify delimiters, you must specify characters that are not used as values in the fields; specifically, the field-delimiter character must not appear in the numeric field values. Therefore, 0–9 and periods must not be used to separate fields. Similarly, the text-string delimiter character must not appear in any of the text strings.

When you use this template file, it creates an extract file that contains the same information as before, but with the new delimiters, as follows:

```
67.8188; 111.6738; 0.0000;"Sewer"; 30
101.1619; 111.6738; 0.0000;"Sewer"; 30
134.0559; 111.6738; 0.0000;"Sewer"; 36
167.7358; 111.6738; 0.0000;"Sewer"; 36
203.8855; 111.6738; 0.0000;"Sewer"; 36
89.4862; 65.2266; 0.0000;"Storm Drain"; 36
129.5653; 65.2266; 0.0000;"Storm Drain"; 36
175.3699; 65.2266; 0.0000;"Storm Drain"; 48
```

Notice that the numeric and text string values are the same as before. The only difference is that the newly specified delimiters are used.

NOTE

AutoCAD automatically uses the comma and apostrophe as default delimiters. Therefore, it is not necessary to specify these values.

Specifying Field Width and Numeric Precision

In the previous template file examples, the second column contained one of two character sets, which looked like the following:

C015000

N004002

These two values indicate to AutoCAD the type of information the field value represents. The character set that begins with a C indicates a text string value, whereas the N indicates a numeric value. The next three characters tell AutoCAD the maximum field width. The last three characters indicate how many decimal places to use when extracting numeric values, which is 2 decimal places in the previous example. In the case of text strings, the last three characters have no meaning, but must be present and must be zero.

WARNING

Even though the last three characters are not used when extracting text strings, they must be present and set to 0.

Because you set these values in the template file, you need to know what type of data—numeric or text string—you are extracting, and its field length. You must then set these values accordingly. For example, if you are extracting a numeric value whose number is 1,000,000, and you want this number to be extracted to four decimal places, you would specify the following character set as a minimum:

N012004

This value tells AutoCAD that the field being extracted is a numeric field that will occupy a maximum of 12 spaces and have a decimal precision of 4. The number one million, carried out four decimal places (with no commas), looks like this:

1000000.0000

Notice that this number occupies 12 spaces. If the number were longer than 12 digits, it would be necessary to adjust the field length accordingly. Otherwise, AutoCAD would simply truncate the extracted value.

To show the effects of setting the numeric and text string character length too short, the template file from the previous exercise has been modified as follows:

```
C:DELIM             ;
C:QUOTE             "
BL:X                N002001
BL:Y                N002001
BL:Z                N002001
OBJECT_CATEGORY     C005000
OBJECT_SIZE         N001000
```

Notice that the field width values and decimal place values are too short to extract the block and attribute values correctly. When this template is applied to the previous drawing file, the extract file results are as follows:

```
67;11;0.;"Sewer";3
10;11;0.;"Sewer";3
13;11;0.;"Sewer";3
16;11;0.;"Sewer";3
20;11;0.;"Sewer";3
89;65;0.;"Storm";3
12;65;0.;"Storm";3
17;65;0.;"Storm";4
```

As you can see, even though the extract file used the same set of blocks, the data extracted does not correctly represent the true values of the blocks and attributes in the drawing.

Additionally, when DDATTEXT or ATTEXT was executed with the modified template file, it issued the following warnings when extracting the data:

```
** Field overflow in record 1
** Field overflow in record 2
** Field overflow in record 3
** Field overflow in record 4
** Field overflow in record 5
** Field overflow in record 6
** Field overflow in record 7
** Field overflow in record 8
8 records in extract file.
```

As demonstrated, it is important that you know in advance what type of data you are extracting, and the field widths necessary to obtain the true value of the block or attribute.

Extraction Data Types

The tag name is the only available extraction data type defined for attributes. Blocks, on the other hand, have a variety of data that can be extracted. To extract each type of block data, you must enter the appropriate field type in the template file. Each block data type begins with BL: and is followed by the character set that specifies the type of block data to be extracted. The following is a list of the various block data types, their definitions, and an example of each. To provide an example of each of the block extraction data types, the data types were added to the template used in the last exercise, and then the data was extracted.

■ **BL:LEVEL N002000.** This value indicates the level of block nesting. Added to the beginning of the template file, the extract file looks like this:

```
1; 67.8188; 111.6738; 0.0000;"Sewer"; 30
1; 101.1619; 111.6738; 0.0000;"Sewer"; 30
1; 134.0559; 111.6738; 0.0000;"Sewer"; 36
1; 167.7358; 111.6738; 0.0000;"Sewer"; 36
1; 203.8855; 111.6738; 0.0000;"Sewer"; 36
1; 89.4862; 65.2266; 0.0000;"Storm Drain"; 36
1; 129.5653; 65.2266; 0.0000;"Storm Drain"; 36
1; 175.3699; 65.2266; 0.0000;"Storm Drain"; 48
```

The BL:LEVEL field is the first field. Notice that all records indicate that each block's nesting level is 1. If these blocks were nested inside other blocks, this value would represent the nested level occupied by the manhole block. For example, if the manhole block were nested inside another block, the record value would look like this:

```
2; 135.2779; 87.4341; 0.0000;"Sewer"; 30
```

■ **BL:NAME C015000.** This value represents the block's name. Added to the beginning of the template file, the extract file looks like this:

```
"MANHOLE"; 67.8188; 111.6738; 0.0000;"Sewer"; 30
"MANHOLE"; 101.1619; 111.6738; 0.0000;"Sewer"; 30
"MANHOLE"; 134.0559; 111.6738; 0.0000;"Sewer"; 36
"MANHOLE"; 167.7358; 111.6738; 0.0000;"Sewer"; 36
"MANHOLE"; 203.8855; 111.6738; 0.0000;"Sewer"; 36
"MANHOLE"; 89.4862; 65.2266; 0.0000;"Storm Drain"; 36
"MANHOLE"; 129.5653; 65.2266; 0.0000;"Storm Drain"; 36
"MANHOLE"; 175.3699; 65.2266; 0.0000;"Storm Drain"; 48
```

The BL:NAME field is the first field. Notice that all records indicate the block definition's name, which in this case is MANHOLE.

■ **BL:X, BL:Y, and BL:Z.** These values represent the block's insertion coordinates and are *always* expressed as WCS values. This is true even with nested blocks.

■ **BL:NUMBER N002000.** This value represents the number of the current extracted block. Added to the beginning of the template file, the extract file looks like this:

```
1; 67.8188; 111.6738; 0.0000;"Sewer"; 30
2; 101.1619; 111.6738; 0.0000;"Sewer"; 30
3; 134.0559; 111.6738; 0.0000;"Sewer"; 36
4; 167.7358; 111.6738; 0.0000;"Sewer"; 36
5; 203.8855; 111.6738; 0.0000;"Sewer"; 36
6; 89.4862; 65.2266; 0.0000;"Storm Drain"; 36
7; 129.5653; 65.2266; 0.0000;"Storm Drain"; 36
8; 175.3699; 65.2266; 0.0000;"Storm Drain"; 48
```

The BL:NUMBER field is the first field. The number is simply a counter, and indicates the order in which the block was selected. As each block's record data is extracted, AutoCAD increases this number in increments of one.

■ **BL:HANDLE C008000.** This value represents the value of the block's handle. Added to the beginning of the template file, the extract file looks like this:

```
"2B"; 67.8188; 111.6738; 0.0000;"Sewer"; 30
"30"; 101.1619; 111.6738; 0.0000;"Sewer"; 30
"3"; 134.0559; 111.6738; 0.0000;"Sewer"; 36
"1C"; 167.7358; 111.6738; 0.0000;"Sewer"; 36
"21"; 203.8855; 111.6738; 0.0000;"Sewer"; 36
"26"; 89.4862; 65.2266; 0.0000;"Storm Drain"; 36
"17"; 129.5653; 65.2266; 0.0000;"Storm Drain"; 36
"12"; 175.3699; 65.2266; 0.0000;"Storm Drain"; 48
```

The BL:HANDLE field is the first field. The handle value, which AutoCAD sets automatically for all objects, remains constant. Consequently, this value can be used to identify the insert objects when you write AutoLISP routines to manipulate these objects.

- **BL:LAYER C015000.** This value represents the block's insertion layer value. Added to the beginning of the template file, the extract file looks like this:

```
"LAYER1"; 67.8188; 111.6738; 0.0000;"Sewer"; 30
"LAYER1"; 101.1619; 111.6738; 0.0000;"Sewer"; 30
"LAYER2"; 134.0559; 111.6738; 0.0000;"Sewer"; 36
"LAYER2"; 167.7358; 111.6738; 0.0000;"Sewer"; 36
"LAYER2"; 203.8855; 111.6738; 0.0000;"Sewer"; 36
"LAYER3"; 89.4862; 65.2266; 0.0000;"Storm Drain"; 36
"LAYER3"; 129.5653; 65.2266; 0.0000;"Storm Drain"; 36
"LAYER4"; 175.3699; 65.2266; 0.0000;"Storm Drain"; 48
```

The BL:LAYER field is the first field. The layer value indicates the layer on which the block is currently inserted. If the block is moved to a new layer, and the block information is extracted again, the value is updated to the new layer. For nested blocks, the layer value is the layer that the nested block is inserted upon within the higher level block.

- **BL:ORIENT N010006.** This value represents the block's rotation angle. Added to the beginning of the template file, the extract file looks like this:

```
0.000000; 67.8188; 111.6738; 0.0000;"Sewer"; 30
0.000000; 101.1619; 111.6738; 0.0000;"Sewer"; 30
0.000000; 134.0559; 111.6738; 0.0000;"Sewer"; 36
0.000000; 167.7358; 111.6738; 0.0000;"Sewer"; 36
0.000000; 203.8855; 111.6738; 0.0000;"Sewer"; 36
0.000000; 89.4862; 65.2266; 0.0000;"Storm Drain"; 36
0.000000; 129.5653; 65.2266; 0.0000;"Storm Drain"; 36
0.000000; 175.3699; 65.2266; 0.0000;"Storm Drain"; 48
```

The BL:ORIENT field is the first field. The rotation angle value is expressed in decimal degrees, even when the angle units are set to another format. If the block is nested in another block, the rotation angle is the sum of its angle and the angle of the higher-level block in which it is nested.

- **BL:XSCALE, BL:YSCALE, and BL:ZSCALE N010001.** These values represent the block's X, Y, and Z scale factors. When added to the beginning of the template file, the extract file looks like this:

```
10.0; 10.0; 10.0; 67.8188; 111.6738; 0.0000;"Sewer"; 30
10.0; 10.0; 10.0; 101.1619; 111.6738; 0.0000;"Sewer"; 30
10.0; 10.0; 10.0; 134.0559; 111.6738; 0.0000;"Sewer"; 36
10.0; 10.0; 10.0; 167.7358; 111.6738; 0.0000;"Sewer"; 36
```

```
10.0; 10.0; 10.0; 203.8855; 111.6738; 0.0000;"Sewer"; 36
10.0; 10.0; 10.0; 89.4862; 65.2266; 0.0000;"Storm Drain"; 36
10.0; 10.0; 10.0; 129.5653; 65.2266; 0.0000;"Storm
➥Drain"; 36
10.0; 10.0; 10.0; 175.3699; 65.2266; 0.0000;"Storm
➥Drain"; 48
```

The BL:XSCALE, BL:YSCALE, and BL:ZSCALE fields are the first three fields, respectively. In this particular drawing, the blocks were inserted with an X,Y,Z scale factor of 10. If a block is nested in another block, the scale factor is the product of its scale and the higher-level block in which it is nested.

■ **BL:XEXTRUDE, BL:YEXTRUDE, and BL:ZEXTRUDE N010001.** These values represent the block's X, Y, and Z extrusion (3D orientation) directions. Added to the beginning of the template file, the extract file looks like this:

```
0.0; 0.0; 1.0; 67.8188; 111.6738; 0.0000;"Sewer"; 30
0.0; 0.0; 1.0; 101.1619; 111.6738; 0.0000;"Sewer"; 30
0.0; 0.0; 1.0; 134.0559; 111.6738; 0.0000;"Sewer"; 36
0.0; 0.0; 1.0; 167.7358; 111.6738; 0.0000;"Sewer"; 36
0.0; 0.0; 1.0; 203.8855; 111.6738; 0.0000;"Sewer"; 36
0.0; 0.0; 1.0; 89.4862; 65.2266; 0.0000;"Storm Drain"; 36
0.0; 0.0; 1.0; 129.5653; 65.2266; 0.0000;"Storm Drain"; 36
0.0; 0.0; 1.0; 175.3699; 65.2266; 0.0000;"Storm Drain";48
```

The BL:XEXTRUDE, BL:YEXTRUDE, and BL:ZEXTRUDE fields are the first three fields, respectively. In this particular drawing, the blocks were inserted with an X,Y,Z in the WCS. Consequently, the X,Y,Z extrusion directions are 0,0,1, respectively. If a block is nested in another block, the extrusion directions represent the actual values in the WCS.

Table 14.1

Extraction Data Types

Block Data Type	Definition
BL:Level	Level of block nesting
BL: Name	Block's name
BL:X/BL:Y/BL:Z	Block's insertion coordinates
BL:NUMBER	Current extracted block's number

Block Data Type	Definition
BL:HANDLE	Block's handle value
BL:LAYER	Block's insertion layer value
BL:ORIENT	Block's rotation angle
BL:XSCALE/BL:YSCALE/BL:ZSCALE	Block's X,Y,and Z scale factor
BL:XEXTRUDE/BL:YEXTRUDE/ BL:ZEXTRUD	X,Y, and Z extrusion (3D orientation)

In this section, you have learned how to extract block and attribute data. In the next section, you learn about extracting other object data.

Obtaining Object Information

The capability to query for object and drawing data is a valuable feature of AutoCAD. With Release 14, querying tools are conveniently grouped together for easy, intuitive access. Additionally, the Object Properties toolbar has been enhanced to make identifying the most common properties of an object as easy as selecting the object itself.

Object Properties Toolbar

With Release 14, AutoCAD's Object Properties toolbar automatically displays the selected object's layer, color, and linetype properties. As additional objects are selected, only properties that are the same for all selected objects are listed. When the selected objects have different properties, such as different layers, the property value is left blank.

The following exercise demonstrates the querying capabilities of AutoCAD's enhanced Object Properties toolbar.

QUERYING OBJECTS WITH THE OBJECT PROPERTIES TOOLBAR

1. Open the 14DWG02.DWG drawing file found on the accompanying CD-ROM. The drawing opens and is displayed. Notice that the Object Properties toolbar lists the layer 0, the color Bylayer, and the linetype Bylayer. This represents AutoCAD's current object-creation mode. If an object were created now, it would be assigned the layer 0 and the color and the linetype of Bylayer.

2. Choose the dashed contour line (the sixth line from the top).

   AutoCAD displays grips along the polyline (see fig. 14.6). Notice that the properties displayed in the Object Properties toolbar now reflect the properties of the selected object.

Figure 14.6

The current object's properties are displayed in the Object Properties toolbar.

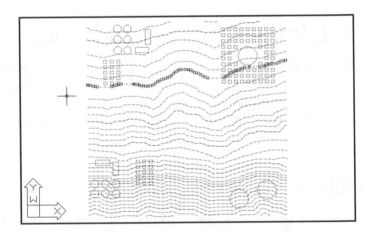

3. Choose the dashed contour line above the one you just chose. AutoCAD displays grips along the polyline (see fig. 14.7). Notice that AutoCAD no longer displays any properties in the Object Properties toolbar. This occurs because the two objects reside on different layers, and have different color and linetype settings.

Figure 14.7

No properties are displayed in the Object Properties toolbar when the two objects have no common properties.

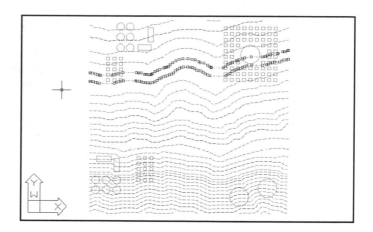

4. Hold down the Shift key, and click twice on the dashed line you originally selected. Make sure you don't select the contour line on a grip—this makes the grip warm instead of deselecting the line.

   AutoCAD deselects the contour line and removes the grips (see fig. 14.8). Because only one object is currently selected, the properties of the object are displayed in the Object Properties toolbar.

INSIDER TIP

I frequently use the DDMODIFY command to list an object's properties. The advantage of using this command is that many of the object's properties are listed and can be edited if necessary. To start the command, choose Modify, Properties.

Figure 14.8

The Object Properties toolbar displays the current object's properties when it is the only object selected.

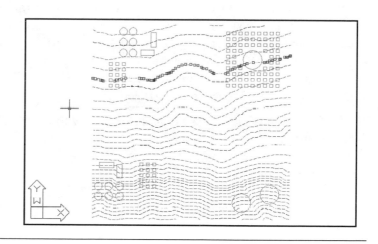

Inquiry Tools

In Release 14, the querying tools are conveniently grouped together in a single location. When you choose Tools, Inquiry, AutoCAD displays all its querying tools (see fig. 14.9). To access one of the tools, simply click on it.

Figure 14.9

Accessing the querying tools from the Inquiry fly-out menu on the Tools pull-down menu.

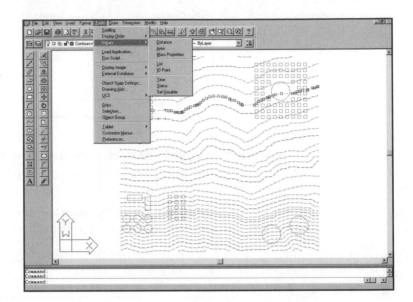

Distance

The DIST command is used to measure the distance between two points in an AutoCAD drawing. When you use the DIST command to query lengths, it's important to realize that this command measures distances three-dimensionally. If you pick two points that are not on the same plane, the overall distance will be based on a 3D vector. Even when you are using Object Snaps, if the objects are not on the same plane, the distance provided will be based on a 3D vector. To ensure that the distance is based on the current two-dimensional UCS, use X,Y,Z point filters when you query distance from 3D objects.

The following exercise demonstrates how to use X,Y,Z point filters to measure a distance two-dimensionally.

MEASURING DISTANCES WITH X,Y,Z POINT FILTERS

1. Continue with the 14DWG02.DWG drawing file from the previous exercise.

2. Press the Esc key twice to clear the grips.

3. From the Tools menu, choose Inquiry, Distance.

4. Using endpoint snaps, snap to the left end of the top blue contour. Then snap to the left end of the blue line below it. AutoCAD displays the following data:

```
Distance = 3767.7248, Angle in XY Plane = 270,
Angle from XY Plane = 2, Delta X = 0.0000,
Delta Y = -3766.3975, Delta Z = 100.0000
```

Notice that AutoCAD indicates that the Angle from XY Plane = 2. This angle is measured up from the XY plane in the Z direction. This data tells you that the distance is a 3D vector, caused by the two contours not being on the same XY plane. The first contour has an elevation of 100; the second, an elevation of 200.

Next, you snap to the same two points while using X,Y,Z point filters.

5. From the Tools menu, choose Inquiry, Distance.

6. Enter **.XY** (the period in front of the XY is necessary).

7. Using endpoint snaps, snap to the left end of the top blue contour.

8. Enter **0** when prompted for the Z value.

9. When AutoCAD prompts for the second point, enter **.XY** again.

10. Snap to the left end of the blue line below the top blue line.

11. Enter **0** when prompted for the Z value. AutoCAD displays the following data:

```
Distance = 3766.3975, Angle in XY Plane = 270,
Angle from XY Plane = 0, Delta X = 0.0000,
Delta Y = -3766.3975, Delta Z = 0.0000
```

Notice that the measured distance is slightly smaller than the first distance you measured. This is the result of using the X,Y,Z point filters and setting the Z value to 0. This distance represents the true horizontal distance.

NOTE

The last distance queried by using the DIST command is saved as a system variable. To view it, type **DISTANCE** at the Command: prompt.

Querying for Areas in Blocks and Xrefs

The AREA command is useful for finding the area of many AutoCAD objects. AutoCAD can find the area of circles, ellipses, splines, regions, closed polylines, or polygon objects. It also quickly finds the length of an open polyline. Using the AREA command's Object option, AutoCAD calculates and lists the object's area and perimeter length.

WARNING

> The AREA command provides both the total length and the total area of an open polyline object. Although the length is accurate, the calculated area is not.

If you select an object that is inserted as a block or xref, however, AutoCAD warns that the selected object does not have an area. How can you calculate the area of objects inserted as blocks or xrefs?

The area of objects inserted as blocks or xrefs can be queried by using the BOUNDARY command. With this command, AutoCAD creates region objects that provide the area and perimeter of block and xref objects.

The next exercise demonstrates how to calculate the area of objects contained within blocks or xrefs.

DETERMINING THE AREA OF XREF OBJECTS

1. Open the 14DWG03b.DWG drawing file found on the accompanying CD-ROM. The drawing opens and displays four objects. The three dashed objects are part of an xref. The rectangle object is part of the current drawing.

Next, you calculate the areas of the xref objects.

2. From the Draw menu, choose Boundary. The Boundary Creation dialog box appears.

3. From the Object Type drop-down list, select Region.

4. Click on the Pick Points button.

5. Pick inside the smaller circle that lies inside the octagon. AutoCAD determines the boundary from the circle object and highlights it.

6. Continue selecting the interior of the remaining xref objects. Pick inside the octagon, but outside the contained circle. Pick the area shared by the octagon and the left

circle. Finally, pick inside the left circle, but outside the octagon. When you finish picking inside the xref objects, all objects are highlighted (see fig. 14.10).

Figure 14.10

The xref objects are highlighted.

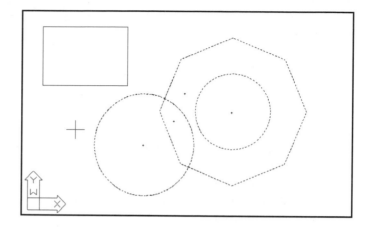

7. Press Enter to end object selection.

AutoCAD notes that the BOUNDARY command created five regions. It created two regions for the circle inside the octagon: one because you picked inside the circle, and the second because you picked inside the octagon but outside the circle. This occurs because Island Detection was enabled in the Boundary Creation dialog box.

After you create the region objects, you can use the AREA command to calculate their area and perimeter. You can also create a single composite region object of the four objects, and calculate its area. This is accomplished by using Boolean operations, as follows:

8. From the Modify menu, choose Boolean, Union.

9 When prompted to select objects, enter **F**. This begins the fence selection method.

10. Select all the region objects except the circle inside the octagon by picking inside the octagon as shown in figure 14.11.

11. Drag the fence line left and pick inside the circle as shown in figure 14.11.

12. Press Enter when you have finished, and then Redraw the screen.

Figure 14.11

The FENCE selection method is used to select the region objects.

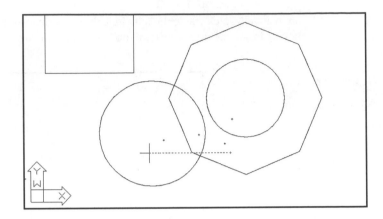

AutoCAD creates a new composite region made up of the three smaller regions, and then it erases the three smaller regions. You can calculate the new region's area and perimeter using the AREA command.

Next, you subtract the remaining circle region from the composite region.

13. From the Modify menu, choose Boolean, Subtract. AutoCAD prompts you to select the objects from which to subtract regions.

14. Choose the composite region, and press Enter.

Next, AutoCAD prompts you to select the regions to subtract.

15. Use the Fence selection method to choose the small circle region, and press Enter. AutoCAD subtracts the circle region from the composite region, creating a new composite region, shown highlighted in figure 14.12.

Next, you use the AREA command to calculate the area and perimeter of the composite region.

16. From the Tools menu, choose Inquiry, AREA.

17. When prompted, enter **O** for Object, and then choose the composite region.

    AutoCAD calculates the region's area and displays it as follows:

    ```
    Area = 405708.1915, Length = 4060.4512
    ```

Figure 14.12

The highlighted composite region.

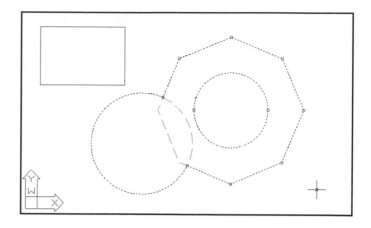

By using this technique, you can quickly determine the area and perimeter of inserted block and xref objects.

Querying with AutoLISP

Two commands, LIST and DBLIST, display object data. The LIST command displays the object data of selected objects. The DBLIST command displays the object data of all objects in the drawing. Both commands are useful for showing information about objects, such as object type, layer, color, linetype, pertinent coordinate values, and in some cases, area and overall length.

Unfortunately, when these commands are used to display object data of a block or xref, only the block's data is shown, not all the objects that make up the block. Although this may be satisfactory in some situations, times may occur when you need more data. For example, how do you find the layer on which an object resides when that object is part of a block or xref?

You can extract data from objects within a block insertion by using a few AutoLISP functions. AutoLISP functions are entered at the Command: prompt, and display an object's data in DXF group code formats.

The next exercise uses the following AutoLISP functions to extract object data:

- `entsel`: Prompts the user to select an entity.

- `nentsel`: Prompts the user to select a nested entity.

- `car`: Returns the first item in a list.

- `entget`: Returns an entity's data list.

NOTE

With Release 13, AutoCAD changed the name of entities to objects. Some AutoLISP function names still refer to an object as an entity, however.

QUERYING AN INSERT OBJECT'S DATA WITH AUTOLISP

1. Open the 14DWG03c.DWG drawing file found on the accompanying CD-ROM. The drawing displays the four objects from the previous exercise.

First, you use the `entsel` function to extract data from the insert object.

2. At the Command: prompt, enter the following, including the parentheses:

   (entsel)

3. When prompted, choose the octagon object. AutoCAD displays the following data:

   `(<Entity name: 1fc0578> (795.9 868.052 0.0))`

The data represents a list of two items that AutoCAD returned. The first item, <Entity name: 1fc0578>, is the selected object's name. The object name you see may be different. The second item is the X,Y,Z pick point coordinates used to select the entity. The pick points in this example are probably slightly different from yours because it is unlikely that you selected the object at the exact same spot.

The object's name is a unique identifier for objects in this drawing. AutoCAD assigns each object this unique identifier when the drawing is loaded (the identifier you see may be different). It represents the object (or entity) name of the insert object. No other object in this drawing has the same name.

Next, use the `nentsel` function to extract data.

4. At the Command: prompt, enter the following, including the parentheses:

   (nentsel)

5. When prompted, choose the octagon object. This time, AutoCAD displays different data information, as follows:

```
(<Entity name: 2050518> (956.579 284.152 0.0) ((1.0 0.0 0.0)
(0.0 1.0 0.0) (0.0 0.0 1.0) (0.0 0.0 0.0))
(<Entity name: 1fc0578>))
```

Notice that the object (entity) has two names. The last name is the same as the name returned by the entsel function. The first name, however, is different. This list of data represents the values of the object nested inside the insert object. The first name is the octagon's object name. The second name simply indicates the object name of the octagon's parent object. In this case, the parent object is an xref insert object.

To return the data list of the octagon object, you need to use the entget function. This function expects an object's name to be passed to it—this is where the car function is used. Next, the car and nentsel functions are used to return the octagon object's name.

6. At the Command: prompt, enter the following, including the parentheses:

(car (nentsel))

7. When prompted, choose the octagon object. This time, AutoCAD returns only the object's name:

```
<Entity name: 2050518>
```

The car function returned the first item in the list, which was returned by nentsel; in this case, it is the octagon object's name. This is the name the entget function needs to use to return the object's data list.

8. At the Command: prompt, enter the following, including the parentheses:

(entget (car (nentsel)))

9. When prompted, choose the octagon object. This time, AutoCAD returns the octagon object's data list, as follows:

```
((-1 . <Entity name: 2050518>) (0 . "LWPOLYLINE") (5 . "23")
(100 . "AcDbEntity") (67 . 0) (8 . "0") (100 . "AcDbPolyline")
(90 . 8) (70 . 1) (43 . 0.0) (38 . 0.0) (39 . 0.0)
(10 1375.09 610.235)(40 . 0.0) (41 . 0.0) (42 . 0.0)
(10 1271.84 859.5) (40 . 0.0) (41 . 0.0) (42 . 0.0)
(10 1022.57 962.749) (40 . 0.0) (41 . 0.0) (42 . 0.0)
(10 773.308 859.5) (40 . 0.0) (41 . 0.0) (42 . 0.0)
(10 670.059 610.235) (40 . 0.0) (41 . 0.0) (42 . 0.0)
(10 773.308 360.97) (40 . 0.0) (41 . 0.0) (42 . 0.0)
(10 1022.57 257.721) (40 . 0.0) (41 . 0.0) (42 . 0.0)
(10 1271.84 360.97) (40 . 0.0) (41 . 0.0) (42 . 0.0)
(210 0.0 0.0 1.0))
```

Notice that the list consists of data grouped together by parentheses. Each group enclosed in a set of parentheses is called a data pair. The first number in each group is an integer that indicates the type of data the remaining values represent. For example, the integer 10 indicates a coordinate value, and groups that start with a 10 represent a coordinate. A 0 indicates the type of object; in this case, a lightweight polyline. The object's layer is indicated by the integer 8.

The values listed represent the actual data values of the octagon object, which resides in an xref. Notice that the octagon is shown as residing on the layer 0, even though the xref was inserted on layer Xref. This is because it resides on the layer 0 of the xref drawing.

NOTE

For a complete list of group codes, look in the AutoCAD documentation under "DXF Group Codes."

Summary

In this chapter, you learned about querying for different types of AutoCAD objects. You learned about using the DDATTEXT command for block and attribute extraction, and about the different extraction formats. You found out how to create report templates, and how to control CDF file delimiters for block data extraction. This chapter showed you how to specify field width and numeric precision, and told you about the different data extraction types for blocks and attributes. You also learned how to quickly query for object data from the Object Properties toolbar, and how to query properly for 2D distances, areas in blocks and xrefs, and how to use AutoLISP to extract an object data list.

Quickly querying objects for data that AutoCAD automatically creates, such as layer, color, and linetype, increases your productivity by providing information you frequently need during an editing session. By querying data that users assign, such as attribute data, you can increase your productivity by automatically extracting large amounts of information you need to complete your work, as when you need to create a bill of materials.

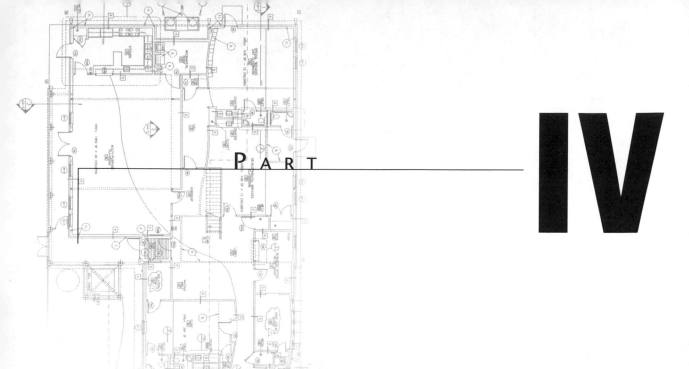

PART IV

ANNOTATING, DIMENSIONING, AND PLOTTING WITH R14

Chapter 15: Paper Space

Chapter 16: Text Annotation

Chapter 17: Drawing Hatch Patterns

Chapter 18: Productive Dimensioning

Chapter 19: Advanced Dimensioning

Chapter 20: Productive Plotting

CHAPTER

15

PAPER SPACE

by Bill Burchard

Paper space is a very powerful feature of AutoCAD. It has the capability to plot a model space drawing without cluttering the drawing with objects only needed for plotting purposes, such as title blocks and sheet borders. You can create a standard size sheet border in paper space and plot it at 1:1 scale. By creating multiple viewports of the model space objects, you can view the objects from different angles. After the views are established, you can move and arrange the viewports in paper space to any necessary position inside the sheet border. All this can be accomplished without compromising the purity of the model space drawing by allowing the project's design model to exist separately from objects only needed for plotting sheets. By using paper space properly, you can quickly and easily design the sheet layouts needed to plot model space objects.

This chapter discusses the following subjects:

- Paper space basics
- Creating paper space viewports
- Setting model space and paper space dimension scales

Understanding the Basics of Paper Space

To maintain a high level of productivity in AutoCAD, properly using model space and paper space is important. This means understanding why you should use paper space and when to use it versus model space. By understanding the circumstances in which the two spaces were intended to be used, you can reduce object editing time and increase productivity.

Why Use Paper Space?

Paper space was developed to make it easy for CAD technicians to create paper plots of CAD drawings. Prior to paper space, model space would be burdened with objects that were specifically needed for plotted sheets. Items such as borders, scales, title blocks, and revision blocks have nothing to do with the actual model; they are only needed on the plotted sheets.

Before the introduction of paper space, problems arose when plotting large model space objects; multiple sheets were needed to show them in their entirety. With multiple sheets came the dilemma of showing only those portions of the model space objects that appeared on a specific sheet. How do you trim the model space objects that extend beyond the sheet's borders without compromising the integrity of the drawing? These were common problems CAD technicians had to deal with.

For example, figure 15.1 shows a preliminary layout for a set of street improvement plans. Notice that the street and underlying contours appear in each sheet's border and title block, which is unacceptable. By using paper space viewports, you can easily remove the model space drawing from areas in which it should not appear.

Figure 15.1

A common problem of plotting sheets from model space is removing the objects that appear in the sheet's borders and title block.

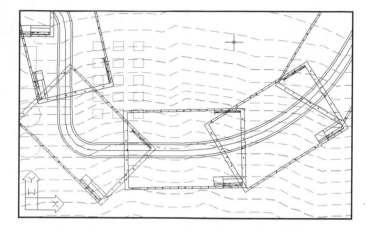

Paper space solved many of these plotting problems by providing a special environment just for plotting purposes. CAD technicians could easily concentrate on the project's design in model space and then change to paper space to create the views necessary to display just the portions of the project needed for plotting, as shown in figure 15.2.

Figure 15.2

Paper space makes it easy to remove model space objects that appear in the sheet's borders and title block.

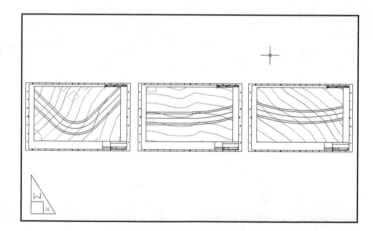

Understanding the TILEMODE System Variable

When talking about paper space and model space viewports, it is necessary to understand the role of the TILEMODE system variable in their creation. Specifically, this variable controls what type of viewport can be created: tiled or untiled.

Tiled viewports are created when the TILEMODE system variable is set to 1 (ON). Untiled—or floating—viewports are created when the TILEMODE system variable is set to 0 (OFF). Tiled viewports are created in model space by using the VPORTS command. Floating viewports are created in paper space by using the MVIEW command.

INSIDER TIP

To quickly switch TILEMODE on and off, double-click the TILE button on the status bar at the bottom of your screen. When the button is grayed, TILEMODE is off. When it is solid, TILEMODE is on.

Tiled viewports, as the name implies, appear as tiles on the screen. They subdivide the original model space viewport (which is a single tiled viewport) into multiple viewports, as shown in figure 15.3. They are fixed and cannot be moved. They never overlap and their edges always lie adjacent to the surrounding viewports. The currently selected tile can be further divided into more tiles or joined with another tiled viewport to create a new larger one.

Figure 15.3

Model space viewports subdivide the screen into smaller tiled viewports. They cannot overlap.

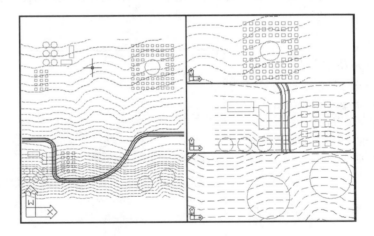

Floating viewports neither subdivide the screen nor remain fixed. They can, however, be copied, resized, and moved, just like any other AutoCAD object. They can even overlap each other, as shown in figure 15.4.

Figure 15.4

Paper space viewports can be copied and resized, and can overlap.

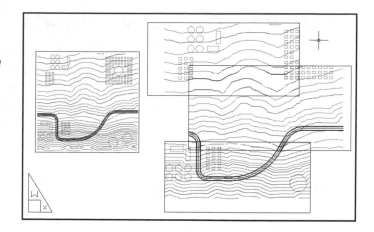

Understanding Limitations of Paper Space versus Model Space

Understanding the limitations of working in paper space is important. Because paper space is intended to make creating plots easier, certain commands that are available in model space don't work in paper space.

For example, paper space is intended to be a two-dimensional environment. Even so, AutoCAD enables you to create three-dimensional objects such as 3D polylines, solids, and extruded objects in paper space. You can even change the position and rotation of the paper space UCS. The limitation is that you cannot change the view to look at three-dimensional objects from different perspectives. Commands such as PLAN and DDVPOINT are disabled in paper space.

In model space, however, not only can you create three-dimensional objects, but you can also modify the model space view to look at these objects from different perspectives. Consequently, model space is where your project design work should be performed.

The limitations of paper space for viewing three-dimensional objects is not a disadvantage. Remember, paper space is intended to be used to create the sheet plots of your model space project. It is not intended to be used for modeling. Therefore, use model space to design your project and use paper space to create your project's plots.

The next section focuses on the special properties of paper space viewports. Here, you learn to use paper space the way it is intended to be used: as an environment for creating sheet layouts for plotting purposes.

Creating Paper Space Viewports

Paper space viewports have unique properties for controlling the appearance of your project's model. By controlling layer visibility, hidden line removal, and model-to-paper space scale on a viewport-by-viewport basis, your finished plot can precisely display the objects necessary, even when you have several viewports on a single sheet. The capability to control how your model space project appears in paper space is a powerful tool.

The MVIEW Command

Creating viewports with paper space is a simple process. After the command is executed, MVIEW prompts for the following information:

```
ON/OFF/Hideplot/Fit/2/3/4/Restore/<First Point>:
Compare MVIEW's prompts with VPORTS' prompts:
Save/Restore/Delete/Join/Single/?/2/<3>/4:
```

Notice that MVIEW's command-line prompts differ from the VPORTS' commands. The differences are due to the varied properties that paper space and model space viewports possess. The most notable differences are paper space's capability to turn viewports on or off and its Hideplot feature.

INSIDER TIP

You can copy MVIEW vport objects just like any AutoCAD entity. This is especially useful for duplicating properties such as zoom factor and display area. Simply copy or wblock an existing vport object.

Hidden Line Removal: Hide Lines versus Hideplot

AutoCAD provides two methods of removing hidden lines. The first involves removing them in model space by using the Hide Lines feature in the Print/Plot Configuration dialog box. The second involves removing them in paper space by using the Hideplot feature of the MVIEW command. Both commands work independently of each other.

The Hide Lines feature in the Print/Plot Configuration dialog box removes hidden lines only in the current space, as the following exercise demonstrates.

REMOVING HIDDEN LINES BY USING HIDE LINES AND HIDEPLOT

1. Open the 15DWG01.DWG drawing file on the accompanying CD.

   The drawing opens in paper space.

2. Click on the Print button from the Standard toolbar.

   The Print/Plot Configuration dialog box opens.

3. Under Additional Parameters, make sure the Hide Lines check box is selected.

4. Under Scale, Rotation, and Origin, make sure the Scale to Fit check box is selected.

5. Under Plot Preview, select Full, and then click on the Preview button.

   AutoCAD displays a plot preview of the drawing.

NOTE

Notice that the arrowheads are not filled in, as shown in figure 15.5. These arrowheads reside in paper space. Also notice that the cylinder's hidden lines were not removed. The cylinder resides in model space. This illustrates that the Hide Lines feature in the Print/Plot Configuration dialog box works only in the current space.

Figure 15.5

Only the arrowhead's fill is removed when the Hide Lines feature is selected from the Print/Plot Configuration dialog box.

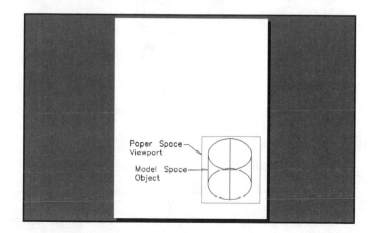

6. Press the Esc key.

   The Print/Plot Configuration dialog box appears.

7. Click on the Cancel button.

8. From the View menu, choose Floating Viewports, Hideplot.

9. When prompted, enter **ON** and then select the viewport.

    AutoCAD turns on the Hideplot feature for the selected viewport.

10. Click on the Print button from the Standard toolbar.

11. Under Additional Parameters, make sure the Hide Lines check box is not selected.

12. Under Scale, Rotation, and Origin, make sure the Scale to Fit check box is selected.

13. Under Plot Preview, select Full. Click on the Preview button.

NOTE

Notice this time that the arrowheads are filled in, as shown in figure 15.6. This is because Hide Lines in the Print/Plot Configuration dialog box was turned off. Also notice that the cylinder has its hidden lines removed. This is because you turned on hidden line removal for the viewport using MVIEW's Hideplot feature.

Figure 15.6

With MVIEW's Hideplot feature, the arrowhead's fill is not removed because they are in paper space. However, hidden lines are removed from the viewport.

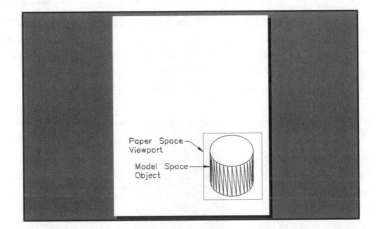

14. Press the Esc key.

    The Print/Plot Configuration dialog box appears.

15. Click on the Cancel button.

The Hide Lines feature of the Print/Plot Configuration dialog box only hides lines in the current space, whether it's paper space or model space. In contrast, the Hideplot feature of MVIEW sets hidden line removal independently for each paper space viewport. Consequently, if you have multiple viewports in paper space and need to hide lines in each one, the Hideplot feature must be turned on for each viewport by specifically selecting each viewport. After a drawing is plotted from paper space, the paper space viewports with Hideplot turned on will automatically remove hidden lines.

INSIDER TIP

In the exercise, "Removing Hidden Lines by Using Hide Lines and Hideplot," the Hide Lines feature in the Print/Plot Configuration dialog box hides the arrowhead's fill. If you want the fill to appear, create a block of the arrowheads and insert it into paper space. When the arrowheads are defined as a block, AutoCAD erases them from model space. Then, instead of using the Hide Lines feature, use MVIEW's Hideplot feature to remove hidden lines in the viewport. This removes hidden lines in the viewport and does not affect the arrowhead fills inserted into paper space.

Aligning Objects in Paper Space Viewports

Paper space viewports can be edited in several ways. You can use grips to scale, move, or resize viewports. Viewports can be copied or erased. You can even create an array of viewports.

Although creating multiple viewports is easy, aligning objects in different viewports can be difficult unless you take advantage of the MVSETUP command.

The following exercise demonstrates how to use the MVSETUP command to align objects in two different viewports.

ALIGNING OBJECTS IN TWO DIFFERENT VIEWPORTS BY USING THE MVSETUP COMMAND

1. Open the 15DWG02.DWG drawing file, found on the accompanying CD.

   When the drawing opens, it displays two viewports. Each viewport shows a different view of the same model space objects. It is important to note that the viewports both have the same scale.

2. Enter **MVSETUP** at the Command: line.

   AutoCAD initializes the MVSETUP routine.

3. Enter **A** to start the Align feature.

4. Enter **H** to start the Horizontal feature.

    AutoCAD prompts for the basepoint. The other viewport will be aligned to this point. If the lower-right viewport is not already highlighted, pick inside it to make it current.

5. With the lower-right viewport current, use endpoint snap to snap the small rectangle as shown in figure 15.7.

Figure 15.7

First, snap to the small rectangle in the lower-right viewport.

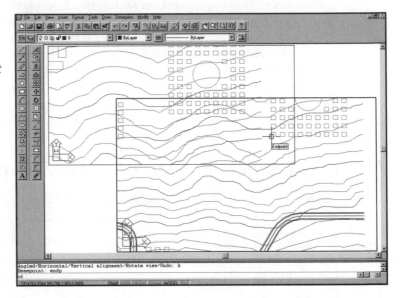

AutoCAD prompts for the other point. Pick inside the upper-left viewport to make it current.

6. With the upper-left viewport current, use endpoint snap to snap the small rectangle as shown in figure 15.8.

Figure 15.8

Second, snap to the small rectangle in the upper-left viewport.

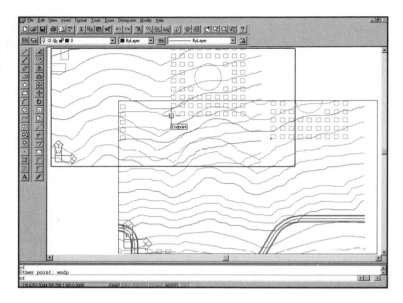

AutoCAD moves the view in the upper-left viewport down and aligns the two small rectangles.

7. Enter **V** to start the Vertical feature.

   Once again, AutoCAD prompts for the basepoint. Pick inside the lower-right viewport to make it current.

8. With the lower-right viewport current, use endpoint snap to snap the same small rectangle shown in figure 15.7.

   AutoCAD prompts for the other point. Pick inside the upper-left viewport to make it current.

9. With the upper-left viewport current, use endpoint snap to snap the same small rectangle shown in figure 15.8.

   AutoCAD moves the view in the upper-left viewport to the right and aligns the two small rectangles, as shown in figure 15.9.

Figure 15.9

The objects in the two viewports are aligned.

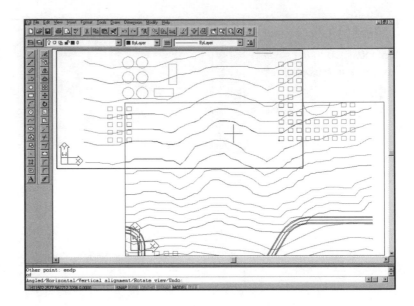

10.   Press Enter twice to end the command.

Notice that the MVSETUP command was started in paper space, but ended in model space. Again, note that the objects in these two viewports aligned perfectly because both viewports have the same scale.

Setting Views in Paper Space Viewports

The purpose of paper space viewports is to create one or more views of your model space project. Typically in paper space, you create a viewport, zoom in to the area of your model that you want to display, and then plot it. Two things you should do when you position the display are:

■   Scale the model space objects in the viewport so they plot out at the proper scale.

■   Save the correctly scaled display as a view in model space.

The following exercise demonstrates how to properly scale model space objects in a paper space viewport and how to save the view once it is scaled.

SCALING MODEL SPACE OBJECTS IN A PAPER SPACE VIEWPORT

1. Open the 15DWG03b.DWG drawing file found on the accompanying CD.

   The drawing opens with TILEMODE set to 0 (off) and in model space. The sheet border is in paper space, and the xrefed objects are in model space. The black box surrounding the xref object is the polyline that was used to XCLIP the xref.

INSIDER TIP

This drawing represents a typical layout for a street improvement plan. In practice, it is a good idea to create a sheet border in paper space and attach the model as an xref. Additionally, each drawing file should contain only one sheet. Avoid having multiple sheets in a single drawing file. By having only one sheet per drawing, you decrease the number of viewports in paper space. The fewer viewports, the faster your drawing regens.

INSIDER TIP

When working with large xref files, use the XCLIP command to display only the necessary model space objects. This reduces regen time and increases productivity.

2. Enter **MVSETUP** at the Command: line.

   AutoCAD initializes the MVSETUP routine.

3. Enter **S** to start the Scale viewports feature.

   AutoCAD prompts you to select the viewports to scale. Notice that AutoCAD switched to paper space.

4. Select the viewport and then press Enter.

   AutoCAD prompts you to enter the ratio of paper space units to model space units. In this case, you want to scale the model space objects to 1:50 (1" = 50').

5. When prompted for the number of paper space units, enter **1**.

6. When prompted for the number of model space units, enter **50**.

   AutoCAD scales the model space drawing to the correct ratio as shown in figure 15.10.

Figure 15.10

The properly scaled model space objects.

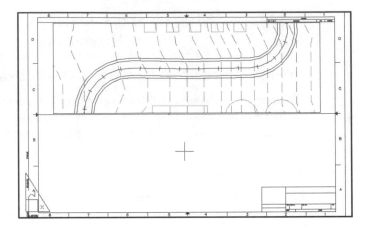

7. Press Enter to end the MVSETUP command.

   With the view properly positioned and scaled, save the view.

8. Enter **V** at the Command: prompt.

   The View Control dialog box is displayed.

9. Click on the New button.

   The Define New View dialog box is displayed.

10. Enter **PLAN** in the New Name text edit box. Be sure the Current Display option is selected and then click on the Save View button. Click on OK.

With the view saved, it is now possible to quickly restore the original view at the proper scale. If the model space objects are panned or zoomed, the view can quickly be restored from the View Control dialog box.

ARNING

You can only use the View Control dialog box to restore a saved view if the viewport is not resized.

Controlling Paper Space Viewport Visibility

Paper space viewports provide the capability to freeze and thaw layers individually. This can be done within the Layers dialog box, from the Layer Control on the Object

Properties toolbar, or by using the VPLAYER command. The advantage of using the Layers dialog box or the Layer Control is that you can simply choose the Freeze/Thaw in current viewport icon to toggle layer visibility on or off. The disadvantage is that the settings only affect the current viewport. In order to set the same layer freeze/thaw properties in multiple viewports, you must make each viewport current and then choose the desired setting. The advantage of using the VPLAYER command is that you can apply the desired freeze/thaw settings to multiple viewports at the same time. Unfortunately, you must type in the layer names.

WARNING

Although you can control a layer's freeze/thaw property in the current viewport, the global freeze/thaw value can override a viewport's setting. If a certain layer is thawed in a viewport but frozen globally, for example, the layer will not appear in any viewports.

The following exercise demonstrates the usefulness of the Layer Control and the VPLAYER command.

CONTROLLING LAYER VISIBILITY IN PAPER SPACE BY USING THE LAYER CONTROL AND THE VPLAYER COMMAND

1. Open the 15DWG04.DWG drawing file on the accompanying CD.

   The drawing opens in paper space (TILEMODE = 0) and displays the two viewports. At this point, it is obvious that there are layers that are not visible in the viewport on the right.

   Next, you determine which layers are frozen in the viewport on the right.

2. Choose the down arrow on the Layer Control.

   The control opens and displays the list of layers as shown in figure 15.11. Notice that the icons indicate that all layers are on and thawed.

Figure 15.11

The Layer Control indicates that all layers are on and thawed.

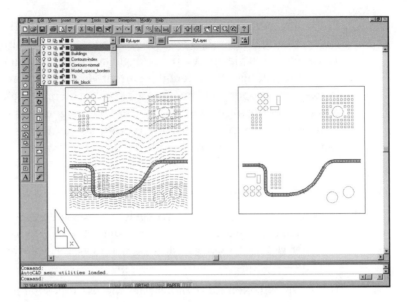

3. Choose the down arrow on the Layer Control to close the list of layers.

4. Double-click the PAPER tile in the status bar at the bottom of the screen.

   AutoCAD switches from paper space to model space, and the right viewport becomes active.

5. Choose the down arrow on the Layer Control.

   The control opens and displays the list of layers as shown in figure 15.12. Notice that the icons indicate that three layers are frozen in the current viewport.

Figure 15.12

The Layer Control indicates that three layers are frozen in the current viewport.

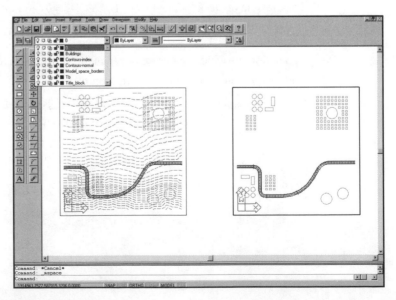

6. Choose the down arrow on the Layer Control to close the list of layers.

7. Double-click the MODEL tile in the status bar at the bottom of the screen.

   AutoCAD switches from model space to paper space.

The next part of this exercise uses the VPLAYER command to list the frozen layers in the two viewports.

8. Enter **VPLAYER** at the Command: prompt.

9. Enter **?** at the Command: prompt.

   AutoCAD prompts you to select a viewport.

10. Select the right viewport.

    The following information is displayed:

    ```
    Layers currently frozen in viewport 3:
    CONTOURS-INDEX
    CONTOURS-NORMAL
    MODEL_SPACE_BORDERS
    ```

    AutoCAD lists the layers frozen in the selected viewport. To list frozen layers in other viewports, repeat steps 9 and 10.

11. Enter **?** at the Command: prompt.

12. Choose the left viewport.

    The following information is displayed:

    ```
    Layers currently frozen in viewport 2:
    MODEL_SPACE_BORDERS
    ```

NOTE

Notice that the VPLAYER command listed the first viewport selected as viewport 3 and the second as viewport 2. Although only two paper space viewports appear in this drawing, the original paper space view is considered viewport 1.

The next steps use the global freeze/thaw layer settings to set both viewports' current freeze/thaw layer settings.

13. Press Enter to end the VPLAYER command.

14. Click on the Layers button.

    The Layer & Linetype Properties dialog box opens.

15. Set the Freeze in New Viewports value to frozen for all layers except layer 0, as shown in figure 15.13.

INSIDER TIP

To view a column's entire heading, click and drag the line separating column titles until the heading is visible.

Figure 15.13

The Freeze in New Viewports value is set to frozen for all layers except layer 0.

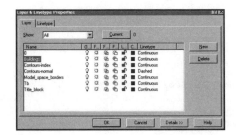

16. Click on OK to accept the changes and close the dialog box.

17. Enter **VPLAYER** at the Command: prompt.

18. Enter **R** for reset.

19. Enter ***** to reset all layers' values to the Freeze in New Viewports values.

20. Enter **S** for Select.

21. Select the two viewports.

22. Press Enter to end the VPLAYER command.

The two viewports' current viewport freeze/thaw values are set to the Freeze in New Viewports values in the Layer & Linetype Properties dialog box. Consequently, only the road alignment is visible, as shown in figure 15.14.

Figure 15.14

The current viewport layer freeze/thaw values are automatically set by using the VPLAYER Reset feature.

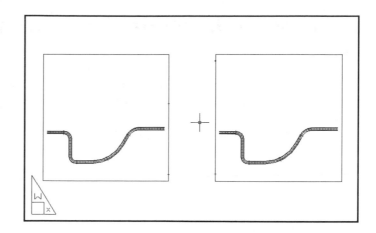

INSIDER TIP

When you have multiple viewports to which you need the same current viewport freeze/thaw values, use the technique of setting the Freeze in New Viewports values to the desired values in the Layer & Linetype Properties dialog box. Then use the VPLAYER's Reset feature to select the viewports and automatically update their current viewport freeze/thaw values.

NOTE

You might have experienced a problem with retaining changes you made to layer values for xref objects after you closed the drawing and reopened it. If you make changes to the layer values of xrefs, and you want those values to be saved with the drawing, set the VISRETAIN system variable to 1. This instructs AutoCAD to save any changes you make along with the drawing.

New Paper Space Features

With Release 14 comes two welcome improvements to working in paper space. First, changing the display in paper space by zooming or panning no longer automatically invokes a regen, which is an important time-saving feature. Second, real-time and transparent zooming and panning are now supported in paper space.

The next section explores AutoCAD's dimensioning tools and explains how these tools work when dimensioning in model space and paper space.

Dimensioning in Model Space and Paper Space

AutoCAD provides a powerful set of dimensioning tools. Using these tools may seem overwhelming in the beginning because of the number of dimension system variables used to control a dimension's properties (approximately 60 different dimension variables exist). Fortunately, most of these system variables are easily controlled through the Dimension Styles dialog box. Although this section is not intended to provide a detailed explanation of how to use AutoCAD's dimensions, it discusses two particular system variables and how they work in paper space and model space.

As a CAD technician, you have the choice of dimensioning objects in model space or paper space. Depending on your company's drawing standards, or the needs of your client, you will probably be required to draw dimensions in one space or the other. Model space objects are typically drawn at real-world scale, however, while paper space viewports display model space objects at a reduced scale. Consequently, when dimensioning in model space, a certain scale factor must be used to correctly determine dimension values. In paper space, however, the reduced scale must be taken into consideration when determining a dimension's value. For AutoCAD to correctly calculate a dimension's value in either space, it relies on two particular system variables.

The variables are:

- DIMSCALE
- DIMLFAC

For information on dimensioning beyond the scope of this chapter, see Chapter 18, "Productive Dimensioning," and Chapter 19, "Advanced Dimensioning."

INSIDER TIP

You can place your MVIEW vport objects on the DEFPOINTS layer to control plotting. The DEFPOINTS layer is created whenever you make your first dimension. One of its unique properties is that objects on it do not plot. By placing the vport on this layer, you don't have to worry about freezing the layer for the vports. Having them available at all times can be quite a time-saver.

Using the DIMSCALE System Variable

The DIMSCALE system variable sets the overall scale for the size of dimension objects. When plotting from model space, it should be set to the intended plot scale. If your final plotted sheet is going to be plotted at 1"=40' (1:40) scale, for example, the DIMSCALE value should be set to 40. Consequently, when dimensions are drawn, AutoCAD will automatically scale the size of the text, arrowheads, and other dimension geometry to the correct size.

But DIMSCALE is a fixed-scale factor. If you have a situation where your plot has two viewports, one at 1"=40' and the other at 1"=20', the viewport with the 1:20 scale ratio will have its dimension geometry two times too big, as shown in figure 15.15.

Figure 15.15

A problem arises if you draw dimensions in viewports with different scale factors.

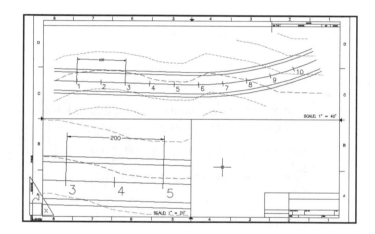

Notice in figure 15.15 that the dimension text in the upper viewport is smaller than the dimension text in the lower viewport. The upper viewport's text size is correct for the intended plot scale of the sheet. The problem is how to account for the different scale factor in the lower viewport.

AutoCAD solves this dilemma with a special value for DIMSCALE. When you draw dimensions in paper space viewports (TILEMODE = 0), set the DIMSCALE variable to 0. This instructs AutoCAD to set the dimension's size relative to the viewports scale factor. This is true for every viewport in paper pace, even if they have different scale factors.

The following exercise demonstrates what happens when DIMSCALE is set to 0 and dimensions are drawn in model space with TILEMODE set to 0.

SETTING MODEL SPACE AND PAPER SPACE DIMENSION SCALES BY SETTING DIMSCALE AND DIMLFAC SYSTEM VARIABLES

1. Open the 15DWG05.DWG drawing file, which can be found on the accompanying CD.

   The drawing shown in figure 15.15 opens.

NOTE

I used the XCLIP command to clip a boundary around the area I wanted to see in the viewport. In this case, instead of inserting the topo as an xref, I inserted it as a block. As you can see, the XCLIP command clips blocks as well as xrefs.

2. Enter **DIMSCALE** at the Command: prompt.

   AutoCAD issues the following prompt:

   ```
   New value for DIMSCALE <40>:
   ```

   This shows that the current value for DIMSCALE is 40. This was the dimension scale factor applied to the dimensions when they were drawn.

3. Press Enter to accept the default value of 40.

4. From the Dimension menu, choose Style.

   The Dimension Styles dialog box opens.

5. Click on the Geometry button.

   The Geometry dialog box opens. Notice under Scale that the Overall Scale value is 40. This is the value of DIMSCALE.

6. Select the Scale to Paper Space check box.

   A check mark appears in the box and the Overall Scale feature is set to 0 and grayed out, as shown in figure 15.16.

Figure 15.16

Scale to paper space is turned on in the Geometry dialog box.

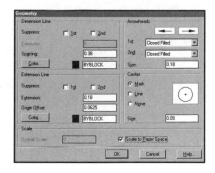

7. Click on OK and then click on OK again to close both dialog boxes.

   The DIMSCALE variable is now set to 0.

Next, you will draw the same dimensions again to view how AutoCAD handles the two viewports' different scale factors.

8. Double-click the PAPER tile in the status bar at the bottom of the screen.

9. Choose the lower viewport if it is not the active viewport.

10. From the Layer Control, select the 10_scale layer to make it current.

11. From the Dimension menu, choose Aligned.

12. Snap to the intersection of the centerline and the number 4 tick mark.

13. Snap to the intersection of the centerline and the number 5 tick mark.

14. Drag the dimension value to just below the existing dimension.

15. Choose the upper viewport to make it active.

16. From the Layer control, choose the 40_scale layer to make it current.

17. From the Dimension menu, choose Aligned.

18. Snap to the intersection of the centerline and the number 4 tick mark.

19. Snap to the intersection of the centerline and the number 5 tick mark.

20. Drag the dimension value above the centerline to about the same position as the existing dimension.

Your drawing should look similar to figure 15.17. Notice that the dimension text you just created is the same size in both viewports. With DIMSCALE set to 0, AutoCAD correctly sized the dimension object's geometry automatically.

Figure 15.17

With DIMSCALE set to 0, the dimension's geometry is scaled correctly.

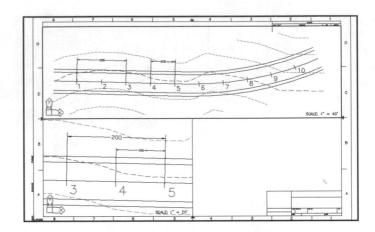

Setting DIMSCALE to 0 works great when you are drawing objects in model space viewports, but how can you instruct AutoCAD to accurately determine the distance between two points when you are in paper space?

AutoCAD has another dimension variable called DIMLFAC that multiplies distances measured in paper space by a viewport's scale factor.

To demonstrate this feature, continue with the previous exercise.

USING DIMLFAC TO SCALE IN PAPER SPACE

1. Double-click the MODEL tile in the status bar at the bottom of the screen.

2. Enter **DIM** at the Command: prompt to automatically set the DIMLFAC value.

3. Enter **DIMLFAC** at the Command: prompt.

   AutoCAD indicates that the current value of DIMLFAC is –40, and it prompts for a new value.

4. Enter **V** for viewport.

5. Select the lower viewport.

   AutoCAD sets the value of DIMLFAC to –20. This value is derived from the viewports scale factor, which is 1/20.

6. Enter **EXIT** to quit the DIM command.

7. Zoom in to the lower viewport.

8. From Layer Control, choose the 0 layer to make it current.

9. From the Dimension menu, choose Aligned.

10. Snap to the intersection of the centerline and the number 4 tick mark.

11. Snap to the intersection of the centerline and the number 5 tick mark.

12. Drag the dimension value below the centerline. Your drawing should look similar to figure 15.18.

13. Close the drawing and save your changes if you want.

Notice that the dimension text you just created is the same size as the previous dimension text you created. More important, notice that AutoCAD calculated the correct distance, even though the measurement was made in paper space. With DIMSCALE set to 0 and DIMLFAC set to –20, AutoCAD correctly sized the dimension object's geometry and correctly determined its length.

Figure 15.18

With DIMLFAC set appropriately, the dimension's distance value is calculated correctly.

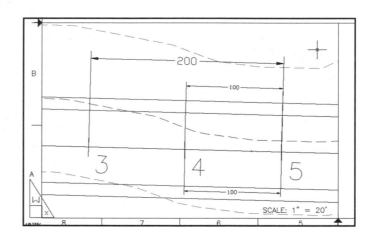

Dimensioning in model space and paper space has advantages and disadvantages. In model space, associative dimensioning automatically updates a dimension as objects in model space are edited. If the dimension is drawn in paper space and the model space objects are edited or change shape, or if the model is moved or rescaled in its paper space viewport, however, the dimensions drawn in paper space will not update. They will have to be edited separately or redrawn.

The advantage of drawing dimensions in paper space is that all dimensions can reside on the same layer. As demonstrated in the previous exercise though, multiple layers are needed for each viewport in which dimensions are drawn. This is necessary so that layers can be frozen or thawed as required to display only the dimensions appropriate for a particular viewport.

Summary

This chapter covered paper space basics and why you should use paper space. You learned about the TILEMODE system variable and the difference between tiled and untiled, or floating, viewports. Comparisons of model space versus paper space were presented, as well as the differences between the Hide Lines and Hideplot. You learned about Release 14's new paper space features, and how to use the MVSETUP command to align model space objects in different viewports. You also learned the value of saving scaled views with the DDVIEW command and how to quickly change multiple viewport's current layer freeze/thaw values. Finally, you learned how to set dimension variables properly to be drawn in paper space viewports or in paper space.

This chapter has shown you how to use AutoCAD 14's Paper Space feature in productive ways. By using the techniques discussed, you can easily control the appearance of your final drawings and ease the time-consuming process of dimensioning, thereby increasing your productivity.

TEXT ANNOTATION

by Francis Soen

Text is a very important part of any drawing. On any given drawing, you may need to draw a single word, a single sentence, or even paragraphs of text. Being able to efficiently draw and edit text directly affects your productivity. In this chapter you learn how to do the following:

- *Draw and edit single lines of text*

- *Define and use text styles to control the appearance of your text*

- *Draw and edit paragraphs of text*

- *Perform a spelling check on your drawing*

- *Invoke Quick Text mode, mapping fonts, and the clipboard*

Drawing Single-Line Text

A single line of text can consist of a single character, a word, or a complete sentence. The easiest way to draw such text is to use the DTEXT command. To insert a single line of text, from the Draw menu, choose Text, Single Line Text. The initial prompt displayed in the command window presents several options:

```
Justify/Style/<Start point>:
```

The default option is to specify the lower-left endpoint, which is otherwise known as the start point, of the new line of text. After picking the start point, you are prompted to supply the height and rotation angle of the text and the new text to be drawn. As you type the text to be drawn, it is displayed on your drawing. If you make a typographical error, you can use the Backspace key to delete the error and retype the text. You signify the end of the line of text by pressing the Enter key, at which point you may begin a new line of text immediately below the line of text just drawn. To stop drawing any additional lines of text, press the Enter key without typing any new text. You may also relocate the text marker (the []) by picking a point with the cursor.

 When you enter text, you can take advantage of the command line buffer to repeat previously entered text by using the up and down arrow keys to scroll through the buffer.

INSIDER TIP

The spacing between successive lines of text is fixed at approximately 1.67 of the text height. This spacing is normally fixed; however, each line of text is a separate object. As such, you can use the MOVE command to re-arrange the lines. You also can pick a new justification point at the Text: prompt prior to typing the new line of text, thus enabling you to override the default line spacing.

Typing the text you want to draw is the easy part. It is also important to know how to format the text according to your needs. The following sections discuss how to choose the correct text height, justification, and text style. You also learn how to continue text below the previous line, use special formatting codes and symbols, and edit text.

In the following exercise, you use DTEXT to add several lines of text to a site drawing.

DRAWING SINGLE-LINE TEXT USING DTEXT

1. Open the IAW drawing ACME.DWG from the accompanying CD. This is a site drawing set up in paper space with a model space scale of 1 drawing unit equal to 100 feet (1:100 scale).

2. Make sure you are in paper space. Choose Named Views from the View menu to restore the view TITLE_BLOCK. Make a new layer named **TEXT** and make it current.

3. From the Draw menu, choose Text, Single Line Text. Using the Style option, set the current style to STANDARD. Using the Justify option, set the justification option to Center and pick the point 29,2.5 as the center point. Specify a height of 0.3 and a rotation angle of 0.

   Type the text **ACME Engineering** and press the Enter key twice.

4. Repeat the DTEXT command. Pick the point 26.75,2 as the start point. Remember, the default justification is left-justified text. Use a height of 0.2 and a rotation angle of 0.

   Type the text **Bakersville Project** and press the Enter key once. Type the text **Legend & General Notes** and press the Enter key twice.

5. Repeat the DTEXT command. Type **M** at the start point prompt, thereby specifying Middle justification.

   You can bypass the Justify option and set the justification directly at the initial prompt. Pick the point 29.5,1 as the middle point. Use a height of 0.2 and a rotation angle of 0.

   Type the text **L10** and press the Enter key twice.

6. Repeat the DTEXT command. Type **R** at the start point prompt to specify Right justification.

   Pick the point 27.8,0.6 as the right point. Use a height of 0.1 and a rotation angle of 0.

   Type the text **1"=100'** and press the Enter key twice.

7. Restore the view ALL. Make the model space viewport active (double-click the Paper button).

8. Issue the DTEXT command. Pick the point 855,1290 as the start point.

   Use a text height of 50, which at a 1:100 plot scale will produce ½" text. Use a rotation angle of 10 degrees.

   Type **Route 101** and press the Enter key twice.

9. The exercise is complete and you may now save the drawing. Figure 16.1 shows the outcome.

Figure 16.1

ACME.DWG with some single line text added.

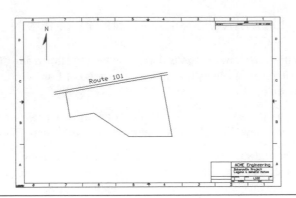

Now that you know how to create new text in your drawing, the following section details how to change text styles in accordance with your needs.

Choosing the Correct Text Height

The hardest part of drawing text is deciding on the correct text height for the scale for which the drawing is set up. Unfortunately, because AutoCAD does not have a built-in mechanism for storing and using the drawing scale to set the correct text height for full-size drawings, it is necessary to take into account the drawing scale in specifying the text height. Use tables 16.1 and 16.2 to help specify the correct text height. To use these tables, go to the row associated with your drawing scale. Then move along the row to the column associated with the height you want your text to have on your plot.

Table 16.1

Text Heights for Architectural Scales

| Drawing Scale | Plotted Text Heights | | | | |
	$3/32"$	$1/8"$	$3/16"$	$1/4"$	$3/8"$
$1/16"=1'$	18"	24"	36"	48"	72"
$3/32"=1'$	12"	16"	24"	32"	48"
$1/8"=1'$	9"	12"	18"	24"	36"
$3/16"=1'$	6"	8"	12"	16"	24"
$1/4"=1'$	4.5"	6"	9"	12"	18"
$1/2"=1'$	2.25"	3"	4.5"	6"	9"

Table 16.2

Text Heights for Decimal Scales

Drawing Scale	Plotted Text Heights				
	$3/32''$	$1/8''$	$3/16''$	$1/4''$	$3/8''$
1:10	0.9375 d.u.*	1.25 d.u.	1.875 d.u.	2.5 d.u.	3.75 d.u.
1:20	1.8750 d.u.	2.50 d.u.	3.750 d.u.	5.0 d.u.	7.5 d.u.
1:50	4.6875 d.u.	6.25 d.u.	9.375 d.u.	12.5 d.u.	18.75 d.u.
1:100	9.3750 d.u.	12.50 d.u.	18.750 d.u.	25.0 d.u.	37.5 d.u.

d.u. stands for drafting units

Choosing a Justification

The default option of DTEXT is to specify the left endpoint, or the start point, of the line of text. Specifying the Style option at the initial DTEXT prompt displays the following prompt:

```
Align/Fit/Center/Middle/Right/TL/TC/TR/ML/MC/MR/BL/BC/BR:
```

Figure 16.2 shows the various justification options and their corresponding locations.

Figure 16.2

The possible justification points for a line of text.

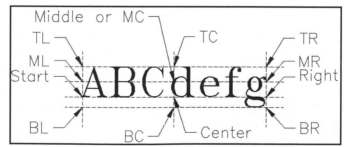

Unlike the justification options illustrated in figure 16.2, the Align and Fit options require that you define two points.

Use the Align option when you want to specify the left and right endpoints of the text and do not care about the resulting height. The text height is automatically set to make the text fit between the specified points. Also, the angle from the first point to the second point is used as the rotation angle of the text.

Use the Fit option when you want to specify the left and right endpoints and the height of the text. To make the text fit between the specified points, the height-to-width ratio of the text characters is varied. Therefore, you may end up with skinny-looking characters on one line and very fat-looking characters on the next.

INSIDER TIP

You can specify a justification option at the primary DTEXT prompt, which eliminates the need for first selecting the Justify option. The most commonly used ones are the default Start point, Right, Middle, and Center justifications.

When the text is initially drawn with one of the alternate justification options specified, it is drawn left justified, as if the default justification were being used. Upon ending the DTEXT command, however, the text is redrawn with the correct justification.

NOTE

You can pick the justification point of a line of text with the INSERT object snap mode.

This concludes the discussion of text justification options. The next section deals with the topic of text styles.

Choosing a Text Style

The appearance of the text drawn by DTEXT is controlled via a named group of settings referred to as a *text style*. The default text style supplied in the prototype drawings ACAD.DWG and ACADISO.DWG is STANDARD. In the template drawings, several text styles are predefined for you. Use the Style option to set the style you want to use to generate the new text. The process of actually defining new and modifying existing styles is discussed in the section "Defining Text Styles," later in this chapter.

Continuing Below the Previous Line

If, after you end the DTEXT command, you want to draw an additional line of text below the last drawn line of text, you can easily do so by issuing the DTEXT command and pressing the Enter key rather than picking a new start point. DTEXT will then draw the new line of text using the style, height, and rotation angle of the previously drawn text.

INSIDER TIP

To help you spot the last line of text drawn, that line is highlighted when you begin DTEXT. The highlighting, however, may not be apparent if the text is too small on the screen.

Using Special Formatting Codes and Symbols

You can do a limited amount of formatting with the DTEXT command. For instance, a line can be drawn under or above the text simply by adding the codes %%u (underlining) and %%o (overlining) to the text as you enter it. The codes act as toggle switches; the first time you include the code in a line of text, it turns that effect on. The second time the code is encountered in the same line of text, the effect is turned off. If the code is not encountered a second time in the line of text, then the effect is continued to the end of the text line but is not continued to the next line. For example, to draw the text shown in figure 16.3, the text you type is **%%uUnderlining%%u and %%oOverlining%%o can be used separately or %%o%%utogether**.

Figure 16.3

Underlining and Overlining can be used separately or together

Using underline and overline formatting codes.

In addition to underlining and overlining, you also can draw symbols that are in the font file, but are not on the keyboard. Table 16.3 shows several formatting codes and the resulting symbols.

Table 16.3

Additional Formatting Codes

Formatting Code	Symbol	Meaning
%%c	Ø	diameter
%%d	°	degree
%%p	±	plus/minus

The codes are not case-sensitive. In addition to the codes in table 16.3, the code %%nnn can be used to draw any character in a font file.

A much easier way of drawing a symbol is simply to use Window's Character Map program.

To use the Character Map program in place of the %%nnn code, simply start the Character Map program (usually found in the Accessories group of programs) and select the font file you have specified in the current text style. Then select the character you want to draw and copy it to the clipboard. You can now paste the character into the text you are typing.

Not all font files contain the same characters, which is why it is important that the font file you choose to copy from in the Character Map program is the same font file specified in the text style you are drawing with in AutoCAD. What the Character Map program actually copies when you choose to copy a character to the clipboard is the character's position number in the font chart. When you paste that character in AutoCAD, the character corresponding to the position number recorded in the clipboard is drawn—if you are using a different font file in AutoCAD, you may end up with a different character altogether.

After drawing and formatting the initial text, you may want to change the wording or appearance of the text. The following section covers the commands you will need to do this.

Editing Single-Line Text

Two commands are of particular use for editing existing text: DDEDIT and DDMODIFY. DDEDIT is quicker to use than DDMODIFY when all you want to do is change the text in one or more text objects. DDMODIFY is slower, but more powerful, than DDEDIT, in that DDMODIFY enables you to change the appearance of the selected text.

Using DDEDIT

From the Modify menu, choose Object, Text to issue the DDEDIT command. After selecting the text object to be changed, the Edit Text dialog box appears displaying the selected text (see fig. 16.4).

Figure 16.4

The Edit Text dialog box of DDEDIT.

Initially, the entire line of text is highlighted and will be replaced by whatever you type. If you want to edit a specific portion of the text, it is necessary to position the cursor at the desired point in the text and pick it. You can then use the Insert, Delete, and Backspace keys to add and delete characters.

If you want to replace a portion of the text displayed in the Edit Text dialog box, highlight the portion to be replaced. The highlighted portion is replaced with any new text you type.

Using DDMODIFY

Choose Properties from the Standard toolbar or Modify menu and select a single text object to issue the DDMODIFY command. The resulting Modify Text dialog box, shown in figure 16.5, enables you to change the text, the style, the justification point, and the various settings that control the appearance of the text object.

Figure 16.5

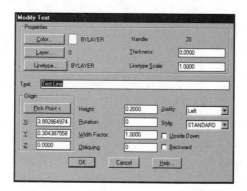

The Modify Text dialog box of DDMODIFY.

See "Defining Text Styles" later in this chapter for a clearer explanation of the text settings that you can change.

In the following exercise, you use DDEDIT and DDMODIFY to change some text in a drawing.

EDITING SINGLE-LINE TEXT WITH DDEDIT AND DDMODIFY

1. Continue to use the drawing ACME.DWG to which you added some text in the previous exercise.

2. Choose Named Views from the View menu. Restore the view TITLE_BLOCK.

3. From the Modify menu, choose Object, Text. Select the text "Bakersville Project." Highlight "ville" and type **field**. The text should look like figure 16.6. Click on OK to make the change. Press Enter to exit the DDEDIT command.

4. Choose Properties from the Object Properties toolbar. Select the text "L100." Press the Enter key to end the selection process. Change the height from 0.20 to 0.30 and click the OK button to effect the height change. The text should look like figure 16.6.

5. You are done making changes to this drawing, so you may now save the drawing.

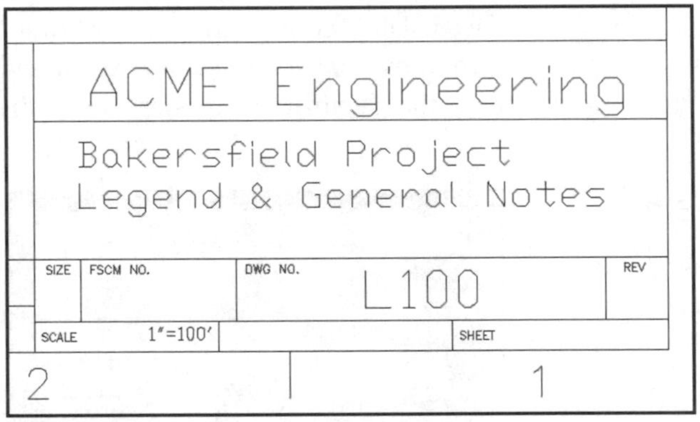

Figure 16.6

Changing text with DDEDIT and DDMODIFY.

Defining Text Styles

A *text style* is a named group of settings that controls the appearance of text in a drawing.

The default text style, and only defined style, in the templates ACAD.DWT and ACADISO.DWT is named STANDARD. You can, however, have as many text styles defined as you want in a drawing (the other template files each have several styles predefined). Text styles are defined and modified with the STYLE command, which is issued by choosing Text Style from the Format menu. Figure 16.7 shows the Text Style dialog box. The various settings within the Text Style dialog box are explained in more detail in the following sections.

Figure 16.7

The Text Style dialog box of STYLE.

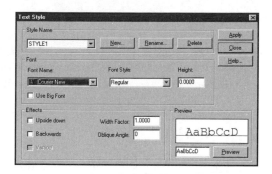

To create a new style, you actually begin by making a copy of the current style. If the current style is not the style you want to begin with, then select the desired style from the list of existing styles (thereby making it the current style).

Click on the New button. Specify a name for the new style, and a duplicate style is created from the selected style. To rename an existing style, select the style from the list of existing styles, click on the Rename button, and enter a new name. To delete an existing style, highlight the name from the list of existing styles, and click on the Delete button. The Standard text style cannot be renamed or deleted.

NOTE

When a text object is created, the style it is created with is recorded with the object. A text style can only be deleted if no existing text objects reference the style.

Text styles are stored in the drawing in which they are defined. If you want to have multiple styles immediately available in a new drawing, define the styles in your template drawings. If you want to import a style from another drawing, insert the other drawing or attach the drawing as an external reference and bind the desired style. (See Chapter 13, "External References," for a complete explanation of binding.)

In defining a new style or modifying an existing style, you must choose a font file, what special effects to enable, a text height, a width factor, and an oblique angle. Choosing these settings and previewing the results of these settings are covered in the following sections.

Previewing the Text Style Settings

The character Preview area enables you to view a sample of the selected style and the results of changing the various settings. To view your own sample text, type your sample text in the text edit box and click on the Preview button.

Choosing a Font and Style

The font file is the file that contains the information that determines the shape of each character. Table 16.4 lists the various types of font files supplied with AutoCAD.

Table 16.4

Various Types of Font Files

File Name Extension	Font Type
SHX	AutoCAD's native font file, known as a shape file
TTF	TrueType font file

The most efficient font files are the shape files supplied with AutoCAD. In addition to the TrueType font files supplied with AutoCAD, the TrueType fonts supplied with Windows and other Windows applications can also be used.

 PostScript files used to be directly usable in earlier versions of AutoCAD. In R14, however, you must first use the COMPILE command to compile the PostScript font file into a shape file. In fact, in earlier versions several PostScript font files were supplied, but none are supplied in R14.

 AutoCAD supports TrueType font families, which means that for some TrueType fonts, you can choose a font style such as regular, italic, bold, or bold italic. Note that not all TrueType fonts have more than the regular style defined.

There are two system variables that affect the plotting of text drawn with TrueType fonts, TEXTFILL and TEXTQLTY. When TEXTFILL is disabled, the characters are plotted in outline form only. If TEXTFILL is enabled, the characters are filled in.

The value of TEXTQLTY affects the smoothness of the characters at plot time. The value of TEXTQLTY can be set from 0 to 100, with the default value set to 50. The higher the value, the better the resolution of the characters, but it will take longer to process the drawing for plotting.

Both system variables can be typed at the Command: prompt, but are easier to access through the Print/Plot Configuration dialog box (see fig. 16.8). TEXTQLTY is set via the Text Resolution text edit box, while TEXTFILL is set via the Text Fill check box.

Figure 16.8

Setting TEXTFILL and TEXTQLTY through the Print/Plot Configuration dialog box.

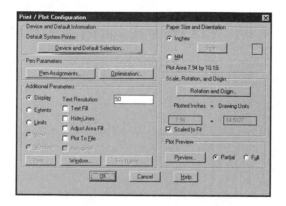

INSIDER TIP

Using the simplest shaped characters will minimize the drawing size and speed up opening and working with the drawing file. The characters in the Simplex and Romans font files are quite simple in appearance and are similar to the simplex characters used in board drafting. Some shape files contain the alphabet of foreign languages, such as GREEKS.SHX, or even symbols, such as SYMUSIC.SHX.

After you change the font file associated with an existing style, upon applying the change, all text drawn with the modified style is updated to reflect the change. If you want to draw text with more than one font file, you must create one style per font file and switch between the styles as you draw the text.

Setting a Height

Also found in the Font area is the text Height setting. The default height of 0 dictates that the user sets the text height at the time the text is drawn. A height other than 0 sets the text height for that particular style to that height. The style is then referred to as a fixed height style and the text height prompt for the DTEXT command is suppressed.

Changing the text height setting of an existing style does not affect the appearance of existing text objects.

Specifying Special Effects

In the Effects section of the Text Style dialog box are the Upside down, Backwards, Vertical, Width Factor, and Oblique Angle settings. These settings are covered in detail in the following sections.

Upside Down, Backwards, and Vertical Text

In the Effects area, you can enable the Upside down, Backwards, and Vertical settings. See figure 16.9 for an example of how these settings affect the appearance of text.

Figure 16.9

The effects of Upside down, Backwards, and Vertical settings on text.

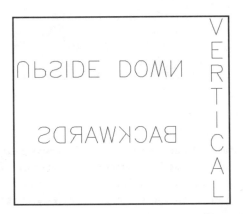

Although the Upside down and Backwards options work with all font files, the Vertical setting only works with SHX files.

INSIDER TIP

If you want to draw text upside down, you don't have to enable the Upside down option. Instead, specify a text rotation angle of 180 degrees. The Backwards option is useful if you want to plot text on the backside of the plot sheet so that the text is readable when viewed from the front. The Vertical option is useful when you need to draw text down the side of a vertical surface, such as a building.

Unlike the font file setting, changing the Upside down and Backwards settings of an existing style does not result in the existing text being automatically updated to reflect the changes. Changing the Vertical setting, however, does affect existing text objects, so you may want to create a new style before changing the Vertical setting.

Setting a Width Factor

The Width Factor determines the width-to-height ratio of the drawn characters. A factor of 1 results in the characters being drawn with the width-to-height ratio defined in the font file used. A factor greater than 1 results in fatter characters, while a factor less than 1 results in skinnier characters. Figure 16.10 illustrates the effects of using different width factors. All three lines were drawn with the same text height.

Figure 16.10

The effects of the Width Factor setting on a line of text.

> Skinny Letters With Width Factor of 0.5
> Normal Letters With Width Factor of 1
> Fat Letters With Width Factor of 1.5

INSIDER **T**IP

Drawing text with a width factor that is less than 1 may make it easier to fit text into an already crowded drawing.

Setting an Oblique Angle

The Oblique Angle setting affects the slant of the characters. It is often used to draw italic text when the characters in the font file being used are not naturally italic. Unlike the text rotation angle, the oblique angle of 0 refers to a vertical direction (see fig. 16.11). A positive text value makes the letters lean to the right, and a negative value makes the letters lean to the left.

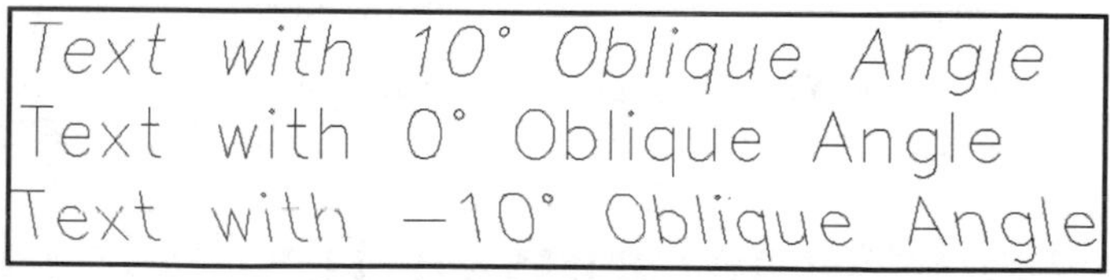

Figure 16.11

The effects of the Oblique Angle setting on a line of text.

> Text with 10° Oblique Angle
> Text with 0° Oblique Angle
> Text with −10° Oblique Angle

In the following exercise, you use the STYLE command to modify an existing style and to create a new style.

MODIFYING AND CREATING TEXT STYLES

1. Continue to use the drawing ACME.DWG. Restore the view TITLE_BLOCK.

2. Issue the STYLE command by choosing Text Style from the Format menu. In the Text Style dialog box, make sure STANDARD is the current style.

3. Select the ROMANS.SHX font file. Click on the Apply button and close the dialog box. Notice how the text you drew in the previous exercise, with the Standard text style, is revised to reflect the font file change (see fig. 16.12).

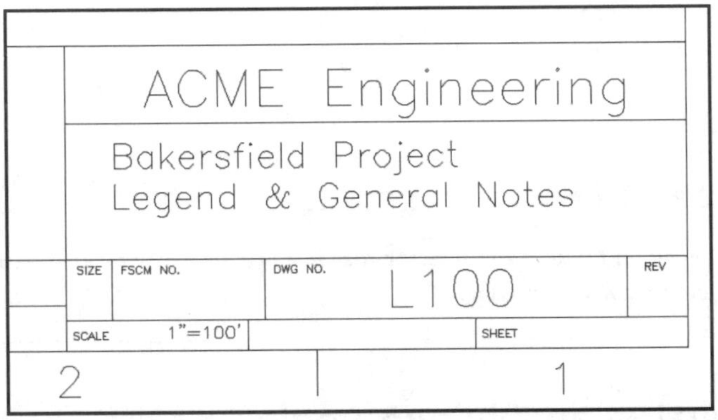

Figure 16.12

Modifying the appearance of text by changing the font file in the text style definition.

ACME Engineering
Bakersfield Project
Legend & General Notes

SIZE	FSCM NO.	DWG NO.		REV
		L100		
SCALE	1"=100'		SHEET	

2   1

4. Repeat the STYLE command. Click on the New button. Name the new style **NOTES**. Initially, NOTES is a duplicate of STANDARD, the style that was current at the time the New button was selected.

5. Choose the TrueType font Courier New, which is a font file that offers several font styles. If you do not have Courier New on your list of available fonts, then choose an alternate font. Choose Bold as the Font Style. Click on the Apply button and close the dialog box. The text style NOTES is now the current text style.

6. After completing the exercise, save the drawing.

Drawing Paragraphs of Text with MTEXT

While the DTEXT command can be used to draw multiple lines of text, each line is drawn as a separate object. Sometimes you will want to draw multiple lines of text as a single unit, such as a paragraph of text. At such times, use the MTEXT command (see fig. 16.13), which is issued by choosing Text from the Draw toolbar or Multiline Text from the Text submenu of the Draw menu.

Figure 16.13

The Multiline Text Editor of MTEXT.

After you issue the MTEXT command, you are prompted to select the first corner point of a window. This window is used to determine the direction in which the mtext object is drawn. When the window is dragged to the right, the mtext object is drawn to the right; when the window is dragged to the left, the mtext object is drawn to the left. Similarly, when the window is dragged upward, the mtext object is drawn upward; when the window is dragged downward, the mtext object is drawn downward. Within the window, the mtext object is drawn with a top left justification. If you want, you can change the justification type to one of eight others: TC (Top Center), TR (Top Right), ML (Middle Left), MC (Middle Center), MR (Middle Right), BL (Bottom Left), BC (Bottom Center), or BR (Bottom Right). These justification types are similar to those available with the DTEXT command (refer to fig. 16.2), except that they apply to the whole mtext object and not just a single line of text.

If you want, you can also choose to use the first window point as the justification point by specifying the Justify option and choosing a justification option. Then choose the Width option and enter the width rather than using the width of the window as the width.

A width of zero will disable the word wrap feature of the Multiline Text Editor, and you will have to press the Enter key every time you want to begin a new line of text.

Several other options appear at the command line that can be set from the command line, but which are easier to set through the Multiline Text Editor dialog box. The Multiline Text Editor is divided into two parts. The bottom part is the screen editor and the top part is divided into three tabs: the Character tab, Properties tab, and Find/Replace tab, all of which are described in detail in the following sections.

INSIDER TIP

If you position your pointer in the screen pointing area and right-click on your mouse, a menu appears that facilitates access to the Undo, Cut, Copy, Paste, and Select ALL operations.

If you have text in an existing ASCII or RTF file, use the Import Text button to import the file into the editor and then edit the text as you want.

Using the Character Tab

The Character tab controls the properties of the text you are drawing. The property settings can be used in one of two ways. First, the property settings control the appearance of the text you type. You also can change the properties of selected text through these settings, thereby creating various special effects. To select text, position the cursor at the beginning of the text, left-click, and then drag the cursor to the end of the text. You can select a word by double-clicking at the start of the word or select the entire body of text by triple-clicking.

Using Special Effects

This section discusses the various effects you can achieve by using the Character tab of the Multiline Text Editor dialog box.

Changing Font File and Text Height

After selecting the text to be affected, you can change the font file to be used and even the height of the text. The text height drop-down list is actually a combination drop-down list and text edit box. You can enter a new text height in the text edit box, or you can also select a height that was previously entered from the drop-down list.

Bold and Italic Text

The Bold and Italic buttons enable you to bold or italicize the text, but only if the chosen font file is a TrueType font. You can use the Underline button to underline any selected text regardless of the font file used. To remove any bold or italic effects, simply select the text again and choose the appropriate button.

Stacking/Unstacking Text

The Stack/Unstack button is used to stack or unstack the selected text. Selected text can be stacked when a backslash character (/) appears somewhere in the text.

Everything to the left of the slash is treated as the numerator and everything to the right is treated as the denominator.

Color Settings

Normally, the color setting is ByLayer, but if you want, you can set a specific color for the selected text with the color drop-down list. Just remember that Text Color controls the pen used with the PLOT command.

Using Special Symbols

Use the Symbol drop-down list to insert the degree, plus/minus, or diameter symbol (see fig. 16.14). To insert any other symbol, choose Other from the list to invoke the Character Map program. Inserting a nonbreaking space prevents the Multiline Text Editor from making a break at that point when deciding where to break the line of text (word wrap feature) to continue to the next line.

Figure 16.14

The Symbol drop-down list in the Multiline Text Editor.

Using the Properties Tab

Choosing the Properties tab enables you to set the text style, justification option, width, and rotation angle of the overall mtext object. Remember that if you use a window to define the location of the mtext object, the justification used is TL, or Top Left, and that the width of the window is the width used for the mtext object.

Using the Find/Replace Tab

Use the Find/Replace tab to search for a specific combination of characters and even to replace the found text with a replacement text string. If the Match Case setting is enabled, only text that matches the case of the find string exactly is found.

If the Whole Word setting is enabled, only words that exactly match the find string are found; otherwise, even words that simply contain the find string are found.

After specifying the settings, use the Find button to start the search.

Editing Mtext Objects

Edit mtext objects with the DDEDIT and DDMODIFY commands as you would edit text objects. If you want to change a property, such as height, of the mtext object, you must select the entire body of text and then change the property. Don't forget, a triple-click selects all text.

Additionally, you can use grips to move or change the width of the mtext object. When you select the grip point that corresponds to the justification point, the mtext object can be moved. Selecting any other grip point enables you to stretch the width of the mtext object.

The next exercise uses mtext to add the notes shown in figure 16.15.

USING MTEXT TO DRAW PARAGRAPHS OF TEXT

1. Continue to use the drawing ACME.DWG. Restore the view ALL. Make sure the paper space viewport is active and the layer TEXT is current.

2. Issue the MTEXT command by choosing the Text tool from the Draw toolbar.

   Specify the point 26,18 as the first corner point. Enter **@4,−1** for the opposite corner point. The Multiline Text Editor dialog box is displayed. Set the height to **0.25**. Enter the text **Notes** and press the Enter key twice.

3. Enter the text. The information on this drawing reflects information gathered as of 2/2/97. Press the Enter key twice.

4. Enter the text. This drawing is a preliminary drawing and should not be used for engineering purposes.

5. Select the text Notes and click on the Underline button. Close the dialog box.

   Figure 16.15 shows the drawing with the MTEXT object added.

Figure 16.15

ACME with an mtext object added.

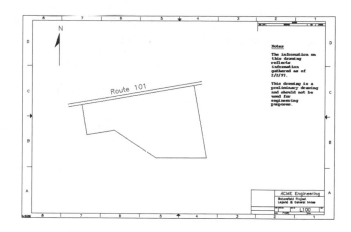

6. For now, you are done modifying this drawing, so go ahead and save your work.

Performing a Spelling Check

To check the spelling of your text and mtext objects, issue the SPELL command by choosing the Spelling tool from the Standard toolbar. Figure 16.16 illustrates the Check Spelling dialog box of SPELL.

Figure 16.16

The Check Spelling dialog box of SPELL.

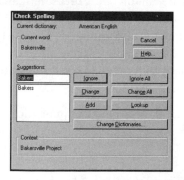

When SPELL encounters an unknown word, the Check Spelling dialog box is displayed, and you must choose to either replace the word, ignore the discrepancy, or add the word to your supplemental dictionary. If no errors are found, a message box appears informing you that the spell check is complete, but the Check Spelling dialog box itself does not appear.

The following exercise takes you through the steps of using the SPELL command to check the text you entered in ACME.DWG.

CHECKING THE SPELLING IN YOUR DRAWING

1. Continue to use the drawing ACME.DWG. Make sure the paper space viewport is current.

2. Issue the SPELL command by choosing SPELLER from the Standard toolbar.

   Use the All option to select all objects. SPELL stops at any word it does not recognize. If you use abbreviations a lot, be sure to add them to your supplemental dictionary.

3. If you want to check the spelling of text in model space, you must repeat the SPELL command with the model space viewport current.

4. This is the last exercise for this chapter, so you may end the drawing if you want.

Specifying the Dictionaries

The SPELL command looks up words in as many as two dictionaries at any given time: a main and a supplemental dictionary. Several main dictionaries are supplied with AutoCAD, with the default being the American English Dictionary. The default supplemental dictionary is SAMPLE.CUS (SAMPLE.CUS contains a number of AutoCAD command words and terms). To change the dictionaries used by SPELL, issue the PREFERENCES command. In the preferences dialog box, change the Main Dictionary and Custom Dictionary File settings under Text Editor, Dictionary, and Font File Names in the Files tab.

Unlike the supplemental dictionary, the main dictionary file cannot be modified or added to. You can, however, add words to and change the supplemental dictionary.

Creating a Supplemental Dictionary

A *supplemental* dictionary file is a simple text file that contains the additional words that you want SPELL to use. The file format is simple—one word per line. You can create as many supplemental dictionaries as you want, but you can only use one at any given time. When you create a supplemental dictionary, be sure to use a CUS file name extension and place it in one of the folders listed in the Support Files Search Path setting in the Preferences dialog box.

Now that you know how to draw single and multiple lines of text, and how to edit the text style and check spelling, you should familiarize yourself with several additional text handling features that are covered in the next section.

Looking at Additional Text Options

The following sections cover several optional text handling features that may prove useful to you. These features will enable you to speed up the display of text, handle missing font files, and insert text files into the current drawing.

Enabling the Quick Text Display

Displaying text, especially text drawn with complex font files, can be time-consuming. When you want to speed up the display of the drawing and do not need to read the existing text, enable the Quick Text mode. You can enable the Quick Text mode through the Drawing Aids dialog box. With Quick Text enabled, text and mtext objects are displayed as simple rectangles. To immediately see the effects of enabling Quick Text on existing text, issue the REGEN command.

Note

Even with Quick Text enabled, new text objects are displayed completely, rather than as rectangles, making adding text easier.

Specifying an Alternate Font File

Font files are not stored with the drawing file. If a font file that is referenced in the drawing is not available when the drawing is opened, an error message is displayed. You are then prompted to choose a replacement font file. If you want to bypass all such error messages, you can specify a font file that is automatically used whenever a needed font file cannot be found. This *alternate font file* is specified by setting the Alternate Font File setting under Text Editor, Dictionary, and Font File Names in the Files tab of the Preferences dialog box. The default alternate font is simplex.shx.

WARNING

A couple of possible problems with using an alternate font occur, however. If the missing font file contains special characters that the alternate font file does not have, the text on the drawing may end up incomplete. Furthermore, because the space that a line of text occupies is dependent on the font file used to generate the text, you may find that the text on the drawing looks out of place or does not fit properly anymore. The best solution is to obtain the correct font files and use them, unless you are sure you have a suitable replacement file.

Mapping Fonts

If you need to specify more than one alternate font file, specify a font mapping file. A *font mapping file* is a text file where each line in the file specifies the font file to be replaced and its substitute font file (separated by a semicolon). The default font map file is ACAD.FMP. You can change the font map used by changing the Font Mapping File setting under Text Editor, Dictionary, and Font File Names in the Files tab of the Preferences dialog box.

The default file ACAD.FMP (the contents of which are listed in the following list) maps the PostScript fonts that were supplied with R13 to their equivalent TrueType fonts.

Cibt__.pfb = CITYB__.TTF

cobt__.pfb = COUNB__.TTF

eur__.pfb = EURR__.TTF

euro__.pfb = EURRO__.TTF

par__.pfb = PANROMAN__.TTF

rom__.pfb = ROMANTIC__.TTF

romb__.pfb = ROMAB__.TTF

romi__.pfb = ROMAI__.TTF

sas__.pfb = SANSS__.TTF

sasb__.pfb = SANSSB__.TTF

sasbo__.pfb = SANSSBO__.TTF

saso__.pfb = SANSSO__.TTF

suf__.pfb = SUPEF__.TTF

te__.pfb = TECHNIC__.TTF

teb__.pfb = TECHB__.TTF

tel__.pfb = TECHL__.TTF

Drawing Text as Attributes

An alternate method to drawing text objects that are to be incorporated into block definitions is to draw attributes. Attributes behave much like text objects but have additional functions beyond displaying text. Attributes are discussed in more detail in Chapter 12, "Creating and Using Blocks."

Dragging and Dropping Text Files

In Windows 95 and NT, you can drag a text file icon from the desktop and drop it into your drawing. AutoCAD will automatically draw the file contents as an mtext object, using the current text settings for the text height, rotation angle, and text style.

Copying Text Using the Clipboard

You also can copy text from any application to your clipboard and then paste the contents into your drawing. If you use the PASTE command, the contents are dropped into your drawing as an embedded object. If you use the PASTESPEC command, you can choose to paste the clipboard contents as text, in which case the text is drawn as an mtext object.

Be prepared to perform some experimenting if you are going to use the clipboard. The clipboard operations depend on OLE (Object Linking and Embedding), which is a constantly evolving feature. Some windows applications support older versions of OLE and may limit what operations you can carry out and how much information you can copy to the clipboard.

Another consideration is that the form in which the data is pasted into your drawing may limit how much information can be pasted from the clipboard. For example, I copied three pages of text from WordPerfect 7.0 onto the clipboard. I then pasted the data into an AutoCAD drawing, but only one page of the text was displayed. But by using PASTESPEC and specifying that the data should be pasted as text, all three pages appeared in the drawing (of course, I lost all the WordPerfect formatting).

Creating Your Own Shape File

You have the option of creating your own shape file containing the characters you want to use. Creating the instructions that define each character is a laborious procedure because you have to break each character into a series of strokes and enter the codes for those strokes into the new font file. In the earlier versions of AutoCAD that did not support the use of TrueType fonts, defining your own shape file was the only way to add to the font files supplied with AutoCAD. With R14 and the support of TrueType font families, it is much more sensible to simply use one of the fonts supplied with Windows. You can also purchase additional fonts from a number of software vendors at a very low cost.

Using the Bonus Text Routines

In the Text submenu of the Bonus menu and on the Bonus Text Tools toolbar, you will find several powerful routines for drawing and editing text (if you do not see the Bonus menu or toolbar, then follow the installation instructions in the "Using Bonus Tools" section of Chapter 11, "Advanced Geometry Editing"). The tools enable you to create some very interesting effects with text and are covered in the following sections.

Adjusting the Width Factor with TEXTFIT

TEXTFIT is issued by choosing Text Fit from the Text submenu of the Bonus menu or from the Bonus Tools toolbar. It is designed to work with text objects only and will not operate with mtext objects. You use TEXTFIT to adjust the width factor of the characters in a text object. After selecting the text object, the following prompt is displayed and a rubber band is displayed:

```
Select Text to stretch/shrink:
Starting Point/<Pick new ending point>:
```

The rubber band is anchored at the left endpoint of the text object. The length of the rubber band represents the distance the line of text is to occupy. The default option is to pick the endpoint of the rubber band, to define that distance. TEXTFIT then calculates and applies a width factor to the text object that will stretch or shrink the line of text to fit the specified distance. Specifying the Starting Point option enables you to move the text to a point you select and then adjust the width factor.

If the selected text was drawn with any justification other than left justification, the point you pick as the endpoint of the rubber band is also used as the new justification point for the text object.

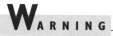

WARNING

> If you have to undo the TEXTFIT command, be careful. TEXTFIT changes the UCS (User Coordinate System) during its operation. Unfortunately, issuing a single U will not undo the effects of TEXTFIT, so you will have to issue several U commands to undo the entire command. If you do not issue enough U commands, you may end up restoring the UCS implemented by TEXTFIT, so always check your UCS when undoing TEXTFIT. Instead of using TEXTFIT, you can use the DDMODIFY command to change the width factor of a selected text object and not have to worry about the status of the UCS.

Creating a Mask with TEXTMASK

TEXTMASK is issued by choosing Text Mask from the Text submenu of the Bonus menu or from the Bonus Tools toolbar. It is designed to work with text objects and will not operate with mtext objects. You use TEXTMASK to create a clear area around the text object. Figure 16.17 illustrates a text object with two lines drawn through the text.

Figure 16.17

Using TEXTMASK to obscure the objects running through a text object.

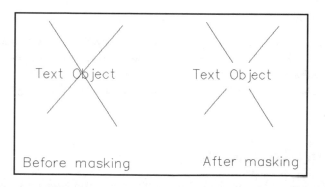

By using TEXTMASK, you can create a clear zone around a text object so that the lines do not obscure the text object. The result of using TEXTMASK illustrated in figure 16.17 suggests that the lines were trimmed. In fact, the lines are still intact. TEXTMASK creates a new type of object named *wipeout*. A wipeout object acts as a barrier that obscures objects that it covers. TEXTFIT draws the wipeout object in such a way as to obscure all objects except the text object. After selecting the text object, the following prompt is displayed:

```
Enter offset factor relative to text height <0.35>:
```

The offset factor defines the size of the wipeout object and is a factor that is multiplied with the text height to obtain the final offset distance (see fig. 16.18).

Figure 16.18

The offset used to size the wipeout object relative to the text object.

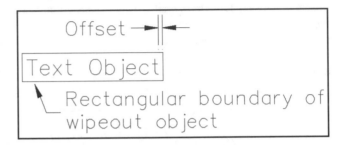

The wipeout object is completely invisible, and the rectangular boundary shown in figure 16.18 is not actually visible. Because a wipeout object is completely invisible, TEXTMASK automatically creates a group to link the wipeout object created with the text object for which it is created. So long as the Object Grouping setting in the Object Selection Settings dialog box is enabled, the invisible wipeout object is automatically selected whenever you select the text object for any editing command.

WARNING

In order for the wipeout object to function correctly, the system variable SORTENTS must be set to 127, which TEXTMASK automatically does. Changing the value of SORTENTS can disable the correct functioning of the wipeout object. SORTENTS is set by choosing the Object Sort Method button of the Object Selection Settings dialog box.

Changing Text with CHT

 CHT is issued by choosing Change Text from the Text submenu of the Bonus menu or Change Multiple Text Items from the Bonus Tools toolbar. It is designed to work with both text and mtext objects. With CHT, you can change the following parameters of the selected text:

- The text height
- The text justification
- The text location
- The text rotation angle
- The text style with which the text is drawn
- The text itself
- The width factor of a text object or the width of a mtext object.

You can use DDMODIFY to change the same parameters that CHT affects; however, the advantage of using CHT is that you can select multiple objects, whereas DDMODIFY can only be used on one object at a time.

WARNING

There seems to be a bug with CHT's Location option (enables you to move the selected object) when an mtext object is selected. With a text object, specifying the Location option enables you to move the object. With an mtext object, the Location option has no effect.

Exploding Text with TXTEXP

TXTEXP is issued by choosing Explode Text from the Text submenu of the Bonus menu or from the Bonus Tools toolbar. It is designed to work with both text and mtext objects. TXTEXP replaces the selected text with a group of polylines. Each character in the text is replaced with a polyline that follows the shape of the original character. The end result of using TXTEXP on a text or mtext object is a group of polylines that resemble the original text characters.

Drawing Text Along an Arc with ARCTEXT

ARCTEXT is issued by choosing Arc Aligned Text from the Text submenu of the Bonus menu or from the Bonus Tools toolbar. It is used to draw text along the outside or inside of an arc (see fig. 16.19).

Figure 16.19

Text drawn along the outside and inside of an arc with ARCTEXT.

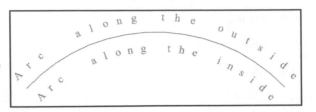

ARCTEXT generates a new type of object, the arctext object. After issuing ARCTEXT, you are prompted to select either an arc or an existing arctext object. Select an arc if you want to draw a new arctext object, and select an existing arctext object if you want to edit the object. After selecting the arc or arctext object, the ArcAlignedText Workshop dialog box is displayed (see fig. 16.20).

Figure 16.20

The ArcAlginedText Workshop dialog box of ARCTEXT.

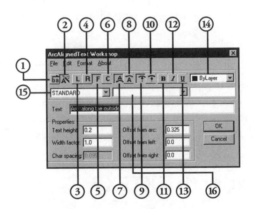

You set the parameters that control the generation of the arctext object with the Format pull-down menu or with the buttons that run along the top of the dialog box. The usage of the controls labeled ① through ⑯ in figure 16.20 is described in the following sections.

Drawing Reverse Text

If you press button ①, the text is drawn backward. This option is similar to the Backwards setting in the Text Style dialog box. The button next to ①, button ②, is inactive as of the time this book was written. Pressing button ② has no effect whatsoever.

Controlling the Alignment

Buttons ③ through ⑥ control how the arctext is placed relative to the selected arc. If button ③ is selected, then the arctext object is positioned relative to the left endpoint of the arc. The offset from the left endpoint is set through the Offset from left text edit box.

If button ④ is selected, then the arctext object is positioned relative to the right endpoint of the arc. The offset from the right endpoint is set through the Offset from right text edit box.

If button ⑤ is selected, then the arctext object is positioned relative to the midpoint of the arc.

If button ⑥ is selected, then the arctext object is positioned relative to both the left and right end points. The offset from the endpoints is set through the Offset from left and Offset from right text edit boxes.

Positioning the Text

You use buttons ⑦ and ⑧ to position the text along the outside ⑦ or the inside ⑧ of the arc. Refer to figure 16.19 for an example of both positions.

Setting the Character Direction

You use buttons ⑨ and ⑩ to choose whether the characters are drawn away from the center of the arc ⑨ or toward the center of the arc ⑩. Figure 16.21 illustrates arctext objects drawn in both directions.

Figure 16.21

Arctext drawn toward and away from the center of the arc.

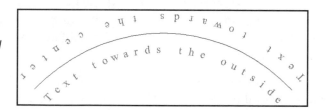

Setting the Typeface

The Bold ⑪, Italic ⑫, and Underline ⑬ buttons are used to set the typeface of the characters and whether the arctext is underlined.

Setting the Color

The color drop-down list (control ⑭) is used to set the color of the arctext. The default color is ByLayer.

Setting the Text Style

The Text Style drop-down list (control ⑮) does not seem to have any effect on an arctext object. You set the font file with the font drop-down list (control ⑯). The text height and width factor of the characters is set with the Text height and Width factor text edit boxes.

Performing a Search and Replace with FIND

FIND is issued by choosing Find and Replace Text from the Text submenu of the Bonus menu or from the Bonus Tools toolbar. It is designed to work with text objects only and will not operate with mtext objects. Use FIND when you want to replace one text string with a new text string. After FIND is issued, the Find and Replace dialog box is displayed (see fig. 16.22).

Figure 16.22

The Find and Replace dialog box of FIND.

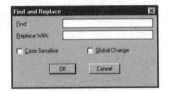

Type the text you are searching for in the Find text edit box. Type the text you want to replace the found text with in the Replace With text edit box. If you want to have the search be case-sensitive, then enable the Case Sensitive setting. If you want to automatically search all text objects in the drawing, then enable the Global Change setting. If the Global Change setting is not enabled, then you will be prompted to select the text objects to be searched.

After you set the parameters for the search, click on the OK button. When the first occurrence of the search string is found, a new Find and Replace dialog box is displayed (see fig. 16.23).

Figure 16.23

The Find and Replace dialog box is displayed when the specified text is found.

The number of text objects that have been found to contain the specified text is displayed in the lower-left corner of the dialog box. Click on the Replace button if you want to replace the found text with the replacement text. Click on the Skip button if you do not want to replace the found text. Click on Auto if you want all occurrences of the found text to be automatically replaced.

Summary

AutoCAD provides a variety of tools to deal with drawing and editing text. This chapter covered the basic steps needed to deal with single lines of text in your drawings, as well as how to add multiple paragraphs of text using the MTEXT command. Editing text and defining and changing text style to control the appearance of text was also covered. But remember, using the simple font files such as SIMPLEX.SHX will make text-rich drawings easier to deal with in the long run.

DRAWING HATCH PATTERNS

by Francis Soen

When you need to fill an area with a repetitive pattern, you can use the
BHATCH command to create an associative hatch object. In this
chapter, you learn how to:

- Specify the pattern to be used and the parameters governing the generation
  of the pattern.

- Define the boundaries of the area(s) to be filled.

- Edit a hatch object.

- Deal with layers and control the visibility of hatch objects.

- Create your own custom hatch pattern.

- Use BOUNDARY to create outlines of complex areas.

Creating Hatch Patterns Using BHATCH

You draw hatch objects whenever you want to highlight an area on your drawing or if you want to convey information pictorially about a specific area on the drawing. For example, you might have a map with different patterns where each pattern represents a distinct type of terrain.

The BHATCH command is used to draw hatch patterns, which are used when you need to fill an area with a repetitive pattern. This section introduces the BHATCH command and also discusses specifying the pattern, defining hatch boundaries, setting attributes, dealing with islands, and using advanced settings.

To issue BHATCH, choose Hatch from the Draw toolbar. The Boundary Hatch dialog box is displayed (see fig. 17.1).

Figure 17.1

Boundary Hatch dialog box of BHATCH.

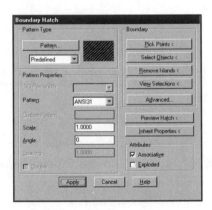

To draw a hatch object, you need to specify the pattern and its parameters, and define the limits of the area to be hatched. These subjects are covered in detail in the following sections.

Specifying the Pattern

The first decision you are faced with is choosing what pattern type to use. You have the option of using one of many predefined patterns, which is the first topic discussed. You can also choose a user-defined pattern, a custom pattern, or imitate an existing hatch object and its parameters. These options are discussed in the sections that follow.

Predefined Patterns

The default pattern type is that of a predefined pattern. AutoCAD comes with a number of predefined patterns. Figure 17.2 shows a sampling of the patterns included with AutoCAD.

Figure 17.2

Some sample hatch patterns supplied with AutoCAD.

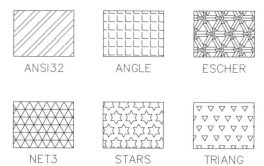

To select one of the predetermined patterns as your hatch pattern, choose the pattern you want from the Hatch Pattern Palette dialog box, which you display by choosing the Pattern button. When you choose a pattern, a sample of the pattern is displayed in the Pattern Type section of the Boundary Hatch dialog box. You can move on to the next available pattern by picking the sample pattern display. Another option is to select the pattern name from the Pattern drop-down list.

Choosing Scale and Angle Settings

After you choose a pattern, you need to set the Scale and Angle settings. The Scale setting is a scaling factor used to scale the pattern's size up and down, much as LTSCALE is used to control the generation of linetypes. The Angle setting enables you to rotate the pattern.

Some of the patterns are designed to represent real building materials and are defined with the appropriate dimensions. The pattern AR-B88, for example, is used to represent 8" × 8" blocks; using a scale factor of 1, the blocks are drawn as 8" × 8" blocks. Other patterns, such as ANSI31, are simply a symbol or linetype drawn in a repetitive fashion. For patterns representing real building materials, a scale of 1 (or thereabouts) should be used for full-size drawings, whereas the scale used for the symbolic patterns should be related to the plot scale for which the drawing is set up. As a general rule, patterns that represent real building materials have an asterisk in the upper-left corner of the sample display.

INSIDER TIP

If you set the scale to too small a value, the pattern can take a while to be generated. If you set the scale to too large a value, the pattern can get so big that you cannot even see a portion of it within the area being filled. Use the Preview Hatch button as you fine-tune the parameters.

Metric (ISO) Patterns

Some patterns are designed for use in metric drawings; their names begin with *ISO* and are near the bottom of the list of predefined patterns. As with the metric linetypes, metric hatch patterns should be used only in metric drawings because the patterns are defined in millimeters and would appear too large in drawings set up in English units. If you do choose to use a metric pattern, the ISO Pen Width setting is enabled. Choosing a pen width sets the initial value for the scale setting equal to the chosen pen width, but you are free to set the scale setting yourself.

Linetype and Color Settings

The hatch object is drawn with the current linetype and color settings. If you want to generate the hatch pattern as displayed in the sample box, make sure that the current linetype is continuous or that you are drawing on a layer with a continuous linetype, using a BYLAYER current linetype setting.

User-Defined Patterns

Another type of pattern, a user-defined pattern, is a simple pattern that consists of one or two sets of parallel lines (see fig. 17.3).

The angle and spacing of the first set of parallel lines is set with the Angle and Spacing settings. A second set of parallel lines can be generated perpendicular to the first set by enabling the Double setting, which you can find in the lower-left corner of the Boundary Hatch dialog box. The spacing for the second set of lines is the same as for the first set (see fig. 17.3).

INSIDER TIP

You can draw a variety of patterns by varying the current linetype with which the pattern is drawn.

Figure 17.3

Two examples of user-defined patterns.

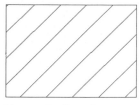

User Defined
Pattern With 1
Set of Lines

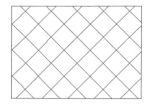

User Defined
Pattern With 2
Sets of Lines

Custom Patterns

Additional hatch patterns, similar to the patterns provided with AutoCAD, can also be defined. The additional pattern definitions are either added to the ACAD.PAT file (or ACADISO.PAT), or each definition is stored in its own individual file (named with a .PAT file name extension). The Individual hatch pattern files are referred to as "Custom Pattern" files. To access one of these custom pattern files, choose the Custom Pattern type, and then specify the file name in the Custom Pattern text edit box.

Specifics on how to create your own hatch patterns are discussed in the section "Creating Custom Hatch Patterns," toward the end of this chapter.

Inherit Properties

If you want to duplicate an existing hatch object in the drawing and the settings used to generate it, choose the Inherit Properties button (located in the lower-right quadrant of the Boundary Hatch dialog box) and select the hatch to be duplicated. The settings for the selected pattern are then retrieved and displayed in the Boundary Hatch dialog box.

Defining the Hatch Boundaries

After a pattern and its settings have been selected, the boundaries of the area to be filled must be defined. The area to be filled has to be completely enclosed by one or more objects (see fig. 17.4). You can define the boundaries either by choosing pick points or by selecting the objects. Both methods are discussed in the following sections.

Figure 17.4

Defining simple areas for hatching with one or more objects.

 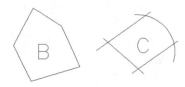

In figure 17.4, Area A is defined with a circle (a closed object). Area B is defined with a series of lines that meet end-to-end. Area C is defined with several lines and an arc that cross over each other and do not meet end-to-end. The objects that define the area to be filled are referred to as *boundary objects*.

Using Pick Points

When you choose the Pick Points button in the Boundary Hatch dialog box, the overall hatch area can be delineated automatically by BHATCH. All you have to do is pick a point inside the area that is to be filled; this point is referred to as an *internal point*. With this method, if multiple boundary objects are used to define the hatch area, the boundary objects do not have to meet end-to-end (refer to Area C in fig. 17.4).

Selecting Objects

A less often used option for delineating the area to be hatched is to choose the Select Objects button in the Boundary Hatch dialog box. With this method, you must select the objects that define the area to be hatched. If more than one boundary object exists, the objects must meet end-to-end, as illustrated by Area B in figure 17.4. This method produces erroneous hatch objects with Area C of figure 17.4 because the boundary objects in that area do not meet end-to-end.

Setting the Attributes

By default, the BHATCH command generates an associative hatch object. *Associative* means that the boundary objects are linked to the hatch object such that when the boundary objects are modified, the hatch object is also modified to conform to the modified boundaries. Furthermore, an associative hatch object's pattern, and the settings used to generate the pattern, can easily be modified with the HATCHEDIT command.

You can choose to disable the Associative setting, but doing so deprives you of the aforementioned advantages when you need to edit the hatch object. Furthermore, you can choose to generate the hatch object as an exploded hatch. By definition, an *exploded hatch* is not an associative object and is not a single object, but rather a collection of lines.

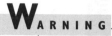

Unless you have a very good reason not to, always use the default setting of generating an associative hatch object. Otherwise, the hatch object will not be modified to conform when you modify the boundary objects.

Sometimes the area you want to hatch is an area with subareas within it. These more complicated scenarios are discussed in the next section.

Dealing with Islands

Enclosed areas within the overall area to be hatched are referred to as *islands*. You can even have islands within islands (see fig. 17.5). Text and mtext objects lying within the area to be hatched are also considered islands.

Figure 17.5

Defining complex areas with islands.

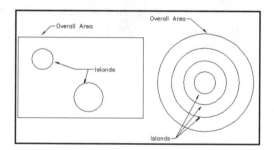

The pick points method for defining the hatch area automatically detects the islands. If you use the select objects method, you have to explicitly select the boundary objects defining the islands for BHATCH to recognize their presence. The islands themselves are defined with one or more objects, just as you would draw the overall hatch area.

The way islands are treated by BHATCH is controlled by the hatch style setting, which is set by choosing the Advanced button in the BHATCH dialog box and then choosing from the Style drop-down list (see fig. 17.6). The three available styles are Normal, Outer, and Ignore. Figure 17.7 shows how the same islands are treated when using the different styles.

Figure 17.6

The Advanced Options dialog box of BHATCH.

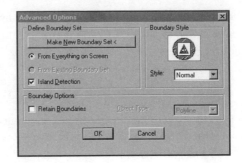

Figure 17.7

Islands using the Normal, Outer, and Ignore hatch styles.

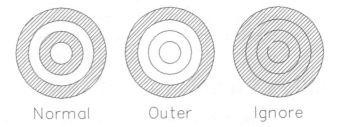

The default style, Normal, is applicable in most situations. It creates alternating bands of hatching. The Ignore style creates a hatch object that is drawn through the islands. With the Outer style, only the outermost area is hatched. The Outer style is useful when you are hatching overlapping areas with different patterns. Figure 17.8 shows such a situation.

Figure 17.8

Using the Outer style to hatch overlapping areas.

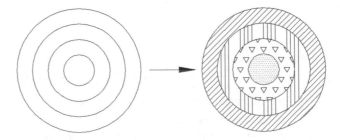

One way to approach the problem of hatching overlapping areas is to pick point 1 and, using the Outer style, hatch the outermost area first. Then pick point 2 and the Outer style, and hatch the next area in, and so on.

BHATCH can also be used on regions. Islands in a region are recognized by BHATCH and are treated according to the current hatch style setting.

In addition to the hatch style settings already discussed, other advanced settings are available to work with in BHATCH.

Choosing Advanced Settings

Choosing the Advanced button displays the Advanced Options dialog box. More often than not, you will not need to change any of these settings.

Define Boundary Set

Normally, the pick points method for delineating the area to be hatched examines all the objects on the screen. You can, however, choose the Define Boundary Set button and explicitly select the objects to be examined for valid hatch boundaries. This option is useful when you have a crowded drawing and want to speed up the algorithm used with the pick points method by restricting the number of objects that are examined.

Style Setting

The Style setting determines how islands are treated. It is discussed earlier, in the "Dealing with Islands" section.

Island Detection Setting

Disabling the Island Detection setting forces the algorithm used with the pick points method to forgo detecting islands. This setting should be left on.

Retain Boundaries Setting

When the hatch area boundary and islands are defined, the areas are automatically delineated with temporary polylines, which normally are removed after the hatch pattern is generated. If you enable the Retain Boundaries setting, the temporary polylines are not removed and are drawn on the current layer. You can even choose to retain the polylines as a region. Enabling the Retain Boundaries option is most useful when the area is delineated by multiple objects and you want a single polyline or region to represent the hatch area. If you subsequently use the AREA command on the resulting polyline(s), or MASSPROP on the resulting region, you can easily determine the area.

The following exercise takes you through the necessary steps of using BHATCH to fill some areas on several details with a pattern.

FILLING IN AREAS WITH BHATCH

1. Open the drawing SOLID.DWG. This drawing contains a 3D solid model. The view you initially see is of paper space with several viewports defined. The viewports themselves are on layer VPORTS, which is frozen.

2. Restore the view ENDVIEW. Make sure that you are in floating model space (double-click on the Paper button, if necessary). Make the Right End view the current viewport by clicking anywhere in that detail. Make a new layer, HATCH, and make sure that it is the current layer.

3. Choose Hatch from the Draw pull-down menu, choose the pattern ANSI34, and set the scale to 1 and the rotation angle to 0. Choose the Pick Points button and pick ① (see fig. 17.9). Click on the Apply button. The results should look like figure 17.9.

Figure 17.9

Hatching the details.

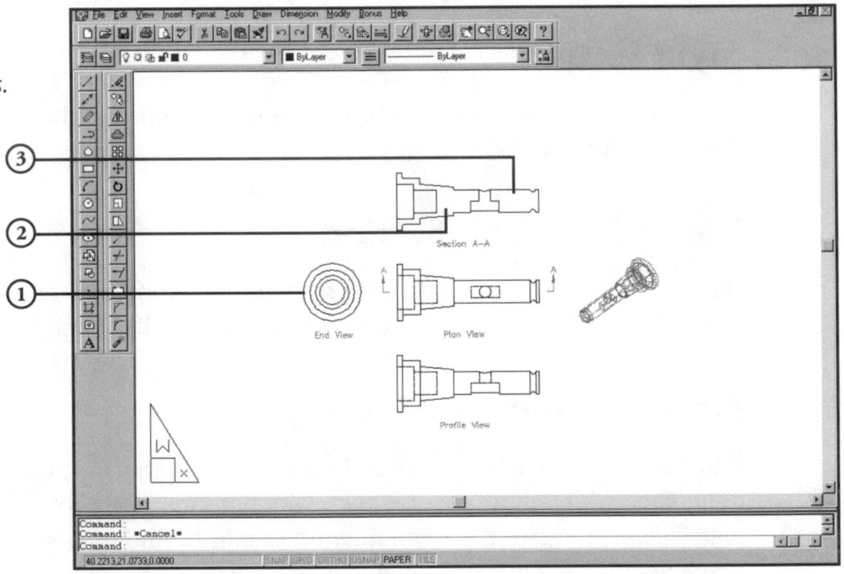

4. Make sure you are in paper space and restore the view SECTION, make floating model space current, and repeat the BHATCH command using the same pattern and parameters as before. Click on the Pick Points button and pick ② and ③ (refer to fig. 17.9). Click on the Apply button. The results should look like figure 17.10.

5. Save the drawing; you are finished with this exercise.

Figure 17.10

SOLID.DWG with the hatch objects drawn.

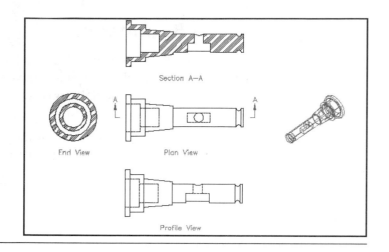

Editing Hatch Objects

To edit hatch objects, issue the HATCHEDIT command by choosing Hatch from the Object submenu of the Modify pull-down menu. The resulting Hatchedit dialog box is similar to the Boundary Hatch dialog box, but with several settings disabled (see fig. 17.11).

Figure 17.11

The Hatchedit dialog box.

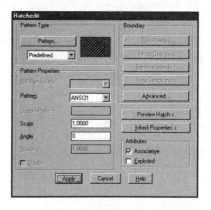

With HATCHEDIT, you can change the pattern of the hatch object or the parameters that control the generation of the pattern. You also can access the Hatchedit dialog box by choosing the Hatch Edit button in the Modify Hatch dialog box (DDMODIFY command).

Editing the Hatch Boundaries

If you stretch or move the boundary objects defining the overall area of an associative hatch object, the hatch object automatically adjusts to fit the modified boundaries. If you move, delete, or stretch any of the islands, the hatch object also is adjusted.

If you delete any of the boundary objects defining the overall hatch area or islands (resulting in an open rather than closed area), the associativity is removed from the hatch object and the hatch loses its capability to adjust to changing boundaries.

WARNING

Islands should *never* be moved beyond the outermost hatch boundary. If you ignore this advice and do so anyway, you may encounter problems later, such as the hatch adjusting incorrectly, move as you continue to edit the hatch or the boundary objects.

Exploding Hatch Objects

You can explode a hatch object into its constituent lines with the EXPLODE command. Exploding a hatch object removes the associativity of the object. Additionally, the single hatch object is replaced by the group of line objects that make up the pattern. Exploding a hatch object does enable you to edit the individual lines of the hatch, but in most cases you lose more than you gain.

Using Object Snap

A hatch object is composed of lines. Therefore, you can use the same object snap modes (such as endpoint or midpoint) on the lines in an associative hatch object as you use on lines.

NOTE

In earlier versions of AutoCAD, a hatch was actually a form of a block, and you could use the insert object snap mode on a hatch. In R14, a hatch is an object in itself and has no insertion point.

The following exercise shows how to modify the hatch objects that you drew in the previous exercise.

STRETCHING THE BOUNDARIES OF THE HATCH OBJECT

1. Continue to use the drawing SOLID.DWG found in the Chapter 17 folder on the accompanying CD-ROM. Restore the view ENDVIEW. Make sure that you are in floating model space and that the current viewport is that of the End View.

2. Choose Hatch from the Objects submenu of the Modify pull-down menu, select the hatch object, change the pattern to ANSI35, and click on the Apply button.

3. Restore the view SECTION. Make sure that the current viewport is that of the Section view. Choose Stretch from the Modify toolbar, and choose ① and ② (see fig. 17.12).

4. Type in the displacement **–0.5,0** for the first stretch point, and press the Enter key for the second stretch point.

5. You are finished with this drawing; save and exit the drawing.

Figure 17.12

Stretching the boundaries.

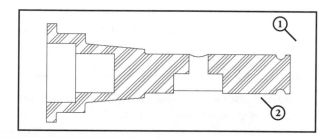

Dealing with Layers and Visibility

There are two methods with which you can control the visibility of hatch objects, layers or the system variable FILLMODE. Both are discussed in the following sections.

Controlling Visibility with Layers

Quite often, the hatch object is drawn on a layer separate from the layer(s) containing the boundary objects. Drawing the hatch object on a separate layer enables you to make the hatch object invisible, while leaving the boundary objects visable, by freezing or turning off the hatch layer. When the time comes to update the hatch object, however, certain consequences must be dealt with because the hatch boundaries have been modified. When you lock the hatch layer and change the boundary objects some consequences will result. The following sections discuss these consequences.

If the hatch layer is frozen and the boundary objects are modified, then the associativity of the hatch object is removed and the hatch object cannot adjust to the changed boundaries.

If the hatch layer is turned off and the boundary objects are modified, the hatch object still adjusts to the changed boundaries. The adjustment is evident when the hatch layer is turned back on.

If the hatch layer is locked and the boundary objects are modified, the hatch object is not adjusted to the changed boundaries; however, the hatch object's associativity remains intact.

To force the hatch object to adjust to the modified boundary objects, first unlock the hatch layer. Then select the hatch object with the HATCHEDIT command and click on the Apply button without making any changes to the settings. If at any time the hatch object fails to adjust correctly to the modified boundaries, you can force AutoCAD to try again by selecting the hatch object with the HATCHEDIT command and clicking on the Apply button without changing any of the parameters.

INSIDER TIP

To avoid accidentally removing the associativity from hatch objects, get into the habit of turning off the hatch layer rather than freezing it.

Controlling Visibility with FILLMODE

 You can control the visibility of all hatch objects in a drawing by setting the FILLMODE system variable. When FILLMODE is turned off (set to 0), all hatch objects become invisible, regardless of the status of the layers on which the hatch objects reside. Of course, you must issue the REGEN or REGENALL command to affect existing hatch objects. The disadvantage of using FILLMODE is that FILLMODE also affects solids, multilines, and wide polylines.

Completely Filling an Area

In earlier versions of AutoCAD, when you wanted to completely fill an area (coloring an area, for example), you either drew solids or generated a hatch with settings that created a dense pattern of hatch lines. In R14, a new pattern has been provided to take care of filling areas: the solidfill pattern. Using the solidfill pattern is much more efficient, in terms of plotting and regenerating the drawing, than the old method of drawing a hatch with settings that result in a dense pattern.

Selecting Hatch Objects

In selecting an associative hatch object, you can choose not only to select the hatch object itself but also to have the boundary objects associated with the hatch object automatically included in the selection. In the Object Selection Settings dialog box (displayed by choosing Selection from the Tools pull-down menu), is a setting labeled Associative Hatch. By default, this option is disabled so that when you select a hatch object, the associated boundary objects are not selected automatically. If you enable the Associative Hatch option, the boundary objects associated with the selected hatch object are automatically included in the selection.

Selecting a hatch object's boundary objects without selecting the hatch object itself can be difficult to do without magnifying the view, turning off the hatch object's layer, or turning FILLMODE off and regenerating the drawing. Another tool is available, however, that you can use to select the boundary objects that can be more efficient at time—*object cycling*.

Using the Direct Hatch Option of HATCH

The older version of the BHATCH command is HATCH. Because it is the older version, it is not located on any of the pull-down menus or toolbars, and must be typed. The major drawback to using HATCH is that it can draw only nonassociative hatch objects.

Despite this, HATCH does have an option that you may find useful: the Direct Hatch option. The Direct Hatch option enables you to define on-the-fly the area to be hatched, removing the necessity to draw the boundary objects before drawing a hatch object. The direct option is most useful when you have a large area to hatch and want to hatch representative patches, not the entire area.

After you issue the HATCH command, choose a pattern, and set the associated settings, you are prompted to select the boundary objects. To invoke the Direct Hatch option, do not select any objects. Press Enter. Then you define the hatch boundary by using options similar to those in the PLINE command. In effect, you are drawing the hatch boundary with a temporary polyline. After you finish defining the area with a closed polyline, the nonassociative hatch object is drawn. If you want, you can even choose to retain the polyline.

In the next section, you learn how to create your own hatch patterns.

Creating Custom Hatch Patterns

It is possible to add new patterns to the ones supplied with AutoCAD. You can add the new patterns (custom hatch patterns) to the file ACAD.PAT (or ACADISO.PAT) or define each new pattern in its own file. ACAD.PAT and ACADISO.PAT are both found in the \ACADR14\SUPPORT directory (also referred to as custom pattern files). If you choose to define each pattern in its own file, the file must have the same name as the pattern and have a file name extension of .PAT. The new custom patterns files should be placed in one of the directories defined in the support file search path (see the PREFERENCES command). Because hatch pattern files are ASCII files, a text editor is all you need to add to ACAD.PAT or to create your own file.

A hatch pattern consists of one or more families of parallel pattern lines. The rules for defining a pattern line are the same as those for defining a new linetype, except that no text or shapes can be included in the definition of the pattern line.

INSIDER TIP

Although the rules for defining a hatch pattern are relatively straightforward, implementing the rules takes time, effort, and patience. A much easier and more cost-efficient solution is to buy the pattern you need from one of several third-party developers (check with your AutoCAD dealer). If you definitely want to define your own pattern, read on.

Defining the Header Line

The first line in any pattern definition is the header line:

```
*pattern-name [, description]
```

The name cannot contain any blanks. The description is optional (as is the preceding comma), and is only used by the ? option of the HATCH command.

NOTE

> If you choose to place the pattern name in its own custom pattern file, you must use the same name for both the file and the pattern.

Defining the Pattern Lines

The header line is followed by one or more pattern line descriptors, one for each family of lines to be drawn, with the following syntax:

```
angle, x-origin, y-origin, delta-x, delta-y [,dash-1, dash-2, ...]
```

The following line descriptor, for example, would result in the hatch shown on the left in figure 17.13:

```
*L45, 45 degree lines @ 0.25 units apart
45,0,0,0,0.25
```

Figure 17.13

Samples of the L45 and TRIANG patterns.

L45   TRIANG

Each family of lines starts with one line, and the line's angle and origin are specified by the first three numbers of the line descriptor. In the preceding example, the first line is drawn at a 45-degree angle through the point 0,0. The family of lines is generated by offsetting each successive line by delta-x and delta-y offsets, with delta-x measured along the line and delta-y measured perpendicular to the lines. In the example, each succeeding line is offset 0 in the x direction and 0.25 in the y direction. With no other dash specifications specified, AutoCAD draws the lines with the current linetype.

The next example is a pattern taken from the file ACAD.PAT, and is shown on the right in figure 17.13:

```
*TRIANG, Equilateral triangles

60, 0,0, .1875,.324759526, .1875,-.1875
120, 0,0, .1875,.324759526, .1875,-.1875
0, -.09375,.162379763, .1875,.324759526, .1875,-.1875
```

In this example, the pattern consists of three families of lines: one family at 60 degrees, another at 120 degrees, and the third at 0 degrees. The dash specifications (the last two numbers in each line) indicate that each line is to consist of a 0.1875 dash and a 0.1875 space repetitive pattern.

You can have as many pattern line descriptors as you want, but each line can be no more than 80 characters long.

Adding Sample Slides

The samples of the patterns displayed in the Boundary Hatch dialog box are slides that are stored in the slide library file ACAD.SLB. If you want a sample of a custom pattern you have added to the file ACAD.PAT to be displayed in the dialog box, you must draw a sample of the pattern, make a slide of the drawing, and add the slide to the ACAD.SLB file (also found in the \ACADR14\SUPPORT directory). The slide file must have the same name as the pattern it represents. See Chapter 23, "Creating Scripts and Slide Libraries," for the commands and procedures used to create slides.

You can use the program SLIDELIB, which is supplied with AutoCAD, to recreate the slide library file ACAD.SLB with your additional new slides. Unfortunately, SLIDELIB cannot be used to add new slides to a library file. In effect, you must recreate the entire library file when you add to it. To recreate ACAD.SLB, you need the original slide files that were used to create ACAD.SLB (and these slide files are not supplied with AutoCAD).

Several third-party packages are available, however, that make managing, deleting from, and adding to a slide library file easier to do.

One such package, a DOS program called MAKSLB21, is provided on the accompanying CD in the Chapter 17 folder. Contact your AutoCAD dealer to see what other packages are available.

Using BOUNDARY to Delineate Areas and Islands

The BOUNDARY command is a variation of the BHATCH command.

BOUNDARY is used to create polylines delineating an overall area and the islands within that area. If you want, you can create a region rather than polylines. The boundary delineation algorithm employed by BOUNDARY is the same as the algorithm employed by BHATCH. The Boundary Creation dialog box is a variation of the Advanced Options dialog box of the BHATCH command (see fig. 17.14). Use Boundary when all you want to do is to delineate an area and its islands but not hatch the area.

Figure 17.14

Boundary Creation dialog box of BOUNDARY.

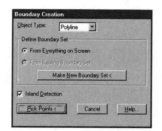

As with the BHATCH command, the overall area and islands must be enclosed by one or more objects.

Summary

Hatching is a powerful tool for clarifying the meaning of your drawing or for conveying information to the reader. It is easy to apply, using BHATCH, and just as easy to edit with HATCHEDIT. Drawing hatch objects on a separate layer is always a good idea. Although you can create your own hatch patterns, buying the pattern you need is usually more cost-effective. In the next chapter, "Productive Dimensioning," you learn about another group of associative objects, the group of dimension objects.

PRODUCTIVE DIMENSIONING

by Michael Todd Peterson

When working in a production environment, one of the more time-consuming and critical challenges is the need to dimension a drawing quickly and accurately. Then, if necessary, you must also be able to modify and correct existing dimensions just as quickly and accurately.

This chapter and Chapter 19, "Advanced Dimensioning," introduce you to various techniques necessary to dimension a drawing quickly and easily. The techniques are the same, regardless of the type of drawing you are working on, whether it is architectural, civil, or mechanical in nature.

This chapter focuses on how to become more productive when dimensioning by using AutoCAD's basic dimensioning tools. Chapter 19 focuses on how to modify existing dimensions quickly. In particular, this chapter focuses on the following topics:

- Productive dimensioning
- Linear dimensions
- Other dimension types
- Leader dimensions
- Paper space and model space dimensioning

Becoming Proficient at Productive Dimensioning

To become proficient at dimensioning a drawing, you need a little practice and a little understanding about some of the various options made available to you by AutoCAD. The most commonly used dimensioning type is linear dimensioning.

Linear Dimensioning

Linear dimensions, of course, define a specific length, whether it is horizontal, vertical, or aligned to the object you are dimensioning. AutoCAD provides you with five different linear dimensioning commands including DIMLINEAR, DIMCONTINUE, DIMBASELINE, DIMALIGNED, and DIMROTATED. Each of these commands is accessed through the pull-down menu (see fig. 18.1), the Dimensioning toolbar (see fig. 18.2), or the Command: prompt. You should access this command using the method you are most comfortable with.

Figure 18.1

The AutoCAD 14 Dimension pull-down menu is where you can select the various dimensioning commands.

Figure 18.2

*The AutoCAD 14
Dimension toolbar
provides you with other
methods of accessing the
dimensioning commands.*

The base linear command DIMLINEAR is fairly straightforward and easy to use. But, you may not be aware of one or two options of the command, which are covered in the next section.

Linear Options

The DIMLINEAR command is based on selecting three points to create the dimension. These points are the start and endpoints, as well as the location of the dimension line. Alternatively, you can create a linear dimension by selecting only two points on the screen under certain circumstances.

When you choose the DIMLINEAR command, you are prompted to select the first extension line. Instead of selecting the first extension line, you can hit Return to select the line you want to dimension. Then, all you have to do is select the line and place the dimension. The endpoints of the dimension are automatically determined from the endpoints of the line.

This option works well when what you are dimensioning is a single line, arc, circle, or polyline segment that is precisely the length you need it to be. This method does not work in paper space but does work on internal lines of blocks and xrefs, simplifying the dimensioning process a bit.

If you use this method with a multi-segmented polyline, the segment you click on will be the segment that is dimensioned. If you use this method with a circle, you can dimension the diameter of the circle with a linear dimension. DIMLINEAR will recognize objects that it cannot dimension and will issue the following informational message: "Object selected is not a line, arc, or circle." Figure 18.3 shows you some example dimensions created with two clicks.

The DIMLINEAR by selection option, however, does not solve every situation for linear dimensions. In instances where using DIMLINEAR with the selection option does not work, you may still need to resort to using construction lines in conjunction with object snap modes. In these cases, AutoCAD Release 14's new tracking feature is very helpful. See Chapter 6, "Creating Drawings with R14" for more information on how to use tracking.

Figure 18.3

Examples of using DIMLINEAR with select object on various types of geometry.

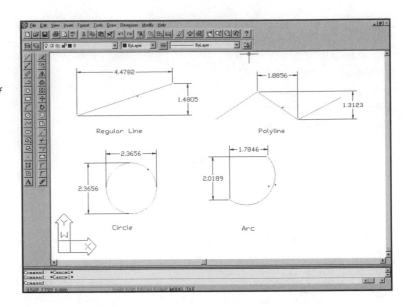

Ultimately, to get more productivity when creating linear dimensions, you need to explore a few more commands. In particular, two to look at are DIMBASELINE and DIMCONTINUE. Both commands are used after creating an initial linear dimension to quickly create additional dimensions. These commands are discussed in the following sections.

Baseline Dimensions

Baseline dimensions are used to quickly and easily create a series of dimensions from a single basepoint. If you want to dimension various objects along a wall, but want all the dimensions to measure from one end of the wall, for example, baseline is the method to use.

To make use of the baseline command, you must create a linear, aligned, or rotated dimension before using the baseline command. After you have the initial dimension, choose Baseline from the Dimension pull-down menu or the toolbar. When inside the command, select the endpoint of the next dimension. Each dimension is then automatically placed above the previous dimension and spaced appropriately. AutoCAD remembers the last dimension placed when using the DIMBASELINE and DIMCONTINUE (to be discussed in the next section) commands. You can perform any non-dimensioning command between the use of DIMLINEAR and DIMBASELINE.

INSIDER TIP

If you want to baseline a dimension that was not the most recently based dimension, you can press the Enter key at the "Specify a second extension line origin or (<select>/Undo):" prompt. This will enable you to select the dimension you want to baseline. This will work with the continue dimension type as well.

Figure 18.4 shows you the click points necessary to create a series of dimensions using the baseline command.

Figure 18.4

A set of baseline dimensions and the mouse clicks that created them.

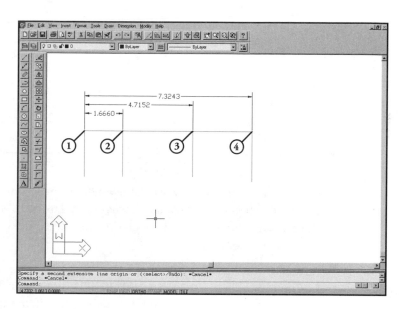

The following exercise shows you how to dimension a steel plate quickly and efficiently using baseline dimensions.

CREATING LINEAR DIMENSIONS BY USING BASELINES

1. Load the drawing 18TUT01.DWG from the accompanying CD.

2. Create a linear dimension from the left end of the block to the center point of the first circle, as shown in figure 18.5.

3. Choose Dimension, Baseline from the pull-down menu.

4. When prompted for the second extension line, select a center object snap mode and select the center of the second circle.

Figure 18.5

The block with the first linear dimension applied.

5. Continue using center snap modes and select the center of the rest of the circles, moving from left to right.

6. When you are finished with the circles, select the endpoint of the upper-right corner of the block. Figure 18.6 shows you the block with all the dimensions applied.

Figure 18.6

The block dimensioned using baseline dimensions.

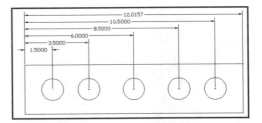

As you can see from this exercise, after you have created the first linear dimension, regardless of whether the dimension was created using DIMLINEAR, DIMALIGNED, or other linear commands, the block is dimensioned quickly with a minimal amount of mouse operations.

To further test the baseline command, try rotating the plate 45° before you create the first dimension. Then, create a DIMALIGNED dimension for the first dimension. When you use the baseline command again, you will see that it works perfectly.

Continue Dimensions

Continue dimensions are very similar to baseline dimensions with one exception—instead of basing all the dimensions off a single point, they are based off the endpoint of the last dimension drawn. Continue dimensions automatically line up the dimension lines to create crisp clean dimensions. For example, a wall is generally dimensioned from centerline to centerline of the components of the wall, such as doors and windows. A continue dimension type makes this very easy, whereas the earlier example of a baseline dimension will base all dimensions off a single point in the wall.

If you have to create a series of dimensions, one after the other on a single dimension line, use the continue command, because it automates the placement of additional dimensions, much like the baseline command did. Figure 18.7 shows you an example of a continue dimension.

Figure 18.7

A set of dimensions showing the use of the continue command.

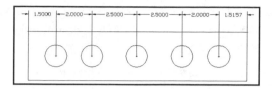

Like baseline, continue dimensions rely on having one linear dimension type already created, followed by the continue dimension command.

For an exercise on how to use this command, repeat the baseline exercise, but use the continue command instead. Both commands work the same way, but just produce different results.

Aligned and Rotated Dimensions

The last two linear dimension types are aligned and rotated. Both of these types are similar to each other in the fact that they are not horizontal or vertical dimensions. Aligned and rotated dimensions are the only linear dimensions where the dimension line is not horizontal or vertical.

Aligned dimensions arrange the dimension line to match the angle produced between the start and endpoints of the dimension. *Rotated dimensions* have the dimension line rotated a specific angle amount before the start and endpoints are selected. Figure 18.8 shows you examples of both types of dimensions.

Figure 18.8

Two dimensions, showing the difference between an aligned and a rotated dimension.

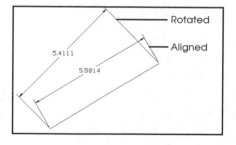

As you can see in figure 18.8, you can use the rotate command to create linear dimensions with any orientation. The aligned command, however, is forced to align itself along the start and endpoints of the dimension. Also note that a different dimension is measured, even though both dimensions use the same endpoints.

The aligned command may be accessed through the pull-down menu, toolbar, or at the Command: prompt. The rotated command, however, is only available at the Command: prompt when you are in the DIM subsystem. You can access the DIM subsystem by typing **DIM** at the Command: prompt. This is the old method for dimensioning in AutoCAD Release 11 and earlier. When in the DIM subsystem, type **ROTATE** to access the DIMROTATE command. When you are done, exit the DIM subsystem to return to the command prompt.

The following exercise shows you how to use the rotate command to create a few dimensions. The exercise also shows you why you need to be careful when using this dimension type, because a rotated linear dimension may end up with a different measured length than the original.

CREATING A ROTATED DIMENSION

1. Load the file 18TUT02.DWG from the accompanying CD. This drawing shows three circles that you are going to dimension from center point to center point.

2. At the Command: prompt, type in the command **DIM** to enter the dimension subsystem.

3. Enter **ROTATE** at the DIM: prompt.

4. When prompted for an angle, enter **38**, which sets the angle of the dimension line.

5. Select the center of the left circle as the start point.

6. Select the center of the middle circle as the end point. The distance between the left and middle circles should measure out to 4.000.

7. Press Enter to bring up the rotate command again. This time, enter an angle of **315** (45° down and to the right).

8. Select the center point of the middle circle as the start point.

9. Select the center point of the circle on the right. Figure 18.9 shows you the three circles dimensioned.

Figure 18.9

A 38-degree and a 45-degree rotated dimension showing what happens when you use the rotate command on a linear dimension.

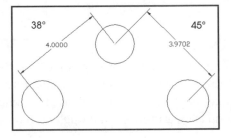

10. When you are finished with the rotate command, type **exit** to return to the standard AutoCAD command prompt.

Other Dimensions

Several other dimensioning types are worth mentioning. These dimension types are not linear and serve specific purposes. Depending on your discipline, you may have a use for some of these types. For example, a mechanical part designer will make heavy use of radius and diameter dimension types, whereas a civil engineer will make use of datum dimension types.

Radius and Diameter Dimensions

Radius and *diameter dimensions* are used to dimension the size of an arc or circle, regardless of the type of object. If you create a polyline with an arc in it, for example, you can use either type to dimension the arc. If you select the Center Mark check box in the Dimension Styles dialog box, the center mark will automatically be used with this type of dimension when the dimension text is placed outside the circle or arc. Other than that, radius and diameter dimension types are straightforward. With these dimension types, you simply pick the arc or circle to dimension, then the dimension line location.

Angular Dimensions

Angular dimensions are used to dimension the angle between two non-parallel lines. Of course, when you dimension angles between two lines, four angles are possible, one on each side of the intersection point of the two lines. Where you place the dimension line determines which angle is measured. Like radius and diameter dimensions, angular dimensions are straightforward as well.

Ordinate Dimensions

Ordinate dimensions are used to dimension a specific coordinate such as a point from a civil survey. For example, a civil survey relies upon a set of three-dimensional data points on which to base a topography. These coordinates are labeled using an ordinate dimension type, which labels the point's exact X and Y coordinates.

When using ordinate dimensions, you may dimension the X or Y axis points, called *datums*. You also have the option to create a leader-like ordinate dimension that has text before or after the coordinate. Figure 18.10 shows you an ordinate dimension.

Figure 18.10

An ordinate dimension showing both X and Y datums.

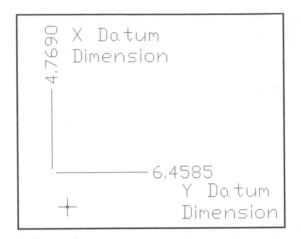

The Ordinate Dimension command is located on the pull-down menu, the toolbar, and at the Command: prompt. When you select this command, you are prompted to select the feature. AutoCAD is looking for you to tell it the coordinate to dimension. After you select the coordinate, you can select the type of ordinate dimension you want to use.

The four types of ordinate dimensions are X datum, Y datum, Mtext, and Text. X and Y datum produce the corresponding coordinate. Mtext pops up the Mtext dialog box so you can add text before and after the Datum dimension. The datum dimension appears as <> in the Multiline Text Editor dialog box. Figure 18.11 shows you the Mtext dialog box when used with the ordinate Mtext option. The Text option enables you to modify the text of the Datum dimension, without having to use the Mtext editor.

WARNING

You should not delete this <> marker or the actual coordinate will not appear in the dimension.

Figure 18.11

The Multiline Text Editor dialog box showing text before and after the ordinate dimension.

The following exercise shows you how to use ordinate dimensions to dimension several survey points. In this exercise, the PDMODE system variable has been set so that points appear as crosses.

USING ORDINATE DIMENSIONS

1. Load the file 18TUT03.DWG from the accompanying CD.

2. Turn on Ortho by double-clicking on Ortho at the bottom of the screen.

3. Choose Ordinate from the Dimension pull-down menu or toolbar if it is open.

4. Using a node object snap mode, click on one of the crosses and place the dimension to the right of the point.

5. Repeat steps 3 and 4, but place the dimension above the cross this time.

6. Repeat steps 3 through 5 for several other crosses so you get a little practice. Figure 18.12 shows you this file with a few ordinate dimensions added.

Figure 18.12

The points dimensioned with ordinate dimensions.

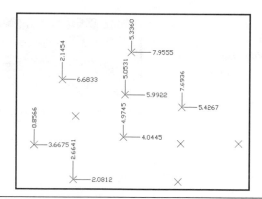

Tolerance Dimensions

Another dimension type is the tolerance dimension. *Tolerances* are used to provide constraints within which you can construct the drawn object. For example, you might construct a mechanical part and specify that its length may be 2.0 CM + or −0.001 CM.

AutoCAD provides you with methods of creating tolerance dimensions. One method is to specify the tolerances in the Dimension Styles dialog box. The tolerances are then automatically added to the dimension text as you place dimensions. The second method is to use the tolerance command and place tolerance symbols on the drawing. The second method is the method discussed in the following section. Figure 18.13 shows a standard tolerance symbol inside of AutoCAD.

Figure 18.13

The tolerance dimension and its parts.

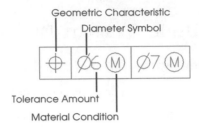

Placing Tolerance Symbols in a Drawing

Under the Dimension menu and toolbars, you find a tolerance option. Choosing this option displays the Symbol dialog box, shown in figure 18.14. The Symbol dialog box is used to select the appropriate type of tolerance you want to use, through the use of industry standard tolerance symbols.

Figure 18.14

The Symbol dialog box enables you to choose the type of tolerance you want to use.

In this dialog box, notice the several different symbols, each representing a different geometric characteristic. When you choose one of the symbols, the selected tolerance method is then placed in the tolerance dimension itself. After you choose a geometric tolerance type and click on OK, you are transferred to the Geometric Tolerance dialog box (see fig. 18.15) where you may then enter the values for the tolerances.

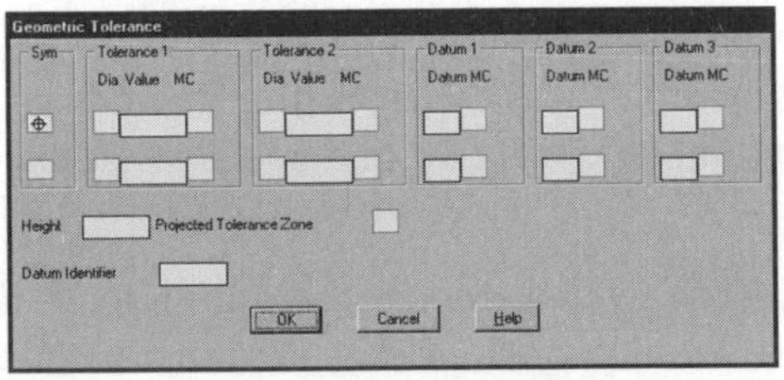

Figure 18.15

The Geometric Tolerance dialog box enables you to specify exact tolerances.

In the Geometric Tolerance dialog box, you can specify values for tolerances 1 and 2, as well as round symbols. You can also specify up to three datums, such as a material condition and a value for that condition. You can also specify height, projected tolerance zones, and datum identifiers.

Leader Dimensions

Leaders are a very popular method of adding notes and pointing out specific aspects of a drawing. A leader is a line with an arrowhead pointing to a specific feature with some sort of text or graphics at the end of the line. For example, you might create a wall section of a house and use leaders to point out specific materials in the section.

A leader is easily created by selecting the Leader command from the pull-down menu. When prompted for the first point, select the point where you want the arrowhead of the leader to appear. Then, you simply draw as many straight leader segments as you like. When you are done, simply hit Return, enter your text, and hit Return twice more to exit the command. This chapter will focus on several more advanced features of leaders, such as using the Mtext dialog box to enter multiline text and using splines instead of straight line segments in your leaders.

Leader Options

When you select the Leader command, you are prompted for a point. This point is, of course, the location of the arrowhead. After you select the start point and then the second point, you are presented with the options for the Leader command. Usually, you type in a single line of text to complete the Leader command. Occasionally, however, you may want to select one of the three options available to you. These options are:

- **Format.** This option enables you to specify a variety of formats for the leader, such as using splines instead of straight line segments, or whether you need to have an arrowhead.

- **Annotation.** This option, which is the default, enables you to control how you place you text in the Leader command.

- **Undo.** This option removes the last line segment you drew in the Leader command.

Format Options

If you select the Format option, you are presented with four types of formats. These types are as follows:

- Splines
- Straight
- Arrow
- None (removing all formatting)

Each option is discussed in the following sections.

Splines Format

The first option is Splines. A spline is a smooth curved line, instead of straight line segments. When you select this option, your leader line is drawn using the AutoCAD Spline command. Note that this is not a smooth polyline, but a true spline.

Straight Format

The Straight option creates a series of straight line segments. You may select either straight or spline, but you cannot have both. AutoCAD does not enable you to draw a leader line with both straight and curved segments. Figure 18.16 shows you one leader with splines and another leader with straight lines.

NOTE

When working with the format options, you can only select either splines or straight line segments. The Leader command is not capable of handling both types of lines in the same leader.

Arrow Format

The Arrow option defines whether an arrowhead is drawn. If you want to change the arrowhead to something other than a standard arrow, you must do so in the Dimension Styles dialog box, discussed in Chapter 19, "Advanced Dimensioning."

Figure 18.16

*A leader with splines
versus one without splines.*

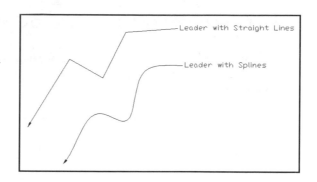

Removing All Formatting

The None option removes all formatting, including arrowheads, and draws straight line segments.

INSIDER TIP

Each of the format options must be set each time you use the Leader command. To combat having to select the options each time you use the Leader command, you might write up a script file or simple LISP routine to create your own Leader command that uses splines if you like using them (see Chapter 22, "Customizing without Programming").

Annotation Options

The annotation options provide you with some control over what is placed at the end of the leader line. When you select the annotation option, you are presented with five options at the command line: Tolerance, Copy, Block, None, and Mtext, which is the default. All text in leaders is now placed using Mtext. If you select this option, you are presented with the Multiline Text Editor dialog box, where all the options of formatting Mtext are available to you. See Chapter 16, "Text Annotation," for more information on the Mtext command.

Three of the four other annotation options enable you to place a variety of objects rather than text at the end of the leader. You can place a tolerance dimension, copy an object from somewhere else in the drawing, or insert a block. Selecting one of these options launches that particular command. The last option is none, which removes all formatting.

The following exercise shows you how to create leaders on a simple architectural wall section.

CREATING LEADERS IN AUTOCAD RELEASE 14

1. Load the file 18TUT04.DWG from the accompanying CD. Figure 18.17 shows you how the drawing should appear at the end of this exercise. Use it as a reference for completing this exercise.

Figure 18.17

The wall section as it will appear at the end of the exercise.

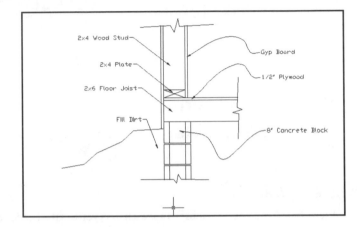

2. On the left side of the wall, create straight leaders by choosing the Leader command from the Dimension pull-down menu or toolbar.

3. When asked for the first point, select a point close to the arrowhead location of the 2×4 Wood Stud leader.

4. Select the second point of the leader, as shown in figure 18.17.

5. At this point, you are presented with the leader options at the Command: prompt. Press Enter to accept the default Annotation Option, which enables you to add text to your leader.

6. Type in **2×4 Wood Stud** and press Enter to complete the leader.

7. Repeat steps 3 through 5 for the rest of the straight leaders shown in figure 18.17.

8. For the spline leaders shown in figure 18.17, again enter the Leader command.

9. Select your start point and a second point so you are presented with the options for the command.

10. Type **F** for the format options.

11. Type **S** for spline. Now the line is a spline. Draw the rest of the line and enter the appropriate text.

Increasing Productivity with Third-Party Programs

At this point, you have seen most of the options available to you for creating standard AutoCAD dimensions. By practicing and using the options that are available to you, you can increase your productivity to some degree in terms of dimensioning. The standard AutoCAD dimensioning commands are by no means slow, but you can increase your speed with a little help.

Many users today make use of third-party programs to help increase productivity in their respective profession. Many of these programs provide automated methods for creating these same dimensions.

An architectural modeling program, for example, enables you to create with one click all the necessary dimensions for a wall, including intersecting wall, door, and window locations, as well as overall dimensions. Then, all you have to do is correct any errors, if they exist. Both Softdesk's Auto Architect and Ketiv's ArchT are excellent examples of programs that automate the dimensioning process.

Other disciplines, such as civil engineering, may make use of programs such as Softdesk's Civil series or Eagle Point Software's civil software. Both packages again automate dimensioning tasks.

In some programs, such as Mechanical Desktop, dimensions are a critical aspect of using the program correctly. In Mechanical Desktop, you must add enough dimensions to the object to fully constrain it (fully define it). Once the object is constrained, the dimensions are parametric, meaning if you change the value of the dimension, the geometry also changes.

This list of third-party programs goes on and on. If you are using a third-party program, explore its dimensioning commands and see how much faster or easier its commands are versus the standard AutoCAD commands.

Dimensioning in Paper Space versus Model Space

When looking at productivity in terms of dimensioning a drawing, one other factor to consider is where you are placing your dimensions. You have two choices in AutoCAD: model space and paper space. Each space has pros and cons.

Pros and Cons of Model Space

Most users today dimension their drawing in AutoCAD. This comes naturally because the drawing is actually created in model space. The advantages and disadvantages are listed and briefly described.

The following are some advantages of creating dimensions in model space instead of paper space.

- Use quick intuitive dimensioning directly on the drawing.

- When using associative dimensioning, you can stretch both the geometry and dimensions at the same time, enabling both the geometry and the dimensions to update at the same time.

- You can use the object selection dimensioning method.

The following are some disadvantages of creating dimensions in model space instead of paper space.

- If you have a sheet with drawings created at different scales, you must use different scale dimensions as well.

- For dimensions to plot correctly, all dimensions must be scaled by a scale factor that is equivalent to the output plot scale.

Overall, the biggest reason to place your dimensions in model space is if you do not understand paper space and how it works. If you are not comfortable working in paper space yet, create your dimensions in model space until you do feel you are ready to work in paper space.

INSIDER TIP

If you work in an environment where you constantly create drawing sheets with varying drawing scales, you should strongly consider using paper space dimensioning methods.

Pros and Cons of Paper Space

With paper space dimensioning, you place your dimensions in paper space, thus separating them from the drawing. Like model space, paper space also has advantages and disadvantages when dimensioning.

The following are some advantages of creating dimensions in paper space instead of model space.

- Paper space dimensions are separate from the drawing, which makes it easy to switch over to model and view a clean drawing.

- All paper space dimensions make use of the same dimension scale factor: 1.

- Dimensions can be placed on sheets more easily with multiple scales.

The following are some disadvantages of creating dimensions in paper space instead of model space.

- You cannot stretch paper space dimensions and model space geometry at the same time.

- You cannot use the object selection dimensioning method.

Ultimately, the decision of whether to use paper space dimensioning depends on your comfort with and understanding of paper space itself. If you are not comfortable with it, continue to place dimensions in model space.

Improving Productivity: Tips and Techniques

The following are a few techniques to help you increase your dimensioning speed when you are creating dimensions. Editing dimensions is covered in the Chapter 19, "Advanced Dimensioning."

- Create keyboard shortcuts for most of the dimension commands. For example, DIMLINEAR can be shortened to DL, which is much quicker to type in. See Chapter 22, "Customizing without Programming," for more on keyboard shortcuts.

- Create a chart of dimension scales for standard plot scales. That way, you create consistency in your drawing throughout your draftsmen.

- Create a variety of dimension styles and save them to AutoCAD Release 14 template files. Then, all you have to do is assign the appropriate style as the current one and begin dimensioning.

- Whenever possible, use the object selection method for dimensioning because it is quickest.

- If you are going to create a series of dimensions, consider using baseline or continue dimensions to help automate and speed up the process.

- If you have a third-party program, consider using that program's dimensioning routines, if it has any. These routines will probably be quicker than the standard AutoCAD commands.

- If you want to create a series of leaders, all using splines, consider writing either a script or LISP routine to enable you to create spline-based leaders quickly and easily. Otherwise, you have to set the spline option each time. See Chapter 22, "Customizing without Programming," for more information.

Summary

Overall, AutoCAD Release 14's dimension commands are fairly productive and much quicker than dimensioning by hand. The key things to remember are:

- Be familiar with all your dimensioning options. Many times, using a different command such as Continue is quicker that using DIMLINEAR.

- Consider using third-party programs to help increase dimensioning speed. You can also consider writing your own dimensioning routines in LISP.

- When possible, use the object selection dimensioning method. Otherwise, you will have to pick the start, end, and dimension line points. In many cases, you may need to create temporary construction lines for dimensioning purposes.

The next chapter delves further into the world of dimensions and covers topics such as dimension styles, as well as editing existing dimensions, where AutoCAD is extremely fast.

ADVANCED DIMENSIONING

by Michael Todd Peterson

One of AutoCAD's best features is its capability to control dimensions in a drawing. In other words, AutoCAD Release 14 provides you with several tools to edit dimensions, as well as control how a dimension appears in the drawing. This chapter focuses on the following topics:

- *Dimension Styles*

- *Style Families*

- *Style Options*

- *Modifying Dimensions*

Defining Dimension Styles

Dimension styles are your primary method for controlling how a dimension appears. By creating a dimension style, you define exactly how that dimension is going to appear in the drawing. This includes the dimension scale, the types of arrowheads, whether or not the dimension lines appear, and if so, what color the dimension lines are.

AutoCAD controls dimension styles through the use of Dimension Variables (DIMVARS). You can control these variables in two different ways. You can use the DDIM Dimension dialog box to access the variables using a graphical interface or you can type the variable at the Command: prompt and assign it a new value. There are approximately 58 dimension variables in AutoCAD Release 14. Most of the time, adjusting the dimension variables through the Dimension Styles dialog box is sufficient (see fig. 19.1). This dialog box is accessible through the Dimension toolbar or styles option of the Dimension menu.

Figure 19.1

The Dimension Styles dialog box enables you to control how a dimension is drawn.

Creating Dimension Style Families

Dimension style families enable you to create a single parent style with smaller variations in the different families. For example, you can create a parent family with a particular font for linear dimensions. Then, you can create a child style of the parent with a different font for radial and diameter dimensions, without having to create a whole new style.

When the parent style is the current style, the child style will be used when that particular type of dimension is used. In the preceding example, if you create a radius or diameter dimension when the parent style is current, the child style will automatically be used instead. This only applies, however, when creating radius and diameter dimensions. If a linear dimension is created, the parent style is automatically used.

There are six different families of dimension style properties that you can use to create child styles from. They are as follows:

- Linear

- Radial

- Angular

- Diameter

- Ordinate

- Leader

Creating the Child in a Style Family

To make use of style families, you must pay attention to how you name your styles. The following steps should be followed to create the child style.

1. Create the parent style first.

2. Create the child style from the parent. Do this by saving the parent style name with a "$#" suffix.

3. Select a family within the child style to adjust. When you select a family for the child, only the dimension style options related to that particular family will be available in other areas of the Dimension Styles dialog box.

4. Adjust the child style properties as you like.

5. Save the child style under a name related to the parent style.

Child styles need to be named after their parents. For example, a parent style can be named ARCH. The child styles of ARCH should be named something like ARCH$1, ARCH$2—using numbers as the suffix. This enables AutoCAD to associate the child styles with the appropriate parent styles.

The following exercise shows you how to make use of style families.

A QUICK USE OF DIMENSION STYLE FAMILIES

1. Load the drawing 19TUT01.DWG from the accompanying CD-ROM.

2. Choose Dimension, Style. The Dimension Styles dialog box appears.

3. In the Name text box, replace STANDARD with the name **CH19**.

4. Click on Save. This renames the current style to CH19.

5. In the Family section of the Dimension Styles dialog box, select the Radial option.

6. Click on the Geometry button to access the Geometry dialog box.

7. Set the Arrowhead to Open 30 for the 1st option. The 2nd option will automatically be set identical to the 1st option.

8. Modify the Dimension Line Color to green.

9. Click on OK to close the Geometry dialog box.

10. In the Name text box, enter **CH19$1**.

11. Choose Save.

12. Under the Current drop-down list, set the current style to CH19.

13. Click on the Save button to save changes to the radial child.

14. Click on OK to close the Dimension Styles dialog box.

15. Select DIMLINEAR and dimension one side of the box in the drawing.

16. Select DIMRADIUS and dimension the circle. Figure 19.2 shows you the resulting drawing. Notice how the differences between the parent and child styles are automatically used, depending on the dimension command used.

Figure 19.2

The box and circle dimension with parent and child styles.

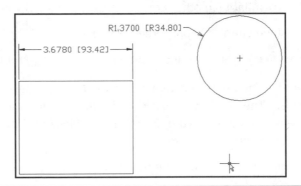

Dimension Style Options

Dimension styles provide you with a method for saving different sets of dimension variables for the various types of drawings you might create. There are many different options for defining how a dimension looks. To help you understand some of these options, figure 19.3 shows you a standard linear dimension with all the parts of the dimension labeled.

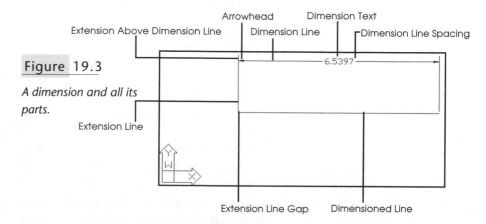

Figure 19.3

A dimension and all its parts.

AutoCAD enables you to define the style options in three different categories, as shown in the following list. When you click on one of these buttons in the Dimension Styles dialog box, a separate dialog box appears.

- Geometry Options
- Format Options
- Annotation Options

Each of these categories is explained in the following sections.

Geometry Options

The Geometry dialog box enables you to control all the dimension system variables related to the geometry of the dimension, except for the text (see fig. 19.4).

The Geometry dialog box is broken down into five distinct areas: Dimension Line, Arrowheads, Extension Line, Center, and Scale.

Figure 19.4

The Geometry dialog box enables you to define the geometry of the dimension.

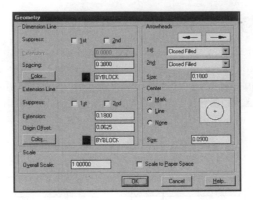

Dimension Line Options

The Dimension Line section controls the appearance of the dimension line. In a linear dimension, this is the line beside or below the dimension text. In certain circumstances, you may want to create a dimension without the dimension line. For example, you may have a short dimension with large text. In this situation, you can suppress the first or second dimension line, or both. This option only takes effect when the dimension text is centered inside of the dimension line. When text is above the dimension line, the suppression options have no effect. The location of the dimension text is controlled under the format options, which are covered in the next section.

The Extension option, which is grayed out by default, is used in conjunction with certain arrowhead types. In particular, the oblique and architectural tick arrowheads make use of this option. When one of these two arrowheads is active, you may adjust the dimension line extension variable, which defines how far beyond the extension lines of the dimension it goes.

Probably the most used dimension line option is that of color. The default color of the dimension line is BYBLOCK, which means the line will take on the color of the dimension as a whole. The only reason to change this color is if you want to have a different line width for the dimension line. For example, you could have a thinner line for the dimension line versus the extension lines.

Extension Line Options

In the Extension Line area of the dialog box, the options perform the same function as those under dimension line. The notable exception is the Origin Offset option.

When you create a dimension, such as a linear dimension, you select two points as the start and end points. These points are considered the origin points and are drawn in as part of the dimension. The origin offset defines the distance above these points that the extension line is started.

Arrowheads Options

The Arrowheads section of the Geometry dialog box provides you with complete control over the arrows. AutoCAD Release 14 provides you with additional standard arrowheads, including architectural tick, open 30, dot blanked, box filled, and a few others. Even with all these new arrowheads, you may want to create your own. To create your own arrowheads, under the 1st and 2nd drop-down lists, select the User Arrow option. This option enables you to select any block as any arrow, as long as that block is already defined in the current AutoCAD drawing. The arrowhead block should be created with an overall size of one unit in AutoCAD so it will be correctly scaled when used in the dimension. It also should be created using the right end of the dimension. The block will be rotated for the left end.

INSIDER TIP

When you create a custom arrowhead, you should save the arrowhead as a block in a template file so it is available to all drawings based on that template. If you prefer, you can also use a block from an xref as well.

Figure 19.5 shows you the dialog box in which you can enter the block name for the arrowhead.

Figure 19.5

The User Arrow dialog box enables you to select custom arrowheads.

The following exercise shows you how to create your own arrowheads.

CREATING YOUR OWN ARROWHEADS

1. Start a new drawing from scratch.

2. Create an octagon using the polygon command. Make the radius of the polygon one unit.

3. Make a block of the polygon with an insertion point at the center of the polygon. Name the block P1.

4. From the Dimension pull-down menu, choose Style.

5. In the Dimension Styles dialog box, click on the Geometry button.

6. In the Arrowheads area of the Geometry dialog box, select user arrow from the 1st drop-down list.

7. In the User Arrow dialog box, enter **p1** as the arrow name.

8. Click on OK to close the User Arrow dialog box.

9. Click on OK to close the Geometry dialog box and return to the Dimension Styles dialog box.

10. Choose Save to save the dimension style changes to Standard.

11. Click on OK.

12. Create a linear dimension. Figure 19.6 shows you a linear dimension created with a custom arrowhead.

Figure 19.6

A linear dimension with a custom arrowhead.

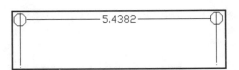

Center and Scale Options

The last two sections of the Geometry dialog box control center marks and scaling. The Center options define how center marks appear when used with radius and diameter dimensions. Probably the most important options in the Geometry dialog box, however, are the Scale options.

There are two scale options: Overall Scale and Scale to Paper Space. The Overall Scale controls how large all the features of the dimension, such as arrowheads, will appear in the drawing. This scale is directly related to the final plot scale for the drawing. For example, if you are plotting at an architectural scale of ¼ inch=1'–0", your scale factor should be 48. This is obtained by taking the denominator of ¼ inch and multiplying it by 12. For a scale such as 1:50, you can equate this to $\frac{1}{50}$=1, so the overall scale factor is 600.

When you set the scale factor, you define a scale multiplier by which all dimension size variables are multiplied. For example, arrowheads default to 0.18 units in size. If you have a scale factor of 48, the 0.18 is multiplied by 48 to arrive at the current size, correctly scaled for plotting.

If you are going to work in paper space, you can leave the Overall Scale factor set to 1 or you can turn on the Scale to Paper Space option. The Scale to Paper Space option sets the dimension variable DIMSCALE to 0. When working in paper space, a default value of 1.0 will be used. In this situation, when you are working in a model space viewport in paper space, you can create a dimension in either space and it will be scaled correctly. This assumes that you have used the Zoom command to correctly scale the geometry in the model space viewport. See Chapter 15, "Paper Space," for more information on paper space and model space viewports.

Format Options

The format options enable you to control the location of the dimension text. When you click on the Format button in the Dimension Styles dialog box, the Format dialog box appears (see fig. 19.7). This dialog box is broken down into four different areas: general, Text, Horizontal Justification, and Vertical Justification. All areas except general control the location of the text in the dimension and are self-explanatory.

Figure 19.7

The Format dialog box showing you the text location controls.

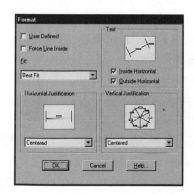

General Controls

The upper-left portion of the Format dialog box provides you with three general controls: User Defined, Force Line Inside, and Fit.

The User Defined option enables you to define how a dimension looks when you actually create the dimension. For example, if you create a linear dimension with the User Defined option enabled, you will be given options such as horizontal or vertical to determine the direction of the dimension. You can create a separate style with User Defined enabled to give you the most flexibility when creating a wide variety of dimensions.

The Force Line Inside option controls the placement of the dimension line when the dimension text is longer than the distance between the extension lines, as shown in figure 19.8. Force Line Inside always assures that a dimension line will appear between the two extension lines.

Figure 19.8

A dimension showing where force line inside is helpful.

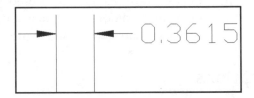

Last, there is the Fit option. This is similar to the Force Line Inside option and is applied in the same conditions. In the Fit drop-down list, you will find six different options. Each option is briefly described in the following list:

- **Text and Arrows.** When this option is selected, both the text and arrows will be forced inside the extension lines, even when there is not enough room for them.

- **Text Only.** When this option is selected, only text will be forced inside the extension lines. Arrows may be pushed outside the extension lines when the distance between the lines is small enough.

- **Arrows Only.** When this option is selected, only the arrows will be forced inside of the extension lines. Text may appear outside the extension lines when the distance between the lines is too small for the text to fit otherwise.

- **Best Fit.** When this option is selected, AutoCAD will try to determine the best method to use to create the most readable dimension. This is the default option.

- **Leader.** When this option is selected, AutoCAD will draw a leader from the dimension line to the dimension text when the distance between the extension lines is small enough to force the text outside.

- **No Leader.** When this option is selected, AutoCAD will not draw a leader when the text is outside the extension lines.

The Format options are generally configured the same for all dimension styles you might use in a drawing. You should try to be consistent with your Format options simply to maintain consistency in your drawings.

INSIDER TIP

In the architectural field, typically dimension text should be above the dimension line. If you adjust an existing dimension with this property by using the Grip feature and drag the dimension to the side, however, a leader is drawn underneath the text. This is typically undesirable and annoying. A quick fix to this is to use the DimOverRide command. Upon requesting this command, the system will ask you for a dimension variable to override. Type **DIMTAD** (DIMension Text Above Dimension), set it to 1, and then select the newly moved dimension with the incorrect leader format. After this is complete, the settings will be returned to normal.

Annotation Options

The Annotation option of the Dimension Styles dialog box enables you to control how the text looks in your dimensions. Figure 19.9 shows the Annotation dialog box.

Figure 19.9

The Annotation dialog box enables you to control how text appears in your dimensions.

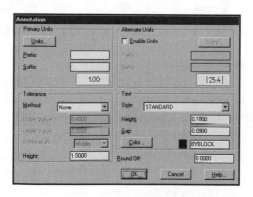

The Annotation dialog box is broken down into four separate sections: Primary Units, Alternate Units, Tolerance, and Text. Each of these areas is explained in the sections that follow.

Primary and Alternate Units

The Primary Units and Alternate Units sections are used to define the units that dimensions will use in their text. Unfortunately, AutoCAD does not automatically set the dimension units to match your Units setting in AutoCAD. So, you must correctly define the units for your dimensions separately.

NOTE

The reason AutoCAD does not automatically use the Units setting from the drawing is because there are additional unit types available to you in the dimensions.

When you click on the Units button, the Primary Units dialog box shown in figure 19.10 appears.

Figure 19.10

The Primary Units dialog box enables you to define units for your dimensions.

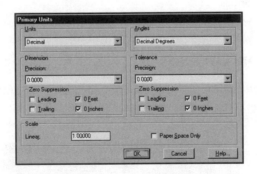

There are two new unit types: Architectural Stacked and Fractional Stacked. The stacked unit types vary from the normal unit types in one way. When you have a fraction in the dimension, the fraction will use AutoCAD's stacking capabilities to create a correctly stacked fraction instead of an inline fraction such as ½. Figure 19.11 shows you a dimension with a stacked fraction.

The dialog box shown in figure 19.10 should look very similar to the Units dialog box discussed in Chapter 3, "Setting Up the AutoCAD 14 Drawing Environment." You can select the type of units as well as the type of angle measurements to use. In both cases, you can specify the accuracy. Of particular interest here are two options: Zero Suppression and Linear Scale.

Figure 19.11

*A dimension showing you
the use of the architectural
stacked unit type.*

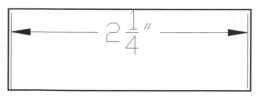

Zero Suppression is used to control when a 0 appears in a dimension. For example, 6' is a valid dimension when in architectural units. But, 6' is easy to confuse with 6", especially if the blueprint of the drawing is not very good. In both cases, the leading or trailing zeros have been suppressed. These dimensions read much easier as 6'– 0" and 0'–6". You can set this up by disabling zero suppression for feet and inches. You can also control zero suppression for leading and trailing zeros such as 0.6 and 6.000.

The Linear scale option is used to adjust how the distance between the start and end points of the dimension is measured. Most of the time, this option is reserved for paper space. In paper space, when you place a dimension, it measures the dimension in paper space units, not model space units.

In a viewport that is scaled to $\frac{1}{4}$"=1'–0", for example, a 4' line will measure 1". This is because of the underlying scale factor difference between paper space and model space. Just as you have to adjust the overall scale factor of a dimension style for model space, you must adjust the linear scale to match paper space. It is calculated in the same way as the overall scale factor. In the above example, a linear scale of 48 is correct.

After you have set your primary units, click on OK to return to the Annotation dialog box. Alternate units are configured in the same way. After secondary units are enabled, they are used to provide a different unit measure for the same dimension. Figure 19.12 shows you a dimension with alternate units.

Figure 19.12

*A dimension showing
alternate units.*

After you have established the units for your dimension, you can further modify the text by adding a prefix, suffix, or both to the dimension. For example, you can further clarify a dimension by using a suffix of CM to indicate centimeters.

Tolerance Types

The Tolerance section of the Annotation dialog box enables you to add tolerances to the end of the dimension text. These tolerances are different from the tolerance command discussed in Chapter 18, "Productive Dimensioning." There are five different types of tolerances. Each tolerance is briefly described in the following list:

- **None.** No tolerances are used in the dimension.

- **Symmetrical.** The tolerance is applied with a high and low limit that are the same. For example, 1.00 +/− 0.1 is a symmetrical tolerance.

- **Deviation.** The tolerance is applied with a high and low limit that can be different. As long as the object is manufactured within the limit, it is acceptable.

- **Limits.** The tolerance completely replaces the dimension. As long as the object is manufactured within the tolerances, it is acceptable.

- **Basic.** No tolerance is used, but a box is drawn around the dimension to help emphasize it.

After you select the tolerance method, you may apply an upper and lower value, as well as justification of the text in the dimension line. Figure 19.13 shows you a dimension with a symmetrical tolerance applied.

Figure 19.13

A dimension showing the use of symmetrical tolerance.

Text Properties

The last section of the Annotation dialog box is the Text section, where you can specify how the text in the dimension will appear. In the Style drop-down list, you can select any previously defined text style. (See Chapter 16, "Text Annotation," for more on how to define a text style.) After you select a style, you can apply other properties to the style, such as height and color. The Height option, in particular, depends on how the text style is defined. If the text style is defined with a fixed height, that height will be used. If the text style's height is 0, the height specified in the Annotation dialog box will be used instead.

Round Off

The last option in the Annotation dialog box is Round Off, which is used to determine how a measured dimension is rounded. For example, if you set the round off to 0.5, all dimensions will be measured to the nearest half unit. A setting of 1.0 will round off to the nearest integer value.

The following exercise ties together all the information you have learned in this chapter so far. It shows you how to quickly and easily set up a complete dimension style for use in AutoCAD.

CREATING A DIMENSION STYLE FOR A MECHANICAL DRAWING

1. Start a new drawing.

2. From the Dimension menu, choose Style.

3. In the Dimension Styles dialog box, rename the style **MECH1**.

4. Click on Save.

5. Click on the Geometry button.

6. In the Center area of the Geometry dialog box, select Line.

7. In the Arrowheads area, select Dot.

8. In the Extension Line area, select Red as the Color.

9. Click on OK to close the Geometry dialog box.

10. Click on the Format button.

11. In the Vertical Justification area of the Format dialog box, select Above.

12. In the Text area, turn off Inside Horizontal and Outside Horizontal.

13. Click on OK to close the Format dialog box.

14. Click on the Annotation button.

15. In the Primary Units area of the Annotation dialog box, click on the Units button.

16. In the Primary Units dialog box, set the Dimension precision to 0.00.

17. In the Angles area, set the Tolerance precision to 0.0.

18. Click on OK to close the Primary Units dialog box.

19. In the Tolerance area, set the tolerance Method to Symmetrical.

20. Set the Upper Value to **0.2**.

21. Set the Text dimension Color to green.

22. Click on OK to close the Annotation dialog box.

23. Click on Save to save the dimension style.

24. Click on OK to close the Dimension Styles dialog box and return to AutoCAD.

25. Create a couple of dimensions in this style. Figure 19.14 shows you a few possibilities.

Figure 19.14

A few dimensions created in the MECH1 style.

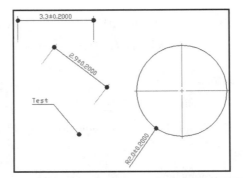

At this point, you would normally create other dimension styles and save them to a template file. For a little extra practice, see if you can create a series of child styles using MECH1 as a parent.

Now that the processes and steps for working with style families have been covered, the following section introduces some important tips that will help you optimize your dimension styles.

Tips for Creating Effective Dimension Styles

The following are a few tips and techniques concerning dimension styles:

■ Create all your necessary styles and save them in a drawing template. That way, you never have to recreate the same styles.

■ Try to create your styles in a somewhat generic fashion so that you can easily modify them.

- When naming your styles, give them names that make sense to you and to others. For example, ARCH14 is easier to understand as an Architectural dimension style for a ¼" drawing than a name such as STYLE1.

- Make use of families when you need to have your dimension styles change slightly when using different dimension types. This saves you from having to set dimension styles every time you change dimension types such as linear or angular.

Modifying Dimensions

After you have created your dimension styles and created a variety of dimensions in your drawing, you will need to eventually be able to modify the dimensions. Some reasons why you might need to modify your existing dimensions include:

- The drawing plot scale changes.

- You make a change to already dimensioned geometry.

- You want to specify a different dimension text and override the AutoCAD measurement.

- You want to reposition the dimension text to help clean up the drawing.

- You want to change the style of a dimension without having to recreate the dimension.

The sections that follow discuss the various techniques for modifying existing dimensions.

NOTE

The rest of this chapter assumes that Associative Dimensioning is turned on. This is controlled through the DIMASO dimension variable, which should be set to On. Without associative dimensioning, you cannot update or modify your dimensions because they are broken down into individual entities and are not considered a dimension entity after they are created.

Leaders, of course, do not make use of associativity and therefore are slightly different when it comes to dimension editing. In most cases, you will simply edit leaders as normal AutoCAD entities.

Grip Editing

One of the most powerful methods of editing in AutoCAD is grip editing. Just like you can grip edit most objects in AutoCAD, you can grip edit dimension as well. Of course, you can only use grip editing if PICKFIRST and GRIPS are enabled and set to a value of 1.

To grip edit a dimension, simply click on the dimension to highlight it. You will immediately see the grip boxes appear on a linear dimension, as shown in figure 19.15.

Figure 19.15

Grip boxes used to edit a linear dimension.

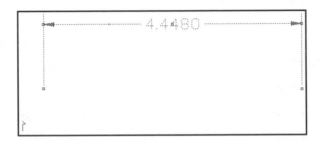

Of course, the exact location and effect of each grip will differ from dimension type to dimension type. Figure 19.16 shows you the grip layout for a radius dimension.

Figure 19.16

The dimension grips for a radius dimension.

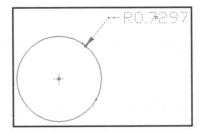

To edit a grip, simply click on one of the blue grip boxes. The box will turn red to indicate it is selected. Then, right-click on the box to view the grip editing pop-up menu shown in figure 19.17.

Most of the time, you will use the Move option to reposition the dimension text, the dimension line, or the start or end points of the dimension. After you select the option you want, simply grip edit the dimension just like you would any other object. See Chapter 10, "Basic Object Editing," for more information on grip editing.

Figure 19.17

Select the type of grip edit you want to use from the grip editing pop-up menu.

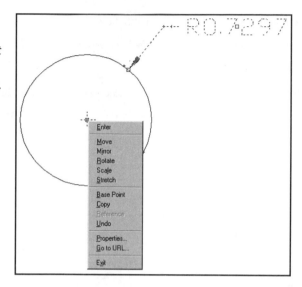

A couple of problems you might encounter are:

- If you select the grip that is nearest to the dimension text and select rotate, the dimension will rotate around the text. You will not rotate the text itself. You must use a special dimension editing command to rotate the text and not the dimension line.

- If you are working with a radius or diameter dimension, you can grip edit the center point of the dimension. If you reposition the center point, the dimension text will change. AutoCAD does not maintain a link between the dimensioned object's center and the dimension itself. Always make sure you move the point back to the center of the dimensioned object.

The following exercise shows you how to make use of grip editing with dimensions.

GRIP EDITING A DIMENSION

1. Load the file 19TUT02.DWG from the accompanying CD-ROM.

2. Turn on a running object snap mode of Endpoint.

3. Click on the one existing dimension to highlight it and show the grips.

NOTE

Pickfirst and grips must both be enabled. They are enabled by default in AutoCAD. If you disabled them, re-enable them for this exercise.

4. Click on the lower-right grip to highlight it.

5. Right-click on the same grip to display the pop-up menu.

6. Choose Copy.

7. Select each corner going to the right to create three more dimensions.

8. Press Esc twice.

9. Click on the dimension farthest to the right.

10. Select the grip at the intersection of the dimension and extension lines and move the dimension up into position, as shown in figure 19.18.

Figure 19.18

The drawing with the first dimension in position.

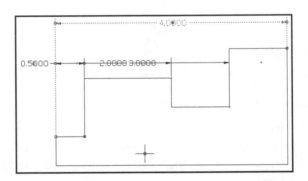

11. Repeat steps 2–10 for the other two dimensions. Figure 19.19 shows you the final dimensioned drawing.

Figure 19.19

The drawing with all dimensions correctly positioned.

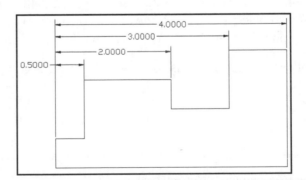

Editing Dimension Text

One of the most common editing tasks for a dimension is the ability to change the dimension text after the dimension has been created. The easiest way to edit the text is to simply choose Object, Text from the Modify pull-down menu. This executes the DDEDIT command. If you select the dimension object, the Multiline Text Editor will appear as shown in figure 19.20.

Figure 19.20

The Multiline Text Editor dialog box when used with a dimension.

The only thing that appears in the dialog box is a <>. This symbol indicates the measured AutoCAD value. To replace the measured value, delete the <> and replace it with the value you want. Otherwise, add the text before and/or after the symbol as you see fit. Just make sure to pay attention to how large the text will be inside the dimension. You don't want to put more text than there is room for.

INSIDER TIP

You can have stacked text in a dimension because of the MTEXT object contained in it. Place a return after the <> text to place the next line below the first. If the text is set to Middle justification, the first line of text will move up and new lines will go below it. If the justification is Above, it will all move up to be above the dimension line. To keep the first dimension line in place and generate any new lines below the first line, place a \X at the end of the first line of text, followed immediately by the second line. Then step any following lines with a return as usual.

When it comes to leaders, the DDEDIT command works just fine for editing the text.

In addition to changing the value of the text in a dimension, you can also rotate and reposition the text. The fastest and easiest way to reposition text is to simply grip edit the dimension. Alternatively, you can also use the DIMTEDIT command, which is accessed by clicking on the Dimension Text Edit button on the Dimension toolbar or by choosing Align Text from the Dimension pull-down menu. For the pull-down menu version, each DIMTEDIT option is listed individually on the Align Text flyout.

DIMTEDIT enables you to reposition the text, as well as align it to the left or right side of the dimension. If you make a mistake, DIMTEDIT also has a Home option that you can use to move the text back to the original position it was in when the dimension was created. The last DIMTEDIT option is Rotate, which enables you to rotate the text of a dimension without rotating the dimension itself.

The following exercise shows you how to edit the text of a dimension.

EDITING THE DIMENSION TEXT

1. Load the file 19TUT03.DWG from the accompanying CD.

2. Choose Object, Text from the Modify pull-down menu and click on the 4.000 dimension. This will bring up the Mtext dialog box.

3. After the <> symbol, add the text **Overall Length**.

4. Click on OK to close the Mtext dialog box. Figure 19.21 shows you the resulting dimension.

Figure 19.21

The dimension with the modified text.

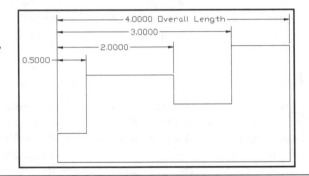

Updating Dimensions

Another popular dimension editing task is to update an existing dimension to the current dimension style. This occurs frequently when users create drawings with many different dimension styles. It is very easy to create dimensions in the wrong style by accident, under this condition.

The three different ways to update the style of a dimension are as follows:

■ Modify the style

■ Update the dimension with DIMSTYLE

■ Revise the dimension with Update.

If you modify a dimension style that is currently in use in the drawing, when you save the style and exit the Dimension Styles dialog box, all dimensions using that style will automatically be updated to the new version. In some instances, you may have to regen the screen to see the changes.

If you want to change a dimension to a different style, you must first set the new style as the current dimension style. You can do this in the Dimension Styles dialog box or use the DIMSTYLE system variable. After the style is set to current, you can choose Dimension, Update or use the Dimension Update tool on the Dimension toolbar. Then, select the dimension and it will be updated to match the new style.

NOTE

There is an inconsistency in AutoCAD with the way updates are handled. The pull-down makes uses of the DIMSTYLE command, whereas the toolbar makes use of the DIM: UPDATE command. Both end up with the same result. Use whichever method you are most comfortable with.

The following exercise shows you how to update AutoCAD dimensions.

UPDATING DIMENSIONS IN AUTOCAD

1. Open the file 19TUT04.DWG from the accompanying CD-ROM.

2. Choose Dimension, Style to open the Dimension Styles dialog box.

3. Set the style 19TUT04 as the current style.

4. Click on OK to close the Dimension Styles dialog box.

5. Choose Dimension, Update.

6. Select all the dimensions in the drawing and press Enter. The dimensions are updated, as shown in figure 19.22.

7. Save the files as 19TUT05.DWG someplace on your hard drive for use in the next exercise.

Figure 19.22

The updated dimensions.

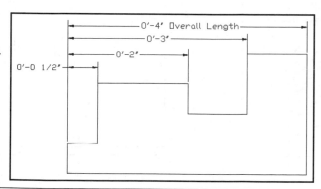

Using DIMEDIT

DIMEDIT is another AutoCAD dimension editing tool. This command is available by typing DIMEDIT at the Command: prompt, or by selecting the Dimension Edit tool from the Dimension toolbar. It is not available from the Dimension pull-down menu.

DIMEDIT enables you to reposition the dimension text back to the home position, rotate the text, and replace the dimension text, just like DIMTEDIT does. What is new is the capability to add an obliquing angle to a dimension. An obliquing angle forces the vertical extensions lines off from vertical by the angle specified. This is more of a cosmetic adjustment to make dimension look more interesting. Obliquing a dimension does not affect the text, dimension line, arrowheads, or origin points. It only affects the extension lines.

The following exercise shows you how to use DIMEDIT.

Using DIMEDIT on a Dimension

1. Continue from the last exercise, or load the file 19TUT05.DWG from the accompanying CD-ROM.

2. Open the Dimension toolbar if it is not open already and select the Dimension Edit tool.

3. At the Command: prompt, type **O** for Oblique.

4. Select all the dimensions in the drawing and press Enter.

5. Enter **85** as the oblique angle and press Enter. Figure 19.23 shows the resulting drawing.

Figure 19.23

The drawing with oblique dimensions.

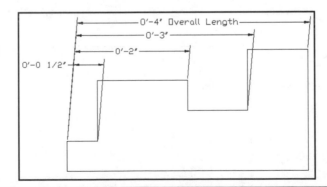

Overriding Dimension Variables

A lesser-known method of modifying a dimension is to override a dimension variable. When you are creating a dimension in a specific style, it is possible to override one or more dimension variables in the style. This enables you to change the color of the dimension text for a couple of dimensions and then revert back to the original if you so desire.

There are several ways to implement dimension variable overriding. The easiest way is to override the dimension variable when you are creating the dimension. Unfortunately, to do this, you must know the name of the dimension variable you want to override. When you select the dimension command, such as DIMLINEAR, simply enter the name of the dimension variable you want to override. Give it the new value and that value will be used until you clear the override. For example, DIMASZ controls the size of the arrowheads. You can override this variable with a larger or smaller value than that found in the dimension style.

To clear a dimension override, you must use the DIMOVERRIDE command, which is available on the Dimension pull-down menu as Override. At the Command: prompt, you will be asked for the dimension variable to override. If you type **Clear** at this prompt, you will clear all overrides and revert back to the original style definition. Alternatively, you can enter any dimension variable, override it, and apply it to existing dimensions.

Overrides stay valid until the CLEAR command is executed, a new style is chosen, or you change the override to another value.

To help you make use of the override command, table 19.1 quickly lists all the dimension variables and what each does.

Table 19.1

Dimension Variables and Meanings

Variable	Function
DIMALT	Enables the use of alternate dimensions units.
DIMALTD	Controls the decimal places used in alternate units.
DIMALTF	Controls the alternate unit scale factor.
DIMALTTD	Number of decimals in a tolerance in an alternate unit.
DIMATTZ	Toggles suppression of zeros for tolerances.

continues

Table 19.1, continued

Dimension Variables and Meanings

Variable	Function
DIMALTU	Unit format for alternate units except for angular dims.
DIMALTZ	Controls suppression of zeros for alternate units.
DIMAPOST	The text prefix or suffix for alternate dimensions except angular.
DIMASO	Enables associative dimensions.
DIMASZ	Controls the arrowhead sizes.
DIMAUNIT	Angle format for angular dimensions.
DIMBLK	Name of block to be drawn instead of regular arrowhead.
DIMBLK1	User defined arrowhead 1.
DIMBLK2	User defined arrowhead 2.
DIMCEN	Enables use of center marks.
DIMCLRD	Color of the dimension line.
DIMCLRE	Color of the extension line.
DIMCLRT	Color of the dimension text.
DIMDEC	Number of decimal places for primary tolerances.
DIMDLE	Controls extension of dimension line when oblique or architectural tick arrowheads are used.
DIMDLI	Dimension line spacing for baseline dimensions.
DIMEXE	Distance extension lines extend beyond the dimension line.
DIMEXO	Extension line offset.
DIMFIT	Placement of arrows and dimension lines inside of extension lines.
DIMGAP	Gap around dimension text.
DIMJUST	Horizontal dimension text position.
DIMLFAC	Global scale factor for linear measurements.
DIMLIM	Generates dimension limits as default text.
DIMPOST	Prefix or suffix for text.
DIMRND	Dimension rounding value.

Variable	Function
DIMSAH	Enables use of user defined arrowheads.
DIMSCALE	Overall scale factor.
DIMSD1	First dimension line suppression.
DIMSD2	Second dimension line suppression.
DIMSE1	First extension line suppression.
DIMSE2	Second extension line suppression.
DIMSHQ	Controls redefinition of dimension when dragged.
DIMSOXD	Suppresses drawing of dimension lines outside extension lines.
DIMSTYIE	Current dimension style.
DIMTAD	Vertical position of text in relation to the dimension line.
DIMTDEC	Number of decimals in a tolerance.
DIMTFAC	Scale factor for text height in tolerances.
DIMTIH	Position of text inside extension lines.
DIMTIX	Draws text between extension lines
DIMTM	Lower tolerance limit.
DIMTOFL	Forces drawing of dimension line.
DIMTOH	Position of text outside of extension lines.
DIMTOL	Appends tolerances to text.
DIMTOJ	Vertical justification of tolerances.
DIMTP	Upper tolerance limit.
DIMTSZ	Size of oblique dimension arrowheads.
DIMTVP	Vertical position of text.
DIMTXTSTY	Text style for the dimension.
DIMTZIN	Zero suppression of tolerance values.
DIMUNIT	Unit format for dimensions except angular.
DIMUPT	Cursor functionality for user positioned text.
DIMZIN	Suppression of primary unit value.

For most of the dimension variables, you may need to look up exactly what values you can use. Many are simply 1 or 0, and others accept text strings like DIMSTYLE does. If you are going to use overrides, though, you need to know which variables you want to override and how you want to override them.

The following exercise shows you how to make use of dimension overrides.

OVERRIDING DIMENSION VARIABLES

1. Load the file 19TUT02.DWG from the accompanying CD-ROM.

2. Erase the first dimension.

3. Choose Linear from the Dimension pull-down menu and create an overall dimension.

4. Select DIMLINEAR again by pressing Enter.

5. At the First Extension line prompt, type in **DIMCLRT** and press Enter.

6. Enter a value of **1** for color RED.

7. Dimension the smaller horizontal lengths of the block, as shown in figure 19.24.

Figure 19.24

The drawing with correctly placed dimensions.

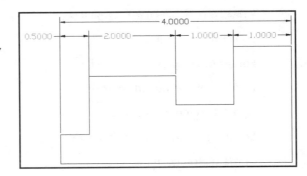

8. Select DIMLINEAR.

9. Enter **DIMCLRT** again and set it back to BYBLOCK.

10. Dimension the right vertical edge of the block. Figure 19.25 shows you the final drawing.

Figure 19.25

The drawing with four overridden dimensions.

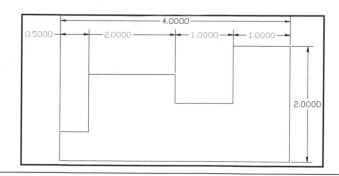

Summary

AutoCAD provides you with a fair amount of control over dimensions through dimension styles. By making good use of templates, you can save your dimension styles and not have to re-create them.

After you create dimensions, of course, you need to be able to edit those dimensions. The primary methods for editing dimensions are grip editing, DDEDIT, and DIMTEDIT. Each gives you various ways of editing the dimension, from text editing to text positioning.

CHAPTER **20**

PRODUCTIVE PLOTTING

by Bill Burchard

The ultimate goal of most AutoCAD drawings is perfecting the final hardcopy output. To reach this goal, contractors use plots to build the project you created in AutoCAD. A good deal of information is available to help you configure your printers and plotters. AutoCAD's Installation Guide, and Autodesk's technical on-demand faxes and online help via their web site, for example, provide a wealth of data. Between this data and that in the manufacturers' guides for printers and plotters, you have the information necessary to properly set up your hardware and software environments.

This chapter does not try to duplicate that information. Instead, the following sections discuss methods for increasing your productivity by using techniques that you can apply to your work regardless of your printer or plotter configuration. By applying the methods and examples presented in this chapter, and by using the associated principles, you will spend less time configuring drawings to be plotted and more time doing productive work.

Specifically, this chapter discusses the following subjects:

- Configuring a plotter
- Setting and saving plotter parameters
- Quickly editing PCP files
- Hiding unwanted objects
- Creating plots
- Using the new Batch Plot utility
- Using script files for multiple plots

Configuring a Plotter

As noted previously, this section does not duplicate the wealth of information already available for configuring printers and plotters. Instead, it discusses methods you should consider when you configure a plotter, to make plotting as easy and intuitive as possible. The specific topics covered here include: naming the configuration, choosing the new network configuration, and configuring for raster plots.

Naming Your Configuration

When you define a new plotter, AutoCAD permits you to name the new configuration with a title containing up to 81 characters. Use a descriptive name, such as the one shown in figure 20.1. This name, HP650c Color Mode - Landscape Orientation, provides enough information to let users know that the configuration is for a Hewlett-Packard HP650c, with color mode selected (as opposed to mono), and with landscape orientation.

Figure 20.1

Use a descriptive name to define plotter configurations.

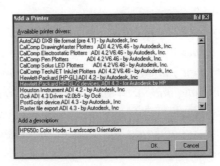

You can include additional information, such as the paper size for which the plotter configuration is set up, and even the location of the plotter, if your office uses several plotters of the same type.

 NOTE

The current printer can be set from the Printer tab in the Preferences dialog box or from the Device and Default Selection dialog box, which is accessed from the Print/Plot Configuration dialog box.

Choosing the New Network Configuration

Release 14 enables you to choose a network printing device, which means that you no longer have to use Autospool to print over a network when you're using AutoCAD's ADI drivers.

NOTE

AutoCAD automatically configures itself for the default system printer. This means that your computer's currently selected default printer, which is chosen from the Windows Printers folder, is the device to which AutoCAD plots.

During the configuration process, AutoCAD asks you to specify the computer port to which the plot should be sent. In earlier releases, the only selections were the Serial port (COM1) or the Parallel port (LPT1). With Release 14, a third choice is available: the Network port (see fig. 20.2).

Figure 20.2

Release 14 offers the new Network port.

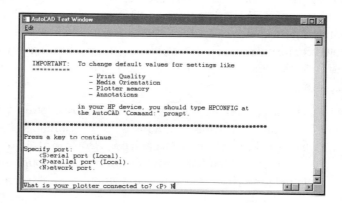

Printer settings (such as paper size and orientation) for your computer's default printer can be controlled from the Print Setup window (accessed through the Windows interface) or through AutoCAD's Print/Plot Configuration dialog box. If you use the dialog box, click on the Device and Default Selection button, and then click on the Change button under Device Specific Configuration.

INSIDER TIP

Use AutoCAD's ADI drivers if they are available for your particular plotters. Autodesk has tested these drivers extensively, and they tend to offer more control over the appearance of your plotted drawings.

Configuring for Raster Plots

A *raster* image is a bitmap image, which is simply a picture that has been divided into a grid. Each element in the grid represents a single color and is commonly called a *pixel* (which stands for *picture element*).

When you configure a plotter with AutoCAD's raster file export driver, AutoCAD prompts you for the grid density. Most of the predefined grid sizes displayed represent those common for computer screens. The standard VGA screen size, for example, is 640×480, which means that the image on the screen is made up of a grid 640 pixels wide by 480 pixels high. Typical AutoCAD computer setups have large screens that allow for denser grids—a common screen grid configuration is 1,024 pixels wide by 768 pixels high.

These densities are fine for computer screens, but might not look very good when plotted. The reason the computer screen density does not work well when plotted is because of the high dots-per-inch (dpi) capability of today's printers. A 600 dpi plotter, for example, is capable of printing 600 pixels in every inch on paper. If you plot a bitmap image that is 640×480 pixels, the printed image will be a little more than one inch wide and less than one inch high. That's not very useful for most poster-size displays.

Of course, you can rescale the bitmap in AutoCAD and stretch it to fill a 24-by-36-inch sheet. The problem with this technique is that the bitmap's pixels also stretch. In this particular case, you would stretch each pixel to a size of about 0.06 inches ($\frac{1}{16}$ inch) wide by 0.05 inches high. The result would be a very rough—or *pixelated*—image, as shown in figure 20.3. Certainly, you would not want to use this configuration to display your work.

Figure 20.3

A low-resolution bitmap image provides a poor-quality product.

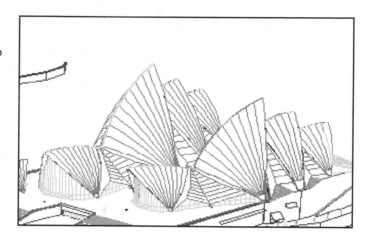

Using AutoCAD Custom Options for Higher Resolution

Fortunately, AutoCAD provides a custom option for the raster file image. Consequently, you can create your own high-resolution bitmaps that produce very crisp, clear output.

Creating bitmaps with large pixel grids does pose one problem, however; the bitmap's file size is correspondingly larger. When you output your bitmap to a 600 dpi plotter, for example, the highest resolution you can choose would have 600 pixels per inch. Therefore, if you were plotting on a 24-by-36-inch sheet, you could create a bitmap grid 21,600 pixels wide by 14,400 pixels high. Unfortunately, the bitmap file would be about 311 MB in size, and that's a tad large for most machines to handle.

NOTE

> To determine the file size of a bitmap image, multiply its width by its height. This gives you a good indication of its size as an 8-bit image (256 colors). To determine the size of a bitmap that is 16 colors (a 4-bit image), multiply its width by its height and then divide that by 2.

Remember not to create a denser pixel grid for your bitmap image than the output device can handle. The extra pixels increase your file's size, but cannot be displayed by the device and will not be used when plotting.

Determining a Bitmap's Pixel Grid Size

When determining a bitmap's pixel grid size, you should determine the grid size based on 100 dpi to 150 dpi. In other words, multiply the width in inches by 100, and the height in inches by 100. This produces the grid density to use. For example, if your bitmap will be plotted on a 24-by-36-inch sheet, use a grid density of 3,600 pixels wide (36 inches times 100 dots-per-inch) by 2,400 pixels high (24 inches times 100 dots-per-inch). The bitmap's file size will be about 8.6 MB. This file size is a little easier to handle than larger files, and the image is still pretty good (see fig. 20.4).

Figure 20.4

An adequate resolution with minimal pixelation can be achieved.

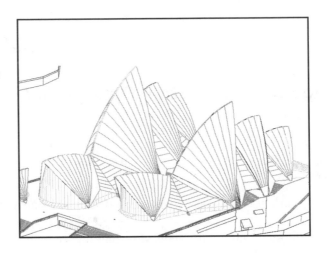

Choosing File and Color Types

AutoCAD offers a choice of four common file types:

- Microsoft Windows Device-independent Bitmap (.BMP)
- TrueVision TGA Format
- Z-Soft PCX Format
- TIFF (Tag Image File Format)

When configuring AutoCAD for raster plots, you must select one of the four file types listed. The reason you must select a file type is because AutoCAD does not send raster images directly to the plotter. Instead, it exports the image as a raster file, which you then import and plot from another application. As a consequence, AutoCAD must know what type of raster file format you need. To determine which file type to select, check the software you intend to use for plotting the image, and use the file type recommended there. For most Windows-based applications, the BMP file type is fine.

AutoCAD also gives you a choice of three color types—Mono, 16-color, or 256-color—for your output. The Mono option creates the smallest files, but the bitmap is black-and-white only. The 16-color option creates the next smallest file size and, because most AutoCAD drawings use less than 16 colors, is usually the best setting. If you are creating rendered images, use the 256-color option to produce the most realistic image.

In this section, you learned about configuring AutoCAD for plotting. In the next section, you learn about fine-tuning plotter configurations from AutoCAD's Print/Plot Configuration dialog box.

Setting and Saving Plotter Parameters

With the latest release of AutoCAD, users now have two choices for defining plot parameter files: PCP and PC2. The original Plot Configuration Parameters (PCP) file format remains the same; the only difference is that AutoCAD now refers to this file format as *Partial* Configuration Parameters. The new PC2 (*Complete Configuration Parameters*) file not only contains the same information as the original PCP file, but also includes detailed plotter configuration information. In other words, the data you create when you configure a plotter is included in the PC2 file.

INSIDER TIP

A convenient way to maintain consistent plotter configurations is to include PC2 files with drawing files that you send to another user.

Generally, it is best to define company-wide standards for pen colors and line widths, as well as for plotter setups. In this way, drawings are consistent in every department and you avoid potential problems in plotting when several departments share drawing files.

When you define unique pen colors and line widths for a particular project, save the settings in a PCP/PC2 file and give the file the same name as the drawing. This is useful when, several months later, another CAD technician must create a plot of the project and has to find the correct PCP/PC2 file to load.

The next section discusses how to edit existing PCP files and determine the plot scale.

Quickly Editing PCP Files

Occasionally, you might need to modify an existing PCP or PC2 file. Using AutoCAD to make significant changes to the file can be quite tedious. To change pen settings, for example, you must click on the Pen Assignments button from the Print/Plot Configuration dialog box, and then choose one linetype at a time and modify its values. The process can be frustrating when you must make the same modification to dozens of pens, setting their linetype to 3 or their pen width to 0.10, for example.

Fortunately, both PCP and PC2 files are ASCII text files. Because they can be opened in any word processor or text editor, you can edit them quickly by using Find and Replace operations.

The following exercise demonstrates how to modify a PCP file quickly, using Windows WordPad. Specifically, the linetype values and some of the pen weights are changed.

QUICKLY MODIFYING PCP FILES, ONE BY ONE

1. From the Windows taskbar, choose the Start button. Then choose Programs, Accessories, WordPad to launch the WordPad application.

2. From the File pull-down menu, choose Open to display the Open window.

3. In the File Name text box, enter ***.PCP**, as shown in figure 20.5, and press Enter. This instructs WordPad to display only files with the PCP extension.

Figure 20.5

When you specify the correct file name in the text box, WordPad returns only PCP files.

4. Open the 20PCP01.PCP file found on the accompanying CD-ROM. The ASCII text file appears.

5. From the Edit pull-down menu, choose Replace to open the Replace window. For the first modification, suppose that you must change the weights of the first 16 pens to 0.10.

6. In the Find what text box, enter **PEN_WEIGHT = 0.010000**.

7. In the Replace with text box, enter **PEN_WEIGHT = 0.10**, as shown in figure 20.6.

Figure 20.6

Replacing the Pen Weight values is easy with a Find and Replace operation.

NOTE

The values entered in the Find what and Replace with text boxes must appear exactly like those values in the PCP files, with the exception of trailing zeros.

To quickly and accurately duplicate the values in the PCP file, highlight a line of text that contains the value to be replaced. Next, use Windows' Copy command (Ctrl+C) to copy the value, and then paste it (Ctrl+V) in the text box.

8. Make sure that WordPad's cursor is at the beginning of the text file, and then click on the Replace button. WordPad now goes to the first instance of the matching value.

9. Click on the Replace button again. WordPad changes the highlighted value to match the value in the Replace with text box, and then finds the next instance of a matching value.

10. Repeat this process until the line weights of the first 16 pens have been replaced by the new value. (Keep the file open. You need it for the next exercise.)

In the next exercise you modify the linetype values, replacing all the 0 linetype values with a value of 1.

USING A GLOBAL SEARCH-AND-FIND OPERATION TO MODIFY PCP FILES

1. Press Ctrl+Home to move the cursor to the beginning of the text file.

2. In the Find what text box, enter **HW_LINETYPE = 0**.

3. In the Replace with text box, enter **HW_LINETYPE = 1**, as shown in figure 20.7.

Figure 20.7

You're ready to replace the Linetype values with a global Find-and-Replace operation.

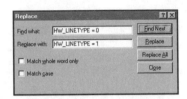

4. Click on the Replace All button. WordPad instantly replaces all 0 linetype values with 1. By using this technique, you can quickly modify PCP and PC2 files.

INSIDER TIP

After you finish editing the file, be sure to save it as a text file—the only type of PCP and PC2 file that AutoCAD recognizes.

This technique can be used with many word processors and text editors, although the commands shown in the preceding exercises are specific to WordPad.

Determining the Plot Scale

Paper space was created to make plotting easier. By creating sheet borders and titles in paper space at a 1:1 scale, and then creating and positioning viewports within the sheet border, you can easily create accurately scaled plots. See the section "Setting Views in Paper Space Viewports" in Chapter 15, "Paper Space," for more detailed information.

In this section, you learned about fine-tuning plotter output by editing PCP and PC2 files. In the next section, you learn about controlling object visibility when plotting.

Hiding Unwanted Objects for Easier Viewing

As a rule, you do not want all objects in a drawing to plot. AutoCAD provides the capability to hide certain objects from view, giving you control over which objects plot. Two methods of hiding objects when plotted are available: Hide Lines and Hideplot. Hide Lines hides objects in model space. Hideplot hides objects in paper space viewports. For more detailed information, see the "Hidden Line Removal: Hide Lines versus Hideplot" section in Chapter 15, "Paper Space."

Using Regions to Hide Objects

In the civil engineering practice, project drawings typically include plans and profiles. The plan views continue from one sheet to the next, and centerline alignments often follow curved paths. When a plan view is continued to the next sheet, it is broken at the current sheet with a matchline. The matchline indicates where the project design stops on the current sheet and continues on the next. For design purposes, the plan view ordinarily is an xref of the entire design model, with only the necessary portion displayed. Until Release 14, it was not easy to hide unwanted objects that extended beyond the matchline. The new XCLIP command solves this problem for xrefs. For more detailed information, see the "Using Release 14's XREF Enhancements" section in Chapter 13, "External References."

The new XCLIP command works only on xrefs and blocks, however. To hide other objects, you still must rely on the tried-and-true methods. The most obvious way to hide unwanted objects is to turn off or freeze the layers on which they reside. This is not always an option, though. When only a portion of an object must be hidden, turning off its layer and hiding the entire object will not work.

One simple way to solve this dilemma is to use the BOUNDARY and REGION commands. The BOUNDARY command quickly creates closed polygons from intersecting objects, and the REGION command transforms these closed polygons into region objects. *Region objects* behave like solid objects. When they are plotted with the Hide Lines or Hideplot features active, region objects hide any objects that are behind them.

The following exercise demonstrates how to hide objects by using the BOUNDARY and REGION commands.

HIDING OBJECTS WITH THE BOUNDARY AND REGION COMMANDS

1. Open the 20DWG01.DWG drawing file found on the accompanying CD-ROM.

INSIDER TIP

It's a good idea to use the BOUNDARY command to create regions because this command does not erase the selected objects used to define the region's boundary. The REGION command *does* delete objects.

2. Create a new layer called Regions and make it current.

Next, you must create the region.

3. From the Draw pull-down menu, choose Boundary to open the Boundary Creation dialog box.

NOTE

The BOUNDARY command is used here to create a new region from the existing green polygon.

4. Choose the Object Type drop-down list, and choose Region.

5. Click on the Make New Boundary Set button.

6. Choose the green polygon, and then press Enter to end the selection process.

7. Click on the Pick Points button.

8. Pick a point inside the green polygon, and then press Enter to end the selection process. AutoCAD creates the new region. In order for the region to hide objects beneath it, the region must be above the objects. Consequently, you must move the region up along its Z axis. This region must be moved to a Z value of 100 because the objects in this drawing have a Z value of 0.

9. Choose the black line that represents the region to activate its grips.

10. Choose one of the grips, and then press Enter to switch the grip edit mode to Move.

11. Enter **.XY** to filter for the X and Y coordinates.

12. Enter the **@** symbol to select the X and Y coordinates of the hot grip.

13. Enter 100 to set the new Z value. This moves the region along its Z axis from 0 to 100.

14. Turn off the Regions layer.

15. Enter **HIDE** at the Command: prompt. AutoCAD regenerates the screen and hides the objects beneath the region, as shown in figure 20.8. The region hides plotted objects with either the Hide Lines or Hideplot features.

Figure 20.8

Objects are hidden beneath the region object after the HIDE command is issued.

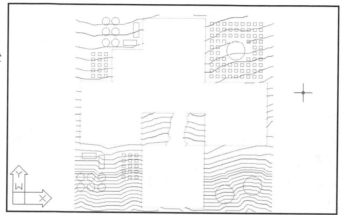

WARNING

Although you can turn off the Regions layer to remove its boundary, you cannot freeze the layer. Freezing the layer also freezes the region, which means that the HIDE command will not work.

If you have objects that you want to display on-screen but that you do not want to have visible when plotted, create a layer called DEFPOINTS on which to place those objects. You can also stop a block from being plotted by placing it on the DEFPOINTS layer, in spite of the internal objects' visibility.

WARNING

AutoCAD creates the DEFPOINTS layer when certain objects, such as associative dimensions, are created. Whether this layer is frozen and off or thawed and on, AutoCAD will not plot any objects on the layer.

By hiding unwanted objects, your plotted drawing will show only the objects you need to show. The next section discusses how to plot the mirror image of your drawing.

Plotting Mirrored Drawings

Many times in producing drawings you are required to provide documents for the sole purpose of making blueprints. The drafting trade in the past used semi-clear medias to give the best possible results for these prints. With today's technologies, you often don't have access to many medias beyond vellum and translucent bond. If you want great-looking blueprints, you need to plot your drawing in reverse.

AutoCAD does not have a native mechanism to plot reverse. However, many plotter device controls provide a mirror option for plotting. This feature typically does exist on older devices, but on the newer plotters you can set the plotter so that every plot produced is flipped. This is a valid solution unless this is a shared plotter—not everyone wants their plots reversed.

In order to create plot files that are mirrored by themselves so you don't have to modify the plotter, you need a way of flipping the AutoCAD view.

You can manually flip the entire drawing about the middle and make your plot and undo the change. This is not recommended, however, because dimensions, hatches, leaders, and so on can change appearance when mirrored.

A quick solution that might work for you is the VPOINT command. Normally VPOINT is set to 0,0,1. This means your perspective is from 0,0 in a 0 X distance, 0 Y distance, and 1 in the Z direction—effectively 1 unit above your drawing looking down. Change this to 0,0,–1; now your view is 1 unit *below* your drawing looking up. Make your plot as needed. When done, set VPOINT back to normal. Changing the drawing perspective is much safer than modifying the drawing objects.

INSIDER TIP

The VPOINT command is unavailable in paper space, and mirroring drawings in AutoCAD is discouraged.

In this section, you learned how to create a mirrored plot. In the following section, you learn how to quickly plot multiple drawings.

Creating Plots

Creating a single plot from AutoCAD is a simple process. But what about printing dozens, or even hundreds of plots? Fortunately, the process of creating plots is repetitious, and computers excel at performing repetitious tasks. By taking advantage of the repetitive nature of plotting, you can easily automate the process of plotting large numbers of drawings.

Using the New Batch Plot Utility

 The latest release of AutoCAD comes with a new stand-alone program called the Batch Plot Utility. With this Visual Basic application, you can easily select multiple drawing files and any associated PC2 or PCP files. The program is easy to use, and you will learn quickly how to have a computer plot multiple files automatically.

One very important feature of this application is that you can save a selection set of drawing files and PC2/PCP files for later use. After you have chosen the appropriate files for plotting, you can save the selection set as a Batch Plot (BPL) file—an ASCII text file that can be viewed by any text editor. The Batch Plot Utility stores the drawing and PC2/PCP file names, along with their paths, in a *comma-delimited file* (CDF). The format of the file is simple, which makes editing it easy if you need to.

Understanding the Format of a BPL File

To gain an understanding of the BPL format, study the contents of this sample BPL file, which is then explained in the text that follows:

```
"*BPL*",3,640,480
"D:\ACADR14\SAMPLE\bflyhse.dwg","D:\ACADR14\bflyhse.pc2"
"D:\ACADR14\SAMPLE\bftitle.dwg",""
"D:\ACADR14\SAMPLE\campus.dwg","D:\ACADR14\campus.pcp"
```

In the first line, the "*BPL*" indicates that this is a Batch Plot Utility file. The 3 is the number of drawings to be plotted, and the 640 and 480 values indicate the screen size of the AutoCAD window in which the file was saved. If you resize this window, the values change accordingly. When the BPL file is opened, the AutoCAD window is resized to the values in the file.

The next three lines list the drawing file names and any associated PC2/PCP files. Notice that the first drawing listed has a PC2 file associated with it. As mentioned earlier, the PC2 file contains PCP file information, as well as information about the plotter to which the drawing is to be sent. The second line lists only a drawing file. When no PC2 or PCP file is associated with the drawing, AutoCAD uses the current plotter and pen settings. The drawing file listed in the last line has a PCP file associated with it. AutoCAD will use this PCP file to determine pen settings but will send the drawing to the current plotter.

INSIDER TIP

For better control when you're plotting drawings, use a PC2 file instead of a PCP file. The PC2 guarantees that your drawing will be sent to the correct plotter with the appropriate pen settings and therefore will be plotted correctly.

The Batch Plot Utility emulates normal Windows selection methods. To select an entire range of file names, for example, you select the name of the first file and then press and hold the Shift key while you select the last file. Windows chooses the two selected files and all files between them. This feature is convenient for selecting a range of drawing file names to be copied into the Batch Plot Utility text box, and can be used also to associate a PC2 or PCP file to a range of selected drawing files.

The following exercise demonstrates how to associate a single PC2 file to all the drawing files listed in the Batch Plot Utility text box.

ASSOCIATING ONE PC2 FILE WITH A RANGE OF DRAWING FILES

1. Start the Batch Plot Utility. The application should be in the same folder as AutoCAD 14. This launches AutoCAD and opens the AutoCAD Batch Plot Utility window.

2. Click on the Open List button to open the Open Batch Plot List File window.

3. Open the 20BPL01.BPL file found on the accompanying CD-ROM. A list of drawing file names appears in the text box (see fig. 20.9).

Figure 20.9

The list of drawing file names in the Batch Plot Utility.

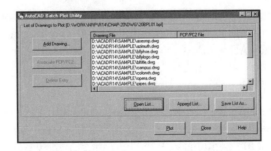

4. Choose the first file in the list.

5. Scroll down to the end of the list.

6. While you hold down the Shift key, choose the last file in the list. All the drawing file names are highlighted.

7. Click on the Associate PCP/PC2 button.

8. Open the 20PC201.PC2 file found on the accompanying CD-ROM. The Batch Plot Utility associates the 20PC201.PC2 file with all the highlighted files (see fig. 20.10). If you were to start the utility at this point, it would plot all the files shown, using the associated PC2 file.

Figure 20.10

The PC2 file is automatically associated with the drawing file names.

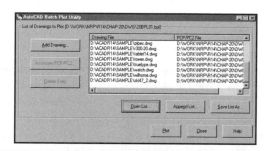

Plotting Different Views with the Batch Plot Utility

One drawback to the Batch Plot Utility application is that, by default, it plots only the drawing's current display. This means that if you want to plot several different areas in the same drawing file, you must make duplicate drawing files and save each view in a different file. Unfortunately, this method uses up disk space and takes time.

A better method is to save the different areas that you want to plot as views. Then follow these steps:

1. Click on the View button in the Print/Plot Configuration dialog box.

2. When the View dialog box opens, choose one of the views.

3. Save the plot setting as a PC2 file. When AutoCAD creates the PC2 file, it saves the current view name.

4. Repeat this process for each saved view.

5. Associate the PC2 files with the drawing in the Batch Plot Utility. The utility will plot all the views from the same drawing.

Using Script Files for Multiple Plots

Script files are commonly used for batch plotting. Although the new Batch Plot Utility is convenient, it is also limited. The technique for plotting different views of a drawing, using PC2 files, works well, but might not meet your needs. The Batch Plot Utility is of no help, for example, if you not only want to plot different views in the same drawing, but also want to turn different layers on and off. Such a task is easy to accomplish with script files, however. Another advantage of script files is that they can be used to execute AutoLISP routines.

INSIDER TIP

Being able to use script files to execute AutoLISP routines was very useful in a recent company project for which we produced more than 1,100 plan and profile drawings. At the end of the project, when it was time to make our plots, we discovered one problem—a block that was inserted in each drawing was the wrong block, and it had several attribute values. I created an AutoLISP routine that extracted the attribute value from the old block, replaced the old block with the new block, and then filled in the attribute values in the appropriate order. The AutoLISP routine was then inserted in the script file, which also plotted all the drawing files.

When you execute an AutoLISP routine with a script file, the script file stops running. To automatically start the script file again, use the following function and argument as the final function when the routine is exited:

```
(command "RESUME")
```

INSIDER TIP

The RESUME command restarts the script file at the appropriate point. On our company project, and using this technique, we replaced the old block with the new block in each drawing, and plotted the 1,100 drawings automatically.

Another technique used for the same project enabled us to create very quickly a script file containing 1,100 unique drawing file names. By using an ASCII text file created with the new Batch Plot Utility along with Microsoft Excel and Word, we were able to develop in only a few minutes a complicated script file containing hundreds of lines.

The following exercise demonstrates how to set up AutoLISP routines to be executed from script files, as well as how to quickly create large script files.

CREATING A SCRIPT FILE WITH THE BATCH FILE UTILITY AND EXCEL TO PLOT MULTIPLE DRAWINGS

1. Start the Batch Plot Utility, which should be in the same folder as AutoCAD 14. AutoCAD is launched, and the AutoCAD Batch Plot Utility window opens.

2. Open the following list of files, all of which appear in the Batch Plot Utility text box:
   - 20DWG02A.DWG
   - 20DWG02B.DWG
   - 20DWG02C.DWG
   - 20DWG02D.DWG
   - 20DWG02E.DWG

3. To save this as a BPL file, first click on the Save List As button. Name the file **MYFILE**.

4. Close the Batch Plot Utility application.

NOTE

The Batch Plot Utility application is used to quickly create an ASCII text file that contains the drawing file names to be plotted, along with their paths. When plotting with scripts, it's useful to have the drawing file's path. The next step opens the BPL file in Excel 5.0. (If you have a different spreadsheet program, use it. Hopefully, it will have the same tools as Excel.)

5. Launch Excel.

6. Open the MYFILE.BPL file. Excel automatically launches the Import Wizard.

7. Set the file type to Delimited, start the import at row 2, and set the File Origin to Windows (ANSI), as shown in figure 20.11.

Figure 20.11

Set the correct values for the first window in the Text Import Wizard.

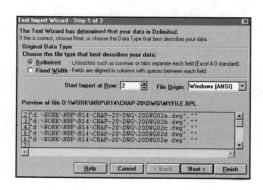

8. Click on the Next button.

9. Set the Delimiters to comma and the Text Qualifier to a single quotation mark, as shown in figure 20.12.

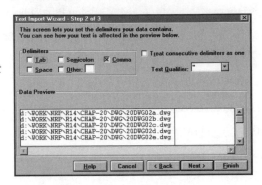

Figure 20.12

The correct values for the second window in the Text Import Wizard.

10. Click on the Next button, and then click on the Finish button. Excel inserts the drawing file names into the first row. Next, you must add the AutoCAD commands the script file will execute. In this particular case, the commands will open each drawing, execute an AutoLISP routine, and then save the drawing.

11. Highlight the first column by clicking on the A button at the top of the column.

12. From the Insert pull-down menu, choose Columns. Excel inserts a new column.

13. Select cell A1, and then type the word **Open**.

14. Move the cursor over the small black dot in the lower-right corner of cell A1 to change the cursor to a small cross.

15. Click and drag down to cell A5. Excel automatically fills all the cells with the word "OPEN."

16. Widen column B by double-clicking the line between the buttons for columns B and C. The cell expands to the width of the text values in column B.

17. Select cell C1. This is where you will enter the name of the AutoLISP routine that will be started from the script. Be sure that the path you type indicates the AutoLISP routine's location on your computer. (The path shown here is just an example.)

18. In cell C1, type the following:

```
(load "d:\\WORK\\NRP\\R14\\CHAP-20\\DWG\\GETNAME.LSP")
```

Be sure to separate subdirectories with two back slashes (\\), and remember to include the parentheses. This line of text loads the AutoLISP application. Even though Release 14 has persistent LISP, it's still a good idea to have the script file load the routine each time a new drawing is opened.

19. In cell D1, type **GETNAME** to execute the AutoLISP routine.

20. In cell E1, type **QSAVE** to save the drawing.

21. Click and drag the cursor across the three cells, C1, D1, and E1.

22. Move the cursor over the small black dot in the lower-right corner of cell E1 to change the cursor to a small cross.

23. Click and drag down to cell E5. Excel fills the cells with the text. Your spreadsheet should resemble figure 20.13.

Figure 20.13

The script file text appears in the spreadsheet program.

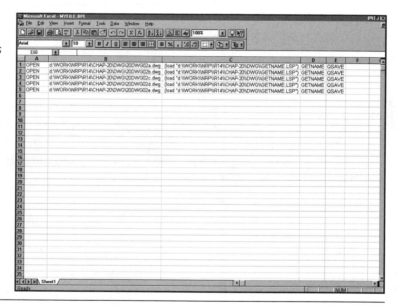

By using AutoCAD's Batch Plot Utility to quickly create a list of drawing file names with their paths, and then importing the file into Excel, you quickly created all the text necessary to plot multiple drawings from a script file. Next, you use Word to change the Excel spreadsheet file into an actual script file that AutoCAD can open and execute.

FINISHING AND RUNNING THE SCRIPT FILE

1. Click and drag across all the cells that contain text to highlight those cells.

2. Choose the Copy button to copy the text to the Windows Clipboard.

3. Launch Microsoft Word.

4. Choose the Paste button.

INSIDER TIP

The text is pasted into the document as a table. If you cannot see all the table's columns, change the page orientation to Landscape. (Choose Page Setup from the File drop-down menu, choose the Paper Size tab, and select Landscape.)

5. Click and drag inside all the cells to highlight them.

6. From the Table drop-down menu, choose Convert Table to Text, choose Paragraph Marks, and then choose OK. The table text is converted to single lines of text, as shown in figure 20.14.

Figure 20.14

The table text converts to single lines of text in the word processor program.

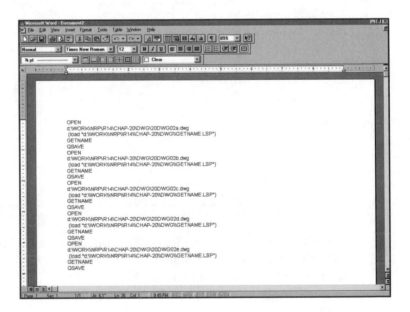

7. Save the file as Text Only. Name the file **MYSCRIPT.SCR**, and save it in the ACADR14\SAMPLE directory. Finally, close Word and Excel, without saving the files.

Next, you will open AutoCAD and run the new script file.

8. Start a new AutoCAD drawing. Before you execute the script file, you must disable two dialog boxes.

9. At the Command: prompt, type **CMDDIA**, and set its value to 0.

10. Next, type **FILEDIA**, and set its value to 0.

NOTE

If dialog boxes to open files or create plots display during a script, they cause the script to halt. This occurs because a script file cannot pass text to a dialog box. Consequently, you must set the FILEDIA and CMDDIA system variables to 0 (off). When you have finished plotting, set them back to 1 (on). You can set the values of FILEDIA and CMDDIA with the script file.

11. Next, type **SCRIPT**.

12. When prompted for a script file name, enter ~ (tilde). The Select Script File dialog box opens.

13. Open the MYSCRIPT.SCR script file you just created. (Be sure to close the file in Word first and remember to save it as Text Only.)

    The script file executes: It opens each drawing in order and runs the AutoLISP routine, which inserts the drawing's name. This script file can be enhanced to plot each drawing automatically. Additionally, if you associate a PC2 or PCP with each drawing before you save the Batch Plot Utility list file, you can use that information as well.

14. After the script file has finished running, remember to reset the CMDDIA and FILEDIA system variables to 1.

The code in the GETNAME AutoLISP routine follows:

```
(defun C:GETNAME (/ DrawingName)
 (setq DrawingName (getvar "DWGNAME"))
 (command "TEXT" "4,4" "0.5" "0" DrawingName)
 (princ)
 (command "RESUME")
)
```

Notice that the last function in the code is the command function. This function executes the RESUME command, which restarts the script file.

So far, this chapter has discussed several ways you can automate the time-consuming tasks associated with plotting in complex situations. Another way you can use your computer to help automate a challenging task is to set up automated plot-file icons. This process is discussed in the following section.

Setting Up Automated Plot-File Icons

In business practice, it is common for someone to ask for check plots of the work you are doing. Creating a plot of a file you are currently working on is easy. But it's a little more difficult when you haven't worked on a project for several weeks, or even months, and then suddenly discover that (in half an hour) you must give the project manager a plot of the five drawings you worked on three months ago.

This situation can be stressful because you must remember where the files were located, open each one, restore the pen settings (of course you created PC2/PCP files, right?), and then send the correct views to the plotter.

You need to set up a way to easily plot your drawing files—ideally, a way that even the project manager can use. Fortunately, Windows 95 and Windows NT provide a simple way to accomplish this task.

The next exercise demonstrates a viable solution. It details the steps involved in creating a folder on your desktop and tells how to create icons in the folder that can launch AutoCAD automatically, open the appropriate drawing, load the correct PC2/PCP file, and plot the drawing.

CREATING JOB FOLDERS WITH PLOT DRAWING ICONS

1. With your mouse pointer over a blank area of your desktop, right-click. A pop-up menu appears (see fig. 20.15).

Figure 20.15

This pop-up menu is used to create a folder on the desktop.

2. Choose New, and then choose Folder. Windows creates a new folder and places it on the desktop.

3. Enter **My Job** as the folder's name. The new My Job folder should be on your desktop (see fig. 20.16).

Figure 20.16

The new My Job folder appears on the desktop.

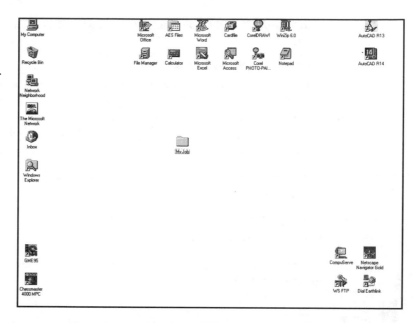

Next, you're going to place copies of the AutoCAD R14 icon in the folder.

NOTE

This next step assumes that you already have the icon on your desktop. If you don't, open Explorer, find the location of the AutoCAD 14 ACAD.EXE file, right-click on it, and drag it over to the desktop.

4. Double-click on the My Job folder to open it.

5. Right-click on the AutoCAD R14 icon, and drag it into the open folder.

6. When prompted, create a shortcut. A copy of the AutoCAD R14 icon should now be in the folder (see fig. 20.17). The icon needs a more descriptive name, so that its task is easily identified.

Figure 20.17

A copy of the AutoCAD R14 icon should appear in the My Job folder.

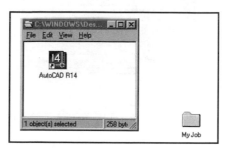

7. With the AutoCAD R14 icon highlighted, press the F2 key. The icon's title can now be edited.

8. Enter **Plot Sheet 1** as the icon's title.

Next, you must modify the properties of the icon. At this point, it is important to understand that you can specify the subdirectory AutoCAD uses as its working directory. And you can assign not only the drawing file that AutoCAD automatically opens, but also a script file that should run automatically when the drawing file is opened.

9. Right-click on the new Plot Sheet 1 icon, and then choose Properties. The Plot Sheet 1 Properties window opens.

10. Select the Shortcut tab.

11. In the Target text box, edit the text to read as follows:

   `D:\ACADR14\acad.exe 20DWG03 /b 20DWG03`

   This command line starts AutoCAD, opens the 20DWG03.DWG drawing file, and then runs the 20DWG03.SCR script file.

NOTE

Make sure that both the drawing file and the script file are in the same directory.

12. In the Start in text box, enter the path on which the 20DWG03.DWG and 20DWG03.SCR files reside. Your Shortcut values should be similar to those in figure 20.18.

Figure 20.18

The new Shortcut values for the Plot Sheet 1 icon.

13. Click on OK to save the changes.

Now, when the icon is double-clicked, it will start AutoCAD automatically, open the 20DWG03.DWG drawing file, and run the 20DWG03.SCR script file.

The script file for this exercise contains the following sequence of commands:

```
;Disable dialog boxes
FILEDIA
0
CMDDIA
0
;Execute PLOT command
PLOT
;Plot Display
D
;Replace configuration from .pc2 file
2
;Enter PC2 file name <D:\WORK\NRP\R14\CHAP-20\DWG\20dwg03>:
20DWG03.PC2
;Accept default for what to plot

;No changes, proceed to Plot
0
;Enable the dialog boxes.
FILEDIA
1
CMDDIA
1
;Quit AutoCAD
QUIT
```

This script file turns off any dialog boxes that might open, plots the drawing by using the 20DWG03.PC2 file, turns on the dialog boxes again, and then quits AutoCAD.

By using this technique, you can create different folders for projects and provide an easy way for anyone to obtain a plot of a particular drawing.

Summary

In this chapter, you learned about configuring a plotter, naming your configuration, choosing the new network configuration, and configuring for raster plots. PCP files and the new PC2 files were discussed, as was the process of setting and saving plotter parameters with these two file formats. You also learned how to quickly edit these files, and you learned a technique for hiding objects with region objects. This chapter introduced the new Batch Plot Utility and discussed how to use it to plot multiple views. Finally, you learned how to use script files for multiple plots and how to set up automated plot-file icons.

By using the techniques discussed in this chapter, you can quickly create plots of your drawing files, automate the process, and maintain a high level of productivity when plotting.

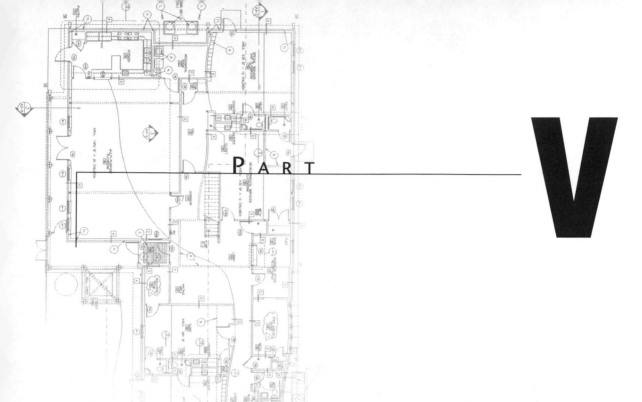

PART V

CUSTOMIZATION AND ADVANCED CONCEPTS

Chapter 21: Introduction to 3D

Chapter 22: Customizing without Programming

Chapter 23: Creating Scripts and Slide Libraries

Chapter 24: Introduction to AutoLISP Programming

Chapter 25: ActiveX Automation

Chapter 26: AutoCAD SQL Environment (ASE)

C H A P T E R

21

INTRODUCTION TO 3D

by Don Spencer

Up to this point in this book, you have been drawing two-dimensional (2D) views of objects that, in their true form, are three-dimensional (3D). This method of designing and drafting is limited because the 2D representations must be interpreted to visualize the 3D object. In addition, 3D objects in a proper form can be used for the following purposes: viewing the model from any vantage point, creating 2D drafting views, visualizing shaded renderings (see fig. 21.1) and photo realistic renderings (images), reading data for FEA, creating animation, checking interference, and extracting manufacturing data. As you can see, using 3D objects can be quite valuable to your palette of AutoCAD. This chapter introduces you to the following topics:

- *X, Y, and Z coordinates in a 3D coordinate system*

- *The user coordinate system (UCS)*

- *The three basic types of 3D modeling: wireframe models, surface models, and solid models*

- *3D views*

- *3D model visualization*

Figure 21.1

A 3D surface model that has been shaded using the Shade command in AutoCAD.

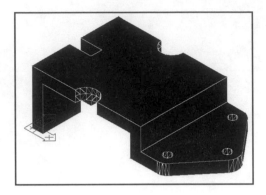

Specifying 3D Coordinates

Understanding how to use the 3D coordinate systems is the key to creating 3D models in AutoCAD. Varied locations must be referenced on a 3D model or in 3D space to effectively use many of AutoCAD's 3D drawing, editing, viewing, and visualization tools.

The Right-Hand Rules

Two right-hand rules govern the 3D coordinate system. These are called "right-hand rules" because, quite simply, you actually use your right hand to determine the information you need to know. The first right-hand rule—Axis Direction—determines the positive axis direction of the Z axis when you know the positive direction of the X and Y axes. The second right-hand rule—Axis Rotation—determines the positive rotation direction about an axis. These rules are explained in the following sections.

Axis Direction

To determine the positive axis direction of the X, Y, and Z axes, place your right hand between yourself and the monitor. The back of your hand should be toward the screen. Point your thumb in the positive direction of the X axis. Next, point your index finger in the positive direction of the Y axis. Last, point your middle finger out of your palm, perpendicular to your thumb and index finger. This last movement indicates the positive direction of the Z axis.

Axis Rotation

To determine the positive rotation direction about an axis, point your right thumb in the positive direction of the axis and curl your fingers into a fist around the axis. Your fingers indicate the positive rotation direction about the axis.

3D Coordinate Input

Specifying 3D Cartesian coordinates (X,Y,Z) is similar to entering 2D coordinates (X,Y). You can enter absolute coordinate values—which are based on the origin— or relative coordinate values—which are based on the last point entered.

For both the World Coordinate System (WCS) and the user coordinate system (UCS), drawing in 3D requires X, Y, and Z values for the coordinate.

Cylindrical Coordinates

Cylindrical coordinate entry is similar to 2D polar coordinate entry, but this entry system includes an additional distance from the polar coordinate perpendicular to the XY plane. With cylindrical coordinate entry, you locate a point by specifying its distance along an angle relative to the UCS X axis and its Z value perpendicular to the XY plane.

For instance, the absolute coordinate 4<30,6 indicates a point four units from the origin of the current UCS, 30 degrees from the X axis in the XY plane, and six units along the Z axis. The relative cylindrical coordinate @2<60,3 indicates a point two units in the XY plane from the last point entered (not from the UCS origin point) at an angle of 60 degrees from the positive X direction. The line extends to a Z coordinate of three.

Spherical Coordinates

Spherical coordinate entry in 3D is also similar to polar coordinate entry in 2D. In this entry system, you locate a point by specifying its distance from the origin of the current UCS, its angle from the X axis (in the XY plane), and its angle from the XY plane. Each value is separated by an open angle bracket (<).

As an example, the coordinate 4<30<60 indicates a point four units from the origin of the current UCS in the XY plane, 30 degrees from the X axis in the XY plane, and 60 degrees up from the XY plane.

XYZ Point Filters

With XYZ point filters, you can extract coordinates from selected points and synthesize a new point using these coordinates. With this method, you can use known points to find an unknown point. On the Command: line use the following format:

```
Command: _line From point: .X
```

AutoCAD Release 14 accepts the following filter selections: .X, .Y, .Z, .XY, .XZ, and .YZ. For example, if you enter .X, you are prompted for the X coordinate and then the Y and Z values.

Defining a User Coordinate System in 3D Space

The User Coordinate System (UCS) provides the means to change the location of the 0,0,0 origin point, as well as the orientation of the XY plane and Z axis. Any plane or point in 3D space can be referenced, saved, and recalled, and you can define as many user coordinate systems as you require.

Usually, it is easier to align the coordinate system with existing geometry than to determine the exact placement of a 3D point. Coordinate input and display are relative to the current UCS, so if multiple viewports are active, they share the same UCS. AutoCAD Release 14 keeps track of the last 10 coordinate systems created in model space and the last 10 in paper space.

Specifying a New UCS

You can define a user coordinate system in one of the following ways:

- Specify a new origin, new XY plane, or new Z axis
- Align the new UCS with an existing object
- Align the new UCS with the current viewing direction
- Rotate the current UCS around any of its axes
- Select a preset UCS provided by AutoCAD

In the following exercise, you will use UCS command options that you might not be using on 2D drawings to define user coordinate systems on 3D objects.

Specifying a New UCS by Using the Z Axis, 3-point, Object, View, and Preset Options

1. Open the 21CAD01.DWG drawing file on the accompanying CD-ROM.

2. Activate the left viewport by picking a point inside its boundaries.

3. Choose View>NAMED VIEWS to initiate the DDVIEW command. Then choose Int and then Restore, to restore the Int view (see fig. 21.2). You have effectively zoomed in to the lower-left corner of the 3D model so that you can better select point locations on the object.

Figure 21.2

The 21CAD01.DWG 3D wireframe drawing opened in AutoCAD.

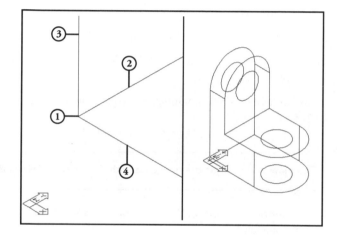

4. Execute the UCS command from the Command: prompt by typing **UCS** and pressing Enter. Then choose the Z axis option.

5. Using the Intersection Object Snap, place the origin point <0,0,0> at the intersection of ①.

6. With the Midpoint Object Snap, choose the midpoint at ② as a point on the positive portion of the Z axis.

7. Launch the UCS command just as you did in step 4 and enter **World** as the default to return to the World Coordinate System.

8. Run the UCS command again just as you did in step 4, and choose the 3-point option.

9. Using the Intersection Object Snap, place the origin point <0,0,0> at the intersection of ①.

10. Using the Midpoint Object Snap, choose the midpoint at ② as a point on the positive portion of the X axis.

11. With the Midpoint Object Snap again, choose the midpoint at ③ as a point on the positive Y portion of the UCS XY plane. You have defined a new User Coordinate System by selecting three points to define a plane.

NOTE

You can define a UCS in 3D space using the 3-point option of the UCS command to specify the new UCS origin and the direction of its positive X and Y axes. The Z axis follows by applying the right-hand rule.

12. Enter the UCS command just as you did in step 4, and enter **World** as the default to return to the World Coordinate System.

13. Enter the UCS command just as you did in step 4, and choose the Object option.

14. Choose the 3D model at ④. The Object option aligns the new UCS with an existing object.

15. Enter the UCS command just as you did in step 4, and choose the View option.

NOTE

The View option aligns the new UCS with the current viewing direction.

16. Restore the Top view by choosing View>NAMED VIEWS to initiate the DDVIEW command.

17. From the Tools pull-down menu, choose UCS, Preset UCS. This enters the DDUCSP command for you.

18. In the UCS Orientation dialog box, choose the Front icon. This is the center picture. Check on the Absolute to WCS dot. Then click on OK.

NOTE

Notice that the UCS icon changes to a box surrounding a broken pencil (see fig. 21.3) when you completed step 18. This new icon appears when the edge of the XY plane of the current UCS is almost perpendicular to your viewing direction or display screen.

Figure 21.3

The UCS icon changes to a broken pencil when the UCS becomes nearly perpendicular to the display screen.

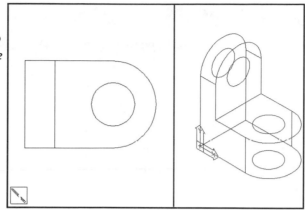

19. Enter **UCSFOLLOW** at the command and set the value to 1 to turn UCSFOLLOW on. Repeat step 17, choosing other Preset UCS settings from the dialog box.

INSIDER TIP

When UCSFOLLOW is turned on, a plan view is generated in the current viewport whenever you change from one UCS to another. UCSFOLLOW can be set separately for each viewport.

You now know how to successfully select a new UCS. The following section explains the use of the UCS icon, which you saw in this exercise.

The UCS Icon

The UCS icon is used to indicate the origin and orientation of the UCS in both 2D and 3D. The UCS icon also can be displayed at the UCS origin point. The same rules applying in 3D as in 2D, with the exception of the broken pencil (refer to fig. 21.3).

After you understand the 3D coordinate system, it is important to know how to create 3D objects in AutoCAD. The following section explains the three major types of 3D modeling and provides exercises on creating 3D objects.

Creating 3D Objects

AutoCAD Release 14 supports three basic types of 3D modeling:

- Wireframe
- Surface
- Solid

Each type has its advantages and disadvantages, depending on the results desired. Each type also uses its own creation and editing techniques, which are explained in this section.

It is not recommended that you mix modeling methods. Each modeling type uses a different method for constructing and editing 3D models, and only limited conversion between model types is available. For example, you cannot convert from wireframes to surfaces or from surfaces to solids.

Wireframe Modeling

A wireframe model is a skeletal description of a 3D object. No surfaces exist in a wireframe model because the model consists only of points, lines, and curves that describe the edges of the object. With AutoCAD 14, you can create wireframe models by positioning 2D (planar) objects anywhere in 3D space. Each object that makes up a wireframe model must be independently drawn and positioned.

In the following exercise, you will create a 3D wireframe by using lines, arcs, and circles. This requires changes to the UCS.

CREATE A 3D WIREFRAME MODEL BY USING LINES, ARCS, AND CIRCLES

1. Open the 21CAD02.DWG drawing file (see fig. 21.4).

Figure 21.4

*The 21CAD02.DWG
drawing contains two
viewports.*

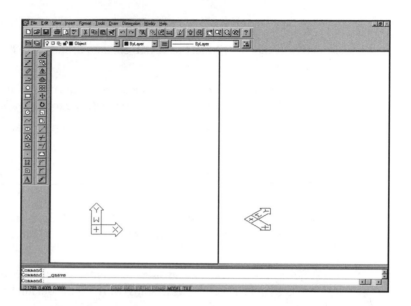

2. Activate the left viewport by picking a point inside its boundaries.

3. Begin the Line command. Draw a line From point: 0,0 To point: 1.5,0 and press Enter to complete the command.

4. Begin the Arc command and press Enter at the <Start point>: prompt. Move the cursor around on the screen and see the following note. Next, at the End point: prompt enter **@0,1.5** for the endpoint of the arc.

Note

Notice that the arc endpoint drag references the current UCS. Arcs, circles, and 2D polylines are drawn parallel to the current XY plane.

5. Begin the Line command, and press Enter past the From point: prompt. Set the length for the line at 1.5, and continue the line To point: 0,0.

6. Choose the Circle command. Using the Center Object Snap, pick the center of the arc as its center point. Enter a radius of **.375** at the default Radius: prompt.

7. From the Copy command, select all the objects. Press Enter and give a Base point or displacement of **0,0**. Press Enter and give a Second point of displacement of **0,0,1**. Press Enter to complete the command.

8. Enter **UCSFOLLOW** at the Command: prompt to make sure UCSFOLLOW is set to 1.

9. From Named UCS, enter the DDUCS command, and make the Back UCS current (see fig. 21.5).

10. With the Zoom command, enter **.5x** to display the objects at one half of the current zoom factor. Next, pan the objects toward the bottom of the screen.

11. Begin the Line command and enter From point: **1.5,0** To point: **1.5,2**. Press Enter to complete the command.

12. Begin the Arc command and press Enter at the <Start point>: prompt.

13 At the prompt End point: enter **@–1.5,0** as the endpoint of the arc.

14. Begin the Line command, and press Enter at the From point: prompt. At the Length of line: prompt, set the line length at **2** to complete the outline of the back of the wireframe.

15. Choose the Circle command, using the Center Object Snap, and pick the center of the arc as its center point. Enter a radius of **.375** at the default Radius: prompt.

Figure 21.5

The UCS in the 21CAD02.DWG drawing references the back plane.

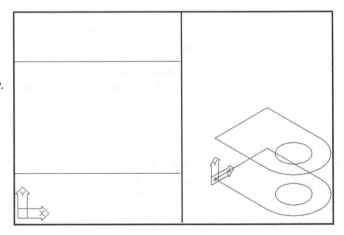

16. From the Copy command, select the objects that you created in steps 11 through 15. Press Enter and give a Base point a displacement of **0,0**. Press Enter and give a Second point of displacement a **0,0,.5**. Press Enter to complete the command.

17. From the Standard toolbar, choose Preset UCS, set to Absolute to WCS, choose the Front icon, and then click on OK.

18. With the Zoom command, enter **.5x** to display the objects at one-half of the current zoom factor.

19. You can now Fillet or Trim, and add additional lines to match figure 21.6. The right viewport also can be used to draw lines, arcs, and circles to represent all the planar edges of the 3D model.

Figure 21.6

The finished 21CAD02.DWG drawing should appear similar to this after you have completed the clean up from step 19.

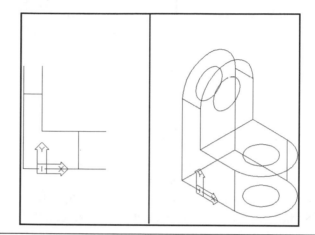

3D Wireframe Objects

AutoCAD also has 3D polylines and splines that can be used to create 3D wireframe objects. These can be drawn continuously over X,Y,Z coordinates.

Surface Modeling

Surface modeling is the most complex—and therefore the hardest to master—of the three modeling types in AutoCAD. AutoCAD's surfaces define not only the edges of a 3D object but also its surfaces.

Surface models are used when the level of detail about physical properties (such as mass, weight, and center of gravity) that solids provide are not needed but you still need the hiding, shading, and rendering capabilities that wireframes can't provide.

AutoCAD's surface modeler uses a polygonal mesh to define the faceted surfaces. The faces of the mesh are planar and can only approximate curved surfaces. Figure 21.7 illustrates how the curved surfaces of the surface model are represented with planar and faceted polygonal meshes.

Figure 21.7

A surface model with faceted surfaces and the boundaries used to define the surface.

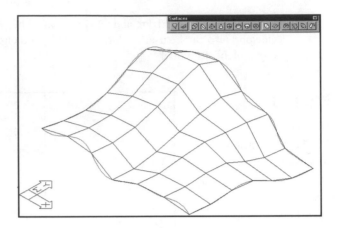

The density of the surface mesh, or number of facets, is defined in terms of a matrix of M and N vertices. These are similar to a grid consisting of columns and rows. M specifies the column position, and N specifies the row position of any given vertex. Surface meshes can be created in both 2D and 3D.

NOTE

Faceted meshes are useful if you want to visualize a 3D model, especially geometry with unusual mesh patterns, such as a 3D topographical model. For true curved surfaces, you need an add-on AutoCAD product called AutoSurf. With AutoSurf, you can create true curved surfaces, and these surfaces can be used to manufacture the model.

Open and Closed Meshes

A mesh can be open or closed. A mesh is open in a given direction if the start and end edges of the mesh do not touch. AutoCAD provides several methods for creating both types of meshes.

Predefined 3D Surface Mesh

Some methods of creating surfaces in AutoCAD can be difficult to use when entering the mesh parameters manually. AutoCAD's 3D command is used to create basic surface shapes. The 3D command is accessed by entering 3D at the Command: prompt. You can also choose the basic surface shapes from the Surfaces toolbar and from the Draw pull-down menu under Surfaces, 3D Surfaces. The 3D command simplifies the process of creating the following 3D shapes: box, cone, dish, dome, mesh, pyramid, sphere, torus, and wedge (see fig. 21.8). These meshes are displayed as wireframes until you use the HIDE, SHADE, or RENDER commands.

Figure 21.8

Basic surface shapes are displayed as wireframes.

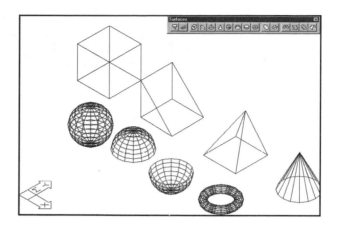

Additional Surfacing Commands

AutoCAD also provides the following surface creation commands: 3DFACE, 3DMESH, PFACE, EDGE, RULESURF, TABSURF, REVSURF, and EDGESURF. A thorough description of these commands is beyond the scope of this introductory chapter. For the following exercise, however, you should know that RULESURF is used to create a surface that is ruled or blended between two selected objects. EDGESURF uses a closed area defined by four edges to blend a surface over the closed area.

In the following exercise, you will use EDGESURF and RULESURF to create irregularly shaped surfaces. You also will control the density of the grid used to define the surfaces.

Using EDGESURF and RULESURF to Create Irregularly Shaped Surfaces

1. Open the 21CAD03.DWG drawing file.

2. From the Standard toolbar, choose NAMED VIEWS, to enter the DDVIEW command. Restore the Edge view.

3. Activate the Surfaces toolbar by choosing, View, Toolbars and checking Surfaces. click on OK.

4. From the Surfaces toolbar, choose the EDGESURF command and pick ①, ②, ③, and ④ (see fig. 21.9).

   You now have defined the four edges of an open surface.

Figure 21.9

These objects are ready to have EDGESURF and RULESURF surfaces defined.

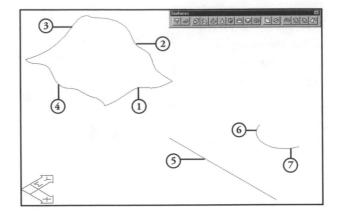

5. From the Erase command, enter an **L** to erase the last object drawn. This removes the surface mesh.

6. Enter **SURFTAB1** at the Command: prompt, and change the value to **12**.

7. Enter **SURFTAB2** at the Command: prompt, and change the value to **18**.

8. Repeat step 4 and refer to the following note.

NOTE

The SURFTAB setting variables are used to control the density of the M and N grid that defines the surface created.

9. Repeat step 2 to restore the Rule view.

10. From the Surfaces toolbar, choose the RULESURF command, and pick ⑤ and ⑥.

The surface now is ruled between the two entities selected. Notice that the SURFTAB1 setting is used for REVSURF (see fig. 21.10).

WARNING

Choosing ⑦ in step 10 usually produces an undesirable result for the Ruled surface. The surface will be crossed over or twisted. To get the desired results as in figure 21.10, the selection points on the objects should be toward the same end. You can verify this by erasing the last object created in step 10 and redoing step 10. This time, choose ⑦ instead of ⑥.

Figure 21.10

The completed edge and ruled surfaces created with EDGESURF and RULESURF.

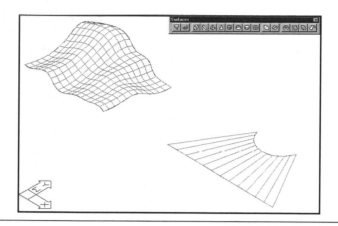

Using Thickness to Simulate Meshes

Thickness is one method of simulating meshes in AutoCAD. The thickness of an object is the distance by which that object is extruded above or below its elevation (see fig. 21.11). Positive thickness extrudes upward (positive Z), and negative thickness extrudes downward (negative Z). A zero thickness means that the object has no extrusion value.

Thickness can be set with the THICKNESS or ELEV commands. The current thickness of objects being drawn remains in effect until the value is changed. AutoCAD applies the extrusion uniformly on an object.

NOTE

A single object cannot have a different thickness for its various points.

Several objects in AutoCAD ignore the current thickness and cannot be extruded. These include 3D faces, 3D polylines, 3D polygon meshes, dimensions, and viewports.

Text objects created with TEXT, DTEXT, and DDATTDEF or ATTDEF also ignore the current thickness. However, you can assign a nonzero thickness to these and other existing objects by using the DDMODIFY, DDCHPROP, CHPROP, or CHANGE commands.

Figure 21.11

After thickness is applied to the objects, the HIDE command is used to show that the object is not a solid.

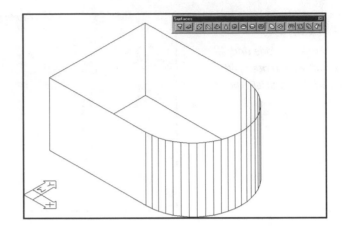

Solid Modeling

Solid modeling with AutoCAD Release 14's ACIS solid modeler is easier and faster than wireframe and surface modeling in AutoCAD. Solid models provide the same display information as wireframe and surface models, and solids also represent the entire volume of an object. You can analyze solids for their mass properties (volume, moments of inertia, and center of gravity), and the data from a solid object can be exported to applications such as CNC or FEA.

The following four types of 3D solid models can be created in AutoCAD:

- Primitive solids
- Composite solids
- Extruded solids
- Revolved solids

Primitive Solids

AutoCAD provides a basic set of solid objects called primitives that includes the following shapes: box, cone, cylinder, sphere, wedge, and torus (see fig. 21.12).

These shapes can be left as they are or can be combined with other solid types to create more complex solids called composite solids.

Figure 21.12

AutoCAD's primitive solids include these shapes.

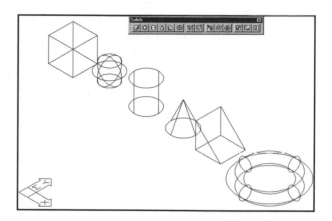

Composite Solids

After you create any solid type, you can create more complex shapes by combining solids. You can join solids, subtract solids from each other, or find the common volume (overlapping portion) of solids with the following Boolean operation commands:

- UNION

- SUBTRACTion

- INTERSECTion

In the following exercise, you will create box and cylinder primitives and apply Boolean operations to these solids to create a composite solid.

CREATING A COMPOSITE SOLID USING BOX, CYLINDER, UNION, AND SUBTRACT

1. Open the 21CAD04.DWG drawing file.

2. Activate the left viewport by choosing a point within its boundaries.

3. Activate the Solids toolbar by choosing, View, Toolbars. Then check Solids from the Toolbars list box and click on OK.

4. Choose the BOX command from the Solids toolbar. Enter **0,0,0** at the Corner of box: prompt. Then enter **1.5,1.5,1** at the prompt for the other corner. You have defined the front lower-left and the back upper-right corners of a 3D solid box.

5. Using the CYLINDER command from the Solids toolbar. Create a cylinder with a center point at 1.5,.75, a radius of .75, and a height of 1.

6. Repeat step 3 to activate the Modify II toolbar.

7. With the UNION command from the Modify II toolbar, choose the box and the cylinder by picking on an edge of each object. Then press Enter to complete the command.

NOTE

With the UNION command, you can combine the total volume of two or more solids into a composite object (see fig. 21.13).

Figure 21.13

The box and cylinder are unioned into one composite solid.

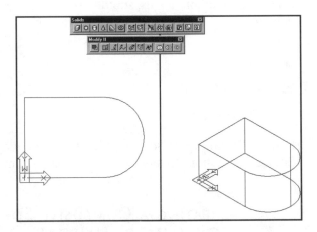

8. From the Solids toolbar, choose Cylinder to create another cylinder with a center point of 1.5,.75 a radius of .375, and a height of 1.

9. Enter the SUBTRACT command from the Modify II toolbar and choose the composite solid created after step 7 by picking on one of its edges. This is the solid to subtract from. Press Enter, then type **L**. to select the cylinder created in step 8 as the solid to subtract. Now press Enter twice.

NOTE

The SUBTRACT command removes the common area of one set of solids from another. Remember that you first choose the solid that you want to keep, then the solid you want to subtract.

INSIDER TIP

You can quickly verify that the .375 radius cylinder created in step 8, was subtracted from the composite model by activating the right viewport and entering the HIDE command (see fig. 21.14).

Figure 21.14

The cylinder is subtracted from the composite solid, and the right viewport is hidden to verify subtraction.

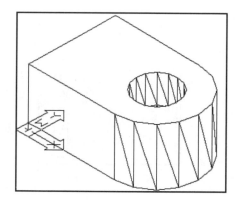

10. Activate the left viewport by choosing a point within its boundaries.

11. From the Standard toolbar, choose Named Views, and restore the Back view.

12. With the UCS command, use the View option to make the current UCS align with the view.

13. With the Zoom command, enter **.5x** to display the objects at one half of the current zoom factor. Next, pan toward the bottom of the view.

14. Enter the BOX command from the Solids toolbar. Enter **0,1,0** as the first corner and **@1.5,1,.5** as the other corner. Notice where the box was drawn in the right viewport. It was drawn on top of the existing composite solid because the Y value for the first corner is 1.

15. From the Solids toolbar, choose the CYLINDER command. Enter a center point of **.75,2**, a radius of **.75**, and a height of **.5**.

16. From the Modify II toolbar, choose UNION. Union the box, cylinder, and composite solids into a single composite solid.

17. Create another cylinder by choosing the CYLINDER command from the Solids toolbar. Give a center point of **.75,2**, a radius of **.375**, and a height of **.5**.

18. From the Modify II toolbar, choose SUBTRACT and select the composite solid as the solid to subtract from. Press Enter and choose the cylinder created in step 17 as the solid to subtract from the composite solid.

You have now created a composite solid (see fig. 21.15) of the same model as the wireframe exercise, shown earlier in the chapter (refer to fig. 21.6).

Figure 21.15

The completed composite solid model appears with the hidden lines removed.

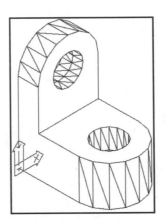

INSIDER TIP

For the preceding exercise, the primitive solids should ideally be created before performing any Boolean operations. Then the two boxes and two .75 radius circles could be unioned in a single operation. The two .375 radius cylinders could then be subtracted from the composite solid, resulting in the same product, but with fewer operations.

Some solid models are more easily defined by finding their shared or common volume. In the following exercise, you will create a composite solid model from two extruded solids using the INTERSECT command.

CREATING A COMPOSITE SOLID WITH THE INTERSECT COMMAND

1. Open the 21CAD05.DWG drawing file (see fig. 21.16).

Figure 21.16

The 21CAD05.DWG drawing contains two extruded solids.

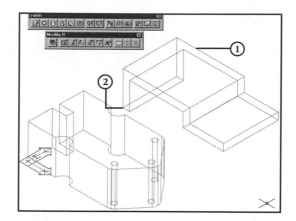

2. Enter the MOVE command, pick ①, and press Enter. Next, pick the intersection ② as the base and 0,0 as the second point.

3. From the Modify II toolbar, choose the INTERSECT command, select both solid models, and press Enter (see fig. 21.17).

Figure 21.17

The completed composite solid model appears like this one.

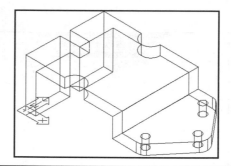

With INTERSECT, you can create a composite solid from the common volume or shared area of two or more overlapping solids. INTERSECT removes the non-overlapping portions and creates a composite solid from the common volume (refer to fig. 21.17).

INSIDER TIP

The INTERFERE command performs the same operation as INTERSECT, but it keeps the original two objects.

Extruded Solids

The EXTRUDE command is used to create solids by extruding (adding thickness to) selected objects. You can extrude closed objects, such as polylines, polygons, rectangles, circles, ellipses, closed splines, donuts, and regions.

In the following exercise, you will extrude a solid from a common profile of an object. Several steps can be eliminated over the use of primitives to create the same complex solid model.

EXTRUDING A SOLID FROM A COMMON PROFILE OF AN OBJECT USING THE EXTRUDE COMMAND

1. Open the 21CAD06.DWG drawing file.

2. Activate the left viewport by selecting a point within its boundaries.

3. Begin the PLINE command from 0,0 to 2.25,0 to 2.25,1 to .5,1 to .5,2.75 to 0,2.75 and close (see fig. 21.18).

Figure 21.18

This closed pline profile will be extruded.

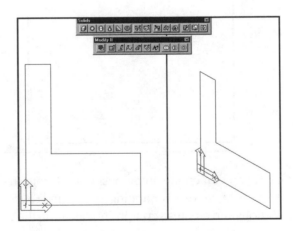

4. Enter the EXTRUDE command from the Solids toolbar and choose the closed pline. Press Enter to continue, and give a Height of Extrusion of 1.5. Then press Enter through the defaults to finish the command (see fig. 21.19).

Figure 21.19

The extruded profile.

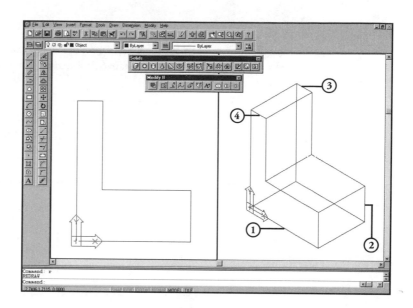

NOTE

> You now have created a solid from the closed pline loop. This solid can be edited to produce the results seen in figure 21.20.

5. Enter the FILLET command and pick ① (refer to fig. 21.19). At the Enter radius: prompt, give a radius of **.75**, and pick ②, ③, and ④. Then press Enter.

NOTE

> This same FILLET command can be used with 2D objects. You will notice however, that you do not have to set a radius before selecting the first edge to be filleted. Additionally, you can select the actual edges to filleted, not the intersecting edges.

6. Complete the model as seen in figure 21.20 by placing the .375 radius solid cylinders concentric with the filleted radii. You can use a Center Object Snap to snap the cylinder's center point to the center of the filleted radii. Refer to the following note.

7. Then SUBTRACT the cylinders from the extruded and filleted complex solid.

NOTE

Remember that circles, arcs, and cylinders are drawn parallel to the XY plane. Cylinders then are given a height in the positive or negative Z direction. You must rotate the UCS to get the desired results.

Figure 21.20

The complete complex 3D solid model appears like this.

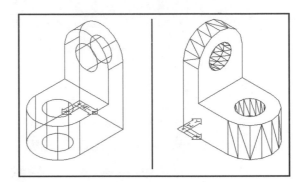

Tapered Extrusions

Tapering the extrusion is useful in specifying an angle along the sides of the extrusion. For example, you could apply this process to create a draft angle needed for a part mold.

WARNING

Avoid using extremely large tapered angles. If the angle is too large, the profile can taper to a point before it reaches the specified height. In some cases, AutoCAD will not complete the command.

Extruding Along a Path

You also can extrude an object along a path (see fig. 21.21). Lines, circles, arcs, ellipses, elliptical arcs, polylines, or splines can be paths. The path should not lie on the same plane as the profile, nor should it have areas of high curvature. If the path contains segments that are not tangent, AutoCAD extrudes the object along each segment and then miters the joint along the plane bisecting the angle formed by the segments.

Figure 21.21

A closed profile and path appear like this with completed extrusion.

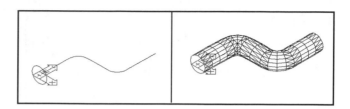

WARNING

You cannot extrude 3D objects or objects contained within a block. Likewise, you cannot extrude polylines that have crossing or intersecting segments or that are not closed.

INSIDER TIP

After the extrusion, AutoCAD deletes or retains the original 2D profile object, depending on the setting of the DELOBJ system variable. Usually you would want the original 2D object to be deleted. The DELOBJ setting should be 1 to delete objects. However, by retaining the profile, you can use it to make mating or slightly modified solid components.

Revolved Solids

REVOLVE is used to create a solid by revolving a closed object about the X or Y axis of the current UCS at a specified angle. Objects also can be revolved about a line, a polyline, or two specified points.

In the following exercise, you will create a revolved solid model from a section profile and subtract holes from the revolved solid model.

CREATING A REVOLVED SOLID MODEL AND SUBTRACTING CYLINDERS

1. Open the 21CAD07.DWG drawing file (see fig. 21.22).

Figure 21.22

A profile to revolve around an axis.

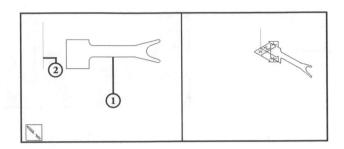

2. Activate the left viewport by selecting a point within its boundaries.

3. Enter the REVOLVE command from the Solids toolbar. Pick the closed polyline ① and press Enter. Then choose the Object option and pick ②. Finally, enter full circle to complete the command.

4. From the pull-down menu, choose the View>3D Viewpoint>Plan View> Current UCS to bring the left viewport into PLAN view relative to the current UCS (see fig. 21.23).

5. With the Zoom command, enter **.8x** to display the objects at 80% of the current zoom factor.

Figure 21.23

The left viewport in PLAN view relative to the current UCS.

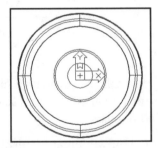

6. From the Solids toolbar, choose the Cylinder command to create a cylinder with a center point of 3,0, a radius of .75, and a height of 1.5.

7. Using the Array command, array the cylinder around the center of the revolved solid at 0,0 for a total of six cylinders.

8. From the Modify II toolbar, select the revolved solid as the solid from which to subtract. Press Enter and choose the cylinders created in step 7 as the solids to subtract from the revolved solid (see fig. 21.24).

Figure 21.24

The completed REVOLVED 3D solid model with cylinder holes removed.

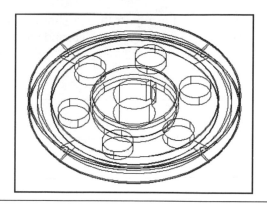

The same rules for closed loops apply to the EXTRUDE and REVOLVE commands. You can use REVOLVE on closed objects, such as polylines, polygons, rectangles, circles, ellipses, and regions. Revolving donuts will give you a solid (not hollow) tube. You cannot revolve 3D objects, objects in blocks, and objects that intersect themselves.

Modifying Solids

As you saw in a previous exercise, solids can be further modified by filleting and chamfering their edges. Some commands on the Solids toolbar also enable you to slice a solid into two pieces or to obtain the 2D cross section of a solid.

Displaying Solids

The ISOLINES system variable controls the number of tessellation lines used to visualize curved portions of the wireframe (see fig. 21.25). The default value is 4, and valid integer values range from 0 to 2047.

Figure 21.25

The completed revolved 3D solid model contains ISOLINES set to 25.

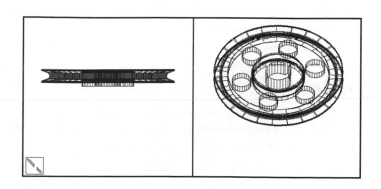

The FACETRES system variable adjusts the smoothness of shaded and hidden-line objects (see fig. 21.26). The default value is 0.5, and valid values range from 0.01 to 10.0.

WARNING

Take care when changing the ISOLINES and FACETRES system variables. Each variable can greatly increase file size and region, hide, shade, and rendering times.

Figure 21.26

The hidden revolved 3D solid model with FACETRES set to 2.

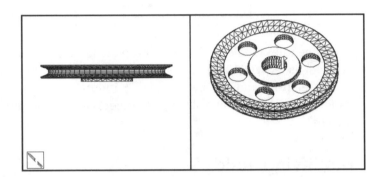

Viewing in 3D

An AutoCAD drawing can be viewed from any 3D location in model space. Objects may be added, edited, and selected in any view. From a selected 3D viewpoint, hidden, shaded, and rendered objects can be better visualized to see height, width, and depth. Parallel projection or perspective view also can be defined.

WARNING

You cannot use the VPOINT, DVIEW, or PLAN commands to change the paper space view. The view in paper space always remains a plan view.

INSIDER **T**IP

You can set up your paper space viewports with any standard and 3D model space view. This a good way of setting up orthographic, auxiliary, and isometric views into a single drawing using one 3D solid model (see fig. 21.27).

Figure 21.27

Multiple views in paper space produce these views of a single 3D solid.

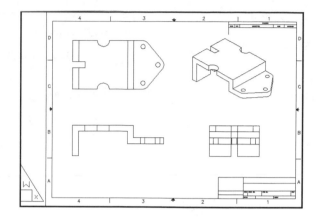

Viewing Direction

Several commands enable you to set a viewing angle for an AutoCAD 3D model. You can set the viewing direction using the following commands:

- DDVPOINT—Displays the Viewpoints Presets dialog box.

- VPOINT—Enables command-line input of viewpoint or rotation of view.

- PLAN—Displays the plan view of a user or world coordinate system.

- DVIEW—Defines parallel projection or perspective views.

In the following exercise, you will set up different views in model space viewports.

DEFINING DIFFERENT MODEL SPACE VIEWS USING DDVPOINT, VPOINT, PLAN, AND DVIEW

1. Open the 21CAD08.DWG drawing file.

 NOTE

You are now looking at a 3D solid model in the WCS, plan, or top view.

2. Enter the DDVPOINT command by choosing View from the pull-down menu and then choosing 3D Viewpoint, Select. The DDVPOINT command activates the Viewpoint Presets dialog box (see fig. 21.28).

Figure 21.28

The Viewpoint Presets dialog box is activated by executing the DDVPOINT command.

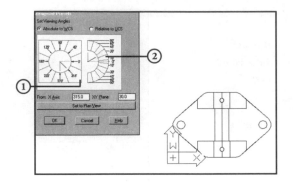

3. Choose ① and then ②.

NOTE

Notice that the value changes as the locations on the dialog box are selected. Viewing angles relative to the X axis and the XY plane are selected by clicking your pointing device inside the image tiles. These values also can be entered directly.

4. Click on to exit the Viewpoint Presets dialog box and to see the resulting view (see fig. 21.29).

Figure 21.29

The DDVPOINT command produces this 3D viewpoint.

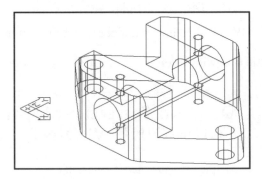

5. Enter the PLAN command by choosing View from the pull-down menu and then choosing 3D Viewpoint, Plan View, and World UCS.

NOTE

Step 5 returns you to the plan view relative to the WCS, which is also the current UCS.

6. Enter the VPOINT command by choosing View from the pull-down menu and then choosing 3D Viewpoint, Rotate.

NOTE

Notice that there is a drag from the crosshair. This enables you to pick an angle from the screen.

7. Enter **135** and then **–30** for the angle from the plane.

NOTE

You are now viewing the 3D model in the opposite direction the model was viewed in step 4. You can use the HIDE command to verify that the –30 is viewing the model from below (see fig. 21.30).

Figure 21.30

The 3D model viewed from below with hidden lines removed.

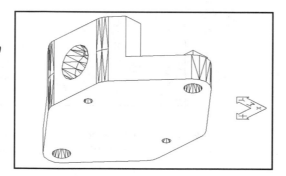

8. From the pull-down menu, choose the View, 3D Viewpoint, Plan View, World UCS to bring the drawing into PLAN view relative to the WCS.

9. Enter the DVIEW command by choosing View from the pull-down menu and then choosing 3D Dynamic View. Then choose the object and press Enter.

10. Enter the Camera option and slowly move the crosshair around the screen.

NOTE

Notice that the object is highlighted as you move around the screen. If you picked a point on-screen at this time, the object would be viewed at the location of the highlighted image.

11. At the Toggle angle in/Enter angle from XY plane prompt, give a value of **35.3** and then press Enter. Now give a value of **–45** at the Toggle angle from/Enter angle in XY plane from X axis prompt, and press Enter again.

12. Continue in the DVIEW command. Choose the zoom option and set a zoom value of 50mm or as needed (see fig. 21.31).

NOTE

You have now defined a view that looks much like the one created in step 4. However, you are still using the DVIEW command to continue using its associated.

Figure 21.31

The 3D view created from the DVIEW command.

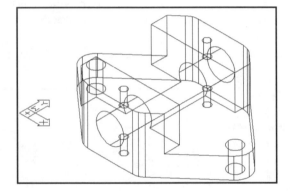

13. Continue in the DVIEW command and enter the Distance option from the DVIEW command. Set a new target distance of 12, and press Enter twice to exit the command.

14. Save this drawing under a new name called VISUAL.DWG. You will be using this view to do the following visualization exercises.

The Distance option in the DVIEW command puts the view into perspective mode. Notice the change in the UCS icon (see fig. 21.32).

Figure 21.32

The perspective view created from the DVIEW command.

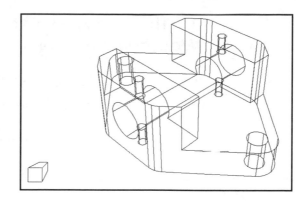

Visualizing 3D Models

One of the main reasons to create 3D surface and solid models, is to better visualize them during the design process and as a completed model. Three commands enable this type of viewing of surfaces and solids:

- HIDE
- SHADE
- RENDER

These commands do involve some limits in their use. For example, you cannot edit hidden-line, shaded, or rendered views.

HIDE

Complex drawings often appear too cluttered to convey useful information. Other times, it might be hard to see the results of a command process on the object. Hiding the background portions of an objects that in reality would be obscured in the current view simplifies the display and clarifies the design.

In the following exercise, you will perform the HIDE command on the VISUAL.DWG drawing.

USING THE HIDE COMMAND TO BETTER VISUALIZE WHAT WOULD BE SEEN ON A TRUE 3D MODEL

1. Use the current drawing VISUAL.DWG, or open the 21CAD09.DWG file.

2. Enter the HIDE command so the view looks like the one shown in figure 21.33.

Figure 21.33

The VISUAL.DWG drawing with hidden lines removed.

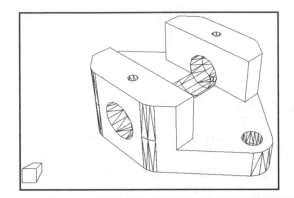

INSIDER TIP

Calculating and obscuring hidden lines can be time-consuming. You can zoom into a part of the drawing to exclude objects or portions of an object from the hide process. You also can hide selected objects in the drawing by using the DVIEW commands Hide option.

SHADE

Flat shading can produce a more realistic image of the model than hidden-line removal. In the shading process, AutoCAD performs a hide before creating a flat, shaded image of the drawing in the current viewport. AutoCAD provides a default light that comes from a single light source located directly behind you (an over-the-shoulder light). Two factors are used to compute the shade (brightness) of each surface:

■   The angle of the surface to the current view

■   The setting of the SHADEDIF system variable

INSIDER TIP

The steeper the angle of the surface to your viewpoint, the darker the surface is shaded. The distance from your viewpoint has no effect on shading.

The higher the value of the SHADEDIF system variable, the greater the contrast in your image. The default for SHADEDIF is 70, but you can specify a value between 1 and 100.

In the following exercise, you will perform four different shading operations.

CREATING A SHADED IMAGE FROM A SOLID MODEL

1. Use the current drawing VISUAL.DWG, or open the 21CAD09.DWG drawing file.

2. From the View pull-down menu, choose Shade and then 256 Color.

3. From the View pull-down menu, choose Shade and then 256 Color Edge Highlight (see fig. 21.34).

Figure 21.34

The VISUAL.DWG drawing can be shaded using the 256 Color Edge Highlight option.

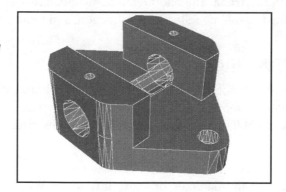

4. From the View pull-down menu, choose Shade and then 16 Color Hidden Line.

5. From the View pull-down menu, choose Shade and then 16 Color Filled.

INSIDER TIP

The SHADEDGE system variable is used to control the different shading methods used in the preceding exercise. By setting this variable to your preferred shading method, you can obtain the desired shading when you enter the SHADE command at the Command: prompt.

Use smaller viewports to speed up the shading process. The smaller the area of screen, the faster the shading process.

NOTE

With the SHADE command, you cannot produce highlights, move the light, or add more lights.

RENDER

Rendering in AutoCAD adds depth and realism to the surface or solid model that a simple hidden-line or shaded image cannot. Rendering is accomplished by means of rendering algorithms, which are mathematical means of relating light, color, and shape. AutoCAD provides the following three types of rendering:

- **Render.** The basic AutoCAD rendering option for best performance.

- **Photo Real.** The photorealistic scanline renderer, which can display bitmapped and transparent materials and generate volumetric and mapped shadows.

- **Photo Raytrace.** The photorealistic raytraced renderer, which uses ray tracing to generate reflections, refraction, and more precise shadows.

Rendered Image

The renderer in AutoCAD 14 is capable of creating photorealistic renderings with the proper material representations, lighting, shadow casting, and backgrounds applied. This capability was added from a Photo Realistic Rendering AutoCAD add-on product for Release 13 called AutoVision.

For your introduction to rendering, you can render your model without adding any lights, applying any materials, or setting up a scene. When you render a new model, the AutoCAD renderer automatically uses a virtual over-the-shoulder distant light much the same as shading uses. As with shading, you cannot move or adjust this light.

In the following exercise, you will use the RENDER command to create three types of renderings. You also will render a file, creating a raster image that can be opened in a paint program to be modified and printed.

CREATING RENDER IMAGES FROM A SOLID MODEL

1. Use the current drawing VISUAL.DWG, or open the 21CAD09.DWG drawing file.

2. From the View pull-down menu, choose Render, Render. This opens the Render dialog box (see fig. 21.35).

Figure 21.35

The Render dialog box.

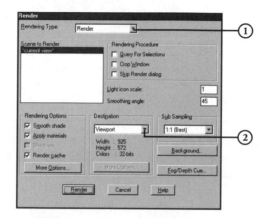

3. Select Render Scene to render the current scene.

4. Re-enter the Render dialog box.

5. Select ① to choose the Photo Real rendering type.

6. Select Render to render the current scene.

7. Re-enter the Render dialog box.

8. Select ① to choose the Photo Raytrace rendering type.

9. Select Render to render the current scene.

Even though no materials and additional lights have been applied, you should notice a difference in the rendering time and the quality of the image. The Photo Raytrace option in the Render dialog box produces the highest-quality image of the three rendering type options. Therefore it takes more time to produce.

10. Re-enter the Render dialog box.

11. Pick ② (refer to fig. 21.35), and then choose File to change the Rendering Destination.

12. Under the Destination portion of the Render dialog box, click on the More Options button to activate the File Output Configuration dialog box (see fig. 21.36).

Figure 21.36

*The File Output
Configuration dialog box.*

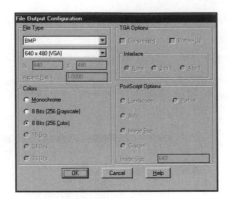

NOTE

The default settings are for a BMP file type at 640×480 resolution and an 8-bit, 256-color depth. You can change the file type, resolution, and color depth in this dialog box.

WARNING

Higher resolution and/or greater color depth results in larger file sizes and longer rendering times.

13. Click on OK to close the File Output Configuration dialog box.

14. Select Render to render the current scene to a file.

15. Assign the name Visual to the render file in the Render File dialog box, and choose Save.

You now have a raster image file that can be viewed, edited, and printed from your favorite paint program that supports the file type chosen.

INSIDER TIP

You can stop the rendering by pressing the Esc key to cancel the command.

The AutoCAD renderer is automatically loaded into memory when you first choose the RENDER command or a render option. To free memory, you can unload the renderer by entering **RENDERUNLOAD** at the command line.

Summary

In this chapter, you learned to how to define X,Y,Z coordinates in a 3D coordinate system. By defining a user coordinate system, you were able to create the three basic types of 3D modeling: wireframe models, surface models, and solid models.

Most exercises emphasized the solid model because this is the easiest and most useful of the three basic types of modeling. You also had the opportunity to try several approaches to modeling with solids.

In addition, you discovered that 3D views are necessary to visualize the design process leading to the project's completion. Without 3D views, it would be nearly impossible to ensure the integrity and accuracy of the 3D model.

Finally, this chapter explored 3D model visualization. By hiding, shading, and rendering your 3D solid or surface models, you were able to visualize your designs like never before.

22

CUSTOMIZING WITHOUT PROGRAMMING

by Michael Todd Peterson

One of AutoCAD's greatest assets is the degree to which this program can be personalized. AutoCAD can be customized by users with little or no programming knowledge, so it's a great tool for users of all skill levels.

Customizing AutoCAD to suit your needs is the best way to increase your productivity. If you can make AutoCAD work in a manner that facilitates your needs, you obviously will be more productive. In fact, AutoCAD is so easy to customize that, in a matter of hours, you can tailor this program to match your working environment.

This chapter focuses on how you can customize accessing commands. The chapter does not, however, discuss the process of adding new commands to AutoCAD. (Adding new commands is covered in Chapter 24, "Introduction to AutoLISP Programming.") In particular, this chapter covers the following topics:

- Creating keyboard shortcuts
- Customizing toolbars
- Customizing menus

Creating Keyboard Shortcuts

The most basic type of AutoCAD customization involves creating keyboard short-cuts, which are one- or two-key combinations that access an AutoCAD command. Keyboard shortcuts offer a powerful way to increase your productivity. For example, when you work with AutoCAD, one of your hands is almost always on the mouse or tablet puck. This leaves the other hand free for typing, so keyboard shortcuts can make accessing commands with your free hand very easy.

In AutoCAD, you can create a keyboard shortcut for any single-step command that can be accessed through the Command: prompt. For instance, you can create a keyboard shortcut for ZOOM, but you cannot create a shortcut for ZOOM WINDOW. This is because ZOOM WINDOW is initiated by accessing two separate commands. The only way you could create this type of keyboard shortcut would be to write a LISP (covered in Chapter 24, "Introduction to AutoLISP Programming") routine or to create a shortcut button on a toolbar.

In AutoCAD, all the keyboard shortcuts are contained in a text file, named the ACAD.PGP file. This file usually is located in the Support directory of your AutoCAD installation, regardless of whether you run the DOS or Windows version of AutoCAD. AutoCAD comes with a predefined ACAD.PGP that has some basic keyboard shortcuts that you may modify to suit your needs.

The process for creating a keyboard shortcut is very simple: modify the ACAD.PGP file and then reload it into AutoCAD. This process is explained in detail in the section that follows.

Modifying the ACAD.PGP File

In this section, you will learn how to modify the ACAD.PGP file to create your own keyboard shortcuts. The ACAD.PGP file should be located in your C:\ACADR14\ Support directory. To add your own custom keyboard shortcuts, you must modify the ACAD.PGP file. To modify the ACAD.PGP file, use any standard text editor, such as Notepad. After you load the file into the editor, you can begin to create your own keyboard shortcuts.

WARNING

As usual, before you make any changes to the ACAD.PGP file, make a backup copy of the original, in case something goes wrong.

Scroll down the ACAD.PGP file until you see the section starting with ";Command alias format:". The term *alias* is another name for a keyboard shortcut. To create an alias, type the shortcut or alias (the shortened command you will use instead of the full command), followed by the command that you want to use in the shortcut. The following code details part of the alias section of the ACAD.PGP.

```
;   Sample aliases for AutoCAD Commands
;   These examples include most frequently used commands. 3F,
   *3DFACE
   A,          *ARC
   AL,         *ALIGN
   AR,         *ARRAY
   AAD,        *ASEADMIN
   AEX,        *ASEEXPORT
   ALI,        *ASELINKS
   ASQ,        *ASESQLED
   ARO,        *ASEROWS
   ASE,        *ASESELECT
   AT,         *DDATTDEF
   ATE,        *DDATTE
   B,          *BMAKE
   BO,         *BOUNDARY
   BR,         *BREAK
   C,          *CIRCLE
   CH,         *DDCHPROP
   -CH,        *CHANGE
```

Notice that letter or symbol combinations act as shortcuts for their ensuing command. "A," for example, is the shortcut for the ARC command. Note also that each shortcut includes syntax containing a comma and an asterisk. You must include both of these characters in all alias commands.

If you scroll through the ACAD.PGP file, you can see all the predefined aliases or shortcuts that come with a standard AutoCAD installation. You can change any of these aliases to suit your needs or personal preference.

NOTE

If you use AutoCAD on a system with a small amount of RAM, limit your use of keyboard aliases to a minimum. Each keyboard alias takes up a small amount of memory, which reduces the total amount of memory available for your work.

After you add all your aliases to the ACAD.PGP file, save the file. The next time you load AutoCAD, the aliases will load automatically.

Changing Aliases within AutoCAD

Under some circumstances, you might want to change an alias without exiting AutoCAD. In this situation, you would follow these steps:

1. Start the standard Windows 95 or Windows NT Notepad text editor application.

2. Load the ACAD.PGP file from the C:\ACADR14\SUPPORT directory.

3. Make any necessary changes to the file, and save it.

4. Exit Notepad and return to AutoCAD.

5. When you enter AutoCAD again, you must re-initialize the ACAD.PGP file to activate the changes. To re-initialize the ACAD.PGP file, use the REINIT command by typing **REINIT** at the Command: prompt. A dialog box appears with options for the REINIT command, as shown in figure 22.1.

Figure 22.1

In the Re-initialization dialog box, you can update your keyboard shortcuts for the current session of AutoCAD.

Under the Device and File Initialization section of the dialog box, select the check box for the PGP File. Then click on OK. AutoCAD will reload the PGP file, and the new command aliases will be available.

As you can see, AutoCAD makes it easy to create as many simple keyboard shortcuts as you need to use the program effectively.

Customizing Windows Toolbars

In the Windows environment, you can use keyboard shortcuts and customizable toolbars to make your workspace work for you. A *toolbar* is a set of icons, each of which represents a specific AutoCAD command. You can customize the toolbars by creating icons of the AutoCAD commands that you use most often.

Creating your own toolbars offers several advantages. First, toolbars enable you to keep your eyes on the screen as you make use of them. If you use a tablet, for example, you would have to look away from the screen while accessing the tablet. Second, using both toolbars and keyboard shortcuts provides the greatest productivity gains from AutoCAD. You obtain the added productivity gains by using both methods because you may access the commands with whichever method is quickest under a particular circumstance. A little practice with using both and you will begin to see where you will use one over another. Figure 22.2 shows AutoCAD Release 14 and its Draw, Modify, Standard, and Object Properties command toolbars.

Figure 22.2

AutoCAD 14 contains four working toolbars: the Draw, Modify, Standard, and Object Properties command toolbars.

Modifying an Existing Toolbar

One of the most powerful advantages of AutoCAD 14 is that it enables you to modify toolbars. The following exercise demonstrates how to add a Polar Array icon to the Modify toolbar.

ADDING AN ICON TO A TOOLBAR

1. Load AutoCAD 14. In AutoCAD's default configuration, the Modify toolbar should be located on the left side of the screen.

2. Right-click on the corresponding button on the Modify toolbar to display the Toolbars dialog box (see fig. 22.3).

Figure 22.3

The Toolbars dialog box appears after you right-click on the Modify toolbar.

3. Make sure Modify is checked in the Toolbars list. Click on the Customize button to display the Customize Toolbars dialog box (see fig. 22.4).

Figure 22.4

The Customize Toolbars dialog box appears after you click on Customize in the Modify toolbar.

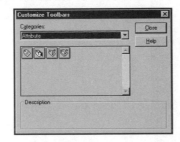

4. Select Modify from the Categories drop-down list. The Customize Toolbars dialog box appears, as shown in figure 22.5.

Figure 22.5

The Customize Toolbars dialog box can be accessed through the Modify toolbar.

5. In the Customize Toolbars dialog box, find the Polar Array button, which looks like a series of green circles arranged in a circle. Click and hold down the mouse button on this button. Drag and drop the button on the Modify toolbar to the location where you want the button to appear. The new Polar Array button appears on the toolbar, as shown in figure 22.6.

Figure 22.6

The Modify toolbar now contains the new Polar Array button.

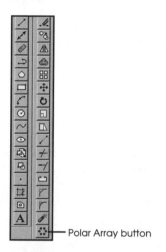

—— Polar Array button

6. Click on Close in the Customize Toolbars dialog box.

7. Click on Close in the Toolbars dialog box. AutoCAD menu files are automatically recompiled, and the changes are made permanent.

You have just customized the standard Modify toolbar and, in effect, have discovered how to add an icon to the toolbar. The following exercise shows you how to remove icons from a toolbar.

Note

In general, it is not a good idea to change the standard toolbars in AutoCAD. If you want to do a lot of customization, create and use your own toolbars. That way, if other users must use your system, they can still find and use the standard commands.

Imagine that you change the toolbar and then realize that you don't want a particular icon on the palette. The following steps demonstrate how to remove an icon from an existing toolbar.

REMOVING AN ICON FROM A TOOLBAR

1. Right-click on the Modify toolbar to display the Toolbars dialog box.

2. Click on the Customize button to access the Customize Properties dialog box.

3. Using the mouse, drag and drop the Polar Array icon off the Modify toolbar, but not on top of another toolbar. This removes the Polar Array icon from the toolbar.

4. Click on Close in the Customize Toolbars dialog box.

5. Click on Close in the Toolbars dialog box. The menus are now recompiled, and the icon is removed.

NOTE

Some icons in AutoCAD 14 have a small black triangle in the lower-right corner. This indicates that the icon is a *flyout* icon. If you click and hold on this type of icon, a flyout— a smaller toolbar—of other related command icons appears. You can add flyouts as a single icon to other toolbars in the same manner as adding individual command icons.

Creating Your Own Palettes

In AutoCAD, you can not only customize existing toolbars, but you also can create your own toolbars. You can place your new toolbar anywhere on the screen or even on other toolbars as a flyout. The following exercise demonstrates the steps used in this process.

You can start this exercise in one of two ways. You may choose whichever method you prefer.

CREATING CUSTOMIZED TOOLBARS

1. Right-click on any button on any toolbar, or choose View, Toolbars. The Toolbars dialog box appears, as shown previously in figure 22.3.

2. Click on the New button to display the New Toolbar dialog box (see fig. 22.7).

3. Type **INSIDCAD** in the Toolbar Name field. This is the name of your new toolbar.

4. Click on OK to create the toolbar. A blank toolbar appears at the top of the screen, as shown in figure 22.8.

Figure 22.7

You can name the new toolbar in the New Toolbar dialog box.

Figure 22.8

The new INSIDCAD toolbar appears at the top of the screen.

 N O T E

The new toolbar might be hard to see because it appears on top of the existing Standard and Object Properties toolbars.

5. Move the new toolbar to the right side of the AutoCAD screen, as shown in figure 22.9.

Figure 22.9

Moving the INSIDCAD toolbar to a new position makes it easier to access.

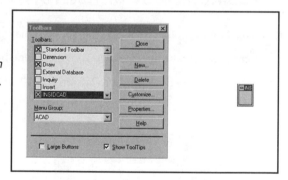

6. Click on the Customize button in the Toolbars dialog box.

7. Add any command from any categories you want to the new toolbar. You can mix and match categories as well.

N O T E

When you create custom toolbars, you have the flexibility to add commands from any and all command categories. Feel free to mix and match commands, because you are not restricted to one category per toolbar.

8. Click on Close when you are finished customizing the toolbar. This saves the toolbar and recompiles the AutoCAD menus. Figure 22.10 shows a possible INSIDCAD toolbar configuration.

Figure 22.10

After customizing, the INSIDCAD toolbar could appear similar to this configuration.

Adding a Flyout to a Toolbar

Now that you have created your own toolbar, you might want to add this toolbar to the Modify toolbar as a flyout. The following exercise takes you through this process.

ADDING FLYOUT MENUS TO TOOLBARS

1. Right-click on the Modify toolbar to display the Toolbars dialog box.

2. Click on Customize to display the Customize Toolbars dialog box.

3. Click on the Categories drop-down list. Scroll down and select Custom to access the custom icons (see fig. 22.11).

Figure 22.11

The Customize Toolbars dialog box enables you to access the custom icons.

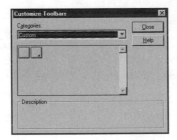

NOTE

AutoCAD 14 now has a Custom Flyout category of commands comprised of toolbars that are existing flyouts already created in AutoCAD. The INSIDCAD toolbar on which you are working does not appear in the list and must be created through the Custom category.

4. Drag and drop the flyout icon with the black triangle in the lower-right corner on the Modify toolbar. This adds a flyout icon to the Modify toolbar, as shown in figure 22.12.

Figure 22.12

The Modify toolbar now contains a blank flyout icon.

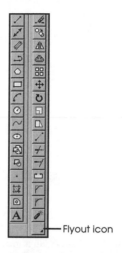

Flyout icon

5. Right-click on the blank flyout icon on the Modify toolbar to display the Flyout Properties dialog box (see fig. 22.13).

Figure 22.13

The Flyout Properties dialog box is displayed by accessing the blank flyout icon.

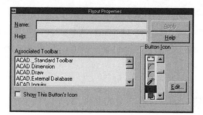

6. Scroll down the Associated Toolbar list until you see the ACAD.INSIDCAD toolbar. Click on and highlight this toolbar so that you can assign it to the flyout.

7. Click in the Name field and type **INSIDCAD** to name the new toolbar.

8. In the Help field, type the following statement to give the flyout a help entry:

   Assorted Commands Added as an Exercise

9. Click on Apply to apply the INSIDCAD toolbar to the flyout icon.

10. Close the Flyout Properties dialog box.

11. Click on Close in the Customize Toolbars dialog box.

12. Click on Close in the Toolbars dialog box to save the menu configuration. Figure 22.14 shows the final Modify tool palette configuration.

Figure 22.14

The final Modify toolbar is configured with the new flyout showing.

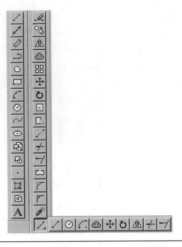

NOTE

As mentioned earlier in this chapter, it is not a good idea to customize the standard AutoCAD toolbars. For a little further practice, see if you can remove the flyout entry that you just created on the Modify toolbar.

The process of creating toolbars is quite simple in AutoCAD 14. Now that you know the steps, try to create a toolbar that contains the commands you use the most. Afterward, place your new toolbar in a convenient location on-screen.

Creating an Icon for a Non-Standard Command

Although the process of creating custom toolbars is straightforward, one problem still remains: not all AutoCAD commands have a toolbar icon for you to use. Additionally, some AutoCAD commands cannot support keyboard shortcuts because they require multiple entries at the Command: prompt. In these instances, you must create your own icon for the commands.

The following exercise shows you how to create a toolbar icon for an AutoCAD command that does not already have an icon on a toolbar. In this example, the REINIT command, discussed earlier, will be added to the INSIDCAD toolbar you created earlier in this chapter. If you have not completed the earlier exercises in this chapter, create your own custom toolbar for this exercise.

NOTE

The ^C^C in the Macro section of the Button Properties dialog box, which you will see in the following exercise, stands for pressing Esc twice in AutoCAD 14. If you press Esc twice, you can get out of any AutoCAD command. When you choose a button that has the ^C^C, it executes a double Esc and then executes the command that follows.

CREATING TOOLBAR ICONS FOR NON-STANDARD COMMANDS

1. Right-click on the INSIDCAD toolbar to display the Toolbars dialog box.

2. Click on Customize from the Toolbars dialog box to access the Customize Toolbars dialog box.

3. In the Categories drop-down list, select Custom to display the custom icons.

4. Drag and drop the blank button on the Modify toolbar. This adds an unassigned button to the palette.

5. Right-click on the blank button that you just dropped. The Button Properties dialog box appears, as shown in figure 22.15.

Figure 22.15

In the Button Properties dialog box, you can create your own custom command buttons for toolbars.

6. In the Name field, type **REINIT** to name the button.

7. In the Macro Box, type **REINIT** after the ^C^C. The button will be associated with the REINIT command when you are finished.

8. In the Button Icon section of the dialog box, you can either choose an existing icon for the button or create your own. For this exercise, you will create your own. Click on the Edit button to display the Button Editor dialog box (see fig. 22.16).

Figure 22.16

The Button Editor dialog box enables you to choose or create your own icon for the new button.

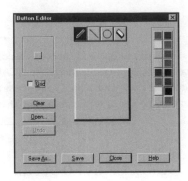

Note

In the Button Editor, you can use the drawing tool at the top of the dialog box to create custom icons. You also can click on the Open button to display a standard windows File Open dialog box. By selecting any BMP format graphic image, you can scale down the image and transfer it to the icon.

You should try to make your image as simple as possible. This will aid in making it as recognizable as possible. It is also suggested that any series of images that you draw follow a consistent pattern or look. This will make your customizations appear as professional as the standard AutoCAD icons.

9. Click on Save after you have created your icon.

10. Click on Close to return to the Button Properties dialog box.

11. Click on Apply to save your changes.

12. Close the Button Properties dialog box to return to the Customize Toolbars dialog box.

13. Click on Close, then Close again to save the changes in the menu file.

14. Place the cursor over the INSIDCAD toolbar and leave it there. The tooltip will eventually appear and confirm that this is the REINIT command, as shown in figure 22.17. Execute the command to verify that it works.

Figure 22.17

The tooltip verifies the REINIT command on the INSIDCAD toolbar.

NOTE

To add commands that require multiple entries at the command prompt, such as ZOOM WINDOW, separate each command with a semi-colon. For example, type **'zoom;w** for this particular command. Note the use of the apostrophe, indicating that the command can be used transparently when chosen from the command button. If you forget the apostrophe, the command cannot be used transparently.

Furthermore, you also can add some simple LISP expressions to these buttons as well. Because this process involves a much more advanced use of these buttons, this book does not cover the steps. Consult the *AutoCAD Customization Reference* for more information on this particular feature.

The Windows version of AutoCAD 14 simplifies the process of creating your own icons. If you use a lot of custom commands in AutoCAD, you should create a toolbar and icons for those commands.

Customizing Menus

At some point, you will need to create your own custom menus in AutoCAD. To do this, you must modify the AutoCAD menu source file and then recompile the menu. This isn't as hard as it sounds, and customizing the menu enables you to create a menu structure that suits your working style. For example, if you created a bunch of AutoLISP routines for AutoCAD and did not want to take the time creating new buttons and icons for each, you could simply create a new pull-down menu for your LISP routines.

Before you begin, you first must understand how the menu items work. To take a closer look, load the ACAD.MNU file in the Support directory (usually C:\ACADR14\SUPPORT) into a text editor, such as Notepad.

The ACAD.MNU file is nothing more than a text file that is easy to modify and use to add features to your AutoCAD menu. Each pull-down menu in AutoCAD is referred to as a POP menu. POP0 is the pop-up menu that appears when you click the third mouse button on a three-button mouse, or when you press the Shift key and right-click with a two-button mouse. POP1 is the File menu. POP2 is the Edit menu, and so on. The following portion of ACAD.MNU lists entries for the Edit menu, or POP2.

```
***POP2
**EDIT
ID_MnEdit    [&Edit]
ID_Undo      [&Undo\tCtrl+Z]_u
ID_Redo      [&Redo\tCtrl+Y]^C^C_redo
             [--]
```

```
ID_Cutclip    [Cu&t\tCtrl+X]'_cutclip
ID_Copyclip   [&Copy\tCtrl+C]'_copyclip
ID_Copylink   [Copy &Link]^C^C_copylink
ID_Pasteclip  [&Paste\tCtrl+V]'_pasteclip
ID_Pastesp    [Paste &Special...]^C^C_pastespec
ID_Erase      [Cle&ar\tDel]^C^C_erase
              [--]
ID_Links      [&OLE Links...]^C^C_olelinks
```

This code represents the Edit menu shown in figure 22.18.

Figure 22.18

The AutoCAD Edit menu is associated with the preceding MNU source code.

The first line of the source code, ***POP2, indicates the position of the pull-down menu. The third line, ID_MnEdit [&Edit], indicates the name of the menu. ID_MnEdit is a unique identifier for the name of the menu. Another occurrence of the word ID_MnEdit should not exist in the MNU file. The &Edit in brackets specifies the word that appears on the AutoCAD menu—in this case, Edit. The ampersand (&) in front of the E means that the E is underlined and can be accessed using the keyboard.

NOTE

Any line in the MNU file that begins with a \\ is a comment and is ignored by AutoCAD.

Following the menu definition is each command included on the Edit menu. The first command on the menu, the Undo command, can also be accessed through the keyboard by pressing Ctrl+Z. The MNU source entry indicates keyboard and menu access:

```
ID_Undo  [&Undo\tCtrl+Z]_u
```

ID_Undo is the identifier for this menu entry, and this entry must be unique. The brackets indicate the actual command name and the underlined character. The \t symbol stands for TAB to space the Ctrl+Z on the right side of the menu. Outside the bracket is the command you would enter at the Command: prompt in AutoCAD. For example, typing **u** at the Command: prompt activates Undo. Because this command is used in the menu file, it must have an underline before the command to make it execute correctly.

WARNING

When editing the MNU file, you must reload the menu to have any changes available. This, however, will delete any customized toolbar modifications you have made via the dialog box system. Be sure to copy your customization out of the MNS file into a temporary text file and transfer to the MNU during editing. That way your toolbar changes will not be lost.

INSIDER **T**IP

The MNU file is a carry-over from the old menu system. This file is not required for AutoCAD menu customization, so you can delete the MNU file (or rename it) and edit the MNS instead. This enables you to save toolbar customization when editing your pull-down menu system. Any changes you make and any toolbar changes will be saved to the MNS file.

Creating Your Own Menu

The following exercise demonstrates how to create a new pull-down menu and add it to your existing AutoCAD menu. After you create the new menu, as shown in the following steps, recompile the menu and exit.

CREATING PULL-DOWN MENUS

1. Copy the ACAD.MNU file to MNU.BAK to make a backup file of the original.

2. Load ACAD.MNU into Notepad.

3. Scroll down the file until you see the section entitled ***Toolbars**, which follows the POP10 entries.

4. Directly after the POP10 entries, add the following lines to the MNU file:

```
***POP11
**INSIDCAD
ID_MnINSIDCAD   [&INSIDCAD]
ID_Reinit [&Reinit...]^C^C_reinit
[--]
ID_Extend [&Extend]^C^C_extend
```

5. Save the new MNU file.

6. In your AutoCAD support directory, delete the ACAD.MNS and ACAD.MNC files. This step deletes the original compiled menu and forces a recompile.

7. Now reload AutoCAD. The new pull-down menu appears after the Help menu.

Adding Commands to the Pop-Up Menu

The following exercise demonstrates how to add commands to the pop-up menu. Because the pop-up menu is accessed through a combination Shift+right-click on the screen, it is very convenient. You can place any commands that you use frequently on this menu; for example, the LINE command would make good sense on this menu.

ADDING COMMANDS TO POP-UP MENUS

1. Load ACAD.MNU file into Notepad.

2. Find the entry marked ***POP0, and then look for the following entry:
   `[Endpoint]_endp`

3. Above this line, type the following entry:
   `[Line]_line`

   This new line adds the LINE command to the menu.

4. Save the file.

5. Delete the ACAD.MNC and ACAD.MNS files from the AutoCAD support directory. This step forces AutoCAD to recompile the menu files.

6. Reload AutoCAD. This recompiles the menus and causes the new pop-up menu to appear.

If you get a little confused while trying to add a new menu, take a few minutes and look over the MNU file for some examples of a menu that has already been done. If all else fails, consult the AutoCAD customization guide for help on customizing the AutoCAD menus.

Summary

This chapter introduced you to many benefits of customizing AutoCAD. Throughout this chapter, you saw how easy it is to create your own toolbars, add your own menus, create your own icons, and even specify where you want AutoCAD to place toolbars when it loads.

After you customize AutoCAD so that it is easier to access the commands that you use most, you almost immediately will begin to see a rise in productivity.

CREATING SCRIPTS AND SLIDE LIBRARIES

by Bill Burchard

The typical CAD technician seldom uses two useful AutoCAD features—script files and slide libraries. Most users consider these two features the realm of the "AutoCAD Guru." That is a shame, too, because they are fairly simple to learn and very useful for performing repetitive tasks.

A script file is simply a series of AutoCAD commands and responses to those commands, saved in an ASCII text file. The easiest way to create a script is to write the AutoCAD commands down on a piece of paper exactly as you enter them into an AutoCAD editing session. Then, use a basic text editor and type each command and its responses on a separate line. Save the file with a .SCR extension and voilá, you've created an AutoCAD script. Script files can easily execute many commands. For example, you can use script files to insert blocks, attach xrefs, draw objects, or plot drawings. Script files are the simplest form of writing programs for AutoCAD.

Slide libraries store a series of AutoCAD images. You can recall these images and automatically display them as a series of slides, creating a slide show. You also can recall them for display in image tile menus. Image tile menus provide a graphic way to show users what AutoCAD function will execute if they select a particular tile.

By using these two features, you can easily and quickly automate your work and increase your productivity.

This chapter discusses the following subjects:

- Using script files to automatically set up your drawing environment
- Using script files to load AutoLISP routines
- Using script files to insert blocks
- Automating commands

Using Script Files

Through Release 13, one use for script files had been to implement batch plotting. Release 14's new Batch Plot Utility begins replacing the use of script files for straight-forward plotting situations. The new utility enables you to easily open a series of drawings, associate a PCP file with each, and then plot each drawing. You can use this routine to automatically plot hundreds of drawings unattended. However, the Batch Plot Utility does have some limitations when dealing with more complicated plotting situations. You can continue to use script files where the Batch Plot Utility falls short, as Chapter 20, "Productive Plotting," discusses.

There are additional uses for script files. You can easily automate repetitive tasks, just by writing simple script files. The remainder of this section discusses a few applications of script files.

Automating Your Drawing Environment

You can use script files to set up your working environment. You can load AutoLISP routines, insert blocks into the block table, load linetypes, and set text styles. You can automate all these functions using a single script file.

NOTE

I find using scripts to set my working environment useful when I'm temporarily working at another CAD technician's station. I simply place the files I need to use on a floppy disk, along with a script file that loads them. Then, when I need to load the files, I execute the script command from the floppy disk. The script will execute and load the appropriate files. Then I'm ready to begin work.

Using Script Files to Load AutoLISP Routines

You can use scripts to automatically load AutoLISP routines. If you have several LISP routines that you frequently use during a drawing editing session, you can create a single script file to load them automatically.

To load LISP routines from a script, you can simply duplicate the LOAD command's syntax in the script file. You also can insert the AutoLISP code directly in the script file. Both methods load the AutoLISP routines.

INSIDER **TIP**

In the following exercise, I use the Notepad program, which comes with both Windows 95 and Windows NT. I use it because it automatically saves files as ASCII text files. You may use any other text editor you prefer, as long as it saves the files as ASCII text files.

In the following exercise, you open an existing drawing for editing. Then, you create a script file that automatically loads three AutoLISP routines. Finally, the AutoLISP routines are used to edit the drawing.

USING SCRIPTS TO LOAD AUTOLISP ROUTINES

1. Open the 23DWG01.DWG drawing file found on the accompanying CD.

2. From the Start button on the Windows Taskbar, choose Programs, Accessories, Notepad. This opens Notepad.

3. In Notepad, enter the following lines:

```
; Define break object at endpoint LISP routine
(defun C:BRE (/) (command "BREAK" pause "F" "ENDP" pause "@"))
; Define break object at intersection LISP routine
(defun C:BRI (/) (command "BREAK" pause "F" "INT" pause "@"))
; Load SBL LISP routine
(_.load "SBL.LSP")
; End script file
```

This file represents a script file. The lines of text enclosed with parentheses is AutoLISP code. When you finish entering the text, be sure it includes the semicolons, slashes, quotes, and parentheses as shown. Also, it's very important to press the Enter key after typing the last line of text. This places the cursor at the beginning of a new blank line just below the last line of text.

4. Save the file in the ACADR14\SAMPLE directory and name it **LOADIT.SCR**. You must use the .SCR extension in naming scripts because this is the only way that AutoCAD recognizes the file as a script file.

INSIDER TIP

Including comments in your code is good programming practice because it helps clarify what your routine is doing each step of the way. In script files, you can enter a comment by preceding it with a semicolon. When AutoCAD encounters a semicolon in a script file, it ignores the text that follows it. Watch out, on the other hand, for blank spaces. Script files are very sensitive to blank spaces. A blank space in a script file represents pressing the Enter key. Too many blank spaces in script files represent the most common problem encountered with scripts that do not execute as expected.

5. At the Command: prompt, type **SCRIPT** and press the Enter key. The Select Script File dialog box opens.

6. From the ACADR14\SAMPLE directory, open the LOADIT.SCR script file you just created. When you open the file, AutoCAD runs the script file, which defines the BRE and BRI AutoLISP routines and loads the SBL routine. Figure 23.1 shows the AutoCAD Text Window, which displays the commands executed through the script file and AutoCAD's responses.

Figure 23.1

The script file loads the three AutoLISP routines.

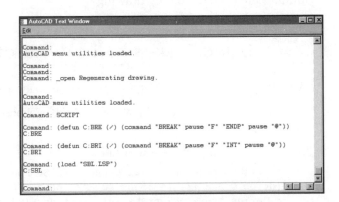

Notice that after AutoCAD loads each routine, it prints C: followed by three letters. The three letters are the command name you type to execute the routine. AutoCAD indicates that it has successfully loaded an AutoLISP routine by printing the routine's command name.

Next, you execute the three routines to verify that they loaded properly:

7. At the Command: prompt, type **BRE** and press the Enter key. The BRE routine executes the BREAK command. It breaks the selected object at an endpoint with a single pick.

8. At the BREAK Select object: prompt, pick the top horizontal line at ①, as shown in figure 23.2.

Figure 23.2

The bubble pick points.

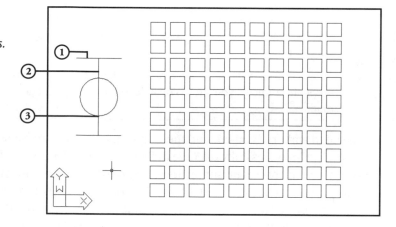

9. Next, at the Enter first point: ENDP of prompt, pick the vertical line at ②.

The BRE routine automatically uses the endpoint snap to break the horizontal line at the point where the vertical line intersects it. You can verify the line is broken by picking it (assuming noun/verb selection is enabled, only the half of the original line you pick will highlight).

Next, you will verify that the BRI routine is working properly.

10. At the Command: prompt, type **BRI** and press the Enter key.

The BRI routine also executes the BREAK command. However, it breaks the selected object at an intersection with a single pick.

11. At the BREAK Select object : prompt, pick the vertical line at ②.

12. Next, at the Enter first point: INT of prompt pick the intersection of the circle and the vertical line at ③.

The BRI routine automatically uses the intersection snap to break the vertical line at the point at which the circle intersects it. You can verify the line is broken by choosing it to highlight it.

Finally, you will verify that the SBL routine is working properly.

13. At the Command: prompt, type **SBL** and press the Enter key.

   The SBL routine uses the SCALE command to resize selected blocks. It scales the blocks from their insertion point. In the current drawing, the rectangles are inserted blocks.

   The SBL routine prompts for a scale factor, and uses the value you enter to scale the blocks.

14. Type **0.5** and press the Enter key.

15. Select the blocks using any standard selection method (including the ALL argument). The SBL routine filters out all objects, except INSERT objects, when it creates its selection set.

   AutoCAD resizes all the selected blocks to half their original size. If you created the script file correctly, you should be able to successfully execute the three AutoLISP routines.

As stated earlier, if you created the script file in the previous exercise correctly, you were able to successfully execute the three AutoLISP routines. If any of the routines failed to work, however, simply look over the data you entered in the script file and make sure it is correct. When you write programs, it is common to have a problem or two when you first try to run it (these little problems are called *bugs*). If you cannot figure out why your script file will not work, check out the 23SCR01.SCR script file on the accompanying CD. It is the correct version of the LOADIT.SCR file you created.

Using Script Files to Insert Blocks

Just as the previous discussion demonstrated how to use script files to load frequently used AutoLISP routines, you can also use script files to quickly load blocks into the current drawing's block table. This makes them immediately available for insertion.

NOTE

Note that in some cases using script files to load blocks can add to the size (number of bytes) of the drawing file—especially if many of the blocks are not used in the current drawing. There are, however, times when this is desirable. They include when the blocks are not locatable via the AutoCAD search path (eliminated typing disk/directory syntax to locate the block), when you're working on another computer and your block library does not exist there (your library is now part of your drawing), and when your network is very slow.

Using script files to load blocks, however, gets a little tricky. That's because you have to use the INSERT command to insert the block. After you select the block's drawing file, AutoCAD expects you to pick the insertion point. If you are only loading the block definitions into the block table, you don't need to insert the block. So then, normally, you cancel the INSERT command when AutoCAD prompts for the insertion point. Unfortunately, script files do not provide a mechanism to cancel an AutoCAD command that is in progress.

You can, however, cancel the current command using a little bit of AutoLISP code. When AutoCAD encounters the code, it passes control from the script file to the AutoLISP code. The AutoLISP code then cancels the current command and passes control back to the script file. It is a simple technique to use, and it provides the capability to automatically load hundreds of blocks into a drawing's block table without having to actually insert each one.

The following exercise demonstrates how to load blocks into the current drawing's block table using a script file. First, you open a drawing that contains no objects, nor block definitions in the block table. Next, you create a script file to load two block definitions into the current drawing. Finally, you verify that the blocks were successfully loaded by viewing them.

USING SCRIPT FILES TO LOAD BLOCKS

1. Open the 23DWG02.DWG drawing file found on the accompanying CD.

Next, you create a new script file.

2. From the Start button on the Windows Taskbar, choose Programs, Accessories, Notepad.

3. In Notepad, enter the following lines:

```
; Insert block
_.insert
; Arrowhead block
```

```
23DWG02a
; Cancel insert command, resume script file
(command \e "RESUME")
; Insert block
_.insert
; Construction bubble block
23DWG02b
; Cancel insert command
(command \e)
```

The lines of text are the commands and AutoLISP code that will load the blocks into the block table without forcing you to actually insert the blocks into model space. The lines of text enclosed with parentheses are AutoLISP code. When you finish entering the text, be sure it includes the semicolons, slashes, quotes, and parentheses as shown. As noted previously, it's very important to press the Enter key after typing the last line of text. This places the cursor at the beginning of a new blank line just below the last line of text.

INSIDER TIP

Notice that an underscore and a period precedes the INSERT command. The underscore indicates that the command name is in English. The period instructs AutoCAD to use the original definition of the command. Always use the period to ensure that you don't inadvertently use a redefined version of the command.

4. Save the file in the ACADR14\SAMPLE directory and name it **BLOCKS.SCR**.

Next, execute the script file and load the blocks.

5. At the Command: prompt, type **SCRIPT** and press the Enter key. The Select Script File dialog box opens.

6. From the ACADR14\SAMPLE directory, open the BLOCKS.SCR script file you just created.

AutoCAD runs the script file, which loads the 23DWG02a.DWG and 23DWG02b.DWG drawing files. Figure 23.3 shows the AutoCAD Text Window, which displays the commands executed through the script file and AutoCAD's responses.

Figure 23.3

The script file loads the blocks into the block table.

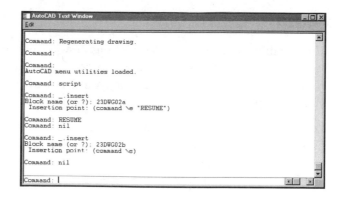

Notice that when AutoCAD loads each block, it does not pause for an insertion point. Instead, it cancels the INSERT command, and then resumes running the script file.

Next, you view the two block definitions to verify that they loaded properly into the block table.

7. From Insert, choose Block. The Insert dialog box opens.

8. Click on the Block button. The Defined Blocks dialog box opens and displays the two blocks you loaded with the script file, as shown in figure 23.4. This verifies that the two blocks have been loaded.

   Once you verify the blocks loaded, click on the Cancel button to exit the Defined Blocks dialog box. Click on the Cancel button again to exit the Insert dialog box.

Figure 23.4

The script file successfully loaded the blocks.

The technique of loading blocks into the block table described in the preceding exercise is very convenient. This technique can also be used if you use template files (which you should) to set up a new drawing, and the template contains dozens of blocks. By using script files to load the blocks, you can automate the process of setting up your template files and increase your productivity.

Automating Commands

The capability to create simple programs in AutoCAD provides a way to automate repetitive tasks. In the previous two script files, you used scripts to load and execute AutoLISP routines. In this discussion, you will use very simple AutoLISP code to launch script files.

You can load AutoLISP commands in AutoCAD by directly entering the code at the Command: prompt. Although you wouldn't want to do that for lengthy routines, it works fine for very simple ones. Routines that consist of one line of code are good candidates to enter quickly at the Command: prompt.

The next exercise demonstrates how to execute a script file from a simple AutoLISP routine. You open a blank drawing that contains a block definition. Then, you use a predefined script file to create a new layer and insert the block. Finally, you execute the script file from a simple AutoLISP routine.

EXECUTING SCRIPT FILES FROM AUTOLISP

1. Open the 23DWG03.DWG drawing file found on the accompanying CD.

2. Enter the following text at the Command: prompt exactly as shown and then press the Enter key:

   ```
   (defun C:TB (/) (command "SCRIPT" "23SCR03.SCR"))
   ```

   AutoCAD prints C:TB after you enter the text to indicate that it has loaded the routine. The script file that the routine executes is as follows:

   ```
   ; Create new layer
   _.layer
   ; Make new layer
   make
   ; New layer name
   title_block
   ; Exit layer command

   ; Insert block
   _.insert
   ; Insert the block named title_block
   title_block
   ; Insertion coordinates
   7,5
   ; X scale
   1
   ```

```
; Y scale
1
; Rotation
0
;Exit script file
```

3. At the Command: prompt, type **TB** and press the Enter key.

    The AutoLISP code executes the script file 23SCR03.SCR. The script file then creates the layer TITLE_BLOCK and makes it current. Finally, it inserts the block, as shown in figure 23.5. You have successfully executed a script file with a simple AutoLISP routine.

Figure 23.5

The script file is started by the AutoLISP command.

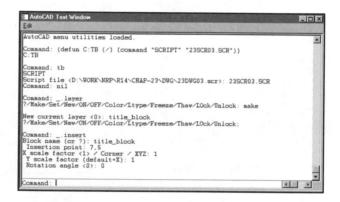

Another situation in which you use AutoLISP to execute script files is when you want to quickly toggle multiple layers on and off. By creating two script files, one that turns layers on and another that turns them off, you can easily modify your working environment.

The next exercise demonstrates how to create two simple AutoLISP routines that execute script files to toggle layers on and off.

TURNING LAYERS ON AND OFF WITH SCRIPT FILES

1. Open the 23DWG04.DWG drawing file found on the accompanying CD. The drawing contains several layers that you will toggle on and off with script files. The script files have already been created. 23SCR04a.SCR turns layers off and 23SCR04b.SCR turns layers on.

Next, you enter the AutoLISP code that executes the script files.

2. At the Command: prompt, enter the following line of code and then press the Enter key:

```
(defun C:LOF (/) (command "SCRIPT" "23SCR04a.SCR"))
```

AutoCAD responds by printing C:LOF. Typing **LOF** at the AutoCAD Command: prompt turns off the layers listed in the script file.

3. At the Command: prompt, enter the following line of code and then press the Enter key:

```
Command: (defun C:LON (/) (command "SCRIPT" "23SCR04b.SCR"))
```

AutoCAD responds by printing C:LON. By typing **LON** at the AutoCAD Command: prompt, you turn on the layers listed in the script file.

The script file that turns on the layers contains the following code:

```
; Turn on layers
_.layer
; Layers on
on
; Layers to turn on
buildings,contour*
; Exit layer command

; Exit script file
```

As you can see, the script file is very simple. It just turns on three layers. The script indicates one of the layers by its complete name and it indicates the other two using a wild-card character. A comma separates the two layer name text values.

4. At the Command: prompt, enter **LOF** and press the Enter key. The layers are turned off.

5. At the command prompt, enter **LON** and press the Enter key. The layers are turned on.

This is a simple, yet useful application of AutoLISP and script files. However, there is one occasion when the script file won't execute properly: when one of the layers you are trying to turn off is the current layer. AutoCAD expects you to respond by indicating that you really want to turn off the current layer. Because the script file does not address the response, AutoCAD halts execution of the script. The simplest way to avoid this problem is to set the EXPERT system variable to 1, which forces AutoCAD to simply turn off the current layer without asking if you really want to do so.

INSIDER TIP

Setting the EXPERT system variable to 1 at the beginning of the script file is a good idea. Then set it back to 0 (its default value) at the end of the script file.

Performing Repetitive Tasks on Multiple Drawings

Script files are very useful for performing repetitive tasks on multiple drawings. For example, you can use the script file you created earlier for inserting the title block, add statements to open and save each drawing, and then use it to insert the title block into multiple sheets. The script can do this automatically by opening each drawing, inserting the block, saving the drawing, and then opening the next drawing.

INSIDER TIP

I have used this feature frequently on large projects where hundreds of drawings were to have the same repetitive things done to them. By creating a script file that opened a file and executed several AutoLISP routines to edit the drawing, then using the script file to plot and save the drawing, I was able to perform hundreds of hours of work automatically. What's especially nice is that most of the work performed by the scripts was done overnight.

For a detailed example of how to quickly create large script files for plotting multiple sheets, see the section titled "Using Script Files for Multiple Plots," in Chapter 20, "Productive Plotting."

Using Slides

Just as new features are overshadowing the usefulness of script files, new software is overshadowing AutoCAD's slide show capability. Although AutoCAD's slide show capability is handy, other software is available that fulfills the same need and is easier to use and less expensive.

However, although AutoCAD may not be the easiest or cheapest software to use for running slide shows, if you already have AutoCAD and know how to use it, you might as well take advantage of what it can do.

Slide shows are simple to create. In fact, all you really need to read is AutoCAD's standard documentation. It does a good job of explaining how to create slide shows. Consequently, this section does not discuss using slides for slide shows.

Slides can also be used to make identifying AutoCAD commands easier. By inserting slides into an image tile menu, you create a graphical user interface where an AutoCAD command is executed by selecting a slide image in a tile, as discussed in the next section.

Creating Image Tile Menus

An *image tile menu* is a dialog box that enables you to execute a command or script file by selecting a tile. More importantly, the image tile menu is easily customized. The image tile menu dialog box displays 20 tiles, and each tile displays a single slide, as shown in figure 23.6. When you choose one of the slide images in a tile, AutoCAD executes the command associated with the tile.

The image tile menu shown in figure 23.6 is the Tiled Viewport Layout dialog box. You open it from View, Tiled Viewports, Layout. By choosing one of the tiles and clicking on OK, AutoCAD creates the tiled viewport arrangement shown in the image tile. The images in the tiles are slides that were made with the MSLIDE command. On the left side of the dialog box is a list of image tile names. Each name is associated with one tile, and a command is executed by selecting either the image tile or its name from the list.

Notice that not all of the tiles have a slide image. When you create an image tile menu to execute commands, it is not necessary to use all of the tiles. In figure 23.6, only 12 layouts are available. Consequently, the remaining unused image tiles are left blank. If selected, they execute no command, since no command is associated with them.

Figure 23.6

The Tiled Viewport Layout image tile menu.

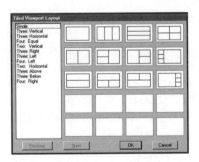

Creating image tile menus involves four basic steps:

- Creating the slides.
- Compiling the slides in a slide library file.

- Editing the ***IMAGE section of the ACAD.MNU file.

- Creating an AutoLISP routine to open the image tile menu.

Probably the most useful purpose of image tile menus is for inserting blocks, which Chapter 12, "Creating and Using Blocks" briefly discusses. By creating a slide of a block and associating the slide with a tile in the image tile menu, you can quickly identify a block from a group of blocks. Then, the block can be inserted by selecting its image tile, which causes AutoCAD to execute the command associated with the tile. In this particular example, the INSERT command would be associated with the tile.

Through the next four exercises, you create an image tile menu that displays images of blocks and inserts a block when you select its associated image tile.

In the following exercise, you open a blank drawing and use it to create the slides for the image tile menu.

INSIDER TIP

When you create the slides, you need to use your judgment to establish the image's appearance. Slides that you use in an image tile menu should fill up most of the tile's area. Also, the image should not be too complex. The complexity of an image becomes lost when you reduce its size to the point that you can place it on a tile.

Also, the tiles have a ratio of 1.5:1. They are 1.5 units wide by 1 unit tall. When you use the MSLIDE command to create a slide, AutoCAD uses the entire screen area. Unfortunately, your screen's ratio is probably not 1.5:1. Consequently, your slide may contain a lot of unwanted blank space. You can easily control the screen ratio by turning TILEMODE off and creating a viewport in paper space that is 1.5 units wide by 1 unit tall. Then edit your image inside the viewport in model space, and position it so the image fills the viewport. Once the image is properly positioned, create the slide.

CREATING SLIDES FOR AN IMAGE TILE MENU

1. Open the 23DWG05.DWG drawing file found on the accompanying CD.

2. Double-click on the TILE button on the status bar at the bottom of your screen. AutoCAD turns off TILE mode. You are now in paper space. Next, you create the viewport that you will use when making the slide images.

3. Choose View, Floating Viewports, 1 Viewport.

4. At the ON/OFF/Hideplot/Fit/2/3/4/Restore/<First Point>: prompt, enter **0,0**.

5. Next, enter **1.5,0**. AutoCAD creates a floating viewport that is the correct ratio for making slide images.

6. Choose View, Zoom, Extents.

    The viewport fills the screen.

7. Double-click on the PAPER button in the status bar at the bottom of your screen.

Now you are ready to create the slides. You will create five slides, one for each sheet size.

8. Choose Insert, Block. The Insert dialog box displays.

9. Select the File button. The Select Drawing File dialog box displays.

10. Open the 23DWG05a.DWG drawing file found on the accompanying CD.

11. Click on the OK button to exit the Insert dialog box. When prompted, type **0,0** for the insertion point and accept the defaults for scale and rotation.

    The 23DWG05a.DWG drawing contains the 8 ½" × 11" sheet size. For purposes of this exercise, large text indicating the sheet size has been inserted. This makes identifying the sheet size in the image tile menu easier. After you create the image, you may edit the original drawing representing each block and erase the text.

Next, you size the image for use as a slide in the image tile menu.

12. Choose View, Zoom, Extents.

13. Choose View, Zoom, Scale.

14. At the Command: prompt, type **0.95X** and press the Enter key. This provides a good size for the slide image, leaving a small white border around the edge of the image.

Next, you create the slide.

15. At the Command: prompt, type **MSLIDE** and press the Enter key. The Create Slide File dialog box opens.

16. Save the slide in the ACADR14\SUPPORT directory and name it 23DWG05a.SLD, the same name as the drawing file. In the File name text box, enter **23DWG05a.SLD**, then choose Save. AutoCAD creates the slide.

17. Erase the inserted drawing. Then repeat steps 8 through 17 for the remaining drawings: 23DWG05b, 23DWG05c, 23DWG05d, and 23DWG05e.

Once the five slides are created, the next step is to combine them into a single file called a slide library.

To create a slide library from the slides, you use the SLIDELIB utility provided with AutoCAD and located in the ACADR14\SUPPORT directory. The utility compiles the slides into one file. To compile the slides, you pass a list of the slide file names to the utility.

A simple way to create the list of slide file names is to shell out of AutoCAD, change to the ACADR14\SUPPORT directory where the slides reside, and issue the DOS DIR command, using the syntax that automatically creates a .TXT file.

NOTE

The SLIDELIB utility creates a copy of the slides and stores them in a library file. Consequently, after you create the slide library, you can delete the original slide files. However, if you intend to add additional slides to the library file, you must re-create the file from scratch. You cannot simply add additional slides to an existing library file. Consequently, you must use all the original slide files to do so. It is a good idea, therefore, to save your original slide files.

The following exercise demonstrates how to create a slide library.

CREATING A SLIDE LIBRARY FROM SLIDES

1. At the Command: prompt, type **SH** and press the Enter key.

2. At the OS Command: prompt, press the Enter key.

   The AutoCAD Shell Active window appears.

3. At the DOS prompt, type the following:
   ```
   CD\
   CD\ACADR14\SAMPLEWORK\NRP\R14\CHAP-23\DWG
   ```

   This makes the ACADR14\SAMPLE directory current, which is where you saved the slide images from the last exercise. Next, you create the list of slide file names.

4. At the DOS prompt, type **DIR *.SLD /b > SLDNAMES.TXT** and press the Enter key.

   The DIR command lists all files that end with SLD, one per line, and stores the results in an ASCII text file called SLDNAMES.TXT.

   Next, you use the SLIDELIB utility to create the slide library file.

5. While still working from the AutoCAD shell Active window, type **SLIDELIB SHEETS < SLDNAMES.TXT** and press the Enter key.

AutoCAD executes the utility, and creates a slide library file named SHEETS.SLB. This is the file name you refer to when you define the image tile menu.

6. Type **EXIT** and press the Enter key. The AutoCAD Shell Active window closes.

After creating the slide library file, the next step is to modify the ACAD.MNU file and add the image tile menu commands.

The commands associated with each tile in the image tile menu are stored in the ACAD.MNU file. The ACAD.MNU file is an ASCII text file. You can edit it using most word processors. After you edit the file, be sure to save it as an ASCII text file.

INSIDER TIP

When editing the ACAD.MNU file, it's a good idea to make a backup copy of it so that if something goes wrong during your editing session, you can recall the original menu file.

The following exercise demonstrates how to edit the ACAD.MNU file and add commands to the image tile menu area.

INSIDER TIP

For this exercise, I use Windows WordPad to edit the menu file. Typically, I prefer to use Windows Notepad simply because I have used it for several years—it's my favorite text editor. Unfortunately, the typical ACAD.MNU file is too large to fit in Notepad.

ADDING IMAGE TILE MENU COMMANDS TO THE ACAD.MNU FILE

1. From the Start button on the Windows Taskbar, choose Programs, Accessories, WordPad.

2. Choose File, Open. The Open window appears.

3. In the File name text box, type ***.MNU** and press Enter. This forces the list box to display only file names that end with *.MNU.

   You are searching for the ACAD.MNU file. It resides in AutoCAD's Support directory.

4. When you find the ACAD.MNU file, select the file to highlight the name and click on the Open button. The ACAD.MNU file is now ready for editing.

Next, you find the location to enter the image tile menu code.

5. Choose Edit, Find. The Find window opens.

6. In the Find what text box, type *****IMAGE**, and then click on the Find Next button.

   AutoCAD displays the ***IMAGE section. This represents the beginning of the image tile menu section. You enter new code at the end of this section.

Next, you enter the image tile menu code.

7. Click on Cancel to close the Find window.

8. Scroll down to display the ***IMAGE section, as shown in figure 23.7.

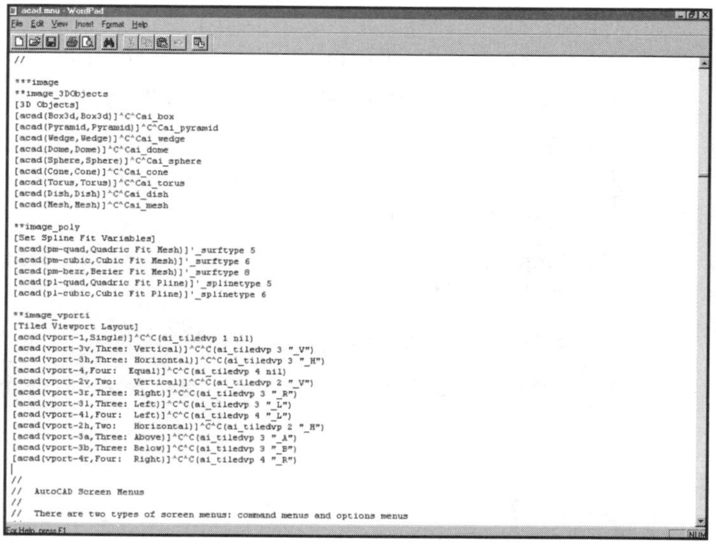

Figure 23.7

The ***IMAGE section of the ACAD.MNU file.

The last image tile menu entry is the section that starts with **image_vporti. Enter the new code following this section.

9. At the end of the ***IMAGE section, enter the following code:

```
**image_sheets
[Insert Sheet Block]
[sheets(23dwg05a,ANSI-A)]^C^C_.script 23scr05a.scr
[sheets(23dwg05b,ANSI-B)]^C^C_.script 23scr05b.scr
[sheets(23dwg05c,ANSI-C)]^C^C_.script 23scr05c.scr
[sheets(23dwg05d,ANSI-D)]^C^C_.script 23scr05d.scr
[sheets(23dwg05e,ANSI-E)]^C^C_.script 23scr05e.scr
```

This code tells AutoCAD the following:

**image_sheets indicates the beginning of a new image tile menu section.

[Insert Sheet Block] is the title that appears at the top of the Image Tile Menu dialog box.

The remaining code tells AutoCAD how to display the slides and what commands to execute when one of the image tiles is selected.

For example, the third line of code listed in the preceding tells AutoCAD to use the SHEETS.LIB file, display a slide named 23DWG05a, and to list the name ANSI-A in the text list at the left of the dialog box. Then, it instructs AutoCAD to cancel any active commands, and finally to execute the 23DWG05a.SCR script file.

The script files have already been created. When executed in AutoCAD, they create a new layer called BORDER, make it current, and then insert the appropriate block.

10.   Save the ACAD.MNU file and close WordPad.

Next, you must reload into AutoCAD the ACAD.MNU file that you just edited.

11.   At the Command: prompt, type **MENU** and press the Enter key. The Select Menu File dialog box opens.

12.   From the Files of type drop-down list, select Menu Template (*.MNU). The ACAD.MNU file appears.

13.   Select the ACAD.MNU file, then click on Open.

14.   When AutoCAD issues the warning, choose Yes to overwrite the .MNS file. AutoCAD recompiles the new menu and loads it.

INSIDER TIP

The warning AutoCAD issues notes that loading the MNU file overwrites the MNS file, which results in the loss of any toolbar customization changes. To avoid this, open and edit the MNS file instead of the MNU file.

The only step left is to create a simple AutoLISP routine to display the image tile menu.

Now that you have created the slide library and saved the commands in the ACAD.MNU file, you simply need to tell AutoCAD to open the new image tile menu you created. A simple way to do this is to define an AutoLISP routine.

The following exercise demonstrates how to create a simple AutoLISP routine to open an image tile menu.

OPENING AN IMAGE TILE MENU WITH AUTOLISP

1. At the Command: prompt, enter the following code:

   `(defun C:SHT (/) (menucmd "I=IMAGE_SHEETS") (menucmd "I=*"))`

   The preceding AutoLISP code uses the MENUCMD function to first load into memory the **IMAGE_SHEETS section you created, then displays the image tile menu.

2. At the Command: prompt, type **SHT** then press the Enter key.

The image tile menu appears, as shown in figure 23.8. To insert one of the blocks, choose it, and then choose OK. AutoCAD executes the appropriate script file, creates a new layer called BORDER and makes it current, and finally, inserts the block.

Figure 23.8

The new image tile menu.

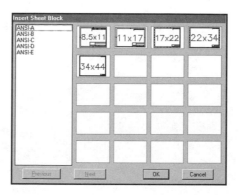

By compiling slides in a slide library, you create a convenient way to store all your slides in one file. By using slides in image tile menus, you can create a graphical user interface that enables you to quickly identify commands and script files you want to execute.

Summary

This chapter discussed using script files and creating slide libraries. You have learned how to use script files to quickly set up your working environment. You discovered how to use script files to define and load AutoLISP routines, and how to load blocks into the block table without inserting the block into the drawing. This chapter showed you how to execute script files from simple AutoLISP commands. You also have learned about image tile menus, and how to create properly scaled slides for them. You found out how to compile those slides in a slide library file. You also learned how to edit the ACAD.MNU file for use with image tile menus, and how to start a script file from an image tile menu.

By using the techniques discussed in this chapter, you can easily create simple programs with script files that can automatically perform repetitive tasks. By using image tile menus, you can quickly identify a script file graphically and start it. The examples you have seen demonstrate how you can perform repetitious tasks quickly and accurately, to increase your productivity.

INTRODUCTION TO AUTOLISP PROGRAMMING

by Michael Todd Peterson

One of AutoCAD's most powerful features is its programming interface. With support for AutoLISP, ADS, ARX, and script programming, you can customize AutoCAD to just about any degree you want.

This chapter focuses on the basics of AutoLISP; its intent is to introduce you to AutoLISP's capabilities. The chapter covers the following topics:

■ *Introducing AutoLISP*

■ *Using AutoLISP for keyboard macros*

■ *Creating a simple AutoLISP routine*

Introducing AutoLISP

AutoLISP is an interpreted language, not a compiled language. An interpreted language is one in which an interpreter converts the source code, or program, into machine language at run time. In AutoCAD's case, the interpreter is built in. A compiled language is one in which a compiler converts the source code, or program, into machine language before you can use the program. An example of a compiled language is C++, which Release 14 uses in its ARX 2.0 programming interface. Another example is C, which AutoCAD uses in the older ADS programming interface, and which it continues to make available in Release 14.

Because AutoLISP is an interpreted language, you can use any text editor you want for creating the AutoLISP routine. Then, to test the AutoLISP routine, you can load it into AutoCAD and run it. AutoLISP routines can be used to automate any of a wide variety of mundane repetitive tasks or they can be used to add functionality to AutoCAD. For example, you may find yourself repeating the same commands over and over again in the same order in your daily work. You may find it more advantageous to spend some time and write an AutoLISP routine that either automates the task or creates a new method of handling the task.

The following is a sample of a simple AutoLISP routine:

```
(defun C:ZI ()
       (command "zoom" ".5x")   ;begin zoom command and its scale
(princ)
)
```

At first, this might look confusing, but it is rather simple. All AutoLISP routines use the same basic features. The preceding routine consists of three parts: a function, a statement or expression, and a command.

A function is a command or series of commands that AutoCAD executes in a particular order. Each function must have a name, so that other functions can call it using that name. The preceding example is one function. A function is defined by the defun statement, followed by the function name. In this case, if C: is used before the function name, then that is the command you can use inside of AutoCAD to run this AutoLISP routine. So, after this AutoLISP routine is loaded, you can run it by typing in **ZI**.

Statements and expressions are a part of a larger function. An *expression* executes one single command or operation. Expressions can do anything from getting a point from the mouse to calculating the sine of an angle. In the preceding example, (command "zoom" ".5x") is the expression. In this example, command function is called. This function executes standard AutoCAD commands. This function executes the Zoom command followed by .5x.

A *command* is a call to another command or function that is either predefined in AutoLISP or predefined in your program. In this case, the (princ) statement is a command calling a predefined AutoLISP command. The princ statement is necessary to have the AutoLISP routine exit correctly without any error messages.

By combining one or more functions, you can create simple to complex AutoLISP routines that can automate many different functions inside AutoCAD.

Formatting an AutoLISP Routine

When you begin to write an AutoLISP routine, the format you write in is rather important. In the preceding example, you will notice that each part of the AutoLISP routine is divided by parentheses. The location of parentheses enables you to define which parts of the program are working at what times. The following is an example of a simple AutoLISP routine showing you how parentheses are being used:

```
(defun C:ZI ()
        (command "zoom" ".5x")
(princ)
)
```

For example, notice that the complete AutoLISP routine is contained within a set of parentheses, as highlighted in this example. A function is contained completely within parentheses as well.

Each function has the option of taking arguments. Arguments are variables that are passed to the function for use at run time. For example, if you have an AutoLISP routine that draws a ten foot long wall, the number 10 would be an argument to the function that generates the wall. Arguments are placed in the bold parentheses in the following example. An *argument* is a value that the calling function passes to the function. For the purposes of this chapter, you do not use arguments.

```
(defun C:ZI ()
        (command "zoom" ".5x")
(princ)
)
```

Then, each statement in the AutoLISP routine is separated completely with parentheses as shown in bold in the following example.

```
(defun C:ZI ()
        (command "zoom" ".5x")
(princ)
)
```

NOTE

The AutoLISP routine is organized with indentations to help clarify visually which statements are part of what commands. You could also write the preceding AutoLISP routine like this:

```
(defun C:ZI ()(command "zoom" ".5x")(princ))
```

As you can see, the first example is easier to read and keep track of.

The last thing that also helps you a great deal as a novice programmer is the addition of comments. If you start a line with a semicolon (;), the AutoLISP interpreter ignores that line. The following example has a comment in it:

```
(defun C:ZI ()
; Call the command function to execute AutoCAD commands
        (command "zoom" ".5x") ;begin zoom command and its scale
(princ)
)
```

Using comments in your programs is highly encouraged. The reason is simple. Say, for example, you write a few AutoLISP routines over the next few weeks. Then, three years from now, you decide to update and increase the functionality of those routines. Those comments in the AutoLISP routines make it much easier to remember what in the world you were doing in this or that routine. Otherwise, you probably would be better off starting from scratch.

NOTE

This chapter only scratches the surface of AutoLISP functionality. For more information on formatting and usage of AutoLISP, see the AutoCAD customization manual shipped with AutoCAD.

What's New in AutoLISP in Release 14?

 Like many other features of AutoCAD, Autodesk basically has left the AutoLISP interface unchanged. The only improvement to AutoLISP comes on the user side, not the programming side. In previous versions of AutoCAD, if you loaded or started a new drawing, AutoCAD would process the ACAD.LSP file and reload all the necessary AutoLISP routines. That's not how it works in Release 14. All the AutoLISP routines remain loaded in memory and become immediately available when the user loads or creates the drawing, resulting in much faster load times and greater productivity for users.

Now that you have an idea of AutoLISP's structure and what's new in AutoLISP in AutoCAD Release 14, you are ready for an introduction to the exact use of AutoLISP through example.

Using AutoLISP for Keyboard Macros

As you saw in Chapter 22, "Customizing without Programming," you could quickly and easily create simple keyboard macros by modifying the ACAD.PGP file. But these keyboard macros had their limitations. For example, you could execute only one command per keyboard shortcut.

In AutoCAD, many commands are combinations of smaller commands. Take, for example, the Zoom command. Before you can use the Zoom command, you must type **zoom**, and then type in an option for the command—only then will it work. In the ACAD.PGP file, you could simplify access to the Zoom command, but not the options. Here comes AutoLISP to the rescue!

You can use the AutoLISP programming interface to develop other keyboard shortcuts quickly and easily, as in the following example:

```
(defun C:ZO ()
        (command "zoom" "2x")
(princ)
)
```

In this example, you define a keyboard macro that executes with the keyboard shortcut ZO. In AutoLISP, this keyboard shortcut is defined as a function. The C:ZO indicates that you can use the ZO shortcut from inside AutoCAD to run the routine.

The (command "zoom" "2x") simply executes the commands in the order you would have to at the Command: prompt to execute the same commands. In this case, the routine enters the Zoom command, followed by the 2x option for the Zoom command.

To see how this works, the following exercise shows you how to load the AutoLISP routine and run it. The AutoLISP routine is provided on the accompanying CD-ROM as the file ZO.LSP. Alternatively, you can type this routine into your favorite text editor and save it as ZO.LSP.

LOADING AND RUNNING A SAMPLE AUTOLISP ROUTINE: ZOOM

1. Load AutoCAD and any sample drawing.

2. Choose Tools, Applications as shown in figure 24.1 to load the AutoLISP dialog box.

Figure 24.1

The Load AutoLISP, ADS, and ARX Files dialog box.

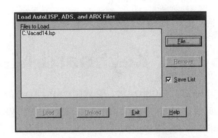

3. Click on the File button, which displays a standard Windows file selection dialog box, as shown in figure 24.2.

Figure 24.2

The Select AutoLISP, ADS, or ARX File dialog box.

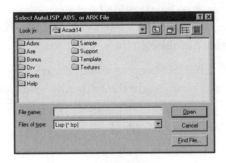

4. Select the ZO.LSP routine from the CD.

5. Click on OK to add the routine to the list.

6. Click on the Load button to load the AutoLISP routine.

7. Type **ZO** at the Command: prompt to execute the AutoLISP routine.

After you load the routine, it stays available (only if persistent AutoLISP is enabled) until you exit AutoCAD or load another routine that uses the same keyboard shortcut.

Creating a Single AutoLISP Routine for Multiple Shortcuts

As you can see, creating keyboard macros is rather easy using AutoLISP. You can generate a single AutoLISP routine to contain all your keyboard macros. Suppose, for example, you want to create a set of macros for the Zoom command and another one that sets your fillet radius to 0. As you know, if you set a radius during the Fillet command, it dumps you out, forcing you to reload it. The following example shows you an AutoLISP routine that has three keyboard shortcuts in it: two Zoom shortcuts and one Fillet shortcut. The fillet shortcut creates a fillet with a radius of 0.

```
(defun C:ZW ()
        (command "zoom" "W")
        (princ)
)
(defun C:ZE ()
        (command "zoom" "e")
        (princ)
)
(defun C:F0 ()
        (command "fillet" "r" "0" "fillet")
        (princ)
)
```

If you load this program into AutoCAD, all three keyboard macros are available to you. This AutoLISP routine is saved on the CD as IACAD142.LSP. To create other keyboard macros, simply use IACAD142.LSP as a template. All you need to know is the exact order in which you must type the commands at the Command: prompt.

Loading an AutoLISP Routine with AutoCAD

Because you have now seen several keyboard macros using AutoLISP, you probably would like to have them available every time you load AutoCAD instead of having to load them with the APPLOAD command. Well, AutoCAD provides just such an interface: the ACAD.LSP routine.

If you do not have an ACAD.LSP file on your system, you must create it. You must place this file in one of your AutoCAD library paths. Usually, the SUPPORT directory works fine.

INSIDER TIP

You may want to search your hard drive to make sure that another ACAD.LSP file is not hiding somewhere. If another ACAD.LSP file is on the system, it may get loaded instead of yours. If you find another one, you can simply add these statements to the end of that file. An easy way to find any available ACAD.LSP file is to use the following short command sequence.

At the Command: prompt type:

(findfile "acad.lsp")

This will return the name and location of the first available ACAD.LSP or nil if none are in the AutoCAD search path. It probably should be the one for you to edit.

To load an AutoLISP routine, simply add the following statement to the ACAD.LSP file:

```
(load "X:/path/LISP")
```

For the preceding statement, $X:$ is the drive where the AutoLISP routine is located, *path* is the location of the file on the hard drive, and *LISP* is the name of the AutoLISP routine without its extension. The path and drive letters are necessary if you save your AutoLISP routine in a directory other than one in the AutoCAD search path. If you do specify a path, make sure you use a forward slash instead of a backslash for specifying your directories. The file will now load automatically every time AutoCAD is loaded.

Creating a Simple AutoLISP Routine

Now that you have seen how to use AutoLISP in a simple context, it is time to look at a more complex example. The following example shows you how you can use an

AutoLISP routine to generate a single wall with BATT insulation. After the code is provided, this section walks you through the entire routine, explaining each section in detail.

The example is saved in completed form on the CD as IACAD14.LSP.

The following is the code for this example:

```
(defun dtr (a)
      (* pi (/ a 180.0))
)
(defun info ()
(setq start (getpoint "\nChoose the start point of the wall: "))
      (setq end (getpoint "\nChoose the end point of the wall: "))
      (setq width (getdist "\nEnter the width: " start))
      (setq halfwidth (/ width 2))
      (setq wallangle (angle start end))
      (setq walllength (distance start end))
      (setq arcsize (/ width 4))
      (setq perpath (+ wallangle (dtr 90)))
      (setq perpath2 (- wallangle (dtr 90)))
      (setq total 1)
      (setq arcnumber 1)
)
(defun drawwall ()
      (command "pline"
             (setq corner (polar start perpath halfwidth))
             (setq corner (polar corner wallangle walllength))
             (setq corner (polar corner perpath2 width))
             (polar corner (+ wallangle (dtr 180)) walllength)
             "close"
             )
)
(defun insulate ()
      (setq arcstart1 (polar start perpath2 (/ halfwidth 2)))
      (while (< total walllength)
             (setq arcenter1 (polar arcstart1 wallangle arcsize))
             (setq arcend1 (polar arcenter1 wallangle arcsize))
             (setq arcenter2 (polar arcend1 perpath (* 2
             ↦arcsize)))
             (setq arcstart2 (polar arcenter2 wallangle arcsize))
             (setq arcend2 (polar arcenter2 (+ wallangle (dtr
             ↦180)) arcsize))
             (command "arc" arcstart1 "c" arcenter1 arcend1)
             (command "arc" "c" arcenter2 arcstart2 arcend2)
             (command "line" arcstart2 arcend1 "")
             (command "line" arcend2 arcend1 "")
             (setq arcnumber (1+ arcnumber))
```

```
                (setq arclength (distance arcstart1 arcend1))
                (setq arcstart1 (polar arcstart1 wallangle (* 2
                ➥arcsize)))
                (setq total (* arcnumber  arclength))
        )
)
(defun C:IACAD14()
        (info)
        (drawwall)
        (insulate)
        (princ)
)
```

This AutoLISP routine is broken down into the following five functions:

■ **DTR.** Converts degrees to radians.

■ **Info.** Collects and generates information for the user.

■ **Drawwall.** Draws the outline of the wall.

■ **Insulate.** Draws the insulation in the wall.

■ **IACAD14.** Executes the routine.

Figure 24.3 shows you the result of running the AutoLISP routine.

Figure 24.3

*A wall created by
executing IACAD14.LSP.*

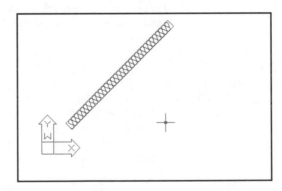

Converting Degrees to Radians with the DTR Function

The first function in the AutoLISP routine is the DTR function. Its source code follows:

```
(defun dtr (a)
     (* pi (/ a 180.0))
)
```

As you can see, it is a fairly simple little function. It is the only function that takes an argument. In this case, the argument is a. This function takes a number that is in degrees and converts it to radians. AutoLISP functions only use radians, so you must make this computation. Look at the second line of the program, which is the one that performs the calculation.

```
(* pi (/ a 180.0))
```

In this equation, pi is multiplied by a/180. In other words, when a degree measure is passed to this function, it is divided by 180 and then multiplied by pi. AutoLISP requires that you place the operator first in the equation, and then follow it with the first and second arguments.

So, the first operator is an asterisk (*), which is multiplication. The first argument is pi, which is 3.14159. Pi is a predefined value in AutoLISP because it gets used so often. Then, in the parentheses, you have the second argument, which is another equation. In this case, the operator is a slash (/), which is division. The first argument is a, the passed variable, and the second argument is 180.0. (180.0 includes the decimal point to ensure accurate floating-point calculations.)

This function is used throughout the AutoLISP routine to calculate the radian equivalent of degrees. As it happens, this is necessary to calculate the angle at which your wall is running.

Gathering Information with the Info Function

The second function in the AutoLISP routine is the information gathering function. In this function, all the necessary information for the routine is gathered or calculated. The following is the info function:

```
(defun info ()
     (setq start (getpoint "\nChoose the start point of the wall: "))
          (setq end (getpoint "\nChoose the end point of the wall: "))
          (setq width (getdist "\nEnter the width: " start))
```

```
(setq halfwidth (/ width 2))
(setq wallangle (angle start end))
(setq walllength (distance start end))
(setq arcsize (/ width 4))
(setq perpath (+ wallangle (dtr 90)))
(setq perpath2 (- wallangle (dtr 90)))
(setq total 1)
(setq arcnumber 1)
)
```

In this function, you set 11 different statements, or expressions. In AutoLISP, you can have something called a variable. A *variable* has a value assigned to it. Each of the 11 statements assigns a value to a different variable for use later in the program. Some statements assign a simple numeric value, whereas others assign the result of a mathematical equation to the variable. Take the first expression for example:

```
(setq start (getpoint "\nChoose the start point of the wall: "))
```

In this statement, you have an AutoLISP command called setq, which is the command to set a variable to a specific value. In this case, the variable is called start. In the parentheses, you have another AutoLISP command called getpoint. The getpoint command returns the x, y, and z coordinates of a mouse click.

The \n is a control code character. Any expression that uses a slash (\) has a control code character after it. In this case, the n represents the newline character. The information following the \n simply prints to the AutoCAD Command: prompt area. Figure 24.4 shows you the Command: prompt area when you run the IACAD14.LSP file and reach this point.

Figure 24.4

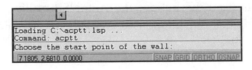

The Command: prompt at the start of the AutoLISP routine.

This statement asks the user to choose the start point of the wall with the mouse or by typing in the coordinates. The x, y, and z coordinates of the start point of the wall are assigned to the variable start.

INSIDER TIP

When you have run the wall routine inside AutoCAD, you can check the value of the variable start. At the Command: prompt, simply type **!start**. This applies to all variables created in this AutoLISP routine. Simply type in an exclamation point followed by the variable name, and AutoCAD displays the value of that variable. A nil value means nothing has been assigned to the variable. Remember this technique—it's invaluable in debugging the program.

The next line of the AutoLISP routine gets the endpoint of the wall in the same manner and assigns it to the variable end. But, the third line does something a little different. The following is the third expression in the function:

```
(setq width (getdist "\nEnter the width: " start))
```

Here, the routine prompts the user for the width of the wall and assigns it to the variable width. What is different here is the getdist command. The getdist command calculates the distance between a chosen point and a stored point. In this case, the width of the wall is defined by the user choosing a point on the screen with the mouse. AutoCAD calculates the distance between that point and the start point of the wall and stores it in the width variable. That is why the start variable appears at the end of this statement.

The fourth statement also does something a little different. The fourth statement is as follows:

```
(setq halfwidth (/ width 2))
```

In this statement, a variable called halfwidth is assigned to the result of an equation. Here, the variable width is divided by 2 and assigned to halfwidth. Later in the AutoLISP routine, it will be necessary to know the halfwidth of the wall.

The fifth statement uses a slight variation on the fourth statement to assign a value to another variable. The fifth statement is as follows:

```
(setq wallangle (angle start end))
```

This line defines the wallangle variable. The angle command calculates the angle between two points, in this case, the start point and the end point of the wall. This value is then assigned to the wallangle variable.

The next two statements in the AutoLISP routine are simple variations. But, look at the eighth statement. Here, the variable perpath is assigned a value. The statement is as follows:

```
(setq perpath (- wallangle (dtr 90)))
```

Here, you are again assigning the result of an equation to a variable. In this case, you are calling another function. Notice the dtr 90 statement in parentheses. This function calculates the angle that is perpendicular to the angle of the wall. In this case, 90 degrees is sent to the dtr function and converted to radians. In the dtr equation, the 90 degrees takes the place of the a variable, which is then added to the wallangle value and assigned to the perpath variable.

The ninth statement performs a function similar to that of the eighth statement, except that it calculates the perpendicular angle in the opposite direction. So, a – operator is used instead of a +.

The tenth and eleventh statements are sometimes called *initialization statements*. All they do is initialize a variable to a value, so that it is not nil. In this case, the total and arcnumber variables are initialized to 1. Why this is done becomes evident later in the routine. Each statement appears as follows:

```
(setq total 1)
(setq arcnumber 1)
```

That completes the info routine. When the AutoLISP routine runs the info routine, either the user inputs or AutoCAD calculates all necessary information. Now, it is time to actually begin drawing the wall. There are two parts to the wall drawing routine. The first part draws the outline of the wall. The second part draws the insulation inside the wall. By far, drawing the insulation is the hardest part of the routine.

Drawing the Wall Outline with the Drawwall Function

The wall outline is handled by the drawwall function. The listing for the drawwall function is as follows:

```
(defun drawwall ()
        (command "pline"
                (setq corner (polar start perpath halfwidth))
                (setq corner (polar corner wallangle walllength))
                (setq corner (polar corner perpath2 width))
                (polar corner (+ wallangle (dtr 180)) walllength)
                "close"
                )
        )
```

In this function, you simply execute a drawing command and calculate all the necessary points. Notice the first statement of function. It is as follows:

```
(command "pline"
```

This statement simply runs the PLINE command. So, the outline of the wall is generated as a polyline. The second statement draws the first point of the polyline. The second statement also assigns that point to a variable called corner. The statement is as follows:

```
(setq corner (polar start perpath halfwidth))
```

In this statement, the variable corner is set to a calculated value. In the parentheses, a polar coordinate is set up. The command polar means you will be using polar coordinate entry methods. So, you have to provide a starting point, an angle, and a distance. In this case, the starting point is the start point of the line, or the start variable. The angle is perpendicular to the wall angle. The distance is half the width of the wall, or the halfwidth variable.

The next statement draws the second part of the line. The statement is as follows:

```
(setq corner (polar corner wallangle walllength))
```

Here, the corner variable is redefined. But, before it is redefined, it is used to calculate the new variable. Again, you are drawing another polyline using a polar coordinate method of entering points. Here, the start point is the corner variable from the previous equation. The angle is now the angle of the wall, or the wallangle variable. This line is drawn to the exact length of the wall, as defined in the walllength variable.

The routine continues over the next two lines to draw the rest of the outline of the wall. The last statement of the routine is simply the close statement to create a closed polyline.

After you draw the outline of the wall, you can begin to draw the insulation inside. The AutoLISP routine contains a function called insulate to draw the insulation. But, before learning about that routine, you should be aware of how the insulation is going to be drawn.

Insulating the Wall

The insulation in the wall is drawn from two different drawing elements: an arc and a line. By drawing arcs up and down both sides and connecting the endpoints, you can create the insulation. The only question is the order in which they are drawn.

Take, for example, the wall shown in figure 24.5. The insulation routine begins by drawing an arc at the lower-right corner of the wall.

Figure 24.5

In this example wall, the insulation routine will start at the lower-right corner of the wall.

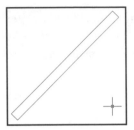

To draw an arc, you must calculate three points. These points will be defined in the routine as arcstart1, arcenter1, and arcend1. Figure 24.6 shows you a blowup of the lower-right corner, with the arc already drawn using the start point of the wall, arcstart1, arcenter1, and arcend1.

Figure 24.6

The example wall with the first arc.

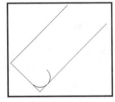

First, the routine must calculate the location of the arcstart1 point. Then, you can simply draw the arc. But, how large an arc should you draw?

When this routine draws insulation, it is dynamic because it will adjust the size of the insulation to match the width of the wall. This is handled by setting the arcsize to be ¼ the width of the wall. If you look back to the info routine, you will see an arcsize variable that calculates this information.

Because an arc is nothing more than a segment of a circle, you can easily calculate the arcenter1 and arcend1 points. You just calculate a point that is one arcsize unit away from the arcstart1 point in the same direction of the wall. You calculate the arcend1 point by using twice the arcsize value. Hence, the arc is drawn.

The next item to draw in the insulation is the arc on the other side of the wall. To make this arc, you first need to find its start point. To make the insulation look good, you can place the start point of the second arc perpendicular to the center point of the first arc, as shown in figure 24.7.

Figure 24.7

The example wall with two arcs.

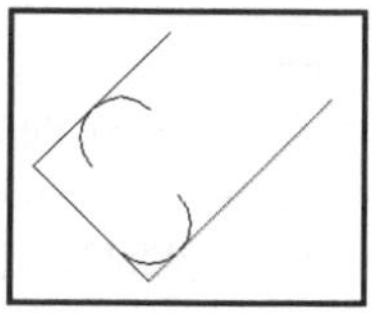

After you calculate the position of the start point of the second arc, you can use a similar routine to calculate the center and end points of the second arc. You can save each of these points to variables named arcstart2, arcenter2, and arcend2.

After you have the second arc, all you have to do is connect the start and end points of the second arc to the end point of the first arc, as shown in figure 24.8.

Figure 24.8

The example wall with two arcs and two lines.

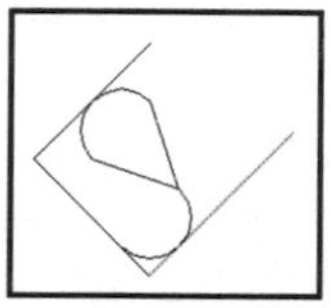

Now, to make that routine repeat, start the first arc next to the previous first arc. Figure 24.9 shows you the wall after the second run of the routine.

Figure 24.9

The example wall after two runs.

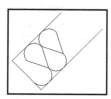

Now that you are repeating the same commands, you must figure out when to stop; otherwise, you will be creating insulation forever.

An easy way to calculate when to stop drawing insulation is to keep track of the number of first arcs that you create. Then, you can calculate the distance from the start point to the end point of the first arc. If you multiply those numbers together, you will get the overall length of the insulation. If you compare the length of the insulation to the length of the wall, you can calculate when to stop the insulation routine.

NOTE

This insulation routine represents one of many different ways you could go about setting up this routine. When you finish this chapter, you may try different methods of creating the insulation to get more practice with AutoLISP programming.

Creating Code for the Insulation Routine

Now that you have an idea of how this insulation routine is going to work, you are ready to look at the code. The code for the insulation routine is as follows:

```
(defun insulate ()
       (setq arcstart1 (polar start perpath2 (/ halfwidth 2)))
       (while (< total walllength)
              (setq arcenter1 (polar arcstart1 wallangle arcsize))
              (setq arcend1 (polar arcenter1 wallangle arcsize))
              (setq arcenter2 (polar arcend1 perpath (* 2
              ➥arcsize)))
              (setq arcstart2 (polar arcenter2 wallangle arcsize))
              (setq arcend2 (polar arcenter2 (+ wallangle (dtr
              ➥180)) arcsize))
              (command "arc" arcstart1 "c" arcenter1 arcend1)
              (command "arc" "c" arcenter2 arcstart2 arcend2)
              (command "line" arcstart2 arcend1 "")
              (command "line" arcend2 arcend1 "")
              (setq arcnumber (1+ arcnumber))
              (setq arclength (distance arcstart1 arcend1))
              (setq arcstart1 (polar arcstart1 wallangle (* 2
              ➥arcsize)))
              (setq total (* arcnumber  arclength))
       )
)
```

The first statement in the insulate routine calculates the start point of the first arc. This statement should look familiar to you by now. The only thing to notice is the distance in the polar command. It is calculated at half of the halfwidth. So, the first start point is halfway between the start point of the wall and the corner, as shown in figure 24.10.

Figure 24.10

*The start point of the
first arc.*

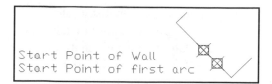

Now that you have the starting point, you are ready to set up the repeating loop. In this case, a while statement will be used. A while statement works by evaluating an equation. As long as the equation is true, the statements inside the while loop will repeat. When the statement becomes false, the loop is broken and the program moves on. The following statements are inside the while loop:

```
(while (< total walllength)
        (setq arcenter1 (polar arcstart1 wallangle arcsize))
        (setq arcend1 (polar arcenter1 wallangle arcsize))
        (setq arcenter2 (polar arcend1 perpath (* 2
   ➡arcsize)))
        (setq arcstart2 (polar arcenter2 wallangle arcsize))
        (setq arcend2 (polar arcenter2 (+ wallangle (dtr
   ➡180)) arcsize))
        (command "arc" arcstart1 "c" arcenter1 arcend1)
        (command "arc" "c" arcenter2 arcstart2 arcend2)
        (command "line" arcstart2 arcend1 "")
        (command "line" arcend2 arcend1 "")
        (setq arcnumber (1+ arcnumber))
        (setq arclength (distance arcstart1 arcend1))
        (setq arcstart1 (polar arcstart1 wallangle (* 2
   ➡arcsize)))
        (setq total (* arcnumber arclength))
```

The first five statements of the while loop calculate the other points necessary to draw the first two arcs. The next four statements draw two arcs, followed by two lines.

Notice in the drawing routines, especially the arc routines, that familiarity with how the arc routine works is important. In the first arc statement, the command arc is executed and the first point is entered. The center option is chosen before the second point is entered.

At this point, you should be able to decipher what is happening in the first nine statements of this function. Next, the arcnumber value is initialized and set. This value counts how many times you run through this routine. Each time you run through the routine, you create one first arc.

The next statement calculates the arclength by calculating the distance between the start and end points of the first arc. Now that you have the arcnumber and the length of the arcs, you can calculate the overall length of the insulation. Notice the last statement of the routine. That is precisely what happens. In the while loop, the variable total is compared to the walllength. If the total variable is less than the walllength variable, the routine will be run again. Otherwise, the routine is ended.

Now, one statement has been skipped. This statement is as follows:

```
(setq arcstart1 arcend1)
```

This statement calculates the position of the start point of the first arc for the next run through of the insulation routine. In this case, the value is set to the end point of the first arc. So, the next time the routine starts, it will begin drawing at the point shown in figure 24.11.

Figure 24.11

The example wall showing the second loop start point.

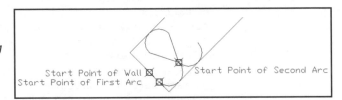

Running the Functions with the IACAD14 Command

All but one of the necessary functions in the AutoLISP routine has been completed. The last function is the easiest; it is the function that runs all the other functions. The code listing is as follows:

```
(defun C:IACAD14()
        (info)
        (drawwall)
        (insulate)
        (princ)
)
```

As you can see, with the use of the C:, this routine is started by the IACAD14 command in AutoCAD, after the routine is loaded. Then, each function is called in the appropriate order. First, you collect the information, so the info routine is called. Second, you draw the outline of the wall, so the drawwall function is called. Third, you call the insulate routine to draw the insulation inside of the wall. Last, you call the princ function to enable the AutoLISP routine to exit gracefully without any errors.

Adding a Dialog Box to an AutoLISP Routine

The IACAD14 routine is fairly decent at this point. But, if you have worked in the Windows environment, you are probably used to being able to type most, if not all, the necessary information for the routine in a dialog box.

Adding one or more dialog boxes to an AutoLISP routine is not necessary, but it makes the routine look more professional and, in many cases, makes the routine easy to use and run.

INSIDER TIP

You should strive to have your AutoLISP routine up and working properly with keyboard entry before you begin to add dialog boxes to it. This makes it easier to debug the routine if errors crop up because of the additional code necessary to create the dialog box(es).

AutoCAD provides you with many tools for creating a dialog box for an AutoLISP routine. But, before you begin to create the dialog box, you must analyze your routine and decide what data the user enters for the routine to work is appropriate for inclusion in the dialog box.

```
(defun info ()
    (setq start (getpoint "\nChoose the start point of the wall: "))
        (setq end (getpoint "\nChoose the end point of the wall: "))
        (setq width (getdist "\nEnter the width: " start))
        (setq halfwidth (/ width 2))
        (setq wallangle (angle start end))
        (setq walllength (distance start end))
        (setq arcsize (/ width 4))
        (setq perpath (+ wallangle (dtr 90)))
        (setq perpath2 (- wallangle (dtr 90)))
        (setq total 1)
        (setq arcnumber 1)
    )
```

The Info routine from IACAD14 shows you all the information that is necessary for the routine to work. As you can see, the user must supply the start and end points of the wall, as well as the overall width of the wall. The start and end points are implemented as getpoint, which requires the user to select a point on the screen with the mouse. The only other information the user supplies is the width of the wall. All three of these items are good candidates for inclusion in the dialog box.

Deciding which information should be retrieved from the user through a dialog box is solely up to you. You may run across instances in which using a dialog box may prove to be cumbersome or unnecessary because it slows down the use of the routine. For example, the ZI function discussed earlier in this chapter is not a good candidate for a dialog box. There isn't any user input. A command such as ZW zoom window is not good either. ZW requires the user to select the two corner points to perform the Zoom Window option. Using a dialog box here would be a waste of time.

Dialog boxes are implemented in a second file called a DCL file. This file is written in a slightly different syntax, called the *Dialog Control Language*. What is nice about this dialog language is that it is shared between AutoLISP, ADS, and ARX for creating dialog boxes. The following code segment is necessary for the dialog box you are going to create for this example. Figure 24.12 shows you the resulting dialog box in AutoCAD 14.

Figure 24.12

The Demonstration dialog box created from the code that immediately follows this figure.

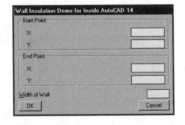

```
cad_box : dialog {
        label = "Wall Insulation Demo for Inside AutoCAD 14";
        : boxed_column {
        label = "Start Point";
                : edit_box {
                        label = "   X:";
                        key = "spx";
                        edit_width = 10;
                        }
                : edit_box {
                        label = "   Y:";
                        key = "spy";
                        edit_width = 10;
                        }
            }
        : boxed_column {
        label = "End Point";
                : edit_box {
                        label = "   X:";
```

```
                                  key = "epx";
                                  edit_width = 10;
                                  }
                        : edit_box {
                                  label = "   Y:";
                                  key = "epy";
                                  edit_width = 10;
                                  }
               }
        : edit_box {
                 label = "&Width of Wall";
                 key = "ww";
                 edit_width = 6;
                 }
        :row{
        : button {
                 label = "OK";
                 key = "accept";
                 width = 8;
                 fixed_width = true;
                 }
        : button {
                 label = "Cancel";
                 is_cancel = true;
                 key = "cancel";
                 width = 8;
                 fixed_width = true;
                 }
        }
   }
```

As you can see, the code for the dialog box looks fairly complex, but it is rather simple to use. The DCL language is very similar to C or C++ in terms of syntax. Brackets surround almost all commands {}. For example, the following code segment shows you one single item in the list.

```
   : button {
                 label = "Cancel";
                 is_cancel = true;
                 key = "cancel";
                 width = 8;
                 fixed_width = true;
                 }
```

As you might guess, this creates a button on the dialog box. Between the brackets are the options for the button, such as width, label, and most importantly, the *key value*. The key value is like a variable in a function in AutoLISP. The key is used to access the data stored in the dialog box. This particular button is the Cancel button.

Let's break down the code for this dialog box succinctly.

```
cad_box : dialog {
        label = "Wall Insulation Demo for Inside AutoCAD 14";
```

The first two lines of the DCL file used in this chapter are shown in the preceding code. The first line: cad_box : dialog is where you give the dialog box a name to call from your AutoLISP routine, in this case, cad_box. The second line is the label, which is the text that shows in the title bar of the dialog box. These two are always required for a dialog box. Everything else is optional for you to use, except for an OK button. You must always include an OK button to give the user a method for exiting the dialog box.

AutoCAD provides you with a set of predefined dialog box parts (called DCL tiles) that you may use. These include items such as text boxes, radio buttons, plain text, and so on. For the dialog box in this example, you will make use of two boxed columns (the start and end point sections of the dialog box) and two buttons. The following is the code for the Start Point section of the dialog box:

```
: boxed_column {
      label = "Start Point";
            : edit_box {
                    label = "   X:";
                    key = "spx";
                    edit_width = 10;
                    }
            : edit_box {
                    label = "   Y:";
                    key = "spy";
                    edit_width = 10;
                    }
      }
```

At the top of the code segment, you will find the boxed column command. Like the dialog box, each boxed column can have its own label, in this case, Start Point. Below that, you see two edit box entries and their properties. The edit boxes give you the type in fields in the dialog box. Each edit box has a label, key value, and width. Additional properties are available if you need them.

NOTE

Refer to the AutoCAD documentation for more on the additional properties of these or any other dialog box feature not covered in this chapter.

Make sure that you note the use of the brackets in this particular code segment. Each edit box has its own set of brackets, as does the boxed column (which contains the edit boxes within its own brackets).

The End Point section is exactly the same. Another edit box is also added to the dialog box, but not inside of a boxed column. This is the width field, as shown in figure 24.12. The last two entries in the code are the OK and Cancel buttons, which are handled very much like the edit boxes.

If you will notice, in the code, AutoCAD creates the dialog box in the order in which the items are presented in the DCL file. You can further control these items by using additional commands such as Column to help lay out the actual location of the DCL tiles.

After you create the code for the dialog box, you must save it in a separate file from the AutoLISP routine with a DCL extension. The file must be located in a directory that is part of the AutoCAD support path or AutoCAD will not be able to load the dialog box. You can control support paths under the Preferences command.

After you save the file, you must add the necessary code and change your AutoLISP routine to make use of the new dialog box.

NOTE

You may need to add the reference to the DCL file to your AutoLISP routine before you get too far into developing the dialog box. You will have to use your AutoLISP routine to access the dialog box and see what it looks like at any given point.

Integrating the Dialog Box Code into the AutoLISP Routine

The following is the wall insulation routine with the new code for the dialog box. New code is shown in bold.

```
(defun dtr (a
        (* pi (/ a 180.0))
)
(defun info ()
        (setq start (list (atof spx) (atof spy) 0.0))
        (setq end (list (atof epx) (atof epy) 0.0))
        (setq width (atof ww))
        (setq halfwidth (/ width 2))
        (setq wallangle (angle start end))
        (setq walllength (distance start end))
        (setq arcsize (/ width 4))
        (setq perpath (+ wallangle (dtr 90)))
        (setq perpath2 (- wallangle (dtr 90)))
        (setq total 1)
        (setq arcnumber 1)
)
(defun drawwall ()
        (command "pline"
                (setq corner (polar start perpath halfwidth))
                (setq corner (polar corner wallangle walllength))
                (setq corner (polar corner perpath2 width))
                (polar corner (+ wallangle (dtr 180)) walllength)
                "close"
                )
)
(defun insulate ()
        (setq arcstart1 (polar start perpath2 (/ halfwidth 2)))
        (while (< total walllength)
                (setq arcenter1 (polar arcstart1 wallangle arcsize))
                (setq arcend1 (polar arcenter1 wallangle arcsize))
                (setq arcenter2 (polar arcend1 perpath (* 2
                ➥arcsize)))
                (setq arcstart2 (polar arcenter2 wallangle arcsize))
```

```
                    (setq arcend2 (polar arcenter2 (+ wallangle (dtr
                    ➥180)) arcsize))
                    (command "arc" arcstart1 "c" arcenter1 arcend1)
                    (command "arc" "c" arcenter2 arcstart2 arcend2)
                    (command "line" arcstart2 arcend1 "")
                    (command "line" arcend2 arcend1 "")
                    (setq arcnumber (1+ arcnumber))
                    (setq arclength (distance arcstart1 arcend1))
                    (setq arcstart1 (polar arcstart1 wallangle (* 2
                    ➥arcsize)))
                    (setq total (* arcnumber  arclength))
            )
    )
    (defun dialdefaults()
            (if (not spx) (setq spx 0.0))
            (if (not spy) (setq spy 0.0))
            (if (not epx) (setq epx 0.0))
            (if (not epy) (setq epy 0.0))
            (if (not ww) (setq ww 0.0))
            (set_tile "spx" (rtos spx))
            (set_tile "spy" (rtos spy))
            (set_tile "epx" (rtos epx))
            (set_tile "epy" (rtos epy))
            (set_tile "ww" (rtos ww))
    )
    (defun CADDIAL ()
            (setq dcl_id  (load_dialog "iacad14.dcl"))
            (if (not (new_dialog "cad_box" dcl_id))(exit))
            (dialdefaults)
            (action_tile "spx" "(setq spx (get_tile \"spx\"))")
            (action_tile "spy" "(setq spy (get_tile \"spy\"))")
            (action_tile "epx" "(setq epx (get_tile \"epx\"))")
            (action_tile "epy" "(setq epy (get_tile \"epy\"))")
            (action_tile "ww" "(setq ww (get_tile \"ww\"))")
            (action_tile "cancel" "(done_dialog)")
            (action_tile "accept" "(info)(done_dialog)")
            (start_dialog)
            (princ)

    )

    (defun C:ddia ( / spx spy spz epx epy epz ww)
            (caddial)
            (drawwall)
            (insulate)
            (princ)
    )
```

As you can see from the code listing, quite a bit of code was added to make the dialog box work. Let's break each new section down, in order of execution. First, the main routine of the program:

```
(defun C:ddia ( / spx spy spz epx epy epz ww)
        (caddial)
        (drawwall)
        (insulate)
        (princ)
)
```

The function name has been changed from IACAD14 to DDIA, which is easier to type in and also to add the DD to indicate a dialog box is now being used. (DD is not necessary; it is just standard practice in AutoCAD.)

In the earlier version of this part of the routine, empty braces followed the command. This is not the case in the modified routine. You will notice a / followed by variables. This simply indicates that the variables listed after the / are available only when this particular function is running. If you try to create this routine without limiting the scope where these variables are used, you will only be able to run the routine once per session of AutoCAD.

To make use of dialog boxes and edit boxes, you must enter information as text strings. But, AutoCAD wants to have the numbers you enter as text strings in floating point format, so later, you must convert from one to the other. If you let the variables listed after the / be available after the routine has run, they will be in the wrong format the next time you run the routine and will cause an error. You will see more about this problem later in the chapter.

Notice that the DDIA command now calls a function called caddial (CAD Dialog) now instead of Info. Let's take a look at this new function.

```
(defun CADDIAL ()
        (setq dcl_id  (load_dialog "iacad14.dcl"))
        (if (not (new_dialog "cad_box" dcl_id))(exit))
        (dialdefaults)
        (action_tile "spx" "(setq spx (get_tile \"spx\"))")
        (action_tile "spy" "(setq spy (get_tile \"spy\"))")
        (action_tile "epx" "(setq epx (get_tile \"epx\"))")
        (action_tile "epy" "(setq epy (get_tile \"epy\"))")
        (action_tile "ww" "(setq ww (get_tile \"ww\"))")
        (action_tile "cancel" "(done_dialog)")
        (action_tile "accept" "(info)(done_dialog)")
```

```
(start_dialog)
(princ)

)
```

Caddial is the main function for creating and handling the dialog box. Notice the first two lines of code in the function. The first line loads the DCL file and assigns its ID (which is defined by AutoCAD at run time) to a variable called dcl_id. The second line verifies that the id is unique, or else the routine exits. Only under rare circumstances will the system incorrectly assign an id and cause and exit here. These two lines plus the (start_dialog) line are all that are necessary to make the dialog box appear. But, additional code is necessary to make the dialog box functional. For each DCL tile (button or text box) in the dialog box, you must assign an event handler so AutoCAD knows what to do with the information the user places in the dialog box.

In the caddial function, this is handled in two ways. First, a function called dialdefaults is called to set all of the tiles in the dialog box to some default value, in this case 0. The following code segment shows you the dialdefaults function.

```
(defun dialdefaults()
       (if (not spx) (setq spx 0.0))
       (if (not spy) (setq spy 0.0))
       (if (not epx) (setq epx 0.0))
       (if (not epy) (setq epy 0.0))
       (if (not ww) (setq ww 0.0))
       )
```

The first five lines of the dialdefaults function set the variables spx, spy, epx, epy, and ww to a default of 0.0, if they are not already defined. Spx and spy are the start point x and y values. Epx and epy are the end point x and y values. Ww is the width variable. After the defaults are set, the control of the routine is returned back to the caddial function.

After the control is returned back to caddial, each tile of the dialog box has a handler created, such as the one shown in the following code fragment.

```
(action_tile "spx" "(setq spx (get_tile \"spx\"))")
```

Here, the command action_tile is used to control what happens when the user enters or makes use of that particular tile. In this case, the tile is the spx tile. If you look back at the DCL file code, find the tile entry with a value named "spx." This is the edit box referred to here. If the user enters any value into the x coordinate start point box, when he leaves the box by clicking somewhere else in the dialog box, or pressing Tab, the second part of the action_tile command is executed.

Here, the value the user typed in is retrieved from the dialog box by the get_tile function and assigned to the variable spx. You may notice the unusual syntax of the get_tile command. This is necessary because of the way the action_tile command works.

An action_tile command is created for all seven tiles in the dialog box. After the action commands are defined, the dialog box is actually started with (start_dialog), which is the last command of the caddial function.

At this point, you may be wondering how the routine proceeds. The answer is in the OK button and Cancel button action_tiles. The Cancel button action_tile command, as shown in the following code, calls the (done_dialog) command, which terminates the routine.

```
(action_tile "cancel" "(done_dialog)")
(action_tile "accept" "(info)(done_dialog)")
```

The OK button, which has a key value of "accept," calls the info routine (which you defined earlier in this chapter), and then calls the done_dialog command to exit the dialog box.

All that is left to complete the sequence is to assign the dialog box values to the variables used in the rest of the routine. This is handled in the first three lines of the Info function:

```
(setq start (list (atof spx) (atof spy) 0.0))
(setq end (list (atof epx) (atof epy) 0.0))
(setq width (atof ww))
```

Here, you will notice that the start, end, and width variables used in the rest of the program are defined. Before, user input at the Command: prompt handled these. Now, the values are coming from the dialog box.

A dialog box can only make use of text strings, so each variable from the dialog box must be converted from text to a numerical format—in this case, floating point. The atof command stands for ASCII to Floating Point, which converts the numbers the user typed in into actual coordinates the system can use. Notice the use of the list command. This is necessary to create the start variable as a point in AutoCAD (which is defined by three coordinates). AutoCAD stores points as a list. So, by creating a list of the x, y, and z points and assigning them to the start variable, the routine can correctly process the rest of the commands and create the geometry.

As you can see from the additions necessary to make a dialog box work in AutoLISP, it may not always be to your benefit to create a dialog box. Even the dialog box created in this chapter has limited uses, because the user must type in the start and end point x and y values.

Going Further

For some practice on your own, do a little research in the AutoCAD customization documentation and see if you can add a Pick button that enables you to quickly pick the point on the screen and return you back to the dialog box where the point you picked will be displayed in the edit boxes. For an example of how to do this, check out BMAKE.LSP in the Support directory of AutoCAD.

There are many features that you can make use of in a dialog box in AutoCAD. This section only covered a few basic ones. Explore the documentation shipped with AutoCAD, which is much more in-depth than what is possible to cover in one chapter here.

Error Handling

The last thing to talk about when creating an AutoLISP routine is error handling. This is one of the more important aspects of writing a good AutoLISP routine. Take the routine you have been studying in this chapter, for example. Think about what could go wrong with it, either due to the way you coded it, or how the user will make use of it. If something does go wrong, how will you handle it?

A good example of an error handling routine might be to check and verify that the coordinates typed in by the user are valid coordinates that can be used by the routine. There are any number of methods to implement this type of error checking. All of them are too involved to cover in this chapter.

When you write a good routine, up to one half or more of the actual code written can be dedicated to correct error handling. Most of the time, this will come from testing and more testing of the routine to find its limitations.

NOTE

Error handling is very important in a routine. The one shown in this chapter is functional, but not really error-proof. This is too complex to cover in this book. Read the AutoCAD documentation sections devoted to error handling to get an idea of how to use it. Then, study the AutoLISP routines shipped with AutoCAD. There are many examples of error handling in each one.

Limitations on the Sample AutoLISP Routine

For all the neat things this routine does, it does have a few limitations. They are:

■ The routine will not draw any insulation if the wall is less than 1 unit long. This occurs because the total variable that is used in the while loop is initialized to 1 before the loop is run. Because a wall that is less than 1 unit long produces a walllength variable of less than one, you never enter the loop. The solution here is to initialize the variable to a value small enough to always be less than the shortest wall length. You must, however, initialize the total variable to some value. Otherwise, AutoCAD will give you a bad function error when it tries to compare the walllength variable to nothing.

■ Depending on the length of the wall, sometimes a part of the insulation may end up outside of the wall. This happens because the length of the insulation is calculated on the lower row of arcs while the upper row is shifted and can sometimes end up outside of the wall. The solution here is to rewrite how the length of the insulation is calculated to include the upper and lower arc rows. This is left as an exercise for you to try on your own.

■ The routine draws all the lines on the current layer. You can set it up to draw the lines on specific layers. Simply add command sequences to change the current layer before the draw portion of the program. Again, this solution is left to you as an exercise.

■ When the routine is running, you will probably notice command after command running by at the Command: prompt. For some people, this is annoying. You can disable this by modifying the IACAD14 routine to turn off the cmdecho system variable before running the routine and turning the system variable back on after the routine is finished. Again, this is left up to you as an exercise.

- The routine's dialog box is rather cumbersome and not particularly useful for the AutoLISP routine. You can modify it to make it more useful or simply get rid of it.

- There isn't any error checking in the routine. There is nothing to stop the user from entering coordinates of AA,BB and having the routine try to work with it. The AutoLISP routine should stop and notify the user if the coordinates are not valid and prompt him to enter the coordinates again in the correct format.

As you can see, you can take an AutoLISP routine and keep adding functionality to it. But, the language is easy enough for you to write simple routines such as this.

INSIDER TIP

Don't expect to be able to write this routine in a couple of hours and don't expect it to work perfectly the first time. This routine took 4.5 hours to develop and about 20 changes to the source code before it worked correctly every time. But, as you can see, this 4.5 hours can be well spent if you can spare it. Eventually, you will save that much time by using this routine.

Summary

The AutoLISP programming interface is a simple but powerful method for you to customize AutoCAD. If you need customized routines, you should consider developing these routines in-house for you to use. If you use the routines a lot, you can load them every time AutoCAD loads by using an ACAD.LSP file. The only question is whether or not you can justify the amount of time necessary to develop the routine.

For many people, they cannot justify the time, or are simply not interested in programming AutoCAD. Fortunately, a whole industry has developed around the prospect of developing custom software for AutoCAD. These products are commonly called third-party products and can significantly enhance the productivity of AutoCAD.

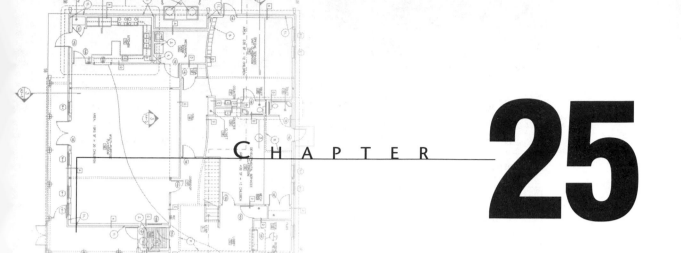

ACTIVEX AUTOMATION

by Surya Sarda

ActiveX Automation is a new feature in AutoCAD Release 14. Using this feature, you can customize AutoCAD and create powerful custom applications by combining AutoCAD objects with objects available from other applications that support ActiveX Automation. With ActiveX Automation, you can develop macros and custom applications by using modern, standard, user-friendly languages such as Visual Basic 5.0. These tools enable you to automate repetitive tasks (such as parameterized part creation). Using ActiveX Automation, you can automatically generate a bill of materials from an AutoCAD drawing file, create an Excel spreadsheet, build a chart, put the chart in a Microsoft Word memo, or mail or fax it—all in one relatively simple application using objects that the different applications expose.

You can create and manipulate AutoCAD objects from any application that serves as an ActiveX Automation controller. Besides Visual Basic 5.0, some of the other popular Automation controllers are Microsoft Visual C++ and Delphi. AutoCAD Automation works with the popular Automation controllers Visual Basic 5.0 and Microsoft Visual C++, but does not work with Delphi.

For simplicity, this chapter refers to AutoCAD ActiveX Automation as *Automation*. As you read this chapter and use Automation, some previous understanding of Visual Basic or programming would be helpful. This chapter covers the following topics:

- Introduction to Automation
- Object Browser and online help
- Writing your first Automation program
- Using Automation with AutoCAD
- Using Automation with other applications

Introducing ActiveX Automation

ActiveX Automation (previously called *OLE Automation*) is a technology developed by Microsoft. AutoCAD ActiveX Automation features provide a modern alternative to AutoLISP, although AutoLISP has a rich set of features and Automation is not intended to replace it. The most popular Automation controller is Visual Basic. Because the exposed objects are accessible from any macro language or tool that can access Automation objects, you can choose a tool based on your current knowledge (rather than learn a new language, such as AutoLISP, for each application).

Programming in Visual Basic is relatively easy. After you learn to program one application in Visual Basic, you can build on this knowledge to program any other application. Visual Basic provides standard functions (such as the math and string-manipulation functions). You have to learn only the AutoCAD-specific functions, and thus can focus on the functionality of your application rather than on the intricacies of the specific macro language. The Automation interface for AutoCAD resembles the Automation interface for Excel and Access. If you already know Excel or Access macro programming, learning AutoCAD Automation programming will be easy.

Visual Basic provides a user-friendly environment for creating a Graphical User Interface (GUI) or front end for your programs. Instead of using AutoCAD Dialog Control Language, you can use Visual Basic to develop the entire user interface. You cannot, however, use Visual Basic to replace AutoCAD dialog boxes or to add new dialog boxes in AutoCAD.

In addition to the languages mentioned earlier (VB and C++), you can use Microsoft Visual Basic for Applications (VBA) as an Automation controller. Microsoft Office 97 components include VBA. As this chapter is being written, more than 50 VBA licenses exist. This number will continue to grow as more and more applications adopt VBA. AutoCAD Release 14 includes a preview version of the program. AutoCAD's VBA is identical to the one in Office 97—except for one major difference: AutoCAD VBA is embedded in AutoCAD and runs *in-process*. This feature helps improve the performance of your applications substantially when they interact with AutoCAD objects. The other advantage of using AutoCAD VBA is that you can use the Automation feature without purchasing full-featured Visual Basic software.

Now that you know what Automation is used for, it is important to cover some of the basic Automation-related terms and definitions that appear throughout the chapter.

Terms and Definitions

You need to become familiar with a few terms before you begin to program. This section attempts to explain the terms in simple language.

An *Automation controller* is the application that controls the server application. For example, AutoCAD is used as a server application with VBA or Visual Basic operating as the Automation controller. The controller initiates the interaction with the server, and server applications respond to the commands issued by the controller application.

An *AutoCAD object* is an element of AutoCAD. Line, UserCoordinateSystem, and Layer are examples of AutoCAD objects. Each AutoCAD object has a set of methods and properties (functions that set or return information about an object), and only the predefined set of functions can be used to program a particular object.

A *property* represents an attribute of an object, and can be read-only or read-write. A program can assign a new value to the read-write properties, but the program can only access the value of the read-only properties.

Methods are functions (such as Move, Copy, Regen, and Save) that perform an action on an object. A method might or might not return a value. Methods can take any number of arguments, any of which can be optional. Arguments are passed by value or by reference.

The AutoCAD object model represents the available AutoCAD objects and their interrelationships. The diagrams shown in figures 25.1 and 25.2 provide an overview of the hierarchical relationship between various objects exposed in AutoCAD.

Figure 25.1

AutoCAD Object Model shows the hierarchical relationship between various objects.

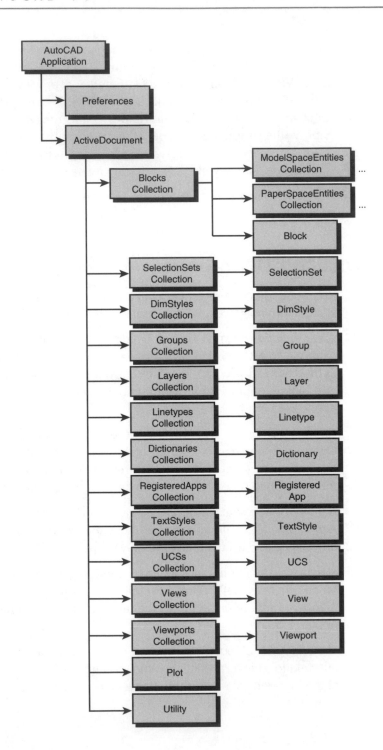

Figure 25.2

AutoCAD Object Model (Part II) shows the hierarchical relationship between various objects.

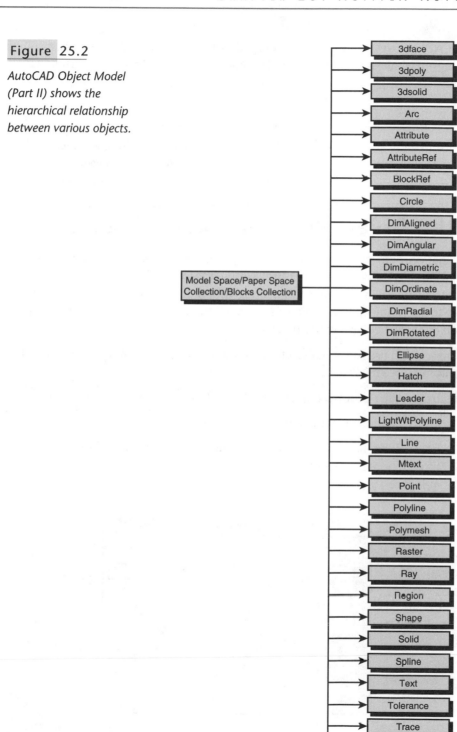

AutoCAD exposes many objects. Luckily, there are tools available that assist you in finding out what each object does and how it can be coded. Next, you will take a look at these tools.

NOTE

The first example in this chapter uses Visual Basic 5.0. You can also use the AutoCAD Release 14 Visual Basic for Applications (VBA) as the development environment.

Using the Object Browser and Online Help

Automation objects can be viewed through an Object Browser that comes with Visual Basic or VBA. The Object Browser enables you to see the complete list of objects available in an application, along with the properties and methods applicable to each object. You can also access online help and a code sample on how to use each particular method or property.

Before you can use AutoCAD's Automation objects, you must reference AutoCAD's type library (see fig. 25.3).

To reference the AutoCAD object type library, follow these steps:

1. From the Project menu, choose References.

2. In the References dialog box, select AutoCAD Object Library or, if it's not listed, choose Browse and select the acad.tlb file in the AutoCAD executable directory.

Figure 25.3

The Object Browser in Visual Basic 5.0 lists the AutoCAD Objects and corresponding methods and properties for each object.

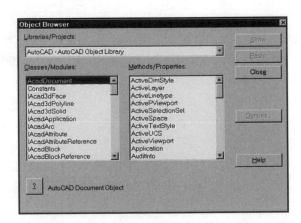

The Browser has undergone significant changes in Visual Basic 5.0. The new Browser in Visual Basic 5.0 resembles the VBA Object Browser (see fig. 25.4).

Figure 25.4

Significant changes are evident in the Object Browser in Visual Basic 5.0.

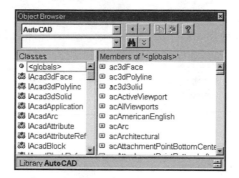

The Object Browser is part of the Visual Basic Editor, also known as *VBA Integrated Development Environment* (IDE) (see fig. 25.5). You use the editor and the tools provided to design the layout of your application, write Visual Basic code, and debug your application. The editor in Visual Basic 5.0 is nearly identical to that in VBA. You can bring up the editor after installing AutoCAD VBA by clicking on the Show IDE item under the VBA menu in AutoCAD. The advantage of VBA is that after you learn about this environment once, you can use it easily with any applications that support VBA.

To display the Object Browser in AutoCAD VBA, choose Object Browser under the View menu of the Visual Basic Editor. As you can see in figures 25.3–25.5, the Object Browser's left column contains the list of objects for the selected application; the properties and methods associated with the highlighted object are displayed in the right column. The Object Browser connects you directly to the online help for Automation. Coding examples for each method and property are included in the help page of the help file. You can use the coding examples to learn more about a particular method or property. You can also use the Object Browser to determine whether a property applies to a particular object.

Figure 25.5

The Visual Basic for Applications (VBA) Editor.

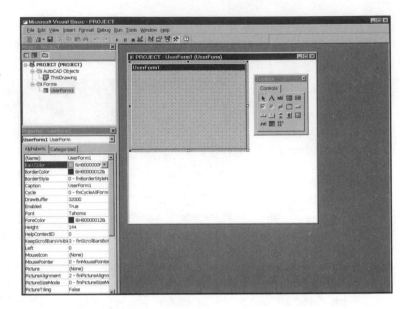

Looking Up Online Help Through the Object Browser

To get to online help for a particular method or property of an object, first highlight the object in the left column, then highlight the item in the right column, and then click on the question mark button. The following exercise shows you how to look up the online help and code sample for Rotate method of BlockReference object. The exercise assumes you have loaded AutoCAD VBA. Confirm this by starting an AutoCAD session and verifying the existence of the VBA pull-down menu.

USING ONLINE HELP

1. Open the VBA pull-down menu and choose the Show VBA IDE command. This will start AutoCAD VBA (Microsoft Visual Basic).

2. Open the View pull-down menu and choose Object Browser. A Classes List and a Members list should now fill the left window on the screen.

3. Scroll down the left column (Classes) and pick the BlockReference object by clicking on IAcadBlockReference.

4. In the right column (Members of 'IAcadBlockReference' list), pick the Rotate method.

5. With these items highlighted, click on the question mark button. Do not select the question mark icon on the Standard toolbar—this brings up help topics for Visual Basic for Applications.

6. The help information for the object is displayed.

7. Click on the green Example hotspot to see a code sample (see fig. 25.6).

8. From the AutoCAD Automation Reference dialog box, open the File pull-down menu, and choose Exit to leave the help screen. From the Microsoft Visual Basic dialog box, open the File pull-down menu and choose the Close and Return to AutoCAD command.

Figure 25.6

The Help page for the Rotate method of the BlockReference object.

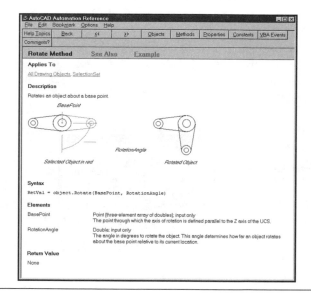

The Object Browser provides a quick method of looking up online help and code samples on how to use a particular method or property in AutoCAD. Becoming familiar with the Object Browser will make creating Automation programs easier and more efficient.

Creating Your First Automation Program

In this section, you learn to write your first simple Automation program. In the following exercise, you will gain insight into how easy it is to write a Visual Basic program. The only way to learn programming is to write programs. Writing a Visual

Basic program entails two major tasks: designing the graphical layout and writing the code.

During the graphical layout step, which does not involve any coding, you use the tools that come with Visual Basic to lay out the user interface for the application. In this step, you can use your imagination to make your application visually appealing.

In the second step, you write the code, using Visual Basic statements. Writing code in Visual Basic is easier than other languages because it is more like English.

AUTOMATION ROUTINE—START AND END AN AUTOCAD SESSION

In this simple exercise, you create the user interface to start and end an AutoCAD session. Then you write the code behind the user interface, and run the exercise to see how Visual Basic can be used to link to AutoCAD. Figure 25.7 shows the finished form you are going to create.

Figure 25.7

The Visual Basic Form for Exercise 1.

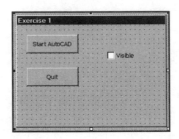

To create this form, follow these steps:

1. Start Visual Basic 5.0.

   The Visual Basic Editor with the default form is displayed. To create the *look* of your application (the way it appears to the user), you will place various buttons from the toolbox on this form.

2. If the Toolbox and Properties dialog boxes are not displayed, open the View pull-down menu and choose the Toolbox and Properties commands.

3. Double-click on the command icon in the toolbox. A button with the caption Command1 appears (see fig. 25.8). Place the cursor over the control button and press and hold down the left mouse button. Drag the control to the upper-left corner of the form.

Figure 25.8

The Visual Basic Form with the first button.

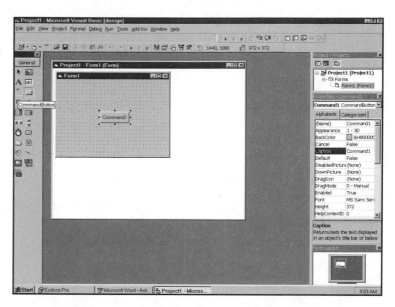

4. Double-click on the command icon to place a second command button. Place the cursor over the control button and press and hold down the left mouse button. Drag the control below the first command button.

5. Double-click on the check box button to place a check box in the center of the form. Place the cursor over the check box button and press and hold down the left mouse button. Drag the control to the right of the two command buttons.

6. Make changes to the property page for each control by highlighting each control and then editing its properties in the Properties window.

NOTE

To change a property, double-click on the property name. This selects the property and highlights its current value. Type a new value for the property.

7. Select Form1 by picking on any open spot on the form. Set the following properties in the Properties window:

Caption: Exercise 1

Scalemode: 2-Point

8. Select the CommandButton1 on the form, and set the following properties in the Properties window:

   Height: 24

   Left: 12

   Top: 12

   Width: 66

   Caption: Start AutoCAD

   Name: cmdStart

9. Select CommandButton2 on the form, and set the following properties in the Properties window:

   Enabled: False

   Height: 24

   Left: 12

   Top: 54

   Width: 66

   Caption: Quit

   Name: cmdQuit

10. Select CheckBox1 on the form, and set the following properties in the Properties window:

    Height: 24

    Left: 114

    Top: 30

    Width: 50

    Caption: Visible

    Name: cmdVisible

At this point, the form should resemble the one shown in figure 25.7.

11. Now, double-click on the Start AutoCAD button and add the following code between the `Private Sub` and `End Sub` lines in the code window:

```
On Error Resume Next
Set acad = GetObject(, "AutoCAD.Application")
            If Err Then
                    Err.Clear
                    Set acad =
                    ➥CreateObject("AutoCAD.Application")
                    If Err Then
                        MsgBox "Unable to connect to AutoCAD"
                Exit Sub
                End If
End If
cmdQuit.Enabled = True
```

12. Open the View pull-down menu and choose Form to switch to the form. Double-click on the Quit button, and add the following code between the `Private Sub` and `End Sub` lines in the code window:

```
acad.Quit
End
```

13. Open the View pull-down menu and choose Form to switch to the form. Double-click on the Visible check box, and add the following code between the `Private Sub` and `End Sub` lines in the code window:

```
acad.Visible = True
```

14. In the Form1 code window, use the Object drop-down list and select (General). The Proc drop-down list will now show (declarations) and the code window will be empty. Type the following line in the code window:

Public acad As Object

15. Now, open the Run pull-down menu and choose Start With Full Compile to run the example.

The statement Public acad As Object declares the *acad* variable as public, so that you can access it from any subroutine. The GetObject function connects your application to AutoCAD, if AutoCAD is already running. This function returns the AutoCAD Application object and stores it in the *acad* variable. CreateObject starts a new session of AutoCAD. AutoCAD stays "invisible" until the "visible" property is set to True. The statement acad.Quit ends the AutoCAD session. To end the application without quitting AutoCAD, just set acad = Nothing. It's a good idea to free up memory associated with objects that will not be used any more; to do so, set those objects to Nothing.

INSIDER TIP

Sometimes, you might want to run AutoCAD in invisible mode. In this way, you can do several operations with only a final display, without having to regenerate the drawing window after each operation. Also, if you are doing a batch-plot sort of operation, you can make your application run faster if AutoCAD is invisible.

The Application object used in the preceding exercise is the top-level object; all the other objects can be reached through the methods and properties of the Application object. To create an AutoCAD block, for example, you must know how the block object relates to the AutoCAD Application object. Now, take a look at the Object Model to understand how the various objects are connected.

Looking at the AutoCAD Object Model

The following exercise shows you how to look at the AutoCAD Object Model, which shows the relationship between the different AutoCAD objects.

LOOKING AT THE AUTOCAD OBJECT MODEL

1. Access the AutoCAD Release 14 online help system by opening the Help pull-down menu and choosing the AutoCAD Help Topics command. This displays the Help Topics:AutoCAD Help dialog box. Select the Contents tab.

2. Double-click on ActiveX Automation, and then double-click on ActiveX Automation Reference.

3. Double-click on Object Model. This hierarchical diagram shows the relationships between different AutoCAD objects.

4. To go to online help for Block reference, click on the BlockReference object. (This takes you to the online help you accessed through the Object Browser, as shown in figure 25.6.)

Now you know how to access help information for Automation objects in a couple of ways—from the Object Browser as well as from the AutoCAD online help file. This knowledge will be useful when you complete the next exercise, which does a simple customization of AutoCAD.

Using Automation with AutoCAD

This section shows how to use Automation to write simple, yet powerful utilities to customize AutoCAD. You can use Automation objects to perform most operations that you would perform interactively. Of course, no one-to-one correspondence exists between the two approaches.

The preceding exercise showed you how to use Visual Basic 5.0 to connect to AutoCAD. The next exercise shows you, step by step, how to create a Visual Basic macro, using AutoCAD VBA to set up top, front, isometric, and right views in paper space.

Setting Up Four Standard Viewports in Paper Space

In this exercise, after connecting to AutoCAD from VBA, you add a *torus* (donut) object, and then create the standard views. Finally, you zoom to fit the torus in each of the views. To be able to do this exercise, you must have AutoCAD VBA installed on your machine. Please refer to your *AutoCAD Installation Guide* for information about installing the AutoCAD VBA Preview.

CREATING A MACRO TO SET UP VIEWPORTS IN PAPER SPACE

1. Start AutoCAD, open the VBA pull-down menu and then choose Show VBA IDE. This starts AutoCAD VBA (Microsoft Visual Basic for Applications).

2. From the Insert menu, choose UserForm. The screen should look similar to figure 25.5.

3. If the toolbox does not appear, go to the View menu and choose the ToolBox command.

4. From the toolbox, click on the command button, and then click once on the form to display the command button.

5. Repeat step 4 five more times, creating a total of six command buttons on the form. Place them so that they do not overlap (see fig. 25.9).

Figure 25.9

VBA Editor with the six command buttons on the form.

6. Click once on each button, and set its properties in the properties sheet as follows:

NOTE

To change a property, double-click on the property name. This action selects the property and highlights its current value.

For CommandButton1, set the following properties:

Height: 24

Left: 18

Top: 12

Width: 60

Caption: Connect

Name: cmdConnect

For CommandButton2, set the following properties:

Height: 24

Left: 18

Top: 48

Width: 60

Caption: Add Torus

Name: cmdAdd

For CommandButton3, set the following properties:

Height: 24

Left: 18

Top: 84

Width: 60

Caption: End

Name: cmdQuit

For CommandButton4, set the following properties:

Height: 24

Left: 108

Top: 12

Width: 60

Caption: Create Views

Name: cmdViews

For CommandButton5, set the following properties:

Height: 24

Left: 108

Top: 48

Width: 60

Caption: Help

Name: cmdHelp

For CommandButton6, set the following properties:

Height: 24

Left: 108

Top: 84

Width: 60

Caption: Cancel

Name: cmdCancel

7. Select the form by clicking anywhere on an open spot on the form. Set its properties in the properties sheet as follows:

Caption: Standard View Creation Utility

8. From the File pull-down menu, choose Save. The Save VBA Project As dialog box is displayed. Type the name **view.dvb** and click on the OK button. (Save intermittently so that you don't lose your work.)

Now that you have laid out the buttons on the form, add the code that is executed when the user presses each button.

9. Double-click on the Connect button and add the following lines of code between the Private Sub and End Sub statements:

```
On Error Resume Next
Set acad = GetObject(, "AutoCAD.Application")
If Err Then

    Err.Clear
     Set acad = CreateObject("AutoCAD.Application")
     If Err Then
             MsgBox "Error in connecting to AutoCAD"
         Exit Sub
     End If
End If
acad.Visible = True
Set mspace = doc.ModelSpace
cmdQuit.Enabled = True
cmdAdd.Enabled = True
cmdViews.Enabled = True
```

10. From the View pull-down menu, choose Object to switch to the form. Double-click on the Add Torus button, and add the following lines of code between the Private Sub and End Sub statements:

```
Dim My_Torus As Object
Dim Center(1 To 3) As Double
Dim EndPoint(1 To 3) As Double
Dim TorusRadius As Double
Dim TubeRadius As Double

Center(1) = 2#
Center(2) = 2#
Center(3) = 0#
TorusRadius = 0.5

TubeRadius = 0.125
Set doc = acad.ActiveDocument
Set mspace = doc.ModelSpace
Set My_Torus = mspace.AddTorus(Center, TorusRadius, TubeRadius)
My_Torus.Update
```

11. Open the View pull-down menu and choose Object to switch to the form. Double-click on the Create Views button, and add the following lines of code between the Private Sub and End Sub statements:

```
Dim Center(0 To 2) As Double
Dim Origin(0 To 2) As Double
Dim Top As Object
```

```
Dim Front As Object
Dim Iso As Object
Dim Right As Object
Dim PSpace As Object
Dim topDir(0 To 2) As Double
Dim frontDir(0 To 2) As Double
Dim rightDir(0 To 2) As Double
Dim isoDir(0 To 2) As Double

Set PSpace = doc.PaperSpace
Origin(0) = 0#
Origin(0) = 0#
Origin(0) = 0#

doc.ActiveSpace = 0

Center(0) = 2.5
Center(1) = 7.5
Center(2) = 0#

Set Top = PSpace.AddPViewport(Center, 5, 5)      'Add the top
➥viewport

Center(0) = 2.5
Center(1) = 2.5

Set Front = PSpace.AddPViewport(Center, 5, 5)   'Add the front
➥viewport

Center(0) = 7.5
Center(1) = 2.5

Set Right = PSpace.AddPViewport(Center, 5, 5)  'Add the right
➥viewport

Center(0) = 7.5
Center(1) = 7.5

Set Iso = PSpace.AddPViewport(Center, 5, 5)  'Add the iso viewport

frontDir(0) = 0              'Set the view direction in the front view
frontDir(1) = 1
frontDir(2) = 0

rightDir(0) = 1              'Set the view direction in the right view
rightDir(1) = 0
rightDir(2) = 0
```

```
isoDir(0) = 1                  'Set the view direction in the iso view
isoDir(1) = 1
isoDir(2) = 1

Front.Direction = frontDir     'Assign the direction values
Right.Direction = rightDir
Iso.Direction = isoDir

Top.Display (acOn)             'Turn the viewports on
Front.Display (acOn)
Iso.Display (acOn)
Right.Display (acOn)

doc.mspace = False        'Equivalent to AutoCAD pspace command

doc.ActivePViewport.ZoomExtents     'Zoom extents

doc.mspace = True        'Equivalent to AutoCAD mspace command

Set doc.ActivePViewport = Iso          'Make the iso view active
Iso.ZoomExtents                        'Zoom extents in iso view

Set doc.ActivePViewport = Right        'Make the right view active
Right.ZoomExtents                      'Zoom extents in right view

Set doc.ActivePViewport = Front        'Make the front view active
Front.ZoomExtents                      'Zoom extents in front view

Set doc.ActivePViewport = Top        'Make the top view active
Top.ZoomExtents                      'Zoom extents in top view

doc.Regen (1)                  'Do a regen in all viewports
```

12. From the View pull-down menu, choose Object to switch to the form. Double-click on the End button and add the following line of code between the `Private Sub` and `End Sub` statements:

    ```
    End
    ```

13. From the View pull-down menu, choose Object to switch to the form. Double-click on the Cancel button and add the following line of code between the `Private Sub` and `End Sub` statements:

    ```
    End
    ```

14. From the View pull-down menu, choose Object to switch to the form. Double-click on the Help button, and add the following line of code between the `Private Sub` and `End Sub` statements:

```
MsgBox (" This is a dummy help")
```

15. In the left list box at the top of the code window, select the (General) section. Add the following lines of code in the (Declarations) section:

```
Option Explicit
Public acad As Object
Public doc As Object
Public mspace As Object
```

16. Now that you have completed writing the code, save the project.

17. To execute the utility, open the Run pull-down menu and choose Run Sub/UserForm (see fig. 25.10).

Figure 25.10

The Run Sub/UserForm entry in the Run menu.

18. Click on the Connect button, and then click on Add Torus and Create Views, respectively. Connect sets up the link to AutoCAD (as explained for the first exercise).

Add Torus creates a three-dimensional torus object. The line *Set doc = acad.ActiveDocument* stores the ActiveDocument object (current drawing) in the *doc* variable. The next line, *Set mspace = doc.ModelSpace*, obtains the ModelSpace collection object and stores it in the *mspace* variable. ModelSpace is usually where AutoCAD adds all the graphical entities, unless you are creating blocks or paper space objects. The next line, *Set My_Torus = mspace.AddTorus(Center, TorusRadius, TubeRadius)*, actually adds the torus. *My_Torus.Update* updates the AutoCAD screen to display the torus.

Create views follows the AutoCAD sequence of creating paper space viewports. First you obtain the paper space collection object and store it in the *Pspace* variable. The line *doc.ActiveSpace = 0* is equivalent to setting Tilemode to 0 in AutoCAD. Then you add each of the four viewports. But you are not finished until you have set the x, y, and z values for the view direction in the viewports. Then you turn on each viewport by using the acOn constant for each viewport. The line *doc.mspace = False* is equivalent to typing Pspace in the AutoCAD command line. The remaining lines in the CreateViews routine perform a zoom extent in each viewport. The line *doc.Regen (1)* is used to regenerate in all the viewports. To regenerate in a single viewport, use *doc.Regen(0)*.

INSIDER TIP

Instead of remembering whether 1 or 0 does a regen in all viewports, use the mnemonic constants. To look them up in the Automation help file, bring up the object model and then, on the top menu, click on Constants.

Running a Macro in AutoCAD VBA

You can run this next exercise as a macro in AutoCAD VBA. Although the full benefits of Macros include record and playback capability (which is not available in AutoCAD), you can run the macro from the command line, or even put it in an AutoCAD menu by following these steps:

RUNNING A MACRO

1. Start AutoCAD, open the VBA pull-down menu, and choose Show VBA IDE. This starts AutoCAD VBA (Microsoft Visual Basic for Applications).

2. Open the Insert pull-down menu and then choose Module. Module1 is displayed in the project window and the code window is now empty.

   Double-click on Module in the project window; the code window appears.

3. Enter the following lines in the code window (see fig. 25.11):

```
Sub My_Macro()
    Load UserForm1
    UserForm1.Show
End Sub
```

   The first line, *Load UserForm1*, loads the form with the buttons. The line *UserForm1.Show* displays the form.

Figure 25.11

VBA window after step 3.

4. To run the macro, switch back to your AutoCAD session and type **VBARUN** (or open the VBA pull-down menu and choose Run Macro).

5. In the Macros dialog box, select Module1 from the Macro Scope list. In the second drop-down list, select MyMacro and then choose Run. The form you created in step 4 of this exercise appears again.

This exercise showed you how to automate tasks in AutoCAD by using VBA. Typically, however, you might use several products to perform various tasks. The next exercise shows you how to use Automation to automate these cross-application tasks. This is where the power of Automation lies, and is what sets it apart from AutoLISP.

Using Automation with Other Applications

You can use the VBA included with Office 97 or a variety of other products, including AutoCAD, to create cross-application programs by using objects from different applications. The following exercise takes you through the steps of creating one such application.

Creating an Application that Links AutoCAD, Microsoft Excel, and Microsoft Word

This exercise shows you how to open a drawing file, tabulate the count of various blocks in MS Excel, and then prepare a memo in MS Word—all in one simple application, using Excel VBA. Note that this exercise works with Excel 7.0, not Office 97 Excel or Excel 5.0. The names of objects supported in each Excel version have changed slightly and some modification in the given code may be required to run on Excel 5 or Office 97 Excel. Figure 25.12 shows the memo that your application creates by using objects from Word, Excel, and AutoCAD.

Figure 25.12

This Word document is based on AutoCAD drawing data tabulated in an Excel chart.

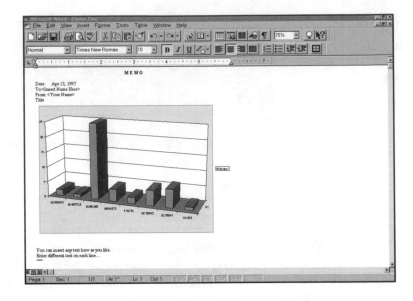

LINKING AUTOCAD, EXCEL, AND WORD

1. Open Microsoft Excel and, from the Insert menu, choose Macro, Module.

2. On the module sheet, add the following code for counting the AutoCAD blocks and tabulating them into the Excel worksheet. (You can also cut and paste the code from the file ew.xls supplied on the CD that accompanies this book.)

```
Public acad As Object
Public excelSheet As Object
Sub CountBlocks()
Dim objMspace As Object
Dim objElement As Object
Dim objExcel As Object
Dim objDoc As Object
Dim intI As Integer
Dim strBlockName(1 To 1000) As String
Dim intNumBlockName(1 To 1000) As Integer
Dim intTotalNumOfBlocks As Integer
Set objExcel = GetObject(, "Excel.Application")
Set objExcelSheet = objExcel.ActiveWorkbook.Sheets("Sheet1")
Worksheets("Sheet1").Activate
On Error Resume Next
Set objAcad = GetObject(, "AutoCAD.Application")
If Err <> 0 Then
        'Set objAcad = CreateObject("AutoCAD.Application")
Exit Sub
End If
```

```
    objAcad.Visible = True
    Set objDoc = objAcad.ActiveDocument
                If Right(ActiveWorkbook.Path, 1) = "\" Then
        DwgName = ActiveWorkbook.Path & "ew.dwg"
    Else
        DwgName = ActiveWorkbook.Path & "\ew.dwg"


    End If
    Set objDoc = objAcad.ActiveDocument
    If objDoc.FullName <> DwgName Then
        objDoc.Open DwgName
    End If
    Set objMspace = objDoc.ModelSpace
    objExcelSheet.Range(Cells(1, 1), Cells(100, 12)).Clear
    intI = 1
    For Each objElement In objDoc.Blocks
        With objElement
            If (.Name <> "*MODEL_SPACE" And .Name <> "*PAPER_SPACE")
            ➡Then
objExcelSheet.Cells(intI, 1) = objElement.Name
strBlockName(intI) = objElement.Name
 intI = intI + 1
End If
End With
Next
    intI = intI - 1
    intTotalNumOfBlocks = intI
    For intI = 1 To intTotalNumOfBlocks
        intNumBlockName(intI) = 0
    Next
   objExcelSheet.Range(Cells(1, 1), Cells(intI, 1)).Font.Bold = True
For Each objElement In objMspace
With objElement
                Found = False
                If StrComp(objElement.entityName,
                ➡"AcDbBlockReference", 1) = 0 Then
                    For intI = 1 To intTotalNumOfBlocks
                        If Not Found Then
                            If StrComp(.Name, strBlockName(intI), 1)
                            ➡= 0 Then
                                intNumBlockName(intI) =
                                ➡intNumBlockName(intI) + 1
                                Found = True
                            End If
                        End If
                    Next
                End If
            End With
            Set objElement = Nothing
```

```
            Next objElement
            For intI = 1 To intTotalNumOfBlocks
                objExcelSheet.Cells(intI, 2) = intNumBlockName(intI)
            Next
            CreateChart (intTotalNumOfBlocks)
            Auto_Wait
            MakeMemos
        End Sub
```

3. Add the following subroutine to create an Excel chart based on the count of the AutoCAD blocks. You can customize your chart by using Excel objects and constants. For this subroutine to work, you must have MS Excel 7.0 installed on your system.

```
Private Sub CreateChart(NumberOfBlocks As Integer)
Dim ChartRange As Object
Static NewChart As Object
Set ChartRange = ActiveSheet.Range(Cells(1, 1), _
    Cells(NumberOfBlocks, 2))
ChartRange.Select
Set NewChart = Charts.Add
NewChart.Activate
With NewChart
        .Type = xl3DColumn
        .SubType = xlNormal
        .CopyPicture xlScreen
End With
End Sub
```

In the preceding routine, you have set the range of input for the Excel chart, added a chart to the Excel Charts collection and made it active. For the new chart object, you have set the type of chart that you want created.

4. Next, you write the code for an auto_wait subroutine. This routine adds an arbitrary wait of four seconds to give Microsoft Excel time to finish creating the chart object before Excel starts the Microsoft Word application.

```
Private Sub Auto_Wait()

        Dim NewHour As Double
        Dim NewMinute As Double
        Dim NewSecond As Double
        Dim WaitTime As Date
        NewHour = Hour(Now())
        NewMinute = Minute(Now())
        NewSecond = Second(Now()) + 4
```

```
        WaitTime = TimeSerial(NewHour, NewMinute, NewSecond)
        Application.Wait WaitTime

End Sub
```

5. Now, write the code that starts Microsoft Word and inserts the chart you created in Excel into the Word document. You can include additional text information, where appropriate, to complete your memo. For this subroutine to work, you must have MS Word 6.0 installed on your system.

```
Private Sub MakeMemos()

    Dim Word As Object
    Set Word = CreateObject("Word.Basic")
    With Word
        .FileNewDefault
        .Insert "M E M O"
        .InsertPara
        .InsertPara
        .Insert "Date:" & Chr(9) & Format(Date, "mmm d, yyyy")
        .InsertPara
        .Insert "To: <Insert Name Here>"
        .InsertPara
        .Insert "From: <Your Name>"
        .InsertPara
        .Insert "Title "
        Word.EditPaste
        .InsertPara   '.Insert Message
        .InsertPara
        .InsertPara
        .Insert "You can insert any text here as you like. "
        .InsertPara
        .Insert "Enter different text on each line...."
        .StartOfDocument
        .EndOfLine 1
        .Bold
        .CenterPara
        .FileSaveAs "C:\Demo.Doc"
        .DocClose
    End With
    Set Word = Nothing
    Application.StatusBar = ""
    MsgBox "The memo has been created and saved.", vbInformation
    Set excelSheet = Nothing

End Sub
```

The preceding code starts Word.Basic application, opens a default document, adds some formatting information, and pastes the chart you created in Excel before saving the document.

Now you are ready to run this exercise.

6.   From the Tools menu, choose Macro, and then select Count_Blocks (see fig. 25.13).

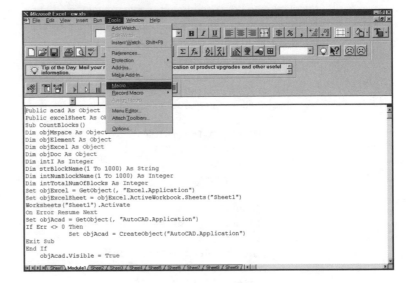

Figure 25.13

Microsoft Excel sheet shows the Macro entry under the Tools menu.

7.   Click on Run, allowing time for AutoCAD to open and create a chart and Word document. This step may take some time to complete.

8.   The Word document is stored as C:\demo.doc. You can change the path in the MakeMemos macro, if necessary.

Notice that you first connect to the running instance of the Excel application by using the GetObject function. The next statements activate Sheet1 on Excel, making it the current sheet, where the count for the blocks is written. Then you cycle through the AutoCAD database, identifying each different block and storing the information in the *strBlockName* variable, as well as writing it on the Excel sheet. Next, you loop through the database again, and add the count for each type of block in the *intNumBlockName* variable.

The CreateChart subroutine creates the chart by selecting the appropriate range. The MakeMemo subroutine starts the Word application and creates the Word document. You can customize this utility for your particular needs.

Summary

ActiveX Automation is a new feature in AutoCAD Release 14 that enables you to customize AutoCAD and create powerful integrated applications. The power of the Automation feature becomes clearly evident when used to integrate automation-compliant applications, such as Microsoft Word, Excel, and Access, with AutoCAD, something that AutoLISP is not well suited for. While AutoLISP is a powerful customization tool for AutoCAD, the Graphical User Interface (GUI) tools available in Visual Basic 5.0 are clearly superior to AutoLISP Dialog Control Language (DCL) and can be used easily to develop well-integrated Visual Basic applications.

In this chapter, you learned how to customize AutoCAD. You learned how to program with the new AutoCAD VBA. The last exercise showed you how to do cross-application macro programming using Excel, Word, and AutoCAD. Knowledge of these new tools will enable you to produce applications that maximize your productivity and enable you to automate tasks.

AutoCAD SQL Environment (ASE)

by Jojo Guingao

AutoCAD SQL Environment (ASE) enables you to link AutoCAD objects to external database files. ASE provides an interface for a two-way data transfer between AutoCAD and external databases, and it enables AutoCAD to associate, or link, non-graphic attributes stored in external programs, such as dBase III, Oracle, and ODBC-compliant databases (such as Microsoft Access), with graphic objects in an AutoCAD drawing. ASE supports the SQL2 standard, which uses environment, catalogs, schemas, and tables instead of the original SQL model of database management system (DBMS), databases, and tables.

This chapter covers the following topics:

- Introducing ASE

- Setting up dBase III, Oracle 7, and ODBC

- Introducing SQL

- Using ASE effectively

- Handling common ASE error messages

Introducing the AutoCAD SQL Environment (ASE)

Autodesk has been providing tools to create "intelligent" drawings for some time. Previous releases of AutoCAD provided an AutoCAD object, known as an attribute, which enables you to store and retrieve text data. As useful as this feature was, however, it was limited only to block entities. In later releases, AutoCAD introduced Extended Entity Data (EED), which enables textual data to be attached to any AutoCAD object. Extended Entity Data has two limitations. First, you can save only 16 KB of information for each object. Second, this increases the size of the electronic drawing file, slowing performance and making it more difficult when working with drawings containing thousands of objects.

Understanding the Benefits of ASE

Many new benefits accompany ASE, including those detailed in the following list:

- Database information can be edited within AutoCAD, and the updated information will be immediately available to your database systems.

- Database information can be edited easily by using AutoCAD selection methods to graphically identify objects that are linked to the data.

- Access to all the columns in a row of a table can be gained with only a single link in the drawing.

- Multiple drawings can link and share the same information.

- A drawing can be linked to many database tables.

- Because the information is external, the table information can be edited independently by the DBMS program. The updated information will be immediately available to the AutoCAD drawing.

Introducing SQL2 Terminology and Concepts

SQL2 is an international standard that compensates for some of the deficiencies in the original SQL standard. Instead of the SQL model based on DBMS, databases, and tables, SQL2 uses environments, catalogs, schemas, and tables. Figure 26.1 illustrates the relationship between these elements of SQL2.

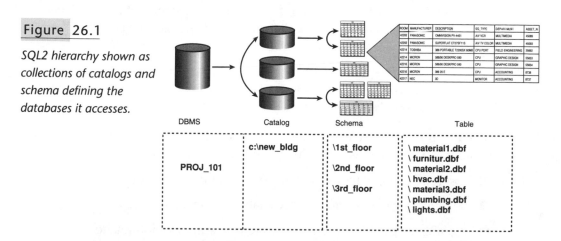

Figure 26.1

SQL2 hierarchy shown as collections of catalogs and schema defining the databases it accesses.

In SQL1, a *database management system* (DBMS) controls the data. A *catalog* is a collection of one or more schemas, and a *schema* consists of one or more database tables held in one location. A *table* contains database information organized in rows and columns, which are referred to as *records* and *fields*.

In SQL2, the environment comprises the DBMS, the databases it can access, and the users and programs that also can access those databases. Environments are part of a hierarchy that includes catalogs, schemas, and tables. More information on using SQL can be found later in this chapter in the section "Understanding the Features and Functions of Structured Query Language (SQL)."

To take full advantage of AutoCAD ASE capabilities, you will need to set up your database properly. This process is discussed in the following section. It is important that you follow each step carefully. Missing any of the steps will result in unsuccessful database connection.

Setting Up Your Database

The process of connecting to a database includes the following steps:

1. Verify that ASE is installed. If you completed a full installation of AutoCAD, then ASE is installed.

2. Run the External Database Configuration Editor to configure your database.

3. In an AutoCAD session, use the ASEADMIN command to make a connection between the database with which you are working and AutoCAD.

4. In the ASEADMIN command, set your Link Path Name (LPN) to specify key columns for the current table identified by its link path.

5. Use the ASEROWS commands to create links between AutoCAD objects and records in the database. Refer to the section "Step 3: Setting Up Your Database Links with AutoCAD Objects" for more information.

6. For those who prefer to use a toolbar, make sure you enabled the External Database toolbar. If not, go to Toolbars under the View pull-down menu, and choose External Database. This is an optional step.

After the links are made to the AutoCAD objects, this data is available for use in a number of ASE functions, including those in the following list:

- Using SQL statements as a criteria to search for information

- Extracting database and AutoCAD data into a text file for reporting purposes

- Combining graphical and textual criteria to search for information

Once you're successful connecting your database to your AutoCAD drawing, you are unleashing the power of "intelligent drawings." Using ASE functionalities, you can combine AutoCAD drawing and database information as your search criteria for finding the right information. For example, suppose you want to show all equipment and office locations where the manufacturer is Compaq. With ASE, this is possible by executing an SQL statement to search the linked database for all occurrences of "Compaq" as the manufacturer. If found, ASE will display its corresponding linked AutoCAD objects.

The preceding steps show the general process of creating a connection between a database and AutoCAD. The remaining headings in this section contain specific procedures for making connections between AutoCAD and the following database applications:

- dBase III

- Oracle 7

- Microsoft Access ODBC-compliant databases

Connecting Using dBase III

The driver for dBase III Plus is a low-level driver that uses an SQL2 interpreter to access the database. Low-level drivers interact with the data directly, which means you only need the database (.dbf) file in dBase III Plus format. You do not need to have the dBase III Plus program installed on your system to access the database files via AutoCAD. To use a dBase III Plus database in AutoCAD, you must use the External Database Configuration Editor (asicfg.exe) to state the location of the database files you plan to use.

In order for ASE to find the database files and character-definition files with which you plan to work, you must specify the database location.

Linking to a dBase III Database

The following procedures can be used to link a dBase III database. This example uses sample database (.dbf) files, which are provided in the Sample directory of AutoCAD Release 14.

The sample database files are located in c:\acad14\sample\dbf. This example is based on an installation of AutoCAD using the default directories.

Figure 26.2

How to define your environment in dBase III.

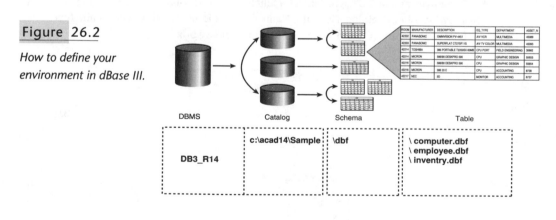

LINKING TO A DBASE III DATABASE

1. Make sure that you have installed the External Database components for AutoCAD. If you complete a full installation of AutoCAD, then these components are included. Refer to the AutoCAD Installation Guide for specific information on installation.

2. Use the External Database Configuration (asicfg.exe) to configure your database. Using Windows 95 or Windows NT 4.0, select the Start button, then choose Programs, AutoCAD R14, External Database Configuration. Using Windows 3.51, double-click on the External Database Configuration icon in the AutoCAD R14 group.

3. The External Database Configuration dialog box is displayed. Click on the Add button. This displays the Select DBMS for new Environment dialog box. Under the DBMS List, select dBaseIII. Go to the Environment Name edit box and type **DB3_R14**, as shown in figure 26.3. Go to the Environment Description edit box and type **R14 Sample Database**. Click on the OK button.

Figure 26.3

Dialog box for creating Environment Name with dBase III.

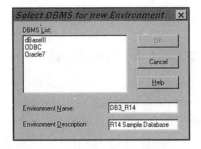

4. The Environment:DB3_R14(DB3DRV) dialog box is displayed. If the Catalog tab is not showing, select Catalog. Go to the Name edit box in the Catalog section and type **Samples**. Figure 26.4 shows the Environment dialog box.

Figure 26.4

The Environment dialog box where Catalog and Schemas are defined.

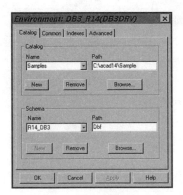

INSIDER TIP

The name you assign to the catalog appears in the Administration dialog box (ASEADMIN command) as one of the choices of catalogs. You can create multiple catalogs, each for a particular set of databases. Pick a meaningful name for the catalog. For example, databases for facility maintenance of the 8000 Broadmoor Street Building could be identified by "Catalog = Broadmoor Street." Likewise, sample databases could be identified by "Catalog = Samples."

WARNING

Catalog names beginning with a numeral or a non-alphanumeric character, such as *1stfloor* or *firstfloor* are not allowed. Numbers and non-alphanumeric characters can be used as long as they do not begin the name (example: *floor1* or *first floor* can be used).

5. Go to the Path edit box in the Catalog section and enter the parent directory for the database file. You can use the Browse button to help identify the proper locations. In this section, you must equate the catalog name with a location of the database files on the hard drive, specifically, the parent directory that contains subdirectories in which the .DBF files are stored.

    For example, if the catalog name was Broadmoor Street, and the database files were located in c:\dbf\broamoor\floor1, the catalog location would be c:\dbf\broadmoor.

6. Click on the New button to save the Catalog information.

7. Go to the Name edit box in the Schema section and type **R14_DB3** as the schema name (refer to fig. 26.4).

INSIDER **T**IP

The schema name should be a meaningful name that identifies a subset of databases or distinguishes one database from another. These schema names are listed in the ASEADMIN dialog box when you select Schemas. For example, if databases for each floor in the 8000 Broadmoor Street building are stored in separate subdirectories based on the floor level of the building, one schema could be set for each floor: "Schema = First_floor," "Schema = Second_floor," "Schema = Third_floor." It is quite acceptable to use the subdirectory name as the schema name, if this helps you to identify the databases to use with the ASE commands. For example, if each database is stored individually in separate subdirectories called Project1 and Project2, the schema names could be "Schema=project1" and "Schema=project2."

8. Go to the Path edit box in the Schema section and type **DBF** as the Schema Path (again, refer to fig. 26.4). The path points to the subdirectory in which the database file or files are located.

NOTE

In the preceding 8000 Broadmoor Street example, if database files exist in the c:\dbf\broadmoor\floor1 and c:\dbf\broadmoor\floor2 subdirectories, and if the catalog name is Broadmoor Street and the schema names are First_Floor and Second_Floor, then the schema locations would be floor1 and floor2.

Figure 26.5

The Common tab of the Environment dialog box is used to specify the language and default catalog and schema.

9. Click on the New button to save the schema information.

10. Select the Common tab of the Environment: DB3_R14(DB3DRV) dialog box to specify the language and the default catalog and schema (see fig. 26.5). In the Language drop-down list, scroll down the list and select English_United States.

11. Click on the OK button to accept the changes.

12. At this point, you should be back at the External Database Configuration dialog box and the environment is now defined. Click on the Test button to verify that you successfully can connect to the dBase III database. A Login dialog box is displayed. Leave the User Name edit box and the Password edit box blank. Click on the Connect button to start the test. A dialog box will indicate that you made a successful connection. On the Connection test passed dialog box, click on the Done button, then the OK button to exit the database configuration.

13. Start AutoCAD.

14. Type **ASEADMIN** at the Command: prompt. The Administration dialog box is displayed. Then, in the Database Objects scroll window, select your environment DB3_R14, and click on the Connect button.

15. In the Connect to Environment dialog box, enter your name and password, and then click on OK. You may choose to leave the name and password fields blank.

16. Select the Catalog button and select the catalog you want to access.

17. Select the Schema button and select the schema you want to access.

18. Select the Table button and select the table you want to access.

You have now successfully connected to dBase III.

Oracle 7 is another DBMS from which links can be made to AutoCAD objects. To use an Oracle database, you must connect to a local or remote Oracle server. The process for connecting using Oracle is provided in the following section.

Connecting Using Oracle 7

The ASI Oracle driver is a high-level driver that translates ASI SQL to the DBMS SQL. SQL statements then are passed to the DBMS engine for processing. You can use either a local or a remote Oracle server to access databases. To use an Oracle database in AutoCAD, you must define the environment in the External Database Configuration editor to specify the location of the database files you plan to use. You also must create an information schema in the Oracle 7 database so that the driver can locate the schemas and tables you want to access.

ASI uses the terms *catalog*, *schema*, and *table* in describing an environment, while Oracle supports the concept of *owners*. Table 26.1 shows the rules that Oracle drivers follow for converting terminology.

NOTE

For more information on the concept of owners, consult the Oracle Reference manual.

Table 26.1

ASI Terminology and Oracle Terminology Equivalents

ASI Terminology	*Oracle Terminology*
Catalog name	Database name or database link
Schema name	Owner name
Table name	Table name

In addition to containing a collection of schemas, a catalog also contains an information schema. An *information schema* is a special group of tables that describes the contents of the tables, including the columns in the various tables, the defined views, and the privileges associated with each authorization identification.

The following exercise details the procedure to link to an Oracle database.

LINKING TO AN ORACLE DATABASE

1. Make sure that you have installed the External Database component for AutoCAD. If you complete a full installation of AutoCAD, then this component is included. Refer to the AutoCAD Installation Guide for specific information on installation.

2. Verify that you have installed Oracle SQL*Net version 2.3 or higher on your client machine. Consult your Oracle manual for more information about how to install SQL*Net.

3. Include the Oracle client directory in your search path. This step depends on which version of Windows you are using, as follows:

   Windows 95: Edit Autoexec.bat, and add this statement:

   PATH=C:\ORAWIN95\BIN;D:\ORAWIN95;%PATH

   Windows NT: Go to the Control Panel, and click on System. Select the Environment tab, and add this variable:

   Variable: **Path**
   Value: **C:\ORAWINNT\BIN;C:\ORAWIN**

4. Close any existing applications and re-boot your system.

5. Create an Information Schema Login ID and Views by doing the following:

WARNING

Please contact your Oracle System Administrator to create these views and the privileges on the views.

This view must be created only once because table views are dynamic.

   5a. Start SQL*Plus or SQL*DBA.

5b. At the SQL prompt, enter the following:

```
CREATE USER INFORMATION SCHEMA IDENTIFIED BY NONE;
GRANT SELECT ON ALL USERS TO INFORMATION SCHEMA WITH GRANT
➥OPTION;
GRANT SELECT ON ALL OBJECTS TO INFORMATION SCHEMA WITH GRANT
➥OPTION;
GRANT CONNECT TO INFORMATION SCHEMA;
```

5c. Log in to an Information Schema.

5d. Connect information schema/password.

5e. At the SQL prompt, enter the following:

```
CREATE VIEW SCHEMATA(CATALOG NAME, SCHEMA NAME, SCHEMA OWNER)
AS SELECT '<DB_NAME>', USERNAME, USERNAME FROM SYS.ALL USERS
WHERE USERNAME <> 'INFORMATION SCHEMA';
GRANT SELECT ON SCHEMATA TO PUBLIC;
CREATE VIEW TABLES(TABLE CATALOG, TABLE SCHEMA, TABLE NAME, TABLE
➥TYPE)
AS SELECT '<DB_NAME>', U.USERNAME, O.OBJECT_NAME, O.OBJECT_TYPE
FROM SYS.ALL_USERS U, SYS.ALL_OBJECTS O
WHERE U.USERNAME = O.OWNER AND
(O.OBJECT_TYPE = 'TABLE' OR O.OBJECT_TYPE = 'VIEW') AND
(O.OWNER <> 'INFORMATION SCHEMA'
AND O.OWNER <> 'SYS'
AND O.OWNER <> 'SYSTEM');
GRANT SELECT ON TABLES TO INFORMATION SCHEMA;
COMMIT;
```

(The database now contains the views INFORMATION SCHEMA.SCHEMATA and INFORMATION SCHEMA.TABLES.)

NOTE

If you are using the default database, the <dbname> is Oracle.

6. Verify that you can connect successfully to your Oracle database. You can use Oracle SQL*Plus to verify the connection.

7. Run the External Database Configuration (asicfg.exe) to configure your database.

8. Add an Environment called **bm_ora7**. Make sure that you select Oracle7 as your DBMS List (see fig. 26.6).

Figure 26.6

When specifying a new Oracle database, a new environment name is specified in the dialog box.

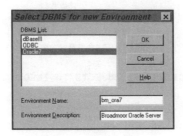

9. In the General tab, enter the base value **broadmoor.world** for locating the server and database to which you want to connect (see fig. 26.7).

Figure 26.7

The Base value in the Environment dialog box should be the same in your TNSNAMES.ORA file.

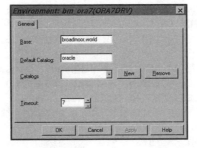

10. Verify your TNSNAMES.ORA (SQL*Net Configuration file) setting, generated by the SQL*Net Easy configuration. Make sure that the setting matches the preceding information. In most cases, this file is located in your Oracle client installation, such as c:\orawin95\network\admin.

11. In the Environment dialog box, enter **oracle** as the default catalog to which you want the driver to connect upon initialization.

12. Enter **7** as your Timeout setting, which specifies the amount of time in seconds that the driver should wait for a lock to be released before informing you of the lock.

13. Click on OK to apply the changes, and close the ASI Environment dialog box.

14. After you define the environment, click on Test to verify that you successfully can connect to the Oracle database. A dialog box will indicate that you made a successful connection.

INSIDER TIP

If you receive an error Operation: System Error, you probably skipped steps 3 and 4.

15. Start AutoCAD.

16. Type **ASEADMIN** in the Command: prompt, select your environment, Oracle7, and click on the Connect button.

17. In the Connect to Environment dialog box, enter your name and password, and then click on OK.

18. Select the Catalog button and select the name of the database you want to access.

19. Select the Schema button and select the user who has access privileges to the database you want to access.

20. Select the Table button and select the table you want to access.

You have now successfully connected to Oracle.

So far, this chapter has shown how to connect using dBase III and Oracle, for which AutoCAD supplies a direct driver. For any other databases, you need to connect using the ODBC interface. An ODBC-compliant database such as Microsoft Access will be used as an example.

Connecting Using ODBC (with Microsoft Access)

ODBC refers to Microsoft Open Database Connectivity (ODBC). ODBC is an implementation of an SQL-based database software interface designed to provide a common data access between Windows applications. You can think of ODBC as a standardized form of Dynamic Data Exchange (DDE) specifically for databases.

Two types of database drivers are supplied with AutoCAD R14: drivers that are used to connect directly to specific database applications, such as Oracle and dBase; and ODBC drivers that are used to connect to any database application with a corresponding ODBC interface. Microsoft and several other third-party developers provide ODBC software packages that contain interfaces for many databases.

The ODBC driver requires two parts: the AutoCAD-supplied ODBC driver, and an ODBC driver manager that is installed into the Operating System. The AutoCAD-supplied ODBC driver communicates with the ODBC driver manager, which in turn communicates with the database application.

To use the AutoCAD-supplied ODBC driver, you first must obtain and install an ODBC driver manager from Microsoft, a third-party provider, or the database application provider. Some 32-bit driver packages are used with Windows 95 or Windows NT, so be sure to obtain a 32-bit ODBC driver manager specific to Windows 95 or Windows NT.

Linking to ODBC-Compliant Databases

The following exercise details the procedure to link to an ODBC-compliant database such as Microsoft Access. In this case, the northwest.mdb available in the Microsoft Access sample directory is used as the sample directory.

LINKING TO MICROSOFT ACCESS

1. Obtain and install the 32-bit ODBC driver for your databases. Microsoft ODBC Driver Kit 3.0 contains several ODBC drivers, including Microsoft Access 7.0.

2. Verify that your database supports an Information Schema. If your ODBC driver does not support Information Schema, you must create one. To verify that your database supports Information Schema, refer to the database documentation.

3. Set up your MS Access database driver in the Windows ODBC Driver Manager by launching the 32-bit ODBC Administrator (odbcad32.exe). You also must set up the Access database driver. Refer to the section "Configuring Windows ODBC Driver Manager" for more information.

4. Run the External Database Configuration Editor (asicfg.exe) to configure your database. Refer to the section "Configuring Your External Database" for more information.

5. Launch AutoCAD and enter **ASEADMIN** in the Command: prompt.

As noted in step 1, sometimes you will need to create your own reference tables. Microsoft Access 7.0 does not support catalogs and schemas, so you must create a new database with two tables to emulate this information. When AutoCAD's ASE commands send requests through ODBC for catalog and schema data, ASE will look to this reference table to locate the actual database tables you plan to use with AutoCAD. The following steps show how to create the new table in MS Access.

NOTE

Refer to the following section, "Creating a Reference Table in Microsoft Access," for more information.

Creating a Reference Table in Microsoft Access

The following exercise shows the process for creating a reference table in Microsoft Access.

CREATING A REFERENCE TABLE IN ACCESS

1. Start Microsoft Access and create a new database. From the File pull-down menu, choose New Database. In this example, the database will be called infsch7.mdb and will be placed in c:\access. Type this name into the File Name edit box located on the New Database dialog box and click on the OK button.

2. The Database: INFSCH7 dialog box is displayed. Make sure the Table tab is selected and click on the New button. If the New Table dialog box is displayed, select New Table—this will bring up a new table in Design View mode. Create two fields; the first is named Catalog_Name and the second is named Schema_Name. Both are assigned Text as the data type.

3. From the File pull-down menu, choose the Save command. When prompted to save the table, name it **Schemata**. Click on the OK button.

4. When asked whether to create a primary key, choose No.

5. From the View pull-down menu, choose Datasheet. Insert the text **Null** in the Catalog Name field. Enter the full path to the database you want to use with AutoCAD in the Schema Name field. You can include as many databases as you need in the table following this format. This example (see table 26.2) uses one of the sample databases, northwind.mdb, that comes with Microsoft Access 7.0.

Table 26.2

Information to be Used for Creating the Table SCHEMATA

Catalog Name	Schema Name
Null	c:\access\samples\northwind

INSIDER **T**IP

Do not include the file extension .mdb in the Schema Name field.

6. From the File pull-down menu, choose the New command, and off the cascade menu, choose Table. If the New Table dialog box is displayed, select New Table—this will bring up a new table in Design View mode. Create the four following fields, specifying the data type Text for each one.

Heading 1	Data Type
Table Catalog	Text
Table Schema	Text
Table Name	Text
Table Type	Text

7. From the File pull-down menu, choose the Save command. When prompted to save the table, name it **Tables**. Click on the OK button.

8. When asked whether to create a primary key, choose No.

9. From the View pull-down menu, choose Datasheet. Insert the following data for each field. Insert the text **Null** for the Table Catalog field, the full path to the database in the Table Schema field, the table you want to use in the Table Name field, and the text **Base Table** for the Table Type. Continue on the next row for the next table you plan to use in AutoCAD. For example, to use the tables Customers and Orders in the sample database northwind.mdb, the values to enter would be as follows:

Table Catalog	Table Schema	Table Name	Table Type
Null	c:\access\samples\northwind	Customers	Base table
Null	c:\access\samples\northwind	Orders	Base table

INSIDER TIP

Do not include the extension .mdb for the database file listed in the Table Schema field.

10. From the File pull-down menu, choose Save Table. Now, open the File pull-down menu and choose Exit Microsoft Access 7.0.

The process is now complete. Figure 26.8 shows the dialog boxes created in this exercise.

Figure 26.8

Sample Microsoft Access Information Schema Database.

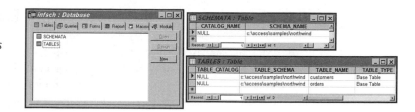

Configuring Windows ODBC Driver Manager

Before you can connect to an SQL database using ODBC driver, you must run the 32-bit ODBC Administrator (odbcad32.exe) to configure the Windows ODBC Driver Manager. You also must set up the Access database driver. The Windows ODBC Driver Manager can be found in your Windows Control Panel.

In the driver manager, you must supply a descriptive data source name in the Data Source Name field for the Access driver, such as ODBC_Access (see fig. 26.9).

WARNING

The ODBC Data Source Name should be the same as your Environment Name.

Figure 26.9

ODBC Data Source Name definition using Windows 32-bit ODBC Administrator.

 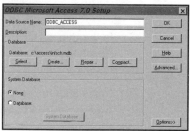

Configuring Your External Database

Before you can use your database application with AutoCAD, you must specify the databases you are using and provide the locations of the database tables. This can be done using the External Database Configuration Editor. The following exercise shows the necessary steps to configure the external database.

CONFIGURING YOUR EXTERNAL DATABASE

1. Run the External Database Configuration Editor (asicfg.exe) to configure your database. Using Windows 95 or Windows NT 4.0, select the Start button, then choose Programs, AutoCAD R14, External Database Configuration. Using Windows 3.51, double-click on the External Database Configuration icon in the AutoCAD R14 group.

2. The External Database Configuration dialog box is displayed. Click on the Add button. This displays the Select DBMS for new Environment dialog box. Under the DBMS List, select ODBC (it should be highlighted). Go to the Environment Name edit box and type **ODBC_ACCESS**. Go to the Environment Description edit box and type **Access7 Database**. Click on the OK button. Figure 26.10 shows the dialog boxes used for steps 1 and 2.

Figure 26.10

Use the External Database Configuration and Select DBMS for new Environment dialog boxes to configure your database.

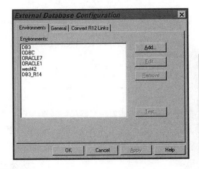
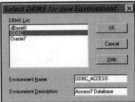

3. In the General tab of the Environment: ODBC_ACCCESS(ODBCDRV) dialog box, select Not Supported in the Set Schema List because Microsoft Access ODBC driver does support an information schema.

4. In the Information Schema box, enter the full path for the information schema, **c:\access\infsch.mdb**, to locate the database to which you want to connect (see fig. 26.11).

Figure 26.11

ODBC_ACCESS has been added to the list of environments, and the correct path name has been entered for the information schema.

5. Click on OK to apply the changes. The ASI Environment dialog box closes.

6. At this point, you should be back at the External Database Configuration dialog box and the environment is now defined. Click on the Test button to verify that you successfully can connect to Microsoft Access database. A Login dialog box is displayed. Leave the User Name edit box and the Password edit box blank. Click on the Connect button to start the test. A dialog box will indicate that you have made a successful connection. On the Connection test passed dialog box, click on the Done button, then the OK button to exit the database configuration.

INSIDER TIP

If you receive an error [Microsoft] [ODBC Driver Manager] data source name not found and no default driver specified, you probably did not configure the Windows ODBC Driver Manager.

7. Launch AutoCAD and type **ASEADMIN** at the Command: prompt. The Administration dialog box is displayed.

8. Select the environment desired from the Database Objects area (in the case of this example, ODBC Access). After you select the name, you will notice that the Environment button is highlighted.

9. Click on the Connect button. A Connect to Environment dialog box appears, with User Name and Password fields. This information is optional. Click on OK to clear this dialog box.

NOTE

Notice that the Catalog button is grayed out. This is because MS Access 7.0 does not support this SQL2 feature.

10. Select the Schema radio button from the Database Objects selection. The database file or files listed in the Schemata table in the reference database you created earlier will appear. Highlight one of the databases listed, and select the Table radio button. The choice of database tables you supplied in the Tables table in the reference database will appear. Select the table you want to access.

You are now successfully connected to Microsoft Access via ODBC.

You now know how to connect AutoCAD to three database applications: dBase III, Oracle 7, and ODBC/Microsoft Access. Depending on which database driver you choose, you will have different capabilities. The various features and capabilities are summarized in the following section.

Understanding the Capabilities of the ASI Database Driver

Table 26.3 is a compilation of the ASI DBMS driver's capabilities, such as features and supported transactions.

Two ways exist by which to verify the capability of the database driver that you are using. In the External database configuration (asicfg.exe), select the database environment and click on the Test button. The second option is to go to the ASEADMIN dialog box, select and connect to an environment, and click on the About Env button.

Table 26.3

Comparison of dBase III, Oracle 7, and ODBC Database Driver Capabilities

Feature	dBase III	Oracle7	ODBC w/Access 7.0
User name	Yes	Yes	Yes
Password	Yes	Yes	Yes
Catalog feature	Yes	Yes	No
Schema feature	Yes	Yes	Yes
Time zone	Yes	No	Yes
Character set names	Yes	No	Yes
Translations	No	No	Yes
Information schema facility	Yes	Yes	Yes

Feature	dBase III	Oracle7	ODBC w/Access 7.0
Catalog definition/ drop catalog	No	No	Yes
Schema definition/ drop schema	No	No	Yes
Table definition/ drop table	Yes	Yes	Yes
View definition/ drop view	No	Yes	Yes
Index definition/ drop index	Yes	Yes	Yes
Translation definition/ drop translation	No	No	Yes
Create assertion/ drop assertion	No	No	Yes
Character set definition/ drop character set	No	No	Yes
Collation definition/ drop collation	No	No	Yes
Domain definition/ drop domain	No	No	Yes
Alter domain	No	No	Yes
Alter table	No	Yes	Yes
Grant/revoke privileges	No	Yes	Yes
Commit work/rollback work	No	Yes	No
Set transaction	No	Yes	No
Set constraint	No	No	Yes
Cursor manipulation (open, close, fetch, next)	Yes	Yes	Yes
Fetches prior, first, last, absolute, relative	Yes	Yes	Yes

continues

Table 26.3, continued

Comparison of dBase III, Oracle 7, and ODBC Database Driver Capabilities

Feature	dBase III	Oracle7	ODBC w/Access 7.0
Select statement: single row	Yes	Yes	Yes
Delete: positioned	Yes	Yes	Yes
Update: positioned	Yes	Yes	No
Delete: searched	Yes	Yes	No
Update: searched	Yes	Yes	Yes
Insert	Yes	Yes	Yes

Converting Release 12 ASE Links to R14 ASE Links

AutoCAD Release 12 supports the original SQL standard format. With AutoCAD Releases 13 and 14, ASE was enhanced by supporting the SQL2 database standard format. This format provides benefits such as simultaneous access to several DBMSs.

The adoption of SQL2 format involves conceptual and environmental changes, including the terms environment, catalog, and schema. These changes in environment also change how ASE defines the database data, as well as its hierarchy, structure, and the methods of access. Due to these changes, R12 ASE links cannot be used in AutoCAD Releases 13 and 14 without conversion.

The following exercise shows how to perform this conversion process. The following R12 tutorial drawing and its databases are used in the exercise. These files are normally found in the tutorial directory of AutoCAD 12:

```
c:\acad12\tutorial\asetut.dwg
c:\acad12\tutorial\dbf\employee.dbf
c:\acad12\tutorial\dbf\computer.dbf
c:\acad12\tutorial\dbf\inventry.dbf
```

AutoCAD Release 14 can read AutoCAD Release 12 ASE link and convert it into AutoCAD Release 14 format. To execute this conversion, an equivalence must take place between Release 12 link terms (DBMS, database, and table) and Release 14 link terms (environment, catalog, schema, table, and link path name (LPN)). The old DBMS name is mapped to the new environment name using the same DBMS driver. The old database name is mapped to the new catalog and schema names. The old tables are mapped to new tables and link path names. Figure 26.12 illustrates the terms and relationships used in R12 with corresponding R14 equivalents.

Figure 26.12

R14 uses different ASE terms than R12.

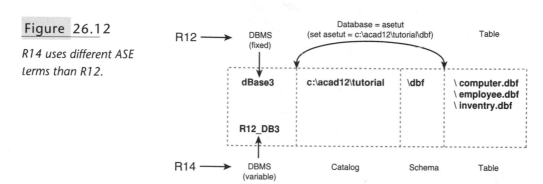

The table name typically is the same table used with the AutoCAD Release 12 drawing. Invalid links resulting from missing linked rows or key columns that have changed will be removed during conversion.

CONVERTING R12 ASE LINKS TO R14 ASE FORMAT

1. Use the External Database Configuration (asicfg.exe) to configure your database. If you are unfamiliar with this process, see the previous section for more information.

2. In the External Database Configuration dialog box, click on the Add button. The Select DBMS for new Environment dialog box is displayed. Under the DBMS List, select dBase III (it should be highlighted). Go to the Environment Name edit box and type **R12_DB3**. Go to the Environment Description edit box and type **Convert R12 Links**. Click on the OK button to save the Environment name.

3. The Environment:R12_DB3(DB3DRV) dialog box is displayed. If the Catalog tab is not showing, select Catalog. Go to the Name edit box in the Catalog section and type **R12DB3**.

4. Go to the Path edit box in the Catalog section and enter the path **c:\acad12\ tutorial.**

5. Click on the New button in the Catalog section to save the new Catalog Name.

6. Go to the Name edit box in the Schema section and type **dbf** as the schema name.

7. Go to the Path edit box in the Schema section and type **dbf** as the Schema Path.

8. Click on the New button in the Schema section to save the new schema name. Click on the OK button to exit the Environment dialog box.

9. In the External Database Configuration dialog box, select the Convert R12 Links tab, if it's not already displayed (see fig. 26.13).

Figure 26.13

The Convert R12 Links tab of the External Database Configuration dialog box is used to map R12 Link information with the new hierarchy in R14.

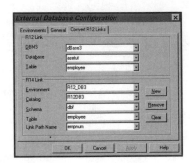

10. Under R12 Link, specify the following for each of the identified edit boxes:

    DBMS: dBase3

    Database: asetut

    Table: employee

11. Under R14 Link, specify the following for each of the identified edit boxes:

    Environment: R12_DB3

    Catalog: R12DB3

    Schema: dbf

    Table: employee

    Link Path Name: empnum

12. Click on the New button to save the conversion of your R12 Link to R14 Link. An ASI Editor dialog box will appear to confirm that you want to proceed with the conversion (see fig. 26.14). Click on the OK button to proceed. Click on the OK button at the bottom of the External Database Configuration dialog box to exit the Database Configuration utility.

Figure 26.14

A dialog box appears to confirm whether you want to proceed with the conversion.

13. Start AutoCAD and use the OPEN command to open c:\acad12\tutorial\asetut.dwg.

14. Type **ASEADMIN** at the Command: prompt. An ASE Warning dialog box is displayed. This lists errors caused by the existence of R12 formatted links in the drawing. Ignore these errors for now and click on the Close button. The Administration dialog box is displayed. In the Database Objects scroll window, select the environment R12_DB3, and click on the Connect button, as shown in figure 26.15. In the Connect to Environment dialog box, leave the name and password fields blank; then click on the OK button. Click on the Catalog button in the Database Object Selection area, then highlight R12_DB3 in the Database Objects scroll window. Click on the Schema button in the Database Object Selection area. Highlight DBF in the Database Objects scroll window. Click on the Table button in the Database Object Selection area.

Figure 26.15

The R12_DB3 environment successfully converted to Release 14 format.

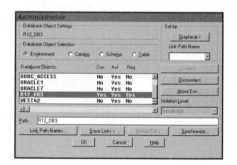

15. Highlight the EMPLOYEE table in the Database Objects scroll window, and click on the Synchronize button (see fig. 26.16).

Figure 26.16

The Administration dialog box displaying existing tables that need to be synchronized.

16.   A dialog box will appear with a warning message, as shown in figure 26.17.

Figure 26.17

A warning message appears stating that the table has the wrong key type.

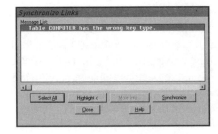

17.   Click on the Select All button to select all the messages, and click on the Synchronize button.

NOTE

This procedure is necessary for the proper conversion of the values or to delete any invalid links. If there is no warning message, then all your R12 information was converted successfully.

18.   If no warning messages are displayed then click on the Close button to exit the Synchronize Links dialog. Click on the OK button to exit the Administration dialog.

19.   Each table must be synchronized. Therefore, you must go through steps 1 through 18 for both the COMPUTER and the INVENTRY tables. In the preceding steps, replace the table name EMPLOYEE with the appropriate table name to synchronize.

NOTE

If a DATE column was used to define key values in the Release 12 drawing and the driver mapped the data type to CHAR, the links to those objects might not get converted and could be lost.

After you synchronize each table, the links should successfully be updated to R14.

Understanding the Features and Functions of Structured Query Language (SQL)

SQL, which stands for Structured Query Language, has become the standard computer database language. The computer program that controls the database, (such as Microsoft Access and Oracle 7) is called the *database management system*. SQL is a comprehensive language for controlling and interacting with a database management system (DBMS), and this tool can organize, manage, and retrieve data stored by a computer database. In fact, SQL works with one specific type of database, called a relational database. Figure 26.18 shows a visual representation of how SQL works.

Figure 26.18

How SQL is used as a tool to request database information.

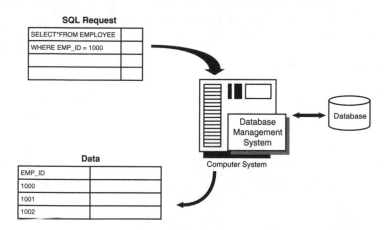

When you need to retrieve data from the database, you can use the SQL language to make the request. The DBMS processes the SQL request, retrieves the requested data, and returns it to you. This process of requesting data from the database and receiving results is called a query (hence the name Structured *Query* Language).

This section contains a quick tour of SQL to illustrate its major features and functions. Included is a sample database to help give you basic familiarity with the SQL language.

NOTE

For detailed information on how to try sample SQL statements from within AutoCAD, see the last exercise in this chapter, "Searching for Database Data Using AutoCAD SQL Editor."

Reviewing a Sample Database: Facilities Management Database

The sample database (bldg18.dbf) in this exercise is a database of an office building detailing the location, asset number, and cost of all computer equipment. The data also includes the room number, equipment manufacturer, and department assignment. The sample database can be found on the CD.

Table 26.4

Bldg18.dbf Sample Database

Room	Manufacturer	Description	EQ_Type	Department	Asset No.	Cost
42202	Panasonic	Omnivision PV-4451	A/V VCR	Multimedia	45089	2600.6
42203	Panasonic	Superflat CT27SF11S	A/V TV Color	Multimedia	45093	2600.6
42214	Toshiba	386 Portable T2200SX 60 MB	CPU Port	Field Engineering	35662	8656.86
42214	Micron	586/90 Deskpro 590	CPU	Graphic design	55653	0

Room	Manufacturer	Description	EQ_Type	Department	Asset No.	Cost
42216	Micron	90 Deskpro 590	CPU	Graphic design	55654	0
42216	Micron	386 20 E	CPU	Accounting	8738	9822.24
42217	NEC	3D	Monitor	Accounting	8737	658.6

Retrieving Data from the Database Using the SELECT Statement

The SQL statement that retrieves data from the database is called SELECT. If you want to list the room number, equipment manufacturer, and the department, the appropriate statement would be:

```
SELECT ROOM, MANUFACTURER, DEPARTMENT FROM BLDG18
```

Table 26.5 displays the results.

Table 26.5

Sample Formatted Output Resulting from Executing the Preceding SQL Statement

ROOM	MANUFACTURER	DEPARTMENT
42202	Panasonic	Multimedia
42203	Panasonic	Multimedia
42214	Toshiba	Field engineering
42214	Micron	Graphic design
42216	Micron	Graphic design
42216	Micron	Accounting
42217	NEC	Accounting

The following list details other valid Select statements:

- Select * from bldg18

- Select * from bldg18, where manufacturer = 'Toshiba'

- Select * from bldg18, where room = '1037'

- Select room, eq type from bldg18, where cost > 700

- Select department, eq type from bldg18, where cost = between 8,000 and 9,000

- Select * from bldg18, where cost = between 1,000 and 8,000 (order by cost)

- Select max (cost) from bldg18

- Select min (cost) from bldg18

- Select sum (cost) from bldg18

Comparison Operators in SQL Syntax

SQL statements contain comparison operators, which are symbols used to describe certain conditions for data. Some of these operators are used in the bulleted list in the preceding section.

The comparison operators and their descriptions are contained in table 26.6.

Table 26.6

Comparison Operators for SQL Syntax

Operator	Description
=	Equals
>	Greater than
<	Less than
>=	Greater than or equal to
<=	Less than or equal to
<>	Not equal to
BETWEEN.. AND..	Between two values

Operator	Description
IN (list..)	Any values in the specified list
LIKE	Match a character pattern
IS NULL	Where the value is null (no value)

Adding Data to the Database Using the INSERT Statement

To create a new record in a table, you must insert the column values by using the SQL statement INSERT. For example, if you want to add a new record in the sample database containing the room number, equipment manufacturer, equipment type, and department, you would type:

```
INSERT INTO BLDG18 (ROOM, MANUFACTURER, EQ TYPE, DEPARTMENT)
VALUES ('42220', 'COMPAQ', 'CPU', 'MULTIMEDIA')
```

Updating the Database Using the UPDATE Statement

Column-specific data can be changed using the SQL statement UPDATE. Columns can be updated individually or globally. For example, to change the cost of the monitor to 8,850, you would type:

```
UPDATE BLDG18 SET COST = 8,850 WHERE EQ TYPE = 'MONITOR'
```

Deleting Data from the Database Using DELETE Statement

Records can be removed using the SQL statement DELETE. Records can be deleted individually or globally. For example, if you want to delete any record(s) that contains equipment from Apple, enter the following:

```
DELETE FROM BLDG18 WHERE MANUFACTURER = 'APPLE'
```

Keep the following points in mind when using the DELETE statement:

- SQL Statements are always case-sensitive.

- You can use Text constants and Wildcard characters. Text fields should be delimited with single quotes, such as 'OBJECTS.'

- The % character is used as a wildcard, which means that it can substitute for any characters. For example, the SQL where clause "Where Firstname Like P%r will find all first names that begin with P and end with r.

Creating a Database Table Using CREATE TABLE Statement

Before you can store data in a database, you first must define the structure of the data. To continue with the example of the Facilities Management database, suppose you want to expand the bldg18.dbf database by adding table data on employee information for each room number. The following list details the data to be stored for each room:

- Room number

- A 25-character last name

- A 20-character first name

- A 20-character title

This SQL Create Table statement defines a new table in which to store the products data: Create Table Employee (Room Integer, Last Name Char[25], First Name Char[20], Title Char[20]).

Calculating Data in the Database

SQL enables you to summarize data from the database through a set of columns. Table 26.9 details some SQL statements that are useful in calculating database information.

Table 26.9

SQL Statements Used to Calculate Database Information

SQL Statement	Description
Select Avg(Cost) from BLDG18	Calculates the average cost of the equipment in bldg18 database
Select Sum(Cost) from BLDG18	Calculates the total cost of the equipment in bldg18 database
Select Min(Cost) from BLDG18	Calculates the lowest equipment cost in bldg18 database
Select Max(Cost) from BLDG18	Calculates the highest equipment cost in bldg18 database

Summary of SQL Syntax

This section has included a lot of information on statements and syntax that can be used to manipulate databases. For quick reference, table 26.10 summarizes the major SQL statements with which you should be familiar.

Table 26.10

Major SQL Statements Used in Data Manipulation and Definition

Statement	Description
	Data Manipulation
Select	Retrieves data from the database
Insert	Adds new rows of data to the database
Delete	Removes rows of data to the database
Update	Modifies existing database data

continues

Table 26.10 continued

Major SQL Statements Used in Data Manipulation and Definition

Statement	Description
	Data Definition
Create Table	Adds a new table to the database
Drop Table	Removes a table from the database
Alter Table	Changes the structure of an existing table
Create Index	Builds an index for a column
Drop Index	Removes the index for a column

So far, you have learned to connect to various databases and include links to databases within your AutoCAD drawings. This chapter also has covered SQL syntax so that you will be able to manipulate data in your database effectively. The following section takes the next step; it discusses how to make productive use of AutoCAD objects and the external database together.

Using ASE Effectively

After you establish your database link in your AutoCAD drawings, the next step to consider is how to combine and use an AutoCAD object and its external database together. This section brings together all the information covered thus far and details the entire process of connecting to external databases and using ASE effectively.

The exercises in this section continue to use the bldg18.dbf database to demonstrate how the database information inside an AutoCAD drawing could be used. To refresh your memory, this is a database of an office building detailing the location, asset number, and cost of the computer equipment. This information includes the room number, equipment manufacturer, and department assignment for each piece of equipment.

Specifically, this section describes how to accomplish the following tasks:

- Set up your database

- Specify the DBMS and database using the ASEADMIN command

- Set your database links with AutoCAD objects

- Display data in the drawings

- Add or delete database records inside AutoCAD

- Search database data

The task of setting up the database and creating and using the links within AutoCAD can be divided into six separate exercises corresponding to the steps in the preceding list.

Step 1: Setting Up the Database

In this example, the drawing and the database reside on the accompanying CD-ROM.

SETTING UP THE EXTERNAL DATABASE

1. Use the External Database Configuration (asicfg.exe) to configure your database. If you are unfamiliar with this process, see the previous section for more information.

2. In the External Database Configuration dialog box, click on the Add button. The Select DBMS for new Environment dialog box is displayed. Under the DBMS List, select dBase III (it should be highlighted as shown in figure 26.19). Go to the Environment Name edit box and type **Project18**. Go to the Environment Description edit box and type **JG Additional Project**. Click on the OK button to save the Environment name.

3. The Environment:Project18(DB3DRV) dialog box is displayed. Go to the Name edit box in the Catalog section and type **Bldg18**. Go to the Path edit box in the Catalog section and enter the path **d:\proj18**. Click on the New button in the Catalog area to save the new Catalog Name.

Figure 26.19

Dialog box for defining your Environment Name after selecting the appropriate DBMS.

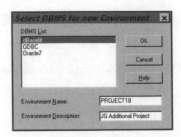

4. Go to the Name edit box in the Schema section and type **Facilities** as the schema name. Go to the Path edit box in the Schema section and type **facmgmt** as the Schema Path. Click on the New button in the Schema section to save the new schema name (see fig. 26.20).

Figure 26.20

The Catalog tab of the Environment dialog box is used to specify the catalog and schema information.

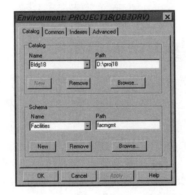

5. Click on OK to apply the changes, and close the ASI Environment dialog box.

6. After you define the environment, click on Test to verify that you successfully can connect to proj18.dbf. A Login dialog box is displayed. Leave the User Name edit box and the Password edit box blank. Click on the Connect button to start the test. A dialog box will indicate that you have made a successful connection. On the Connection test passed dialog box, click on the Done button, then the OK button to exit the database configuration.

Step 2: Setting Up Your DBMS and Database

After you configure your database, you must tell AutoCAD which DBMS you are using and where to find the databases. This step is facilitated by the ASEADMIN command.

SPECIFYING THE DBMS AND DATABASE USING THE ASEADMIN COMMAND

1. Start AutoCAD and use the Open command to open d:\proj18\facmgmt\bldg18.dwg.

2. Type **ASEADMIN** at the Command: prompt. The Administration dialog box appears, as shown in figure 26.21.

Figure 26.21

The Administration dialog box appears when you enter ASEADMIN at the Command: prompt.

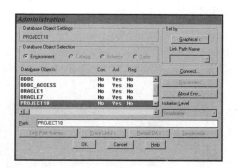

3. In the Database Objects scroll window, scroll down the list and select the environment Project18, and click on the Connect button. In the Connect to Environment dialog box, leave the name and password fields blank; then click on the OK button. Click on the Catalog button in the Database Object Selection area. Highlight Bldg18 in the Database Objects scroll window. Select the Schema button in the Database Object Selection area. Highlight Facilities in the Database Objects scroll window. Select the Table button in the Database Object Selection area. Highlight Bldg18 in the Database Objects scroll window as shown in figure 26.22.

Figure 26.22

Multiple tables are displayed for every database environment defined.

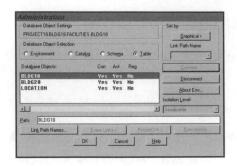

4. Select the Link Path Name button at the bottom of the Administration dialog box. The Link Path Names dialog box is displayed. In the Key Selection area, select Asset_No (that row will highlight), and then click on the On button.

5. In the Link Path area, go to the New edit box and type **ASSET_NO**. (Note, do not include the period as part of the name.)

6. Make sure that you click on the New button to register the new link path name successfully (see fig. 26.23). Click on the Close button to exit the Link Path Name dialog box. Click on the OK button to exit the Administration dialog box.

Figure 26.23

Creating Link Path Name by selecting the unique identifier for the database.

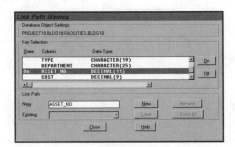

Step 3: Setting Up Your Database Links with AutoCAD Objects

One of the most powerful features of ASE is the link that you can create between a graphic entity and a row in a table. This link enables you to create a two-way data flow: data changed in the table can update the values of displayable attributes in a drawing, and AutoCAD can change data stored in the table.

The process of making the object data links with the AutoCAD objects can be both manual and automated. Linking from the Rows dialog boxes involves selecting a specific record and then picking the AutoCAD object. You can link multiple entities to the same row, and you can link multiple rows to the same entity. Often, rows from multiple tables link to one entity. The only restriction is that each row must have a unique key value.

This exercise links bldg18.dbf using the Asset No. column as the primary key because the asset number is unique to each record.

LINKING AN OFFICE FLOOR PLAN DRAWING WITH THE BUILDING DATABASE

1. Continuing with the bldg18.dwg drawing, type **ASEROWS** at the Command: prompt. The Rows dialog box is displayed. In the Condition edit box within the Select Rows area type **ROOM=42317**, as shown in figure 26.24. This specifies the room number to which you want to link. Here, the Room value 42317, which is located on the left portion of the drawing, is used.

Figure 26.24

The room number is entered in the Rows dialog box to search the database for each occurrence of Room 42317.

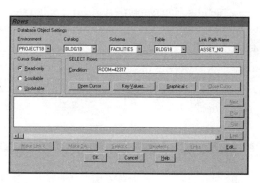

2. Press Enter to confirm the value you specify. ASE will return all occurrences of Room 42317 in the database. In this example, nine records belong to this room.

3. Click on the Make Link button to link the current record to the AutoCAD object that matches the room number 42317. The dialog box is temporarily cleared and you're prompted to select the graphic object that will be linked to the current database row. Select the AutoCAD text object identifying room 42317. Press the Enter key to end object selection. The Rows dialog box will reappear (see fig. 26.25) and if the link is successfully created, a confirmation message saying 1 link(s) created will appear at the bottom of the dialog box.

Figure 26.25

The ASE Rows dialog box appears displaying the database information linked to the AutoCAD objects.

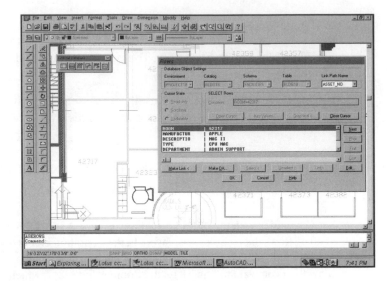

4. Click on the Next button to go to the next record to which you want to link. Repeat step 3 to create the link. You can repeat the preceding steps if you want to link with more AutoCAD objects.

5. To verify that the link was created, type **ASELINKS** at the Command: prompt and select the object that contains the link.

6. In the Links dialog box, click on the Row button to view the associated database information (see fig. 26.26).

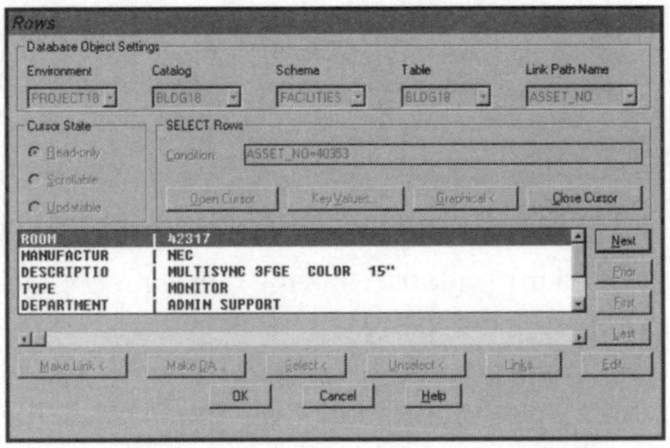

Figure 26.26

The Rows dialog box shows the associated database information.

Step 4: Displaying Data in the Drawings

After you link your external database to your AutoCAD drawing, you can prompt ASE to display the data. Using the links set in a drawing, you can display column data in the drawings, display data using graphics selections, and select entities based on a table query.

This can be accomplished in ASE using the Displayable Attributes function in ASEROWS. This function enables you to display the value of a particular row and column in the drawing. The user must determine how the row and column will appear.

Continuing with the current example, use the steps in the following exercise to display, on the AutoCAD drawing, the information linked to Room 42317.

DISPLAYING THE INFORMATION LINKED TO ROOM 42317

1. Continuing with the bldg18.dwg drawing, type **ASEROWS** at the Command: prompt. Click on the Graphical button.

2. When prompted to select the object, select the object 42317. The screen should display the current record linked to that object.

3. Click on the Make DA button to create the displayable attributes.

4. In the Make Displayable Attribute dialog box, identify each column to display by selecting each column in the Table Columns list box and by clicking on the Add button or double-clicking on the desired column (see fig. 26.27).

Figure 26.27

Select columns to display using the Make Displayable Attribute dialog box.

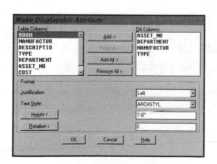

5. Once all the columns are identified, adjust text object characteristics in the Format area as desired. Click on the OK button and identify the insertion point of the attributes. The Rows dialog box reappears. Click on the OK button to exit the dialog box. The displayable attributes will now be visible on the drawing. (See figure 26.28 for the resulting display.)

Figure 26.28

Room 42317 in the AutoCAD drawing displays the information contained in the selected columns.

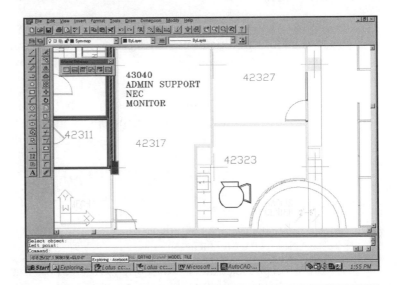

Step 5: Adding or Deleting Database Records Inside AutoCAD

Now that you have linked your external database to your AutoCAD drawing, the database information is available within your current drawing session. With ASE, you do not need a DBMS system to manipulate the database information. ASE provides a two-way data flow, manipulating the graphic objects from the table and manipulating the table from the graphic objects.

Suppose you have a new Compaq computer and must add the information in the database. The following exercise shows the steps involved in adding a new database record.

ADDING A DATABASE RECORD

1. Continuing with the bldg18.dwg drawing, type **ASEROWS** at the Command: prompt. Select Updatable in the Cursor State area.

2. Click on the Edit button. The Edit Row dialog box appears. This dialog box serves as a template that lists all the columns in which you must enter the information, as shown on figure 26.29.

Figure 26.29

The Edit Row dialog box enables you to create or modify external database information.

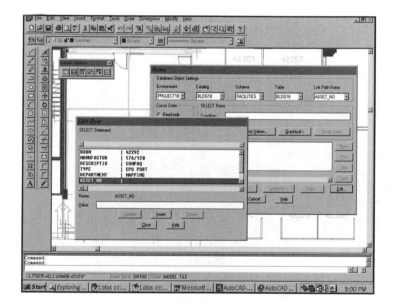

3. Type the column's data into the Value edit box and press the Enter key. Repeat this for each column until the template is filled out.

4. Click on the Insert button to insert the row in your database. The message `Row is inserted` appears at the bottom of the Edit Rows dialog box. Click on the Close button and then click on the OK button to exit the Rows dialog box.

Next, suppose you want to delete all the obsolete equipment in your office, such as the Canon equipment. To delete a database record, follow these steps:

DELETING A DATABASE RECORD

1. Continuing with the bldg18.dwg drawing, type **ASEROWS** at the Command: prompt. Select Updatable in the Cursor State area.

2. In the Condition edit box in the SELECT Rows area, type **manufactur='CANON'** to specify the equipment you want to delete in the database.

3. Press Enter to confirm the value you specify. ASE will return all occurrences of all equipment manufactured by Canon in the database. In this example, one record belongs to Canon.

4. Click on the Edit button. The Edit Row dialog box appears with the current record information, as shown in figure 26.30.

Figure 26.30

The ASE Edit Rows dialog box appears containing the search result executed in the ASE Rows dialog box.

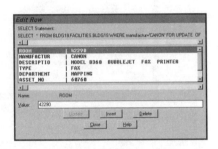

5. Click on the Delete button, and click on OK to confirm the deletion of the current record. The message `Row is deleted` appears at the bottom of the Edit Rows dialog box.

INSIDER TIP

If the Delete button is disabled, the Cursor State is set as Read-Only. You must change the Cursor State to Updatable to be able to edit your database.

6. Click on the Close button on the Edit Row dialog box. The record disappears from the Rows dialog box. Click on the OK button to exit the ASEROWS command.

Step 6: Searching Database Data Using AutoCAD SQL Editor

You can use the AutoCAD SQL Editor to search for data using SQL statements as your criteria. For example, the following exercise shows the steps involved in searching for all the Apple Computer equipment.

SEARCHING FOR DATABASE DATA USING AUTOCAD SQL EDITOR

1. Continuing with the bldg18.dwg drawing, type **ASESQLED** at the Command: prompt. The SQL Editor dialog box is displayed. In the SQL edit box within the SQL Statement area, type **select * from bldg18, where manufactur='APPLE'**.

2. Click on the Execute button to process the SQL statement. As shown in figure 26.31, the computer will return all the records that match the SQL criteria you specified.

Figure 26.31

The SQL Cursor dialog box displays the search result executed from the SQL Editor dialog box using an SQL statement.

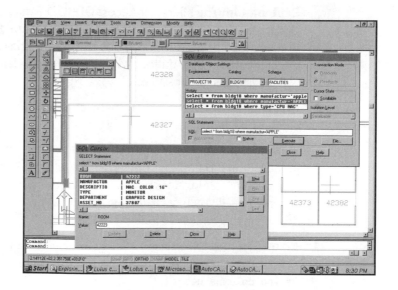

Dealing with Common Problems and Error Messages

This section discusses some of the common problems and error messages that can occur when using ASE. Each of the following is an explanation of the possible reasons or suggested ways to solve the problem.

- **Error:** The messages `Error: Can't prepare the SQL statement` or `Error: Insufficient Memory` appear.

  Explanation: These errors can occur when you attempt to create a link to a table in an Access 7.0 database if the table being linked to contains OLE Object or Memo fields. These two data types are not supported, so it is not possible to create a link to any of the fields in a table that contains either of these two data types.

- **Error:** Using Microsoft Access, when selecting Open Cursor in the ASE Rows dialog box, the Cursor State option Updatable is grayed out.

  Explanation: The Microsoft Access ODBC Driver does not support the Updatable Cursor feature. To determine the capabilities of the ODBC driver, bring up the ASEADMIN dialog box, connect to the ODBC driver, and then select the About Env. button. With this driver, the feature Update: Positioned will be listed as not possible.

- **Error:** `Can't get list of database objects` appears when loading a catalog or schema.

  Explanation: This error occurs if the information in the Environment section in the External Database Configuration Editor (asicfg.exe) is incorrect. Make sure that the catalog alias points to the parent directory of the schema. In other words, if you have a catalog called Cat and a schema called Data, the actual database files are located by the path.

- **Error:** The messages `Error: Table is unaccessible, wrong format of <filename>.dbf file` or `Error: Table is unaccessible, can't get a list of the columns description` appear.

  Explanation: These errors occur when you select a table in the Administration dialog box if the database file is in an incompatible format for use with dBase III. The .DBF file is most likely in dBase IV format.

■ **Error:** The message R12-R14 ASE Conversion: Object has no links appears.

Explanation: This error can occur when you use the ASELINKS command when you click on the entity to verify that the R12 link is recognized. Your existing R12 links are not automatically recognized in R13. You must convert the link in order for the Link Path Names to be recognized.

■ **Error:** The system can't find LPN for R12 DOR.

Explanation: This error can occur when you open an existing drawing and select Administration for ASE if the drawing file that you opened contains an existing R12 ASE link. To eliminate this error, use the External Database Configuration Editor (asicfg.exe) to convert existing R12 ASE links to R13 ASE links.

Summary

This chapter explained how to get the most out of the AutoCAD SQL environment. In addition to explaining how to connect to dBase III, Oracle 7, and ODBC (Access) database applications, this chapter provided an overview of the basics of SQL syntax. Exercises were provided to help you understand how to use ASE effectively to link to and display database information. Finally, common error messages and problems were presented, along with explanations and suggestions on how to solve them.

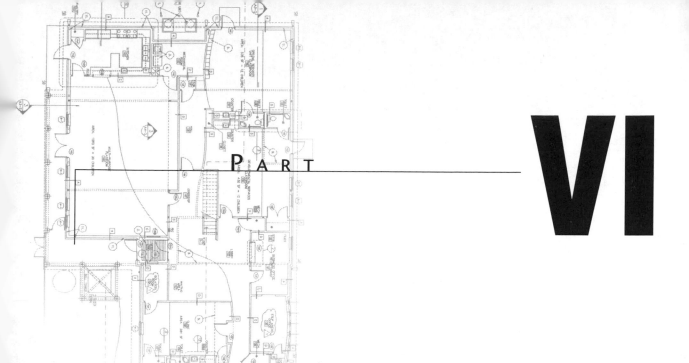

PART VI

CAD on the Internet

Chapter 27: Publishing on the Web

Chapter 28: Project Collaboration over the Internet

CHAPTER 27

PUBLISHING ON THE WEB

by Mark Sage

With the integration of Internet access functionality into Release 14, AutoCAD has become "web-enabled." At the same time, Autodesk's WHIP! technology has "CAD-enabled" the web. The merger of these two technologies delivers very powerful tools to web-savvy designers. In this chapter, you learn how to integrate these exciting new capabilities into your current engineering practices. Useful information to help further your understanding of the Internet is also included. Exercises in this chapter help you learn how to use AutoCAD's Internet functionality to:

- *View AutoCAD DWG or DWF files from your web browser.*

- *Open, insert, or save drawings over the web from within AutoCAD.*

- *Embed Uniform Resource Locators (URLs) within drawings.*

- *Save drawing files in the vector-based, highly compressed Drawing Web Format (DWF).*

- *Place DWF files into HTML pages.*

Sending CAD Data Over the Internet: What's It All About?

The World Wide Web has become a pervasive medium for computing. For many firms, the role of the Internet as a serious business tool has not yet been made clear, with numerous web sites implemented strictly for marketing purposes. Yet, for creators and users of CAD data, the Internet provides an environment that greatly benefits the engineering community. From a CAD perspective, the web is the ideal mechanism for facilitating collaborative design and real-time communication.

Ask 100 people to define the Internet and you are likely to receive 100 different answers. That's because the web is something different to everyone. To one person it may be a valuable research tool, to another an e-mail system, and someone else may consider it strictly as an entertainment media. The Internet is all these things and much, much more. For you and your colleagues, using the World Wide Web offers the opportunity to expand the reach of your business.

The Internet and the World Wide Web deliver powerful tools and new ways to enhance the virtual reach of your business. With these new Net tools, you can offer potential customers immediate access to technical drawing data, specifications, or other key project data.

Internets versus Intranets

The Internet is a global network made up of other networks that communicate with each other consistently. People using the Internet can access services from other computers. Much of the resources available through the networks are free. The services available on the Internet include:

- HTTP (HyperText Transfer Protocol). Used to receive hypertext content that links to other content on the web

- FTP (File Transfer Protocol). Used for getting files

- E-mail

- UseNet news groups and discussion forums

- World Wide Web

An intranet offers services similar to those previously noted, but is an internal corporate network. Instead of being hooked up to the world, an intranet is an internal corporate resource. The purpose of an intranet is to deliver internal information about the company's resources to each employee. Intranet access is secure and typically limited to designated employees with external access prevented by a *firewall*.

Impact of the Internet on CAD

The Internet has a wide variety of uses, and new capabilities emerge on a daily basis. As previously noted, the web is used for marketing, software distribution, retail sales, stock trading, entertainment, market research, e-mail, and more. Companies with a presence on the web (a web site) deliver information to a global audience, saving time, the cost of materials, and shipping and handling. Web users get the benefits of rapid access to information they need at little cost. The Internet lends itself particularly well to communicating technical information (such as CAD drawing information) or data about sophisticated products (such as AutoCAD Release 14). Most important, the Internet can deliver information targeted at an audience with interests similar to yours.

Manufacturers' information is becoming widely available online in electronic formats, ready to be inserted into a CAD drawing. Designers and manufacturers save time while improving accuracy and overall project quality. Online training programs improve the skills of designers while reducing the cost of keeping current with changing technologies.

Direct Benefits of the Net for CAD

With Internet-enabled Release 14, multiple designers at various locations can view, redline, or edit your drawings in real-time. This new technology is highly beneficial, facilitating the coordination of large or small projects. With AutoCAD Release 14, you can access .DWG files anywhere in the world at any time via the Internet. No more waiting for a drawing file to arrive by overnight courier. This immediate access reduces cycle time and travel costs while increasing quality through enhanced communications. Bids for new projects can be searched, solicited, and submitted online, opening up new opportunities for companies that may not have had the resources to previously participate in such processes. Questions and proposals are e-mailed, and the time saved is put to better use in refining the bid. A product portfolio of the firm's successful projects can be converted into a web site. This expands the audience for your services, resulting in greater market exposure and potentially higher revenues.

Understanding the Capabilities of a Web-enabled AutoCAD Release 14

The web enabling of AutoCAD actually began with the AutoCAD Release 13 Internet Publishing Kit (IPK). The IPK included some utilities for accessing .DWG files across the Net of the *WHIP!* Plug-In for Netscape Navigator, and the capability to create DWF files from inside Release 13. With Release 14, some key elements of the IPK have been integrated into AutoCAD, resulting in a more seamless, Internet-friendly product. A web-enabled AutoCAD Release 14 includes components divided into the following three categories:

- Applets
- Toolbars/Menus
- Help System

Each of these categories is examined in the following sections.

Release 14's ARX Internet Applets

AutoCAD Release 14 contains four separate demand loaded ObjectARX applets that web-enable the product:

- **BROWSER.ARX.** Invokes the Launch Browser function.
- **INTERNET.ARX.** Contains the code for accessing DWG files on the Internet.
- **DWFIU.ARX.** Delivers the functionality for embedding and managing URLs in the drawing file.
- **DWFOUT.ARX.** Supports the creation of DWF files.

In combination, these applets comprise the AutoCAD Internet Utilities. By default, these files get installed into the root ACADR14 directory (you may have a different AutoCAD directory name). Because these applets are based on ObjectARX, they can be updated asynchronously from AutoCAD or each other. Given that the web changes so rapidly, this design enables each component to include the latest technology.

Toolbars/Menus

Access to most of the Internet Utilities (such as the OpenURL or AttachURL commands) is available either through the Command: line or Toolbar. Unfortunately, no partial pull-down menu entries are provided with Release 14. The only web-related function available by pull-down is the creation of DWF files. The Files pull-down menu provides support for creating DWF files under the Export option. As with all file formats created by the Export dialog box, no icon is provided. DWFOUT is the command-line equivalent of the Export|DWF menu function. For more information, please refer to the section "Creating DWF Files with the DWFOUT Command," later in this chapter.

NOTE

The Internet Utilities Toolbar will only be installed if Full or Custom installation is selected.

Release 14's Internet Utilities toolbar includes nine icon buttons as shown in figure 27.1. Each icon includes a helpful tooltip description.

Figure 27.1

The AutoCAD Internet Utilities toolbar. Pausing the cursor over the icon displays the associated tooltip.

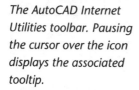

Help System

 New to this version of AutoCAD is the capability to connect directly to the Release 14 home page at Autodesk (if so defined). In the Help pull-down menu is the new item, Connect to Internet. When chosen, the system's configured web browser is launched, and the system changes focus to your web browser. Complete context-sensitive help for the Release 14 Internet functionality is built in to the AutoCAD Help system. As shown in figure 27.2, online help is available for all the web-enabling features of AutoCAD Release 14.

NOTE

Only Netscape Navigator 3.0x, Navigator 4.0 (Communicator), or Microsoft Internet Explorer 3.0 browsers are supported by AutoCAD Release 14.

Figure 27.2

AutoCAD Release 14's Help system includes support for the Internet functions.

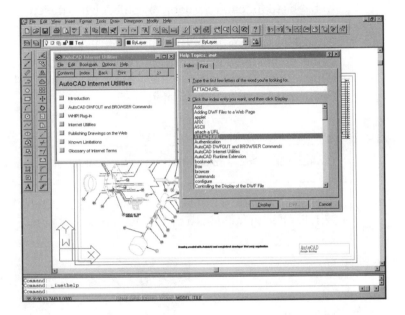

Viewing Design Data on the Web

It is essential to have the capability to view design data, such as drawing files, on the web if you are going to add the Internet to your arsenal of design tools. With the extensive incorporation of the *WHIP!* technology into Release 14's graphics pipeline, Autodesk furthers your ability to accomplish this key task. AutoCAD Release 14 supports the launching of your web browser from inside the product and creates web-friendly DWF files. In addition, Autodesk offers browser plug-ins that support viewing of DWG (Autodesk View) and DWF (*WHIP!* Release 2) files.

BROWSER Command: Release 14's Connect to Internet Feature

The Browser command launches the Internet web browser that is associated with .HTM in the system registry. This command is available from the Help pull-down

(Connect to Internet), the Standard toolbar menu, or the Command: prompt. When invoked from the toolbar or the pull-down menu, the Browser command does not prompt for a location (URL). A system variable (INETLOCATION) contains the URL address that the browser will invoke.

When the Browser command is issued at the Command: prompt, the command window shows the following:

```
Location <www.autodesk.com/acaduser>:
```

At this point you may press Enter to accept the default location or type in a new address. AutoCAD then launches the web browser, and your browser then goes to the specified location (URL).

INSIDER TIP

AutoCAD won't launch a new instance of your browser if the browser is already running. Your browser will go to the URL specified by AutoCAD's INETLOCATION system variable. You can use your browser's Back button to return to the location that was active prior to using AutoCAD Release 14's Browser command.

Understanding DWF Files

AutoCAD Release 14 writes (but does not read) DWF files. In essence, a DWF file is like an electronic plot—it facilitates the viewing of CAD drawings on the World Wide Web. DWF is a file format for viewing CAD data published to the web through your Internet browser. DWF is not intended to be a CAD file format used to create engineering documents, but to publish them. As previously explained, Autodesk (and other software companies) offer web browser plug-ins that support viewing of DWG and DWF files.

The Drawing Web Format was developed because current, widely accepted, two-dimensional vector file standards did not address the needs of Internet-aware applications and because existing commercial formats are too closely tied to specific proprietary data structures to support the exchange of illustrations among systems.

Specifically, the Drawing Web Format was developed for the following purposes:

- Archival of drawings in an openly accessible and application-independent format.

- Transmission of drawings over a variety of mediums, especially the Internet's World Wide Web.

- Open exchange of drawings between DWF-generating applications and DWF-viewing applications.

- To enable users of illustration applications to self-publish their work on the World Wide Web and to add functionality to their drawings by embedding hyperlinks (URLs).

What Is DWF?

DWF is intended for the efficient viewing of CAD drawing data on the web (an electronic plot). DWF is not intended for the interchange of higher-level data between applications. *DWF* is a file format for the standardized description of two-dimensional, vector-based drawings and illustrations.

The primary features of DWF files are:

- **Application independence.** Because DWF files incorporate a generalized two-dimensional vector format rather than using the data structure details of a specific application, DWF provides application independence.

- **Compatibility.** DWF files provide for compatibility by having established a common, extensible syntax for the exchange of two-dimensional graphical data between applications that generate drawings and viewing applications that read DWF files.

- **Simplicity.** Through the use of a flexible syntax that requires minimal information for simple cases while allowing a graceful escalation of information required for more complex drawing descriptions, DWF maintains simplicity.

- **Robustness.** Fully supported features of DWF include lines, polylines, polygons, polytriangles, markers, images, circles, arcs, wedges, ellipses, Bézier curves, text, visibility, Gouraud shading, texture mapping, 31-bit data precision, layer control, view control, clip regions, variable transparency, and international character sets.

- **Extensibility.** DWF delivers extensibility through the use of mechanisms built into the specification and through a set of rules for DWF file-reading programs that allow for unforeseen extensions.

- **Compact size.** Especially critical for Internet transmission, DWF includes a data compression method that minimizes duplication of geometric information.

- **Embedding mechanism.** DWF includes a mechanism for the attachment of any kind of data (with a link or an embed operation) to the format.

- **URL hyperlink support.** DWF supports the embedding of World Wide Web hyperlink URLs into the drawing data.

The preceding list summarized the main features of a DWF file. The primary benefits of using the DWF file type are described in the following section.

Benefits of DWF

You should note several benefits of using the DWF file format. The main advantages are summarized as follows:

- **Speed.** DWF allows rapid download and viewing.

- **Accuracy.** With 32-bit precision, drawing detail is maintained.

- **Security.** Proprietary drawing data can be kept safe.

- **Ease of Use.** Creating, publishing, and viewing DWF files is simple to do.

Speed

DWF files are vector-based, making them more efficient than bitmaps or other file formats for storing and displaying design information. In addition, DWF files are transmitted in compressed form, further reducing download time. As a result, DWF drawings are faster to download and faster to use. Panning and zooming are virtually instantaneous because there's no need to reload images or access the server.

Accuracy

AutoCAD Release 14 supports creating DWF files with up to 32-bit precision, ensuring that your designs can maintain the detail you expect with AutoCAD. Within the DWF file, vector data is stored as lines, arcs, and circles, as opposed to the individual pixels found in bitmap file formats such as GIF and JPEG. Vector images are a more efficient and robust method for storing precise, detailed graphic information, such as technical illustrations and CAD drawings.

Security

DWF supports both secure and open data. For liability reasons, electronic transfer of engineering data has been fairly limited. DWF files don't expose all the drawing file data to the public. This means that you can showcase your work, yet maintain ownership of the intellectual property contained within the drawing file.

Ease of Use

Creating DWF files with AutoCAD Release 14 is a simple matter, as shown later in the chapter. Publishing DWF files to the web is quite easy as noted in the section titled "Publishing Your Drawings on the Web." Viewing DWF files with Autodesk's *WHIP!* browser tool is an intuitive and straightforward process.

The DWF File Specification

DWF files are organized into three main sections:

- **File identification header.** Enables applications to easily determine the DWF file version.

- **File data block.** The file section containing drawing data.

- **File termination trailer.** Indicates the end of the DWF data sequence—normally the end of the file.

Data in the file header and the trailer is in readable ASCII text. Data in the file data block is delimited by operation codes (opcodes) and argument data used by the opcodes (operands). The two types of opcode-operand pairs are: readable ASCII text and coded binary.

All DWF operations have a readable ASCII opcode/operand form, and most operations also have a coded binary opcode/operand form. By using the proper opcode form, you can create a file that is humanly readable (ASCII), one that is more efficient from a processing and storage point of view (binary), or (more commonly) a mixture of both types (ASCII and binary).

An application reading a DWF file may not understand a set of opcodes, especially when the application reading the file outdates the application that created the file. For this reason, DWF is designed to enable a file reader to skip most opcodes. For the file reader to skip an opcode, it must know the length of its operand. DWF has three categories of opcodes:

- Single-byte opcodes that must be recognized (for efficiency reasons) and thus cannot be skipped. A reader application need not implement these opcodes but must be able to compute their operand length (which requires that the opcode be recognized). If a single-byte opcode is unrecognized by a DWF reading application, the rest of the file cannot be read.

- Extended ASCII opcodes (humanly readable) that have delimited and nestable operands. By following some simple rules, a reader can safely skip such an opcode/operand pair without understanding the operation or its contents.

- Extended binary opcodes that indicate their operand length so that a reader can easily skip past the unknown operation and data.

For more information on the DWF file specification, a complete copy of the *WHIP!/* DWF Developers Toolkit is available for downloading at no charge from the Autodesk web site.

Viewing DWG Files

Now that the DWF file format has been covered, it's time to discuss the role that DWG files have on the web. First, it is important to reiterate that DWF does not supplant the DWG format. Remember that DWF is like an electronic plot file, containing only the information needed to convey the visual representation of the drawing. DWG files contain greater amounts of drawing data (object associations, xdata, styles, and so on) and in a higher order of precision. Both formats have their proper place on the web.

The viewing and use of DWF files can be considered an important tool for the communication of drawing information on the Internet. DWG files are essential components of any corporate intranet. The bandwidth and performance constraints of the Internet do not necessarily apply to an intranet. Also, due to the inherently secure nature of an intranet, issues surrounding protection of the intellectual property contained in DWG files are minimized. In an intranet setting, the use of DWG files facilitates internal collaborative design work.

The following example illustrates the role each file format plays in the design process. During the initial phase of a project, the internal development team creates the basic product design by using Release 14. An interdepartmental team reviews the initial design (DWG file) on the corporate intranet using their browser and DWG viewing plug-in. Comments are made via e-mail or by directly editing the DWG file using AutoCAD. Once approved, ownership of the project is passed to the Engineering department, which elects to subcontract various elements. The drawing file is converted to DWF, and a notice is placed on the company web site soliciting bids for certain aspects of the project. Prospective bidders view the DWF file on the web and submit their proposals accordingly.

Tools for Viewing DWG Files on the Web

Numerous tools are available for viewing DWG on the Internet. A preview version of the Autodesk View DWG Plug-in that delivers functional DWG viewing support is include with the Release 13 Internet Publishing Kit. An enhanced version of the View DWGX Plug-in (Release 1.2) also supports redlining and other DWG viewing capabilities such as layer control. Release 1.2 of the DWGX Plug-in is included with Autodesk Work Center and requires that a client version of Autodesk View be installed on the host PC. The Autodesk DWG View Plug-in has an interface similar to that of *WHIP!*, as shown in figure 27.3.

Figure 27.3

The DWG View Plug-in supports a right-click user interface menu.

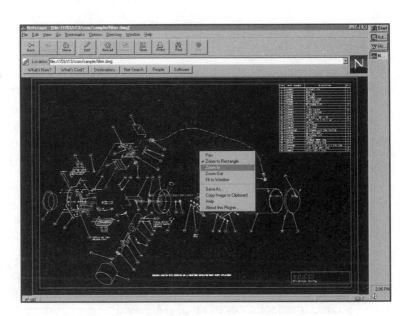

SoftSource's Vdraft plug-in adds support for viewing DXF in addition to DWG and DWF files.

WARNING

DWG performance issues: Be judicious about which DWG files you choose to publish on the Internet. Unlike DWF, the DWG file format is not "web" friendly. Features such as streaming and compression are the domain of DWF. Also please recognize that the average DWG file is very large, resulting in lengthy load times for clients who access the Internet with a low-speed modem.

Viewing DWF Files with *WHIP!*

DWG has limitations that reduce its usefulness as an Internet-based design collaboration medium. To overcome this limitation, AutoCAD Release 14 supports generation of DWF files. In this section, we will study *WHIP!*, Autodesk's DWF web browser viewing tool. Again, please remember that DWF does not replace DWG files.

The *WHIP!* Browser Tool

The *WHIP!* Plug-In and ActiveX Control are Autodesk's Internet tools for viewing DWF files on your web browser. *WHIP!* Release 2 is written to the WIN32 API specification, which means that the Plug-in and Control support the Windows 95 and Windows NT operating systems only. Support of other platforms has not been readily forthcoming from Autodesk. However, Autodesk does offer a developer's toolkit that enables independent developers to port the plug-in to other platforms.

NOTE

I expect that we will see independently developed DWF browser plug-ins on the market sometime soon.

How to Get the *WHIP!* Browser Tool

Autodesk makes *WHIP!* available for download at no charge from their web site. You can obtain *WHIP!* Release 2 by pointing your browser to `http://www.autodesk.com/products/autocad/whip/whip.htm`. The *WHIP!* home page contains download, installation, and user guide information.

What's New in *WHIP!* Release 2

Even if you are familiar with *WHIP!*, you may not know about several new features in *WHIP!* Release 2. Named Views and DWF View Coordinates are two new features of Release 2 and are discussed in the following sections.

Named Views

Some DWG files have named views for use with AutoCAD. With AutoCAD Release 14, the named views are passed along to the DWF file. Any named views that are present in the DWG file (when the DWF file is generated) are recorded in the DWF. For convenience, if the named view INITIAL is not already specified in the DWG, this named view is automatically placed in the DWF file. The INITIAL view for the DWF matches the view of the DWG when the DWFOUT command is issued. Named views of DWF files are available via a pop-up dialog box off the *WHIP!* Release 2 right mouse button menu.

WHIP! Release 2 incorporates support for named views into the right-click menu. Right-clicking a DWF file pops up the *WHIP!* menu. The Named Views menu option only appears when the loaded DWF file contains named views. Choosing Named Views from the right button menu displays a modeless dialog box that lists previously defined views to select from, as shown in figure 27.4. This option only appears when the loaded DWF file contains named views. Double-clicking on the named view positions the browser to that view. You can also single-click a named view and then click on OK to select that view and dismiss the dialog box. Alternatively, you can click on Cancel to dismiss the dialog box.

Figure 27.4

The WHIP! *Release 2 Named View selection dialog box.*

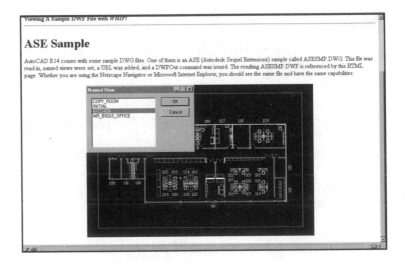

DWF View Coordinates

DWF file coordinates can be determined when viewing a DWF. Position the drawing to a desired view by panning and zooming. Issue the About *WHIP!* command from the right mouse button menu. One of the items listed, current view coordinates, is shown in figure 27.5. These coordinates can be noted and used in HTML files.

Figure 27.5

The WHIP! *Release 2 About* WHIP! *dialog box displays the DWF view coordinates.*

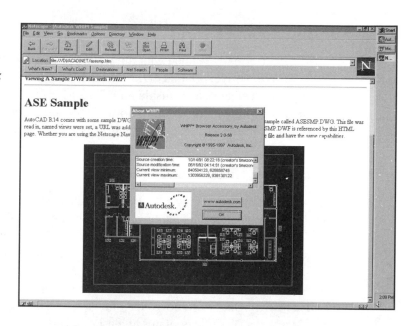

The *WHIP!* Release 2 Interface

When the cursor is over the *WHIP!* window, pressing the right mouse button will display a menu. The menu enables you to select from various "modes" of operation. A discussion of each mode follows.

INSIDER TIP

Viewing DWF files with Netscape Navigator is made possible by having the server-side software export the drawing/x-dwf MIME type. If the server-side software is Microsoft's Internet Information Server, however, this is not always the case. In some *WHIP!* installations the MIME type has to be registered on the *client* side for Netscape Navigator. This problem appears to be a rare occurrence and is machine specific. Should you encounter this problem, complete the following procedure: For example, in Navigator 3.0x, access the Options pull-down menu, select the Helper tab located under the General Preferences menu option. Click on the Create New Type button. At the Mime Type field, enter **drawing**. In the Mime Subtype field, enter **x-dwf**. For the Unknown Action field, enter the file extension as **dwf**. Click on OK.

Pan and Zoom Features

By now you are already familiar with the *WHIP!* display driver menu. In addition to the normal *WHIP!* driver options, *WHIP!* Release 2 adds support for a Fit to Window function. When selected from inside an HTML, the DWF file being viewed fills the entire browser window. To return to normal viewing, select the Back button from either the *WHIP!* Release 2 menu or your browser's toolbar.

Highlighting URLs in DWF files

When you right-click and toggle the Highlight URLs check item, *WHIP!* identifies all the URLs in a drawing by highlighting a box over each URL region. This enables you to see where URLs are before navigating. To avoid matching the color of the background or geometry in the DWF file, the box is drawn in alternating light-gray, dark-gray, and clear colors. Rendering in the clear color enables you to see the geometry underneath the box. To remove the boxes, right-click again and select Highlight URLs again to remove the check. The Highlight URLs menu item is available when a DWF file contains at least one URL.

NOTE

When viewing a DWF file contained in an HTML document that is being displayed in a scrollable frame, only the URLs directly under the Highlight URLs right-click menu box flash. The problem only exists in frames that are scrollable. By setting "scrolling" to "no" in the frame definition code, the problem disappears.

INSIDER **T**IP

A keyboard accelerator exists for *WHIP!* URL highlighting. Holding down the Shift key acts as a shortcut for highlighting URLs. Releasing the Shift key is a shortcut for dehighlighting.

Using SaveAs

If you right-click and select SaveAs, you can save the DWF file to your local hard drive. You may choose to save the DWF file in one of three formats: DWF, DWG, or Windows Bitmap (BMP). If you select DWG, *WHIP!* copies the DWG file used to generate the DWF, provided that the DWG file is available. The SaveAs menu item becomes available after the streaming of the DWF file completes.

NOTE

When looking for a DWG file, *WHIP!* looks in the directory where the DWF file is stored. The DWF file and DWG file must all reside in the same directory for this feature to work. Should the file not exist in the same directory, an error message is generated that indicates that the DWG file is not available and the SaveAs fails.

Printing DWF Files from Your Browser

You can print a DWF file in two different ways: from the *WHIP!* Release 2 menu and from the Browser menu. If you right-click over a window containing a DWF file and select Print, the currently visible view is sent to the printer using the standard system controls. *When you use* WHIP!*'s Print menu item, only the DWF file prints.* Using your browser Print button results in the entire HTML file—including the embedded DWF file—to print. When printing using the browser menu item, you have the option to force the background color of the DWF file to white via the Print dialog box.

In this section you have studied how to view DWF-based CAD data on the web with Release 2 of *WHIP!* In the next section, you will learn how to use the Internet to bring DWG data into AutoCAD Release 14.

Accessing CAD Data from the Web in Release 14

As mentioned previously in this chapter, new features of Release 14 enable you to access CAD data from the web. Before you can take advantage of these capabilities, however, you must modify the appropriate AutoCAD settings for your web use.

Configuring Release 14 for Internet Access

If you want to change where the Launch Browser button takes you, the value of a new Release 14 system variable, INETLOCATION, must be modified. To use Release 14's Internet Utilities, AutoCAD must be properly configured for Internet access. The INETCONFIG command provides a convenient method for configuring AutoCAD's Internet access capabilities. A discussion of these commands follows.

The INETLOCATION System Variable

Release 14's default URL information is stored in a profilable system variable, INETLOCATION. You may store a different URL default for each saved profile. You can easily modify the default value (URL address) of this variable, which AutoCAD passes to your browser. To change the URL invoked by the BROWSER command, type **INETLOCATION** at the Command: prompt. You will be prompted as follows:

```
New value for INETLOCATION <www.autodesk.com/acaduser>:
```

Type in the new URL you want to have your browser go to when launched by AutoCAD.

INSIDER TIP

You can choose to type http:// at the beginning of the URL if you want. The Release 14 Browser command checks for the presence of http://, ftp://, and file:/// prefixes. If none of the standard Internet prefixes exist, AutoCAD will attach http:// to the URL for you. This handy little feature is both a time-saver and a convenience tool, enabling you to type in the URL in the manner you are accustomed.

INETLOCATION can also be changed from Preferences in the Files tab as seen in figure 27.6.

Figure 27.6

Modifying the profilable INETLOCATION system variable enables you to change the default URL launched by the Browser command.

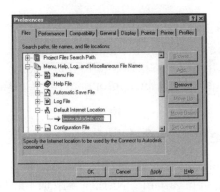

The following exercise takes you through the necessary steps to modify Release 14's "home" URL.

MODIFYING RELEASE 14'S "HOME" URL
IN PREFERENCES

1. From the Tools pull-down menu, choose Preferences.

2. Select the Files tab.

3. Scroll to the Menu, Help, Log, and Miscellaneous File Names entry as shown in figure 27.6.

4. Expand the selection by double-clicking.

5. Select and expand Default Internet Location by double-clicking on the entry.

6. Replace the default entry www.autodesk.com/acaduser with the *WHIP!* home page URL. Type in **www.autodesk.com/products/autocad/whip/whip.htm**.

7. Click on OK.

You have now successfully changed the Browser default to the *WHIP!* home page.

Another command used in modifying AutoCAD's Internet access capabilities is INETCFG. The INETCFG command is examined in the following section.

Configuring Your Internet Connection with INETCFG

INETCFG is used for setting user name, password, and other Release 14 Internet connection information. Choose the Configure Internet Icon from the Internet Utilities toolbar, or enter **inetcfg** at the Command: prompt. You can also access the INETCFG command by clicking on the Options button on the OPENURL, SAVEURL, and INSERTURL dialog boxes. The Internet Configuration dialog box, where you must enter all relevant information, is shown in figure 27.7.

Figure 27.7

The Internet Configuration dialog box simplifies the process of readying Release 14 to access the web.

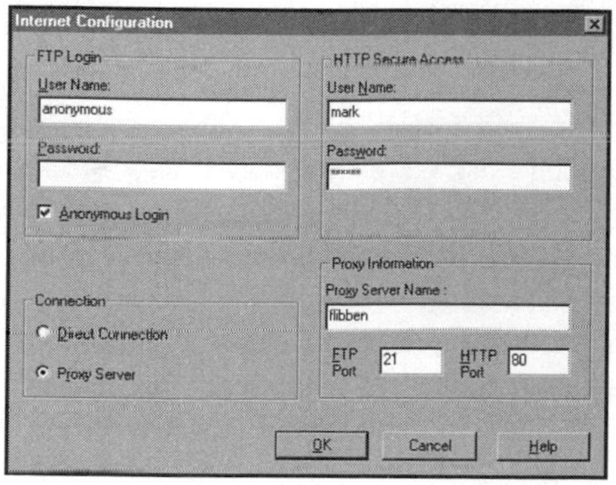

The following list discusses the areas in the Internet Configuration dialog box that require configuration information:

- **FTP Login.** If Anonymous Login is selected, the user name "anonymous" is used with no password. When you are logging in to a secured FTP server that contains DWG files you want to access via the OpenURL, InsertURL, or SaveURL commands, however, turn off the Anonymous Login feature. Enter your user name and password for that server in the spaces provided.

- **HTTP Secure Access.** If you regularly access HTTP URLs that require authentication, enter your user name and password. If you leave these values blank, you will be prompted to enter your user name and password when necessary.

NOTE

AutoCAD does store your user name for the FTP and HTTP logins, but not your password between sessions. Each new AutoCAD session requires you to enter your password when entering secured sites.

- **Connection.** Select the type of access method used for logging on to the Internet. The options are as follows:

  - **Direct Connection.** If you connect to the web through an Internet Service Provider (ISP), typically via a dial-up function, select Direct Connection. Direct connections do not require that you perform proxy configuration.

  - **Proxy Server.** If you connect to the Internet through a proxy server, you will need to select the Proxy Server option and configure Release 14's Internet access functions as documented in the Proxy Information section of this list.

NOTE

A *proxy server* is a machine that serves as a gateway between a company's internal intranet and the external Internet. A proxy server typically runs on a firewall machine, providing secure access to the outside world for people inside the firewall. The proxy server provides various services, mainly caching of requests and a secure means of accessing data. If you don't know if you are using a proxy server, you can look at the proxy settings in your browser (in Netscape Navigator 3.0x, choose the Options menu, then Network Preferences, then the Proxies tab) or contact your network system administrator.

- **Proxy Information.** This function configures Release 14's Internet access through a proxy server user environment. If a proxy server is in use at your site you will need to enter the following information:

  - **Proxy Server.** Enter the Proxy Server name. Your network system administrator can supply you with a valid machine name.

  - **FTP Port.** The default FTP port is automatically set. You can select another port by entering its number in the FTP Port text box. Your network system administrator can supply you with a valid port number.

  - **HTTP Port.** The default HTTP port is automatically set. You can select another port by entering its number in the HTTP Port text box. Your network system administrator can supply you with a valid port number.

Extending Your Reach to Drawing Data on the Web

The first step to publishing your AutoCAD designs on the web involves creating a new drawing or opening an existing drawing, embedding URLs (if desired), and saving the drawing as a DWF file. With AutoCAD Release 14 you can extend your access to CAD data beyond the desktop and LAN to the Internet. Commands that let you open, insert, and save AutoCAD drawings over the web are included in AutoCAD Release 14.

You can open an AutoCAD drawing from the web as though it resided on your local area network or hard disk. Think of the Internet as just another network drive which you can connect to for accessing drawing data. Release 14's Internet functions extend access to CAD data beyond the desktop or network. With http, ftp, and Release 14, you can access drawing files anywhere on the Internet.

When you are connected to the Internet through a proxy server, the AutoCAD Internet Utilities cannot transfer files (Open, Insert, or Save) using FTP.

Using HTTP and the OpenURL Command

Use the OpenURL command to Open a drawing from the Internet. The OpenURL command in Release 14 can be invoked from the Open DWG from URL icon in the

Internet Utilities toolbar or at the Command: prompt. Once invoked, a "special" file open dialog box is presented, as shown in figure 27.8. In the Open DWG from URL text box, enter the URL of the file you want to access and then click on the Open button. The Open DWG from URL box supports entering an URL in the following formats:

```
http://servername/pathname/filename.dwg
ftp://servername/pathname/filename.dwg
file:///drive|/pathname/filename.dwg
```

The Open DWG from URL text box also features a drop-down list as shown in figure 27.8. This drop-down list maintains a history of previously used URLs, which is very handy should you repeatedly visit a site.

INSIDER TIP

The URL text in the drop down list can also be edited before pressing the Open button. If you are re-visiting a site but want to open a different drawing, you can just edit the drawing file name. What a time-saver that is!

Figure 27.8

The Open DWG from URL dialog box includes a handy drop-down URL history list.

INSIDER TIP

You can use the Browser (Connect to Internet) button to find a web site containing a drawing you want to open. After you identify a web site, copy the URL from your browser and paste it into the Open DWG from URL dialog box.

Clicking the Options button in the Open DWG from URL dialog invokes the INETCFG command, enabling you to change your Internet configuration settings. After entering an URL and clicking on OK, AutoCAD displays the Remote Transfer dialog box. The Remote Transfer dialog box is also displayed during inserting or saving a drawing to an URL. You can terminate the transfer by clicking on the Cancel button.

NOTE

> AutoCAD Release 14's Internet Utilities do not check to confirm that an Internet connection exists. If you're not connected to the Internet and you attempt to connect to a web location, the Transfer Status dialog box will display 0 bytes and 0% complete until you click on the Cancel button or the transfer times out.

The following brief exercise shows you how to open a sample DWG file located at the Autodesk web site.

OPENING A DRAWING FROM A WEB SITE

1. Select the Open from URL icon in Internet Utilities toolbar.

2. Enter the following URL into the Open DWG from URL text box:

   `http://www.autodesk.com/exercise/colorwh.dwg`

3. Press Enter.

Using InsertURL to Insert a DWG File into Release 14

The InsertURL command performs an insert of a drawing accessed from the Internet into AutoCAD. You can insert an AutoCAD drawing—a block, for example—from the web into your current drawing session with the InsertURL command. The InsertURL command is accessed by choosing Insert from URL from the Internet Utilities toolbar or by entering **inserturl** at the Command: prompt. The dialog box for InsertURL appears very similar to the Open DWG from URL dialog box. The URL formats supported by OpenURL apply to the InsertUrl function as well. After the DWG file has completed downloading, Release 14's normal INSERT behavior commences.

NOTE

> You cannot insert a drawing into itself.

Using FTP and SaveURL to Save a DWG to the Web

With Release 14's SaveURL command, you can write a DWG file to a location on the web. From the Internet Utilities toolbar, select Save to URL or enter **saveurl** at the

Command: prompt. Again, a dialog box similar in form to that used by the Open and Insert URL commands appears. Enter the URL in the Save DWG to Internet text box and then click on the Save button. You must enter an URL in the following format (http and file schemes are not supported):

```
ftp://servername/pathname/filename.dwg
```

If you click on the Browser button, you can use your browser to find a web site. After you identify a web site, you can copy its URL from your browser and paste it into the Save DWG to URL dialog box. After you click on OK, AutoCAD displays the Remote dialog box while it saves the drawing to the web site. The Save to URL dialog box also includes access to the INETCFG command via the Options button.

You can change your Internet configuration settings while in the Save to URL dialog box by clicking the Options button. Selecting Options runs the INETCFG command, enabling you to change your Internet configuration (such as login name or password) settings.

 NOTE

AutoCAD Internet Utilities cannot transfer files using FTP when you are connected to the Internet through a proxy server.

Using Drag and Drop to Open or Insert DWG Files

A great productivity enhancement included with Release 14 is the DWF Drag and Drop feature. Rather than having to execute the Open or Insert URL command and type in the web address, Release 14 enables you to drag the DWF and drop the parent DWG into your current AutoCAD session.

While viewing a DWF file, you can open or insert the original DWG file in AutoCAD by dragging the DWF image from Netscape into AutoCAD.

 NOTE

For drag and drop to work, the DWG file used to create the DWF file must exist in the same directory as the DWF file at the time you drag and drop.

To open a DWG in AutoCAD using drag and drop, follow these steps:

1. Press and hold the Ctrl and Shift keys simultaneously.

2. Click on the DWF image and drag it into AutoCAD.

3. Release the mouse button and then release the Ctrl and Shift keys.

To insert a DWG into a current AutoCAD drawing session using drag and drop, do the following:

1. Press and hold the Ctrl key.

2. Click on the DWF image and drag it into AutoCAD.

3. Release the mouse button and then release the Ctrl key.

Autodesk's Data Publishing (ADP) division has a service comprised of an online catalog of mechanical parts called PartSpec OnLine. Subscribers to this service can drag a needed part into an active AutoCAD session. ADP provides a method for you to sample this functionality. The following exercise illustrates how to implement these steps using a real file and dragging it into AutoCAD.

DRAGGING A FILE FROM PARTSPEC ONLINE INTO AUTOCAD

1. At the Command: line, enter **INETLOCATION**.

2. Type the ADP URL **http://data.autodesk.com/adpon2.htm**.

3. Click on the Browser (Launch Browser) button.

4. Register as a user of this site if you haven't already done so. Once your form is complete then select the SUBMIT button and go to step 6.

5. If you are registered, then click on the blue PartSpec Online ICON in the center of the screen.

6. Enter your Username and Password in the dialog box and click on the OK button.

7. You should now be at the Part Spec Online Home Page (`http://data.autodesk.com/partspec/partspec.htm`).

8. From the Select a Manufacturers frame (left side frame), choose ADEPT TECHNOLOGY, INC. (see fig. 27.9).

9. Select 4-AXIS SCARA ROBOTS. A listing of Adept's robots appears.

10. Select the ADEPT 1850 PALLETIZING ROBOT. The part frame becomes active, revealing product information.

11. Select the View Window tab from the part information frame on the right.

12. Choose Top from the View Control.

13. Press and hold the Ctrl and Shift keys simultaneously.

14. Click on the DWF image and drag it into AutoCAD.

15. Release the mouse button and then release the Ctrl and Shift keys.

16. Change focus to Release 14 by using the Windows Alt+Tab key combination.

17. Follow the Insert prompts at the AutoCAD Command: line.

Figure 27.9

Release 14's DWF Drag and Drop feature simplifies accessing DWG files from the Internet.

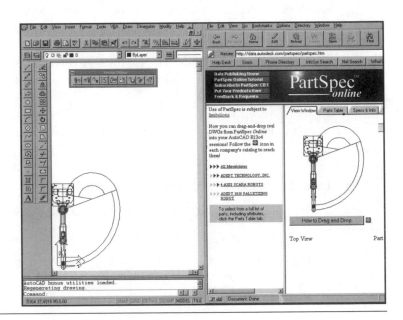

Publishing Your Drawings on the Web

Now that you have mastered viewing and accessing DWG or DWF files with Release 14 and the Internet, the time has come for you to start creating some of these files yourself and publishing them onto the Internet. So how do you do this in such a manner that protects your investment in the drawing file data? How can you create enough interest in your data that people come to your site? This section presents an informative discussion regarding the considerations and decisions involved in publishing CAD data on the web.

Strategies for a Secure Web Site

Your site should be partitioned for different levels of access. For example, you should have one level assigned for general public access, another access level for prospective clients and yet another for existing clients or subcontractors. You can configure your firewall software to limit general public access while delivering greater levels of access to your customers and total access to your own employees. A comprehensive discussion of firewall software and security issues is provided by Netscape on their web site.

DWG-DWF File Co-location

Autodesk recognizes the need for you to be able to adequately protect the intellectual property contained in the DWG files of your creation. To facilitate this need, the DWF to DWG drag and drop functionality has a very simple yet sophisticated security mechanism. When a DWF file is created, the file name of the parent DWG is embedded into the DWF file header. Only the file name is embedded, and all path information is stripped out. When AutoCAD receives a notification of an Internet-based drop event, Release 14 searches the directory location passed to it during the notification process for the parent DWG file. Should the DWG file be located in the same directory as the child DWF file, then AutoCAD proceeds with the appropriate Open or Insert function. Should the parent DWG file *not* be located in the same directory as the DWF, however, the operation will abort with a file not found error.

Hence, it is a simple matter for you to control which DWG files you make available for downloading by visitors to your web site. This activity is controlled by either including or excluding the parent DWG file from the directory containing the child DWF. This system allows for maximum flexibility and controlled access. With your firewall software, you can place your most sensitive DWG files (and associated DWFs) in those directories with the highest degree of secured access.

Creating Web-friendly CAD Files

Now that you have a handle on how to protect your data, you can start building files. This section studies how to embed links into DWG files and then create web-friendly DWF files.

Attaching an URL

The ATTACHURL command embeds a hyperlink onto an object in the Release 14 drawing file. You can attach an URL either to objects or areas in a drawing. When you view the resultant DWF file and select the object or area, you are hyperlinked to the site identified by the attached URL.

As previously noted, you can attach URLs in drawings in two ways: by objects and by area.

When you attach an URL by objects, AutoCAD places a rectangular URL area around each object. The URL is attached as xdata (extended entity data) to objects in the drawing. For each object with an URL attached there is a separate xdata entry. If you attach many individual objects to an URL, your AutoCAD DWG file will contain many bits of xdata attached to each selected object.

When you attach an URL to an area, AutoCAD creates a rectangle around the area you specify and stores the rectangle on a special layer called URLLAYER. *Don't delete this layer*. For each URL attached there is xdata, just as when you attach using the by object mode, but your AutoCAD DWG file will contain large areas attached as xdata and not individual objects.

INSIDER TIP

Deciding whether to attach by area or object is sometimes confusing. I have found that attaching by area works well for sections of contiguous geometry. Also, when I want to attach a hyperlink to area where no geometry exists, attaching by area is the only viable method. When geometry is distributed throughout the drawing, attaching by objects is the best method.

Embedding Links

One of greatest features of the ATTACHURL command is that the specified URL does not have to refer to an *absolute* address. ATTACHURL also supports the capability to embed *relative* URLs. This means that you can create a DWF file that links to another DWF that displays a detailed section of the referenced drawing. For example, you may have a master drawing containing a parts list. Each part entry can have an URL attached to it that references another DWF which displays the individual part details.

The following exercise walks through the process of using the ATTACHURL command to attach an URL to an area of a drawing.

USING ATTACHURL TO ATTACH AN URL TO A DRAWING

1. Open the drawing filter.dwg supplied on the accompanying CD-ROM.

2. From the Internet Utilities toolbar or Internet menu, choose Attach URL, or enter **attachurl** at the Command: prompt.

   AutoCAD prompts you to attach an URL by defining an area or selecting objects.

3. Select Area by entering **a** at the Command: prompt.

4. Pick the top-left corner of the area defined by ① and the lower-right corner of the second row defined by ②, as shown in figure 27.10.

5. At the Enter URL prompt, enter **filter2.dwf**.

AutoCAD creates a rectangle and stores the polylines defining the area on the special layer, URLLAYER.

Figure 27.10

Using the AttachURL by Object option places a rectangle into the drawing.

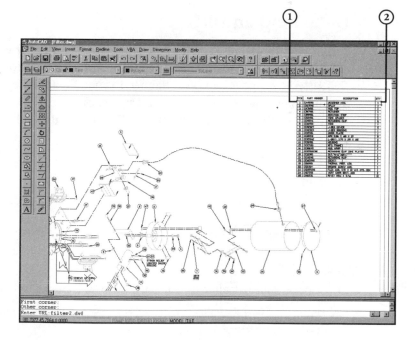

6. Save the drawing file with the changes as filter.dwg.

Don't worry about the file not existing yet. You'll create that file and the appropriate DWF counterparts in a minute.

NOTE

You may also select objects before invoking the ATTACHURL command, and then respond to the URL (Area/Objects) prompt with Area. AutoCAD will automatically place a rectangle around the extents of the objects you selected.

WARNING

The ATTACHURL command creates a rectangular entity on a layer named URLLAYER and then attaches the URL string to the new area entity as xdata. You can destroy the hyperlink information in your drawing if you tamper with URLLAYER! You should not freeze, lock, or change the visibility of URLLAYER. Do not edit or delete the area entities on URLLAYER, nor attach URLs to them using the ATTACHURL command. If you turn off the visibility of URLLAYER for normal viewing of your drawing, it should be turned back on before using the DWFOUT command.

Detaching an URL

Just as you may want to embed an URL in a file, you may also want to detach an already embedded URL (for instance, when a hyperlinked URL address has changed). DETACHURL removes an URL attached to an entity in the drawing file. You detach an URL from objects (or areas) in a drawing to remove the hyperlink to a web site identified by the attached URL. AutoCAD detaches the URL xdata (extended entity data) from the object in the drawing.

The following is an exercise to show you how to use the detach an URL from a drawing file.

USING DETACHURL TO REMOVE AN URL FROM A DRAWING FILE

1. Open the file detachurl.dwg from the CD-ROM included with this book.

2. From the Internet Utilities toolbar, choose Detach URL, or enter **detachurl** at the Command: prompt.

AutoCAD prompts you to select the objects associated with the URL you want to detach.

3. Select the area object AREAURL and the object OBJECTURL by using an object selection method, such as picking the objects or drawing a selection window around the text.

NOTE

When you detach an URL from the object (OBJECTURL), AutoCAD removes the URL stored in the object's xdata. When you detach an URL from an area (AREAURL), AutoCAD deletes the rectangle that represents the area from the URLLAYER layer.

4. Save the file as detachurl.dwg to your local hard drive.

Listing URLs

The LISTURL command displays the URLs attached to objects or areas in a drawing. The following exercise shows you how to use this command.

USING THE LISTURL COMMAND TO DISPLAY EMBEDDED URLS

1. Open the drawing file filter.dwg, which you saved in the earlier ATTACHURL exercise.

2. From the Internet Utilities toolbar, choose List URLs, or enter **listurl** at the Command: prompt.

3. Select the area containing the URL you attached in the earlier "Using ATTACHURL to Attach an URL to a Drawing" exercise with a crossing window.

   AutoCAD lists the URL filter2.dwf in the command and text windows, as shown in figure 27.11.

Figure 27.11

LISTURL displays the URL address attached to the selected drawing objects or areas at both the Command: line and in the Release 14 Text Window.

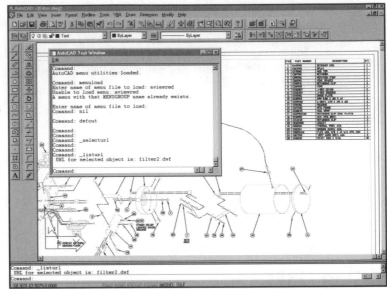

Keep this drawing loaded; it will be used in the next exercise.

Selecting Objects and Areas with URLs Attached

You can select all objects and areas that have URLs attached with the SELECTURL command, as shown in the following short exercise. AutoCAD puts all objects and areas that have URLs attached into the current selection set so you can edit them. This feature comes in handy when you need to update all of the hyperlink addresses attached to objects in your drawing.

SELECTING ALL OBJECTS AND AREAS WITH URLs ATTACHED USING SELECTURL COMMAND

1. From the Internet Utilities toolbar, choose Select URLs or enter **selecturl** at the Command: prompt.

   AutoCAD selects all objects that have URLs attached.

NOTE

To list all the URLs in a drawing, use the SELECTURL command to select all objects with attached URLs and then use the LISTURL command to list the URLs.

Creating DWF Files with the DWFOUT Command

To create a DWF file with Release 14, use the DWFOUT command. The EXPORT function also supports creation of DWF files. Release 14 has an easy to use DWF Export Options sub-dialog box that facilitates creating DWF files, as shown in figure 27.12. The various settings in the dialog box are discussed in the following section.

Figure 27.12

The DWFOUT dialog box makes creating DWF files a simple task.

Precision and File Size

You can set the precision of your DWF files between 16 and 32 bits, with the default being 20 bits. For parts drawings and basic architectural drawings, using 16-bit precision gives you 40 percent smaller DWF files. With 16-bit precision, you can get as much as an 8-to-1 compression ratio when you compare the size of the original DWG file to the resulting DWF file.

For simple drawings, little visual difference exists. For more complex drawings and fine details, however, you'll need higher precision.

Using 20-bit precision produces a file 16 times more precise and only about 20 percent larger than a 16-bit file, but about 30 percent smaller than a full 32-bit file.

Background Color and File Size

The DWF file uses the background color from the original drawing file. To keep file size down, you can use a default color map and reduce file size by 1 KB. This savings is usually only beneficial to DWF files smaller than 5 KB. You can only use the default color map if the background color is black or white. By combining the use of a black or white background and 16-bit precision, you can reduce the size of your DWF files.

The Geometry Written to the DWF File

The geometry written to the DWF file is what the *WHIP!* display driver has in its display list. If the current view is a zoomed area of a larger drawing, then any geometry outside of the zoomed area isn't included in the DWF file. Commands that affect the visibility of geometry on-screen, such as VIEWRES, FACETRES, DISPSILH, and HIDE, also affect the contents of the DWF file.

WARNING

Currently, DWFOUT does not function from paper space. DWFOUT only works in model space and only exports data from the current model space viewport. The EXPORT method of creating a DWF file will work in paper space but you will only get the objects that are in paper space.

DWF files can be created from AutoCAD with either the DWFOUT or EXPORT command. You save a DWF file when you want to publish an AutoCAD drawing to the web in drawing web format. When creating DWF files in a batch process, use the text-only mode of the DWFOUT command by turning the FILEDIA system variable off (FILEDIA controls whether the file system dialog is displayed). If FILEDIA is set to 1 (on), an Explorer dialog box displays after entering the DWFOUT command at the Command: prompt. If FILEDIA is set to 0 (off) the text mode is active.

The following exercise focuses on creating a DWF file.

CREATING A DWF FILE BY USING THE DWFOUT AND EXPORT COMMANDS

1. Open the filter.dwg file, which you created in the ATTACHURL exercise.

2. Choose Export from the File pull-down menu (or type **DWFOUT** at the Command: prompt). As with other Export file types, a toolbar icon does not exist for this command. The DWF format is listed in the Files of Type list box in the EXPORT dialog box. The Options button activates the same sub-dialog box of options as in the DWFOUT dialog box (not the tabbed options dialog box normally displayed in the Export command). The DWFOUT Options dialog box has a Help button that is tied to AutoCAD's help file.

3. Accept the default DWF file name filter.dwf as displayed in the DWF File Save As dialog box. The current drawing file name with a .dwf extension is used as the default.

4. If you want to control the precision of the file, you must click on the Options button, then select either low (16-bit precision) or high (32-bit precision) detail. The default, 20-bit precision (medium), is sufficient for most files. The higher the precision, the larger the file. For the purposes of this exercise, you can accept the default precision value of medium.

5. If you want a compressed DWF file, you must click on the Options button, then select Compress File (it's on by default). Add compression to the DWF file by accepting the Yes default value.

6. Click on OK to exit the DWF Export Options sub-dialog box.

The DWF Export options are saved in ACAD14.CFG; therefore, the options chosen are saved between AutoCAD sessions.

Click on OK to exit the Create DWF File dialog box, thus creating the DWF file.

NOTE

The name of the drawing used to create a DWF is stored in the header of the DWF. The path of the drawing is not stored in the DWF and the file name is case-sensitive. This information is stored to give the Internet Utilities, the *WHIP!* plug-in, and Control for ActiveX drag-and-drop functionality when a DWF and DWG are located in the same directory.

In the next exercise, the DWF file—filter2.dwf—linked to by filter.dwf has to be created. This is the file called from the hyperlink that you attached to the parts list entry in filter.dwg.

CREATING A HYPERLINKED DWF FILE BY USING THE DWFOUT AND EXPORT COMMANDS

1. Open the file filter2.dwg included on the CD-ROM supplied with this book.

2. Type **DWFOUT** at the Command: prompt.

3. Click on the Options button to activate the DWFOUT dialog box.

4. Accept all the default values in this dialog box by clicking on OK.

5. Click on the OK button on the Create DWF file dialog box.

   You've created the second DWF file, filter2.dwf.

To recap, you utilized the ATTACHURL command to create a relative URL that references another DWF file. When you load the filter.dwf into your browser and select the parts list entry containing the hyperlink, your browser will automatically load the file filter2.dwf. This simple example shows how you can use the power of Release 14's Internet tools to create a useful method for navigating complex drawings on the web.

Creating the Effective CAD-oriented Web Site

A great web site is like a well-designed building: you always know where you are and where to go. The entrance into the web site is the home page. It welcomes the visitor, makes them want to stay, and guides them to what they seek. Done well, the home page guides visitors where the publisher wants them to go. This section covers how to embed CAD data into an HTML and delivers some insights on how to build a web site.

Creating Web Pages Containing CAD Data

Because DWF and DWG are not considered standard MIME types, adding CAD data to an HTML requires a bit of effort. This section outlines the structure and methodology of properly embedding DWF files. If you use Autodesk's DWGX View plug-in, the same structure also applies to embedding a DWG file.

Adding DWF Files to HTML Pages

After you have created a DWF file, you can add it to a web page by adding special tags into the HTML document. There are two ways in which you can associate DWF files with HTML files: embedding and referencing. When "embedding" a DWF file into a HTML page, <object> and <embed> tags are used. Referencing is done through a traditional HREF tag.

NOTE

To publish your web pages to the Internet, you must have an Internet connection. If you already have an Internet connection, ask your Internet Service Provider or Webmaster how to put your files on the Internet server.

Object and Embed Tags

When embedding a DWF file into an HTML file the following two tags are used: <object> and <tag>. The <object> tag is used for Microsoft Internet Explorer. The <embed> tag is for Netscape Navigator. Netscape Navigator ignores the Microsoft Internet Explorer references and vice versa. These tags are specific to their respective browsers even though the embed tag is nested within the object tag. In the sample HTML provided, some of the parts are specific to DWF, that is, hardcoded, while others are under your control.

As you see in the exercise that follows, the parts of the <object> tag for the Microsoft Internet Explorer include:

- **classid.** The classid value is specific to *WHIP!*. *Do not change this value.* The value specified is used to distinguish *WHIP!* from other controls for ActiveX.

- **codebase.** The URL specified in codebase is hardcoded to identify where users of the Microsoft Internet Explorer get updates of the *WHIP!* ActiveX Control. The current version of the control is 2.0-76, which is expressed as 2,0,14,76 (the 14 indicates that the control is R14 compatible). Do not change this value except for intranet-only scenarios. In the case of intranet usage of Internet Explorer, the file whip.cab can be downloaded to the local site. For these situations ONLY, the codebase portion of the object tag should be changed to reference the local copy instead of the whip.cab file on the Autodesk FTP site.

- **id.** The id portion enables you to give each DWF reference a unique id that can be referenced by Java and JScript. This can be changed as desired. This is not to be confused with the classid.

- **width.** The horizontal size of the DWF file object measured in pixels. You may modify the value of this field at your discretion.

- **height.** The vertical size of the DWF file object measured in pixels 300. You may modify the value of this field at your discretion.

- **param name.** Identifies the type of parameter you are specifying for the object tag.

- **Filename.** This parameter is required. You *must* specify the DWF file name in the value portion.

- **View.** This parameter is optional. The value portion is where you specify an initial view (in logical coordinates) for your DWF file. The initial view is specified by four values: left, right, bottom, and top.

- **NamedView.** Also an optional parameter. Specifies a valid named view for the DWF file in the value portion.

- **UserInterface.** The UserInterface parameter is optional. The value portion is where you specify whether or not the *WHIP!* right-click menu and cursor are on or off.

The parts of the <embed> tag for Netscape Navigator include:

- **name.** This optional value gives each DWF reference a unique name that can be referenced by Java and JavaScript. Unlike the name="Filename" item on the Microsoft Internet Explorer <object> tag, this value can be changed as desired.

- **src.** A required value used to specify the actual name of the DWF file being embedded.

- **pluginspage**. Specifies an URL where users who do not have the *WHIP!* plug-in can go to download the plug-in. *Do not change this value except for intranet-only scenarios.*

- **width.** The horizontal size of the DWF file object measured in pixels. You may modify the value of this field at your discretion.

- **height.** The vertical size of the DWF file object measured in pixels. You may modify the value of this field at your discretion.

- **view.** This portion is optional and specifies an initial view (in logical coordinates) for your DWF file. The initial view is specified by four values: left, right, bottom, and top.

- **namedview.** Also an optional field. Used to specify an initial view for your DWF file.

NOTE

The initial view is specified by using the name of the named view. If the specified named view has not been defined in the DWF file, the option is ignored. Either a NamedView or a View (not both) may be used to specify an initial view. The specified initial view overrides the initial view that is stored inside the DWF file. The parameters are case-insensitive.

These instructions explain how to embed a DWF file into an HTML document by adding special tags using an ASCII text editor. In this exercise, you will be using an

HTML template to simplify the process for adding a DWF to an HTML page. The exercise will show you how to use this template for DWF embedding.

EMBEDDING A DWF FILE INTO AN HTML DOCUMENT

1. Start your text editor and create a DWF—HTML template by copying the following code as it appears in the following code. The template uses "dummy" names and values as placeholder references. In this exercise, you will replace the placeholder text with actual file names and values.

NOTE

You should save the DWF—HTML template code into a separate file (I named my template dwftags.htm) before proceeding to step 2.

```
<object
 id="dwfname"
 classid="clsid:B2BE75F3-9197-11CF-ABF4-08000996E931"
codebase="ftp://ftp.autodesk.com/pub/autocad/plugin/
whip.cab#version=2,0,14,76"
 width=600
 height=400>
<param name="Filename"  value="dwfname.dwf">
<param name="View"      value="10000+30000+20000+40000">
<param name="NamedView" value="viewname">
<param name="UserInterface" value="on">
<embed name="dwfname"    src="dwfname.dwf"
 pluginspage="http://www.autodesk.com/products/autocad/whip/
 ➥whip.htm"
 width=600
 height=400
 view="10000+30000+20000+40000"
 namedview="vicwname"
 userinterface="on">
</object>
```

2. Open the sample HTML document in your text editor, filter.htm, supplied with this book's CD-ROM.

3. Insert the DWF—HTML template (created in step 1) into the HTML document at the point ① specified in figure 27.13. This is the location following the page description title that you want the DWF file to appear in the document.

4. Modify the merged text as follows:

Figure 27.13

① *shows where the DWF file will appear in the document.*

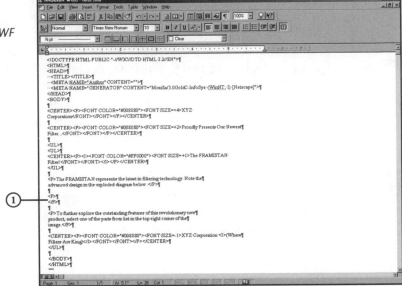

NOTE

This step shows you how easy it is to change the DWF file reference and image size using the HTML template.

- Change the width of the DWF object by replacing the width= value of 600 with a value of **400**. (Do this for both the <object> and <embed> tags.)

- Change the height of the DWF object by replacing the height= value of 400 with a value of **300**. (Do this for both the <object> and <embed> tags.)

- Globally replace dwfname with **filter**.

- Replace viewname with **initial**.

- Replace the value 10000 with **860000000**.

- Replace the value 30000 with **1270000000**.

- Replace the value 20000 with **530000000**.

- Replace the value 40000 with **800000000**.

5. Save the file in HTML format.

6.   Load and view the file in your browser.

Your completed file should appear as shown in figure 27.14

Figure 27.14

The HTML page as it appears after successful completion of the exercise.

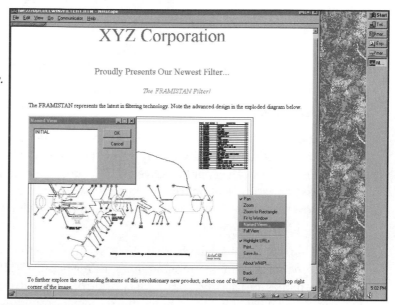

Referencing with HREF Tag

Referencing a file using the HREF tag is a common method of associating non-HTML files (for example DWF or JPG files) with an HTML file. Using an HREF tag causes the DWF file to appear as a link in the HTML page. When the link is selected, the DWF file occupies the entire window available to the HTML file. The other parts of the HTML file are not visible, so the DWF file does not appear to be "embedded" as part of the current HTML file.

The format used in an HREF tag is as follows:

```
<A HREF=http://myserver/myfile.dwf>myfile.dwf</A>
```

URL Format Information

The general format of a Uniform Resource Locator (URL) is:

```
http://www.company.com/path/file.suffix#option=value
```

where the suffix is typically html, htm, or dwf. For the purposes of DWF, the HREF tag option portion can be any of the following:

- target
- namedview
- view

Each of these options is explained in the following sections.

Target Option

The target option indicates that the current link is to be loaded into a specified frame window. In a CAD web site, you may want to embed DWF files into HTML pages using frames. Frames can separate active HTML pages containing DWF files from static pages such as a navigational bar. A frame is a window into a specific URL. The frame window name specified by a target must begin with an alpha-numeric character, for example, target=mywindow.

Working with frames can be tricky, but DWF files support certain "magic" window frame names to simplify programming a CAD-based HTML page. Magic window frame names are used by HTML targets inside of a frame to initiate specific behavior. Some magic window frame names have special properties. These magic window names begin with an underscore and are summarized in table 27.1.

Table 27.1

DWF Magic Window Name Options and Descriptions

Name	Description
target="_blank"	The link loads in a new blank window.
target="_self"	The link loads in to the same window the link is in. This link is only useful for overriding a globally assigned target, which is different than the current window.
target="_parent"	The link loads in the immediate frameset parent of the current document. It defaults to "_self" if the document has no parent.
target="_top"	The link loads in a full window and exits the frame. This option is useful for leaving your site or exiting a deep frame nesting.

NOTE

Any targeted window name beginning with underscore that is not one of the preceding options will be ignored.

Namedview Option

The namedview option specifies a particular named view of a DWF file reference by using an existing named view already inside the DWF file. If a named view does not exist in the DWF file, the namedview option is ignored.

View Option

The view option specifies a particular view of a DWF file reference by using DWF file coordinates.

You can specify a #option=value item by itself, that is, without the preceding URL information, and have that option apply to the current instance. URLs of this type are always preceded by the # symbol.

NOTE

Microsoft Internet Explorer does not support the view, namedview, and user interface HREF tag options.

Adding DWF Files as a MIME Type

To get your Internet server to recognize DWF files so that *WHIP!* gets invoked, you need to ask your Webmaster to add a new MIME type to your Internet server. The server software MIME environment needs to have a new data type **drawing/x-dwf** with the extension as **dwf** added. MIME types enable files to be opened by "helper" applications on web browser clients, such as Microsoft Internet Explorer. Users who have not added the MIME type but try to view DWF files from their own servers experience the Torn icon. If you experience the Torn icon, you must also add the MIME type and then clear your browser cache to achieve correct results.

If you are using the Netscape FastTrack Server, follow these steps to add the new MIME type:

1. Search your drive(s) for the file mime.types.

2. Open each instance of the file with Notepad or another ASCII text editor.

3. Add the text **type=drawing/x-dwf exts=dwf** to the file (at the bottom of the file is OK).

4. Save the file and repeat for each instance of the mime.types file just to be safe.

5. Fully apply the changes by using your server software. Alternatively, you could shut down and reboot the server.

If you are using Microsoft's Internet Information Server 2.0, you can find instructions for adding MIME types at:

```
http://www.microsoft.com/kb/articles/q142/5/58.htm
```

Currently, MIME types for Internet Information Server (IIS) must be added manually to the registry. At this time, no graphical interface for adding MIME types exists. IIS installs the most common MIME types by default, but MIME types for new applications such as *WHIP!* are not among those added by default.

MIME entries can be added to the following registry location:

HKEY_LOCAL_MACHINE\SYSTEM\CurrentControlSet\Services\
InetInfo\Parameters\MimeMap

To add an entry, open the MimeMap key and choose Edit Value or Add Value. The MIME information needs to be placed in the Value Name box. You should set the data type for the entry to REG_SZ and leave the string field blank. The following is an example of a MIME entry:

```
drawing/x-dwf,dwf,,1:REG_SZ:
```

The unused field is represented by an extra comma between "dwf" and the letter "l" (lowercase L). The extra comma must be included for the MIME type to work correctly.

Elements of a CAD-oriented Web Site

Some basic elements comprise a good CAD web site. These elements, which are explained further in the following sections, are common to most compelling sites and include:

- Company Background
- Portfolio
- Feedback

Company Information

Including background information about your company helps paint a picture of a successful firm to do business with. Focus on presenting company information in a "lightweight" format. That is, don't get too heavy on the surface because you don't want to bore visitors to your site with dry corporate data. You can always place the detailed company information in secondary pages linked to the main page. Visitors who are interested in getting more data can "double-click down" to the more detailed pages.

Portfolio

Use your web site to market your company by posting a portfolio of your work. Use the AutoCAD Release 14 Internet tools and the exercises included in this chapter to create HTML pages containing DWF files representing your best work. Make certain to include customer testimonials, awards, press releases, published articles, and related marketing materials. You want visitors to download or print this type of prestigious information. Your site could attract audiences that you may never have anticipated, so blow your own horn and strut your stuff, but be sure to have compelling, valuable, CAD-based content to complement your marketing.

Feedback Mechanisms

Providing a method for eliciting feedback from visitors to your web site is critical. This method can be as simple as including "mailto" options or as sophisticated as a registration site and chat room. You want people to ask questions about your services or products, so have the infrastructure in place to rapidly provide a brief recognition of any e-mail sent. If you can budget the resources, a method for delivering answers in a timely fashion goes a long way toward building great customer relationships.

Use a registration form to elicit profile information of visitors to your site. You might consider offering some type of "freebie" to encourage registration. Building a profile of the visitors to your site provides invaluable insights into the needs of your customer base.

Marketing Your Work

Your web site is your company's presence on the World Wide Web. There are major advantages to having your own site, if you know how to attract the right audience. A fundamental rule is to publish something of value for your audience. You want your site to compel prospective clients to visit and explore. Including information that is free, educational, and useful to your audience always works well. Having links to other CAD related sites of interest (such as `http://www.autodesk.com`) also increases the value of your site. In your site, provide promotional cues leading to areas where an exchange of value can take place, like a sale of a product or service. An architectural firm may feature home designs, or a lighting manufacturer can include DWG data for insertion into drawings. For a design firm, having a CAD-oriented web site opens countless possibilities for expanding your market.

You can take the following steps to ensure that your site can be found easily by those you want to attract:

- Register your site with all the popular search sites. Some sites will automate this process for you from one location on the net.

- Print the URL of your site on your business cards, brochures, and advertisements just as you would your phone number and e-mail address.

Another good reason to have a web site is to provide your employees with remote access to company information, and through it, to the Internet for business reasons. Remote access is especially valuable for field personnel in construction, manufacturing, and sales.

Now that you've envisioned your web site, how do you create it and where do you put it? Fortunately, you have many options to match your enthusiasm, need, and budget. The next section examines some of these options.

Building a Web Site

An entry-level webmaster might consider using one of the online services offered by CompuServe or America Online. These vendors have simple facilities for creating and maintaining basic web sites for a monthly fee. However, these vendors offer a very limited amount of space on their server, which may make it difficult for you to build the type of CAD web site you want.

What if you want to create a more sophisticated site than America Online or CompuServe provides, but don't want to spend a lot on a professional web designer? Many excellent web site authoring packages are available that automate HTML code generation. These modern Windows-based tools support drag-and-drop HTML page construction and are highly visual in nature. Despite many packages having automated page creation features, you still have to embed DWF files into your CAD-oriented HTML pages. Check out Netscape Communicator or Microsoft's FrontPage as basic examples of this functionality.

So maybe this all sounds easy and wonderful, but you're too busy drafting to spend any time building a CAD-based web site. What can you do? Perhaps you should consider hiring a professional web design firm to create your site. If you can afford it, this strategy has numerous benefits. The cost can vary from several thousand to hundreds of thousands of dollars. An experienced web site design firm can really help you showcase your designs and get your message across to your audience.

Self-Hosting Your Web Site versus Using an ISP

The effort you invest in creating your own site can grow with your requirements and budget. You do not need to wait because the sophistication of your site can grow along with your needs. After you've created your site, where do you put it? The simplest method may be for you to start by renting a partition on a server with an Internet connection, and expand as presence grows. You also have the option of setting up your own server or maintaining your home page with a service provider. Many Internet Service Providers offer this option, as do major online proprietary services. If you want your own server, turnkey systems are available from Sun Microsystems, DEC, and others that include the hardware and software you need. Keep in mind that you will still have to arrange for your server to be "plugged in" to the network, and the cost for this can vary widely depending on the speed of your connection. Visitors to your site generally will not tolerate slow response time—even if your content is very compelling.

As a web publisher or intranet manager, you want to have your site linked to the net via a T1 connection. A T1 connection can be either shared with others (fractional T1) or dedicated solely to your server. Your connection decision should be based on balancing the cost against the traffic you anticipate on your site. If you expect thousands of visitors, or *hits*, per day or during peak times, you may need a dedicated T1 or faster. If you can't afford a T1, you should consider hosting your site with a service provider that has a link to the Internet backbone. Satellite services are also available for Internet and intranet publishers.

Utilizing "Push" Technologies

So now that you have a site on the web, how do you keep your clients, contractors, or other visitors apprised of changes to the drawing information displayed on your HTML pages or drawing files required for a specific project? Keeping subcontractors in sync or customers informed of changes to your web site can be a difficult task. A simple solution to this situation can be handled through site registration and offering an e-mail service notifying clients of any changes to the site. In addition, more sophisticated solutions involve utilizing software that implements Internet "push" technology. In essence, a push application sends updated information (such as revised DWG files) to subscribers that have set a filter requesting that they receive changes to these files.

For example, say you are a general contractor involved in coordinating numerous subcontractors on a large airport construction project. Changes to the base DWG file occur on a nearly daily basis, and you must get these updates out to the field each day. By using a push server (such as Marimba's Castanet Transmitter), you can "push" updated drawings on a daily (or hourly) basis to each subcontractor. This new Internet technology is becoming very commonplace. Both Netscape's Communicator NetCaster feature and the forthcoming Active Desktop of Microsoft's Internet Explorer 4.0 have embraced push functionality.

INSIDER TIP

Push technology can be a great asset to your web site. I believe that all industries that depend on staying in synch with distributed information must utilize this technology.

Using Other Web Tools

For those of you who are serious about using the Internet and AutoCAD, this section discusses the additional plug-ins and development tools that you can add to control Internet data in Release 14 and at your web site. The web changes so rapidly that some of this information may be out of date by the time you read this book. Therefore, you can use this section as a guide and expect updates to have occurred since this book was written.

Java

Java is the programming language of the web and is highly platform-independent and similar in structure to the C/C++ languages, but without the dependencies on pointers. You can integrate Java routines into your existing AutoCAD programming environment.

Using Java and JavaScript with DWF Files in HTML Pages

To Java enable HTML pages containing DWF files, you have to add two tags— <script> and <form>—to the HTML file. As mentioned earlier in this chapter, the <embed> tag has a name=*"drawingname"* reference parameter. This reference is very important for Java development because Java functions reference the <embed> tag's name parameter. These references are contained in the <script> portion of your HTML file.

If you want to set control buttons to manipulate the DWF file, you have to use the <form> tag. Again, Java references the <embed> tag's name= parameter when calling a function to activate the navigational control button.

With the <embed> tag name= reference properly used, you can use the <script> and <form> tags to implement a great deal of interactivity to your web pages. DWF files and *WHIP!* can be manipulated with Java. You can use Java to extract named views from DWF files. With Java it is also possible to embed links to the named views into an HTML page. With some elementary programming skill you can build an interactive navigational front end to your CAD-based web site.

AutoLISP

You can use AutoLISP to manipulate URLs attached to objects or areas in an AutoCAD DWG file. This section details some of the basic mechanisms available to AutoLISP programmers.

Integration with AutoLISP

The AutoLISP Internet functions require that the Internet Utilities be loaded to operate. Two handy functions when working with URLs and AutoLISP are *seturl* and *geturl*.

Use the seturl function to attach an URL to an object. This function requires two variables to be passed to it: the entity name and the URL string.

The counterpart to seturl is geturl. Use geturl to return the URL string attached to an object.

Accessing URL Information Using AutoLISP

Two AutoLISP functions, *allurls* and *pickurls*, provide a powerful environment to aid in accessing URL information. Scroll a list of all the URLs contained in a DWG file to the AutoCAD Command: line with allurls. Use pickurls to scroll a list of all the URLs contained in a selection set. Neither function removes duplicate URL data from the list.

Important Formats and Plug-ins

No CAD-oriented Internet environment is complete without a number of plug-ins or controls. The following sections discuss some of the plug-ins that are useful when working with CAD data on the web.

VRML2

VRML2, or Virtual Reality Modeling Language Revision 2, is a recent update to the Internet's three-dimensional graphics communications protocols. VRML is used to present a three-dimensional navigational view of a web site. You can consider a VRML "room" the 3D evolutionary equivalent of a 2D HTML-based web page. In a year or two, VRML may become the defacto interface standard for navigating the Internet.

Perhaps some analogies of basic behavior will help you understand the similarities between HTML and VRML a bit more. VRML expands the two-dimensional interface of HTML into three dimensions. Like HTML, VRML supports hypertext links (targets or anchors). Selecting a link embedded into an HTML page can send you to another web site located elsewhere on the Internet. With VRML, selecting a 3D object (such as a door) can transport you to another VRML room located somewhere else on the Internet. Also like HTML, VRML supports inlines (objects embedded into the page that are not native to the page itself). With an HTML page, the DWF file does not have to reside in the same location as the text for the HTML page itself. The same paradigm exists for VRML; in essence, any object containing a hyperlink (for example, the door) can exist in a location (directory, server, web site, and so on) separate from the VRML file.

INSIDER TIP

If you want to experiment with VRML2 browsing, I suggest obtaining a copy of CosmoPlayer from Silicon Graphics (`http://webspace.sgi.com/cosmoplayer/download.html`). Cosm oPlayer is the premier VRML 2.0 browser tool, compliant with the VRML 2.0 specification, and supports interpolators, script nodes, sensors, and 3D sound. SGI & Netscape have entered into a partnership to integrate Live3D with CosmoPlayer. If you want to explore the 3D world of the net, you should get CosmoPlayer.

PDF

If you are going to create an engineering document web site, you may have a need to create portable document format (PDF) files. PDF encapsulates a business document into universal, platform-independent file format. Adobe Acrobat is a PDF creation tool that, according to Adobe marketing materials, "enables you to create and share business documents on a cross-platform basis while they maintain their original look and feel."

NOTE

According to Adobe Systems, "Acrobat software is the fastest way to publish any document online." That very well may be, but putting the hype aside for a moment, I do find that viewing PDF files is useful and may be required at certain web sites. The free Adobe Acrobat Reader enables you to view, navigate, and print PDF files across all major computing platforms.

You can download the Acrobat Reader from the Adobe Systems web site at: `http://www.adobe.com/prodindex/acrobat/readstep.html`. For more information on Acrobat, contact Adobe at `http://www.adobe.com/prodindex/acrobat/main.html`.

Marimba Castanet

Castanet automatically distributes and maintains software applications and content within a company or across the Internet. The Castanet Transmitter (server) and Castanet Tuner (client) work together to keep software and content always up-to-date. Create a "channel" and place it on a Castanet Transmitter. Castanet automatically distributes, installs, maintains, and updates the channel, all via the Internet. Castanet can support any type of channel: internal corporate applications, multimedia consumer channels, and more.

Hyperwire

The Kinetix division of Autodesk has a product called Hyperwire that enables you to create dynamic, interactive, 3D content and harness the power of Java without writing a single line of code. This product is a boon for those of us who want to create cool interactive web sites, but don't want to get bogged down with writing Java code. Kinetix claims that, "Hyperwire is a powerful 3D authoring tool that integrates seamlessly with 3D Studio MAX and other VRML applications." Hyperwire can be used to manipulate DWF files and *WHIP!*. Check out the AutoCAD Internet Publishing Kit for a great example of Hyperwire controlling *WHIP!* and displaying DWF files.

NOTE

I consider Hyperwire another product in the realm of visual development tools (such as Symantec's Visual Café or Microsoft's Visual Basic) that have become so popular of late.

For more information, visit the Kinetix web site at `http://www.ktx.com/hyperwire/hwhome.html-ssi`.

QuickTime

QuickTime is the multiplatform, industry-standard multimedia architecture used by software tool vendors and content creators to create and deliver synchronized graphics, sound, video, text, and music. QuickTime is an excellent choice for "author once, playback anywhere" multimedia. Numerous development tools exist for creating QuickTime files. To find out more about QuickTime and associated development tools, point your browser to `http://quicktime.apple.com`.

Shockwave

Shockwave is a family of multimedia authoring tools and players, designed to give you a wide range of interactive experiences on the web. The Shockwave player is used by many web authors for presenting interactive multimedia display and content. One drawback to Shockwave is that it is a proprietary Macromedia format supported only by their products (such as Director). Creating Shockwave files requires that you use a Macromedia application. For more information, check out `http://www.macromedia.com/shockwave/intro.html`.

Summary

In this chapter, you have learned how to use a web-enabled Release 14 to view, access, and publish CAD to the web. You now know how to use the Internet Utilities to open, insert, or save DWG files to the Internet. In addition, you have also learned about attaching URLs to objects in your DWG files and how to link one file to another. This chapter has also discussed the ins and outs of publishing CAD data on the web with Release 14.

Hopefully, your appetite for building a web site has been whetted. The next chapter, "Project Collaboration over the Internet," studies a live site and provides an in-depth analysis of what it takes to manage an effective CAD web site.

Happy surfing!

PROJECT COLLABORATION OVER THE INTERNET

by Mark Sage

By its nature, project design is a collaborative process. From concept to final construction or manufacturing, a varying range of disciplines are involved in bringing an idea to reality. Each member of the design team has specific processes to follow and standards to apply. Effective management of the project design process requires timely communication and rapid distribution of design standards.

This chapter discusses how the World Wide Web benefits the design process by facilitating communication and delivering a collaborative environment. The chapter also covers some important Internet collaboration tools for the design and engineering space. Finally, this chapter examines a design firm that has embraced Internet technologies. You will study the business reasons that led them to become a leader in their field through use of the web. The firm's CAD web site is examined here, with discussion of the problems and issues encountered, how they were overcome, and what the web has meant for their business. The discussion wraps up with a tour of the site itself. Specifically, this chapter covers the following topics:

- Coordination and the iterative design process

- Collaborative Internet technologies

- Case study background: Architekton

- Site implementation

- Going live online

- Taking the Architekton tour

Coordination and the Iterative Design Process

Constant communication between disparate (possibly distant) parties such as consulting engineering firms, subcontractors, and suppliers is essential to a successful venture. In most cases, many firms, individuals, and sources are involved with the project. During the project design phase, a development team establishes the basic product design. A review and reiterative approval loop, perhaps involving external agencies, follows. Finally, ownership passes to engineering, who may contract with consulting engineering firms. At each step in the process design changes will occur. Coordinating and communicating changes to the design is critical to keeping a project on schedule and costs under control.

Throughout the project life cycle, distribution of design, and structural, construction, or manufacturing standards becomes an issue. By facilitating collaboration through rapid communication of design intent, you eliminate much of the reiteration involved. Coordinating engineering document flow and revision has always been a headache, even for companies with deep pockets. The web, in conjunction with the proper graphical Internet client technologies, brings powerful tools for managing, viewing, accessing, and publishing CAD data for clients and agencies alike. Web servers provide central drawing management control and distribution mechanisms.

Real-Life Coordination Problems

Have you ever experienced the following scenario?

A general contractor contracts with your engineering firm to supply a set of drawings for a specific aspect of a building project. Numerous other portions of the project (including HVAC, electrical, structural, and lighting) are subcontracted to other consulting engineering firms.

You submit completed plans to the general contracting firm, invoice your client, and begin work on another project. Without your knowledge, the structural engineer alters the main load-bearing supports to meet new safety standards. After a few days, a call from the general contractor alerts you to the structural change. He is falling behind schedule and needs updated drawings immediately for your portion of the project. You put your current project on hold and address the issues arising from the structural changes made to the previous building project. A new cycle of engineering work begins while the deadline approaches for your existing project.

In a nearly perfect world, you would submit revised plans and return your focus to the "back-burnered" project. But this is real life, and Murphy's Law seems to always take precedence. Due to the structural modifications, the HVAC ducting has been rerouted, and you have to update your drawings again. By the time you resubmit final, final, *final* drawings, the number of hours you have spent on the project has nearly tripled. Not only that—your current project is past deadline and the client has had to slip his schedule.

Do you know what this situation sounds like to me? Very expensive! Just try getting another job from the client who had to slip his schedule.

Using the Internet to Facilitate Coordination

How could such a problem be obviated? With better and more timely communication between the disparate parties, all the project delays could have been avoided. Even when you use the telephone, faxes, and e-mail, the communications cycle is still imperfect. Real-time collaboration is the solution. An Internet (or a private intranet) with the visual benefits of the web supports the collaborative design process in ways not addressed by any other technology.

With the web, changes to CAD data can be communicated immediately on a global basis. The use of web technologies as a foundation for design collaboration creates a "follow the sun" engineering environment. Properly implemented, a good CAD project web site delivers worldwide access to relevant drawing data, immediately communicating design changes to affected parties.

Staying on Top of Projects

Examine how the previous scenario plays out when you use web technologies as a central point of communication. The following case is hypothetical, but based on real technologies and experiences.

Day 1—8:30 a.m. A week before the project deadline for engineering drawings, the general contractor and structural engineer simultaneously receive high-level information on their desktops about new structural safety regulations. Servers utilizing Push technologies such as Marimba Castanet, BackWeb, or the Point Cast Network deliver information in real time, based on the client's profile settings. The profile acts as a filter, enabling you to select the kind of information and discussion topics that interest you.

Day 1—8:45 a.m. Detailed data retrieved from the web by using a search engine like Digital's Alta Vista, or Infoseek, indicates that the new earthquake safety regulations will affect the building project.

Day 1—9:15 a.m. The structural engineer fires off an e-mail to the regulatory agency representative, asking about the new rules' impact on the current design.

Day 1—10:00 a.m. The engineer receives a confirmation by e-mail that the safety standards apply to his project.

Day 1—10:30 a.m. Realizing that major structural design changes are necessary, the engineer points his web browser to the project web site, and fills out an online Engineering Change Order (ECO) request form.

Day 1—10:45 a.m. Having received a completed ECO request form, the general contractor's project management system automatically generates a notification of a pending ECO.

Day 1—11:00 a.m. The notice, indicating a potential change to the central drawing database, is sent via e-mail or a "push" server to involved or interested parties.

Day 1—11:30 a.m. A threaded discussion of the design impact begins, using web browser tools and groupware, such as Lotus Notes or Novell GroupWise. Electronic whiteboard software, such as Netscape's CoolTalk and Autodesk View, is used in a collaborative redlining session. The whiteboard session enables the consulting engineers to visualize that potential structural changes will impact the HVAC design.

Day 1—1:00 p.m. The participating engineers agree to implement changes to the structural plans, and approve the ECO. The structural revisions are scheduled for delivery to the project web server by beginning of business tomorrow.

Day 1—1:30 p.m. Having current information, the consultants and contractors e-mail their internal resources, shifting focus to their next scheduled project.

Day 2—9:00 a.m. The design revisions are uploaded to the project's central drawing database server, and are reviewed and approved by the project coordinator. New DWF files of the structural drawings are generated and posted, along with the associated DWG, to the web server. Notification of the new postings, including the appropriate URLs, is e-mailed or pushed to the project participants.

Day 2—10:00 a.m. The consulting engineers download the revised drawings and continue their work. The project work stays on schedule and finishes on time.

In the preceding situation, the web played a crucial role in the design process. Internet technologies were used to facilitate design team collaboration and keep the project on track. From a business perspective, the return on investment for using the World Wide Web as a CAD design collaboration tool is easily justified.

Collaborative Internet Technologies

The web facilitates collaboration in ways never before possible. As a graphical interface to the Internet, the World Wide Web has spurred development of new tools designed to increase business communications and enable people separated by distance to work more closely together. This section discusses some important Internet-based tools and technologies that will help you expand your business into the virtual cyber realm.

Redlining Tools

Now, having viewed DWF and perhaps DWG files with your browser and plug-ins, you want to make some changes to the drawing file.

As this is being written, during the early stages of the AutoCAD Release 14 cycle, few applications can handle native Release 14-based drawing files. Until developers deliver support for the Release 14-based DWG files, you will have to use the R13 drawing file format. AutoCAD Release 14 has a SaveAs R13 feature to ease this transition.

With redlining tools, you can mark up a drawing without changing the base file. Redlining data typically is saved to a specific layer or a separate file. The following section highlights a number of different redlining utilities and plug-ins you might want to investigate.

Autodesk View: The Autodesk View Plug-In

Release 1.2 of the Autodesk View plug-in component is free of charge, but requires that a runtime version of Autodesk View Release 1.2 be installed on the computer. Unlike *WHIP!*, the Autodesk View plug-in supports layer control, paper space views, and xrefs. One shortcoming of View 1.2 is the lack of Release 14 DWG file support. The forthcoming Release 14-compatible release of View will incorporate Autodesk's Whip display list, which is based on Heidi technology.

The combination of Autodesk View (desktop application) and the Autodesk View plug-in creates a powerful redlining tandem. The Netscape plug-in supports DWG and DXF, reading files into your browser for manipulation (see fig. 28.1). Redlining is performed with Autodesk View, but the plug-in enables you to see the redlining information.

SoftSource Vdraft Internet Tools

SoftSource offers two Netscape plug-ins: one for viewing DWG and DXF files, and another that adds support for HTML links and Simple Vector Format (SVF) files, a proprietary format. The SoftSource plug-ins are free for noncommercial purposes, and cost $50 for commercial use. Both versions include navigational controls (zoom, pan, layer visibility) and vector graphics.

Figure 28.1

Redlining an AutoCAD DWG with Autodesk View 1.2 and the View plug-in combination aids in the collaborative design effort.

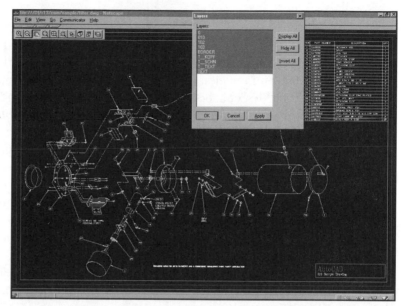

Whiteboarding

Internet-based whiteboard applications enable multiple sites or users to collaborate on projects in real time. Using one of these applications is just like using the whiteboard at work. "Markers" are used to call out areas of interest or write notes on the board. Most whiteboard applications support simultaneous telecommunications access and mark up of documents. You are able to talk on the phone with your colleagues while visually communicating with them. Whiteboard applications facilitate communication through engineering document collaboration, and "virtual" meetings.

To date, none of the whiteboard applications reads native engineering document formats such as DWG or DWF. At this point, the technology is limited to using screen captures of drawings—which, surprisingly, works quite well. Nevertheless, with the rapid changes occurring in Internet applications, this too will change. Before long, DWF or DWG redlining tools will probably be integrated into whiteboard applications. Following are some of the more popular applications to consider:

- Microsoft NetMeeting
- Netscape Communicator
- PictureTel GroupBoard/GroupShare

Microsoft NetMeeting

NetMeeting is an Internet whiteboard application supplied with Microsoft Internet Explorer 3.0. The product enables users to work together by sharing applications, exchanging information between shared applications through a shared clipboard, transferring files, collaborating on a shared whiteboard, and communicating with a text-based chat feature. NetMeeting supports Internet *telephony* (phone communications), application sharing, and data conferencing. The whiteboard program is a drawing program that enables the display and sharing of graphic information with other people during a conference session. The data-conferencing feature enables two or more users to work together and collaborate in real time over the web, using application-sharing whiteboard, and chat functionality. The Internet phone feature delivers point-to-point audio conferencing over the web, so that voice calls can be placed to associates around the world. With the application-sharing feature, your colleagues will be able to see the drawing information on your machine. With NetMeeting, you can "share" your local copy of AutoCAD Release 14 with conference participants. The chat tool is a text-based medium for communicating with conference participants.

Netscape Communicator

The latest iteration of Netscape's web browser—Communicator—includes Collabra group discussion software, and Netscape Conference real-time collaboration software. Also included in Netscape Communicator is support for *extranets*—features that extend corporate intranets beyond the firewall. With Netscape Communicator, it is possible to communicate and share information over the Internet with partners, suppliers, and customers.

Netscape Conference brings tight integration of collaboration tools—including whiteboard, chat, and file transfer—into the Messenger (e-mail) and Navigator (browser) components. With Conference, "virtual" conferencing sessions increase communication. As shown in figure 28.2, participants can sketch or redline on a collaborative whiteboard, browse documents, and share data anywhere in the world. Also, as with other similar collaborative tools, meeting participants can converse by telephone, using the Internet instead of paying long distance connection charges.

Figure 28.2

Communicator's whiteboard includes sophisticated markup tools.

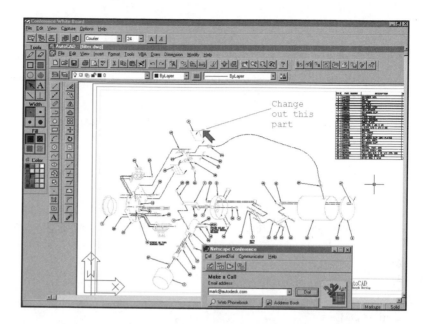

Netscape Collabra is a tool that facilitates the creation and management of threaded discussions. Like the AutoCAD Forum on CompuServe, a Collabra discussion forum is an electronic "room" where people can discuss key issues, solicit input, and communicate decisions. Collabra's discussion-group management features enable you to specify whether to ignore or watch specified topics, and to conduct advanced searches for information across forums.

PictureTel GroupBoard/GroupShare

GroupBoard supports multiple-site video conferencing, and an electronic whiteboard and flipchart. The whiteboard component of GroupBoard enables collaborative viewing, annotation, highlighting, and editing of files and presentations. More than just a simple whiteboard application for the Internet, the product supports the TWAIN interface, allowing for scanned paper documents to be imported for collaborative mark-up and revision. Additional features include the capability to import many graphics and presentation formats, and the create and save multiple "pages" functions as an electronic flipchart.

GroupBoard brings easy-to-use information-exchange tools to the Internet-based collaborative experience. The tools contained in this product add a familiar element to virtual meetings. Colleagues scattered over great distances can interact more naturally. The result is greater collaboration, improved decision-making, and increased group productivity.

A superset of GroupBoard is the GroupShare product. GroupShare offers full application sharing, not just screen sharing. As with Microsoft's NetMeeting, only one PC needs to be running a particular application, such as Release 14; another meeting participant can work with Release 14 as if it were local. Users swap control of AutoCAD with the click of a mouse. A shared Clipboard enables participants to cut and paste images back and forth. Meeting participants can record notes in GroupShare's Message window. For this technology to work, each member of the conference must have a local copy of GroupBoard and GroupShare installed on his or her local machine.

E-Mail

The life blood of all Internet collaboration and communication is electronic mail. Whether you use AOL or a more sophisticated Internet-based system, e-mail has the distinct advantage of immediacy, compared to overnight package delivery or standard postal services. Typically more exact than telecommunications, the written word provides an opportunity to clearly articulate one's thoughts. Many industry analysts consider e-mail the "killer" application of the Internet.

With today's improved e-mail technologies, one can embed a multiplicity of data types in a document. Electronic mail has evolved from an ASCII format into a rich communications medium. With Netscape's e-mail tool, it is possible to send colleagues HTML pages that contain DWF files. Embedding HTML in e-mail is part of the Internet technological evolution.

Case Study Background: Architekton

Among design firms that have adopted Internet technologies for enhancing collaboration, one company stands out: Architekton. This company has fully embraced the web, deriving immense business benefits from the Internet. What follows in this section is a case study of Architekton: how they came to use the web, the benefits it has brought their clients, how it has helped their business grow, and the tools they have used. Whether you are very interested in using the web or already have set up a corporate site on the Internet, this in-depth study should provide information that helps you to better understand how you can increase design project collaboration by using the Internet.

Company Information

Founded by four architects in 1989, Architekton's practice has expanded in a relatively short time. It is rare for a design firm to rapidly build a portfolio of successful endeavors, especially by tackling a wide variety of projects ranging from civic and public works to fuel-delivery facilities. How did they accomplish this feat? By implementing cutting-edge technologies to address business needs, cultivating a reputation for superior service, and delivering high-quality designs for projects that require highly integrated, technical systems.

Company Philosophy

Architekton views design and service as inextricable components of each project. From Architekton's viewpoint, the marketplace demands both speed and personalized attention. One aspect of the firm's personality is their willingness to go beyond the boundaries of architectural practice. Diversity is the foundation of the Architekton philosophy. To quote the Architekton home page, that philosophy is "to engage all areas of architectural production to respond to clients' needs, and provide superior service by maintaining a leading role in the integration of technology and practice."

Their organizational structure enables lateral, rather than top-down, project management. Many individuals in the firm become involved as they are consulted for their areas of expertise. Architekton believes this management style is effective, and has repeatedly proven its value in numerous projects. It is rare to find such an organizational structure in an architectural office; yet, this environment has been instrumental in meeting the needs of multidisciplinary projects.

Technical expertise is a key element of the company's success; there are no technophobes at Architekton. The company is among the most technically advanced practices in the West. Use of CAD and Internet technology facilitates collaboration at every stage of the design process. Advanced technologies such as 3D modeling are used to accelerate the design process and to enhance communication.

Market Locations and Business Expertise

With offices in the Phoenix, San Francisco, and Seattle markets, the firm can respond quickly to demands for their expertise. Architekton's corporate headquarters in Tempe, Arizona, offers a full range of services: architecture, planning, fuel services, multimedia, and corporate identity services. A Phoenix office complements the Tempe location, supporting their fuel industry business. The San Francisco office handles Media, Design, and Planning projects for both domestic and international markets. The Seattle area location provides architecture, fuel services, and personal communication system (PCS) design, as well as a full range of Internet and intranet media solutions.

Architekton offers more than just architectural services. Their current business model is divided into the following five major areas:

- Architecture
- Fuel delivery
- Internet services
- Multimedia
- Personal communication system design

Architecture

Architekton's architectural practice covers a wide range of projects and is the primary service the company offers. The firm has expertise in civic and public projects, as well as in residential design.

Fuel Delivery Systems

Architekton has developed technical systems expertise associated with retail fuel facility designs, and has actively marketed these skills. Architekton carved a unique niche in the fuel industry design field, clearly differentiating themselves from their competition.

Internet Services

Architekton's investment in the web has paid huge dividends for their clients and for the company itself. The Internet services offered by this case study are based on solutions designed to improve client communication. The firm developed a complete Internet site, from which an assortment of web-based solutions are made available to clients.

Architekton has leveraged their internal Internet and technological expertise into a business unit that provides client services based on Internet technology. The offering of Internet-based document distribution services is rare for an architectural firm. Architekton approaches distribution of engineering documentation over the web in a unique manner, offering solutions to clients whose business depends on timely dissemination of information.

Multimedia

By adopting cutting edge technologies for their marketing and communication materials, Architekton cultivated skills in multimedia authoring and development. Whenever an adopted technology successfully aids collaboration or communication, a business effort grows up around it. Architekton's client base for multimedia projects has expanded beyond architectural services to efforts such as interactive kiosks and other services.

Personal Communication System Design

Architekton entered a new market niche servicing the design and engineering needs of the *Personal Communications Services* (PCS) industry. Leveraging their technical systems expertise, Architekton can deliver accurate and timely engineering documentation. Keys to success in this market will be determined by their role in facilitating the permitting process.

Basic Business Case

Architekton, because it views the Internet as a revolutionary way to communicate with clients, has developed interactive tools with which consultants and clients can share information.

Why did an architectural design firm get into the business of using Internet technology? By offering World Wide Web–based Internet solutions to their clients, Architekton improves their own work-flow processes. Architekton developed a method for communicating current engineering standards for their client base. By building interactive web sites for their clients, they were able to simplify distribution of standards and changes. These standards are delivered to any consultant with a connection to the Internet in any geographic region.

Architekton principal Joseph Salvatore, AIA, is a chief proponent of Internet use for their clients. "One of our clients has a major presence in the Southwest with numerous convenience stores and gas stations," said Mr. Salvatore. Architekton had been working with this client for some time, developing prototype drawings, prototype buildings, working with existing building types, and placing them on specific sites.

Before becoming a client, the company came to Architekton seeking a solution to a problem distributing documents to consulting engineers throughout the West. According to Mr. Salvatore, "The problem they were having is that the consultants they use were not always using the most current engineering documents. Consultant A would have documents dated one day, while consultant B would have different documents from the previous day."

In this case, drawings were always changing because of new equipment, new technology, or new materials. With a large number of consultants spread throughout the country, keeping up with changes is extremely difficult. Prior to acceptance of the Internet as a business solution, engineering document distribution was tedious and inaccurate. The typical distribution scenario consisted of FedEx packages, bulletin boards, sending floppy disks through the mail, and telephone follow-up.

Giving an example of the severe nature of the problem their clients faced, Mr. Salvatore states, "It's been to the point where our client's engineers go out to their site and they're looking at the buildings. Their superiors come out and look at the site and say, 'What happened to the changes we made? Why weren't these incorporated?' That creates a lot of problems for our clients."

Before the engineering industry became automated through the use of computers, project schedules were significantly longer. Such protracted schedules were the norm due to limited communications technologies. It took a greater period of time for engineering data to circulate to members of the design team.

Automation and modern communications technologies compresses the design cycle. Adopters of technological innovations benefit from advances in automation by having the ability to rapidly respond to changes in client criteria.

Building the Support Infrastructure

Laying the infrastructural groundwork for a web site is not a simple task. Researching the various Internet products and platforms alone can consume vast quantities of time. Adding to this effort is the continuously changing Internet product landscape. Every few months great upheavals take place in web technology. It seems that advances in feature sets or technologies are so rapid that we can never keep up.

The facilities Architekton uses for their Internet Media services are based on an exhaustive research effort. They evaluated both Unix and Windows NT as networking platforms, ultimately deciding on Windows NT. Scott Harden, Architekton's Director of Internet Media Solutions, states, "The decision to use NT was based on the direction the industry appears to be performing future development on." In many respects, the choice of NT over Unix was a difficult one. Unix, a tested and proven operating environment for Internet server technology, offers strong reliability. The deciding factor for Architekton's selection of NT was simplified networking. "However, NT offered a simplified networking solution to my limited knowledge in networking," said Mr. Harden.

Windows NT was the platform of choice for sites that were integrating back-end databases to front-end web sites. "With the amount of information we were trying to distribute, the utilization of databases is only a short time away," Mr. Harden concluded.

Architekton finally selected the following equipment and operating environment:

- Main web server and FTP server

    Pentium Pro 200 server

    128 MB of RAM

    8 GB of storage in RAID arrayed drives

    Windows NT

- Mail server

    Pentium 90

    32 MB of RAM

    Windows NT Server

- Cisco router

- Multiple UPS

- Dedicated T1 Internet line for network connectivity

Implementation

This section examines processes and decision points Architekton went through before attaining a satisfactory implementation. First, you will study the machinations Architekton went through as they built their own internal site. Next, you will look at the process Architekton used to go online. Finally, the section explains what Architekton did after the system was up, what changes they made, and why.

Site Planning

Architekton's process for web-enabling (setting up a web site) an established client entails a series of steps before the site gets published on the Internet. According to Mr. Harden, the first and most important step is much like architecture, designing how the information that the site will offer will be presented to the visitor.

Scott Harden explains the firm's first attempt at using the Internet for document distribution: "My process began as solving a document distribution problem between ourselves and our client. The original solution was to utilize the FTP (file transfer protocol) space allocated to us by our local ISP (Internet service provider) as a virtual file directory between offices. This solution, however, was marginal due to the fact that additional communication was essential (via phone or e-mail) to ascertain the exact files required and at what time they would be placed on the FTP site."

The initial use of FTP and a hosted environment actually created another layer of complexity in the current problem. Staying synchronous with the client proved more difficult than relying on existing methods of document acquisition and distribution. Architekton then considered expanding their FTP-based Internet solution to the web. "In search of a more efficient and autonomous solution," Mr. Harden states, "I explored the use of the web as a medium for distributing project documentation between ourselves and clients. The web offered us a method by which we could not only give access to the files available on the FTP site, but also offer visual previews of the information prior to download."

Content Creation

The site framework was developed next. "This is the interface through which the users will interact with the site," Scott explains. After the interface is completed, the process of uploading the working content into the framework takes place. With Architecture/Engineering-related sites, the information being incorporated into the site is usually drawings, specifications, and equipment information. "The amount of effort involved in this step is relative to the amount of information that is to be contained on the site," according to Mr. Harden.

With Architekton's Internet-based business model, one person or one source controls the documents that are uploaded to the project web site. All the building types and drawings are uploaded by Architekton to the hosted site. Architekton is responsible for making all the drawing corrections as they occur, and for updating the site. With a project-oriented web site, consultants all over the country immediately have access to the latest and most current drawings, eliminating the mistakes that can occur when consultants and drawings are out of synch.

"The Internet has enabled creation of a central database for drawing information where everyone can access the most current information," says another principal of Architekton, Arny Bailey, AIA. "The days of 'as changes occur they have to make sure they distribute all of the changes to the consulting architects' is gone. That doesn't have to happen anymore," said Mr. Bailey.

Publishing

As Architekton developed their first client site, they published the following four main sections:

- Construction Drawings
- Construction Specifications
- Equipment Documentation
- Contact List

Each section was created with links to the actual files as well as previews of the data. "With the limitations of the web (images/file size), we were restricted to low-quality images representing the actual drawing sheets," said Mr. Harden. The use of raster images to preview the contents of engineering drawings has a number of serious drawbacks. To be useful, the raster (GIF or JPG) imagery would have to be fairly large. The use of large images increases the size of the HTML page, which results in painfully slow load times. No wonder they call it the worldwide wait! Also, the visual fidelity of the drawing is seriously compromised with a bitmapped (raster) image.

Autodesk recently addressed the market need for a compact, yet accurate method of publishing CAD data to the web by developing the Drawing Web Format (DWF) file specification. DWF files can be embedded in HTML pages and viewed with the *WHIP!* browser tool. *WHIP!* is based on the same technology used to accelerate AutoCAD Release 14 display operations. "When Autodesk offered the beta *WHIP!* plug-in, I tested its value in displaying drawings, and it eventually became an integral part of the site," claims Scott Harden. "The dynamic ability to preview drawings solved the last major hurdle in creating an efficient method to review and distribute construction data between consultants and clients," he adds.

With the completion of the first phase of the project, Architekton's client was amazed at how simple the process of distributing engineering information had become. During the implementation, Architekton had also been marketing the web site to some of their corporate clients. Based on favorable responses from other customers, Architekton decided to offer Internet Media as a service.

Going Live Online

When a site has been fully developed internally and tested off the web, it is ready to be published online. Architekton offers both site hosting and site development services. One of the services Architekton continues to offer is an ongoing maintenance contract for any modifications or upgrades.

Site Host Issues

The question faced by every company wanting to establish a presence on the web is whether to build and maintain a site yourself, or outsource it. Many models will work—the problem is picking the right one. You can start out with an ISP-hosted page, build it into a site, and then move it internally as your confidence and expertise increase. Perhaps your company is big enough to already have a site on the web, but you want to add CAD collaboration functionality to it. Other firms have started out by self-hosting a web site, and then, recognizing that their own value lies in providing content, gradually turn it over to a third party for maintenance. Or you might find that using a service from an outside vendor provides greater returns on your investment.

The value of a service such as Architekton's lies in the firm's experience. Architekton offers not only experience in the building industry, but also technological experience in the Internet. "We have developed solutions that are based on solving problems for architects and engineers and have applied them to working relationships between ourselves and our clients," notes Scott Harden. The services offered by Architekton can help smaller companies succeed in a competitive environment that is based on rapidly changing technology. These systems are tools to help firms expand their business from a focus on regional markets to one of competing on global projects.

Client Educational Issues

One of the biggest issues that companies such as Architekton face is the client's lack of computer or Internet knowledge. The rapid changes in Internet technology pose additional barriers to client education. Getting clients trained to use these new systems can be a formidable task. According to Mr. Harden, "Several firms that had minimal computer knowledge and resources had to be trained on the Internet and the web." Be sure to budget adequately for training your CAD operators. Given the investment your firm makes when it embraces Internet technologies, maintaining operator productivity is essential to success.

In response to use of the Internet for design collaboration, Architekton has added another client service. Mr. Harden notes, "One of the services we have added, in addition to the Internet Media products, is Change Management Consulting. This way, we offer the ability for implementing the new communication system, and the qualified training to help clients fully utilize the potential."

Maintenance

Maintaining an active web site presents new issues for you to address. Internet technology changes so rapidly that it is difficult to keep systems current. If you are an experienced web surfer, you will notice that many sites regularly change their visual appearance and content. Consider dedicating some time each quarter to maintaining your site.

Staying Fresh

Keeping content fresh and compelling is essential if you want your web site to draw new customers and encourage people to return. To keep a site from going stale, you must make a commitment to updating a site on an ongoing basis. A CAD-oriented web site's focused approach makes it easier to refreshen than some other sites. Target the following areas for regular refreshing:

■ **Change the Look and Feel**—Change the background, layout, and fonts to keep your web pages looking new. Try setting aside some time every few months to complete this update. The beauty of HTML is that you don't need to change the underlying structure of the page to accomplish this task. A simple search-and-replace operation on the image files and font types embedded in the HTML content can bring about a whole new look. Consider changing the location of graphics and repositioning navigational aids. Even the most rudimentary HTML editing software can greatly simplify the task of moving images. Keep the site style consistent!

- **Add Information about New Projects or Services**—Don't wait for a regularly scheduled update to include information about a new client service or add to your Project Portfolio! Get information out to your clients as rapidly as possible. You may find that creating internal project documents in HTML form makes it easier to move them quickly to the web.

- **Add New Links**—When you come across an interesting site that might have value for your clients, add a link from your site to that page. You no doubt can work out a reciprocal arrangement with the site to which you are linking.

Adopting and Integrating New Technologies

New design collaborative environments are becoming available for the web daily. You need to develop a process for adding the most valuable of these tools to your site. If you have been through an update or upgrade of your AutoCAD system, you probably already have one in place! All you have to do is modify it appropriately to address the unique aspects of web software. At a minimum, your process should include the following steps:

- **Research**—Many suppliers of Internet technologies are firms that do not have established reputations. In today's rapidly changing world, that shouldn't be a deterrent. With new companies springing up everywhere, spend some time studying the vendor's background and product offerings. The web is a researcher's dream. Use it to gather applicable information about both the vendor and technology.

- **Evaluation**—Install the software or hardware locally, and put it through a rigorous testing cycle. Evaluate the tool for functionality, stability, and usability. Many of the new collaboration tools are released in Beta form on the web and might not be very stable. Be prepared for crashes and anomalous behavior. When a product is in full release, it should have gained the stability you expect of a production drafting tool. If not, move on to another supplier; there are many to choose from.

- **Integration**—Adding a new feature to your site requires careful integration; you must update affected pages and notify clients that it's available. Whether you are adding something simple, such as a registration form, or something with the complexity of push technology, the integration must minimize disruption of your current services. Remember to update all pages that will be affected. There is nothing worse than a site full of broken links or pages that don't function properly. Alert site visitors and clients to your new feature by updating your home page. Consider sending e-mail notices to clients as well. Your implementation will go relatively smoothly if you carefully integrate the product into your existing site.

Taking the Architekton Tour

This section examines Architekton's use of Internet technologies in a real-life situation. A complete exercise follows, in which you navigate to the Architekton web site, study the layout, browse portfolios and personnel resumes, view drawings, and engage in collaborative design.

Navigating the Architekton Site

Before you visit this web site, make certain that you have all the tools necessary to effectively view the site. The Architekton site is optimized for Netscape Navigator or Microsoft Internet Explorer. If you don't have either browser, you should download one of them immediately. Netscape is pervasive and available on a wide variety of platforms. Navigator is available for download at `http://www.netscape.com/comprod/mirror/client_download.html`. You need two plug-ins also: Autodesk's *WHIP!* (`http://www.autodesk.com/products/autocad/whip/whipdwn.htm`) and Adobe's Acrobat Reader, which is available from their web site at `http://www.adobe.com/prodindex/acrobat/readstep.html`.

Type the URL for the Architekton web site, `http://www.architekton.com`, in the address field of your browser, and press Enter. Add a bookmark to this site because you may return periodically to this page.

Depending on the speed of your connection, the page should load relatively quickly. This is an important point to consider. When a visitor first comes to your site, you want your home page to load quickly. Keeping the size of home pages small not only helps bring customers into the site, but also overcomes bandwidth limitations and connection speeds. Cool, animated GIFs and AVI movies are eye-catching additions to a web site, but consume tremendous amounts of bandwidth.

Studying the Site Layout

The structure of Architekton's site provides insight into the effective presentation of CAD-related services and technologies to the architectural and engineering marketplace. The sequence of pages, links, and content flows logically. It is important to keep site navigation simple and structured. No single page overwhelms you with information, and links to related materials are presented at each level.

Navigational aids and supporting hyperlink text are always present to simplify moving about the site. As you can see in figure 28.3, the Architekton site is structured in a straightforward fashion, which makes it simple to use. You never seem to get so many pages deep that you become disoriented.

Figure 28.3

The relatively flat structure of the Architekton site simplifies site navigation.

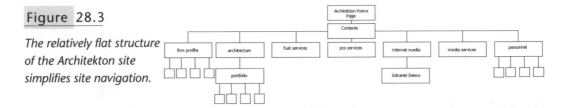

Home Page

Amazingly enough, Architekton doesn't present an information-laden home page. Rather, this site starts off in a very understated manner. The folks who put together this site figure that you came there on purpose, and didn't just "surf on in." The home page alerts you to any special plug-ins or tools necessary for visiting the site.

Visually, the site consistently places hyperlinks in the lower-left portion of the HTML page. The home page provides links to help you obtain the prerequisite plug-ins or browsers. In keeping with Architekton's penchant for superior service, this approach is useful. So many sites make no effort to inform you up front of the site's requirements.

To continue to the contents page, select the graphic image or the highlighted hyperlinked text.

Contents Page

The contents page briefly informs you of Architekton's services and directs you to select an area of expertise to obtain additional information (see fig. 28.4). Topics you can select from include the firm's areas of expertise, a firm profile, and personnel information.

Figure 28.4

Site navigation is facilitated through the use of image tile button highlighting.

A vertical row of colored images is presented on the left side of the screen. To the left of each image is highlighted hyperlink text. As the cursor passes over each image, the image comes to life as a jump button. A JavaScript routine embedded in the HTML page handles the slick button highlighting. Another useful feature is the inclusion of a mailto function on the main page itself.

This page might take a while to load, even on a T1 line.

Browsing the Informational Material

Now that you understand the site layout, you will study the messages and informational content the site provides, starting with Architekton's profile information. Select the firm profile image with a single click.

Firm Profile

The profile page provides some data related to the company and its strengths. The content presented here is limited, at best. In keeping with the style of previous pages, hyperlinks are located in the lower left. Each office link takes you to a page containing a brief overview of the Architekton office.

Take a look at what one of these links has to say. To select Architekton's main office, which is located in Tempe, Arizona, click on the Tempe link.

Here you find more detailed information about the client services that Architekton offers from its headquarters. To help you navigate, the service images are on the left side of the page, with links to other office locations in the lower-left quadrant.

As a drill, check out the Architecture section. Select the image button containing the rendering of a building.

Architecture

After the page has loaded, it is almost disappointing. There seems to be a dearth of information about the company's architectural strengths. Rather, the content seems more of a vision statement. In the center of the page is a link titled "portfolio." Follow that link by selecting it.

Several projects are displayed in a horizontal list of scrollable image tiles. Select the leftmost image button.

You see a definitive description of the project, the Tempe Police Substation, along with a series of hyperlinks representing various views of the structure. Select the Floor Plan hot link, as shown in figure 28.5. A DWF file of the AutoCAD drawing is loaded so that you can study the floor plan and layout of the substation.

Use the Pan and Zoom functions of *WHIP!* to navigate around the drawing. Note that many of the important structural details have been omitted (for security reasons, and to protect the intellectual property of the design firm). Remember that in public sites, you don't want to publish anything that compromises earnings capacity or contractual agreements. Architekton recognizes that the function of a portfolio section is to sell the firm, not to enlighten their competition.

The other view choices on the page are 3D renderings of the police substation. Select the Entrance link to see a sample rendering of the entryway to the finished building. Renderings help the viewer visualize the completed structure. While you are here, you might want to explore other examples in the portfolio section. To do so, use the navigational scroll bar of image tiles to select another project.

Figure 28.5

WHIP! enables you to zoom in quickly and pan around the building's floor plan to study details.

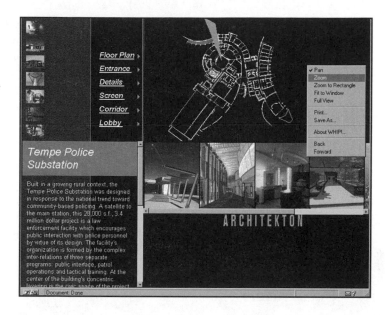

Fuel Services

Next, you will investigate the Fuel Services area of Architekton's web site. Select the image tile of a Texaco Service Station to jump to this page. As mentioned earlier, Architekton is a leading provider of architectural and client services to the petroleum industry. The Fuel Services page contains an in-depth discussion of their expertise in the areas of technical systems, rendering, and permitting. The page also includes links to various petroleum producers.

PCS Services

Going down the vertical navigation bar, select the image of the cellular telecommunications transmission tower. A brief narrative covering Architekton's involvement in the PCS design field is loaded into your browser. By now, you should have noticed that each of the pages provides a handy link to the page on Architekton's personnel. This is smart use of a web page, encouraging visitors to investigate the qualifications of the firm's principals.

Internet Media

Next stop on your site tour is the Internet Media page. To display the page, select the image of office colleagues collaborating on a project. This page contains detailed information about the firm's web services, and numerous links. The wealth of information probably is due to the degree of experience Architekton has in this discipline. As with other pages, a small list of links to useful external sites (including Autodesk's) is included. You will come back to this page later in this chapter and study it in more detail.

Media Services

To reach the Media Services page, select the image tile (the next-to-the-bottom tile) in the navigational bar. After the page has loaded, a description of Architekton's multimedia services is displayed. Note that the page features a brief description of multilingual services. As we become globally connected through the Internet, serving the international market becomes more economically feasible. Architekton is positioned to take advantage of this growing opportunity, and makes it known on their web site.

Personnel

The last portion of the site to browse is the personnel portfolio. Select the image tile located at the bottom of the navigation bar to link to the personnel page. Using an interface similar to that of the architectural portfolio, a horizontal row of scrollable images is displayed. Each image tile consists of a color photograph of an Architekton principal—a very nice touch in what might otherwise be a dry résumé presentation. By selecting a picture, you bring up a brief résumé of that individual.

All design and engineering firms should consider implementing a visual system for the personnel portfolio. Doing so shows dedication to the Internet as a serious business platform, and helps to build prestige while giving visitors a sense of the firm's stability.

Viewing Drawing Data

Now that you have browsed through an external CAD-based web site, it is time to thoroughly evaluate what an intranet-based CAD project web site should look like. Select the Internet Media Services image button to return to that page. The Internet Media contains an image-button hyperlink called "Example," as shown in figure 28.6. Select that link to bring up the sample intranet page you will reviewing in depth.

Architekton uses this site to show prospective clients the type of high-quality Internet services they provide. As you tour this demonstration intranet, please remember that Architekton generates revenue from their expertise in this area and can develop a site for your firm.

Figure 28.6

Architekton's intranet CAD web example differentiates itself from the main site pages with an alternative look and feel.

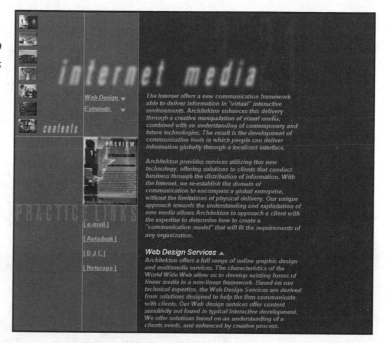

The design and navigation of this site is different from that of the other Architekton pages. The different look and feel serves to separate the technological demonstration area from the actual site content.

To move deeper into the demo site, from the home page (`http://www.architekton.com/internet/demo/home.html`) select the `services` hotlink. The navigational system includes a vertical index frame to the left of the page, a horizontal frame with tabs across the top, and a central document window frame. The following indices are listed in the vertical navigation frame and covered in this section:

- Updates
- Drawings
- Specs
- Equipment
- Contacts
- EDI

Updates

As noted earlier in this chapter, keeping track of the latest changes to current projects is always a difficult task. With a properly managed intranet, an update section can always supply the most current engineering documentation to those in the field. Architekton has chosen to make the update mechanism the most highly visible aspect of this intranet example. The Updates tab is the first navigational entry in the site. Select the Updates tab at the top of the screen, as shown in figure 28.7.

Figure 28.7

A horizontal set of tabs is added to the sample intranet interface to facilitate rapid navigation.

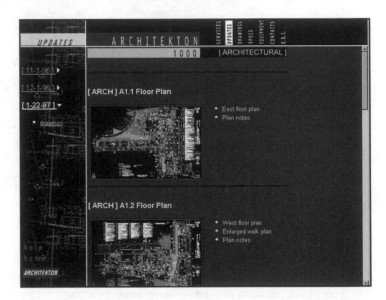

The newly loaded page replaces the vertical categorical selections on the left frame with a date-oriented index. Select the first date entry (11–1–96); the vertical index frame exposes links to categories that contain updated documents. The main portion of the document window reveals a list describing each of the updates. The description frame contains hotlinks to each of the related documents. By selecting the first document, you bring up a page with a GIF image of the updated drawing. Text on the image's right notes the changes that have been incorporated into the drawing. Selecting the image brings up the DWF file for detailed viewing. Sadly, in this demonstration site, there are no links to the drawing details noted on the update page. In a live site, links to the drawing views are essential.

Drawings

For users of engineering documentation, one of the Internet's greatest benefits is that it facilitates creation of a repository for globally retrievable CAD data. With a centralized database of AutoCAD drawings, managing project drawings can be simplified. The embedding of DWF files—derived from project .DWG files—in HTML pages enables the user to view the drawing before opening it for editing.

Select the Drawings tab located at the top of the horizontal frame. The main HTML frame presents the visitor with sample information describing the nuances of previewing and accessing drawing data from the site. The vertical index frame reflects drawings of various building types. As you can see in figure 28.8, selecting the 1000 series building type link displays a series of indexed entries including architect, millwork, structural, and m.e.p (Mechanical/Electrical/Plumbing). The main HTML frame displays a rendering of the building, along with descriptive text.

Figure 28.8

Embedding DWF files in HTML pages supports rapid access to AutoCAD drawing data.

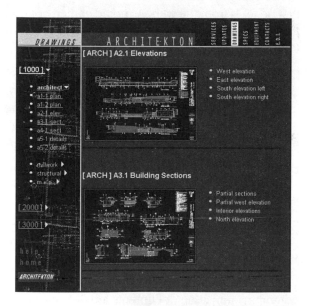

From a usability standpoint, this is an excellent system for navigating a company's large volume of architectural production drawings. This style might not work as well for mechanical assemblies or manufacturing drawings.

To study the architectural drawings, clicking on the architect hotlink reveals another set of indexes. This time you see a list of various plan, elevation, and sectional views, as well as index entries for detail drawings. The main HTML frame conveniently contains GIF thumbnail images of each drawing in the index. Select the a3-1 sect. index entry. The main frames jumps you to the appropriate thumbnail image tile. If you prefer, use the main frame to scroll the images.

To view the drawing dynamically, click on the GIF image tile. The main frame is updated to include the DWF file of the raster image. The top of the frame conveniently contains a title of the drawing that you're viewing. Little things count in cases like this, and Architekton's use of the title is handy.

Specs

Construction specification is another aspect of engineering document distribution that benefits from the web. As noted earlier, concurrent dissemination of construction specifications was an arduous, tedious task until the World Wide Web became CAD-enabled.

Click on the SPECS tab, located in the top horizontal frame. The index bar lists construction specification document indexes for two service areas: fuel and building. A live site might have many different entries here, depending on the business model. Because you are interested in the construction specifications for building projects, click on the building link in the vertical index frame.

By selecting the building link, you bring into the vertical frame an index that refers to sections of the construction document displayed in the document window. Clicking on the index reference (see fig. 28.9) causes the desired section of the construction specification document to be displayed in the central frame. The specification text can be scrolled with the vertical bar on the far right of the document window.

Whether on an intranet or an external web site, links to document sections are common. Many long documents are difficult to navigate, however, without excessive use of the Back button. In the case of Architekton's sample CAD site, frames containing the link references simplify navigation. The process of building frame links is automated by most HTML software packages, including Communicator and Front Page. Use of the frame index technique is heartily recommended for posting complex or lengthy documents.

Figure 28.9

Browsing a complex construction specification is simplified by using indexes linked to the document.

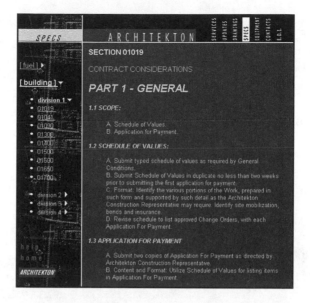

Equipment

For many design disciplines, tracking and managing equipment-related information is troublesome. Suppliers continually update their product lines, regularly introducing models and making others obsolete. New vendors also emerge, forcing changes to current documents and standards. As the Architekton sample site demonstrates, a complete CAD intranet should maintain current information about all equipment (and suppliers) used in their construction or engineering documents.

Select the EQUIPMENT tab from the horizontal top frame to display the site's equipment standards section. Again, the vertical index frame changes—this time to reflect references to various equipment manufacturers—while the document viewing frame introduces you to this area. Choose the first equipment vendor from the list—Star—to invoke the Adobe Acrobat Reader plug-in. As shown in figure 28.10, the Acrobat Reader enables you to view manufacturer-specific product information about the equipment used by the various building projects.

Using Acrobat to view equipment documents is helpful because they contain both text and graphics. Other solutions (such as Hummingbird's Common Ground) exist, but the PDF format from Adobe is well-established. Another solution is to use Autodesk's Design Blocks or Part Spec products from their Data Publishing Division. As you saw in Chapter 27, "Publishing on the Web," PartSpec online even supports drag-and-drop operations of mechanical parts directly into the AutoCAD Release 14 editor across the web.

Figure 28.10

The Acrobat Reader presents documents in their original format, mixing text and graphics for web-based viewing.

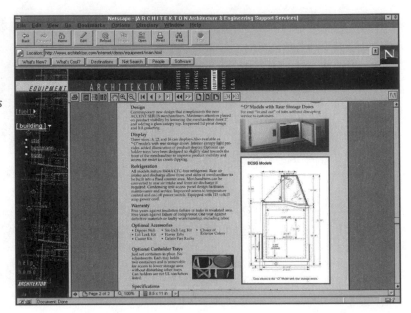

Contacts

A nice touch in the CAD intranet example developed by Architekton is a Contacts page. A current contact database, centrally available to all members with access to the intranet, is a great productivity tool. Maintaining contact information is always time consuming and often a redundant operation (because many individuals keep separate databases). Select the CONTACT tab located in the upper horizontal frame to activate this page.

The Contacts sample page index lists consultants and corporate contact options. Selecting the corporate contacts link reveals Architekton as a selection option. Click on Architekton to expose a list of contact information in the document window frame. The vertical index frame enables you to jump from contact to contact. Selecting the name of Scott Harden (Architekton's Director of Internet Media Services) displays his contact information. To send Scott an e-mail telling him how much you enjoy his demonstration intranet CAD site, click on his name in the main document frame, as shown in figure 28.11.

Figure 28.11

Having mailto functions for each contact streamlines the process of reaching a client or contractor.

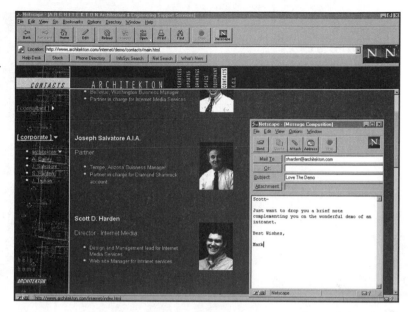

EDI

Production of quality construction drawings is what CAD is all about. As you have seen throughout this chapter, maintaining and distributing a set of standards for creating production drawings can be a difficult process. In concert with their clients and consultants, Architekton establishes a complete and exact set of standards for drawing data.

Select the EDI tab from the horizontal navigation frame. The vertical navigation frame displays a lengthy index of entries tied to the online EDI document. The main document window displays the EDI standards text (see fig. 28.12). To scroll through the document, use the vertical bar on the frame's right side. It is much more convenient to use the index frame to move through this section.

Scroll through the index frame, using the vertical bar located just to the right of the index links. Select the Sheet Order link. The main document jumps to the Sheet Order section, which displays information related to this topic. You might want to pick other topics to further study this document.

Providing this degree of detail in an online format helps to ensure a high-quality drawing. As changes to the EDI standard occur, push technology makes updating the page and informing site users of those changes a simple matter.

Figure 28.12

Online access to CAD drafting standards through an intranet increases drawing quality.

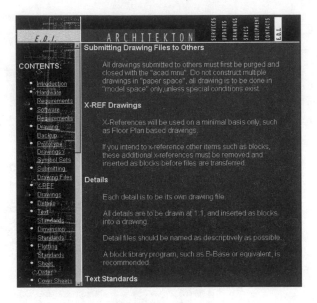

Summary

In this chapter, benefits of the web for the design process were detailed. Hopefully, you have gained an understanding of how the Internet facilitates communication and delivers a collaborative environment. Although brief, this look at some important Internet collaboration tools for the design and engineering space should raise your interest.

The case study of Architekton showed how a design firm that has embraced Internet technologies experienced success and growth. The business reasons that led to their becoming a leader in the field through use of the web tools were described. I believe that if implemented correctly, your firm can benefit from use of the Internet as well.

By studying the firm's CAD web site, you learned of issues you will confront and saw a solid structure for a site of your own. The sample CAD Internet site tour covered web navigation and features. In conclusion, here is an important message: the web is now CAD-enabled, AutoCAD Release 14 is web-enabled, and it is time for your design firm to become Internet-enabled!

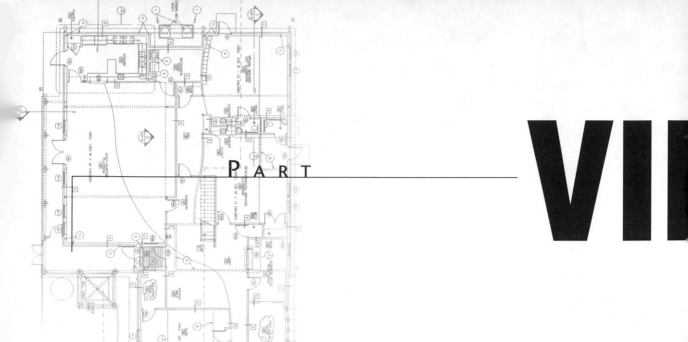

PART VII

REFERENCE MATERIALS

Appendix A: AutoCAD 14 Bonus Pack Reference and Tutorials

Appendix B: System Variables Reference

Appendix C: Dimensioning Variables Reference

Appendix D: Exercise Index

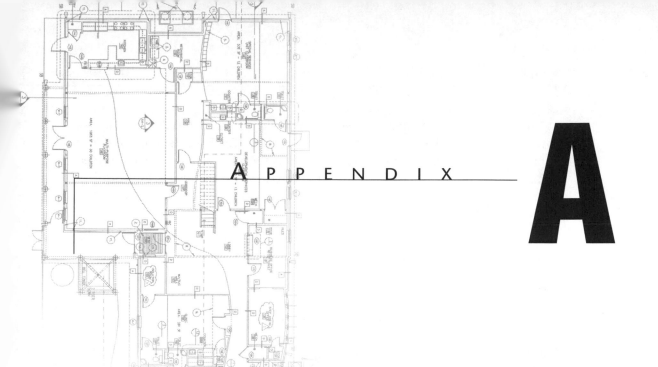

A P P E N D I X   **A**

AutoCAD 14 Bonus Pack Reference and Tutorials

by David M. Pitzer

AutoCAD Release 14 ships with a large group of tools collectively called the Bonus Pack. These tools consist of AutoLISP routines and executable AutoCAD Runtime Extension (ARX) functions. The Bonus Pack is located in the \Bonus\Cadtools folder. This folder is created during either a Full installation or a Custom installation that specifies the "bonus" option. The Bonus pull-down menu and the three Bonus toolbars referred to in the exercises in this appendix are defined in the files ac_bonus.mnu, which is loaded automatically if the folder \Bonus\Cadtools exists. If you decide to install the Bonus Pack after the initial AutoCAD R14 installation, ensure that the \Bonus\Cadtools folder is placed in AutoCAD's search path using the Environment tab of the Preferences dialog box. Loading the ac_bonus.mns file using AutoCAD's MENULOAD command will also cause the ac_bonus.lsp file to be loaded, enabling all of the bonus features.

Table A.1 lists all the tools contained within the Bonus Pack. The table lists the tool name, command-line name, and a brief description. The Help item on the Bonus pull-down menu provides more complete information for each bonus feature. Keep in mind that although these features have been tested and are free of problems, they are not officially supported by Autodesk. Make sure you have backup copies of any critical drawings before using these features.

The asterisk next to some of the bonus routines' names means there is a tutorial for this routine in the second half of this appendix.

Table A.1

Bonus Pack Reference Table

Bonus Routine Name	Command Name	Description
	Layer Tools	
CHANGE TO CURRENT LAYER	LAYCUR	Changes the layer of one or more selected objects to the current layer.
FREEZE OBJECT'S LAYER	LAYFRZ	Freezes layer of selected object(s).
*ISOLATE LAYER	LAYISO	Isolates the layer of one or more selected objects by turning all other layers off.
LOCK OBJECT'S LAYER	LAYLCK	Locks layer of selected object.
MATCH OBJECT'S LAYER	LAYMCH	Changes the layer(s) of selected object(s) to match layer of a selected object.
*TURN OBJECT'S LAYER OFF	LAYOFF	Turns off layer of selected object(s).
TURN ALL LAYERS ON	LAYON	Turns all layers on.
THAW ALL LAYERS	LAYTHW	Thaws all layers.
UNLOCK OBJECT'S LAYER	LAYULK	Unlocks layer of selected object.

Bonus Routine Name	Command Name	Description
*LAYER MANAGER	LMAN	Manages layer settings. Saves and restores layer configurations as "layer states" that can be modified, recalled, or renamed within an AutoCAD session. Layer states are saved within the drawing file but can also be exported to or imported from external *<filename>*.LAY files.
	Text Tools	
*ARC ALIGNED TEXT	ARCTEXT	Places a type of text entity along an arc.
EXPLODE ATTRIBUTES TO TEXT	BURST	Explodes blocks and then converts their attribute values to text entities.
CHANGE MULTIPLE TEXT ITEMS	CHT	A mini "text-property editor" to edit individual or global text attributes including height, justification, location, rotation, style, width factor, and text string.
FIND AND REPLACE TEXT	FIND	Finds and replaces text string values.[1]
GLOBAL ATTRIBUTE EDIT	GATTE	Globally changes attribute values for all duplicate blocks.
*FIT TEXT BETWEEN POINTS	TEXTFIT	Shrinks or stretches text by picking new start and end points.
*MASK OBJECTS BEHIND TEXT	TEXTMASK	Creates an invisible rectangular frame around text objects masking underlying objects.

continues

Table A.1, continued

Bonus Pack Reference Table

Bonus Routine Name	Command Name	Description
EXPLODE TEXT TO LINES	TXTEXP	Explodes dtext entities into lines and arcs that then can be given thickness.
Draw Tools		
*QUICK LEADER	QLEADER	Draws quick associative leaders with preset options.
ATTACH LEADER TO ANNOTATION OBJECT	QLATTACH	Attaches leader object to Mtext, Tolerance, or Block Reference object.
DETACH LEADER FROM ANNOTATION OBJECT	QLDETACHSET	Detaches leader object from Mtext, Tolerance, or Block object.
GLOBAL ATTACH LEADER TO ANNOTATION OBJECTS	QLATTACHSET	Globally attaches leader object to Mtext, Tolerance, or Block objects.
*REVISION CLOUD	REVCLOUD	Creates a freehand polyline of sequential arcs to form a revision cloud.
WIPES OUT AREA OF DRAWING	WIPEOUT	Covers area defined by a polyline with current background color.
Modify Tools		
EXTENDED CLIP	CLIPIT	Allows isolated clipping of an area of an external reference or block defined by a polyline, arc, or circle. Display of area outside the clipping area is removed.

Bonus Routine Name	Command Name	Description
EXTENDED CHANGE PROPERTIES	EXCHPROP	Changes similar properties of multiple objects.
EXTEND TO BLOCK	EXTBLK	Extends object ends using a block entity as boundary edge.
EXTENDED TRIM	EXTRIM	Trims all objects at a cutting edge specified by a selected polyline, line, circle, or arc.
*MOVE COPY ROTATE AND SCALE	MOCORO	Moves, copies, rotates, and scales object(s) with a single command.
MULTIPLE POLYLINE EDIT	MPEDIT	Performs a PEDIT on multiple polylines. Converts lines and arcs to polylines.
*MULTIPLE ENTITY STRETCH	MSTRETCH	Allows multiple crossing windows and/or crossing polygons to define objects for stretch operation.
TRIM TO BLOCK	TRMBLK	Trim object(s) using block as cutting edge.
EXTENDED EXPLODE	XPLODE	Provides control of all the properties of the component entities of a block(s) during explode. Entity selection methods can be individual or global for objects such as polylines, meshes, and blocks.
Miscellaneous Tools		
READ COORDINATE DATA	ASCPOINT	Reads coordinate data from an ASCII file and generates either a continuous string of Lines, a Polyline, a 3D Polyline, Points, or copies of a specified object(s) at the coordinate points.

continues

Table A.1, continued

Bonus Pack Reference Table

Bonus Routine Name	Command Name	Description
LIST ATTRIBUTES AND ATTRIBUTE VALUES	BLK_LST	Loads four separate AutoLISP block commands:
		BLKTBL Lists the block table showing the block definitions in the current drawing.
		BLKLST Lists the definition of user-selected block.
		CATTL Lists all the attributes, both constant and variable, of a user-selected block.
		ATTLST Lists all attributes in a block insertion, reading the constant ones from the block definition and the variable ones from the block.
LIST BLOCK ENTITIES	BLOCK?	Lists the entities in a block definition.
BONUS POPUP MENU	BONUSPOPUP	Loads and unloads the bonus pop-up menu utility. Once loaded, the utility enables you to select a pull-down for use as a pop-up menu. Alt+right-click selects the pull-down menu to be used; Ctrl+right-click pops up the menu.
CONVERT POLYLINES TO LWPOLYLINES	CONVERTPLINES	Concerts all pre-R14 polylines to lightweight polylines.[2]
COUNT BLOCKS	COUNT	Counts, itemizes, and displays the number of insertions of each block in the selected objects or the entire drawing.

Bonus Routine Name	Command Name	Description
BLOCK CROSS REFERENCE	CROSSREF	Searches block definitions for references to a specified layer, linetype, dimstyle, mlinestyle, or block and reports the names of all blocks that contain at least one reference to the specified object.
EXPORT DIMENSION STYLES	DIMEX	Exports named dimension styles and their settings to an external, <filename>.DIM file.
IMPORT DIMENSION STYLES	DIMIM	Imports named dimension styles from a <filename>.DIM file.
CREATE A TEMPORARY SELECTION SET	GETSEL	Creates a selection set of objects from a specified layer of a specified object type. All layers and/or all object types may be specified.
CONVERT JULIAN DATE	JULIAN	AutoCAD Julian/calendar date conversion utilities including calendar to Julian; calendar date and time to Julian; Julian date to calendar date; Julian date to AutoCAD calendar date/time; and Julian to day of week.
PACK 'N GO	PACK	Copies all files associated with a drawing (fonts, xrefs, and so on) to a specified location.
LISP PROGRAM CHECK	PQCHECK	Checks AutoLISP programs for mismatched parentheses and closing quotes in a group.
CREATE A SELECTION SET	SSX	Returns a selection set either exactly like a selected entity or, by adjusting the filter list, similar to it.

continues

Table A.1, continued

Bonus Pack Reference Table

Bonus Routine Name	Command Name	Description
EDIT SYSTEM VARIABLES	SYSVDLG	Edits and saves system variables on the fly.
ATTACH XDATA	XDATA	Attaches extended entity data (xdata) to a selected entity.
LIST ENTITY DATA	XDLIST	Lists extended entity data (xdata) associated with an object.
ATTACH XDATA	XDATA	Attaches extended entity data (xdata) to a selected entity.
EDIT ACAD.PGP FILE	ALIASEDIT	Create, modify, and delete AutoCAD command aliases in ACAD.pgp file.
AUTOCAD BATCH PLOTTING UTILITY	EBATCHP	Plots multiple AutoCAD drawings on one or more devices automatically.
FONT CONVERSION UTILITY	TTC2TFF	Converts TTC (collection of TrueType fonts) files to TTF files.
TRANSLATE AN R13 DXF FILE TO R12	DXFIX13	An external, open, programmable application that generates ASCII or binary CXF files compatible with any release of AutoCAD.
LOAD ARX COMMANDS INTO REGISTRY	DLINIT	External application that enables a third-party developer or CAD administrator to load ARX commands into the registry during product installation or AutoCAD deployment.
DRAWING DATABASE TEXT FORMAT TRANSLATOR	DBTRANS	Translates textual data (encoded as 8-bit values) contained in a drawing between various formats.

Bonus Routine Name	Command Name	Description
COUNT COMMANDS, REITERATIONS AND ELAPSED TIME	CMDCOUNT	Counts commands and the number of times they were invoked in successive AutoCAD sessions.
CONVERT AUTOCAD CONFIGURATION FILES	CFGCONV	Converts CFG and INI files created for Release 13 into CFG and REG (registry) files readable by Release 14.
AHP TO HLP CONVERTER	AHP2HLP	Builds a Windows help file from an R13 AutoCAD Help file or a pre-R13 ASCII Help file.

[1]Does not apply to block attributes or multiline text entries.

[2]This command displays the message: ***Warning: This will convert all polylines to lightweight unconditionally. It removes all xdata on existing polylines and may cause third-party applications reliant on this data to fail.

Bonus Pack Tutorials

The following tutorials demonstrate a sampling of the tools found in the Bonus Pack. Not all of the options or features of these representative tools are necessarily included in these short exercises. Please refer to the Bonus Help facility found on the Bonus pull-down menu for the options available with each of these and the other Bonus Pack tools.

LAYER MANAGER

1. Open the drawing APP-1.DWG from this book's CD-ROM.

2. Start Layer Manager by: a) clicking on the Layer Manager tool from the Bonus Layer Tools toolbar, b) choosing the Bonus pull-down menu, then Layers/Layer Manager, or c) entering **lman** and pressing Enter at the Command: prompt.

3. The Layer Manager dialog box appears. If necessary, place the screen pointer in the title bar of the dialog box, click and drag the box to the position shown in figure A.1. Notice in the bottom-left corner that the current layer state is titled PLAN-ONLY.

Figure A.1

The Layer Manager dialog box.

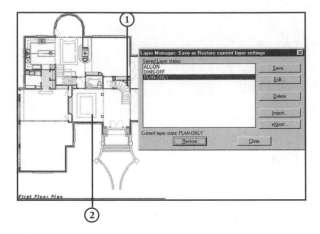

4. With the Layer Manager dialog box still displayed, highlight the ALL-ON layer state, and then click on Restore.

   Note that the ALL-ON layer state makes all layers visible.

5. Highlight the layer state DIMS-OFF and click on Restore. Note that the dimension layers are turned off.

6. Close the Layer Manager dialog box.

7. Using AutoCAD's Layer Control drop-down list on the Object Properties toolbar, turn off the layer BRTITLES.

8. Select Layer Manager to display the Layer Manager dialog box again. Create and save the current layer state by clicking on the Save button. Save the current layer state as NO-NOTES. Select and Restore the layer state NO-DIMS.

9. Restore the layer state NO-NOTES and note the layer BRTITLES is not displayed.

10. Delete the layer state NO-NOTES by clicking on the Delete button and clicking Yes in the Warning dialog box.

11. Finally, restore the layer state PLAN-ONLY and close the Layer Manager dialog box.

NOTE

Layer states may be saved to and restored from an external file as well.

12. Leave this drawing open if you plan to continue in the next exercise.

LAYER TOOLS

1. If necessary, open the drawing APP-1.DWG from this book's CD-ROM.

2. Select the Isolate Layer bonus feature by: a) clicking on the Isolate Object's Layer tool from the Bonus Layer Tools toolbar, b) choosing the Bonus pull-down menu, then Layers/ Layer Isolate, or c) entering **layiso** and pressing Enter at the Command: prompt.

3. At the Select object(s) on the layer(s) to be ISOLATED: prompt, pick the stairway at ① in figure A.1 and then press Enter.

4. Note that all layers except the layer you picked are turned off. Undo the last operation by entering **u** and pressing Enter.

5. Select the Turn Object's Layer Off bonus feature by: a) clicking on the Turn Object's Layer Off tool from the Bonus Layer Tools toolbar, b) choosing the Bonus pull-down menu, then Layers/ Layer Off, or c) entering **layoff** and pressing Enter at the Command: prompt.

6. At the Options/Undo/<Pick an object on the layer to be turned OFF>: prompt, select the object at ② in figure A.1. Note that the layer of the object picked, ARHEADER, is turned off.

7. With the prompt in the preceding step still active, enter **u** and press Enter to turn the ARHEADER layer back on. End the command by pressing Enter.

    Leave this drawing open if you plan to continue to the next exercise.

REVISION CLOUD

1. If necessary, open the drawing APP-1.DWG from this book's CD-ROM. Restore the view REVISE.

2. Select the Revision Cloud bonus feature by: a) clicking on the Revision tool from the Bonus Standard toolbar, b) choosing the Bonus pull-down menu, then Draw/Revision Cloud, or c) entering **revcloud** and pressing Enter at the Command: prompt.

3. At the Arc length/<Pick cloud starting point>: prompt, pick a point near ① in figure A.2 and guide the cursor in a counterclockwise direction to surround the objects following the path shown in figure A.2. AutoCAD draws the revision cloud along the path automatically as you outline the revision, and closes the cloud when you get within an arc length distance from start point.

4. Close this drawing without saving changes.

Figure A.2

Revision Cloud.

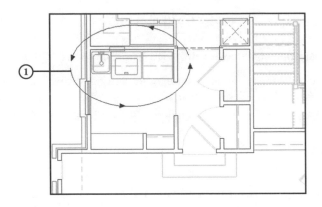

MULTIPLE ENTITY STRETCH

1. Open APP-2.DWG from the book's CD-ROM. Check that Layer1 is Thawed, On, and Current and that Layer2 is Frozen.

2. Start the Multiple Entity Stretch bonus feature by: a) clicking on the Multiple Entity Stretch tool on the Bonus Standard toolbar, or b) selecting the Bonus pull-down menu, then Modify/Multiple Entity Stretch, or c) entering **mstretch** and pressing Enter at the Command: prompt.

   The following prompts appear:

   ```
   Define crossing windows or crossing polygons...
   CP(crossing polygon)/<Crossing First point>:
   ```

3. Form the two crossing boxes at the ends of boxes 1 and 3 as shown in figure A.3. Then press Enter.

Figure A.3

Multiple Stretch.

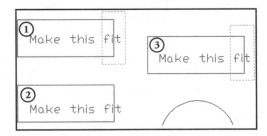

4. Respond to the following prompts as follows:

   ```
   Remove objects/<Base point>: pick anywhere in the drawing area
   Second base point: @0.75,0
   ```

The bonus routine stretches the two rectangles. Note in the previous step you could have entered the stretch distance using direct distance entry or you could have stretched the boxes dynamically with a click and drag motion.

Your drawing should now resemble figure A.4.

5. Leave this drawing open if you plan to continue with the next bonus tutorial, otherwise close the drawing without saving changes.

Figure A.4

Your image should resemble this figure at the end of the Multiple Entity Stretch exercise.

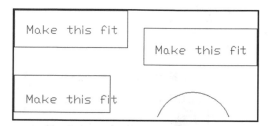

FIT TEXT BETWEEN POINTS AND ARC TEXT

1. Continue from the previous bonus tutorial or open drawing APP-2.DWG from the book's
   CD-ROM. Check that Layer1 is Thawed, On, and Current and that Layer2 is Frozen.

2. Start the Text Fit bonus feature by: a) clicking on the Text Fit icon on the Bonus Text Tools toolbar, b) choosing the Bonus pull-down menu, then Text/Text Fit, or c) entering **textfit** alnd pressing Enter at the Command: prompt.

   The following prompt appears:

   `Select Text to stretch/shrink:`

3. Pick the text in box 2. The following prompt appears:

   `Starting Point/<Pick new ending point>:`

4. Position the cursor to the right and pick near ① in figure A.5.

   The bonus routine fits the text as shown in figure A.5.

5. Start the bonus Arctext feature by: a) clicking on the Text Along Arc icon on the Bonus Text Tools toolbar, b) choosing the Bonus pull-down menu, then Text/Arc Aligned Text, or c) entering **arctext** and pressing Enter at the Command: prompt.

   The following prompt appears:

   `Select an Arc or an ArcAlignedText:`

Figure A.5

Fit text between points.

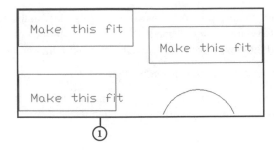

6. Pick the arc. The ArcAlignedText Workshop dialog box appears as shown in figure A.6.

Figure A.6

The ArcAlignedText Workshop dialog box.

7. In the ArcAlignedText Workshop dialog box, enter the following values: Text height: **0.2**, Offset from arc: **0.2**. Leave all other values at their default settings. In the Text edit box, enter the following text: **Fit this text along an arc**. Click on the OK button.

   The bonus routine fits the text along the arc as shown in figure A.7.

Figure A.7

Text along an arc.

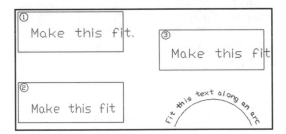

8. If you want to continue in these tutorials, leave this drawing open. Otherwise, quit AutoCAD without saving changes.

QUICK LEADER

1. Continue from the previous bonus tutorial or open drawing APP-2.DWG from the book's CD-ROM. Check that Layer2 is Thawed, On, and Current and that Layer1 is Frozen. Your drawing should resemble figure A.8.

Figure A.8

Placing a Quick Leader.

2. Start the Quick Leader bonus feature by: a) clicking on the Quick Leader tool on the Bonus Standard toolbar, b) choosing the Bonus pull-down menu, then Draw/Leader Tools/Quick Leader, or c) entering **qleader** and pressing Enter at the Command: prompt.

   The following prompt appears:

   ```
   First Leader point or press Enter to set Options:
   ```

3. Ensure that ORTHO mode is off, then select the points ① and ② in figure A.8, and press Enter. At the Enter Leader text: prompt, type in the following two lines of text: **Lorophytum** (press Enter) **pitzerii** (press Enter), then press Enter again. AutoCAD places the leader and text as shown in figure A.9.

Figure A.9

Adding a Quick Leader.

4. If you plan to continue in these tutorials, leave this drawing open. Otherwise, quit AutoCAD without saving changes.

TEXT MASK

1. Continue from the previous bonus tutorial or open drawing APP-2.DWG from the book's CD-ROM. Check that Layer2 is Thawed, On, and Current and that Layer1 is Frozen. Your drawing should resemble figure A.9, resulting from the previous tutorial.

2. Start the Quick Leader bonus feature by: a) clicking on the Text Mask tool on the Bonus Text Tools toolbar, b) choosing the Bonus pull-down menu, then /Text/Text Mask, or c) entering **textmask** and pressing Enter at the Command: prompt.

   When the following prompt appears, accept the default value of 0.35 by pressing Enter.

   ```
   Enter offset factor relative to text height <0.35>:
   ```

3. At the Select Objects: prompt, pick the "Conference Table" text items and press Enter. AutoCAD creates the text mask as shown in figure A.10.

Figure A.10

Creating a text mask.

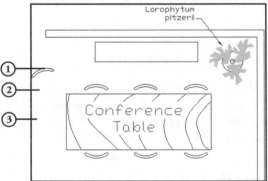

4. If you plan to continue in these tutorials, leave this drawing open. Otherwise, quit AutoCAD without saving changes.

MOVE COPY ROTATE

1. Continue from the previous bonus tutorial or open drawing APP-2.DWG from the book's
CD-ROM. Check that Layer2 is Thawed, On, and Current and that Layer1 is Frozen. Your drawing should resemble figure A.10, resulting from the previous tutorial.

2. Start the Move Copy Rotate bonus feature by: a) clicking on the Move Copy Rotate tool on the Bonus Standard toolbar, b) choosing the Bonus pull-down menu, then Modify/Move Copy Rotate, or c) entering **mocoro** and pressing Enter at the Command: prompt.

3. At the Select Objects: prompt, pick the chair at ① in figure A.10 and press Enter.

4. At the Base point: prompt, pick near ②. The following options prompt appears:
   `Move/Copy/Rotate/Scale/Base pt/Undo/<eXit>:`

5. Choose the Move option by entering **m** and pressing Enter. At the Second point of displacement: prompt, move the cursor and pick near ③. The options prompt returns.

6. Choose the Rotate option by entering **r** and pressing Enter. At the Rotation angle: prompt, move the cursor to orient the chair as shown in figure A.11 and pick. The options prompt returns.

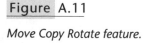

Figure A.11

Move Copy Rotate feature.

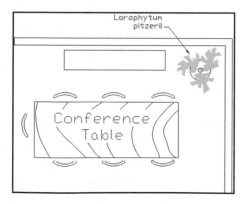

7. End the Move Copy Rotate feature by pressing Enter.

8. This completes the tutorials for the Bonus Package. Quit AutoCAD without saving changes to the drawing.

Icons on the three Bonus Toolbars are shown in figure A.12.

Figure A.12

Bonus Package toolbars.

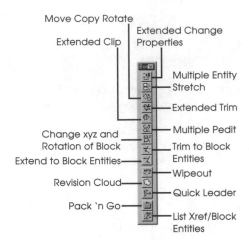

Move Copy Rotate

Extended Change Properties

Extended Clip

Multiple Entity Stretch

Extended Trim

Multiple Pedit

Change xyz and Rotation of Block

Trim to Block Entities

Extend to Block Entities

Wipeout

Revision Cloud

Quick Leader

Pack 'n Go

List Xref/Block Entities

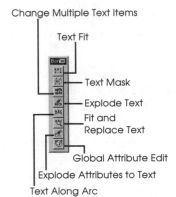

Change Multiple Text Items

Text Fit

Text Mask

Explode Text

Fit and Replace Text

Global Attribute Edit

Explode Attributes to Text

Text Along Arc

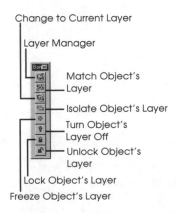

Change to Current Layer

Layer Manager

Match Object's Layer

Isolate Object's Layer

Turn Object's Layer Off

Unlock Object's Layer

Lock Object's Layer

Freeze Object's Layer

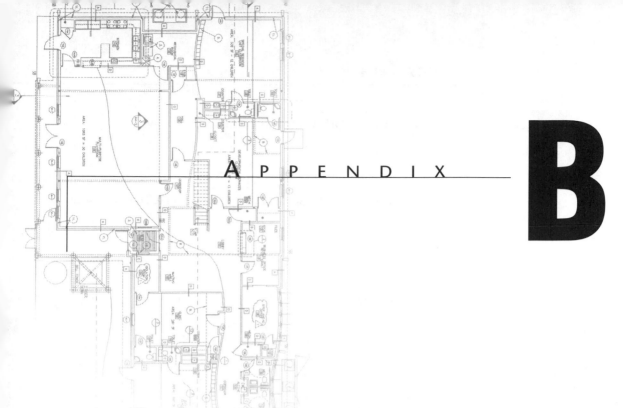

SYSTEM VARIABLES REFERENCE

A

ACADPREFIX   Stores the directory path, if any, specified by the AutoCAD environment variable, with path separators appended if necessary.

ACADVER   Stores the AutoCAD version number, which can have values such as 14 or 14a.

AFLAGS   Sets attribute flags for ATTDEF bit-code.

ANGBASE   Sets the base angle 0 with respect to the current UCS.

ANGDIR   Sets the positive direction from angle 0 with respect to the current UCS.

APBOX   Turns the AutoSnap aperture box on or off.

APERTURE   Sets object snap target height, in pixels.

AREA   Stores the last area computed by AREA, LIST, or DBLIST.

ATTDIA   Controls whether INSERT uses a dialog box for attribute value entry.

ATTMODE   Controls display of attributes.

ATTREQ   Determines whether INSERT uses default attribute settings during insertion of blocks.

AUDITCTL   Controls whether AUDIT creates an ADT file (audit report).

AUNITS   Sets units for angles.

AUPREC   Sets number of decimal places for angular units.

AUTOSNAP   Controls the display of the AutoSnap marker and SnapTips, and turns the AutoSnap magnet on or off.

B

BACKZ   Stores the back clipping plane offset from the target plane for the current viewport.

BLIPMODE   Controls whether marker blips are visible.

C

CDATE   Sets calendar date and time.

CECOLOR   Sets the color of new objects.

CELTSCALE   Sets the current global linetype scale for objects.

CELTYPE   Sets the linetype of new objects.

CHAMFERA   Sets the first chamfer distance.

CHAMFERB   Sets the second chamfer distance.

CHAMFERC   Sets the chamfer length.

CHAMFERD   Sets the chamfer angle.

CHAMMODE   Sets the input method by which AutoCAD creates chamfers.

CIRCLERAD   Sets the default circle radius.

CLAYER   Sets the current layer.

CMDACTIVE   Stores the bit-code that indicates whether an ordinary command, transparent command, script, or dialog box is active.

CMDDIA   Controls whether dialog boxes are turned on for PLOT and external database commands.

CMDECHO   Controls whether AutoCAD echoes prompts and input during the AutoLISP (command) function.

CMDNAMES   Displays the name of the currently active command and transparent command.

CMLJUST   Specifies multiline justification.

CMLSCALE   Controls the overall width of a multiline.

CMLSTYLE   Sets the multiline style.

COORDS   Controls when coordinates are updated on the status line.

CURSORSIZE   Determines the size of the crosshairs as a percentage of the screen size.

CVPORT   Sets the identification number of the current viewport.

D

DATE   Stores the current date and time.

DBMOD   Indicates the drawing modification status using bit-code.

DCTCUST   Displays the path and file name of the current custom spelling dictionary.

DCTMAIN   Displays the path and file name of the current main spelling dictionary.

DELOBJ   Controls whether objects used to create other objects are retained or deleted from the drawing database.

DEMANDLOAD   Specifies if and when AutoCAD demand loads a third-party application if a drawing contains custom objects created in that application.

DIASTAT   Stores the exit method of the most recently used dialog box.

DISPSILH   Controls display of silhouette curves of body objects in wireframe mode.

DISTANCE   Stores the distance computed by DIST.

DONUTID   Sets the default for the inside diameter of a donut.

DONUTOD   Sets the default for the outside diameter of a donut.

DRAGMODE   Controls display of objects being dragged.

DRAGP1   Sets regen-drag input sampling rate.

DRAGP2   Sets fast-drag input sampling rate.

DWGCODEPAGE   Stores the same value as SYSCODEPAGE (for compatibility reasons).

DWGNAME   Stores the drawing name as entered by the user.

DWGPREFIX   Stores the drive/directory prefix for the drawing.

DWGTITLED   Indicates whether the current drawing has been named.

E

EDGEMODE   Controls how TRIM and EXTEND determine cutting and boundary edges.

ELEVATION   Stores the current elevation relative to the UCS for the current space.

EXPERT   Controls whether certain prompts are issued.

EXPLMODE   Controls whether EXPLODE supports nonuniformly scaled (NUS) blocks.

EXTMAX   Stores the upper-right point of the drawing extents.

EXTMIN   Stores the lower-left point of the drawing extents.

F

FACETRES   Further adjusts the smoothness of shaded and rendered objects and objects with hidden lines removed.

FILEDIA   Suppresses display of the file dialog boxes.

FILLETRAD   Stores the current fillet radius.

FILLMODE   Specifies whether objects created with SOLID are filled.

FONTALT   Specifies the alternate font to be used when the specified font file cannot be located.

FONTMAP   Specifies the font mapping file to be used.

FRONTZ   Stores the front clipping plane offset from the target plane for the current viewport.

G

GRIDMODE   Specifies whether the grid is turned on or off.

GRIDUNIT   Specifies the grid spacing (X and Y) for the current viewport.

GRIPBLOCK   Controls the assignment of grips in blocks.

GRIPCOLOR   Controls the color of nonselected grips (drawn as box outlines).

GRIPHOT   Controls the color of selected grips (drawn as filled boxes).

GRIPS   Controls use of selection set grips for the Stretch, Move, Rotate, Scale, and Mirror grip modes.

GRIPSIZE   Sets the size of the box drawn to display the grip in pixels.

H

HANDLES   Reports whether object handles can be accessed by application.

HIGHLIGHT   Controls object highlighting; does not affect objects selected with grips.

HPANG   Specifies the hatch pattern angle.

HPBOUND   Controls the object type created by BHATCH and BOUNDARY.

HPDOUBLE   Specifies hatch pattern doubling for user-defined patterns.

HPNAME   Sets a default hatch pattern name.

HPSCALE   Specifies the hatch pattern scale factor.

HPSPACE   Specifies the hatch pattern line spacing for user-defined simple patterns.

I

INDEXCTL   Controls whether layer and spatial indexes are created and saved in drawing files.

INETLOCATION   Stores the Internet location used by BROWSER.

INSBASE   Stores insertion base point set by BASE.

INSNAME   Sets a default block name for DDINSERT or INSERT.

ISAVEBAK   Improves the speed of incremental saves, especially for large drawings in Windows.

ISAVEPERCENT   Determines the amount of wasted space tolerated in a drawing file.

ISOLINES   Specifies the number of isolines per surface on objects.

L

LASTANGLE   Stores the end angle of the last arc entered.

LASTPOINT   Stores the last point entered.

LASTPROMPT   Stores the last string echoed to the command line.

LENSLENGTH   Stores the length of the lens (in millimeters) used in perspective viewing for the current viewport.

LIMCHECK   Controls creation of objects outside the drawing limits.

LIMMAX   Stores the upper-right drawing limits for the current space.

LIMMIN   Stores the lower-left drawing limits for the current space.

LISPINIT   Specifies whether AutoLISP-defined functions and variables are preserved when you open a new drawing.

LOCALE   Displays the ISO language code of the current AutoCAD version.

LOGFILEMODE   Specifies whether the contents of the text window are written to a log file.

LOGFILENAME   Specifies the path for the log file.

LOGINNAME   Displays the user's name as configured or as input when AutoCAD is loaded.

LTSCALE   Sets the global linetype scale factor.

LUNITS   Sets linear units.

LUPREC   Sets the number of decimal places displayed for linear units.

M

MAXACTVP   Sets the maximum number of viewports that can be active at one time.

MAXOBJMEM   Controls the object pager.

MAXSORT   Sets the maximum number of symbol names or file names sorted by listing commands.

MEASUREMENT   Sets drawing units as English or metric.

MENUCTL   Controls the page switching of the screen menu.

MENUECHO   Sets menu echo and prompt control bits.

MENUNAME   Stores the MENUGROUP name.

MIRRTEXT   Controls how MIRROR reflects text.

MODEMACRO   Displays a text string on the status line.

MTEXTED   Sets the name of the program to use for editing MTEXT objects.

O

OFFSETDIST   Sets the default offset distance.

OLEHIDE   Controls the display of OLE objects in AutoCAD.

ORTHOMODE   Constrains cursor movement to the perpendicular.

OSMODE   Sets running object snap modes using bit-codes.

OSNAPCOORD   Controls whether coordinates entered on the command line override running object snaps.

P

PDMODE   Controls how point objects are displayed.

PDSIZE   Sets the display size for point objects.

PELLIPSE   Controls the ellipse type created with ELLIPSE.

PERIMETER   Stores the last perimeter value computed by AREA, LIST, or DBLIST.

PFACEVMAX   Sets the maximum number of vertices per face.

PICKADD   Controls additive selection of objects.

PICKAUTO   Controls automatic windowing at the Select Objects prompt.

PICKBOX   Sets object selection target height.

PICKDRAG   Controls the method of drawing a selection window.

PICKFIRST   Controls whether you select objects before or after you issue a command.

PICKSTYLE   Controls use of group selection and associative hatch selection.

PLATFORM   Indicates which platform of AutoCAD is in use.

PLINEGEN   Sets how linetype patterns are generated around the vertices of a two-dimensional polyline.

PLINETYPE   Specifies whether AutoCAD uses optimized 2D polylines.

PLINEWID   Stores the default polyline width.

PLOTID   Changes the default plotter based on its assigned description.

PLOTROTMODE   Controls the orientation of plots.

PLOTTER   Changes the default plotter, based on its assigned integer.

POLYSIDES   Sets the default number of sides for POLYGON.

POPUPS   Displays the status of the currently configured display driver.

PROJECTNAME   Stores the current project name.

PROJMODE   Sets the current Projection mode for trimming or extending.

PROXYGRAPHICS   Specifies whether images of proxy objects are saved in the drawing.

PROXYNOTICE   Displays a notice when you open a drawing containing custom objects created by an application that is not present.

PROXYSHOW   Controls the display of proxy objects in a drawing.

PSLTSCALE   Controls paper space linetype scaling.

PSPROLOG   Assigns a name for a prologue section to be read from the acad.psf file when you are using PSOUT.

PSQUALITY   Controls the rendering quality of PostScript images.

Q

QTEXTMODE   Controls how text is displayed.

R

RASTERPREVIEW   Controls whether drawing preview images are saved with the drawing and sets the format type.

REGENMODE   Controls automatic regeneration of the drawing.

RE-INIT   Reinitializes the I/O ports, digitizer, display, plotter, and acad.pgp file.

RTDISPLAY   Controls the display of raster images during realtime zoom or pan.

S

SAVEFILE   Stores current auto-save file name.

SAVENAME   Stores the file name.

SAVETIME   Sets the automatic save interval, in minutes.

SCREENBOXES   Stores the number of boxes in the screen menu area of the graphics area.

SCREENMODE   Stores a bit-code indicating the graphics/text state of the AutoCAD display.

SCREENSIZE   Stores current viewport size in pixels (X and Y).

SHADEDGE   Controls shading of edges in rendering.

SHADEDIF   Sets the ratio of diffuse reflective light to ambient light.

SHPNAME   Sets a default shape name.

SKETCHINC   Sets record increment for SKETCH.

SKPOLY   Determines whether SKETCH generates lines or polylines.

SNAPANG   Sets snap and grid rotation angle for the current viewport.

SNAPBASE   Sets snap and grid origin point for the current viewport.

SNAPISOPAIR   Controls the isometric plane for the current viewport.

SNAPMODE   Turns Snap mode on and off.

SNAPSTYL   Sets snap style for the current viewport.

SNAPUNIT   Sets snap spacing for the current viewport.

SORTENTS   Controls object DDSELECT sort order operations.

SPLFRAME   Controls display of spline-fit polylines.

SPLINESEGS   Sets the number of line segments to be generated for each spline-fit polyline.

SPLINETYPE   Sets the type of spline curve to be generated by PEDIT Spline.

SURFTAB1   Sets the number of tabulations to be generated for RULESURF and TABSURF.

SURFTAB2   Sets the mesh density in the N direction for REVSURF and EDGESURF.

SURFTYPE   Controls the type of surface-fitting to be performed by PEDIT Smooth.

SURFU   Sets the surface density in the M direction.

SURFV   Sets the surface density in the N direction.

SYSCODEPAGE   Indicates the system code page specified in acad.xmf.

T

TABMODE   Controls use of the tablet.

TARGET   Stores location of the target point for the current viewport.

TDCREATE   Stores time and date the drawing was created.

TDINDWG   Stores the total editing time.

TDUPDATE   Stores the time and date of the last update/save.

TDUSRTIMER   Stores the user-elapsed timer.

TEMPPREFIX   Contains the directory name for temporary files.

TEXTEVAL   Controls the method of evaluation for text strings.

TEXTFILL   Controls the filling of Bitstream, TrueType, and Adobe Type 1 fonts.

TEXTQLTY   Sets the resolution of Bitstream, TrueType, and Adobe Type 1 fonts.

TEXTSIZE   Sets the default height for new text objects drawn with the current text style.

TEXTSTYLE   Sets the name of the current text style.

THICKNESS   Sets the current thickness.

TILEMODE   Controls access to paper space and the behavior of viewports.

TOOLTIPS   Controls display of tooltips.

TRACEWID   Sets the default trace width.

TREEDEPTH   Specifies the number of times the tree-structured spatial index may divide into branches.

TREEMAX   Limits memory consumption during drawing regeneration by limiting the number of nodes in the spatial index (oct-tree).

TRIMMODE   Controls whether AutoCAD trims selected edges for chamfers and fillets.

U

UCSFOLLOW   Generates a plan view whenever you change from one UCS to another.

UCSICON   Displays the user coordinate system icon for the current viewport.

UCSNAME   Stores the name of the current coordinate system for the current space.

UCSORG   Stores the origin point of the current coordinate system for the current space.

UCSXDIR   Stores the X direction of the current UCS for the current space.

UCSYDIR   Stores the Y direction of the current UCS for the current space.

UNDOCTL   Stores a bit-code indicating the state of the UNDO feature.

UNDOMARKS   Stores the number of marks that have been placed in the UNDO control stream by the Mark option.

UNITMODE   Controls the display format for units.

USERI1–5   Stores and retrieves integer values.

USERR1–5   Stores and retrieves real numbers.

USERS1–5   Stores and retrieves text string data.

V

VIEWCTR   Stores the center of view in the current viewport.

VIEWDIR   Stores the viewing direction in the current viewport.

VIEWMODE   Controls viewing mode for the current viewport using bit-code.

VIEWSIZE   Stores the height of the view in the current viewport.

VIEWTWIST   Stores the view twist angle for the current viewport.

VISRETAIN   Controls visibility of layers in xref files.

VSMAX   Stores the upper-right corner of the current viewport's virtual screen.

VSMIN   Stores the lower-left corner of the current viewport's virtual screen.

W

WORLDUCS   Indicates whether the UCS is the same as the World Coordinate System.

WORLDVIEW   Controls whether the UCS changes to the WCS during DVIEW or VPOINT.

X

XCLIPFRAME   Controls visibility of xref clipping boundaries.

XLOADCTL   Turns demand loading on and off and controls whether it loads the original drawing or a copy.

XLOADPATH   Creates a path for storing temporary copies of demand-loaded xref files.

XREFCTL   Controls whether AutoCAD writes external reference log (XLG) files.

DIMENSIONING VARIABLES REFERENCE

DIMADEC Controls the number of places of precision displayed for angular dimension text.

DIMALT Controls use of alternate units in dimensions.

DIMALTD Controls the number of decimal places in alternate units.

DIMALTF Controls scale factor in alternate units.

DIMALTTD Sets the number of decimal places for the tolerance values in the alternate units of a dimension.

DIMALTTZ Toggles suppression of zeros in tolerance values.

DIMALTU Sets the units format for alternate units of all dimension style family members except angular.

DIMALTZ Controls the suppression of zeros in alternate unit dimension values.

DIMAPOST Specifies a text prefix or suffix (or both) to the alternate dimension measurement for all types of dimensions except angular.

DIMASO Controls the creation of associative dimension objects.

DIMASZ Controls the size of dimension-line and leader-line arrowheads.

DIMAUNIT Sets the angle format for angular dimensions.

DIMBLK   Sets the name of a block to be drawn instead of the normal arrowhead at the ends of dimension lines or leader lines.

DIMBLK1   If DIMSAH is on, specifies a user-defined arrowhead block for the first end of the dimension line.

DIMBLK2   If DIMSAH is on, specifies a user-defined arrowhead block for the second end of the dimension line.

DIMCEN   Controls drawing of circle or arc center marks and centerlines by DIMCENTER, DIMDIAMETER, and DIMRADIUS.

DIMCLRD   Assigns colors to dimension lines, arrowheads, and dimension leader lines.

DIMCLRE   Assigns colors to extension lines of dimensions.

DIMCLRT   Assigns colors to dimension text.

DIMDEC   Sets the number of decimal places displayed for the primary units of a dimension.

DIMDLE   Sets the distance the dimension line extends beyond the extension line when oblique strokes are drawn instead of arrowheads.

DIMDLI   Controls the spacing of dimension lines in baseline dimensions.

DIMEXE   Specifies how far to extend the extension line beyond the dimension line.

DIMEXO   Specifies how far extension lines are offset from origin points.

DIMFIT   Controls the placement of text and arrowheads inside or outside extension lines based on the available space between the extension lines.

DIMGAP   Sets the distance around the dimension text when the dimension line breaks to accommodate dimension text.

DIMJUST   Controls the horizontal position of dimension text.

DIMLFAC   Sets a global scale factor for linear dimensioning measurements.

DIMLIM   When turned on, generates dimension limits as the default text.

DIMPOST   Specifies a text prefix or suffix (or both) to the dimension measurement.

DIMRND   Rounds all dimensioning distances to the specified value.

DIMSAH   Controls use of user-defined arrowhead blocks at the ends of the dimension line.

DIMSCALE   Sets the overall scale factor applied to dimensioning variables that specify sizes, distances, or offsets.

DIMSD1   Controls suppression of the first dimension line.

DIMSD2   Controls suppression of the second dimension line.

DIMSE1   Suppresses display of the first extension line.

DIMSE2   Suppresses display of the second extension line.

DIMSHO   Controls redefinition of dimension objects while dragging.

DIMSOXD   Suppresses drawing of dimension lines outside the extension lines.

DIMSTYLE   Sets the current dimension style by name.

DIMTAD   Controls the vertical position of text in relation to the dimension line.

DIMTDEC   Sets the number of decimal places to display in tolerance values for a dimension.

DIMTFAC   Specifies a scale factor for text height of tolerance values relative to the dimension text height set by DIMTXT.

DIMTIH   Controls the position of dimension text inside the extension lines for all dimension types except ordinate.

DIMTIX   Draws text between extension lines.

DIMTM   When DIMTOL or DIMLIM is on, sets the minimum (or lower) tolerance limit for dimension text.

DIMTOFL   Controls whether a dimension line is drawn between the extension lines, even when the text is placed outside.

DIMTOH   Controls the position of dimension text outside the extension lines.

DIMTOL   Appends tolerances to dimension text.

DIMTOLJ   Sets the vertical justification for tolerance values relative to the nominal dimension text.

DIMTP   When DIMTOL or DIMLIM is on, sets the maximum (or upper) tolerance limit for dimension text.

DIMTSZ   Specifies the size of oblique strokes drawn instead of arrowheads for linear, radius, and diameter dimensions.

DIMTVP   Controls the vertical position of dimension text above or below the dimension line.

DIMTXSTY   Specifies the text style of the dimension.

DIMTXT   Specifies the height of dimension text, unless the current text style has a fixed height.

DIMTZIN   Controls the suppression of zeros in tolerance values.

DIMUNIT   Sets the units format for all dimension style family members except angular.

DIMUPT   Controls options for user-positioned text.

DIMZIN   Controls suppression of zeroes in the primary unit value.

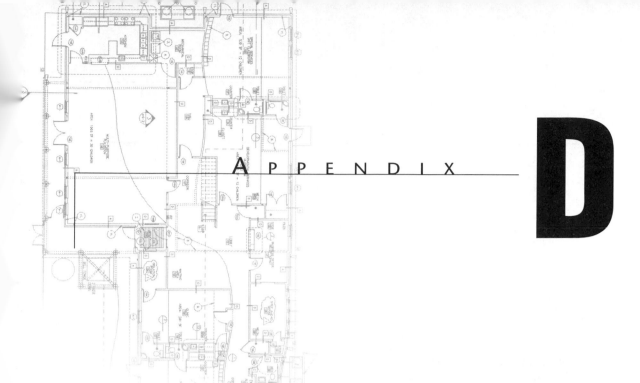

A P P E N D I X **D**

EXERCISE INDEX

Exercise Title	Page Number
Chapter 1	
Displaying and Hiding Toolbars with the TOOLBAR Command	13
Controlling Layer Properties from the Layer & Linetype Properties Dialog Box	15
Creating, Deleting, and Renaming Layers	16
Performing Operations on Groups of Layers	18
Building More Sophisticated Layer Filters	19
Using the Make Object's Layer Current Command	22
The Advantages of "Toolbar Editing"	24
Changing Properties with Match Properties Command	28
Editing Grip-Selected Objects with a Shortcut Menu	31
Using Real-Time Pan & Zoom	32

continues

continued

continues

continued

continues

continued

continues

continued

continues

continued

INDEX

Symbols

2D compound objects, 353-354
2D objects
  command, FILLET, 639
  UCS, aligning, 195-197
3-View ellipses, drawing, 237-238
3D coordinates
  cylindrical, 619
  inputting, 619
  right-hand rules
    axis direction, 618
    axis rotation, 619
  spherical, 619
  UCS, defining, 620
3D models
  commands
    HIDE, 649-650
    SHADE, 650-651
  visualizing, 649
3D objects
  creating, 624
  extruding, 641
  wireframe, 627

3D solid models, 632
3D viewpoints, drawings, viewing, 644
3D work objects, trimming, 332
3DPOLY command, polylines, 252

A

absolute coordinates
  features, 186
  polar, 187
  rectangular, 187
acad variables, public, 745
acad.dwt
  backing up, 109
  default values, storing, 98
ACAD.LSP routines, AutoLISP, 706
ACAD.PGP files
  aliases, 660
  modifying, 658-659
accelerator keys, priorities, 118
accelerators, *see* keyboard
  accelerators

I

O

S

V

REGISTRATION CARD

Inside AutoCAD 14

Name _____ Title _____

Company _____ Type of business _____

Address _____

City/State/ZIP _____

Have you used these types of books before? ☐ yes ☐ no

If yes, which ones? _____

_____

How many computer books do you purchase each year? ☐ 1–5 ☐ 6 or more

How did you learn about this book? _____

Where did you purchase this book? _____

Which applications do you currently use? _____

_____

Which computer magazines do you subscribe to? _____

_____

What trade shows do you attend? _____

_____

Comments: _____

_____

_____

Would you like to be placed on our preferred mailing list? ☐ yes ☐ no

☐ **I would like to see my name in print!** You may use my name and quote me in future New Riders products and promotions. My daytime phone number is: _____

New Riders Publishing 201 West 103rd Street ◆ Indianapolis, Indiana 46290 USA

Fold Here

New Riders

Tell us what you think and receive a FREE computer book catalog!

Thank you for purchasing this book. New Riders wants to continue to provide timely, accurate information on subjects in which you are interested. To do that, we need to hear from you. Please take a minute to complete and return this postage-paid form. In return, we'll send you a free catalog of all our computer books on topics ranging from networking to web technologies to graphics applications.

Name:_____ Title:_____

Company name:_____ Type of business:_____

Address:_____

City/State/Zip: _____

E-mail address:_____ Phone number: _____

❑   Please contact me with information on how I can become an author or technical writer with New Riders.
❑   I'd like to keep up to date on new books from New Riders. Please add me to your electronic mailing list.

How many computer books do you purchase a year?   ❑ 1   ❑ 6-10   ❑ 2-5   ❑ 10 +

Where did you purchase this book?
❑ Bookstore/Superstore   ❑ Catalog/Mail order
❑ Electronics/Software store   ❑ Internet
❑ Office supply store   ❑ Trade show
❑ Other_____

How did you learn about this book?   ❑ Book review in _____   ❑ Advertisement in _____
❑ Found while browsing in bookstore   ❑ Internet
❑ Catalog   ❑ Other _____

How would you rate the overall content of this book?
❑ Very Good   ❑ Satisfactory
❑ Good   ❑ Poor

What is your level of experience with the technologies/applications covered in this book?
❑ Beginner   ❑ Advanced
❑ Intermediate   ❑ Expert

How many New Riders books do you own?   ❑ 1   ❑ 2-5   ❑ 6-10   ❑ 10+

Why did you buy this book? _____
_____

Which chapters did you find most valuable? _____
_____

Which chapters did you find least valuable? _____
_____

What types of chapters or topics would you like to see in future editions of this book? _____
_____

Did you find the CD-ROM to be a valuable addition or companion to the book?   ❑ Yes   ❑ No   ❑ Not Applicable

What would you like to see added to the CD-ROM to make it of more value to you?_____
_____

What industry publications do you read consistently? _____
_____

What trade shows/conferences do you attend regularly? _____
_____

Which types of software packages do you use regularly?
❑ CAD   ❑ Electronic commerce
❑ Windows NT (version _____)   ❑ Communications
❑ C/C++   ❑ Novell NetWare/IntranetWare

- ❏ Database
- ❏ Multimedia applications
- ❏ Java
- ❏ 3D graphics
- ❏ Desktop publishing
- ❏ Web servers
- ❏ Networking applications
- ❏ Animation
- ❏ Image editing

- ❏ HTML
- ❏ 2D graphics
- ❏ Web publishing
- ❏ Perl
- ❏ Visual Basic
- ❏ Windows 95
- ❏ Web browsers
- ❏ Macintosh
- ❏ Other _____

Do you hold any of the following certifications?

- ❏ MCT
- ❏ MCP
- ❏ MCSE
- ❏ Other _____

- ❏ MCSD
- ❏ CNE
- ❏ MCNE

- ❏ ECNE
- ❏ Compaq ASE
- ❏ MCPS

Comments:_____

❏ I would like to see my name in print! You may use my name and quote me in future New Riders products and promotions. My daytime phone number is _____

Source Code: 1-56205-755-3

_____

_____

NO POSTAGE
NECESSARY
IF MAILED
IN THE
UNITED STATES

BUSINESS REPLY MAIL
FIRST-CLASS MAIL   PERMIT NO. 9918   INDIANAPOLIS, IN

POSTAGE WILL BE PAID BY ADDRESSEE

NEW RIDERS PUBLISHING
201 W 103RD STREET
INDIANAPOLIS IN 46290

MACMILLAN COMPUTER PUBLISHING USA

A VIACOM COMPANY

Technical Support

If you need assistance with the information provided by Macmillan Computer Publishing, please access the information available on our web site at **http://www.mcp.com/feedback.** Our most Frequently Asked Questions are answered there. If you do not find the answers to your questions on our web site, you may contact Macmillan User Services at **(317) 581-3833** or email us at **support@mcp.com.**

Getting Started with the CD-ROM

This page provides instructions for getting started with the CD-ROM.

Windows 95/NT Installation

Insert the disc into your CD-ROM drive. If autoplay is enabled on your machine, the CD-ROM setup program starts automatically the first time you insert the disc.

If setup does not run automatically, perform these steps:

1. From the Start menu, choose Programs, Windows Explorer.

2. Select your CD-ROM drive under My Computer.

3. Double-click SETUP.EXE in the Contents list.

4. Follow the on-screen instructions that appear.

5. Setup adds an icon named CD-ROM Contents to a program group for this book. To explore the CD-ROM, double-click on the CD-ROM Contents icon.